MW00824757

LOUISIANA

The Land and Its People

QUEEN OF THE WEST

*The Spanish Flag
of Leon and Castile
1492-1541*

*Fleur-de-lis of Bourbon
France
1672-1762*

*Union Jack of Great Britain
1763-1779*

*Spanish Flag at the time
of the Treaty of Paris
1763-1803*

*The Tricolor
of the French Republic
November 30, 1803-
December 20, 1803*

*Louisiana Statehood Flag
(Unofficial)
1812*

*The Bonnie Blue Flag
of the Republic of West
Florida
September 1810-
December 1810*

American Flag 1803-1818

*American Flag
Present*

*National Flag of Louisiana
1861*

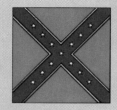

*The Southern Cross
Confederate Battle Flag
1862-1865*

*The Stars and Bars
The First Confederate
National Flag
March 4, 1861-
March 1, 1863*

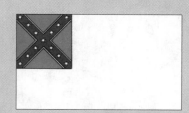

*The Stainless Banner
Second Confederate
National Flag
March 1, 1863-March 4, 1865*

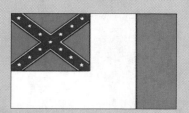

*The Third Confederate
National Flag
After March 4, 1865*

LOUISIANA
The Land and Its People

FIFTH EDITION

Dr. Sue Eakin
Retired Professor, Department of History
Louisiana State University at Alexandria

Manie Culbertson
Retired Junior High School Social Studies Teacher
Louisiana Public Schools

Martha Long
Belle Chasse Middle School Social Studies Teacher
Louisiana Public Schools

Illustrations by
James Forrest Culbertson

PELICAN PUBLISHING COMPANY
GRETNA 2007

The word "Pelican" and the depiction of a pelican are trademarks of Pelican Publishing Company, Inc., and are registered in the U.S. Patent and Trademark Office.

ISBN: 1-58980-303-5

First edition, January 1986
Second edition, first printing, August 1986
Second edition, second printing, January 1987
Second edition, third printing, October 1988
Second edition, fourth printing, October 1989
Third edition, first printing, January 1992
Third edition, second printing, July 1992
Third edition, third printing, December 1992
Third edition, fourth printing, February 1993
Third edition, fifth printing, August 1997
Fourth edition, first printing, August 1998
Fourth edition, second printing, August 1999
Fourth edition, third printing, May 2000
Fourth edition, fourth printing, April 2003
Fifth edition, first printing, January 2007

Printed in Canada

Published by Pelican Publishing Company, Inc.
1000 Burmaster Street, Gretna, Louisiana 70053
1 2 3 4 5 6   10 09 08 07 06

CONTENTS

State amphibian:
Green tree frog

State bird:
Brown pelican

State colors:
Blue, white, and gold

State crustacean:
Crawfish

State dog:
Catahoula leopard dog

State drink:
Milk

State flower:
Magnolia

State wild flower:
Purple iris

State fossil:
Petrified palmwood

State freshwater fish:
White perch

State fruit:
Cantaloupe

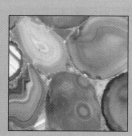

State gemstone:
Agate

State insect:
Honeybee

State instrument:
Accordion

State reptile:
Alligator

State tree:
Bald cypress

MESSAGE TO YOUNG LOUISIANIANS

How much do you know about the state in which you live? Many of you have lived here all of your lives, and you have probably taken your surroundings for granted. This year you will have the opportunity to learn more about this wonderful state and your Louisiana heritage.

What do you picture when you hear the name "Louisiana?" Do you think about the beautiful waterways, or the moss-covered trees, or the great fishing and hunting, or the cotton and sugarcane fields, or the first French settlement, or the exciting sports events? You may not picture any of these things. Since different people may view the same environment in different ways, it is unlikely that your picture is exactly like anyone else's.

Historians also picture history in different ways. All history is written or told or pictured by human beings. Each has a unique viewpoint of the personalities and events of the past. History cannot be separated from its author. Southern history has been dominated by historians from outside the area who have not pictured the South accurately. Thus, grossly unfair images have been left in the minds of the entire population. Various groups have each written their own histories. Often these histories adds their own distortions and slanted views. What is not included in history is as important as what is told in determining bias.

With the present communication explosion, readers will hear from many more historians. Each will have his or her own version of history to tell.

The authors of this book have simply done their best not to exclude any group and to include only factual information. We have tried to provide you with an accurate history as free from bias as humanly possible. Like other human beings, we see the history through our viewpoint. That said, we have tried to give you the basic facts of Louisiana history. Of that you are the judge.

Social scientists get their information from many sources: books; maps; articles in professional journals, magazines, or newspapers; local governmental offices; television; radio; photographs; minutes of meetings of clubs and organizations; official and personal archives; record books and scrapbooks; diaries; cemeteries; courthouse records; museums; interviews with knowledgeable persons; historical markers; almanacs; brochures; genealogical material; artifacts; and natural and man-made structures.

There are two basic sources of information from which to learn the Louisiana story. These are **primary,** or firsthand, **sources,** and **secondary,** or secondhand, **sources.** Primary sources are original works. Letters, diaries, autobiographies, and documents of a person give us a picture of what the person was like. Other examples of primary sources are historical documents and eyewitness accounts of events. We also learn from such secondary sources as a book about Huey Long by T. Harry Williams. We view secondary materials through the eyes of the author instead of having the opportunity to interpret them ourselves.

Many words are associated with Louisiana. In this book some of these terms have been used with a slightly different meaning. **Gumbo** and **jambalaya** (JAM bə lä yə) are two of Louisiana's famous foods. Both dishes are mixtures of a variety of ingredients. **Potpourri** (pō poo RĒ) originally referred to a stew, but now it is the name given to a miscellaneous mixture. These terms are used in the text to cover a variety of study activities. Jambalaya activities put the facts of a subject area together. You get involved in further study with potpourri activities. Gumbo activities bring the topic up-to-date. Coup de main (coo duh MANG) is a term used to describe the custom of neighbors getting together to build a house, to shear sheep, or to do other work. This term describes the study of the entire subject by the whole class. **En partie** (en par TĒ), meaning "partly" in French, is used for the study of a part of a subject area. **Lagniappe** (lan YAP) means something extra. Old-time Louisiana merchants gave small gifts to their best customers. Throughout this book, many extras have been added for you.

Your study of Louisiana will include a discussion of many of the questions that troubled Louisiana's citizens during its years of growth. Some of the questions are not fully answered. Other questions that must be solved if Louisiana is to continue to move forward now face the state. Finding a solution to such problems may be in your future. Those who built and preserved this state have left it for you. In a few short years you will take your place making decisions for the welfare of Louisiana. Learning the Louisiana story is your first step in preparing to take this responsibility.

LOUISIANA

The Land and Its People

PART ONE
In the Beginning

CHAPTER 1

THE GEOGRAPHIC SETTING

4

The story of the land of Louisiana and its people is unique. The state's geography has shaped the history of Louisiana more than that of most states. Its location at the mouth of the greatest river in North America, the Mississippi, sets Louisiana apart. The state has the meeting of rivers, marshes, and swamps with gulf waters and barrier islands. There are

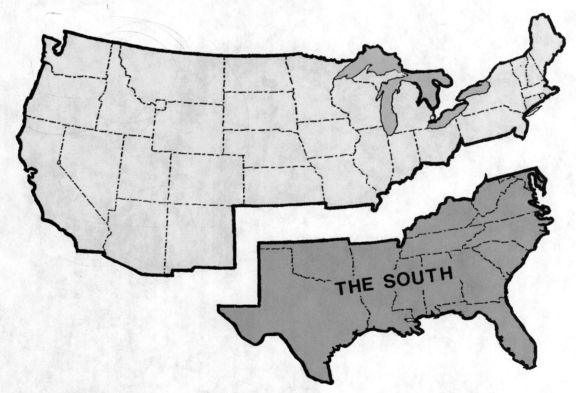

THE SOUTH

Louisiana, the boot-shaped state, is part of the Deep South.

Overleaf: *Discovery of the Mississippi by de Soto.*

bountiful forests and wildlife and rich soils with many minerals. The relatively mild climate affords long growing seasons. All that nature has so generously provided Louisiana offers the opportunity for a good life.

The Land

The first settlers who came here in 1699 had to plan their lifestyle around this special site they found at the mouth of the Mississippi. Imagine what it was like when the first Frenchmen arrived in the New World.

It had taken more than two months for the first Europeans to cross the Atlantic Ocean.

The first who saw the land near the **Gulf of Mexico** looked at the low marshlands. Marsh grass was shoulder-high. Cane grew ten feet tall. Armies of mosquitoes buzzed overhead. Long-legged egrets pecked for food at the water's edge and across the marshlands.

The newcomers found that it was almost impossible to walk in the **marshes**. The watery mud stuck to their feet and made walking a problem. There were places where grass and other plants grew on soft peat or extended out onto the water. The marshlands would clearly not be a good place to construct shelters.

Later as the Frenchmen explored this land, they found a baffling maze of **inlets,**

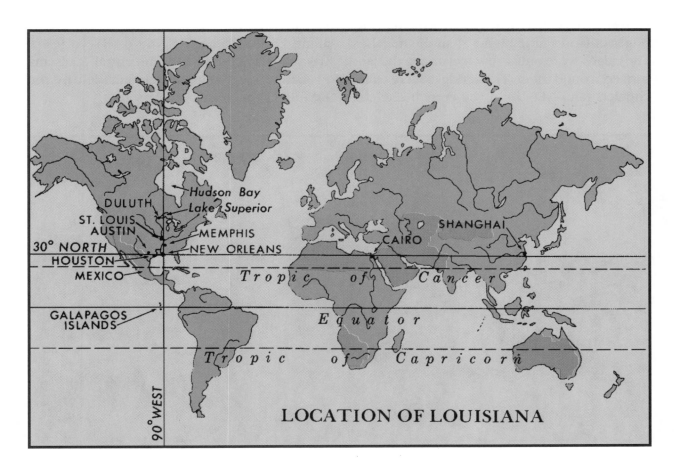

LOCATION OF LOUISIANA

bays, and **swamps**. The marshes were filled with waterways. Snakes slithered through the grass and across the water. Alligators could be mistaken for floating logs. Logs were sometimes mistaken for alligators.

Even with so much water everywhere, the newcomers found that it was hard to find drinking water. Most of the water in plentiful supply tasted of salt. The water at the coast was a mixture of saltwater and freshwater called **brackish**. There were really three kinds of water in the area—**saltwater, freshwater,** and brackish water.

When they neared the southwestern corner of the Louisiana coast, they saw twisted live oak trees on the **barrier beaches**. These beaches were the result of the water building up ridges of land a little higher than the marshes. The ridges were only a few feet above the land surface around them. These ridges were called **cheniers** (shə NEERS) by the French. The che-

niers are really old beaches of the Gulf of Mexico. They are an important mark showing where the Gulf extended at one time.

Upstream, along the Mississippi River and its **tributaries,** they knew that the land was very rich. The **alluvial soil** had been carried by the river waters many miles downstream from its origin far to the north. As they settled this land they learned how fast and fine the crops grow in the soils near the Mississippi and other rivers and streams. Those who came to the Red River found a **reddish-brown soil** that was equally rich.

Large natural levees were built along the old channels as the river changed its course. Some of the best farmlands in the state are located on these old Mississippi natural levees along **Bayou Teche** (BY you or BY yo tesh). **Bayou Boeuf** (bef or buf) in central Louisiana probably flows in an old channel left by the **Red River** thousands of years ago.

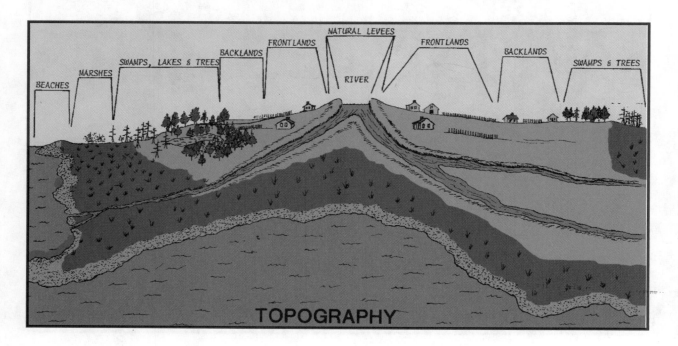

TOPOGRAPHY

Standing on the natural levees, the early settlers looked out over the **floodplains**. This area was subject to **flooding**. The floodplain of the Mississippi River is more than fifty miles wide in places. Twenty-five miles is its minimum width in Louisiana. Early settlers realized that the floodplains were not desirable for building homes except on high spots provided by natural levees.

As the French visitors left the Mississippi and explored this land that comprises the state, they found **sandy clay hills** covered with trees. Both east and west of the river there were hills. They found that the farther north they went, the higher the land became.

The highest point of land they found was **Driskill** (dris KILL) **Mountain** in Bienville (bi EN vil) Parish. It is really not a mountain. It is only a hill and reaches 535 feet above sea level.

When explorers left the hills, they saw great stretches of flatland. In years to come it would be discovered that Louisiana is one of the flattest states in the nation. The whole state is in the Gulf Coastal Plain. Farther to the west of the river, farther than the settlers went at first to lay out farms and build houses, were stretches of flat grasslands, or **prairies**. Prairies appeared like giant tables. The settlers roamed all over the area looking for better land.

Strange as it may sound, Louisiana is very young in measurements of **geological age**. The formation of Louisiana took millions and millions of years, but it is young in comparison to some other states. Not many states' deposits are more than one hundred million years old. There have been many changes in our land during these years.

Louisiana was built by one layer of sediment forming on top of another. The oldest

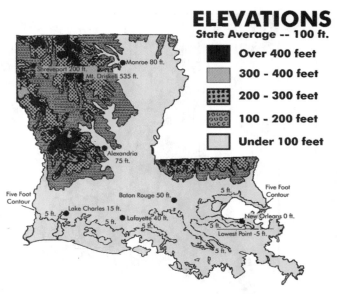

ELEVATIONS
State Average -- 100 ft.

■ Over 400 feet
▨ 300 - 400 feet
▦ 200 - 300 feet
▨ 100 - 200 feet
□ Under 100 feet

layer is left on the bottom. Other layers are added, one by one. The youngest layer lies on top. In this way much of the state was built by streams and the ocean. Such action continues and builds up land today.

Two opposing actions are always at work. These actions cause the **sinking of the land** in the southern part of the state while there is the **rising of the land** in North Louisiana. North Louisiana hill country rises in elevation a little each century. These dual processes go on very slowly all of the time.

During the past few years, Louisiana has been decreasing very slightly in size every year. **Delta** land, which is a deposit of sediment, is being eaten away by the Gulf. Islands being eaten away by the waters are becoming smaller. Most of Louisiana's shoreline is retreating, or receding. Over the long term however, the Mississippi, Ouachita, Red, and other rivers are building layer upon layer of deposits in Louisiana. This action takes place primarily in the floodplain, marshes, and

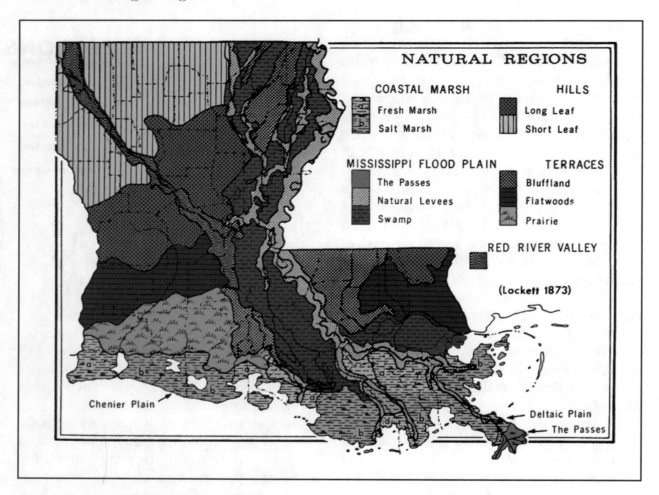

NATURAL REGIONS

COASTAL MARSH
  a Fresh Marsh
  b Salt Marsh

HILLS
  Long Leaf
  Short Leaf

MISSISSIPPI FLOOD PLAIN
  The Passes
  Natural Levees
  Swamp

TERRACES
  Bluffland
  Flatwoods
  Prairie

RED RIVER VALLEY

(Lockett 1873)

Chenier Plain

Deltaic Plain
The Passes

shallow Gulf waters. Many acres of new delta, marshes, and **wetlands** are being built every year in the Atchafalaya Bay.

Lagniappe—*Wetlands*. Any place that water stands for a good part of the year and usually has trees and plants that thrive in wet soil is **wetland**. That is a United States government classification since 1990. The federal government regulates and protects them and will fine you if you harm them. Louisiana claims forty percent of all coastal wetlands and about one fourth of the total United States wetlands. Rare vegetation and wildlife depend on **wetlands**.

En Partie 1 (Studying a Part). 1. What problems did the settlers encounter? 2. How was Louisiana built? 3. What is Louisiana's geological age? 4. What geological action is going on today? 5. Define these key words and phrases: (a) barrier islands (b) bays (c) bottomland (d) brackish (e) chenier (f) coastline (g) delta (h) elevation (i) floodplain (j) geologic age (k) inlet (l) latitude (m) longitude (n)

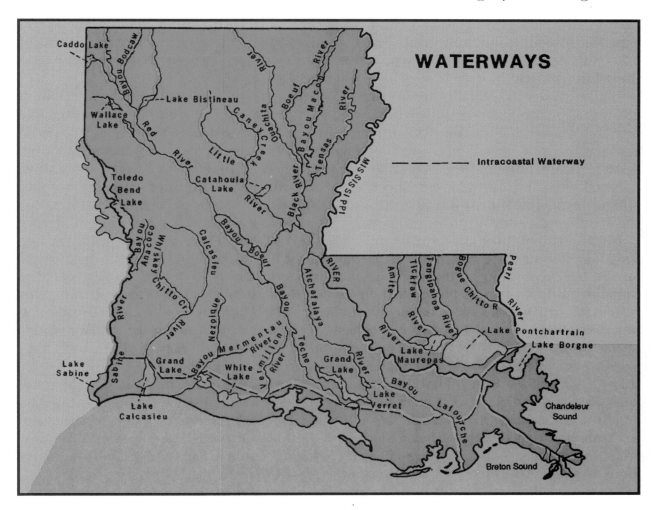

marsh (o) natural levee (p) natural region (q) shoreline (r) swamp (s) terraces (t) time zone (u) tributaries (v) wetland.

The Waterways

The great **Mississippi River** dominated the land. The river got its name from the Algonquin (al GON kwin) Indians—"miss" for "big" and "sipi" for "water." It is the most important single feature of the landscape of Louisiana and one of the largest drainage systems in North America. It is the longest river on the North American continent. The Mississippi extends 2,348 miles from its origin in the north to where it pours into the Gulf of Mexico in Louisiana. The Mississippi formed a vast north-south highway for travelers as far away as Canada. The Indians felt the overwhelming power of the "Big River." They called it the Father of Waters.

At the mouth the river waters spread out toward the Gulf of Mexico through three narrow channels. These passes form a pattern that resembles the outspread foot of a bird. For that reason geologists have called this a **birdfoot delta.**

The great river has made Louisiana rich by creating new land out of sediment. Lands near the Mississippi River are rich with mud, silt, clay, and sand deposited by overflowing waters. Huge amounts of sediment are dumped into the Gulf every day. About two million tons of sediment are deposited by the Mississippi each day.

The Mississippi River appeared more than a million years ago. The present course of the Mississippi River appeared between one thousand and five hundred years ago. In its rush to the sea, the Mississippi has not always remained in one channel. In fact, the river has changed channels many times. Louisiana maps show old Mississippi River channels shaped like snakes. Even today the river is constantly at work trying to redirect its path.

As the Mississippi changed its course, it left Louisiana veined with **bayous** and **lakes.** Sometimes the Mississippi formed great loops around parts of the land. In time some of these loops became cut off from the rest of the river. The length of the river was reduced by about fifty miles each time it straightened its course by cutting across a big bend. Each of these loops of water became what is called a **cutoff lake.**

Early settlers heading northward up Red River found it impossible to navigate the river for miles. Clogging the river was the **Great Raft.** The Great Red River Raft extended from above Natchitoches to near the state's boundary with Arkansas. Logs and brush had fallen into the river and collected in the water over the centuries. Water, spreading out in both directions from the river, filled low places on both sides of Red River. When the flood was over, the water was trapped in these low places. The water remained there. These areas became **raft lakes.**

Like the Mississippi River, the Gulf of Mexico has changed its points of contact with the shore. The action of the waters built up sediment deposits. Sometimes the water overran the land. Then, when it fell back to its own seabed, some of the water stayed in low spots. These formed **lagoonal** and **deltaic lakes.**

A location on a waterway was essential for the pioneers. The waterways were the settlers' highways. They were the link of the wilderness with civilization. To have access to New Orleans was vital. Early settlers often struggled with the problem of navigation on shallow streams. Some were used for navigation only out of necessity. Even then, they were not dependable.

There were many other important water resources in Louisiana. There was abundant rainfall. They treasured countless springs in the hills for their drinking water. The new settlers could usually find a good water supply for their homes.

The state's water resources are more abundant than in most other states. There are 3,593 square miles of water in a land area of 43,566 square miles, making the state thirty-first in size in the U.S. Louisiana has more water surface than any other state. Louisiana has between five thousand and eight thousand miles of navigable waterways. The daily flow of the state's rivers is more than 450 billion gallons.

Early settlers encountered water problems in Louisiana, however. **Waterpower** was badly needed to turn the wheels of early gristmills and, later, for cotton gins and sawmills. Louisiana had the lowest potential waterpower of any of the states. Water creates waterpower when it flows from a high place to a low one, creating waterfalls. To obtain such waterfalls early settlers had to dam streams. This provided enough water force to turn the wheels.

En Partie 2 (Studying a Part). 1.(a) What is the most important waterway in Louisiana? (b) Justify your answer. 2. What is the bird-foot delta? 3. Name some of the kinds of lakes in the state. 4. Why did the early settlers live along waterways? 5. What makes this state water-rich? 6. Name the state's main (a) rivers and (b) bayous.

The Forests

Vast virgin forests existed when the early settlers came from France. The forests covered 85 percent of the land. The forests represented rich resources beyond anything they had dreamed.

The riches of available lumber could bring wealth. Tar, pitch, and other products from the forests could be sold to the motherland. Huge timbers were needed by France in building ships.

Beautiful live oak and cypress trees were hung with *iti shumo,* or "tree hair," according to the Choctaws. The Frenchmen called it *barbe a l'espagnole,* or "Spanish beard." Later, the Americans would call it **Spanish moss.** It draped on the trees near the coast. As the settlers moved north, they found less of it. Newcomers found the moss useful in various ways. They used it in horse collars, ropes, mattresses, and pillows. It was also used with mud to form insulation for their homes. The resulting product was called **bousillage** (bōō zē YÄZH).

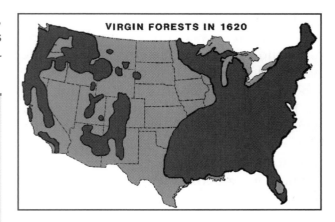

VIRGIN FORESTS IN 1620

In the forests the settlers found many kinds of **wild berries, roots,** and **nuts.** They gathered **pecans, walnuts,** and **hickory nuts. Grapes, plums, persimmons, acorns,** and **sunflowers** were all gifts of nature. **Muscadines, blackberries, dewberries,** and **wild strawberries** added to their diet. They gathered the roots of **sassafras** trees to make tea. They powdered the dry leaves to **make filé** (fee lay). Leaves and nuts provided **dyes.**

No doubt the newcomers realized that the advantages of the abundant forests far outweighed the disadvantages.

En Partie 3 (Studying a Part). 1. How much of the land was covered with forests? 2. How did the forests present problems? 3. How did the first settlers use the forests? 4. What else did they find in the forests?

Wildlife and Fish

Louisiana's location on the Mississippi Flyway provided many dividends. Each year, the pioneers saw about 55 percent of all the species of birds known on the North American continent.

The woods were filled with wild creatures. **Wild turkeys, wolves,** and **deer** found food and shelter in the underbrush. **Wild horses, hogs,** and even **cattle** roamed the woods. They had been brought to this land by European explorers, and their offspring had multiplied. **Quail, squirrels, doves, rabbits,** and similar game offered the settlers tasty food. **Bears** provided fat.

The Louisiana marshes serve as nurseries for a large percent of the fish in the northern Gulf of Mexico. The settlers found that they could catch a variety of freshwater fish in the many waterways. Fish from coastal waters included **shrimp, oysters, crabs,** and **sea turtles**. **Frogs** were everywhere. **Loggerhead snapping turtles,** the largest freshwater species in the state, weighed as much as fifty pounds. They provided much food for the early settlers.

En Partie 4 (Studying a Part). 1. What types of wildlife and fish did the settlers find? 2. How did they use nature's gift of wildlife and fisheries? 3. What is the Mississippi Flyway?

MISSISSIPPI FLYWAY

Climate and Weather

Scientists describe the climate as **humid** and **subtropical**. Louisiana has plenty of moisture; long, hot summers; and relatively short, mild winters. The state's climate is chiefly determined by three factors: the state's location on the Gulf of Mexico, its subtropical latitude, and the huge land mass to the north.

There are really two **seasons** in Louisiana—summer and winter. Fall and spring are too brief to notice. August, with an average of eighty-two degrees, is the warmest month. January, the coldest month, averages about fifty-three degrees. During most Louisiana winters there is no snow even in the northern part of the state.

The average temperature near the coast is nearly seventy-one degrees. The state average temperature is about sixty-seven degrees. In the northern part of the state the average is sixty-four degrees. South Louisiana has fewer extremes in temperature. North Louisiana has hotter summers and colder winters. The farther away from the Gulf settlers went, the greater the extremes in climate they encountered.

Louisiana's mild climate allows a long **growing season**. It was very important to grow as

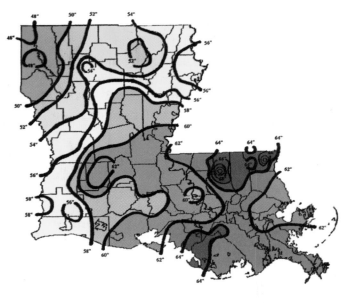

Mean Annual Precipitation.

much food as possible between the last killing frost in the spring and the first killing frost in the fall. The last killing frost in North Louisiana is around March 31. The first killing frost in North Louisiana is expected around November 1. Near the coast the growing season ordinarily is from February 1 to December 15.

About fifty-six inches of rain **(precipitation)** fall each year. Still, there were droughts occasionally. In fact, Louisiana has had serious droughts. These usually occur in the northern part of the state.

The heaviest rains fall along the Gulf Coast. Most rainfall occurs in March and December and the least amount in September and October. **Thunderstorms** are a part of the weather pattern in Louisiana.

Moisture in Louisiana is an everyday occurrence. Heavy dew falls over the land bringing small amounts of moisture. The high **humidity,** or mugginess, can be very uncomfortable. It is impossible to see through dense fog that often covers the coast.

Louisiana weather can be violent. New settlers were sometimes harassed by winds strong enough to sweep away their hard-built houses. Most fear the two deadly storms—**hurricanes** and **tornadoes.**

Hurricanes come out of the Gulf between June and November. Most hurricanes come in September. The hurricane winds may blow across a wide expanse of land tearing down trees and buildings. Rarely do the storms extend far inland. Heavy rains following hurricanes are sometimes as destructive as the high winds. Another problem is created by the lashing of the Gulf waters by the hurricane. This causes high waters from the Gulf to wash onto the shore. The low-lying coastal areas suffer most from the storm's fury when the sea waters cover the ground, sometimes to depths of fifteen feet. Usually, they average about one every four years.

Tornadoes sometimes seem to come out of nowhere. The dark funnel clouds with whirling winds are terrifying to see. The tornado's destructive path is narrow, usually about one-fourth of a mile wide. In the spring and fall the settlers were on the lookout for these deadly funnels in the sky. If they were in the northern part of the state, they had even more reason to watch for them, especially in March, April, and May.

En Partie 5 (Studying a Part). 1. Describe Louisiana's climate. 2. Describe Louisiana's unique weather conditions. 3. Compare North and South Louisiana climate. 4. Why is Louisiana said to have two seasons? 5. Why is it important to know the extremes in temperature rather than the averages? 6. Compare tornadoes and hurricanes. 7. (a) What is the growing season? (b) Why is Louisiana's favorable? 8. Explain the relationship between climate and the way people live. 9. (a) Why do some plants grow in South Louisiana which do not grow in North Louisiana? (b) Why do plants vary in their blooming seasons?

Lagniappe—*State Divisions.* Every other state has counties but Louisiana has parishes. The Roman Catholic Church defines church districts as parishes so during the French Colonial period Louisiana was divided up by the church. It now has sixty-four, with French, Spanish, English, and many Indian names. Each parish has a parish seat and courthouse, usually in the largest town or city. Officials of the parish have their offices there.

Coup de Main
(Completing the Story)

Jambalaya (Putting It All Together)

1. Relate the geography of our state to its history.

2. (a) Analyze what this land had to offer the first settlers. (b) Analyze the challenges they met.

3. (a) Describe the relationship between the settlers and their environment. (b) Explain the importance of each of these

resources to man: (1) soil (2) vegetation (3) water (4) wildlife and fisheries.

4. Justify the settlers' choice of staying near the coast.

5. Identify some of the geographic characteristics of the part of Louisiana where you live.

6. Compare North and South Louisiana in these areas: elevation, rainfall, soils, climate, vegetation, special or unusual characteristics, waterways, and growing seasons.

7. Map work: (a) Label Louisiana's border states. (b) Label waterways that serve as boundaries. (c) Mark the latitude and longitude of the state. Show (d) the coastline, (e) the shoreline, and (f) the longest distance across the state. Give the measurements for (d), (e), and (f). Label (g) the Five Islands, (h) the highest point, and (i) the major cities.

8. Complete this chart about Louisiana:
a._____planet
b._____hemispheres
c._____continent
d._____country
e._____section of the U.S.
f._____time zone
g._____plain
h._____shape of state
i._____percent water
j._____rank in size
k._____area in square miles

9. (a) In what ways has the appearance of this land changed since the first settlers arrived? (b) How has technology changed our environment?

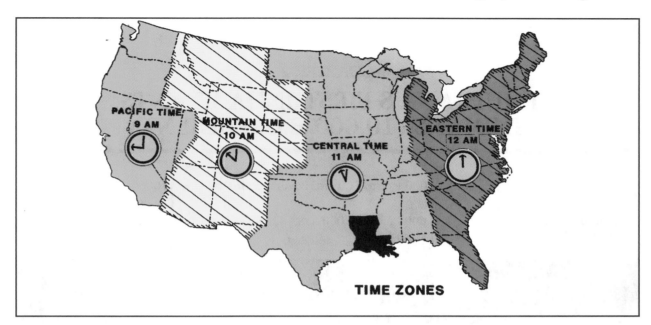

TIME ZONES

Potpourri (Getting Involved)

1. Find examples of architecture, economic activity, or any other examples that show relationships to the environment.

2. Locate pictures that show the advantages and disadvantages of living in different parts of Louisiana.

3. Compare the problems caused by weather in Louisiana with those in Colorado.

Gumbo (Bringing It Up-to-Date)

1. Identify specific ways of living that would be affected if modern ways of controlling our environment were removed. Identify some of the things over which we have no control or practically no control.

2. Relate geography to your daily living—food, clothing, shelter, health, occupation, and recreation.

3. Explain how the Louisiana environment has changed since the first settlers came.

4. Display pictures that look most like Louisiana.

5. Plan a trip to some spot in Louisiana. Describe the people, vegetation, land surface, crops, livestock, waterways, and any other important points.

6. Research: What does Louisiana need that it does not have? What does the state not have in the right amount or the right kind?

CHAPTER 2

LOUISIANA'S FIRST INHABITANTS: INDIANS (10,000 B.C.-PRESENT)

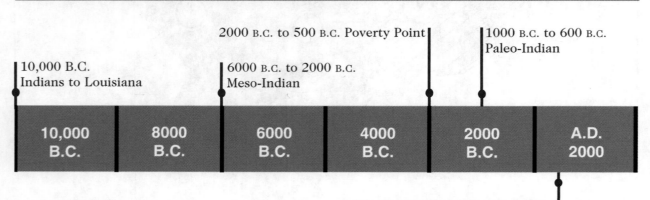

10,000 B.C.
Indians to Louisiana

6000 B.C. to 2000 B.C.
Meso-Indian

2000 B.C. to 500 B.C. Poverty Point

1000 B.C. to 600 B.C.
Paleo-Indian

| 10,000 B.C. | 8000 B.C. | 6000 B.C. | 4000 B.C. | 2000 B.C. | A.D. 2000 |

1514 Beginning of Historic Period

A.D. 400 to A.D. 1542 Coles Creek – Plaquemine – Mississippi – Caddo

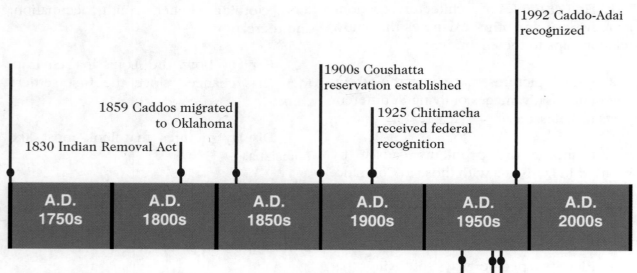

1992 Caddo-Adai
recognized

1900s Coushatta
reservation established

1859 Caddos migrated
to Oklahoma

1925 Chitimacha
received federal
recognition

1830 Indian Removal Act

| A.D. 1750s | A.D. 1800s | A.D. 1850s | A.D. 1900s | A.D. 1950s | A.D. 2000s |

1972 Louisiana established an office of Indian affairs

1981 Federal recognition of Coushattas

1982 Tunica-Biloxi reservation established

LOUISIANA'S FIRST INHABITANTS

When the first Europeans came to this land that became Louisiana, there were people living here. These were **Indians,** or Native Americans. Their lifestyle was so different from the Spanish, the French, and the English that each group of newcomers called them "uncivilized." To be civilized was to be like themselves—European. The Indians spoke different languages, worshiped different gods, and wore fewer clothes than the Europeans of that day. The Europeans measured everything by what was familiar to them. On this basis they labeled these people "savages."

Scholars studying the Louisiana Indians have provided us with some interesting facts. It was probably as far back as **10,000** B.C. that the first ones came to Louisiana. Indians have been in the state for about twelve thousand years, if this date is correct.

Scholars name two periods of Indian residence:

(1) **The prehistoric period.** The prehistoric Indians lived in the state from about 10,000 B.C. to A.D. 1514. The coming of the white man to Louisiana ended this period. This time is called prehistoric, since there are no written records.

(2) **The historic period.** For Louisiana, this period started around 1514. From the beginning of this period, we have written accounts by the Europeans.

LOUISIANA'S PAST

A.D. 1542 to Present	Historic	
A.D. 400 to A.D. 1542	Coles Creek - Plaquemine - Mississippian - Caddo	
500 B.C. to A.D. 400	Tchefuncte - Marksville	
2000 B.C. to 500 B.C.	Poverty Point	
6000 B.C. to 2000 B.C.	Meso-Indian	
10000 B.C. to 6000 B.C.	Paleo-Indian	

Lagniappe—*Terminology.* The **Indians** of Louisiana as everywhere are addressed as Indians, more often than the term **Native-Americans.** Literature of the Inter-Tribal Council and that of most newspapers and magazines freely uses that term. As many others search for the proper term, either term is acceptable for the inhabitants that greeted the explorers and settlers when they arrived at the New World, the North American continent. Their tribal names give distinction within the Inter-Tribal Council. **Indian** is clearly designated as the name at their casinos and reservation headquarters, and it appears in their newspaper ads.

Indians in General

The Arrival of Indians in Louisiana. Most authorities believe that the first Indians

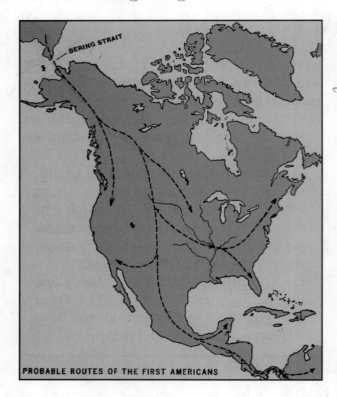

PROBABLE ROUTES OF THE FIRST AMERICANS

crossed the narrow Bering Strait, an extensive land bridge that connected Siberia and Alaska. At the time the Indians crossed from Asia into North America, the world was in the midst of the Ice Age.

The first Indians were probably hunters. For thousands of years after reaching the American continent, they spread southward, very likely in pursuit of game. In this manner, they made their way into present-day Louisiana.

Not all of the Indians who came to Louisiana came from the same place. The exact **migration patterns** cannot be traced. Some came when the entire tribe decided to move into the area. Others left their large groups and came in small groups.

Tribes. Many different Indian tribes lived in Louisiana. The first Indians lived in groups of four or five families. These groups were called **bands**. The bands grew into larger groups called tribes. In turn the large tribes joined together to form loose **confederacies**. The list of tribes included in a confederacy was not always the same.

The **tribal organizations** varied little. There was a chief in most family or kinship groups. These groups lived and traveled together. Some tribes had both a war chief and a peace chief. All tribes had a shaman, or medicine man. Usually the shaman was an old Indian man thought to have magical powers in curing the sick. He often "drove off evil spirits" to make the patient well. The shaman served at religious and other solemn ceremonies of the tribe.

Classification. Scholars studying the Indians of the entire North American continent, have divided Indians into groups. One classification is based on how the Indians lived. There are ten of these culture groups. Louisiana Indians are classified as **Southeastern Indians**.

Language. Each Indian group had its own special characteristics. There were similar characteristics among groups, too. For instance, many Indian tribes spoke similar languages. In the United States, there were forty-eight language families with different dialects.

Relationship to the Environment. One thing that all Indians had in common was their dependence on nature. Indians in early Louisiana obtained the necessities of life from the environment. Their food, shelter, and clothing came from the wilderness.

Food. What the Indians used for food depended heavily on what was available in their living area. Louisiana Indians had roots, herbs, berries, seeds, and nuts of

Louisiana Indians walking along a bayou.

many kinds. Wild game and fish were plentiful. South Louisiana Indians had saltwater fish as well. Indians in northwestern Louisiana hunted buffalo. The buffalo later disappeared from the area.

Homes. Indian homes differed, too. Indian homes in Louisiana changed according to the period of time and the culture. Some of the houses were round and some were rectangular. There were no tepees in Louisiana, however.

Scalping. The Indians' practice of scalping enemies sounds shocking. Indians felt it essential to prove one's ability as a warrior. Some thought that the head of the enemy must be cut from the body or the person would be reborn and could fight again. These "trophies" were displayed in very much the same way a sportsman collects trophies today.

Contributions of the Indians. These people passed on to the white man their knowledge of **how to survive in this land.** They made life much easier for the early settlers. Their help enabled the Europeans to avoid the risks of learning the hard way. **Where to secure foodstuff, what and when to plant in Louisiana soil, how to deal with insects,** and **how to handle the many problems of everyday living** were learned from the Indians. They showed the Europeans **new foods.** Indians taught them how to make use of the wild game of the forests and the abundance of fish in Louisiana waters. They taught their **skills in hunting, fishing,** and **trapping** to the white man.

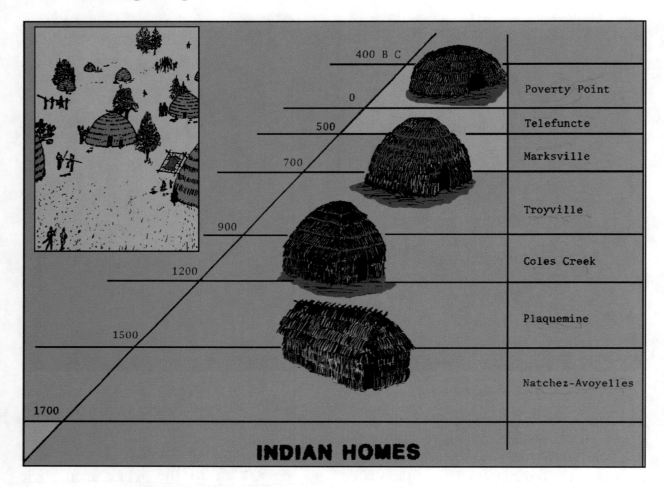

INDIAN HOMES

400 B C

0

500

700

900

1200

1500

1700

Poverty Point

Telefuncte

Marksville

Troyville

Coles Creek

Plaquemine

Natchez-Avoyelles

Indians taught the Europeans **how to live with the "floating land"** on the coast. The Indians pointed out **dyes** to be found in the forests. They showed the Europeans **herbs** and other seasonings—bay leaf, cayenne, and wild cherry. They recommended **teas** for medicine such as that made from sassafras roots. They made **filé** from the sassafras leaves. Indians showed the Europeans the way to travel on the bayous in a light boat—the **pirogue** (pē RŌ or PĒ rogue). Newcomers learned about **mud baths** from the Indians, too.

Many Indian **words** have become place names in Louisiana. These include Natchitoches (NAK i tosh), Caddo (KAD O), Atchafalaya (ə CHAF ə lĭ ə), Istrouma (is TROO mə), Opelousas (op ə LŌŌ səs), and Ouachita.

En Partie 1 (Studying a Part). 1. (a) Identify the two periods of Indians. (b) Identify the event which marks the end of one and the beginning of the other. 2. Explain: Not all Louisiana Indians lived in Louisiana at the same time. 3. (a) How did their ancestors probably come to the New World? (b) From where? (c) When? (d) Why? 4. Why can't the

Excavated artifacts displayed at the museum at Marksville.

typical Louisiana Indian or the typical Louisiana Indian house be described? 5. To which general United States Indian group do Louisiana Indians belong? 6. (a) Why did Indians live in tribes? (b) What is a tribe? (c) A confederacy? 7. List contributions made by the Indians. 8. Describe Louisiana Indians in general.

Sources of Indian History

We are largely indebted to **archaeologists** for what we know about prehistoric Indians. These scientists have excavated the sites of Indian **villages, burial grounds,** and **fortifications.** They have also studied **middens,** deposits of refuse, or garbage, that accumulated near residences, and **mounds,** structures built by Indians. Louisiana is rich in such findings.

Until very recently Indian sites were not protected by Louisiana law. As a result, much of the evidence left by Indians has been lost forever. Countless sites have been destroyed. It is now unlawful to dig into, alter, or take anything from a site of Indian artifacts on state or federal land without a permit. Other laws seek to protect the remaining sites.

Lagniappe—*Archaeological Sites.* The **Registry of State Cultural Resource Landmarks** lists archaeological sites for the state of Louisiana. Property owners and the state protect them from vandals, destruction, or unprofessional digs. Permits can be granted to archaeologists and researchers with proper tools.

Choctaw village near the Tchefuncte.

The earliest accounts of Louisiana Indians were left by members of Hernando (er NÄN dō) de Soto's 1540s expedition. More than a century and a half passed before other Europeans left records of their observations. Henri de Tonti (TÔN tē) and other members of Robert Cavalier (ka və LYĒR) de La Salle's (deh lə SAL or lə SÄL) expedition, missionary priests, and others left their records.

Indians themselves depended upon oral history. The Indians passed on stories of the past from one generation to another by one person telling it to another. Therefore, the story taken from the spoken words of Indians themselves was entangled with **legends** as the story was passed down. Many of the legends were shared by different Indian groups.

En Partie 2 (Studying a Part). 1. (a) How have we obtained information regarding prehistoric Indians? (b) How complete is this information? 2. How do archaeologists work? 3. Where are Indian artifacts found? 4. How is our Indian heritage protected by the government? 5. (a) How have we obtained information about historic Indians? (b) How accurate is this information?

Prehistoric Period

The way of life, or **culture,** of prehistoric man in Louisiana passed through three major periods. Each lasted thousands of years.

① **Paleo-Indians.** The first culture to develop in Louisiana came in the **Paleo-Indian era** (PĀ lē ō). Scientists have found sites dating back to the earliest Indian cultures.

The Paleo-Indians moving into this land of Louisiana did not find the same plant and animal life that we know today. The western half of the Louisiana area was probably one vast prairie. Large **buffaloes, mammoths, mastodons, horses, sloths,** and **peccaries** roamed over the rich land. The only coastal areas where the Indians could live were slightly high places like beach ridges, natural levees, and river terraces. The presence of water, salt, chert (a rock used for arrowheads), and an abundance of animal and plant life for food made it possible for the Indians to live in Louisiana.

Louisiana's Paleo-Indians had the simplest of social organizations. They were **nomads**—people who migrated with the seasons—who needed only temporary shelter. They made these shelters with tree branches, grass, and hides.

Big-game hunting was an important part of the lives of the Paleo-Indians. They developed weapons and fine spearpoints according to their needs.

② **The Meso-Indians** (MES ō), or **Archaic Indians.** After thousands of years, the way of life of prehistoric man in Louisiana changed. Nobody is sure why this change occurred. Perhaps the large game animals that had furnished a food supply became extinct. Possibly new groups of people arrived in Louisiana. For whatever the reason, around 5000 B.C., a new cultural period called the **Archaic era** replaced the old Paleo-Indian era.

Archaic man was a **hunter,** but he depended more on gathered foods than the people who came before him. Archaic man also had more **tools.** He fashioned scrapers, knives, axes, choppers, picks, and drills from stone, or sometimes from bone. He also made flint points that were put on darts and hurled by using a spear thrower or atlatl (AT əl AT əl). He produced stone beads, stone pipes, and stone mortars and pestles with which to grind seeds and nuts. It was Archaic man who tamed the **dog.**

He was still **nomadic.** However, he stayed longer than before at one place before moving on. He did not go as far from home as his ancestors had.

The climate was warmer during the Archaic Age, which followed the Ice Age. Indians found some of the same plants and animals that we know today. There were **different animals** than Paleo-Indians had known. Rivers and smaller streams were filled with fish, mussels, and clams. Louisiana had more lush **grasslands** than today. Large deltas and coastal marshes were developing along the Gulf coast. Natural levees developed higher and higher as the streams flooded their banks with sediment brought from the north.

There were many choices to replace the big-game diet of the Paleo-Indians. These Indians enjoyed Louisiana shellfish. Large quantities of oysters, clams, and many other kinds of seafood were available from the coast. Indians ate large numbers of deer and wild turkey. The alligator was also used for food.

It is believed that these Indians probably heated rocks and then dashed them with water to make steam to cook their food. Archaeologists found large deposits of fire-cracked gravel, suggesting that the Indians used the red-hot rocks to bake or steam their food. Large numbers of intact snail shells found in the area suggest that the people steamed the snails and then removed the cooked flesh without breaking the shells. Since this was a preceramic period, these people did not have pottery vessels for cooking over fire.

In the late 1960s archaeologists discovered mounds of these Indians at four locations in the southeastern part of the state. The locations are on Avery Island and in or near Baton Rouge. In the 1990s other mounds were found in Lincoln, Ouachita, and St. Landry parishes.

Building on these mounds started about 5,400 years ago. These people lived at these sites over hundreds of years. They are about 1,900 years older than the mounds of Poverty Point and elsewhere in Louisiana. Therefore they make up the oldest known earthen structures in North America.

The Neo-Indians. The final cultural era of the prehistoric period in Louisiana was called Neo-Indian. It lasted from 2000 B.C. to 1600 A.D. During this era, the Indians learned to make **pottery.** They regularly built shell and earthen mounds. They began to use the **bow** and **arrow** for hunting. The development of **farming** was the most important event that occurred in the Neo-Indian era. Some Indians learned how to plant crops for food, allowing them to settle down in one place. Corn, beans, and squash were important crops.

The **Poverty Point** Indian culture belonged to the Neo-Indian period. The political and religious center for the entire culture was located in Louisiana. These Indians were located at Poverty Point on the west bank of Bayou Macon (MAY son) in West Carroll Parish at Epps. Macon Plateau is a stretch of ground fifteen to twenty feet higher than the surrounding Mississippi Valley.

It was here that these people chose to lay out their city. The Indians built earthen ridges shaped like half-moons. There were six of these. They also built a series of six dirt terraces about one hundred feet wide. This was where they lived. Their palmetto-covered homes were round. They measured about fifteen feet in diameter and looked something like warm-weather igloos. It is estimated that as many as five or six thousand people lived in the village at Poverty Point.

On the west side of the village, the Poverty Point Indians built an amazing **mound.** It was about six hundred feet long and seventy feet tall. It was joined to a terrace by a long, flat platform twenty feet high. A ramp or stairway led from the platform to the top of this mound. All this the Indians built by hand. The Indians loosened the dirt with shells or stones. Then they filled baskets and animal hides with the loose dirt. The unbelievable fact is that 530,000 cubic yards of earth were moved in those baskets! The Indians constructed 11.2 miles of ridges in a geometrical design. It probably took several generations to complete the site.

These Indians used stone choppers and knives for cutting meat. They cleaned the hides of deer and other animals with stone scrapers. These scrapers were used for digging, also. Poverty Point residents did not use the bow and arrow but had spears and darts. Bolas were made with five or six heavy weights or plummets. The weights were tied to leather thongs or animal fiber and used for catching large birds like ducks, geese, turkeys, and other small animals. The Indians held the leather strings, whirled the weight around the head, and hurled it at the bird or animal. The weights wrapped the cords around the head or legs of the living target.

Mound of the Marksville Indians.

The Poverty Point culture lasted from about 2000 B.C. to 700 B.C. Archaeologists have estimated that this village was built nearly three thousand years ago. The Poverty Point culture flourished for over one thousand years at this site. By 700 B.C. it had virtually disappeared. This was probably the last time that Louisiana Indians built such massive earthworks or traded over such a large area. At its peak the Poverty Point village may have been the largest community in the entire area now covered by the United States.

The Poverty Point residents lived a thousand years before the cliff dwellers in Colorado, New Mexico, and Arizona. Their territory spread over Louisiana, Mississippi, and Arkansas. Even the Mayan and Toltec Indian cultures in Mexico and Central America either had not begun to develop or were only in the beginning stages. The culture of Greece was just beginning to develop. Old Testament prophets like Elijah, Isaiah, and Solomon were alive. Yet the Poverty Point people planned in a way we think of as modern. Their **earthwork, planned village, clay figurines, stone beads,** and **pendants** were very advanced. Many of the things done by the Indians at Poverty Point have been compared with those of the Indians of Mexico and Central America.

Artifacts recovered from the site are on display at the Poverty Point Museum. They are also shown in the Masur Museum of Art in Monroe, the Louisiana State Exhibit Museum in Shreveport, and the Smithsonian Institute in Washington, D.C.

The next Indian culture built in Louisiana was the **Tchefuncte** (che FUNK tə) culture. These people lived from 500 B.C. until A.D. 200. The Tchefuncte Indians lived in family groups with a simple lifestyle. This group of Indians was the first to make large amounts of pottery. Most of these Indians lived in the coastal areas and in the lowlands. Clams made up a big portion of their diet.

The **Marksville Indians** represented another tribal group. They built larger, more permanent settlements than the state's earlier Indians. The Marksville Indians were influenced by the Hopewell culture, which was centered in Ohio and Illinois. They built dome-shaped mounds in which they buried their dead.

The Prehistoric Indian Museum at Marksville is located on the Avoyel (ə VOI yel) prairie. The museum displays specimens of articles found in the many mounds left by these Indians. This museum visually tells the story of these Indians of the lower Mississippi Valley from about 400 B.C. until modern times.

Before the historic period, other Indian cultures developed. The Indians lived much like the Indians who had been here before them. The people lived peacefully—hunting, fishing, and gardening.

En Partie 3 (Studying a Part). 1. Make a time line of the prehistoric Indian cultures found in Louisiana. 2. Give some of the outstanding characteristics of each of the prehistoric groups. 3. (a) Locate Poverty Point on a map. (b) Describe Poverty Point culture. (c) What amazing job did the Poverty Point Indians accomplish? 4. How did life change for prehistoric Indians?

Historic Indians

When the Europeans arrived, the prehistoric era of the Indians ended. The historic period began around 1514. This means that there were now written records about the Indians. The first explorers found many tribes and bands of native people already living here. It has been estimated that **twelve to fifteen thousand** Indians made the area their home when the first explorers set foot in Louisiana.

Scholars in the past have assigned historic Louisiana Indians to various groups. Usually these groupings were based on language. Modern Louisiana Indians have traced their ancestry and made their own groupings. The Inter-Tribal Council of Louisiana, the organization of Indians which handles concerns of their people, names Louisiana's historic Indian groups. The Council's groups include the Atakapa (ə TAK ə paw), Caddo or Kadohadacho (KAD ō hə dä choh), Chitimacha (chit ə MÄCH ə), Choctaw (CHOK taw), Coushatta (kə SHAT ə), Koasati (ko ə SÄ tē), Houma (HOO mə or HŌ mə), and Tunica (TŪ ni kə).

The **Atakapa** area extended from Bayou Teche to the Sabine River and from Opelousas to the coastal marshes. This large group included the **Opelousas**. They were semi-settled, agricultural people. They established their villages along waterways. In 1942 all known villagers of the last Atakapa village were dead.

The **Caddo (Kadohadacho)** applied collectively to an important group of approximately twenty-five tribes. The **Adai** (Ā dï) tribe lived near the present site of Robeline. The Caddo area covered the present states of Arkansas, Louisiana, and Oklahoma. Their culture was different from other Louisiana groups in several ways. They allied themselves with the plains cultures. Unlike the others, they readily accepted horses. They were known for their beautiful pottery. Because of increased interference by whites, the Indian agent purchased their lands. The Caddos migrated to Texas. Life there was no better. Finally, on August 1, 1859, the Caddos migrated to the Indian territory in Oklahoma. By the end of the nineteenth century, the importance of the Caddos as a distinct tribe was at an end. Survivors merged with other tribes.

The **Chitimachas** inhabited two villages. One group was located along the upper reaches of Bayou Lafourche near the Mississippi River. The other group was located on Grand Lake and in the Bayou Teche area. The **Chawasha** (chə WASH ə), **Tensas** (TEN saw), and the **Washa** (WASH əw) were Chitimacha tribes. When the Cajuns moved into their territory in the 1760s, they often married the Chitimachas. Within a century full bloods became scarce. Cajun French was spoken by the Indians, and they converted to the Roman Catholic church.

The **Choctaw** was the second largest tribe in the southeastern United States. The Choctaws served as guides for the European expeditions across Louisiana. This relationship resulted in many Choctaw words being used as place names throughout the state.

Prior to 1778 Choctaw communities moved from north-central Louisiana to LaSalle, Rapides, Jackson, and Grant parishes. Choctaws lived in the vicinity of two sawmill towns—Jena and Eden. Other Choctaw communities were scattered throughout the Florida parishes north of Lake Pontchartrain.

The Choctaws migrated to the west of the Mississippi in search of farmland and peace. Between 1801 and 1830 they were methodically negotiated off their tribal homelands. A considerable number remained in Mississippi.

Smaller bands migrated to northern and central Louisiana. The **Jena Band of Choctaw** live northeast of Alexandria.

The **Coushattas (Koasatis)** migrated through Georgia, Alabama, Mississippi, Louisiana, and Texas in search of unclaimed land. They looked for a place to reestablish their peaceful agricultural way of life.

By the beginning of the Civil War in 1861, some 250 Coushattas had settled along the Calcasieu River near Kinder. Their peaceful and prosperous existence was again lost when American settlers became interested in Coushatta lands. In 1884 most of the Coushattas remaining in Louisiana moved to a site fifteen miles east of the Calcasieu River and three miles north of Elton in Allen Parish.

The French explorer La Salle first encountered the **Houma** tribe in 1682. The meeting was in the area now known as Wilkinson County, Mississippi, and West Feliciana (fə lish i AN ə) Parish, Louisiana, near Angola. This was the first known contact with Europeans. When the French returned to the area in 1700, half of the

Red River dugout canoe.

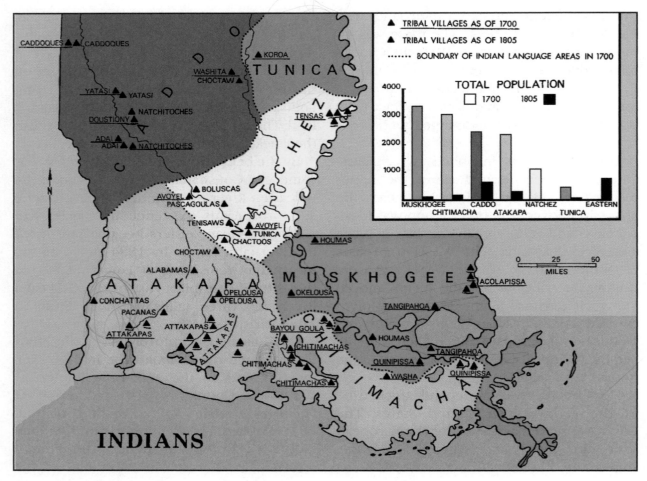

Historical tribal locations.

Houma tribe had died of abdominal flu. During much of the 1700s they migrated from place to place searching for a suitable location for resuming their agricultural economy. They settled briefly on the Mississippi River near Donaldsonville. From 1820 to 1840 the Houmas migrated farther south until they reached the Gulf of Mexico. They settled along the bayous and swamps in Terrebonne (TER ruh bô or TER bon) and Lafourche (lə FOORSH) parishes. The Houmas shared this territory with the French Acadians and gradually adopted the French language and Catholic religion. Tribes which apparently merged with the Houmas include the **Acolapissas** (ak ə la PI səs), **Bayougoulas** (bə yoo GOO lə), **Mugulasha** (MŌŌ gōō ləh shə), **Quinapissa** (ki nə PI sə), and **Tangipahoa**.

Tradition and early records indicate that the **Tunica** tribe lived in northwestern Mississippi and neighboring parts of Arkansas. Parties were scattered throughout northeastern Louisiana to boil salt that they traded. They had a village on the Ouachita as late as 1687. In 1706 they feared attacks by the Chickasaws and other Indians allied with the English. The Tunicas abandoned their villages and moved to the Houma townsite opposite the mouth of the Red River. They soon rose against their hosts, killed more than half, and drove the rest away.

Sometime between 1784 and 1803 they again abandoned their villages. They moved up the Red River to the Marksville prairie. There they settled on a strip of land formerly owned by the **Avoyel** Indians. This land was recognized as the Indians' Reserve. Their mixed-blood descendants have continued to occupy the land. A part of them went farther west and joined the Atakapas, and another part moved to the Chickasaw Nation in Oklahoma. They settled there along the Red River.

The **Biloxi** (bi Luk si) was a Siouan (SUE ən) tribe. In 1763 they settled near the mouth of the Red River. They must have soon moved to the neighborhood of Marksville. Later they sold or abandoned this site. They moved to Bayou Rapides (rap PEDZ). From there they moved to the mouth of the Rigolet de Bon Dieu (RIG uh lē ēz bôn dew). Finally, between 1794 and 1796, they crossed to the south side to Bayou Boeuf below a band of Choctaws.

On May 5, 1805, they sold their lands. However, the Biloxis remained in the immediate neighborhood. They gradually died out or fused with the Tunicas at Marksville and Choctaws where they still reside. A large group moved to Texas.

Each Indian group included several tribes. The territory claimed by each group had no specific boundaries. However, the territory claimed by each was recognized by the others. Within such territories one basic language was spoken. All the people felt a sort of kinship, which exerted an influence against fighting within their group. Groups speaking the same language often banded together to form a confederacy. They stood together against outside tribes with different languages and different customs.

By 1700 most of the Indians no longer built mounds. They lived in small villages along the rivers and streams. They mostly farmed. However, they continued to hunt, fish, and gather.

The coming of the Europeans brought quick changes in the Indian culture. Most, if not all, Indians developed a trade system with the Europeans. The Indians furnished salt, horses, furs, and other goods for them. The white men gave the Indians glass beads, bottles, guns, ammunition, knives, ceramics, bells, and bracelets. Whiskey was traded to the Indians for their furs. The white man's diseases, such as measles and smallpox, killed many Indians. The Indians no longer were the only humans here. The Europeans took more and more of the land. Thus, Indians lost their freedom to live as they chose. They could no longer move as they wished in the vast wilderness. Since Louisiana Indians were located between the French and the Spanish, both groups attempted to control Indian trade and secure the Indians as allies in conflicts with each other. Tribes combined to survive the advance of the Europeans.

Finally, the United States government tried to protect the Indians to some extent. Mistreatment of the Indians by some

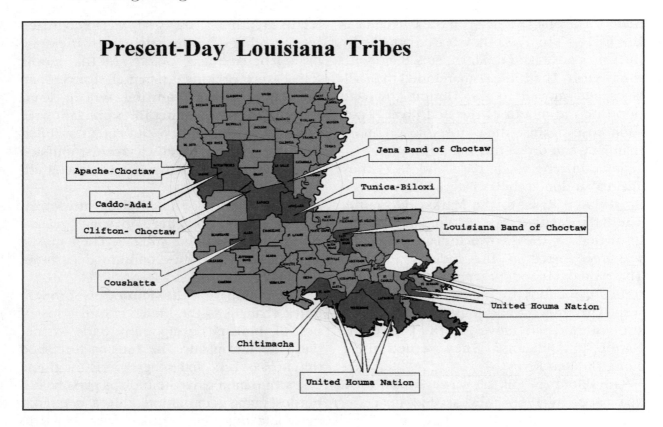

Present-Day Louisiana Tribes

Jena Band of Choctaw

Apache-Choctaw

Tunica-Biloxi

Caddo-Adai

Louisiana Band of Choctaw

Clifton- Choctaw

Coushatta

United Houma Nation

Chitimacha

United Houma Nation

whites, trespassing by whiskey traders and unlawful hunters, and other offenses finally brought action. Indian agencies were established. Dr. John Sibley was appointed United States Indian agent for Louisiana in 1805. He lived at Natchitoches.

After the Louisiana Purchase in 1803, more white settlers began pushing into the Indian territory. The ancient domain of the Indians began to slip completely from their grasp. In May, 1830, Congress passed the Indian Removal Act. Funds were provided for the government to **relocate** the Five Civilized Tribes from their lands east of the Mississippi. Some Indians moved through the state on their way to Oklahoma Indian territory. Some ended their westward walk in Louisiana.

During this time some Indian groups granted away most of their homelands.

Life changed for many Louisiana Indians with the arrival of the lumber companies sometime around 1900. The Indians benefited when they were hired by lumbering companies. At the same time they were victimized by these companies. They purchased Indian lands for pennies an acre. Gradually the Indians lost most of their lands.

Lagniappe—*Indian Reservation.* The **Bureau of Indian Affairs** is the arm of the federal government established to aid and protect the Indians. The reservations are acres of land held in trust for the Indians by the United States government. They provide room for residences and businesses, as well as recreational spaces.

The intermarriages of Indians and other ethnic groups brought changes in Indian life. The cultural patterns of the Indians changed. The French language was adopted by some groups. The Roman Catholic religion replaced the traditional Indian beliefs. Even the basic economics of Indians changed. They learned that cash was more desirable than land, and in some cases their lands were sold.

The story for each tribe differs slightly, but the pattern was much the same. Most of them migrated from one place to another looking for a location for a peaceful home. In so doing, they united with other groups, and some lost their identity. Thus present-day Indians have had problems documenting their existence.

En Partie 4 (Studying a Part). 1. Why is this period called "historic"? 2. Approximately how many Indians were here when the explorers came? 3. How did (a) the white man affect the Indian's life? (b) Indians affect the white man's? 4. (a) How was life different for historic Indians? (b) How was it the same?

Present-Day Indians

Before 1970 the census takers classified the people. Most Indians were grouped as nonwhite. Now each person counted classifies himself.

Many Louisianians are of partial Indian descent. However, very few full-blooded Indians live in the state now. Louisiana had nine state-recognized tribes in 1996. There are a few other small Indian groups scattered throughout the state.

The recognized groups include the following: **Chitimachas** at Charenton (sha reen DON), **Coushattas** at Elton, **United Houma Nation** at Dulac, **Jena Band of Choctaw** at Jena, **Apache-Choctaw** at Ebarb, **Clifton-Choctaw** at Gardner, **Tunica-Biloxi** at Marksville, **Caddo-Adai** at Robeline, and **Louisiana Band of Choctaws** at Baker. Of these, only four receive federal recognition and benefits given to such recognized tribes. These are the Chitimachas, Coushattas, Tunica-Biloxis, and Jena Band of Choctaw.

All of these Louisiana Native Americans have a long history of struggling to gain recognition as sovereign nations. With that designation there are certain benefits. Each tribe has its own identity and its own government. State laws do not apply on federally recognized reservations. This means that these sovereign nations are independent and may enter into contracts. Each tribe has to document that it has had a continuous form of government for generations. It has to establish the genealogy and tribal history, and it must still have a language.

The **Chitimacha** received federal recognition in 1925. The reservation had existed since 1919. This is the only group of Louisiana Indians which lives on or near the homeland of their ancestors. About 863 Chitimachas live on the reservation at Charendon near Baldwin in St. Mary Parish. Chitimachas continue to make beautiful cane baskets. In 1993 the tribe's Cypress Bayou Casino opened.

In the early 1900s the **Coushatta** reservation was established at Elton. In 1981 it received federal recognition. There are 680 tribe members, but all of them do not live on the reservation. The Coushatta—or Koasatis as they were once known—have their own language, which is purely oral. The language has never been written. The tribe is known for its pine needle baskets. In January, 1995, the Coushatta Grand Casino opened at Kinder. The tribe has a flourishing aquaculture industry. The Coushattas work their own rice fields. They now display and market their artistry in the retail complex located on the reservation.

The largest group of Indians in the state is the **United Houma Nation**. There are 17,950 tribe members in southeast Louisiana. Prior to 1765 the Houmas traded with the French explorers. As a result, the United Houma adopted French as its first language. Most Houmas speak French. This tribe is known for the baskets, hats, mats, and fans they weave with palmetto. Also notable are the tribe's moss dolls, wood carvings, and culinary skills.

The **Tunica-Biloxi's** 150-acre reservation near Marksville was established in 1982. About 283 Indians live there. There are 707 people on the tribal rolls. The ones not on the reservation are living elsewhere, not necessarily in Louisiana. The Tunica-Biloxi is the state's only tribe that operates a conservation lab for its cultural artifacts. The tribe was the second one to open a land-based casino. The Grand Casino complex in Avoyelles opened in mid-1994.

Jena Band of Choctaw is perhaps the smallest tribe in Louisiana. There are 188 residents on the reservation. Only twelve members still speak fluent Choctaw, and they are teaching it to the younger generations. The Jena-Choctaws plan a casino. The tribe has a contract pending with the state.

Coushatta Indian.

The **Apache-Choctaw** tribe descends from the Lipan Apache slaves who married into the Choctaw tribe. It now has about nine hundred members.

Clifton-Choctaws have been in the central Louisiana area since the early 1800s. There are approximately five hundred members.

Caddo-Adai is the newest tribe. It was recognized by the state in 1992. However, the Caddo-Adai may be the oldest residents of this area. They have been recorded in the Natchitoches area since 1529.

Several Indian tribes have taken steps toward regaining ownership of much of Louisiana's state-owned, as well as privately owned, lands in a legal fight. The Caddos have filed lawsuits. They sued for the difference in what they were paid for their land and what it was worth at the time they gave it up. They have won one suit and lost one.

In 1977 the Chitimacha Tribe of Louisiana filed a suit against eighty-two defendants. The tribe wanted to recover damages for the occupancy of what is allegedly the property of the Chitimachas. The suit asked for oil, gas, and mineral leases and titles to lands in St. Mary Parish. According to their claims, this land is their original territory. The suit claimed that the land is subject to the protection of acts between the Chitimacha tribe and the French crown in 1767 and the Spanish crown in 1777. The acts were carried forward by the Louisiana Purchase, according to the suit filed. The lands include the center of the ancient Chitimacha tribal territory. The Chitimachas lost this suit.

Most Indians in Louisiana have lost their old ways of life. After World War II they entered the labor forces and merged with American life. They live like their white neighbors. Many Louisiana Indians are bilingual. Some speak at least four languages. These languages include various Indian languages as well as French and English. Interest has been shown in preserving the Indian languages, tribal songs, dances, and crafts such as basket-weaving.

The future seems much brighter for Louisiana's Native Americans. Since the Indian involvement in the gaming industry, a better standard of living has been possible for some. The dangers of gambling, however, could easily outweigh the short-term benefits.

Lagniappe—*Indian Schools.* Indian children were not permitted to attend public schools in Louisiana until the sweeping changes of desegregation. In the 1960s, Indian children were no longer relegated to black schools, if any were provided. The Choctaws had a Louisiana-supported school in Huey Long days, followed by one for the Chitimachas supported by U.S. Indian funds. Mrs. Charles Penick became well known as the education advocate for Indian children and brought many improvements. Rural schools in poor parishes provided little schooling for children of any race and funds were not available to improve the situation. Today, the reservations are better tended and financed. Some have a building and an attendant available to children when the school bus brings them home. Poor educational opportunities did not prevent many skills being taught by the elders. Many Indians have had higher education offered after time in the armed forces, where they have conducted themselves with honor and distinction. Indian children, as others, are schooled under the **LEAP** program of tests.

Louisiana established an office of Indian affairs in 1972 to help meet the needs of the Indian communities. The office is also responsible for working with the federal, state, and local governments on matters pertaining to Indians. Since May 1975 the Inter-Tribal Council of Louisiana has provided the leadership to meet the needs of the state's Indians.

En Partie 5 (Studying a Part). 1. Locate and name Louisiana's Indian reservations. 2. Why are the pre-1970 population figures inaccurate? 3. Why have Louisiana Indians received more publicity in the 1990s than ever before? 4. How has this development affected their lives? 5. Describe Indian life in the state today.

Present-day Louisiana Indians are still questioning the rights of the white man to this land. In 1774 the French writer and explorer **Le Page du Pratz** (le pazh du PRĀ) recorded the feelings of a Natchez Indian chief, Tattooed Serpent, about the same subject.

Why . . . did the French come into our country? We did not go to seek them: they asked for land of us because their country was too little for all the men that were in it. We told them they might take land where they pleased, there was enough for them and for us: that it was good the same sun should enlighten us both, and that we would walk as friends in the same path; and that we would give them our provisions, assist them to build and to labor in the fields. We have done so; is not this true? What occasion then had we for Frenchmen? Before they came, did we not live better than we do, seeing we deprived ourselves of a part of our corn, our game, and fish, to give a part to them? In what respect, then, had we occasion for them? Was it for their white, blue, and red blankets? We can do well enough with buffalo skins which are warmer—our women wrought feather blankets for the winter, and mulberry-mantles for the summer; which indeed were not so beautiful; but our women were more laborious and less vain than they are now. In time, before the arrival of the French, we lived like men who can

be satisfied with what they have; whereas at this day we are like slaves, who are suffered to do as they please.

Coup de Main
(Completing the Story)

Jambalaya (Putting It All Together)

1. Describe how life changed for Indians from prehistoric to present days. Include changes in (a) transportation, (b) animal life, (c) ways to make a living, (d) ways to meet basic needs, and (e) education.

2. Identify by name and location the early and modern Louisiana Indians.

3. Explain how geographical factors affected the way Indians lived, where they settled, and how they made a living.

4. Explain the reasons it is a problem to get a true picture of Louisiana Indians.

Potpourri (Getting Involved)

1. Prepare a map of Louisiana showing (a) location of prehistoric Indian sites, or (b) location of historic sites.

2. Make a model of (a) an Indian village, (b) an Indian house, (c) an Indian tool, (d) an animal trap used by the Indians, or (e) one or more Indian weapons.

3. Demonstrate how Louisiana Indians (a) farmed, (b) secured food, (c) made

arrowheads, (d) played games, (e) dressed, (f) danced, (g) talked, (h) cooked, or (i) made pottery.

4. Research (a) carbon-14 dating, (b) Indian warfare, (c) the practices of medicine men, (d) Indian legends, (e) forms of amusement, (f) Indian music, or (g) the history of any tribe.

5. On a map trace the migration of an Indian tribe.

6. Produce a mural, film, or play on (a) the history of Louisiana Indians from their origin to present or (b) the struggles between the Indian and the white man.

7. Compare and contrast the Indians in Louisiana with Indians from other areas.

8. Pretend that you are (a) an Indian boy or girl in Louisiana before the first Europeans arrived, (b) the first European to visit Louisiana, or (c) an Indian being driven westward by the white man. Write a letter or diary entry describing your feelings.

Gumbo (Bringing It Up-To-Date)

1. Research (a) Louisiana's present Indians, telling how and where they live, (b) a Louisiana Indian tribe from the time it left the state until today, (c) lawsuits involving Louisiana Indians, (d) Louisiana's Indian reservations, or (e) the role of federal and state governments in present-day Indian affairs.

2. Prepare an exhibit or bulletin board entitled (a) "Indians—Then and Now" or (b) "Indians Today."

3. Research Louisiana's Indian gaming industry. Relate it to gambling in the rest of the United States.

Lagniappe—*Racial Identity.* This textbook has chosen the term **black** to identify Africans or persons of African descent. Negro and colored are terms used in the past and various groups have declared those to be undesirable names. Afro-American and African-American are also used, though that would not reflect the origin of the islanders. In Louisiana, during the time of slavery and until the early 1900s, Negro was an acceptable term. The Society for the Advancement of Colored People brought colored into popularity in its activities. This term was replaced by blacks in today's integrated society and appears in the media as the proper and acceptable name for those of African descent.

In newspapers and magazines, black is often used. The term African-American is still often heard on television, in particular newscasts and at award shows. So many television performers are blacks and no reference is made to any name in the situation comedies.

This text distinguishes between blacks, Indians, or Native-Americans, and immigrant populations that are sometimes people of color. It is the intent of the choice of the word black to be used as a generic term covering persons of African descent in narration of historical events and today's operations and plans. Negro or Negroes is not used.

CHAPTER 3

LOUISIANA'S EXPLORERS (1519-1687)

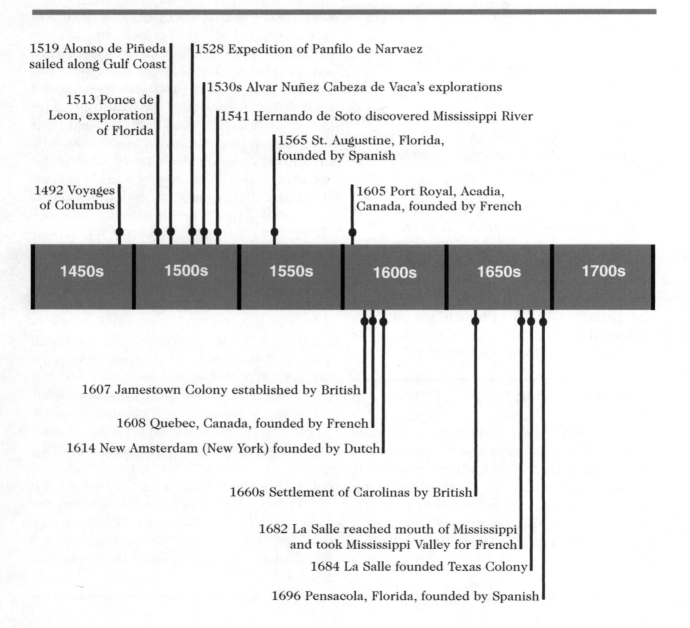

1519 Alonso de Piñeda sailed along Gulf Coast

1513 Ponce de Leon, exploration of Florida

1492 Voyages of Columbus

1528 Expedition of Panfilo de Narvaez

1530s Alvar Nuñez Cabeza de Vaca's explorations

1541 Hernando de Soto discovered Mississippi River

1565 St. Augustine, Florida, founded by Spanish

1605 Port Royal, Acadia, Canada, founded by French

| 1450s | 1500s | 1550s | 1600s | 1650s | 1700s |

1607 Jamestown Colony established by British

1608 Quebec, Canada, founded by French

1614 New Amsterdam (New York) founded by Dutch

1660s Settlement of Carolinas by British

1682 La Salle reached mouth of Mississippi and took Mississippi Valley for French

1684 La Salle founded Texas Colony

1696 Pensacola, Florida, founded by Spanish

LOUISIANA'S EXPLORERS

If the Vikings or others visited the North American continent earlier, it was not they who ushered in a New Age with their voyages. It was Christopher Columbus in 1492. He triggered an explosion of adventurers and explorers from Europe. Suddenly, they were out to discover what the rest of the world was like. Columbus himself had set out to find a new water route to the Orient. He thought that if he were to sail far enough to the west, he would come to Asia. He had no idea that great continents lay between Europe and Asia.

In the latter half of the 1400s, Europeans needed new and better ways of trading with the Orient. That was reason enough to believe that the nation which could solve that problem could earn vast wealth. For several hundred years Europeans had wanted many products from Asia. Sugar, glass, iron, cutlery, rugs, pepper, cloves, cinnamon, nutmeg, porcelain, and silk were some of the products they sought. They did not produce these items for themselves. An almost endless market was there for all of these items. This one fact provided incentive to navigate unchartered seas in hopes of reaching Asia.

The discovery of the New World was the result. This discovery marked the introduction of the modern era and the colonization of the New World. For two centuries European nations tried to outdo each other in claiming a share of the New World continents.

During this time, many European countries sent men to find out more about the land across the sea. Two hundred years after Columbus set foot in the Western Hemisphere, the Louisiana colony was settled. Only two countries—Spain and France— sent men to explore what is now Louisiana.

The Spanish Explorations

Columbus's voyages gave Spain claim to the islands of the Caribbean and changed the course of Spanish history. Gold was found in Mexico and Peru, and there were promises of even more. **Hernando Cortes** (kar TEZ) captured the vast treasures of Montezuma in Mexico. **Francisco Pizarro** (fran THEES co pē ZÄR ō) conquered the Incas in Peru and gained tremendous stores of gold and silver. The hope of great wealth brought other explorers. The desire for riches was not the only reason people came to the New World, however. Friars and priests also came because they

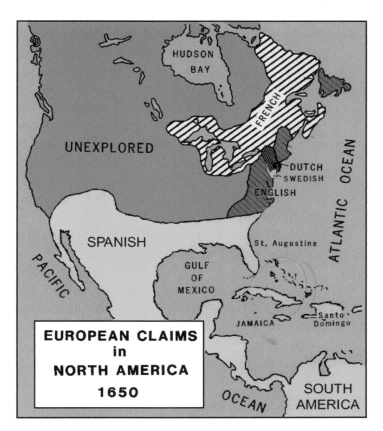

EUROPEAN CLAIMS in NORTH AMERICA 1650

wanted to spread Christianity. Other Spaniards came to escape the harsh rules of both the church and government. Others sought adventure and fame. The Spanish, then, have been described as coming to the New World for the "three Gs"—gold, God, and glory.

By 1500 the colonies that had been started in the West Indies by Spain became the bases from which numerous explorers sailed. Spaniards went to the mainland of both North and South America in search of wealth in the form of gold, silver, and precious stones. Several of the many exploring journeys or expeditions of the early 1500s had a direct impact on the history of Louisiana.

Piñeda's Journey. In 1519 the governor of Jamaica sent **Alonzo Alvarez de Piñeda** (ä LŌN sō ĂL vä räs pē NYĀ dä) to explore the Gulf of Mexico from Florida to Vera Cruz, Mexico. As his fleet sailed along the coast, he made maps of the area and showed the rivers he had discovered. Piñeda went ashore in several unnamed spots along the way. Piñeda reported that the entire coast from Florida to Vera Cruz was part of the mainland. He described the Indians as peaceful. Piñeda's map showed that the all-water route to the riches of the East was not anywhere in the Gulf area. The voyage was also important because it gave the first account of the landmass of the New World.

De Narváez's Expedition. In 1527 the king of Spain gave **Panfilo de Narváez** (pan FĒ lō dä när VĂ eth) a grant to explore and settle all land between the Cape of Florida and Rio de las Palmas (probably the Rio Grande). Early in 1528, the expedition of four hundred men, eighty-two horses, and four ships left Cuba and landed on the west coast of Florida to search for gold.

Alvar Nuñez Cabeza de Vaca (ÄHL var NOON yez käh BĀ sä dä VÄH cäh), the treasurer of Narváez's trip, was to look after the king's interest. Narváez and his men suffered many hardships. They lost their way in the swamps and forests of Florida and almost died of starvation.

They built five crude horsehide boats. Narváez and eighty weary and sick Spaniards were about halfway to their destination in November 1528 when a storm drove them to land. The coast where they found themselves was probably about where Galveston, Texas, now stands.

While most of his men slept ashore that night, Narváez stayed aboard ship. During the night, he was blown to sea. He was never seen again.

After five years of living under severe circumstances, there were only a few survivors. One of these men was Cabeza de Vaca. Other survivors were Castillo (kas TĒ yō), Dorantes (dō RAHN tes), and Estevan (es TAY vähn) or Stephen, a skillful black slave. By chance, they came to be looked upon as medicine men and were treated royally by their Indian captors.

The Spaniards left their captors and walked to Mexico City. It took eight to ten years to make the trip. In July 1536 Cabeza de Vaca, Estevan, and the other survivors finally reached Mexico City.

Hernando de Soto's Travels. De Soto was a veteran of the Spanish expeditions. He had been a lieutenant of Pizarro when they robbed the Incas of Peru. He was soon getting ships, men, and supplies ready to sail for Florida. It was done largely at his own expense.

On April 6, 1537, de Soto began his trip with one of the largest and best-equipped outfits that ever set sail for the New World. They were also used as lookouts. There were

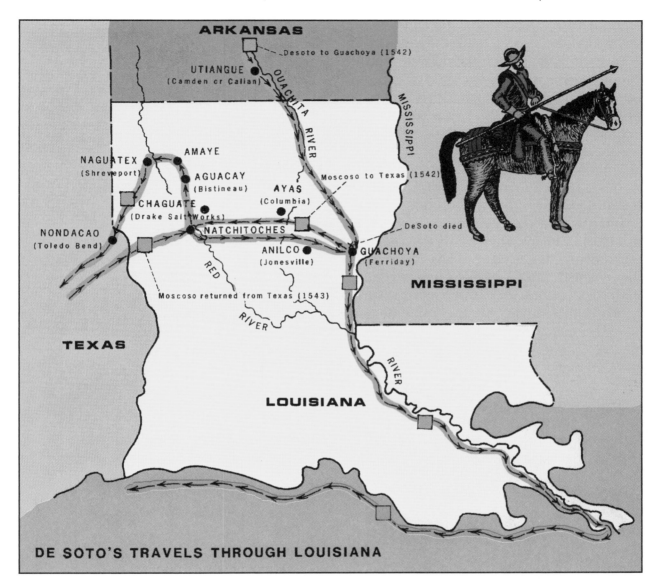

DE SOTO'S TRAVELS THROUGH LOUISIANA

about six hundred men, including twelve priests, in the party. The assemblage made a spectacular sight.

De Soto planned for everything. Such things as iron for saddlebows, spades, pickaxes, crates, ropes, and baskets, as well as many other tools, were aboard ship. The cargoes included about one hundred horses and some hogs to supply meat for the explorers.

De Soto took bloodhounds for running down escaped Indian slaves.

After visiting Havana, they finally left on May 12, 1539. On the last day of May they reached Florida. Three days after they arrived in Florida, de Soto sent some of his men to claim the land for the king of Spain. For the next few days, the ships were unloaded. Then de Soto ordered the ships to return to Cuba so that the men would not be able to use the ships to desert.

Early in the journey de Soto found a young Spaniard from the Narváez expedition. His name was Juan Ortiz (wahn ör TEEZ). Ortiz served as interpreter and helped de Soto make friends with some of the Indian chiefs.

The Spaniards had to fight their way through the country because most of the Indians were hostile. Frequently the Spaniards used their fierce dogs to frighten or kill the Indians. They also took food from the Indians. When the Indians learned that the Spanish soldiers had a big advantage with their horses, they shot the horses from beneath the riders. By the time de Soto reached the Mississippi River, more than half of his men and horses had been lost.

After two years of wandering, on May 8, 1541, the men looked through an opening in the pine forest and saw before them a mighty river. They had discovered the **Mississippi River.** They did not realize that they had found something more important than gold. Instead, they saw it as a problem; it would be difficult to cross the broad expanse of water in their search for gold.

De Soto had his men build rafts with which to cross the river. On the western side of the river, they marched through what is now Arkansas. After spending the winter in the area, they continued their journey to reach the Gulf.

Burial of de Soto.

This trip took them into present-day Louisiana. Researchers believe that de Soto and his men stopped at places in Louisiana now known as Jonesville, near Lake Bistineau (BIS tə nō); the town of Columbia; and Drake's Salt Lick near Winnfield.

Just three years after the journey started, forty-two-year-old de Soto died of a fever at an Indian village called Guachoya (WÄ CHOI yəh). This was near the present town of Ferriday, Louisiana. His body was first buried inside the walls of their little fort at the mouth of the Arkansas River. Then, when it was feared that the Indians would find the newly made grave and realize that the Spanish leader was dead, his body was dug up. It was placed in the trunk of a hollow tree, weighted down, and buried in the Mississippi River.

Luis de Moscoso (LŌŌ ēs deh mōs KŌ sō), who had been with de Soto in Peru and was the commander of one of the galleons of the expedition, became the leader. After spending the winter in Guachoya, they started down the river on July 2, 1543. About 350 soldiers and twenty-five Indian servants with thirty horses and eighteen hogs spent twenty days getting to the Gulf coast. By staying close to the coastline, they reached the Spanish colony located where the city of Tampico, Mexico, is today. Approximately 312 men reached Mexico City.

De Soto and his men found no gold, but de Soto is acknowledged as the discoverer of the Mississippi River. Knowledge of the great river spread throughout the European world. Firsthand accounts helped spread information about the trip. At least four original accounts of de Soto's travels exist.

The Spaniards failed to see the great value in the land they explored. Henceforth, they lost interest in the land that they might have claimed. For a century and a half, the Indians continued to live undisturbed by Europeans. It remained for another nation—France—to claim and settle the land that was to become the state of Louisiana.

En Partie 1 (Studying a Part). 1. What were the goals of the Spanish? 2. Why were the explorations of Piñeda, de Vaca, and de Soto important? 3. Why were the Indians hostile toward the Spanish? 4. Why was de Soto's discovery of the Mississippi River far more important than the finding of gold would have been? 5. Give reasons that the Spanish explorers should be connected to Louisiana history.

French Explorations

The history of Louisiana has its origins in the ambitions of Louis XIV and the French settlers in Canada. French expeditions spread from Canadian settlements to the Mississippi Valley in the latter part of the seventeenth century.

New France was the land now known as Canada. The French started settling it only a year after the English planted their first settlement at Jamestown, Virginia. The Frenchmen strung their settlements out along streams far into the wilderness. They came down the St. Lawrence River and into the Great Lakes. That gave them an easy way to travel to other sections of the continent.

The French were concentrating on the fur-trading business. Rich Europeans clamored for furs to adorn themselves. The price was high enough for the fur business to compete with gold mining as a sure road to wealth. Fur traders kept pushing farther westward and southward. They made agreements with Indians covering areas of the vast wilderness where rich furs could be obtained.

Fur trading did not encourage large groups of settlers. A number of Frenchmen became **coureurs de bois** (ku RĀER də bwä), or **woods runners**. These people lived with the Indians or lived like the Indians. They trapped animals and sold furs. Their enterprises naturally led them into every stream, and they heard about the "Great Water" from the Indians. Curiosity about where the river went stirred the explorers into searching for the answer.

Marquette and Joliet's Trip. In 1673 Gov. Louis Frontenac of Canada ordered **Fr. Jacques Marquette** (zhak mär KET), a Jesuit priest, to go with **Louis Joliet** (LŌŌ i JŌ li a), a fur trader, on an exploration of the Mississippi River. (The French always took priests along to Christianize the Indians.) They followed the Mississippi to the mouth of the Arkansas River, but they were afraid to go farther because of possible trouble with the Spaniards. They returned by way of the Illinois River after a four-month journey. Their trip had shown that the Mississippi flowed southward.

The Journeys of René-Robert Cavelier, Sieur de La Salle (lə SAL). La Salle, a rich fur trader, heard tales about the Mississippi River. He decided to try to do what no other white man had done; he would follow the great river to its mouth. He hoped to set up a string of forts and to find a passage across the continent to the Pacific Ocean and the Far East. He also hoped to attract the fur trade of the Great Lakes region to Louisiana. La Salle had made an agreement to help finance the trip himself in exchange for trade rights.

There was another reason for La Salle's trip. The king of France, Louis XIV, wanted a harbor for French ships on the Gulf of Mexico. Spain, France's enemy, had gold and silver mines in Mexico that the king wanted to reach. In 1679 he became very angry when Spanish warships on the Gulf of Mexico captured a French ship. The king, therefore, wanted La Salle to find a harbor so French ships could harass the Spanish.

On February 6, 1682, La Salle, at the age of thirty-nine, began the historic journey. With him were his long-time friend and business partner, **Henri de Tonti,** and a priest, **Father Anastase Douay** (äh nähz TAH sē dōō Ā). With a small band of fifty-six people, they started at the Great Lakes and journeyed toward the Mississippi. Upon reaching the Mississippi, they started their canoe caravan down its long and twisting path toward the Gulf of Mexico. As they went along, they selected locations for forts and gave names to the places where they stopped. It took them more than two months

Sieur de La Salle.

La Salle takes possession of Louisiana in April 1682.

to make the journey. Finally they reached the mouth of the river and landed.

With great ceremony, on April 9, 1682, La Salle set up a cross bearing the coat of arms of France. It was inscribed "Louis the Great Reigns." It was erected amid shouts and the solemn chants of the priest leading the mass. Then, standing near the cross, La Salle read his speech. He announced the naming of the new land **"Louisiane"** for Louis XIV, king of France. The party chanted the "Te Deum (tə DĒ əm)," a song of praise to God, and they sang the song of France. Then they fired their muskets into the air. With suitable words in honor of the king, La Salle claimed for King Louis XIV of France the Mississippi River and all the land drained by the river and all its tributaries. He buried a metal plaque marking the spot. In this manner, he set up a claim to territory already explored by Spain.

La Salle was pleased with the results of his trip. He was eager to tell the king of his discoveries. As rapidly as possible, he returned to Canada and then crossed the ocean to France. He told King Louis about the Mississippi. He explained that if a French colony were established at the mouth, it would be easy to attack the Spaniards and take their wealth.

King Louis was so pleased that he approved La Salle's plan to build a fort near the mouth of the Mississippi River. He named La Salle governor of all the lands that he had claimed for France. The king outfitted four ships, gave La Salle four hundred colonists, and sent him to make a settlement where he had set up the cross.

The four ships bearing La Salle's colonists sailed from France July 24, 1684. They took a course toward the West Indies. La Salle quarreled constantly with Beaujeu (BŌ zhə), the naval commander who was in charge of the ships. At Santo Domingo La Salle became ill, and the trip to Louisiana was delayed six weeks.

The expedition missed the mouth of the Mississippi. The river waters pour into the Gulf of Mexico through three narrow passages that were not so well defined in 1684 as today. Some historians say that La Salle may have wanted to go closer to Mexico and its silver mines. Whatever the causes, La Salle and Beaujeu missed the Mississippi River entirely.

La Salle's party, in the three remaining ships, sailed four hundred miles farther to the west. They landed at Matagorda (MAT ə gôR də) Bay in what is now Texas on February 15, 1685. A storm came up suddenly and sank one ship. Another was grounded. That left only one ship. Beaujeu lost no time in returning to France in it. Beaujeu took about forty settlers with him. They took items badly needed by those left behind—priceless guns and ammunition, food, supplies, and clothing. La Salle and about two hundred settlers were left stranded in an area of hostile Indians.

In 1685 La Salle directed the construction of a fort at Garcitas (gar SĒ təs) Creek. He named it Fort St. Louis. With scant supplies, La Salle and the little colony, which had dwindled to about forty-five people, survived for two years. La Salle hoped to get to Canada and seek help for the colony. Canada was 1,500 miles away. Twice, La Salle and a party started out but finally had to return to Matagorda Bay. It was March 1687 when a third and final attempt was made.

On March 18, 1687, La Salle was assassinated. Many stories exist about the assassination. At least one reason given for his assassination is strange indeed. According to that version, La Salle's men were sitting around a campfire eating wild game that they had roasted. La

Salle's nephew was in the group. A quarrel arose over who was to have the privilege of eating the marrow from the bones of the animal. In the fight that followed, the nephew was killed. Nobody wanted to tell La Salle. They knew that they would pay with their own lives. Therefore, they killed La Salle when he returned to the camp.

Another version has it that La Salle's murder was planned by angry followers. According to this story, the assassin had slashed the heads of La Salle's nephew, his servant, and an Indian guide while they were sleeping. When La Salle came upon the scene, he was murdered.

When the Spanish heard rumors that a French settlement had been established in

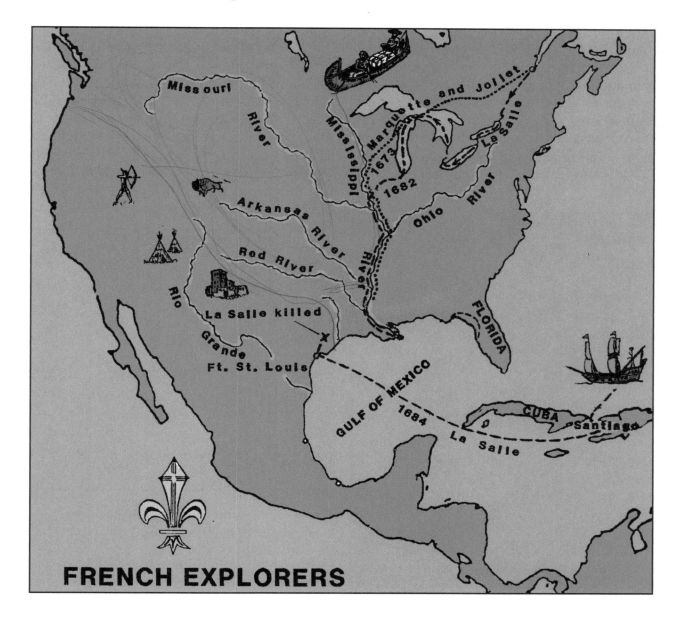

FRENCH EXPLORERS

Texas, they sought to find it. Four expeditions went to search for La Salle's colony. In 1689 a Spanish party found the ruins of the doomed settlement on Matagorda Bay. It is known that many of the handful left at Fort St. Louis had died of disease long before La Salle was killed. It is believed that the Indians killed all except a young man and some young children.

One of the survivors of La Salle's second expedition kept a diary, which provides information about La Salle's trip. The story of how La Salle's friend **Tonti** received his nickname is included. The name "Iron Hand" was given to Tonti by the Indians. While serving in the French army, he had lost his hand in battle. He received his nickname because of a metal device that replaced his hand.

Tonti and La Salle had long been partners in a fur-trading business. They operated from a post on the Great Lakes. Tonti was in Canada when La Salle was in trouble with his new settlement, Fort St. Louis in Texas. He became alarmed about La Salle's failure to report and took an expedition down the Mississippi River to find him. For two years, Tonti searched and was unable to find any trace of La Salle. He left a note written on bark with an Indian chief somewhere near the mouth of the Mississippi River.

La Salle made a place for himself in Louisiana history as well as in the history of the world. He was the first man to fully explore the Mississippi from its upper waters to its mouth. La Salle was the first white man to appreciate the size and importance of the Mississippi Valley. It was because of his efforts that the French eventually became interested in colonizing the great Mississippi Basin.

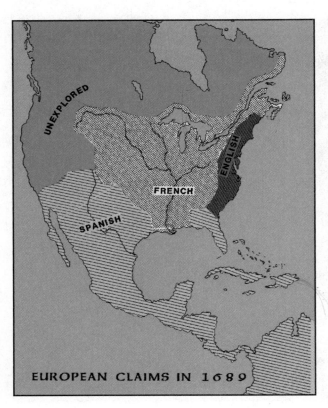

EUROPEAN CLAIMS IN 1689

En Partie 2 (Studying a Part). 1. What were the purposes of La Salle's expedition? 2. Describe the ceremony at the mouth of the Mississippi River when the land was claimed for France. 3. (a) What was the name given the land? (b) Why? 4. What area did he claim? 5. Why did the French king assist La Salle in his plans to settle Louisiana? 6. Who was Tonti? 7. Why did La Salle fail to find the Mississippi? 8. Describe La Salle's second expedition. 9. What happened to La Salle? 10. What was the importance of La Salle's explorations?

Coup de Main
(Completing the Story)

Jambalaya (Putting It All Together)

1. Make a chart using the following headings. In chronological order, fill in the information. Explorer; Country; Date; Purpose; Area Explored; Results.

2. On a map, trace the routes of the Louisiana explorers and show the territory claimed by La Salle.

3. Which European country had the first claim to Louisiana?

4. Which European country next explored Louisiana?

5. (a) Which country had the best claim? (b) Justify your answer.

6. What is the relationship between the following?

a. deVaca's journey	Narváez's journey
b. Coronado's expedition	Louisiana explorations
c. Tonti	La Salle
d. de Soto	Moscoso
e. de Soto	Indian trouble
f. Explorers	Poor travel and communication
g. Explorers	Westward travel
h. Goal of exploration	Success

Potpourri (Getting Involved)

1. Imagine that you made one of the trips with a Louisiana explorer. Give reasons why you were selected. Tell about your experiences. Include the preparations for the trip.

2. Pretend that you were an Indian boy or girl who watched the landing of a ship loaded with an exploring expedition. Tell what you saw, how you felt, and how you greeted the visitors. Tell how you were treated by them.

3. Describe the lifestyle of the *coureurs de bois*.

4. Make a model of (a) the type ships used by the explorers or (b) Fort St. Louis.

5. Make a time line showing various expeditions, settlements, and wars during the period of exploration of Louisiana. Show what was happening in the rest of North America and/or the world.

Gumbo (Bringing It Up-to-Date)

1. Report on any part Louisiana has in current explorations.

2. Compare: (a) La Salle's trip with a trip in space, (b) the support given to the early explorers by people from their home countries with the support given to the space programs in the United States and Russia, (c) the reasons for interest in the New World with the reasons for interest in space, or (d) the preparation for a trip by an early explorer with preparations for a space trip.

3. Research the archaeological findings of recent years of any of the expeditions.

Overleaf: *St. Denis confers with the Natchitoches Indians.*

PART TWO

During the French Colonial Period

n.b.Wright

CHAPTER 4

FRENCH COLONIZATION (1699-1713)

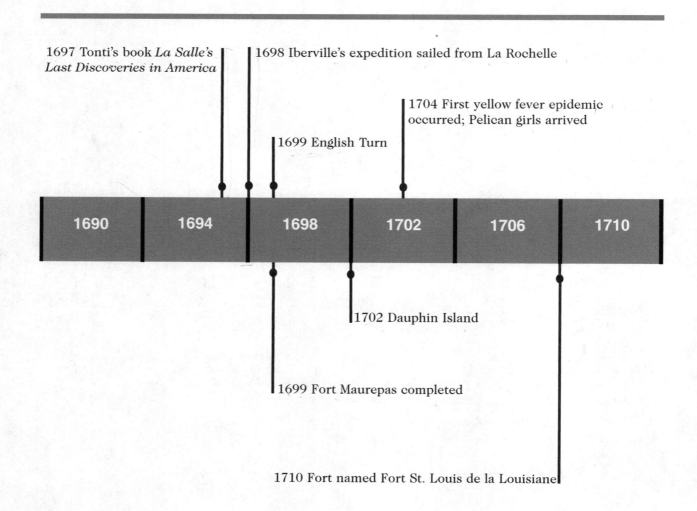

1697 Tonti's book *La Salle's Last Discoveries in America*

1698 Iberville's expedition sailed from La Rochelle

1704 First yellow fever epidemic occurred; Pelican girls arrived

1699 English Turn

| 1690 | 1694 | 1698 | 1702 | 1706 | 1710 |

1702 Dauphin Island

1699 Fort Maurepas completed

1710 Fort named Fort St. Louis de la Louisiane

FRENCH COLONIZATION

By 1690 France was at war in Europe. That was three years after La Salle died. The peace treaty was signed in 1697. Because of the war and the spending of Louis XIV, France had no money for foreign investments. **King Louis XIV** had constructed a palace at great cost at Versailles. To plant a colony required vast sums of money. France could not afford to settle its Louisiana colony. Yet, if France did not take possession of the land, other nations could claim Louisiana.

One book was written by La Salle's friend **Henri de Tonti**. The book *La Salle's Last Discoveries in America* was published in

King Louis XIV of France.

1697. Tonti gave reasons why France should hasten to cinch its claim to Louisiana by planting a colony there. The colony would be located at the mouth of the Mississippi River. It would be close to the silver mines of Mexico. From the colony, France could seek to capture these mines. Along the coast Louisiana had a wealth of fur-bearing animals. Louisiana, at the mouth of the Mississippi, was the gateway to Canada, which the French owned. The colony would prevent their rival, England, from settling in the area. Such arguments excited the French people about France establishing a colony in the Mississippi Valley.

The other enthusiastic explorer was **Father Louis Hennepin**. He had been on one of La Salle's expeditions. Later he became a subject of Great Britain. He wrote two books, which were published in England. In his books Hennepin urged England to place a colony at the mouth of the Mississippi River. These books had great influence on the decision to send another expedition to settle Louisiana.

Already there were signs that the English were preparing to settle Louisiana. They were locating settlers to send and were outfitting ships. Other nations were also showing interest in Louisiana. Among them was the Netherlands.

The Count de Pontchartrain (pôn chär TRAIN), the minister of the marine in France, supported the establishment of a colony. He knew that whoever controlled the lower Mississippi River Valley would control the "back door" to the entire continent. He convinced King Louis XIV that France had to send colonists to Louisiana as quickly as possible.

Iberville, Louisiana's First Governor

Iberville's Selection. Tonti and others had already asked that they be allowed to lead an expedition to Louisiana. These offers were rejected. Instead, the minister started the search for the most suitable leader available. Finally, he selected a young Canadian. The twenty-seven-year-old man was **Pierre Le Moyne, Sieur d'Iberville** (pē AIR leh MWAHN syur dē ber vil).

Iberville was from a large wealthy family. Charles Le Moyne and Catherine Primot had eleven children. Four of the sons became famous. The two most famous contributed to the development of Louisiana. They were Iberville and **Jean Baptiste** (jhon bap TĒST), known as **Bienville**.

Iberville's Expedition. Pontchartrain asked Iberville what he needed for his task. The list included the ships, people, and supplies for accomplishing the mission. The lieutenant asked for an eight-month supply of provisions for the ship. He required goods for six months for the fort that he planned to build in Louisiana.

About three hundred men began the voyage. The group included Iberville's eighteen-year-old brother, Bienville. As was the custom on all French expeditions, a priest went along. With Iberville and his party was **Father Anastase Douay.** The priest had been with La Salle on his first expedition down the Mississippi River to claim the territory. Father Douay could speak several Indian dialects. It was a very useful skill for one traveling in the New World.

Ten crewmen had either died on the voyage from France or were seriously ill with yellow fever. Iberville replaced them with some tough pirates. He hired a guide, Laurent de Graaf, who had explored the northern Gulf coast earlier. Iberville got information about this new land from de Graaf and the pirates.

Iberville, trained as a naval officer, kept careful records of the voyage. He took notes day by day. It is from his journal that we learn about this first settlement.

The French convoy went into the harbor at **Pensacola** on January 26, 1699. The fog lay heavy over the coast. The French were surprised to find that a large number of Spanish boats filled the harbor. Iberville dropped anchor out of range of cannons

Bienville.

that might be fired from the shore. To his surprise the Spaniards caused no problems. They were half-starved and sick. Iberville pretended to be searching for some lost Canadians. He was glad to learn about the surrounding country from the Spanish settlers. A few days later the Frenchmen sailed on along the coast to the west. The ship that had guided them from the islands returned to Santo Domingo.

On January 31, 1699, Iberville wrote that he had anchored at **Mobile Bay**. In the area he slept on an island, which he christened **Massacre Island** (MAS ə ker). It was renamed **Dauphin** (daw FIN) later.

Iberville's expedition island-hopped as it continued along the Gulf coast. They made soundings and took notes. At last, on February 10, 1699, they arrived at **Ship Island** in Biloxi Bay. It was so named because it had a natural harbor.

Iberville's expedition went farther west following a string of barrier islands. He named **Horn** and **Cat** islands. The "cats" were probably raccoons or opossums.

On February 13, 1699, Iberville and Bienville visited the **Biloxi Indians** on the mainland. There were three men and two women in the group. They chanted words of peace. Iberville gave them gifts and walked with them to their canoes. The Indians made a bread called sagamite from maize for Iberville and his men. The next day the Indians came in their canoes. By this time Iberville was able to persuade three of them to come aboard the ship. To do so, he left his brother Bienville and two other men as hostages with the Indians on shore. They smoked the calumet, or peace pipe. Then Iberville shot the cannon for them. The Indians told him about a great river to the west. They said that it could be reached by a short land journey. They called the river Malbanchia. They agreed to guide him to it. On the appointed day they failed to appear.

Some of the Indians Iberville saw wore only loincloths. Others wore breechcloth leggings, moccasins, and feather headdresses. Some wore necklaces of bone and the bills of flamingos. Others wore nose rings and earrings. These were the Biloxi Indians, a peaceful, friendly people.

En Partie 1 (Studying a Part). 1. Why were the French interested in the Mississippi Valley? 2. Why did France wait many years after La Salle's death before sending colonists? 3. Why were the Le Moyne brothers especially well prepared to begin a settlement? 4. Who headed the expedition?

The Mississippi River Trip

The Frenchmen knew that locating the Mississippi River would be difficult. The low, flat marshlands made the task hard. It was not easy to navigate among the many small islands covered with grass and tall reeds.

About the middle of February 1699 Iberville decided on a plan to find the river. One of the officers would remain at Ship Island with the fleet. Iberville and Bienville would go in one boat. Sieur de Sauvole (syur deh sō VŌL), who was an officer, and Father Douay would go in another. The search party was to return within six weeks. If it did not, Surgeres, one of the crew, would return to France in the *Marin* if provisions ran short.

On February 27, 1699, Iberville set out with two large boats and two canoes. About forty-eight men started the trip. They took

Mississippi River.

provisions for twenty days. They sailed along the coast to the west. They very carefully watched for a sign that they were approaching the great river. The fog, heavy rains, lightning, and winds made the job very difficult.

They approached the river by sailing from the Gulf into what is now known as the North Pass. After four days, on March 2, 1699, Iberville discovered fresh water. The stream became much wider. It had a swift current. As he reached the widest part, Iberville knew that this had to be the Mississippi.

The next day Iberville continued upstream. After four days, he met some **Houma Indians**. They provided him with guides. The Indians showed them a short path leading to a small bayou.

Indian friends sent word to the **Bayougoulas** and **Mongoulachas** (Mon gōō LA chə) that the French were on their way. These Indians lived not far from Bayou Plaquemine (PLAK ə min). Iberville's expedition received a very warm welcome. They were even invited to smoke the peace pipe at a nearby village. The Bayougoulas pointed out the crescent in the river to Iberville. They thought that this would be a good spot for a settlement. (The spot that the Indians pointed out is the site of present-day New Orleans.)

A description of the French and Indians meeting is given in the *Journal of Paul du Ru* (dew rew):

Everybody dresses up to meet the Bayougoulas. Beards are trimmed and fresh linen put on. Here is the landing place. Our vessels assemble to enter the port in order. The landing begins. The whole bank is black with savages who sing the Calumet to us. M. de Bienville is in the escorting canoe; M. de la Ronde is in the wooden canoe which he calls *Hardy* and M. Chateauguy (shə tō GĒ) in another wooden canoe, all with flags at the stern and all firing shots. We arrive in good form.

Iberville was still not sure that he had found the Mississippi. When he saw the Mongoulacha chief wearing a blue coat, his doubts were erased. Father Douay had told Iberville that Tonti had left his Montreal blue coat with the Indian chief. He also told him that Tonti had left a letter with the Indian chief. It was to be given to the first white men who came by. The chief did not give the letter to Iberville. He thought Iberville was a Spaniard.

The Frenchmen moved up the river. They came to a spot on which a red pole about thirty feet tall stood. It marked the boundary between the Bayougoulas and the Houma Indians. The Indians called the red stick "istrouma" in their language. The French called it **"baton rouge"** (red stick) in theirs.

The next day the Indians took the French through a sharp turn in the river. This place was called **Pointe Coupee** (kōō PĒ), (cut point). The Frenchmen traveled for two more days. They reached the Houmas village.

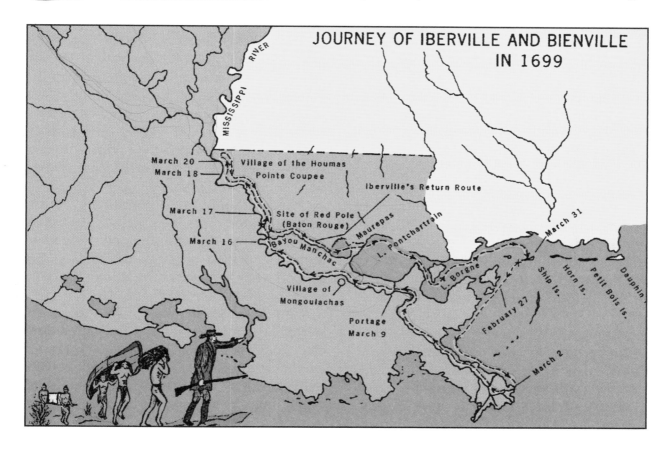

There they feasted. In turn they gave presents to the Indians. The chief of the Houmas told Iberville that Tonti had been to their village twice. Once he was on the way to the mouth of the river. Again, he came when he returned to the north.

Iberville and Bienville did not return together to Ship Island. Instead, Iberville chose to take the shortest route home. He went through **Bayou Manchac** (MAN shak). It connects the Mississippi with a lake. Iberville named it **Lake Maurepas** (mōr ē PÄ) for the son of the minister of the marine of France. From Lake Maurepas, he sailed into a larger lake. Iberville named it **Lake Pontchartrain** for the minister of the marine. Iberville found that waterways connected Lake Pontchartrain with the **Gulf of Mexico**. He sailed through them. Then he went through the Gulf waters back to Ship Island in Biloxi Bay.

Bienville, Sauvole, and the others returned the same way they had come. They went down the Mississippi River. Then they sailed out into the Gulf of Mexico and sailed east to Ship Island. Bienville's crew stopped at the Mongoulacha village to get **Tonti's letter** to La Salle. The Indians had hidden it in a hollow tree thirteen years before. For that reason, they called it "the speaking bark." The letter was final proof that the Frenchmen had found the Mississippi River. Iberville recorded a copy of Tonti's letter in his journal.

Although we have neither heard news concerning you nor seen signs of your presence, I do not doubt God will crown your affairs and your enterprise with success. I desire it with all my heart, for you do not have a more loyal servant than myself, who sacrifices everything to find you.

The two brothers arrived back at the starting point within a few hours of each other. It was just one month after starting the trip.

En Partie 2 (Studying a Part). 1. After landing, what expedition did Iberville and Bienville undertake? 2. What was the proof that they had reached their destination?

Settlement of the Colony

Fort Maurepas. Iberville selected a site on Biloxi Bay for building a fort. The French had planned to set up a colony on the Mississippi River. However, Iberville decided to place the settlement on Biloxi Bay instead. He was not sure that the ships could go through the passes at the mouth of the river. The fort was needed to secure supplies from the ships. The area was low and marshy on the coast, so he carefully selected the highest ground. It was a quiet bay. He thought there would be shelter from the winds.

Construction began on April 8. By May 1, 1699, the fort was completed. The small square fort had four bastions. On these were mounted twelve guns. A ditch was dug around the fort for protection. Iberville named it Fort Maurepas.

Many activities helped to get the colony started. Twenty-five men were ordered to clear land. Then they planted peas and beans so they would have food. Livestock were unloaded from the ships. There were bulls, cows, hogs, and fowl, including turkeys. Priests ministered to the newcomers, who

FORT MAUREPAS

worked to construct their fort. When the ships were unloaded, Iberville recorded the inventory. There were "eight casks of completely rotten peas, two kegs of spoiled bacon which had not been salted, two barrels of flour which was like dust and had soured."

Friendly Indians. Several Bayougoula braves came to the fort. Later, they returned with the chiefs of five nations. They presented Iberville with the calumet of peace and honored the French officers in their own way.

Iberville and his men gave the Indians mirrors, combs, glass beads, guns, hats, rings, and other things. Iberville's presents to the Indians also included shirts, stockings, hatchets, knives, and blankets.

The French gave the Indians picks and shovels. They showed them how to make ax handles. The Indians taught the French how best to plant seeds. They also taught them how to care for plants. They showed the Frenchmen many foods that they could find in the forests. Another important thing the Indians taught the French was the art of making "dug-out" canoes. These were canoes dug out of a single log. The Indians gave the French bearskins. The French built a good relationship with almost all of the Indians. They were not successful with the **Natchez** and the **Chickasaws,** however.

Bienville started learning about the Indians as soon as he set foot in the New World. He traveled in canoes with Indian guides. He carefully studied the Indian languages and dialects. By the time he had made a trip with the Mongoulacha guide up the river, he was able to understand the language. He could speak it with some ease.

Iberville's First Return Trip. After Iberville was sure he had arrived at the Mississippi, he was relieved. Once he planted a settlement, he decided to return to France. It was necessary to get supplies and enlist new colonists. He was eager to report to the king. He had accomplished his mission "to find the Mississippi River and chart it and to establish a fort." Iberville left Sauvole in charge. Bienville was made second in command.

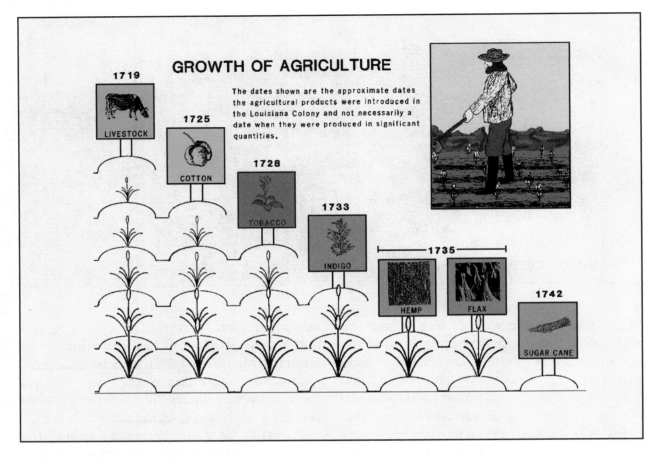

GROWTH OF AGRICULTURE

The dates shown are the approximate dates the agricultural products were introduced in the Louisiana Colony and not necessarily a date when they were produced in significant quantities.

1719 — LIVESTOCK
1725 — COTTON
1728 — TOBACCO
1733 — INDIGO
1735 — HEMP / FLAX
1742 — SUGAR CANE

Iberville selected seventy-five of the best men and six cabin boys to remain at Fort Maurepas. He took the other men with him to man the ship. He sent a ship to Santo Domingo to secure supplies for those left at the fort. He left enough provisions with them to last six months. On May 4, 1699, he departed for France. He reached France on July 2, 1699.

Difficulties at Fort Maurepas. As leader while Iberville was gone, Sauvole had a terrible time. Keeping the men working and the fort in order were his biggest problems. Coping with deserters and threats of desertion were a constant burden. He was to look for a better location for building a permanent fort. Keeping friendly with the Indians was highly important. Moreover, it was necessary to improve the area around the fort.

Many of the colonists did not like to farm. That first year few crops were planted. Their gardening efforts did provide some food. The colonists were surprised at their success with lettuce seeds. Eighteen days after planting, they were amazed to find the lettuce ready to eat. Later the hot sun burned the crops. They did not like the hard work of growing food. Actually, the land around the fort was not good for farming. The colonists preferred to hunt, trap, or search for gold and other precious metals. They wanted wives to make homes for them.

The marshy area became so dried out that there was not even good drinking water available. There was no rain at all during that first July, and men became ill due to lack of good drinking water. The suffocating heat was almost unbearable. There were alligators, which frightened the settlers, and there were many snakes. Fungus grew on furniture and clothes in the hot, humid climate. Worms and insects plagued the Frenchmen. The vicious mosquitoes and hostile animals added to their discomfort. Sudden tropical gales, uncertain water currents, and uneasy footing in the marshes presented untold problems. The colonists were frustrated and discouraged. They drank liquor excessively.

Bienville's Explorations. Bienville went on an exploring trip to the mouth of the Mississippi River. He went by way of the lakes and Bayou Manchac.

In May 1699 while Bienville was exploring, he learned from some Indians near Lake Pontchartrain that a group of Indians had been attacked by some Englishmen. The threat of attacks by the Indians or the English was always present. Bienville worked at winning the friendship of the Indians.

The English Turn. On September 15, 1699, Bienville was about eighteen miles below the present site of New Orleans. He was shocked to see a big ship flying an English flag. He signaled the pilot to stop. Bienville was surprised to see Capt. Lewis Banks, a person he had known in Canada. Banks said he was looking for a place to start a settlement. The quick-thinking Frenchman informed Captain Banks that he was trespassing on French soil. Bienville told him to turn back without delay. He also told him that there were many Frenchmen at the settlement just around the bend of the river. Captain Banks turned his boat around and left. Because of the incident, that point on the river is called *Détour des Anglais* (dā toor dez ÄYN glā), or **English Turn**. Today there is a historical marker at the spot. Historians have wondered what would have happened if the English had not turned back.

Iberville's Return. In France Iberville was given much encouragement. He was supplied with full equipment for a second voyage. His brother Chauteuguay, aged seventeen, joined Iberville for his return trip. He was also joined by two other kinsmen—**Louis Juchereau de St. Denis** (LŌŌ I JŌŌ cher rō deh saint dee KNĒĒ) and **Pierre de Boisbriant** (pē AIR BWÄ brē änt).

As soon as Iberville reached the settlement at Fort Maurepas on January 8, 1700, he heard bad news. In fact, he received the news even before he left his boat anchored in Biloxi Bay. Sauvole came aboard Iberville's ship to report. He told what had gone on in the colony during Iberville's absence. Four men had died, he said. He had heard also that two priests had been killed by the Natchez Indians. This brought concern that the colonists at the mouth of the Mississippi might be cut off from the north country by hostile Indians.

Iberville listened to Sauvole tell about how Bienville had met the English and turned them back. The English presence alarmed Iberville. He thought that the powerful English might well return to challenge the French claim to Louisiana.

Fort de la Boulaye (deh lah BŌŌ lā). Iberville left Sauvole in charge of Fort Maurepas and made another trip to the Mississippi River. With him were Bienville, St.

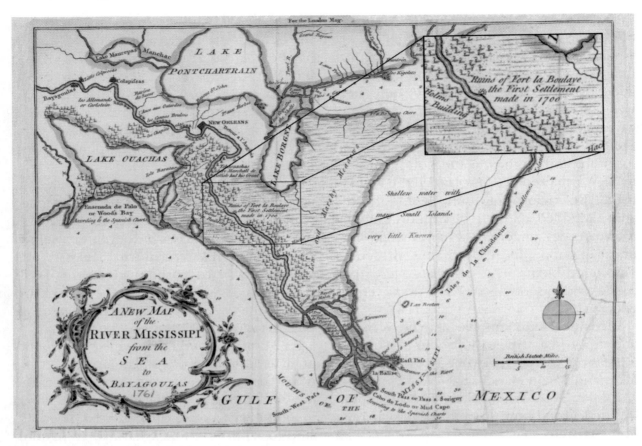

Location of Fort de la Boulaye.

Denis, and sixty men on two barges. Their most important business on this expedition, however, was the building of a fort. The fort was intended to protect France's claim to the Mississippi River.

Iberville selected the site. It was about fifty miles above the mouth of the river. Workers built a small blockhouse and powder magazines of red cypress. The house was twenty-eight square feet. Five or six cabins remained to be constructed according to the plans. They were to have roofs of palm leaves. A Frenchman who saw the place kept a journal. He said that the fort was "only an idea here in the midst of the Mississippi woods." The fort was named Fort de la Boulaye. It was completed in February 1700.

The little fort was equipped with four four-pound guns and two eighteen-pound guns. A moat twelve feet wide was dug around the fort. It was the first European settlement in what is now the state of Louisiana. Fort de la Boulaye was abandoned several years later.

While the fort was being built, some Frenchmen from Canada arrived. Tonti had heard that the French were settling the territory. He decided to find out for himself what was being done. With him were fifty men, ten canoes, and a cargo of furs. Tonti had visited the Natchez Indians on the way. He told Iberville that it was not true that the Natchez had killed two French priests. He remained at the fort for three days before he, Bienville, and Iberville left together to sail up the big river. Iberville and Bienville returned, leaving Tonti at the present site of Natchez, Mississippi, among the **Chickasaws**. Iberville thought that this spot would make a good place for a settlement. Tonti understood the mission of going among the powerful tribe of the Chickasaws. It was necessary to try to build better relationships for the French.

After Iberville returned to Fort de la Boulaye, he became ill with a fever. For a while he rested at the fort before returning to Fort Maurepas. Bienville was left in command of the new fort.

Iberville's Second Departure. Sauvole remained in charge at Fort Maurepas. There were 123 men left at the fort. The ailing Iberville sailed for France at the end of May 1700.

Exploration of the Red River. Because King Louis XIV had ordered Iberville to locate mines in the colony, Sauvole sent twenty-five men to search in the area near the Spanish territory. Bienville and St. Denis went through Old River to reach the Red River. Bienville and his party came upon the Indians called Natchitoches, or "Chinkapin-eaters."

Life at Fort Maurepas. Things did not go well while Iberville was away. There were threatening signs from Indians stirred up by the English. Canadians, coming into the territory with their furs to trade, alarmed the settlers. They needed all the fur-trade business of the lower Mississippi Valley.

Supplies at Fort Maurepas were getting low. The settlers could not depend on the shipments from France. They came only now and then. The settlers had little success with their game-hunting or their farming. As a result, food was scarce. The peas, beans, maize, and other vegetables did not grow well in the coastal soils at Biloxi. The colonists were often ill, and there was no medicine. Once a ship that was to bring

Iberville.

medicine left the medical supplies in the warehouse in France. The crew forgot to load them on the ship. Nearly a third of the fort's settlers died within the first two years.

Sauvole's Death. On August 22, 1701, Sauvole died of yellow fever. Bienville, then twenty years old, was left to run the colony. Bienville had been living at Fort de la Boulaye. After Sauvole died, Bienville left to take charge of Fort Maurepas. Only 150 persons remained in the colony. St. Denis took Bienville's place at Fort de la Boulaye.

Iberville's Arrival. In December 1701 Iberville returned from France.

Fort St. Louis de la Mobile. While in France Iberville had gained permission from the king to move the fort to a more suitable site. He first moved most of the settlers to Dauphin Island (Massacre Island) in early 1702. Iberville later selected a higher and healthier site for the new fort. Bienville began construction of a new fort at Mobile Bay. That site had a good harbor and better farmlands.

The new fort was named Fort St. Louis de la Mobile. Within the fort walls were quarters for the commandant, a house for the officers, a guardhouse, a chapel, and a storehouse for supplies. Barracks for soldiers and homes for the settlers were built outside the fort. The new fort was much larger than Fort Maurepas. Fort St. Louis de la Mobile became the capital of the Louisiana colony.

A group of soldiers were left at Fort Maurepas and another post was established on Dauphin Island. Iberville, the founder of Louisiana, had now completed four settlements—Fort Maurepas, Fort de la Boulaye, Fort St. Louis de la Mobile, and Fort Dauphin Island. A few plantations and farms had been established along the banks of the Mississippi River.

En Partie 3 (Studying a Part). 1. (a) Where did the French settle? (b) When? (c) Why? 2. (a) Show the changes in the location of the capital. (b) Which locations were in the present state of Louisiana? (c) In which states were the others located? (d) Why is this information included in a study of Louisiana? 3. What was the story of English Turn?

Change of Governors

Spanish Warnings. Arriola (är rē Ō lə), the Spanish governor of Pensacola, demanded that the French leave Fort Maurepas. The peppery governor had earlier tried to get Mexican officials to help him get rid of the French on the Gulf coast. The Mexicans refused. At that time Sauvole was acting governor of Louisiana. Sauvole had flown an English flag over Fort Maurepas to deceive the Spanish leader. The Mexicans then promptly sent help to the Spanish governor, Arriola, to attack the "English" settlement at Biloxi and destroy it.

Governor Arriola reached Biloxi with four ships and four hundred men. He captured a boat that was flying an English flag and found that all aboard were Frenchmen. They told him about the strength of the French colony. Arriola decided not to attack. He sent a letter to Sauvole instead. In the letter, he wrote that the French were in violation "of the treaties" which gave Spain claim to the land. Arriola claimed that the treaties applied not only to Biloxi but to all the land bordering the Gulf of Mexico. Arriola threatened several more times. Then he sailed away.

A storm wrecked Arriola's ships. One wreck drifted toward Biloxi. When the

French from the fort sailed out to see what was floating in the water, they found Arriola clinging to his wrecked ship. He was half-naked and ill from his ordeal. Some of his men were left marooned on the islands in Biloxi Bay.

Sauvole sent a rescue party to take the governor and his surviving men to Fort Maurepas. There they provided a feast, wine, and fresh clothes. Then the French escorted the Spanish back to Pensacola. The French were amused by this incident.

Iberville's Final Trip. By the spring of 1702, the colony was badly in need of supplies. Iberville decided he must return to France. He left on April 27. With him was the Jesuit priest Fr. Paul Du Ru. A new war, Queen Anne's War, had broken out in 1701. Iberville was needed in France to serve in the French navy. He tried to get more soldiers and settlers to send to Louisiana. However, the mother country was too busy fighting to send help.

Iberville was still weak from his six-year fight with what some historians have called yellow fever. When he became well enough, he was placed in command of a fleet belonging to France and Spain. The two countries were allied in the war against England. He was expected to capture the English colony Carolina. Iberville reached Havana in 1706 and was to complete plans to attack Carolina. Before he could do so, he died.

Problems. There were many serious problems in the colony. There was much illness and a lack of medicine. The deadly fevers often killed settlers. After 1702 the settlements in the Louisiana colony grew very slowly.

Most of the colonists were soldiers. Many of the men deserted and joined the English in Carolina. A number of the men took Indian women as mates during the first years at Fort Maurepas. Neither the French leaders nor the Indians approved of the situation. Iberville had pleaded with France to send families who would till the soil. Most of the settlers who came, however, were adventurers and fortune-seekers. They expected to get rich easily. They were not willing to put forth the effort or make the sacrifices necessary for survival in the colony. They had not dreamed of the hardships they would have to endure.

Lagniappe—*Creoles.* The word **Creole,** once defined as child born in the New World colony and taken from the Spanish **crillo,** has developed into new meanings. That first child, Jean Francois LeCamp, was Creole. Today the term is applied to the descendants of early settlers. They are a blend of French, Spanish, Black, Indian, and Caucasian—no accurate lines drawn. A museum is being established and a major study of Creoles is in progress in the Natchitoches area. Creole is applied to cooking, recipes, architecture, music, festivals, beautiful people, and countryside. Louisiana boasts of the Creole life style in nationally distributed advertising campaigns.

Until the arrival of the **Pelican girls** in 1704, there had been no French mates for the colonists. The bishop of Quebec shipped twenty-three young women to the Mobile colony on the *Pelican.* They were chaperoned by Mlle. Boisrenaud (mad ə mə ZEL BWA rə nō). They were to become wives of some of the men. The women soon threatened to leave. They did not like the food, especially the Indian maize. They wanted

French bread. Bienville's housekeeper taught them how to use maize. She taught the women to grind the corn into meal for cornbread. They also learned to make hominy, grits, and succotash.

Arriving with the Pelican girls were two nuns and a curate (religious leader). Seventy-five soldiers and four families of artisans also arrived on the *Pelican*. There was another addition to the population in 1704. The first Creole, Jean Francois LeCamp (jhon frähn SWAH luh KAMP), was born in the colony.

Almost all of the settlers were extremely unhappy with their living conditions. The homes of the colonists were crude and poorly built. They resembled Indian huts with thatch roofs. The shipments of supplies from France never arrived regularly. Once the situation became so desperate that the Spanish in Pensacola came to the rescue with provisions.

France was in serious financial trouble. It had no money to spend on the Louisiana territory. The colony had not brought the riches the French officials had expected. King Louis XIV and his officials had ordered the soldiers to search for pearls and for gold and silver mines. The French government tried to promote such schemes as having the settlers tame buffalo or raise silkworms.

There was no relief for the settlers. In 1705 thirty-five persons, including Tonti, died of yellow fever. Malaria and dysentery were common.

Complaints about Bienville. The dissatisfied settlers constantly quarreled among themselves. They also complained about Bienville. Iberville's death seemed to encourage them to attack Bienville fiercely. Even the priests joined the attackers. They sent angry protests to France about their young governor.

Bienville statue, New Orleans.

There were so many charges against Bienville that the king sent a man named **Diron d'Artaguette** (dē RON dar ta GET) to investigate Bienville's performance as governor. Bienville was ordered to return to France for questioning. Before Bienville was to leave, d'Artaguette cleared him of all blame. A dishonest official in France had been stealing money that Bienville had been accused of taking. Bienville remained as governor.

Fort St. Louis de la Louisiane. It was decided to relocate Fort St. Louis de la Mobile. There was always the danger of Indian attacks on the fort. The site was also subject to flooding. The flood of 1709 was the immediate cause of the move. About 1710 the fort was moved closer to Dauphin Island and Biloxi. The name was changed to Fort St. Louis de la Louisiane. It became the capital of the colony.

Bienville. Bienville remained as governor until 1713. At that time a new governor was appointed. Bienville, although cleared by the investigator, had been retained in the position only until a new governor could arrive at Mobile.

Bienville had been in his teens when he arrived in Louisiana in 1699. He had no experience in governing. Yet with all of the problems involved, Bienville was able to keep the colony in existence for a decade.

En Partie 4 (Studying a Part). 1. Analyze problems of the colony. Include government. 2. (a) Why did Iberville earn the title "Founder of Louisiana?" (b) Justify the title. 3. Why were there complaints about Bienville?

CHAPTER 5

LOUISIANA UNDER PROPRIETORS: CROZAT AND LAW (1712-1731) 5

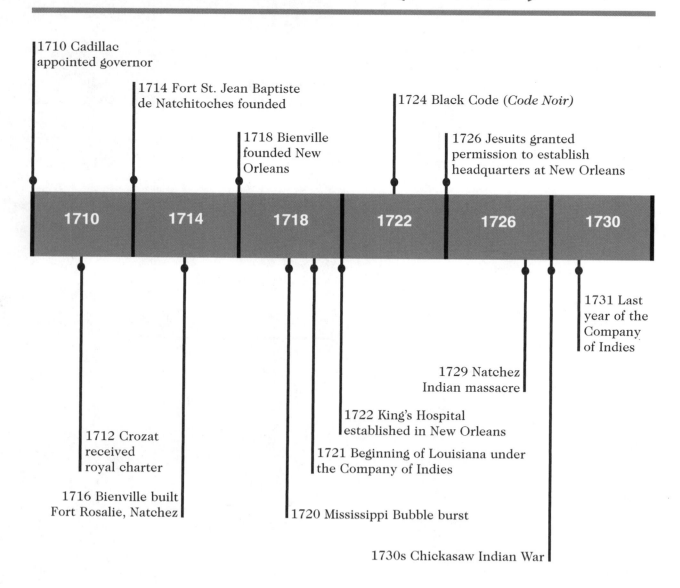

1710 Cadillac appointed governor

1714 Fort St. Jean Baptiste de Natchitoches founded

1724 Black Code (*Code Noir*)

1718 Bienville founded New Orleans

1726 Jesuits granted permission to establish headquarters at New Orleans

| 1710 | 1714 | 1718 | 1722 | 1726 | 1730 |

1731 Last year of the Company of Indies

1729 Natchez Indian massacre

1722 King's Hospital established in New Orleans

1721 Beginning of Louisiana under the Company of Indies

1712 Crozat received royal charter

1716 Bienville built Fort Rosalie, Natchez

1720 Mississippi Bubble burst

1730s Chickasaw Indian War

LOUISIANA UNDER PROPRIETORS

Crozat's Commercial Venture

France was in such financial distress that the government could no longer support the colony. Louis XIV and his officials concluded they must turn over the colony to private enterprise. A wealthy merchant, **Antoine Crozat** (ÄHN twähn krō ZÄH), agreed to take Louisiana as a commercial venture.

Crozat's Commercial Monopoly. At age fifteen, Crozat, a peasant's son, became a clerk in a commercial firm. At thirty-five, they made him a partner. He married his partner's daughter and became the owner of the business on the death of his father-in-law. He dealt in slaves and other trade with Africa. Primarily interested in making more money, he became very wealthy. Crozat thought there were huge profits to be made in Louisiana through trade and the mining of precious metals.

Crozat received a royal charter on September 14, 1712. It granted him the sole right to carry on trade in the Louisiana territory for fifteen years. Crozat agreed to send two shiploads of colonists and supplies to Louisiana each year. For nine years France was to allow him a sum of money to pay the soldiers and colonial officers. After that the expenses were to be borne by Crozat. The king was to get the "royal fifth" from the proceeds from mining and from any precious stones found. Crozat also had to follow the laws of France in Louisiana. In addition, he was to own all factories started by him. He was also given all the land he could cultivate. He was the only one who could import slaves from Africa. Crozat held exclusive right to trade in all hides and furs except beaver skins. Beavers were protected in Canada because they were used in place of money.

Appointment of Cadillac. Antoine de la Mothe Cadillac (lə MŌT kä DĒ yak or kad ə LAK) had been appointed as governor May 5, 1710. He was bitter about his appointment. He did not arrive in Mobile until March 17, 1713. Sixty-seven years old, he had made a glorious reputation for himself. A career soldier, Cadillac had served the king over twenty years. He traveled to France before coming to Louisiana. Cadillac's wife chaperoned twelve girls who made the trip from Paris.

Cadillac had founded Detroit, the chief fur-trading center in all the Western world. He had expected to live the rest of his life there. Detroit was much more advanced than Mobile at that time. Living there was much more comfortable than on the raw frontier.

When Cadillac arrived, the settlers first learned about the removal of Bienville as governor. It took several weeks and sometimes months for news from the capital to reach the distant posts. Most of the settlers did not object when they did hear the news of Bienville's removal.

In 1712 there were only about three hundred non-Indians in Louisiana. These settlers lived along the Gulf coast and along the Mississippi River. Probably fewer than fifty Europeans were in the present state of Louisiana. There were two companies of soldiers, with about fifty men in each. Between seventy and eighty Canadians employed by the king completed the makeup of the colony.

From the moment he saw the colony, Cadillac criticized it. He seems to have planned to compensate for his misery by getting rich off treasures in Louisiana. He traveled to the Illinois country hoping to find

French Colonial Government

King

Governor

Superior Council

Crozat's Plans. Crozat started his new business venture by sending over two shiploads of new settlers. They were mostly people expecting to get rich quickly. Most of them made poor settlers. Volunteers had stopped coming to the colony. Criminals, debtors, and orphans were almost the only ones coming. Crozat offered free passage to settlers. Soldiers were allowed to bring their families. In 1716 a royal decree returned all land grants to the royal domain so that the land could be given to new settlers.

Crozat's dream of obtaining riches from Louisiana commerce depended heavily on the sale of Louisiana furs. His plan was to sell all supplies to the settlers and buy their pelts for the European market. To drive better bargains, he obtained monopolies.

St. Denis's Trip. Once Crozat undertook the Louisiana project, he moved quickly. He shipped tons of merchandise for trade to the capital at Mobile. Crozat had plans to start trade with Mexico. He finally succeeded in getting Cadillac to appoint a representative to go to Mexico. Cadillac chose St. Denis, who was then in charge of Fort de la Boulaye.

Cadillac could not have made a better choice than St. Denis. He was a heroic figure to the Indians living in western Louisiana. St. Denis already knew the vast stretch of land to the west very well. He spoke several Indian languages as well as Spanish and French. He respected the Indians and helped them in times of need. Rarely has there been such a gifted salesman as St. Denis. He had the polish and skill needed by a diplomat.

Cadillac had received a letter from Father Hidalgo (ē DAL gō), a Spanish priest. Father Hidalgo had once worked with the Tejas (TAY häs) Indians. The priest asked the French to send missionaries to minister to the Tejas

silver mines. All he found were lead mines. Crozat grew angry at Cadillac's lack of leadership in developing Louisiana's trade. He filed complaints against the governor with French authorities.

Superior Council. A new set of officials was sent to Louisiana with Cadillac. The Superior Council, appointed for three years, was established as an advisory body. The council consisted of the governor, the intendant, and two agents who were to represent Crozat's interests. The attorney general used the Custom of Paris laws. These were the written laws and legal customs of Paris and the surrounding area.

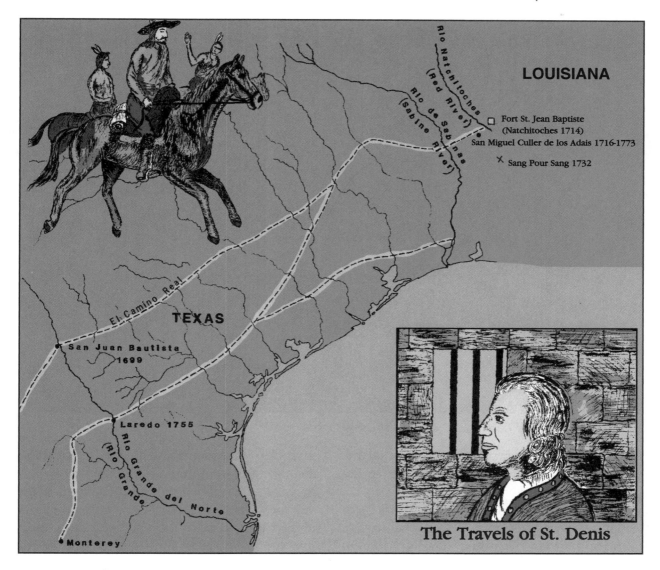

The Travels of St. Denis

because his own government would not allow Spanish priests to cross the Rio Grande into the land of the Tejas. The letter provided an excuse for St. Denis's presence in Spanish Texas. He was to establish trade relations with the Indians along the way and obtain a trade agreement with the Spanish.

Natchitoches in 1714. St. Denis's first stop was with the Natchitoches Indians on the Red River. He signed a treaty with them.

Then he built a storehouse for his goods. After that he left some of his men at the village. They were to form a garrison on the Red River against the Spanish. They were to guard the goods left in the warehouse. A fort, **Fort St. Jean Baptiste de Natchitoches,** was later established at the garrison. The storehouse became a trading post, and an important settlement grew around it. This was Natchitoches, the oldest permanent

A modern replica of Fort St. Jean Baptiste.

settlement in the present state of Louisiana. The post extended French influence in that part of the colony.

After a short while St. Denis started for Mexico with a pack train. He and twenty-five men took a load of goods. He sold goods to Indians all the way to the Rio Grande del Norte. Some Tejas Indians agreed to guide St. Denis and his party to San Juan Bautista (sähn bə TĒĒs tə).

After months he was ready to cross the Rio Grande del Norte into Mexico. It was a very daring thing to do. The Spanish were ready to shoot any stranger who dared to cross the boundary. A presidio, or Spanish fort, guarded the boundary. St. Denis was not fazed.

On July 18, 1714, St. Denis arrived at the mission of San Juan Bautista. He became the guest of the commandant of the presidio. There may have been a deal between them, and they discussed trade. Perhaps St. Denis offered him a share of profits from a trade agreement. Supplies from France and Spain were never enough for early settlers. They were so far away from rulers that perhaps they felt that they had a right to secure goods wherever they could.

The viceroy (Spanish authority) chose Capt. Domingo Ramon (rah MÔN) to lead an expedition to reestablish Spanish occupation of the land of the Tejas Indians. St. Denis was chosen as second in command. On February 17, 1716, they left with a group of sixty-five. The party included about a dozen priests, twenty-five soldiers, and the families of the soldiers. By late 1716 they were in the land of the Tejas. They established four missions in a line leading toward the Red River.

Captain Ramon and St. Denis traveled into Louisiana for talks with French officials. They were told that the French had no desire to interfere with Spanish control of Texas. Not trusting the French, the Spanish built two more missions close to French territory. One was at the present site of San Augustine, Texas. The other was at what is now Robeline, Louisiana. The **mission San Miguel de Linares de los Adaes** (mi GEHL lē NAH rēs lohs Ä daze) was erected only fifteen miles west of the French settlement of Natchitoches.

In January 1719 war broke out in Europe between France and Spain. The king of France directed his forces in the colony to move against Spanish holdings. The governor of Louisiana sent out scouting parties to determine the strength of Spanish defenses for the missions in Texas. When the French scouts arrived at the mission San Miguel in June 1719, one priest and one soldier stationed there surrendered.

The Frenchmen began to gather booty at the mission. Chickens escaped from a pen and ran under the Frenchmen's horses. The horses threw their riders. The trouble with the chickens was the only trouble the Frenchmen had. Seven scouts had driven the Spanish out of East Texas. This is sometimes called the "Chicken War."

Los Adais or Los Adaes (both spellings apear in historical records). In the spring of 1721, the Spanish returned to reoccupy East Texas. Spain claimed Red River as their eastern boundary. Near the mission San Miguel, the Spanish built a new presidio, or fort. They named it Nuestra Señora del Pilar de los Adaes (noo EH strah pē LAHR). They left more than one hundred well-supplied soldiers there. The fort and the settlement that grew around it were called Los Adaes. It became the official capital of Texas and remained so for fifty years.

The person in charge of the western area of French Louisiana was St. Denis. St. Denis became commandant of Fort St. Jean Baptiste in 1722. St. Denis agreed to keep his traders east of the Red River. He protested the location of a Spanish fort on French soil.

Child King. Louis XIV died September 1, 1715. During the last months before the king died, little was done for Louisiana. **Louis XV**

Duke of Orleans.

had been named by the old king to take his place. He was the five-year-old grandson of Louis XIV. To actually carry on the government until Louis XV was thirteen, France was ruled by three **regents**. One of these was the duke of Orleans, the child-king's uncle.

Fort Rosalie. The Natchez resented the coming of the white man to their lands. From time to time, this resentment resulted in Indian violence against the European settlements. Still, Bienville was usually successful in maintaining a friendship with them. It was Bienville who established Fort Rosalie at the present Natchez in 1716. It was named for the wife of the Count de Pontchartrain. The fort was constructed on holy ground of the Natchez and further infuriated the Indians.

A series of wars broke out after the founding of Fort Rosalie. The first Natchez attack against the French at Fort Rosalie occurred in 1716. In the background, the English were pushing the Indians to take action.

Cadillac's Departure. Cadillac was a notably poor governor of the Louisiana colony. He offered no leadership for the struggling colony. The settlers blamed him for their hardships. Crozat blamed Cadillac's inefficiency for his failure to secure profits from Louisiana. Cadillac carried on a feud with Bienville. There was a story that Bienville had refused to marry Cadillac's daughter. Cadillac himself hated the colony. In 1716 he was transferred

Bienville building Fort Rosalie.

to another post. In Canada and Detroit Cadillac had been successful. As governor of Louisiana he was a failure. Bienville was appointed temporary head of the colony again.

Governor Lepinay. The new governor was **Jean Michiele, Seigneur de Lepinay** (mi SHEL SĒN yēr LA pē na). He arrived in less than a year with fifty colonists and more soldiers. He decorated Bienville with the Cross of St. Louis, awarded him by the king of France. As additional recognition for his service to France, he was presented with the title to Horn Island, an island in Biloxi Bay.

Lepinay was also a failure. Almost immediately his conflicts with Bienville divided the colonists into two opposing factions. One faction was pro-Bienville. The others were on Lepinay's side. When the English heard that the French were quarreling, they took advantage of the conflict. They found ways to make inroads into the Indian trade.

Crozat's Failure. Five years after starting his venture Crozat was bankrupt. Lepinay's problems had only made Crozat's problems worse. Crozat asked the king to release him from his agreement. That was done in August 1717.

Why did Crozat fail in his Louisiana venture? The monopolies did not work. The settlers had no money with which to buy. Besides, Crozat's goods were overpriced. Nobody else was free to generate trade. This caused commerce to grind to a halt. The small vegetable trade with the Spanish ceased because the colonists were not allowed to own seagoing vessels. Crozat expected to make large profits from trade with Mexico and the Spanish islands. This trade was closed to him. The slave trade did not prove profitable, either. Few colonists had the money required to buy slaves.

It did not occur to Crozat to cultivate friendships with Indians. He did not realize that this was extremely important. He stopped giving trinkets, which the Indians had learned to expect.

English traders from Carolina consistently paid the Indians higher prices for furs. Naturally, the Indians chose to trade with the English. The Spanish at Pensacola also offered the Indians more for their furs. That wasn't all. Both the English and Spanish sold European goods more cheaply to the Indians.

Crozat also neglected agriculture in his search for quick riches. He had expected to develop mining in the northern reaches of the Louisiana colony. This, too, failed.

There was another investor waiting to take over the Louisiana colony. Perhaps he would learn from Crozat's mistakes.

The child king, Louis XV of France.

En Partie 1 (Studying a Part). 1. Why did King Louis XIV wish to get rid of the colony? 2. Describe Crozat's efforts to get rich from Louisiana. 3. What type of people came? 4. Describe government under Crozat. 5. Why was a post established at Natchitoches? 6. (a) Who was St. Denis? (b) What was his mission in Spanish territory? 7. Describe the settlements of Los Adaes and Fort Rosalie. 8. Why was Crozat's venture a failure?

John Law's Mississippi Bubble

John Law's Plan. Redheaded John Law was no ordinary man. By the time he was twenty, he had already gambled away a fortune. He was a playboy in Scotland. After he killed a man in a duel, he fled to France.

John Law took pains to cultivate the rich and powerful. Among those he charmed was the duke of Orleans. The duke was the most powerful man in France as regent for young King Louis XV. With France in financial chaos, the duke of Orleans was looking for a solution. He turned to John Law.

In 1716 John Law established the Bank of France. Large quantities of paper money were printed. In 1717 the paper money of the Bank of France was accepted throughout France. He became the director general of his Royal Bank of France. John Law was at the peak of power in 1718. It was a year later that he got the idea of obtaining riches from Louisiana. His scheme became known as "The Mississippi Bubble."

He vowed that he could turn Louisiana into a source of wealth for France. The duke

John Law.

gave him a monopoly in the colony for twenty-five years.

Company of the West. John Law organized the Company of the West in 1717. The new company took over the Louisiana colony. Law had much the same arrangement as Crozat, as well as the right to select a governor. His territory included the Illinois country, which had not been included in Crozat's charter.

Law sold stock in his Company of the West. Frenchmen excitedly bought it. Law could hardly keep up with the demand for his stock. Not only everybody in France who had any money to invest, but also some outside its boundaries bought shares in the company.

Settlers for John Law's Louisiana. John Law was a great promoter. He advertised the Company of the West in Germany, Switzerland, Italy, and Holland. He told the people that Louisiana was a "land of milk and honey." All over France, people were told of the wonderful venture.

The Company of the West was required to send six thousand whites to the Louisiana colony every year. Also, they were to send three thousand slaves yearly. John Law tried many ways to get settlers. He started a big advertising campaign. He put out giant handbills, posters, circulars, and broadsides. All described the wonderful opportunities in the colony. Such an inviting picture of Louisiana was painted that many poor people were convinced. Many French people mortgaged or sold their homes to seek their fortunes in Louisiana. They left France to become pioneers, homesteaders, prospectors, or miners.

In August 1718, eight hundred colonists arrived in three ships. Among them was Le Page du Pratz, one of Louisiana's first historians. So many came to the colony that the population increased from seven hundred to five thousand by 1721. The advertising led these people to expect too much. When they found that they could not produce four crops a year, they felt cheated. They knew that John Law had lied to them. Friendly Indians did not do most of the work as John Law had promised. The new settlers sent gloomy reports to France. People no longer chose to move to Louisiana.

Thereafter, the main sources for the Louisiana population were the prisons and houses of correction in France. Petty **criminals** were brought to the colony. They had been given the choice of Louisiana or prison. Some who chose prison were forced to come anyway. Some of these criminals were women. The wives and children of convicts were allowed to come to Louisiana with their husbands and fathers. Girls from **orphans'** homes were sent to become wives of the settlers. Officials were ordered to kidnap people to send to the colony. The streets were searched for prospective settlers. Grace King, a Louisiana writer, described it as "dogcatcher's work." She said that servants and children were taken from the streets. **Beggars** and **idle persons** were forced to go. These actions caused so much hatred in France that even the word "Louisiana" became distasteful. This did not help in attempts to recruit volunteers.

A law was passed in 1720 prohibiting vagabonds and criminals from going to Louisiana. The experiment in emptying prisons for settlers had not worked. The ones already in the colony proved that they did not change their habits by coming to the New World. They had begun to settle in the

This Indenture made the 13th day of July in the year of 1757 between John Ezelle of the one party and Isaac Colbert of the other party. The said Isaac Colbert doth hereby promise to serve the said John Ezelle from the date above; for the term of seven years. In Return, the said John Ezelle doth promise the said Isaac Colbert to pay for his passing, and to find him meat, drink, clothing, and lodging, with other necessaries during the said term; and at the end of the said term, to give him one whole year's provisions of corn and fifty acres of land, according to the laws of the country. In witness whereof, the said John Ezelle and Isaac Colbert have put their seals on the date above written.

frontier towns to gamble, drink, and fight.

The company tried several other methods to get colonists. Wealthy noblemen received **large grants** of **land** called **concessions.** Individuals of lesser wealth were given smaller grants called **habitations.** Concessionaires (grantees) were expected to bring over many settlers to develop their grants. Some did develop their grants. Few grantees came themselves. Diron d'Artaguette was granted the land where Baton Rouge now stands. Bernard de La Harpe received land in the Natchitoches area. Other offers were made to attract settlers. Free passage, food, equipment, and supplies were sometimes furnished.

Some **indentured servants** were brought into the colony. These were persons whose passages were paid by prospective employers. The servants worked for a specified number of years to pay for their passages.

Being an indentured servant was not much different from being a slave. Yet the New World's promise of a better life caused some hard-pressed people to accept indenture. Seven years of hard labor were usually necessary to repay the cost of passage. Yet the master could add years for such offenses as running away. Meantime most of the indentured servants arrived on crowded ships under the watchful eye of the ship's captain. These ship captains created a lively business for themselves. They crowded as many indentures as possible to bring on the ships. Once here, they sold the labor contract for a price to a settler. Often housed in a barn and set to work at menial tasks, the servant found that he or she had paid a high price for the journey to Louisiana.

New settlers found life in the colony vastly different from that pictured by the Company of the West. After the miseries of the months-long trip, they needed time to restore their energies. Yet they were faced with cutting down trees and building their own shelters. Supplies from France were scant, and they were forced to fish, hunt game, and search for edibles in the forests.

Probably the most successful settlers were those who came from outside France. The French who could have been successful colonists did not come. Most French peasants did not believe that they would be better off in the new country. Most Germans wanting to come to the New World chose the new colony of Pennsylvania instead of Louisiana. However, some German peasants did accept John Law's offer. So did some Swiss. Some Germans arrived in 1721. Nine hundred sixty-five left France. Two hundred arrived in Louisiana. They became some of the colony's most valuable settlers.

Bienville Governor Again. One of John Law's first actions was to replace Governor Lepinay. In 1718 Bienville once more became governor.

Founding of New Orleans, 1718. One goal of the company was to establish a port to handle the fur commerce on the Mississippi. La Salle, Iberville, and Bienville all had thought that if France were to control the entire Mississippi Valley, the chief settlement should be on the Mississippi River. For a long time Bienville had wanted to establish a settlement at a certain point. The site was on Lake Pontchartrain. Bienville wanted New Orleans to overlook that "beautiful crescent of the river." The chief engineer, Le Blond de la Tour (luh BLON lah TOOR), did not approve of the place that Bienville had selected. Other engineers were consulted and agreed with de la

Tour that it was a poor site. Bienville's choice was a low, marshy strip of land.

In spite of the engineers, Bienville had his way. In February 1718 Bienville had eighty men—slaves, prisoners, and a few carpenters—clearing the site, digging drainage ditches, and making the place ready for new settlers. He named the new city *Nouvelle-Orléans* (no VEHL or noo VEHL, New Orleans) for the duke of Orleans.

The first building that finally took shape was a hut covered with palmetto palms. It became Bienville's headquarters. Other crude huts similar to those of the Choctaws were built. The huts could not stand the damp heat, and winds ripped off the roofs. Flooding was a regular event. Then fire destroyed some of the huts. Hurricanes swept many away. The little village was rebuilt every time, and New Orleans survived.

Snakes, mosquitoes, and water seeping up through the marsh soil made New Orleans something less than appealing. The muddy streets often looked like canals. For three years the little village was almost deserted. City engineers recommended that a new site be found. Bienville persisted in making New Orleans the capital. He finally convinced French officials.

Bienville set about constructing a new city with a master plan in 1721. **Adrien de Pauger** (pō ZHĀ), the royal engineer, worked with Bienville in laying out the city. With a gridiron pattern, the large blocks were laid out along the banks of the river. The plan was shaped like a parallelogram. The settlement was four thousand feet long by 1,800 feet wide. A public square beside the river was to be used as a parade ground and for ceremonial occasions. The square was called the **Place d'Armes** (plas duh ÄRMS). The space around the public square was to be occupied by barracks for the soldiers, a church, a residence for the priest, and a prison. This eleven-by-seven-block rectangle is known today as the *Vieux Carré* (vyōō kä RAY), or **French Quarter**.

In 1721 there were 470 people living in New Orleans. Of these, 145 were free Frenchmen, sixty-five were French women, and thirty-eight were children. There were twenty-nine indentured servants, 172 black slaves, and twenty-one Indian slaves. Most of the people in the area lived just outside the city. Indigo plantations were worked by nearly 1,800 slaves. There were Acolapissa and Choctaw Indian settlements on and around the land occupied by present-day New Orleans. About 350 families of Houma Indians lived there until 1720.

En Partie 2 (Studying a Part). 1. Why was the Company of the West organized? 2. Tell the John Law story. 3. How were settlers obtained? 4. Describe the settlement of New Orleans.

Change of Management

Company of the Indies. By 1719 the Company of the West was expanded to include five other companies. The company received a new name: Company of the Indies. It purchased the trading rights of the East India, China, Africa, Senegal, and West Indies companies. This gave the company control of practically all foreign trade of France, including the slave trade. Again shares of stock sold rapidly.

In 1719 the company bought the sole

Indian traders.

right to coin money for France for a period of nine years. It also bought the right to collect all French taxes. Directors of the company were given large land grants in the Louis-iana colony. They were supposed to settle that land. Very few of the directors came across the sea to the New World colony. However, some sent settlers to their lands.

Plans were made to bring many more settlers. The company also planned to establish new settlements, to promote agriculture, to extend trade, and to send currency to the colony.

German Settlement. German settlers located just north of the new settlement of New Orleans. This became known as *Côte des Allemands* (the German Coast) (Coat dayz äl lə MAHN or DEZ AL monds). The Germans established small farms. The hard-working, thrifty people produced a great deal of food.

They actually saved New Orleans with food from their farms. This German settlement among the French and Indians has retained its identity as the Lower and Upper German Coast. This area is located in St. Charles and St. John the Baptist parishes.

Bursting of the Mississippi Bubble: 1720. John Law was made comptroller general of France in 1720. His company, the Company of the Indies, was teetering at the verge of collapse. In France paper money was everywhere. Even the government refused to accept it. Stockholders began to withdraw their deposits from the Bank of France. The bank could no longer allow withdrawals by depositors. John Law was frantic. He combined the Bank of France with the Company of the Indies in hopes of saving both. The bank was abolished by the French government. The company was broke. Its stock became worthless. John Law fled France in women's clothing to escape death from angry mobs of people. All had lost their investments.

There was no sound basis for John Law's claims that large profits could be made from Louisiana at that time. There was no reason that his moneymaking scheme should have worked. The people did not realize that mere paper with no real wealth or value behind it was not good money. Gold and silver had not been found. There would never be any precious metals from the colony. Tar, pitch, and forestry products produced in Louisiana did not compare with those produced in France. There were few laborers skilled in preparing lumber products. The lumber industry that Law planned would someday exist in Louisiana. However, that was more than a century away.

Louisiana under the Company of the Indies: 1721-31. The Company of the Indies was left in control of Louisiana. The French government did not wish to take on the company's debts and expenses. They did not want to be responsible for the colony, either.

A new policy was established for managing the colony. This was done in cooperation with the French government. In 1722 the French government granted an annual subsidy of three hundred thousand livres to the company. It was to pay the four directors of the colony. It was also to cover the cost of military fortifications.

With this assistance from France, Bienville, as governor, tried to place the colony on a sound footing. He went to France to confer with officials on how this could be done. The king wanted a successful colony. During Bienville's absence in 1723, Boisbriant was acting governor.

Black Code, or *Code Noir.* Enough slaves arrived during the time of Crozat and Law that it was necessary to have written laws concerning them.

Bienville formulated the **Black Code,** or *Code Noir.* The provisions of this code were collected from rules and customs governing slaves under France and Spain. Bienville in 1724 put the rules which had been found workable into law. These laws were to govern relations between the slaves and their masters. The code dealt with other problems as well.

The first article of the *Code Noir* expelled Jews from the colony. Other articles prescribed religious instruction in the Roman Catholic faith. The code ordered that Sundays and all holidays be given to the slaves as days off. Masters were made responsible for moral instruction of slaves.

The code forbade mingling of the two races. Masters were absolutely forbidden to force marriage between slaves. The children of slaves were to belong to the master of the mother. If the father were a slave and the mother a free woman of color, the children were to follow the condition of the mother and be free. Slaves who were husband and wife could not be seized or sold separately when belonging to the same master. Children under the age of fourteen could not be taken from their parents. Other provisions were included in an effort to protect slaves from cruel masters.

Four articles of the Black Code dealt with provisions for the feeding and clothing of slaves. The code stated that old and sick slaves must be cared for by their masters:

In case they should have been abandoned by said masters, said slaves shall be adjudged to the nearest hospital, to which said masters shall be obliged to pay eight cents a day for the food and maintenance of each one of these slaves; and for payment of this sum said hospital shall have a lien on the plantation of said master.

Slaves could not own property. They were forbidden to carry weapons except for hunting. Slaves of different masters could not assemble in crowds. Branding with the fleur-de-lis was the severe penalty for those who violated the code. If a slave struck his master or mistress or their children so as to make a bruise or draw blood, they were to suffer capital punishment. All acts of violence on the part of slaves against free persons were to result in severe punishment to the offenders. This could mean death. Theft of horses, cows, or other valuable property could also result in the death penalty. A runaway slave who was gone for as much as one month had his ears cut off. He was also branded on the shoulder with the fleur-de-lis. If he tried to run away a second time, he was hamstrung and branded on the other shoulder. The third offense meant death.

The Louisiana slave laws seem cruel by today's standards. They were very lenient for that time. The code was signed by Bienville during March 1724 in the name of the king. It was the last important act of Bienville under the administration of the Company of the Indies.

Lagniappe—*Cattle and Stock.* Establishing law and order in the colony included efforts to ensure a food supply. Cattle and stock were tended in order to reproduce for a herd. No one could slaughter cows, sows, or ewes without permission. Senseless killing of animals carried severe penalties, even death. Male animals could be slaughtered for food. The Company of the Indies made stringent rules to protect the colonists.

Bienville's Troubles. Disaster struck the struggling little town of New Orleans on September 11, 1722. The first recorded hurricane destroyed thirty-four huts and the makeshift church and rectory. A small fleet of vessels sank in the Mississippi. One ship loaded with grain, fowl, and produce ran aground. There was a shortage of food and a quickness of tempers. The people were very angry, and Bienville again became their target.

The citizens complained about Bienville for many reasons. One concerned the land that he had ceded himself. He chose some choice river property about eight miles long on the east side of the Mississippi. He also got a large tract on the west side. After the French government told him that this act was unethical, he gave up part of his land. The part he kept was about the size of today's downtown section of New Orleans.

Another source of trouble was the jealousy existing between different factions in the colony. Two different political groups grew in the colony—the pro-Bienvilles and the anti-Bienvilles. Those against him blamed him for all of the colony's problems. The Company of the Indies blamed him because the colony had brought no profit. The king and those around him seethed with anger at the same question. Why had France received so little for such huge investments?

Part of the political trouble in the colony

was due to the custom of sending officials to French colonies with overlapping duties. The offices of governor and *ordonnateur* (or don nat TEUR) represented such a problem. The duties of each official were neither clearly defined nor clearly separated. It was a constant source of trouble. There was so much trouble that it took stronger police protection to maintain order.

Finally, a secret committee of investigators headed by Jacques de La Chaise (zhak lah shāz) arrived in the colony. The mission of the committee was to investigate the actions of Bienville. On February 16, 1724, Bienville was recalled to France in disgrace to answer charges against him. Boisbriant acted as governor while he was gone. Not only was Bienville removed from office, but every kinsman and partisan of his was likewise removed. Bienville was banished from the city that he had founded. He was awarded an annual pension of 750 livres.

For the first time since the colony had been founded, not a single member of the Le Moyne family had any part in the governing of the colony. The officials hoped that the changes would bring peace to the colony. Bienville's policies were no longer in use.

En Partie 3 (Studying a Part). 1. What was the Company of the Indies? 2. Why did Law's bubble burst? 3. What was the Black Code? 4. Describe Bienville's troubles.

More Changes

The New Governor: Périer. Etienne Périer (Ā tē en PĀ ri ā) replaced Bienville in 1726. He found that he could not satisfy the complainers any more than Bienville had. The new governor worked to improve the economy. He succeeded in bringing in new settlers. However, some of them did not make good colonists. Périer stressed agriculture and urged the settlers to produce indigo and tobacco. He brought in specialists to advise planters on these crops. However, for plantations to produce these crops, more labor was needed than a family could supply. The only answer they had was to purchase slaves. Most of the colonists were too poor to invest in slaves.

Périer tried to bring profits from **forest products** to the company and to the settlers. Unlimited resources of virgin forests were at hand. The settlers could produce such products as tar, pitch, masts, and lumber needed in France and the West Indies. Many forest products were needed for shipbuilding in France. However, there were so few craftsmen experienced in preparing these products for market that this industry did not succeed. Shipbuilding itself was encouraged in the colony. Very skilled carpenters were needed, but there were few in the colony. So not much was accomplished by Périer in his attempts to improve the economy.

Périer sought to increase **commerce**. He felt that could be done between the French-owned islands of the West Indies and Louisiana. The Louisiana settlers needed to buy coffee and sugar from the islands. The islanders badly needed lumber and food produced in Louisiana. Ships to carry goods and money for investment did not exist in the colony. Therefore, Périer had no success with those plans either.

Périer tried to improve **transportation** and **communication.** Both were very difficult during the French period. Waterways in these years were the arteries of the colony. Travel for any distance had to be by water. Settlers were responsible for keeping the waterfront to their property clear of obstructions. A variety of watercraft was used on inland bayous and creeks. Interior posts were linked to New Orleans by waterways. There were no bridges. Cattle or horses moved overland. They were made to swim bayous and rivers. Fear of Indians caused settlers to travel in convoys.

Horseback was a major mode of overland transportation. Usually this was only for short distances. Those families able to afford them bought carriages. Two-wheeled carts were used for short overland hauls. These vehicles were of little use unless there were good roads. Only buffalo and Indian trails existed. These paths ran mostly alongside streams. Périer required all landowners along the Mississippi to build roads in front of their property.

Mail came from France irregularly. It was simply placed aboard ships carrying supplies. The same was true of mail from colonists to their homeland. So valued were these early communications from the colony that an interesting custom started in France. One sheet of each letter from Louisiana was given to each related family to preserve.

The Ursuline Nuns. In 1726 the Jesuits were granted permission to establish headquarters in New Orleans. They were to secure the service of the Ursuline nuns. In September 1726 the Company of the Indies made a contract with the Ursuline sisters to furnish twelve nuns for the colony. The following February 1727 the nuns sailed from France.

The nuns were given eight arpents of land, a house, and eight blacks to till their land. While they waited for their house to be built, they were temporarily housed at Bienville's residence. The permanent convent was completed in 1734.

The nuns served in the hospital and gave religious instruction to the girls of the colony. They also taught the girls to raise silkworms and make the silk into cloth. The nuns taught them how to make dresses with the cloth. Most importantly, the nuns and the girls provided a refining influence on the frontier population. It was the nuns who sheltered the girls of good character and gave them useful training to become wives of the colonists.

Casket Girls. In the fall of 1727 the first of the *filles à la cassette* (fē yē ə lə kə SET) arrived in New Orleans. They were the famous "Casket Girls." The girls were volunteers who came to become wives of the settlers. They were not, of course, the first women to come to the colony. They simply received more publicity because of the small pieces of luggage that they brought with them. They carried small portable trunks, or *cassettes,* which were given to them by the company. Each girl brought two dresses, two petticoats, six headdresses, and underwear. The carefully selected girls were placed in the care of the nuns. The girls remained in the convent until they were married. They were locked up at night. During the day they walked through the streets if the weather permitted. That way the men could meet the girls. The actual choice of a husband was left to each girl. Still, she had to choose from the suitors approved by the nuns. Within a few weeks, all were married.

Soldiers who married the casket girls were rewarded. Each one received his discharge from military service, a plot of land, a cow, provisions, and a rifle.

The French and Indian Troubles. Most

Indians of Louisiana came to bitterly resent the French. The **Natchez** were particularly hostile. The hostility of the Indians toward the French was encouraged by the English on one side and the Spanish on the other. The Indians saw the French overrunning lands that they had always considered their own. The Indians felt that the Frenchmen were driving away the wild game from the forests. Moreover, the French had sometimes outraged the Indians with acts of ruthlessness. There were other reasons. There was not a steady supply of trinkets and gifts expected by the Indians. The English were always in a better position to trade with the Indians. The English studied the Indians to find out what they wanted. They tried to supply these wants. The English made the best deals for the Indians. The French did not give them enough for their furs, and they charged too much for their goods.

For several years, the Natchez had been at peace with the French. By 1729, three hundred French settlers made their homes in Natchez territory. That year the Natchez

Casket girls.

massacre occurred. It was started by the high-handed act of Captain Chepart (shā PAR), the commander of **Fort Rosalie.** Chepart had already been scolded by the French officials for his conduct toward those under him. He made impossible demands on the Natchez Indians, ordering them to abandon White Apple, their most important village.

Chepart wanted to build his own plantation on a choice Indian plot. This land was the site of the Indians' burial ground and temple. To make matters worse, Chepart demanded a portion of their harvest.

The Natchez held a council and sent word to other Indians to join them in an effort to destroy the French. The Natchez struck in late November 1729. The Frenchmen at Fort Rosalie were massacred. Women, children, and black slaves were taken as prisoners. About 250 Frenchmen and a dozen Indians were killed. Around three hundred women and children were captured. The Indians burned Fort Rosalie and all buildings belonging to the French.

News of the Natchez massacre reached New Orleans on December 2. An exhausted refugee who had been in the woods when the massacre took place had made his way to New Orleans. The details of the massacre increased the panic and horror of the colonists. Within a few days the report of the massacre was confirmed by several other people who had escaped. Only three of the white men at the fort had survived. It was rumored that this was only the beginning of a general Indian war against the French. New Orleans was believed to be in danger. A moat was dug around the city. Guards were posted at its four corners. Word was sent to France for help. Messages were sent to outlying settlements. Emergency refuges were planned for the women and children.

Governor Périer sent a detachment of regular French troops and militia under the engineer Broutin (brū TAN). These were joined by a force from the French post at Pointe Coupee. They were ordered to make a bold, sudden strike against the Natchez to rescue the French women and children. Ammunition was sent from the Illinois post. Seven hundred Choctaw warriors joined the French against the Natchez. The Avoyels, Tunicas, and other small tribes joined the French, also. After days of battle, on March 1, 1730, the French found that the Natchez had deserted Fort Rosalie.

Périer's attacks on the Natchez did not subdue them. Instead, it drove them into desperate, widely scattered groups. These continued to harass the French.

After the Natchez massacre, there was rumor that the blacks and Indians were planning an uprising. Blacks were given a choice—hanging or attacking Indians. Eighty blacks armed with knives, hatchets, and bayonets ambushed a small settlement of peaceful Indian farmers. The blacks killed seven or eight innocent Indians. After this incident there were strained relationships among the whites, blacks, and Indians. Each group was suspicious of the others.

The Tunica Indians caught four Natchez braves and took them to New Orleans. They publicly burned them alive in an elaborate ceremony. Other Natchez Indians murdered the Tunica chief and destroyed the rest of the Tunica nation.

It was August 10, 1730, before French soldiers arrived in New Orleans. They brought French military strength up to between one thousand and 1,200 regular troops and militia. On January 28, 1731, Périer secured the surrender of the small fort of the Natchez located at Sicily Island. The Natchez had taken refuge at Sicily Island after the Natchez massacre.

The French king sent delegates to Louisiana to investigate the Indian policies of Périer. They reported that the evils growing out of Périer's policies were without remedy. Most of the Indians were now hostile to the French due to Périer's cruelty to the Indians. The only way to improve the situation, the delegates reported, was to return Bienville as head of the colony.

Last Year of the Company of the Indies: 1731. The Company of the Indies finally gave up its charter on July 1, 1731. It would not have expired for another eleven years. The Natchez massacre caused the company to request permission to surrender control over the Louisiana colony. The directors had learned the same lesson that Crozat had learned. Colonies were too expensive for private investors. Colonies, to be successful, required the vast resources of a nation. The directors had done all they could to generate profits from the Louisiana colony. They felt that Louisiana would develop slowly. It would take a long time before Louisiana could even be self-supporting.

En Partie 4 (Studying a Part). 1. What were the changes made by Périer? 2. (a) Who were the Ursuline Nuns? (b) The Casket Girls? 3. Describe French-Indian troubles. 4. Why did the Company of the Indies give up its charter?

Mural depicting the Company of the Indies.

Contributions of John Law

Even though John Law had created havoc in France, he had done some lasting good for Louisiana. The colony had grown from seven hundred persons (five hundred whites and two hundred blacks) when John Law took control. When the Company of the Indies, begun by Law, finally left Louisiana, there were 7,500 persons in the colony, including about 2,500 slaves and five thousand whites. The potential for agriculture was reflected in the production of crops, such as indigo, along the Mississippi plantations.

France learned important lessons. France learned that it must provide sufficient troops to protect the settlers from Indian raids. Settlers also needed protection from the English and Spaniards. Since France could not afford the expense, the settlers would have to pay for their own protection. Only settlers of good character who were willing to work must come to the colony. No more criminals would be allowed. France needed to supply funds to construct public buildings. The colony must grow its own food and not depend upon France. Large numbers of slaves were needed to clear the forests and develop agriculture.

Trading posts were established at New Orleans and at some inland ports in the colony. New Orleans had grown into a bustling trading center. In 1719 a fort had been built on the present site of Baton Rouge. Further explorations of the colony were made during mining expeditions.

John Law and his companies had done great things for Louisiana. However, the commercial life and prosperity of the colony were on the verge of ruin in 1731 when the Company of the Indies withdrew.

En Partie 5 (Studying a Part). 1. What contributions did Law make to the colony?

LOUISIANA: A ROYAL COLONY (1732-1763)

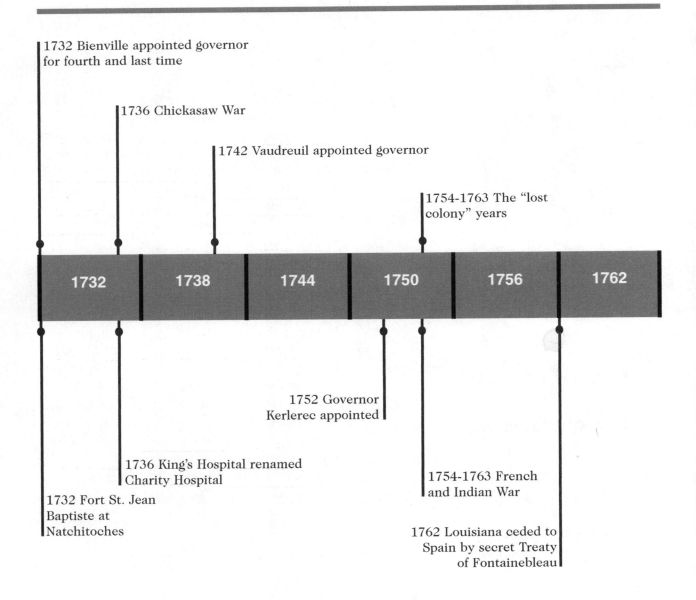

1732 Bienville appointed governor
for fourth and last time

1736 Chickasaw War

1742 Vaudreuil appointed governor

1754-1763 The "lost
colony" years

| 1732 | 1738 | 1744 | 1750 | 1756 | 1762 |

1752 Governor
Kerlerec appointed

1736 King's Hospital renamed
Charity Hospital

1732 Fort St. Jean
Baptiste at
Natchitoches

1754-1763 French
and Indian War

1762 Louisiana ceded to
Spain by secret Treaty
of Fontainebleau

LOUISIANA: A ROYAL COLONY

Bienville's Fourth Term

For the next thirty-one years, Louisiana was a royal colony. It was once again under the direct control of the king. Périer remained as governor for two years, then resigned.

Bienville's Last Term as Governor. By this time the colonists—even some of those who had opposed him—wanted Bienville back as governor. Perhaps it was the Natchez massacre that caused some of them to want the old Indian fighter back at the head of the colony.

In September 1732 Bienville was appointed governor for the fourth and last time. When he arrived in New Orleans from France on March 3, 1733, there was great rejoicing at his return.

Bienville, like Périer, realized that the Louisiana colony must become self-supporting. The settlers must have ways to make their living. Also, Bienville knew that **agriculture** was the place to begin.

Agriculture was a critical matter. An experimental farm had been in existence for a long time near New Orleans. Tobacco and indigo were being tried to find a staple crop. Bienville added experiments with cotton, hemp, flax, and silk to see if one of these would be right for Louisiana. It had long since been proven that rice, corn, and vegetables could be produced readily. These were essential for the use of the settlers. There was not enough produced with which to build an export business.

The colony had to have a crop to sell for cash. To find a marketable crop for the Louisiana settlers to produce was difficult. There was a scarcity of seed in the colony. There was never enough labor. The lack of sufficient numbers of farm animals and improved farm implements was an obstacle. To farm the land for the first time, virgin forests had to be cleared. The soil had to be broken up and prepared in rows for planting. Horses, mules, and oxen were in short supply. Under such conditions, progress beyond simple subsistence was very slow indeed.

It was possible to sell forestry products to France and the islands of the French West Indies. The quality of these products was below standard due to the lack of experienced craftsmen to handle the production. Therefore, the prices obtained for these products were low. Shipping costs, on the other hand, were high.

Bricks were made in Louisiana, but they were too soft and crumbly for marketing overseas. They were also too bulky to make exporting them profitable. They were useful only for colonial buildings.

With the unending financial troubles in France itself, there was no way for the colony to be unaffected. Only a few metal coins circulated in the colony. The colonists were left to trade mostly without money. They resorted to the barter system. Trade with the Indians was a matter of barter. Certain goods such as bear oil, tobacco, or corn were used as a standard of measurement.

Health Care. The King's Hospital had been established in 1722 in New Orleans. It took care of the military. Male nurses were used there until the Ursuline nuns took charge. The Ursulines provided nursing services from 1727 until the end of the French period.

In 1736 Jean Louis, a former sailor, left a

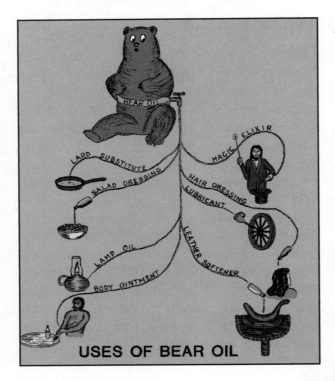

USES OF BEAR OIL

compounded medicines from a variety of plants and homegrown herbs. She is believed to have been the first female pharmacist in America.

More Indian Troubles. Indian troubles continued to plague Louisiana. The bitterness following the Natchez massacre lived on for years. A few Natchez warriors survived to cause trouble for the French. In one of the continuing acts of revenge against the French, a band of Natchez Indians attacked Fort St. Jean Baptiste at Natchitoches in 1732. St. Denis, the commandant, did not respond to their assault. As a result the band of Natchez Indians burned alive a French woman they had captured just outside the fort. The French pursued the attackers to a lake just west of Cloutierville. The French

fund for the establishment of a hospital for the poor. Dr. Prat, who had been in charge of the King's Hospital for years, was placed in charge. In 1759 a new building was built. It was named *Maison de Charite* (MA zon day CHAIR ə tē ē), or **Charity Hospital**.

There was a problem of contagious diseases in Louisiana. Apparently a separate hospital was established for smallpox cases. It was thought that the diseases were brought in from Santo Domingo. A crude system of quarantine was used. People with contagious diseases were separated from patients without such diseases.

Treatment was hindered by the limited knowledge of medicine. Medicines were compounded on the spot from native medicinal herbs and plants. Dr. Prat established a garden of medicinal plants. One of the Ursuline nuns, **Sister Xavier** (zā vi er),

Mural depicting modern Charity Hospital in New Orleans

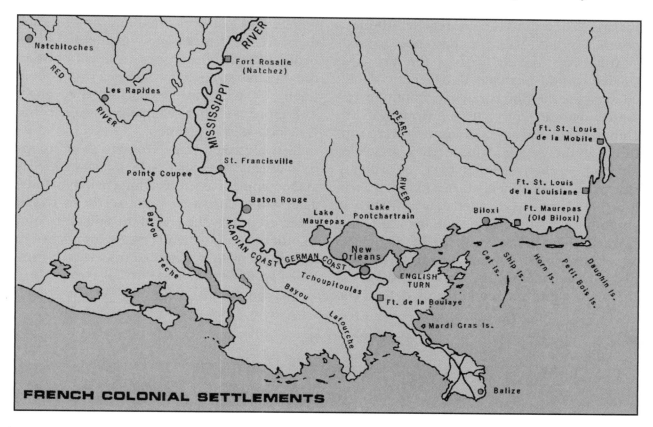

FRENCH COLONIAL SETTLEMENTS

and their Indian allies killed every Natchez warrior. After this battle, the lake and the hill rising above it were called *Sang pour Sang,* or "Blood for Blood."

There were other Indian groups who harassed the colonists. The **Choctaws** divided their loyalties between the French and the English. All Indians expected a flow of gifts from the European nations. With France's lack of funds, the supply of trinkets was too small to keep the Indians satisfied.

The Chickasaw War. The Chickasaws disliked the French. They enjoyed a close relationship with the English settlers to the east. When French traders went among the Chickasaws and obtained some of their

trade, the English were angry. They insisted that the Indians tell the French traders to stay out of Chickasaw territory. Perhaps it was for that reason that the Chickasaws murdered several French traders.

Bienville wanted to punish the Chickasaws for helping the Natchez. He ordered the Chickasaws to give up the Natchez refugees who lived with them. The Chickasaws refused. Bienville planned an attack.

In May 1736 Bienville assembled a force of over five hundred whites and forty-five free blacks. He ordered Pierre d'Artaguette, a commandant in Illinois, to meet him with an army in the Chickasaw country. Bienville left from New Orleans with his forces, which had been joined by six hundred Choctaw

Indians. When d'Artaguette reached the rendezvous point, Bienville had not arrived. D'Artaguette looked for him for ten days. Unable to find Bienville, d'Artaguette decided to attack the Chickasaws without him. His forces overran one village. However, the commandant and some of his men were captured at the second village they attacked. Meanwhile, Bienville had been delayed by stormy weather. When he and his men finally arrived, Bienville decided to attack. He was soundly defeated. The Indians had not harmed their prisoners prior to Bienville's attack. Afterward, d'Artaguette and fifteen of his men were slowly burned to death.

France could not endure this defeat. The French had lost over one hundred of its soldiers to the Chickasaws. Its defeat at the hands of the Indians was a critical blow in the nation's struggle for survival on the continent. French prestige demanded revenge. Therefore another campaign against the Chickasaws was planned.

Bienville asked France to send more troops to Louisiana. There had to be military supplies and equipment assembled for a march in force against the Chickasaws. Not to do so would mean eventually the end of the French colony. In order to secure the necessary supplies from France, Bienville was forced to delay the campaign against the Chickasaws for two years.

The campaign lasted until 1739. The French

Travel through the marshes was difficult.

built a fort where Memphis, Tennessee, stands today. About 3,500 men assembled and prepared for battle. Their preparations lasted so long that soldiers died and provisions ran short. When all was ready, Bienville was relieved of command. The French government sent the Sieur de Novilles (syur) to take his place. The war of the French against the Chickasaws finally ended in a stalemate. Neither side could claim victory. Instead, the French and Indians signed a peace treaty. The Chickasaws continued to harass the French colony even after the treaty was signed.

Bienville's Last Years. During the war there was no chance for progress on the home front. Louisiana settlers were drafted into the army. This required leaving their farms for months. The normal commerce that brought supplies from the Illinois country to Louisiana was destroyed. Hostile Indians made trade down the river a risky business. Inflation in the colony brought problems.

Storms and hurricanes in semitropical Louisiana came as predicted during certain seasons. There were always the periods of flooding after the winter rains. **Weather problems,** along with the **war,** the **lack of money, inflation,** and the poor **state** of the **economy,** caused great discontent among the colonists. Again the blame was centered on Governor Bienville.

Bienville, too, must have grown weary of so much criticism over so many years. He never recovered from the grief and humiliation of the Chickasaw defeat. The king was especially frustrated about the failure of Bienville's Indian policy. He wrote to the minister of the marine, begging to be recalled. After nearly forty years of service in Louisiana, the **Father of Louisiana** retired. He handed over the authority to the Marquis de Vaudreuil on May

10, 1743, and left Louisiana forever. He died in Paris in 1767 at the age of eighty-seven.

En Partie 1 (Studying a Part). 1. Describe Bienville's governorship. 2.(a) Why was he called the Father of Louisiana? (b) Justify the title.

End of the French Period

Vaudreuil, a Most Unusual Governor. Pierre Francois de Rigaud, Marquis de Vaudreuil (RĒ gō vō DRĀ Y), was appointed

Governor Vaudreuil.

governor April 27, 1742. Vaudreuil was reared in all the luxury that New France could provide. After joining the army as a young man, he received the rank of major at the age of twenty-two. He led an expedition against Indians in Canada and became a hero. He was awarded the highest honor in the French army, the Cross of St. Louis, at age twenty-six. Before he was thirty, he was appointed governor of one of the largest settlements in Canada. At thirty-nine years of age he was named governor of Louisiana.

Vaudreuil's outlook on being governor of Louisiana was different from the previous governors. His years in the colony were known for the governor's **lavish entertainment, elegant ceremonies,** and **military display.** Vaudreuil was the man who made New Orleans the "City that Care Forgot." He led an elite society that imitated the court at Versailles as much as possible. Vaudreuil formed a miniature court around the governor's office. His distinction of manner, his generosity, and his personal grace seemed to cast a direct reflection of the glory of Versailles. There was more entertainment and display during Vaudreuil's service in Louisiana than the colony had ever known. Some people resented this display of wealth.

Vaudreuil at first tried to be friendly with the **Indians.** He could not afford the required gifts, and he could not sell for cheaper prices. The European wars cut off contact with France for much-needed supplies. He did not receive enough trade items. The continual prodding of the Indians by the English resulted in harassment of the French colony. A group of Choctaws favorable to the English attacked the German settlements on the Mississippi River above New Orleans. Settlers were driven from their homes. Some were murdered. In 1748 Vaudreuil led an unsuccessful expedition against the Chickasaws. In 1752 the Chickasaws attacked French settlements again. Vaudreuil with his seven hundred men burned villages. Finally the Indians sued for peace.

The new governor tried to bring **financial order** to the colony. He removed the old paper money at a value much less than its face value. The colonists who held this money lost a great deal in the change to a new series of money.

Like all of the earlier governors, Vaudreuil tried to improve **agriculture.** Farming was the mainstay of the colony. Agriculture was aided by the immigration of planters from Santo Domingo. Indigo and tobacco were staples there. The new governor experimented with sugarcane. An unsuccessful effort was made to manufacture syrup and sugar. The wax of the myrtleberry was still an important article of trade. The wax was produced for candles and other purposes. Vaudreuil wanted to try cotton as a staple crop. This was done, but removing the seed from the cotton required many slaves working for many hours.

The colony was still small and struggling. A **census** taken in 1744 showed three thousand white inhabitants, eight hundred soldiers, and over two thousand slaves in the colony. On September 3, 1749, there was another setback. A hurricane destroyed crops, domestic animals, and buildings in the lower Mississippi area.

During his last years as governor, Vaudreuil was preparing for the next war against the English, the **French and Indian War.** The victor would dominate the North American continent. Louisiana defenses had to be improved. Defense of the Mississippi Valley would play a large part in the war.

The forts and military defenses of the colony had long been neglected. The neglect was at least partly due to the lack of funds with which to maintain and supply them. There were never enough troops to protect the settlers on the frontier in inland Louisiana. Vaudreuil finally received enough scarce money to improve the defenses of the colony.

Vaudreuil made worthwhile **contributions** to the colony. He started Louisiana's first flood-control efforts and its first formal police regulations. He required all owners of property along the Mississippi River to maintain a levee and a public road along the levee.

Governor Kerlerec.

In spite of the war in Europe and Indian troubles, the colony at last seemed to be prospering. With his social background, Vaudreuil brought an elegance to New Orleans that had never been there before. Louisiana—and New Orleans before he came—had an image of mud, heat, and mosquitoes. Vaudreuil gave the little port and the colony a boost with the social life he led. He provided a more inviting image.

Vaudreuil was appointed governor of Canada on June 8, 1752. Vaudreuil's appointment proved that the king was impressed with his tenure in Louisiana. He remained in New Orleans until February 3, 1753. He had to wait for his replacement. The vessel on which Vaudreuil sailed for France was stuck on a sandbar at the mouth of the Mississippi. His trip was delayed for six weeks.

Governor Kerlerec. Louis Billouart, Chevalier de Kerlerec (bē loo WAR kair LĀ rek) was appointed governor April 1, 1752. As usual the new governor did not arrive in Louisiana until months later.

Kerlerec was a military man. He had served in the French navy twenty-five years. As governor, he was concerned about defense of the colony and built a palisade around New Orleans.

A **religious "war"** between the Jesuits and the Capuchins (KAP ə chins), two groups of Catholic religious orders, went on during Kerlerec's administration. The war concerned spiritual supremacy in Louisiana. In 1717 the Capuchins had arrived in Louisiana. Nine years later, the Jesuits arrived. There was a struggle for power. Each claimed authority over all religious orders in the colony. The colony divided itself into religious factions. The

Capuchins ultimately prevailed, and in 1764 the Jesuits were forced to leave Louisiana. They disbanded in 1773, only to reorganize in 1814 and return to the state. The Jesuits remain in Louisiana today.

Kerlerec became governor at one of the most critical points in the colony's history. France was fighting for its colonies in America. Battles were not fought in Louisiana, but Louisiana was greatly affected by the **French and Indian War.** Louisiana was practically a "lost colony" from 1754 to 1763.

Cajun Mardi Gras.

France sent no settlers, money, or supplies. The colony was neglected and abandoned by the French government. By the end of Kerlerec's years in the colony, France had entirely lost interest in Louisiana.

New Ownership. On November 3, 1762, **France ceded all the colony west of the Mississippi River and the Isle of Orleans to Spain.** The secret treaty was signed at Fontainebleau, France. The king of France gave Louisiana to his cousin, the king of Spain, to keep Louisiana from being taken by England. It was to repay Spain for helping France during its war against England.

After Louisiana had been ceded to Spain, Kerlerec continued to act as governor. Kerlerec was notified a year later that Jean Jacques d'Abbadie had been appointed to replace him.

Contributions of the French. To begin with, the French achieved a **permanent settlement.** Sailing across the Atlantic in ships of that day was enough to discourage all but the most hardy. Water was scarce and bad. Food stored for the long journey was spoiled. People were so crowded that there was barely room for sleeping on the floor. Storms of great power imperiled the ships. Pierre Clement Laussat (KLĀ mahn lō sä) wrote in his record:

The weather became foul; and the seas very high. There was rain, strong winds, squalls, roaring waves, and water 38 to 48 fathoms deep. The brig rolled and pitched. No bottom at 100 fathoms. The prolonged and deafening noise of the sea; the impact of the waves as they broke against the side of the frail vessel; their sudden and furious eruptions as high as the tops of the sails, from which they fell back in torrents that flooded the deck; and the distant whistling of the wind—this was our most distressing situation.

The mosquitoes, fevers that plagued the people living in the lowlands, Indians who came out of nowhere and attacked the Frenchmen—these hardships came with the wilderness. Hard manual work in the struggle to clear woods and construct shelters was not for the lazy. France itself was in deep financial trouble. It could hardly do justice to the colony overseas. Yet, with all those problems, France founded and sustained Louisiana.

The Catholic **religion** was the only religion legally permitted under the French. The French approach to religion is still a part of Louisiana.

There are many other gifts. The **customs** of the French people—the folkways—became a part of Louisiana. *Bouche-ries* (BŌŌ shə rē), or hog-killings, *cochons de lait* (KŌ shon dā lā) (roasting suckling pigs over a slow fire), and Mardi Gras are only a few of the best known. Not so well known but even more important, perhaps, are the **skills** of craftsmen passed down through generations. These include skills from carpentry to sewing. French **cooking** has remained a part of Louisiana. The French gave us their **patterns** of **inheritance** and of settling the land. Their **music** and **art** left their marks.

One French contribution to Louisiana was a lasting influence on food.

A most obvious contribution is the French language with its many variations. Place names are often in French. Courtboullion (KŌ Ō be Ō yon) and countless other **French words** remain in the language of Louisianians.

One of the gifts of the French was their **outlook on life** that helped them endure. This was the *joie de vivre* (zwah duh VĒV rə) or "joy of living." To work hard and well was of first importance, yet to be cheerful and happy was essential. Louisiana inherited from the French a habit of laughter, dancing, high spirits, and love of being together with friends and family. The French manner of turning drudgery into a festive event has become a way of life in Louisiana. Many Louisianians have adopted the French motto *Laissez les bons temps rouler* (lay zay lay bawn tawn rou lay)—"Let the good times roll." For nearly three hundred years the rollicking spirit of our French ancestors has influenced Louisianians, whatever their roots.

En Partie 2 (Studying a Part). 1. How was Vaudreuil an unusual governor? 2. Why was the colony neglected by France? 3. (a) What was the Treaty of Fontainebleau? (b) In what year was it made? 4. Why was Louisiana given to Spain? 5. Why did Louisiana become a political pawn?

France had lost the war. Therefore, it was being forced to give up the colony that it had founded in Louisiana. France was completely expelled from the mainland of North America. For these reasons, French prestige declined all over the world.

Coup de Main
(Completing the Story)

Jambalaya (Putting It All Together)

1. Why was it difficult for the people of Europe to obtain reliable information about Louisiana?

2. List (a) economic problems of the colony, and (b) government problems.

3. Cite reasons France (a) failed in Louisiana and (b) is owed a debt of gratitude.

4. (a) Analyze French-Indian relations (b) colony-France relations, and (c) France-other countries relations.

5. What was life like for the colonists? Shelter? Food? Recreation? Health care? Religion? Hardships?

6. (a) Why were slaves brought to Louisiana? (b) When? (c) How many?

7. Why were the rivers the main routes of transportation?

8. On a map, locate all settlements made by the French. Put the date of settlement by each. Circle the capitals.

9. Compare Louisiana under Crozat, under John Law, and under the king.

10. Trace the growth of the Louisiana colony.

Potpourri (Getting Involved)

1. (a) Prepare an illustrated time line of the French colonial period, or (b) draw cartoons of the main events of the French period.

2. Construct an authentic model of (a) an early French fort, (b) a French colonial home, (c) a pirogue, or (d) a flatboat.

3. Prepare a map showing place names given by the French.

4. Dramatize (a) Iberville's journey, (b) the importation of slaves to Louisiana, (c) the treatment of Indians, (d) a fur-trading trip, (e) the Natchez massacre, (f) the arrival of the Casket Girls, (g) a voyage of unwilling settlers, or (h) life in the colony.

5. Interview La Salle, Iberville, Crozat, Bienville, and John Law concerning the failure of the French in Louisiana.

Gumbo (Bringing It Up-to-Date)

1. Relate present-day Louisiana to the French colonial period. How is Louisiana's present social and cultural background a reflection of its French heritage of the colonial period?

2. Report on what is being done to preserve Louisiana's French heritage.

3. Compare Law's venture with present land scams.

Overleaf: *The historic Presbytere on Jackson Square in New Orleans.*

During the Spanish Colonial Period

SPANISH COLONIAL LOUISIANA (1762-1770)

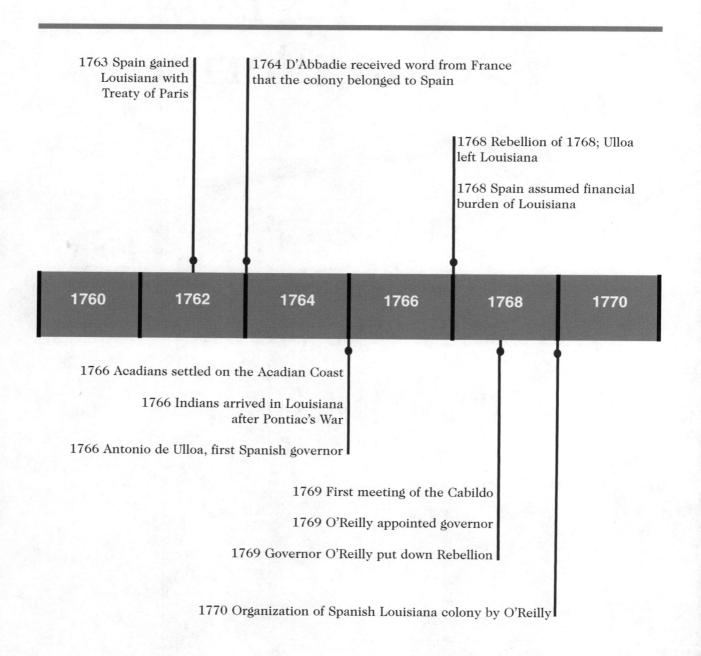

1763 Spain gained Louisiana with Treaty of Paris

1764 D'Abbadie received word from France that the colony belonged to Spain

1768 Rebellion of 1768; Ulloa left Louisiana

1768 Spain assumed financial burden of Louisiana

1760   1762   1764   1766   1768   1770

1766 Acadians settled on the Acadian Coast

1766 Indians arrived in Louisiana after Pontiac's War

1766 Antonio de Ulloa, first Spanish governor

1769 First meeting of the Cabildo

1769 O'Reilly appointed governor

1769 Governor O'Reilly put down Rebellion

1770 Organization of Spanish Louisiana colony by O'Reilly

SPANISH COLONIAL LOUISIANA

The French and Indian War ended in 1763 with the Treaty of Paris. France was completely expelled from the mainland of North America. The British received Canada and all of the French territory east of the Mississippi except the Isle of Orleans. Spain officially received the French territory west of the Mississippi and the city of New Orleans. Louisiana now belonged to Spain.

The Colony in Limbo

The Louisiana colony went through a period when it was treated as though it belonged to no one. The Spanish had a policy of *mañana* (mon YAH nə, Spanish for tomorrow), meaning that they would take the colony over when they got around to it. In the interval, France continued to send officials to govern the colony. All the time they complained about spending more money on the colony that did not belong to them.

D'Abbadie: French Governor. Kerlerec remained as governor until late 1763. Jean Jacques d'Abbadie (dah bə DE) replaced him. The king intended that d'Abbadie remain in the position until Spain took possession of the colony.

D'Abbadie found the colony in a terrible condition. He complained of the disorder "long existing in the colony." He referred to the "license" of the people as having had too much freedom for too long. There was a shortage of all kinds of supplies. He did what he could to restore trade and strengthen defenses. He tried to relieve the distressed French colonists without any support from France.

On September 30, 1764, d'Abbadie received official word from France that the

Governor d'Abbadie.

colony belonged to Spain. He was ordered to make the transfer. This was nearly two years after the secret treaty ceded the colony to Spain. It was not until d'Abbadie posted an announcement on the door of the church, in the custom of the times, that the Louisiana people learned of the transfer.

The people reacted in horror to the news. They were French! The idea of changing their flag, laws, language, and customs made them furious. They were angry that the king had given them to Spain. Louisianians were also fearful. For a long time stories had circulated about the treatment by the Spanish in Mexico, Florida, and the West Indies.

Critical Times in the Louisiana Colony. France was no longer concerned. Even though Spain owned the colony, there was no sign of the Spanish. Louisiana colonists had to manage for themselves.

A mass meeting was held in New Orleans. Every district of the colony was represented. A petition protesting the action was drawn up to send to King Louis XV of France. A leading merchant of New Orleans, **Jean Milhet** (mēl Ā) was sent to France to present the petition to the king.

Five months after d'Abbadie received the order to transfer the colony, he died suddenly of a stroke on February 4, 1765. An officer from Spain had not yet arrived to accept possession of the colony.

Aubry in Control. Captain Charles Philippe Aubry (fē LĒP Ō brȳ), commander of French troops in the colony, was the next highest ranking official. He was now in charge of Louisiana. He had no official authority except as an army officer. Aubry had no instructions from France. France did not appoint a successor to d'Abbadie. Spain was expected to take control of the colony at any moment.

The only money in use, French paper money, went down in value. Many citizens were financially ruined because of this. The French government would not redeem the money at face value. Rumors were that the money would be completely worthless under Spain. It was well known that Spain kept rigid control of the commerce of its colonies. Without such controls French merchants had been able to develop a brisk and thriving trade at the port of New Orleans. This trade appeared to be doomed under Spain.

Almost every Frenchman wanted the colony to remain under France. It was easy to stir the people to rebel against Spain.

Month after month went by with no sign that Spain was planning to take possession of Louisiana. The people began to think that

Church at Acadian Village Museum, Lafayette.

Milhet's trip to Europe had been successful. They were getting used to the news of Spain's ownership.

Ulloa's Announcement. Five months after d'Abbadie's death, **Antonio de Ulloa** (an TŌ nē ō dā ōōl YŌ ə) wrote a letter to the Superior Council. In it he stated that he was the new Spanish governor of Louisiana. The letter, dated July 10, 1765, was from Havana, Cuba. He wrote that he would be arriving soon to assume his duties.

Weeks and then months went by. Still the Spanish did not take control. The French flag still flew over the government buildings in New Orleans. French troops were still in New Orleans. Aubry was still in authority. It was over three years after Louisiana was given to Spain when the Spanish governor finally arrived in New Orleans.

En Partie 1 (Studying a Part). 1. What were the results of the French and Indian War? 2. Describe the atmosphere in the colony. 3. Describe the changes in governing officials. 4. (a) How long was it before the colonists learned the news? (b) How did they learn? (c) What was the reaction? (d) What action did they take? 5. (a) Why did Spain delay in taking control? (b) What did France think about the delay? 6. Why were conditions in the colony critical? 7. What did Jean Milhet do? 8. What news was received about the change in authority?

The Acadians' Migration to Louisiana

Arrival of the Acadians. In the midst of the gloom and depression, a party of strangers arrived in the colony. Twenty Acadians came to Louisiana in 1764. They had been exiled from their homes for almost ten years. They came from the peninsula of Acadia. The group settled in the area from near present-day Breaux (brō) Bridge to Loreauville (LORE o ville). In 1766, 224 Acadians were settled along the Mississippi River in a section that was called "the Acadian Coast." (In time the Mississippi River settlements in St. James and

Ascension parishes became known as the Upper and Lower Acadian coasts.) In 1767, 210 were forced to settle at Fort St. Gabriel. Another 149 in 1768 settled at Fort San Luis de Natchez. In 1769 some Acadians settled near other family members along the Acadian coast. These French migrants from France came in seven different boats, and all were treated well by the Spanish.

About fifty years before Louisiana was transferred to Spain, Acadia, a large peninsula on the east coast of Canada, had been ceded by France to Great Britain. The transfer was made at the end of Queen Anne's War. The British then changed the name of the province, **Acadia,** to **Nova Scotia** (New Scotland).

It was over four decades later when the French and Indian War started. The British were afraid that the Acadians would not fight against their fellow Frenchmen. They thought the French in Nova Scotia might even give aid to them. The English governor of Acadia demanded that the French settlers swear their loyalty to England. They were also told that they must leave the Catholic church. They might have been willing to sign their allegiance to England had they not been asked to leave their church. When the Acadians refused to meet the governor's orders, the English drove about six thousand persons from their homes. The English took over the small farms of the Acadians. They burned their houses and fields and sent the Acadians out to sea in crowded boats.

In 1755 the Acadians were deported from their homeland. Families and friends were separated. The Acadians went in different directions seeking new homes. Some went to Canada. Others headed for France. Some stopped at the British colonies along the Atlantic coast. Others went farther south to the West Indies. Many made their way to Louisiana.

Most of them were poverty stricken. D'Abbadie requested funds with which to assist them in settling in Louisiana. They were supplied with tools, livestock, and food from government stores in New Orleans. The refugees received grants of land along Bayou Teche and in the prairie section farther west.

Aubry had a difficult time finding supplies when some of the Acadians arrived. He went to the royal storehouse in New Orleans and got what he could. Each family was given food, clothing, a gun, and gun powder. Aubry sent them to settle on the lower Bayou Teche.

The intendant of New Orleans, Navarro, was surprised to find on the lists of arrivals on two of the ships that there a large number of single girls of marriageable age aboard. He checked further to find that sixteen stowaways were aboard the *St. Remy* and twelve on *La Amistad*. In addition, there were young sailors manning the boats who wanted to marry pretty Acadian girls. These men of the Spanish military had a problem. If they married while in service, their brides would not be eligible for government subsidies.

Without checking with Spanish authorities, Navarro published new rulings. He knew how much the Spanish wanted new settlers. Stowaways and sailors had a right to settle in the Louisiana colony. Any bachelor marrying an Acadian girl would enjoy the same rights as other family heads. This meant they would be eligible for government subsidies. Thus, Navarro arranged for twenty-three marriages.

Longfellow's poem *Evangeline*. Henry Wadsworth Longfellow wrote the epic poem

Statue of Evangeline, St. Martinville.

Evangeline about the expulsion and wanderings of the Acadians. He described the Acadian country of Louisiana. Today the land remains much as he described it. According to legend, the poem is based on the story of a real couple, Louis Arceneaux (ÄR cə nō) and Emmeline LaBiche (lə BEESH). Others say that there were many couples separated in the tragic situation encountered by Evangeline and Gabriel in the poem.

"Evangeline's" grave and statue can be found in the old Atakapas Cemetery. The home of "Gabriel" is now the Acadian Museum in Evangeline State Park at St.

Martinville. The Evangeline Oak, the meeting place of Evangeline and Gabriel, is near Bayou Teche.

Louisiana named a parish Evangeline, and another one was named Acadia for these people who added so much to Louisiana.

En Partie 2 (Studying a Part). 1. Describe the migration of the Acadians to Louisiana. 2. How were they treated by the Spanish? 3. What story is told in the poem *Evangeline?*

Ulloa's Administration

Arrival of Ulloa. The first Spanish governor was Antonio de Ulloa. He arrived on March 5, 1766, in a drenching rain to take possession of Louisiana. Captain Aubry formed his few troops in the public square to receive the new governor. Ulloa had only ninety soldiers with him. This was hardly enough to impress the colonists with his position as head of state. His small stature did not help his image. He had a reputation throughout Europe as being one of the outstanding scholars of his generation. Ulloa was a mathematician, scientist, and writer. This was of no interest to the colonists.

He did not take control immediately. Instead, Aubry continued to be in charge. He left New Orleans without lowering the French flag and raising the red and yellow colors of Charles III. French citizens, already confused, were more than puzzled at his failure to do so.

Ulloa was a practical man. The distaste of the colonists for a Spanish governor was clear to him. He had expected the French troops under Aubry to serve for Spain. They refused. With so few troops Ulloa felt it

Governor Ulloa.

unwise to assume complete control of the colony. Orders were issued in Aubry's name, but they were under Ulloa's direction. The arrangement proved to be very awkward. The Spanish government planned to allow the French a period of adjustment to their new government. Ulloa was told that Louisiana would be governed differently from other Spanish colonies. He was also advised to leave things as they existed under the French as much as possible.

Ulloa did not report to the Superior Council. Nor did he respond when the governing body asked for his commission or credentials. Since he ignored the body, it refused to accept Ulloa's authority. Members of the Superior Council were unhappy over this show of disrespect to their position. Worse, it increased the colonists' fears about Spanish rule.

With Aubry, Ulloa visited the interior posts and settlements. He stayed longer at Natchitoches than any other place. There he studied how he could establish communication with Mexico.

He ordered a **census** taken. There was a total of 5,552 white people and about the same number of Negroes. The many Indians living in Spanish Louisiana were not counted.

Ulloa left New Orleans in September 1766 without explanation. He went to the **Balize**. Ulloa raised the Spanish flag and established residence there. In late spring he was still at the Balize. Ulloa did not explain to the Superior Council nor anybody else why he did this. Had he done so, he might have found the people more tolerant. Aubry and other officers made trips to the Balize to report to Ulloa. Aubry issued orders from New Orleans. Ulloa conducted scientific experiments while he waited.

Trade Regulations. On September 6, 1766, Ulloa received new orders from Spain. No French ship was permitted to enter the port without first obtaining a permit from a Spanish official. Agents of foreign vessels were required to furnish lists of the goods aboard the ships. This list had to include the prices for which the goods were to be offered for sale. If the prices were too high, the agent was not allowed to unload. When the agent left port, he had to take a minimum of one-third of his cargo in products of the colony. In the spring of 1768, more regulations were issued. Only Spanish ships could be used in commerce. Trade was restricted to Spanish ports.

French ships had continued coming in and out of the port of New Orleans. They brought goods from Europe that the colonists needed. Spain's new regulations meant that henceforth Louisiana would only trade with the mother country. Spanish colonists were not allowed to trade with other Spanish colonists. Supplies desired by the colonists could not be obtained from Spain. They wanted goods from France. Even worse, the regulations confirmed the worst fears of French businessmen. They thought that the new orders were an indication that more restrictions on trade would follow.

New Orleans was a prospering small port by the 1760s. A group of the city's businessmen had taken advantage of opportunities to build a lively commerce. The economy of the little capital was largely dependent upon this trade. Now it seemed that it was going to be destroyed. Spanish trade regulations were too strict. They were afraid that their businesses would be ruined by these regulations.

Formal Possession. Ulloa planned to officially take over Louisiana from the French at the Balize. When Aubry protested, he decided to wait until more Spanish troops arrived. At the Balize Ulloa and Aubry signed a document called the *Toma de Posesion* (TŌ mä day po ze si ŌN) on January 20, 1767. It was an agreement to divide control of Louisiana between France and Spain. This joint rule would last until more soldiers arrived from Spain. The dual arrangement was known to both French and Spanish officials. They made no protests.

On December 4, 1767, Ulloa was still living at the Balize. By then he felt called upon to make an announcement. He announced that Juan Joseph de Loyola would become minister of finance on January 1, 1768. Spain was finally relieving France of the financial burden of the colony. This was five years after the colony became Spain's property.

Ulloa's Wedding. Another reason for Ulloa's delay in officially taking over New Orleans was his forthcoming wedding ceremony. He had been waiting for his bride, Doña Francisca Ramirez de Laredo y Encalada from Peru. She and Ulloa had been married by proxy, a privilege of royalty alone. Ulloa waited seven months for her to arrive. Although they were officially married, a marriage ceremony was performed by Ulloa's chaplain at the Balize when she arrived.

Nothing could have done more harm to Ulloa's acceptance by the French people. The idea of the governor of Louisiana being married in such a simple way upset them. The social elite in New Orleans were insulted. They felt that there should have been feasting, dancing, and celebrating. Even the religious leaders criticized Ulloa's marriage. They felt that it should have been performed in a church in New Orleans. Since Vaudreuil's term as governor, New Orleans society had rarely been without a celebration of some sort. A big wedding would have offered the opportunity for another celebration.

To make matters worse, Ulloa and his wife never joined the New Orleans social circle. The wives of the leading citizens would not call on her. They thought Ulloa's new wife was even more cold, haughty, and exclusive than her husband. The bride had brought attendants and friends with her from Peru. She plainly preferred their company. She did not even attend mass with the New Orleans people. Ulloa's bride only spoke Spanish. Her inability to speak French may have caused her to remain with her own group. He may have thought that participation in New Orleans' social functions was unimportant. If so, he was not prepared to be governor of Louisiana.

Problems. Ulloa used some of the gold and silver he brought with him to pay the soldiers of France under Aubry. Even that attempt to help the colony met with disappointment. The French were distressed that the French paper money was worth only one-fourth its face value under the Spanish.

The financial situation had worsened. Ulloa forbade illegal trade. Commerce in New Orleans was paralyzed. Spain's new commercial regulations increased the problems. Only Spanish wines could be imported. That made the Frenchmen furious.

Underneath all of their honest, legitimate complaints against Spain was the unalterable fact that the colonists were French. Being French, they dreaded being the subjects of the Spanish king. Their hopes faded when they got the news about their petition. Jean Milhet returned to New Orleans in late 1767. After an absence of two years, he announced the failure of his mission. Bienville tried to help. However, even the elderly former governor was not granted his request for an audience with the king. Bienville and Milhet then called on the prime minister, but were unsuccessful.

Plot of Revolutionists. Finally, French leaders, officials, officers of the armed forces, merchants, and planters met. At this meeting they made secret plans to get rid of Ulloa. The acknowledged leader was Nicolas Chauvin de Lafreniere (shō VAN lä frä NYAIR), attorney general of the province. Nicolas Denis Foucault (fou KŌ), first judge of the Superior Council, was one of the principal leaders.

Others were Lafreniere's brother-in-law, Joseph Villeré (vēl ā RĀ), and the Milhet brothers, Jean and Joseph.

On October 28, 1768, at eight o'clock in the morning the colonists met in New Orleans. De Noyan (nwä YÄN), a nephew of Bienville, led a band of armed men from the Acadian coast. Villeré led another group from the German Coast. Colonists came from below New Orleans. About four hundred people assembled. French soldiers under Aubry refused to fight the rebels. Aubry advised Ulloa and his wife to leave their official residence and go to a Spanish warship in the harbor.

Expulsion of Ulloa. Leaders of the angry people presented a **petition** against Spanish rule to the Superior Council on October 29, 1768. It was signed by 560 of the leading men of the colony. The next day, the Superior Council voted in favor of the petition. The council had no authority under Spain. Nevertheless, it ordered Ulloa to leave the colony within three days. Aubry protested. It did no good because he did not have sufficient troops to suppress the rebellion. Ulloa had sent the few Spanish soldiers he had to various inland ports over the colony. The troops he had been promised had not arrived.

Aubry was caught in a bad position. He had written back to France before this incident, "My position is most extraordinary. I command for the King of France and at the same time I govern the colony as if it belonged to the King of Spain."

The Spanish warship was not able to leave the port of New Orleans immediately. Ulloa left it and boarded a French ship instead. Before the ship was to leave, a curious incident was said to have occurred. Some historians say that the ship was set adrift by young Frenchmen before daylight on November 1, 1768. The young men were returning from a party late at night. They cut the rope that moored Ulloa's ship to the wharf. Afterward, Ulloa angrily ordered the captain to sail for Havana, Cuba. Another version simply states that Ulloa left New Orleans in a French sailing vessel headed for Havana. Historians state that threats to cut the ropes had been received.

When Ulloa arrived at Havana, he sent to Spain a report of the Louisiana mob action against him. It brought quick response. Spanish officials, furious at the insult, were determined that Spain would be avenged. The French leaders would be punished. The Spanish flag would be respected by the Louisiana French.

Meanwhile, the Superior Council again ruled Louisiana. The council sent a petition to the king of France asking him to take control of Louisiana. Although he refused, rebel leaders and their friends felt that they had succeeded. Ulloa was gone from the colony. The leaders rejoiced, sang patriotic songs, and cheered King Louis.

The revolution had happened without the Louisiana leaders foreseeing the position in which they would find themselves. The colony belonged to Spain. That they knew. However justified they felt in their anger, they were now at the mercy of Spain. They had insulted Spain by expelling Ulloa. However much at fault Ulloa had been, he represented Spanish authority in a Spanish colony. France had turned a deaf ear to their pleas.

Second Petition to France. Another meeting of French leaders was held in New Orleans. The group drew up a second petition to King Louis XV. It was called "Memorial to the Planters and Merchants of Louisiana on the Events of October 29, 1768." The Louisiana French asked France not to give the colony to Spain. The petition recited the story of the colony under France. It repeated the loyalty of the people to France.

Three men took the document to France. King Louis paid no more attention to the second petition than he had paid to the first. All France wanted was to wash its hands of the expensive colony. France did not wish to anger its ally Spain.

Revolution of 1768: Aubry. While the revolutionists were taking their petition, Captain Aubry sent his report of these events. The series of acts against Spain were now called the Revolution of 1768. Aubry had no sympathy for his fellow French. He called leaders of the revolution "twelve firebrands." He sent a report to France blaming Ulloa for what had happened. He also stated that "it is no pleasant mission to govern a colony which undergoes so many revolutions."

Last Appeal. The leaders of the rebellion were spurned by France. Now they realized that their very lives were at stake. In desperation they appealed to the English, who now owned Pensacola. The English would have nothing to do with the situation. They refused to offend Spain over Louisiana.

Finally, the leaders considered independence. They could establish a republic in Louisiana. They knew that an independent republic could not survive without the support of a powerful nation. France, England, and Spain would be against the independent republic. This being so, the leaders realized that it could not last.

En Partie 3 (Studying a Part). 1. Describe the arrival and action of the first Spanish governor. 2. Explain reasons for the colonists' fear. 3. (a) What was done to protest? (b) Who were the leaders? (c) Did Milhet succeed in his mission? 4. What was Ulloa's relationship with the Superior Council? 5. How did the new trade regulations affect the colonists? 6. What were some of the problems Ulloa faced? 7. Under what circumstances did Ulloa leave? 8. What other plans did the revolutionists have?

The Establishment of Spanish Rule

Alejandro O'Reilly's Arrival. Lt. Gen. Alejandro (ə lā HÄN drō) O'Reilly was an impressive military man. He was born in Ireland but moved with his parents to Spain when he was ten years old. O'Reilly had saved King Charles' life in 1765 during a raid in Madrid. He received the king's commission appointing him governor and captain general of the province of Louisiana on April 16, 1769.

On August 17, 1769, O'Reilly arrived at the Balize with more than two thousand men and twenty-four ships. This was a show of power to support his authority. It had been eight months since Ulloa had left. The colonists were amazed that the king of Spain had sent one of his highest officers and one of the greatest generals of Europe to Louisiana.

O'Reilly had orders to put down the Louisiana rebellion. The leaders of the revolution tried to get people to resist the new Spanish governor. The colonists paid no attention. In such a crisis, three of the leaders of the revolution met O'Reilly at the Balize.

Jackson Square, formerly the Plaza de Armas, in New Orleans.

These were Lafreniere, Pierre Marquis (mär KĒ), and one of the Milhets. They wanted to make known their willingness to live under Spain. O'Reilly entertained the visitors at dinner. He treated them so courteously that they admired him. The rebel leaders thought that O'Reilly was not going to hold their past actions against them.

O'Reilly's Entry into New Orleans. O'Reilly's dramatic entry with his display of military force was a big contrast to Ulloa's arrival. This display was meant to impress Louisianians with the power of Spain. On August 18, 1769, a great colorful ceremony was held at the Plaza de Armas (PLAH thā deh ÄR mähs), or French Place d'Armes. The colony was formally transferred by Aubry to O'Reilly. Amid the roll of drums and the blare of trumpets, O'Reilly's two thousand soldiers, in full uniform, watched the flag ceremony. The French flag was lowered, and the Spanish flag was raised high on the staff.

Arrest of Conspirators. O'Reilly lost no time in arresting the twelve leaders of the revolution. For his information about them, he called on Aubry. The French people bitterly resented Aubry's part in the actions against his fellow Frenchmen.

O'Reilly quickly took measures to secure justice against the revolutionists. He invited ten ringleaders of the revolution to his house. As they arrived, one at a time, he had them arrested. They were taken to different places of confinement. They were not allowed to communicate with one another. The French considered this to be treachery on O'Reilly's part. One of the rebels, Joseph Villeré, did not accept the governor's invitation.

The People's Reaction. The people of New Orleans were in a state of frenzy. They closed themselves up in their homes. Many prepared to leave the colony and seek refuge with the British. O'Reilly finally realized the extent of their fears. He issued a statement pardoning all persons except those arrested. Three days later a meeting was held so that citizens could pledge allegiance to Spain. If they refused, they were required to leave the colony. O'Reilly sent officers to the military posts in the interior. This was so that citizens there could take the oath of allegiance to Spain. Most took the oath.

Punishment of Rebels. Spanish law defined a traitor as anyone "who labors by deed or word to induce any people or any provinces under the domination of the king,

Governor O'Reilly.

to rise against his majesty." The law stated that traitors were to be put to death.

The trial of the rebel leaders was carried out according to Spanish law. It lasted for several weeks. There was no trial by jury. Each of the accused was examined separately. So were the witnesses. Judges made the decisions. No one questioned the fact that the rebels were attempting to get rid of Spanish rule. One defense used by the rebels was that Spain had not taken legal possession of the colony. Therefore, they argued, they had not broken any Spanish laws. The judges ruled that the revolution was carried out on Spanish soil. They were, therefore, under Spanish law.

O'Reilly pronounced the sentences. Joseph Petit (pā TĒ) was sentenced to prison for life. Balthasar de Mason (BAL thǝ sar MĀ sone) and Julien Doucet (ju li EN dōō SĀ) got ten years. Jean Milhet and Pierre Poupet (pē AIR poo PAY) got six. Hardy de Boisblanc (BWÄ blän) also got a prison sentence. Villeré was declared "infamous" (disgraced). Five were sentenced to be hanged. They were Lafreniere, de Noyan, Caresse (kǝ RES), Marquis, and Joseph Milhet. The public hangman was instructed to destroy any revolutionary documents belonging to the group.

No Frenchman would act as hangman, in spite of the large reward that had been offered for anyone who would serve. The leaders sentenced to be hanged were execut-ed by a firing squad of Spanish soldiers. Those sentenced to jail were sent to a huge prison called Morro Castle at Havana, Cuba. Later, they were pardoned by Charles III of Spain at the request of the French ambassador.

Not only were the leaders executed or imprisoned, but their property was seized by the Spanish government. These men were the wealthiest business and political leaders of Louisiana. Most of them were related. Their wives and children were left with nothing.

Aubry's Fate. Aubry left for France. At least that is what was said in the colony. His ship wrecked off the coast of France on February 17, 1770. Aubry drowned. Many colonists felt that he got what he deserved.

"Bloody O'Reilly." O'Reilly was soundly hated by the French in Louisiana. He was called "Bloody O'Reilly." Yet, as tragic as the revolution was for its leaders, O'Reilly was sent to Louisiana for one purpose. He was to punish these leaders. Spanish honor had to be upheld and respected.

Rebellion was in the air—and not merely in the Spanish colonies. The English colonies on the east coast were seething with rebellion.

Spain was having trouble with two other colonies. She felt the need to get Louisiana colonists under control. Spain also wanted the treatment of the revolutionists in Louisiana to serve as a warning to all others who might be thinking of rebelling against Spanish authority.

The Contributions of O'Reilly. O'Reilly changed the government from French to Spanish. His reorganization cut the expenses to half of what they had been under the French. O'Reilly employed attorneys to write a set of laws under which Louisiana would

Patriot leaders are executed by O'Reilly.

be governed. This set of laws came to be known as the **O'Reilly Code**. All laws, orders, and decrees were published in Spanish after December 1, 1769. The form of government established by O'Reilly was used throughout the Spanish period.

General O'Reilly abolished the Superior Council. In its place he formed another group, the **Cabildo**. It was composed of ten members. The governor presided. Most of the members were from New Orleans. O'Reilly ordered that a suitable building be constructed for the new government.

Then the general appointed **comman-**

dants for each district in the colony. These were selected from among the French residents. They were in charge of most minor official matters involving persons living at their posts. The commandant was responsible for the preservation of order; the upkeep of levees, highways, and bridges; and the policing of slaves. He also enforced locally the royal decrees and ordinances passed by the Cabildo.

O'Reilly visited interior forts. The Spanish general knew that the colonists had given him the unflattering nickname "Bloody O'Reilly." He said that he was going to the distant forts to show the colonists that he did not have "horns, hoofs, and spiked tail." O'Reilly appointed a surveyor for each district. The French had not made **surveys** to determine exact boundaries of property. This led to many disputes. The Spanish recorded property boundaries. The surveys aided farmers by establishing land titles. The surveying of land was one of the most important contributions made by the Spanish.

On February 18, 1770, O'Reilly's **land ordinance** was issued. It remained unchanged until the 1790s. It was O'Reilly's system of homesteading. The attractive offer is believed to have been the reason for the large increase in population during the Spanish period. The ordinance provided that each newly arrived family be given a tract of six to eight arpents of frontland on a river or bayou. The tract was forty arpents in depth. The grantee had three years to build a levee and drainage ditches. A road behind the levee with bridges over ditches also had to be constructed. Within three years the grantee had to clear the entire front to a depth of two arpents. A fence had to enclose the cleared land and all improvements had to be maintained.

A new **census** was taken under O'Reilly's orders. New Orleans had 3,190 persons. Of these, 1,225 were slaves, and one hundred were free people of color. In the whole colony there were 13,538 people. At least half were slaves.

O'Reilly continued the **trade policies** issued by Ulloa. However, he did urge Spain to allow the colony to trade with Cuba. Spain could not use lumber from the colony, but Cuba was in need of it. Spain allowed the colony to trade with Cuba in 1777.

O'Reilly vowed to break up the practice of "going to Manchac." This was a common expression in Louisiana. It referred to the trade between the colonists and the English located on Bayou Manchac. This unlawful trade commenced after the English gained possession of the land east of the Mississippi in 1763. Here the English traders sold supplies needed by planters and merchants of New Orleans. Such trade became even more important when the Spanish banned French ships from the port of New Orleans. Goods from Europe had to be secured if the Louisiana business was to prosper. Under these conditions much smuggling developed.

O'Reilly forbade the **importation** of **West Indies slaves**. He required that slaves imported be those from Africa. This way they would not have adopted voodoo. Slaves transported to the islands practiced this strange cult. Fresh from their homeland, slaves could be trained to better suit the needs of settlers. They would not absorb any ideas of freedom that might exist among the island slaves.

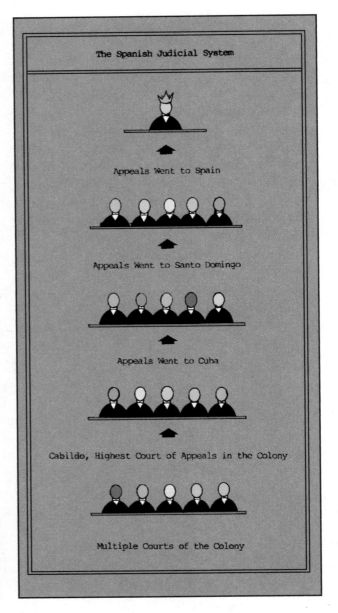

The Spanish Judicial System

Appeals Went to Spain

Appeals Went to Santo Domingo

Appeals Went to Cuba

Cabildo, Highest Court of Appeals in the Colony

Multiple Courts of the Colony

During the seven months O'Reilly was in Louisiana, he made other changes. Shortly after he arrived, he started sending the military troops that he had brought with him back to Spain. He organized about one thousand men in the colony into a **military unit**

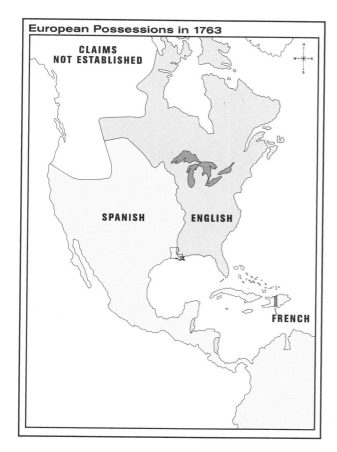

European Possessions in 1763

CLAIMS NOT ESTABLISHED

SPANISH

ENGLISH

FRENCH

were strictly religious divisions. O'Reilly changed the jurisdiction of the Catholic church in Louisiana from Canada to the bishop of Santiago de Cuba.

The first meeting of the Cabildo was held on December 1, 1769. At this meeting O'Reilly transferred the office of governor to **Unzaga**. He had brought the well-trained Unzaga with him for the purpose of making him governor. O'Reilly stayed a while after Unzaga took the position to be sure that the colony was on sound footing. After O'Reilly completed the work that he was assigned to do, he left Louisiana. He sailed back to Spain on October 29, 1770.

En Partie 4 (Studying a Part). 1. Describe the arrival of O'Reilly. 2. How was O'Reilly's takeover different from that of Ulloa? 3. (a) What did some of the leaders of the revolution do when O'Reilly arrived? (b) What were the results? 4. (a) What part did Aubry play? (b) How did the French feel about him? 5. What happened to the leaders of the revolution? 6. Relate the action taken with the establishment of Spanish authority. 7. Describe the government set up by O'Reilly. 8. What else did he do?

for defense. It made the people feel more in control of their own fate rather than being under the heel of "foreign" troops. Another step he made was to divide Louisiana into twenty-one **parishes**. O'Reilly's parishes

SPANISH RULE UNTIL 1800

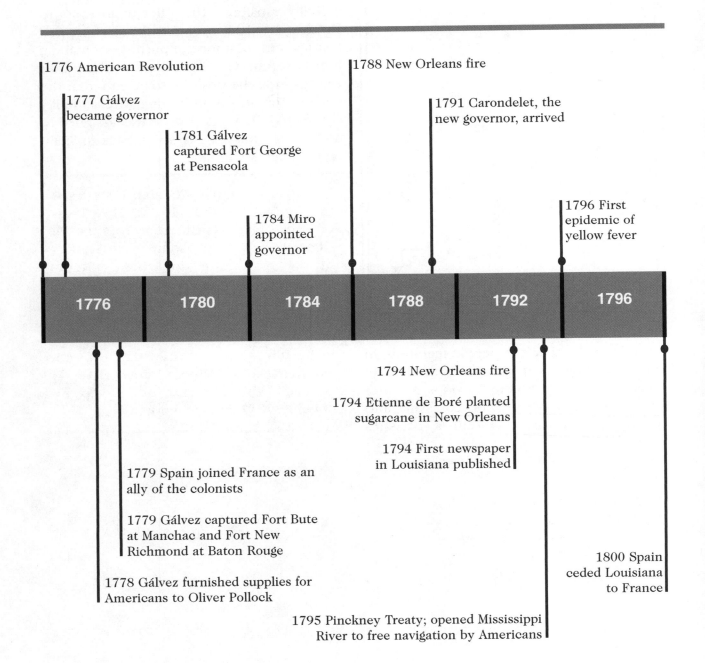

1776 American Revolution

1788 New Orleans fire

1777 Gálvez
became governor

1791 Carondelet, the
new governor, arrived

1781 Gálvez
captured Fort George
at Pensacola

1796 First
epidemic of
yellow fever

1784 Miro
appointed
governor

1776	1780	1784	1788	1792	1796

1794 New Orleans fire

1794 Etienne de Boré planted
sugarcane in New Orleans

1794 First newspaper
in Louisiana published

1779 Spain joined France as an
ally of the colonists

1779 Gálvez captured Fort Bute
at Manchac and Fort New
Richmond at Baton Rouge

1800 Spain
ceded Louisiana
to France

1778 Gálvez furnished supplies for
Americans to Oliver Pollock

1795 Pinckney Treaty; opened Mississippi
River to free navigation by Americans

SPANISH RULE UNTIL 1800

Spanish Administration

Unzaga's Rule. Unzaga was an elderly man when he came to the colony with O'Reilly. He had been a colonel in the troops at Havana, Cuba. He was a mild-mannered Spaniard for whom O'Reilly had prepared the way. Unzaga's marriage to a French woman helped him become a part of the population. He was well liked by the colonists. He also continued to appoint Creoles to important positions in the government.

The governor did not go out of his way to find violations of Spanish law. He ignored the illegal trade situation going on with the English in Manchac. Unzaga knew that he must gain the friendship of the French citizens of Louisiana. Stopping the trade would ruin his chances of doing so. He allowed English merchants to establish stores in New Orleans as well.

Louisiana became prosperous under Spain, which helped the people accept Spanish rule. Hard money was introduced when Spain used silver to pay the cost of officials and others needed in the colony. Trade improved. French paper money, worth one-fourth of its face value, soon disappeared.

In 1771 the king of Spain made plans for a **public school** in the colony. Manuel Andres Lopez de Armesto (ar MES tō) and three assistants came to New Orleans as schoolmasters. They were to introduce the Spanish language and instill loyalty to Spain. The school failed because the French parents would not send their children. Most of the children who attended were those of Spanish officials.

Under the French only the Roman Catholic church was allowed in the colony. The Spanish were even more dedicated to the **Catholic church**. The people spoke French, so they wanted French-speaking priests. None of the Spanish priests spoke French well.

The **American Revolution** was brewing among the thirteen English colonies on the Atlantic coast. Unzaga strengthened the militia in case of British attack during the revolution.

In 1776, a forceful young militarist, **Don Bernardo de Gálvez** (ber NAR dō day GĀL vāz), became commander of Spanish troops in Louisiana. He quietly aided the American

Governor Unzaga.

colonists by sending them the supplies that he could spare.

In 1776 Unzaga was promoted to captain general of Caracas, Venezuela. This was the same year the English colonies declared their independence. Unzaga left the colony in March 1777. He had seen the bad feelings against the Spanish gradually disappearing.

Military Governor: Gálvez. Gálvez became governor in 1777. A brilliant young military officer of the age of twenty-nine, Gálvez came from a line of prominent military men in Spain. He had already gained military experience in Portugal and Mexico. His father was viceroy of Mexico. His uncle became president of the Council of the Indies.

The military operations of Gálvez dominated life in Louisiana during much of his administration. Gálvez was an ambitious young military officer. He could see possibilities of capturing English possessions across the Mississippi River. He would thereby gain recognition and promotions. The Spanish officials favored the American colonists because they considered England a powerful rival.

As long as Spain remained neutral, Gálvez secretly aided the American revolutionists. So did other Spanish officials in Louisiana. They lent money to the colonists. They allowed American agents to make New Orleans their headquarters. The agents helped the colonists obtain guns and ammunition for use against the British. Military supplies were shipped to New Orleans. Then these supplies were shipped up the river to **George Rogers Clark**. Clark became a hero of the American Revolution who saved the western land for the United States. **Oliver**

Pollock was one of the most active of these American agents in New Orleans. He was the fourth largest financier of the Revolution. Pollock also helped Clark by securing credit to buy supplies locally.

Lagniappe—*Oliver Pollock.* Pollock was an active agent in obtaining military supplies to fight the British. He aided **George Rogers Clark** in securing financing and supplies. Pollock went to debtor's prison and lost all he had to support the Revolution. After buying his way out of prison, he made enough money to start over.

James Willing, a rebelling colonist, conducted a **raiding expedition** down the Mississippi and into British territory. Apparently he was on an errand for the Continental Congress. He attempted to persuade the people of West Florida to support the colonists. Those who did not agree to take an oath to support the United States suffered. Willing looted the plantations in West Florida and destroyed or took much of their belongings. Later he tried to dispose of his stolen goods in New Orleans.

In early 1778 Gálvez offered homes to the British refugees from West Florida. These people were left homeless because of Willing's raid. Many of these people who fled to New Orleans were able to return to their homes.

On May 8, 1779, Spain joined France as an ally of the colonists three years after the Declaration of Independence. The decision was very important to Louisiana. Gálvez then had reason to attack the English across the river. War disrupted the normal development of the colony.

Governor Gálvez.

When Spain joined the rebelling colonists, Gálvez saw his opportunity. He placed Don Martin Navarro (nä VÄR rō), the intendant, in charge of civil affairs in Louisiana. Then he marched on the nearest English forts. He had planned to attack earlier, but a hurricane sank all of his vessels. In 1779 he quickly captured **Fort Bute** at Manchac.

A week later he captured Fort New Richmond at **Baton Rouge**. He did this by deceiving the British. Some of his men hid in the woods during the night and pretended to be ready to attack. The British wasted their ammunition during the night. Meanwhile Gálvez moved some of his men to the other side of the fort. At daylight on September 21, 1779, he started the attack.

It ended in the afternoon. The British commander surrendered. He gave up the fort at Baton Rouge and **Fort Panmure** at Natchez to Gálvez. This Spanish victory prevented the British from getting a stronghold on the lower Mississippi. For this achievement the young Gálvez was promoted to brigadier general.

Spanish vessels captured several English gunboats on the lakes and on the Mississippi. Next, Gálvez headed for **Mobile**. This time a tropical storm struck. Several ships went aground, and many men and guns were lost. It took a month to regroup. Gálvez captured Fort Charlotte at Mobile from the English in 1780. For this achievement he was rewarded with a promotion to major general.

On May 10, 1781, Gálvez captured Fort George at **Pensacola.** It was then the strongest fort in the Floridas. This victory established Spanish control over East Florida. The battle had gone on for more than a month. The Spanish appeared to be losing. A lucky shot from a Spanish cannonball caused the powder magazine inside Fort George to explode. With part of the fort walls destroyed, the Spanish were able to storm the fort. The English surrendered. Gálvez was then given new titles that were even more imposing than the old ones: Knight Pensioner of the Order of Charles III, lieutenant general, and finally, captain general of Louisiana and Florida.

A few months after the fall of Pensacola, fighting in America ended. As a consequence of Gálvez's victories, Spain received the Floridas when peace was made in 1783. This marked the end of the American Revolution. The military genius of Gálvez was recognized and rewarded. The fighting

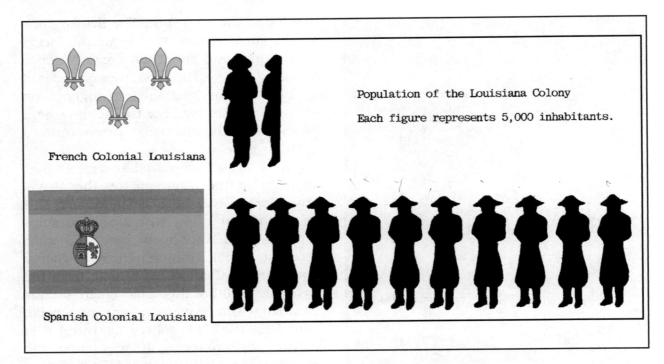

French Colonial Louisiana

Spanish Colonial Louisiana

Population of the Louisiana Colony

Each figure represents 5,000 inhabitants.

spirit and ability of Louisianians were demonstrated.

Civil Affairs. During Gálvez's absence the war had overshadowed routine civil affairs. Now for the first time, Spain separated the Louisiana colony from Cuba.

Although Spanish citizens were encouraged to come to the colony, few came. The **Isleños** (is LĀ nyos) ("Islanders") from the Canary Islands migrated to the colony. They found homesites around St. Bernard and Bayou Lafourche. One group settled on the Amite River. A total of 1,582 Canary Islanders had migrated by 1779. **Spaniards** from Malaga, Spain, settled at New Iberia on the Teche. Five hundred settled at New Iberia. Acadians continued to come into Louisiana. The **1784 census** showed a total of 32,114 white and black, slave and free, in the colony.

A Spanish royal decree in 1778 encouraged settlers to come to Louisiana. The head of each family was given a land grant of five arpents fronting a stream. He could own as far back as he could clear. The allotment also included one bushel of corn for each adult and half a bushel for each child for the first year. Each family received a hoe, an axe, a scythe or sickle, a spade, ten hens and a cock, and a two-month-old pig.

During Gálvez's years as governor Spain granted more freedom of trade to the French businessmen in New Orleans. They were allowed to trade with the French West Indies. Then Spain went even further in freedom of trade. Trade was allowed with France for a period of ten years. Gálvez encouraged trade by reducing the export and import duty. For two years ships were duty-free. Plans were made for a customhouse, too. The Spanish, then, learned to favor trading with the French to "going to the Manchac."

Gálvez was given the highest prize the Spanish king could give him in colonial administration. He was named viceroy of Mexico. Louisianians hated to see the brilliant young military man and his Creole wife, Felicie de St. Maxent d'Estrehan, leave the colony. Gálvez has been called Louisiana's first Creole folk hero. Galveztown was named for him. He died in Mexico in 1786 of a fever. He was only thirty-eight years old.

En Partie 1 (Studying a Part). 1. What was Unzaga's attitude toward trade with the English? 2. What part did Louisiana play in the revolt of the American colonists? 3.

Governor Miro.

Trace the action of Gálvez during the American Revolution.

Major Crises

Governor Miro: 1784. The next governor of Louisiana was one of the mildest mannered and most progressive the colony ever had. He was **Don Estevan Miro** (ME rō). Brigadier General Miro had been on the military expeditions with Gálvez. He served as acting governor in 1780 during Gálvez's absence. He was a well-educated man who spoke both French and Spanish. Miro married a Creole, Marie Celeste Elenore de Macarty. His marriage helped him win the goodwill of the people.

Miro's administration was outstanding. Miro relaxed restrictions against the colonists' trade with Americans up the Mississippi River. A hospital for the treatment of leprosy (Hansen's disease) was established in Iberville Parish.

Miro encouraged Americans to settle in the area now called the Florida parishes. Most of these settlers were **Protestants**. They did not have to become Catholics. In the rest of Louisiana settlers had to pledge allegiance to Spain and practice Catholicism. In 1785 the **Post of Ouachita** (Fort Miro, Monroe) was established by Don Juan Filhiol (fil HOIL). In the 1790s Col. Abraham Morehouse of Kentucky took settlers to the Ouachita River Valley. They settled on the land grants of Bastrop and Maison (MA zon) Rouge.

A **census** was taken in 1788 by Miro's administration. The Spanish colony had 43,111 residents. Blacks numbered 19,945. Within the limits of present-day Louisiana

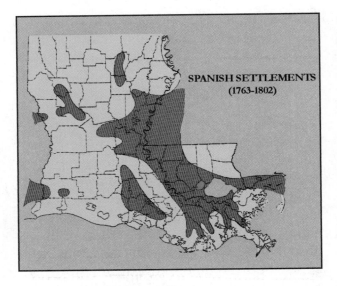

SPANISH SETTLEMENTS
(1763-1802)

admirable speed he supplied tents for the homeless people. He dispatched ships to the United States to obtain food. All restrictions on American trade on the Mississippi River were removed so that the homeless could be helped.

Don Andres Almonester (än DREZ al mō NES ter), the richest man in the colony, helped pay to replace the buildings destroyed by fire. The Cabildo, the St. Louis Cathedral, the Presbytere, Charity Hospital, a new governor's house, the public school, the church of the Ursuline convent, and sheds for an outdoor

there were thirty-four thousand persons. The population of the entire colony had more than doubled since the Spanish took over.

Most of the residents of the colony lived in and around New Orleans. New Orleans was a busy port town. About forty boats at a time could be seen anchored at the docks. When it rained, sewage floated into the narrow streets. The town was infested with insects and reptiles.

New Orleans Fire. On Good Friday, March 21, 1788, 856 buildings valued at 2.6 million dollars went up in flames in New Orleans. Over a thousand people were left without homes. The fire started in a private chapel in the home of an official. It was caused by a lighted candle falling against lace draperies. In five hours almost all residences and government buildings had been destroyed.

It was told that the Capuchins would not ring the church bell because it was Good Friday. The bells would have called the city's volunteer firefighters.

In this disaster, Miro became a hero. With

The Cabildo.

market were built. The new structures featured Spanish architecture. There were courtyards, ironwork, high ceilings, balconies, and arched windows and doors.

Spanish Plot Against the United States. Miro saw the possibility of Spain's securing the land between the Allegheny Mountains and the Mississippi River. Settlers who crossed the mountains into the frontier of Tennessee, Kentucky, and other areas felt neglected.

Miro contacted well-known Americans to interest these resentful settlers in starting a movement to obtain Spanish annexation of this United States territory. Miro's most active agent was **Gen. James Wilkinson** of the United States Army. Thus, Wilkinson received pay from both the United States Army and Spain at the same time. Some historians think that he was a traitor to the United States. Others think that he was trying to get trade advantages in New Orleans for the Kentucky settlers.

Inquisition Crisis. Spain was undergoing an Inquisition—a type of church court—to search out heretics and punish them. The Inquisition seized and tried people who had opinions contrary to those of the Catholic church. Fr. Antonio de Sedella was sent to Louisiana to carry out such a mission. Miro forced him to return to Spain. Because of Miro's action, there was no Inquisition in Louisiana.

Other Efforts of Miro. Miro did as much as he dared to relax the strict Spanish trade regulations. Miro taxed imports and exports at a lower rate than previously used. He permitted limited trade with Americans.

Miro made every effort to secure the goodwill of the **Indians**. The Indians were able to play the Spanish against the Americans to the east. Miro ignored Spanish rules so that he could get along with the Indians. He allowed agents to bring in some American goods from Georgia and the Carolinas to trade with the Indians. The American traders gave the Spaniards many worries. They made better deals with the Indians. Miro met with the Choctaws, Chickasaws, and Alabamas at Mobile and signed treaties with them. He promised to help protect their land.

Miro's Departure. Miro was old and tired and ready to return to Spain. After many requests fell on deaf ears, finally he was granted permission to go home. The people over whom he had ruled for seven years regretted his leaving.

Francisco Luis Hector, Baron de Carondelet (ector kä rôn dē LĀ). Governor Carondelet arrived December 30, 1791. He was a veteran in government service. Carondelet did not speak English. He did have a lot of ability and energy. He quickly won the friendship and respect of the Creoles.

Effect of French Revolution. Carondelet was governor during a period of crisis. George Washington had been inaugurated as president of the United States in 1789. That same year, France broke into revolution. The French people in Louisiana had sympathy for the people in France. The king of Spain did not want the new French ideas about liberty to be brought to Louisiana. No one could own any coin, clock, or other article that showed the figure of Liberty.

After Louis XVI was beheaded, Spain declared war on France. Carondelet's troubles increased. The ideas of "liberty, equality, and fraternity" of revolutionary France caused problems in the colony in spite of the king's warnings. Frenchmen in the New

Governor Carondelet.

boats patrol the Mississippi River. This, he wrote to Paris officials, was to impress the citizens with the power of the government. These precautions were necessary to check any inhabitants whose sympathies with the French revolutionists might be too strong.

Many French royalist refugees came to Louisiana to escape the Reign of Terror in France. Carondelet encouraged them to come. He hoped that their tales of horror would discourage the sympathizers in the colony. Large land grants on the Ouachita River were made to two of these royalists. The Baron de Bastrop received more than thirty square miles of land. The Marquis de Maison Rouge received a vast stretch of land on the river. Newcomers were granted land in West Florida and other parts of the colony. They had to take the oath of allegiance to Spain. If Protestant, they could not erect churches or worship publicly.

Trade. Carondelet restricted navigation of the Mississippi River. He hoped that residents along the river would ask that their area belong to Spain. The use of the river was very important to them. The navigation of the Mississippi was the bait Carondelet offered.

Merchants from the Atlantic states had become an important part of the commercial life of the port of New Orleans. Western produce came down the Mississippi for outside markets. Imports went up the river to the westerners. Spanish authorities were unable to prevent the sale of American goods to planters on the lower Mississippi. The problem continued for many years.

Carondelet was liberal in interpreting and enforcing Spanish law. Despite existing Spanish laws, he allowed Louisiana residents to trade with Americans. He also

Orleans theater had the orchestra play the national anthem of France. Carondelet issued a proclamation to silence the sympathizers. They were not allowed to discuss or read aloud any printed matter about the French Revolution. Those who did so were fined or sent to the prison of Morro Castle. Carondelet forced about seventy persons to leave the colony. He sent six of the leaders of the French rebels in Louisiana to prison to silence them.

The governor took further measures to deal with the dangerous situation. He reorganized the military and repaired fortifications around the city. He even had a few

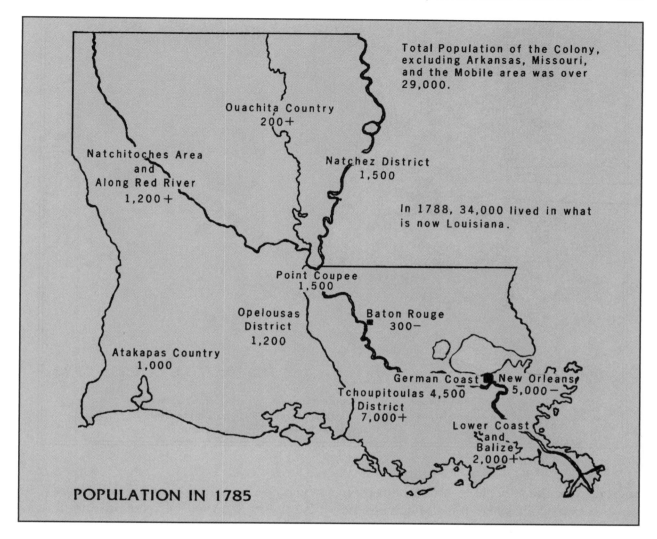

Total Population of the Colony, excluding Arkansas, Missouri, and the Mobile area was over 29,000.

Ouachita Country
200+

Natchitoches Area and Along Red River
1,200+

Natchez District
1,500

In 1788, 34,000 lived in what is now Louisiana.

Point Coupee
1,500

Opelousas District
1,200

Baton Rouge
300−

Atakapas Country
1,000

German Coast
Tchoupitoulas 4,500
District
7,000+

New Orleans
5,000−

Lower Coast and Balize
2,000+

POPULATION IN 1785

allowed foreign ships to enter the port as Spanish. Spain was not in a position to supply the colony. The people were grateful for the governor's policy allowing some **free trade**. It helped to improve the welfare of the colony.

Agricultural Development. Agriculture was the basic industry of the planters along the lower Mississippi. In the early 1790s a new insect attacked the **indigo** crop, the chief staple. In three years these insects almost

destroyed that crop. During the crisis the idea of planting **sugarcane** was revived. Until this time Spain had not allowed the sugar industry to thrive. This was probably because sugar was a staple of Spanish islands. Spain did not want Louisiana to compete against them.

Sugar planters had migrated from Santo Domingo to Louisiana. They were accustomed to raising cane as a staple. Now they lent their help to the Louisiana effort. The refugees taught local planters how to plant

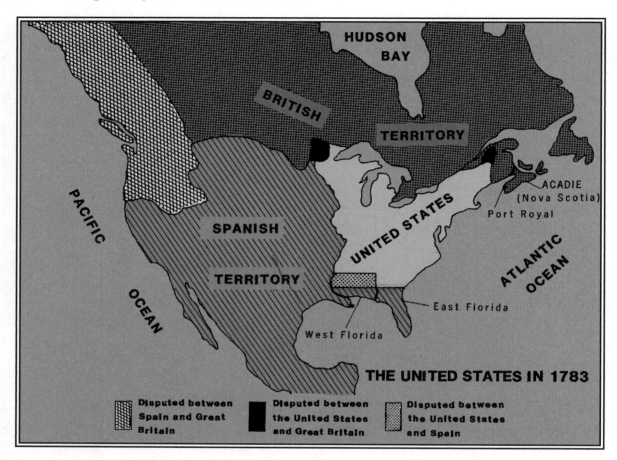

THE UNITED STATES IN 1783

Disputed between Spain and Great Britain

Disputed between the United States and Great Britain

Disputed between the United States and Spain

and cultivate the cane. They also taught them how to construct sugar mills and manufacture high-quality sugar.

In 1794 **Etienne de Boré** (bō RĀ) planted sugarcane on his plantation (now Audubon Park in New Orleans). In 1795 de Boré started the profitable sugarcane industry when he succeeded in granulating sugar. In that year he produced a sugar crop worth twelve thousand dollars. Sugarcane rapidly became a major crop. After sugar was granulated, more land and slaves were acquired. Sugar mills were built. Sugar-producing plantations increased in number.

Once Spain had agreed to buy all of the

tobacco the colony could produce. In 1790 the Pointe Coupee District produced nearly seventy-five thousand pounds of tobacco. During this period Spain reduced considerably the number of pounds of tobacco it would buy from Louisiana. Now there was no market for the tobacco in Europe. Prices fell, and the growers were forced to find a new crop that could be sold at a profit. It was at this time that **cotton** began to take the place of tobacco as one of the staple crops of Louisiana.

En Partie 2 (Studying a Part). 1. What part did Miro play in trying to get United States territory for Spain? 2. Describe the first New Orleans fire. 3. What did Miro do when Spain attempted to prosecute non-Catholics? 4. (a) What European revolution was going on during Carondelet's administration? (b) What effects were felt in Louisiana? (c) How were they handled?

Continued Challenges

Unrest. In spite of all the problems, the population of the colony steadily increased. Secret societies that aimed at returning Louisiana to France still existed in New Orleans. The city gates were closed at an early hour to prevent outsiders from coming into town. A system of syndics was established. The syndics were men living no more than nine miles apart serving as citizen-guards. A commandant was in charge. Any signs of rebellion, such as gossip or talk about plans against the government, were to be reported. Travelers were questioned. Whatever important knowledge that they might have was to be written down and reported.

The Pointe Coupee Slave Rebellion. The French Revolution was felt in Santo Domingo. Slaves rebelled on the island. A series of terrible massacres of whites followed. Tales of these events reached Louisiana. When the slaves in the Pointe Coupee District heard about these happenings, they got ideas.

A plot developed on the plantation of Julien Poydras (poi DRÄS). He had the reputation of being a very humane slave owner. Slaves on other plantations joined in the plot. Three white men were participants also. The rebellion was to take place on April 15, 1795. On that day slaves were to kill their masters.

Plans changed quickly when the slave leaders quarreled. One of the leaders chose to have his wife inform the parish officials about the plans. The officials put the ringleaders, including the three whites, into prison. Some slaves attempted to free the prisoners. Fighting broke out. Twenty-five people were killed. About sixty were captured. Twenty-three slaves were tried and hanged at various points along the river. Their bodies were left on public display for several days as a warning to other rebels. Thirty-one slaves were whipped. The three white men were forced to leave Louisiana.

Slave Problems. White people of the colony were so fearful of slave **revolts** that they asked Carondelet to stop the entry of slaves into Louisiana. Slaves were not permitted to come into the colony from Santo Domingo after 1792. However, the import ban was temporary.

The French Black Code of 1724 regulated slavery during the early part of the Spanish period. In 1784 more stringent **regulations** were adopted. Slaves were not permitted to carry dangerous weapons. They could not sell anything without written permission from the master. They were not allowed to purchase intoxicating liquor. They could not assemble except in small groups under white supervision. Spanish regulations required that slaves have instruction in religion. But this regulation was not enforced. Marriages of slaves were encouraged, but the slaves were not enthusiastic about marriage. They felt that marriage was another type of bondage.

In 1790 the Spanish government called for better **treatment** of slaves. Colonial officials did not comply. They argued that lenient treatment would lead to insubordination and insurrection. On the whole, self-interest of masters dictated the care of the slaves. The food, clothing, and shelter provided depended upon the master.

At times bands of **runaway** slaves were a cause of fear to settlers. Slaves organized under capable leaders. The forests and swamps made it rather easy for a slave to run away. Some ran away when they were faced with a task that they did not wish to perform. Often they were looking for family members located on other plantations. Most were seeking freedom. Hunger and loneliness usually caused most of them to return. Runaway slaves lived by stealing from storehouses on plantations and in New Orleans. They did not hesitate to commit murder to avoid being caught. Planters used several different methods to catch them. Squads of soldiers, or militia, were sometimes sent out to trace runaways. Sometimes the masters themselves looked for the slaves. In 1784 a military expedition was used to capture an armed band of runaways. Over fifty were caught. The four ringleaders were hanged and the rest imprisoned.

The Second Fire. A second fire destroyed much of New Orleans on December 8, 1794. The destruction was caused by some boys playing with fire. A high wind helped the fire spread rapidly. In about three hours forty city blocks were destroyed. Two hundred buildings were leveled. Only two stores escaped destruction. Many people were left homeless. A smaller portion of the city burned than had burned six years before. However, the money value of the losses was greater than in the first fire. The loss of foodstuff was so great that there was danger of famine. Carondelet did all he could to assist the people.

One public building of great importance was not burned. This was the **St. Louis Cathedral**. The earlier cathedral had been destroyed by the fire of 1788. The new structure was completed in 1794. It was dedicated on Christmas Day.

After these two fires almost wiped New Orleans out of existence, little of French architectural influence remained. The buildings erected after the fires were of Spanish architecture. They were mostly made of brick, with roofs of tile. The only surviving French building in the Vieux Carré, or French Quarter, was the **Ursuline convent**. This ancient building survives today.

First Newspaper. The first newspaper in Louisiana was published in 1794. It was called *Le Moniteur de la Louisiane (Louisiana Monitor)* (lee MAHN ih toor deh loo zee AHN). It was a weekly written in French. The Spanish government sponsored it as the official journal of the colony. This means that government documents were printed in the paper. The journal included royal decrees and ordinances. At that time official documents were written in both Spanish and French.

Indians. Carondelet did not work simply to maintain peace with the Indians. He signed military protection treaties with the Chickasaws, Creeks, Cherokees, Talapouchas (tal ə PUSH əs), and the Alabamas. The Spanish policy was to use Indians as allies in wars against Spain's rival nations.

Carondelet's Canal. One outstanding project of Carondelet was the digging of an immense canal leading into New Orleans from Bayou St. John. This waterway, Carondelet wrote to Spanish officials, would drain the city of stagnant waters. Since New Orleans was on such low ground, flooding was always a great problem. It would permit small vessels to reach New Orleans from the Gulf of Mexico by sailing through Lake Pontchartrain. Local planters contributed their slaves for a period of time to help dig the canal. The canal was named for Carondelet.

Life in Spanish Louisiana. A Catholic bishop reported to the king that only about one-fourth of the people of New Orleans attended church. There were rarely enough priests. The bishop wrote to the king explaining that these people were ripe for rebellion.

There were few schools. The Ursulines maintained a school for girls. The bishop complained that the French language was used there. There were private schools for both boys and girls. Most parents could not afford private schools or tutors. Consequently, most children received no education at all. At the time of the great fire in 1788, four hundred boys and girls were being taught "reading, writing, and ciphering" in eight private French schools. Spanish officials tried to induce public schools to teach the Spanish language in order to instill loyalty to Spain. They failed because French parents did not send their children to the public school. With so few students, the school was turned over to the Catholic church in 1789. There were no colleges in Louisiana. French fathers who could afford to do so sometimes sent their sons to college in France.

Life in Spanish Louisiana was more comfortable than it had been in the early years under the French. Farming, crafts, and trade had developed to provide colonists with more home furnishings. Still, medical practice was crude, and modern sanitation was unknown. The population had grown. Commerce at the port continued to increase, attracting more and more attention from Europe.

Entertainment was simple. There were theatrical performances in New Orleans. Cafes or coffeehouses were favorite meeting places of the men. There were card games, billiard tables, and drinks in the cafes. Business deals were often arranged at these places. Dances and parties were held in private homes. Hunting and fishing were favorite sports for men. Both men and women played cards.

Possession Problems. Americans had tried to secure Louisiana for the United States for a long time. Various plans had been devised to accomplish this. The Spanish were well aware of this. Problems between the Americans and Spanish officials over this effort continued until the end of the Spanish period.

Like Miro, Carondelet continued to try to obtain the area between the Allegheny Mountains and the Mississippi River for Spain. His efforts were unsuccessful.

The Pinckney Treaty. Spain was losing power among the nations during these years. When the news reached Spain that John Jay of the United States had gone to England to discuss a treaty, Spanish officials were worried. They thought the two nations were plotting against Spain. Spain wanted the friendship of the United States. The American meeting with England made Spain more receptive to discussions with the United States about such matters as navigation on the Mississippi River.

In 1795 Thomas Pinckney, the American minister in Spain, was able to conclude a very favorable treaty with Spain for the United States, known as the Pinckney Treaty. It opened the Mississippi River to free navigation by Americans. Americans acquired the valuable **right-of-deposit** for a three-year period. At the end of that period Spain was to decide whether to renew it. American businessmen could use warehouses at New Orleans for goods awaiting later shipment to markets elsewhere. There was no charge for this service. Spain also agreed to keep in check the Indians under its control who had been attacking Americans. The treaty set the northern boundary of West Florida at thirty-one degrees north latitude.

The time came to carry out the provisions of the Pinckney Treaty. Carondelet and **Don Manuel Gayoso de Lemos** (gäh YŌ sō LAY mōhs), the commandant at Fort Panmure at Natchez, had no intention of doing so. Spain had held onto the Natchez area, which had been ceded to the United States by the Pinckney Treaty. Gayoso claimed he was at Fort Panmure to defend against an attack by the British from Canada. A United States commissioner, Andrew Ellicott, was to survey and mark out the boundary between the United States and Spanish West Florida.

Ellicott received only excuses from Carondelet and Gayoso. An uprising of the Americans resulted in 1797. Carondelet and Gayoso resisted to the point of war. Gayoso was once forced to take refuge in Fort Panmure. The American commissioner declared that he would repel by force any attempts to imprison American citizens in Natchez. The anger of the people was such that no matter what Gayoso tried, there could be no peace. He and Carondelet had stirred up resistance because they refused to honor the Pinckney Treaty.

Finally Gayoso granted the requests of the Americans to honor the treaty. The Spanish surrendered the post at Natchez. The West Florida boundary at the thirty-first parallel was finally surveyed. It was marked as the international boundary between American and Spanish possessions.

Carondelet's Last Years in Office. European conditions prevented Spain from devoting much time or attention to the development of Louisiana. Agriculture remained the principal industry. Cattle-raising continued in the southwestern part of the colony. The Spanish government could not find a market for all the tobacco produced. In spite of Spanish neglect, the colony prospered to a degree.

Before Carondelet ended his career as governor, there had been one crisis after another. In 1795 a French crew had captured the Balize. Naturally, that frightened the colonists. Within a few months the Spanish regained control. Commerce was also a problem. Robberies were so frequent on the unlighted streets of New Orleans prior to 1796 that something had to be done. Also, Carondelet feared that the many friends of the French Revolution in Louisiana might cause trouble. For those reasons he put lights and watchmen on the streets of New Orleans for the first time. Oil lamps were hung by chains at the corners. In 1796 he organized a regular twenty-four-hour police force for New Orleans. There were thirteen *serenos* (watchmen). They called out the hour and the state of the weather. This was the practice in Europe. Police were called at night only in case of alarm. Carondelet placed a tax of nine reales (12½ cents) on every chimney to provide funds for improvements. He ordered the people of Baton Rouge to rebuild their levees.

Carondelet carried out the laws and punished violators. He removed officials who did not perform their duties well and replaced them with others who would.

What was described as the first epidemic of yellow fever visited New Orleans in 1796. Morales (MŌ rāl is), the intendant, wrote back to Spain that it was a disease known in America as "black vomit."

Louisiana, in spite of many problems, prospered under Carondelet. He was given a promotion and sent to Quito (early name of Equador) in 1797.

En Partie 3 (Studying a Part). 1. What measures did Carondelet take to improve life in New Orleans? 2. How did the slave revolt in Santo Domingo affect Louisiana? 3. What was the right-of-deposit? 4. (a) What treaty did the United States sign with Spain? (b) How did it affect the colony?

Last Years of Spanish Rule

Short-Term Governors. There were three other governors before the end of the century. They were Gayoso, **Casa Calvo** (KÄ sə KÄL vō), and **Salcedo** (säl THĀY dō). These last three governors shared a common problem. Navigation of the Mississippi River dominated the administration of each of them. Americans upstream evaded the Pinckney Treaty's provision for right-of-deposit in New Orleans. The use of the river and the need of the facilities at the port for free trade heightened the interest of the United States in securing New Orleans for itself.

Don Manuel Gayoso de Lemos became Carondelet's successor on July 30, 1797. Born in Spain, Gayoso was forty-five years old when he became governor of Louisiana. Ten years earlier, the army lieutenant colonel had been assigned to Natchez as commandant.

A year after he arrived in Louisiana, Gayoso published the policies he planned to pursue in the colony. He felt some order had to be introduced in making grants of land and in admitting immigrants. He sent instructions to commandants at the various posts: "Commandants are forbidden to grant land to a new settler coming from another spot where he has already obtained a grant. Such a one must either buy land or obtain a grant from the Governor himself."

Gayoso demanded that settlers who were single remain so at least four years and work "in some honest and useful occupation" before they could receive a land grant. An

Governor Gayoso.

Spanish architecture in New Orleans.

exception could be made if the individual "should marry the daughter of an honest farmer with his consent, and be recommended by him." Only married people could receive land grants at once. No Protestants were to receive land grants. The size of the land grant varied according to the number of productive household workers. Religious freedom for Protestants was granted to the first generation only. Their children had to become Catholics.

Trouble over navigation of the Mississippi continued in 1798. Spain refused to renew the right-of-deposit for another three years. That caused renewed agitation in the West. Americans were in favor of the seizure of New Orleans. They were determined to continue free navigation of the Mississippi.

Gayoso, at the age of forty-eight, died of yellow fever on July 18, 1799, during an epidemic. He had done a satisfactory job during a very troubled time for the colony.

Don Francisco Bouligny (bōō lēg NĒ) served as acting governor after Gayoso's death. He was commander of Spanish troops in the colony. He had come over with O'Reilly and was primarily a military man. He had fought with Gálvez. Bouligny served from July 18 to September 13, 1799. Nothing of importance happened during his short term.

Sebastian Calvo de la Puerta y O'Farril, Marquis de Casa Calvo was sent from Havana as the newly appointed governor. Casa Calvo had come to Louisiana with O'Reilly when he was eighteen. He had not remained in the colony, however. His appointment was only temporary. He was to serve until the Spanish king named a permanent governor.

Carondelet had temporarily stopped the entry of slaves from foreign countries. In 1799 planters of lower Louisiana requested that Governor Casa Calvo allow the free trade of slaves. The cabinet in Spain allowed five thousand slaves to be sent to the colony duty free. The cabinet resolved "not to go farther" in extending the privilege. This action satisfied the planters.

During Casa Calvo's term, negotiations were underway for Spain to return the colony to France. With Napoleon rising to power at the same time, a new factor was affecting the destiny of Louisiana. This factor was the yearning of the French people for their one-time American empire. Napoleon wanted the Louisiana colony back for France.

Casa Calvo left for Cuba when the next governor arrived. **Juan Manuel de Salcedo** was appointed governor October 24, 1799, but he did not arrive until the middle of June 1801.

Salcedo was an old military man. His son was a Spanish officer in Louisiana. It was said that this son dictated most of Salcedo's policies as governor.

Change of Ownership. On October 1, 1800, Spain ceded Louisiana to France. The secret **Treaty of San Ildefonso** (il dā FON sō) was signed on that date. The treaty was kept secret for some time. France made no immediate preparations to take over the colony.

During Salcedo's entire term of office, France owned the colony. Salcedo had one important duty to perform. He was to assist in the formal transfer of Louisiana from Spain to France.

Contributions of the Spanish. The major contribution of the Spanish was in administration, which established a badly needed stable economy. A sound financial base was laid. Gold and silver coins were brought by the Spanish to the colony. The Spanish piece of eight (*real*) became the model for the United States silver dollar. The efficient governors provided a dependable framework of government for settlers. The population increased. New Orleans developed into a sizable city and important port. Spanish architecture is still evident in New Orleans, Natchitoches, and elsewhere in the state. The beautiful ironwork of the Vieux Carré has been appreciated since Spanish colonial days. The Spaniards made a most valuable contribution in surveying property lines and establishing firm boundaries. The Spanish also left their place names. Their peppery cuisine is one of the reasons Louisiana is noted for its delicious foods.

Louisiana's French and Spanish inheritance makes our state unique. No other state in the United States has the same background.

En Partie 4 (Studying a Part). 1. What was the problem that dominated the administration of the last three Spanish governors? 2. (a) What were the provisions of the Treaty of San Ildefonso? (b) When was it signed? 3. Identify reasons that Spain ceded the Louisiana territory to France. 4. Summarize the contributions of the Spanish.

Coup de Main
(Completing the Story)

Jambalaya (Putting It All Together)

1. Summarize the Spanish period by naming the main events in chronological order. Make a topic sentence with each main event.

2. Describe the conditions of the following under Spanish rule: (a) slaves, (b) agriculture, (c) trade, (d) religion, (e) standard of living, (f) money exchange, (g) education, and (h) health care.

3. Map work: (a) show the territory in dispute between Spain and the United States from 1783 to 1795, (b) label Spanish settlements in Louisiana, (c) show boundaries of Spanish Louisiana, and (d) label the Floridas.

4. Compare progress under the French and under the Spanish.

5. Analyze reasons Spanish governmental practices strengthened the colony.

Potpourri (Getting Involved)

1. Compare Longfellow's poem with the true story of the Acadians.

2. Trace the route of the Acadians.

3. Research the reasons Longfellow happened to write *Evangeline*.

4. Make an Acadian house model, or dress a doll as a typical Acadian.

5. Prepare a time line of events for the years 1762 to 1803.

6. Conduct a forum to contrast O'Reilly with Gálvez—their personalities, their administrations, and their reputations. Show how events in history altered their careers.

7. Write a series of letters to someone in France from a well-to-do Creole, tracing the feelings of the French toward the Spanish.

8. Debate: "The Spanish contributed more to the development of Louisiana than did the French," or "The right-of-deposit should not have been given."

9. Stage a council between Indian chiefs and Spanish officials. Include all aspects of Spain's Indian policy.

10. Relate the effects of the Revolution of 1768 with later revolutions in the rest of the world.

Gumbo (Bringing It Up-to-Date)

1. Report on ways the Acadians are preserving their heritage.

2. Show the Acadian influence on modern Louisiana and the rest of the world.

3. Conduct an imaginary tour of Acadian country.

4. (a) How have the Spanish buildings in New Orleans been preserved? (b) What is the present status of preservation?

5. Compare (a) the Spanish hard specie with present-day United States money, or (b) Spain's control over the right-of-deposit with present shipping arrangements at the port of New Orleans.

6. Show the Spanish influence in present-day Louisiana.

Overleaf: *Gen. Andrew Jackson (on white horse) was the hero of the Battle of New Orleans.*

From 1800 until 1860

LOUISIANA IN TRANSITION (1800-1812)

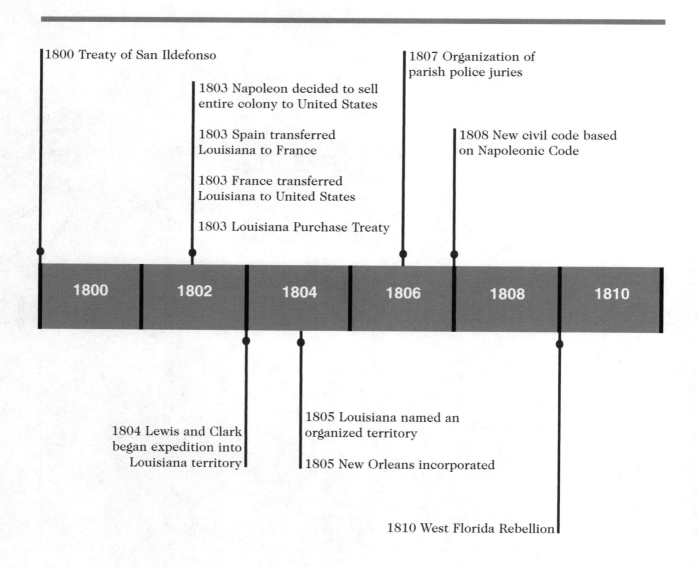

1800 Treaty of San Ildefonso

1803 Napoleon decided to sell entire colony to United States

1803 Spain transferred Louisiana to France

1803 France transferred Louisiana to United States

1803 Louisiana Purchase Treaty

1807 Organization of parish police juries

1808 New civil code based on Napoleonic Code

| 1800 | 1802 | 1804 | 1806 | 1808 | 1810 |

1804 Lewis and Clark began expedition into Louisiana territory

1805 Louisiana named an organized territory

1805 New Orleans incorporated

1810 West Florida Rebellion

LOUISIANA IN TRANSITION

New Owner: France

Plans of Napoleon. The French Revolution brought many years of chaos to France. Finally, Napoleon Bonaparte, one of the most remarkable men in history, became ruler of France. One of Napoleon's ministers, Talleyrand, had been exiled in the United States for a time. He encouraged Napoleon to get a foothold on the North American continent for France again.

The people of France had always regretted losing the Louisiana colony. Some of the French in Louisiana still hoped that they would belong to France again.

Spain had held the colony for almost forty years. During most of this time, the power of Spain had been declining. Even though the colony had been prosperous during the 1790s, Spain still could not afford Louisiana.

Treaty of San Ildefonso. Napoleon had a study made of the Louisiana colony. He received the results of the study in September 1800. Less than a month later, he closed a deal with Spain. France, with the Treaty of San Ildefonso, received a bargain. On October 1, 1800, the treaty was signed giving Louisiana and the Floridas to France. In return, Napoleon promised to create a kingdom in Italy for the son-in-law of the Spanish king, Charles IV. This agreement was kept secret for almost two years.

The treaty was not ratified by the king. Charles IV balked until it was agreed that France would never give up Louisiana to any other country. This, too, was kept secret. On March 21, 1801, a second treaty was negotiated at San Ildefonso.

Delay in the Occupation of Louisiana. When the secret Treaty of San Ildefonso was worked out between Spain and France, France agreed to wait six months before claiming Louisiana.

Meanwhile, someone leaked information about the treaty to United States Secretary of State **James Madison.** He, in turn, informed President **Thomas Jefferson. Robert Livingston,** United States minister to France,

Napoleon Bonaparte.

remained in doubt about what he regarded as a rumor. He asked Talleyrand. The French minister assured him that no final settlement had been made concerning Louisiana. The Americans were afraid to have someone as powerful as Napoleon take possession of such a large part of North America.

By the time Napoleon was ready to take charge of the colony, it was 1802. Then it was necessary for him to send military troops to Santo Domingo. Napoleon thought that this island was the key to the new French empire he wanted. Unfortunately events in Santo Domingo caused Napoleon to change his mind. Slaves led by Toussaint L'Ouverture (tōō SAN loō ver TUR) were in revolt on the island. Napoleon sent his brother-in-law Gen. Charles Victor Emmanuel Leclerc to get the situation under control. General Leclerc and twenty thousand troops had landed at Santo Domingo in January 1802. In a yellow fever epidemic most of the soldiers died. General Leclerc died on November 2, 1802. The slave revolt became more violent. Napoleon knew that war with England was coming. With these and other problems Napoleon had to delay plans to deal with the Louisiana colony. Spain continued to control it.

En Partie 1 (Studying a Part). 1. (a) Why did France want Louisiana back? (b) Who was the leader of France? 2. Why did Spain consider giving up Louisiana? 3. How did France obtain Louisiana? 4. What were two agreements made by Napoleon in his deal with Spain? 5. Why was ratification of the treaty delayed? 6. Relate the revolution in Santo Domingo to the occupation of Louisiana by France.

The Purchase of Louisiana

The right-of-deposit. The ongoing conflict over the right-of-deposit in New Orleans reached a crisis on October 16, 1802. **Morales,** the Spanish intendant at New Orleans, withdrew the right-of-deposit.

Up river American farmers had found a way to avoid paying duty to store their products in Spanish warehouses. They stopped at plantations above the city and sold their produce to traders. There they unloaded produce for whoever would buy. Many flatboats unloaded their goods before reaching New Orleans. The planters liked it that way. This was an open violation of the letter and spirit of the right-of-deposit. Morales resented this. The only way he could break it up was to withdraw the right-of-deposit.

People living west of the Mississippi River and in the upper valley of the river were intensely angry at Spain. **President Jefferson** wrote to the United States minister to Spain instructing him to impress upon Spanish officials the serious crisis provoked by Morales. The withdrawal of the right-of-deposit and navigation rights on the river gave them no outlet for marketing their crops.

The entire trade of the American West passed through New Orleans. Business in New Orleans had doubled in the five-year period ending in 1798. This was due to the use of the city's facilities. The total value of exports leaving New Orleans in 1803 was over two million dollars.

Whatever reason Morales had for his actions, he could not foresee the chain of events his action would set in motion. He could not predict the final outcome: the purchase of Louisiana by the United States.

New Plans. Radicals in Congress proposed measures that could lead to war. President Jefferson and others preferred to try diplomacy. It was **Robert Livingston** whom Jefferson instructed to buy the Isle of Orleans for a maximum price of ten million dollars. The president sent **James Monroe** as a special diplomat to assist Livingston in dealing with Napoleon and French officials.

Meanwhile, England was reportedly planning to seize Louisiana rather than allow France to occupy it.

Napoleon was reconsidering his earlier plans. He knew that war with England lay ahead. He feared that England would seize Louisiana when the conflict started. He also feared that the United States would form an alliance with England if he did not satisfy them regarding navigation on the Mississippi River. Napoleon needed money for the impending war. He did not wish to extend himself with this overseas empire and risk losing control in Europe. Despite heated opposition from his inner circle, Napoleon decided to sell.

United States–France Negotiations. On Sunday, April 10, 1803, Napoleon decided he would sell the entire colony to the United States. He put the sale of Louisiana in the hands of his minister of finance, Barbé-Marbois (BÄR bā mär BWÄH).

Livingston and Monroe were startled to find that not only the Isle of Orleans but all of the Louisiana colony could be purchased. The United States representatives explained that they were authorized to negotiate only for the Isle of Orleans and the Floridas. At that time, transportation between Washington and France was by sailing vessel, which took many weeks. It would take too long to reach Jefferson for approval. Therefore, without consulting their government, Livingston and Monroe proceeded.

Negotiations continued. Napoleon set the selling price at a minimum of fifty million francs (ten million dollars). The wrangling over the price went on for about two weeks. Finally, the arrangements were made for the United States to purchase the Louisiana colony for **fifteen million dollars**. That amounted to about four cents per acre.

The Louisiana Purchase Treaty was signed on **April 30, 1803**. News reached the United States July 3, 1803.

In the United States there was the problem of getting Congress to approve the purchase of the territory. The purchase would more than double the land area of the nation. President Jefferson had all along believed in sticking closely to the words of the Constitution. Of course, the Constitution said nothing about the nation's buying Louisiana.

New England politicians strongly opposed it. They said that it violated the Constitution. They argued that the price was too high. They were also sure that adding so many "foreigners" would destroy the Union. Even so, Congress approved the purchase. However, the nation had to secure the great amount of money required. The United States finally borrowed the money from Holland and England to pay France for Louisiana. With the interest added, the total cost ran around twenty-seven million dollars.

The signing of the Louisiana Purchase.

Spain protested the sale of Louisiana. The king demanded that Napoleon revoke the sale. Spanish officials pointed out that it violated the agreement made earlier with Napoleon. Napoleon had agreed never to give up Louisiana to any other country. The differences between the two countries were eventually resolved, however. Finally Spain approved the sale. This came a month after the formal transfer of the colony to the United States.

In the meantime Napoleon had trouble convincing fellow Frenchmen that this was best. The French very reluctantly gave up their dreams of restoring their American empire.

En Partie 2 (Studying a Part). 1. Why was Louisiana important to the United States? 2. Why did Spanish officials withdraw the right-of-deposit? 3. What drastic action were some radicals in Congress considering in response? 4. (a) Identify the principal leaders responsible for the Louisiana Purchase. (b) What was the part each played? 5. Why did Napoleon change his mind? 6. Explain the complications that arose because of lack of communication. 7. Give the details of the Louisiana Purchase. 8. What was the reaction to the purchase?

French Possession

Occupation by France. Napoleon planned for France to occupy Louisiana as though the nation would own it forever. **Pierre Clement de Laussat,** a young career colonial official, became governor. He arrived in the colony March 26, 1803. This was just two weeks before Napoleon made his decision to sell Louisiana. Laussat was not informed of events going on relating to the Louisiana Purchase.

Lagniappe—*Laussat's Account.* Pierre de Laussat arrived in Louisiana in March 1803, expecting to serve as governor for France. He accepted the colony from Spain and published the laws based on the **Napoleonic Code.** He wrote a journal describing his life during these events leading to the sale of

Governor Pierre Laussat.

Louisiana to the United States. On December 20, 1803, Louisiana became a United States Territory by Laussat's handing over keys and the French flag.

For months after his arrival Laussat heard nothing from France. He did not know the reason that Gen. Victor Leclerc and the soldiers had not arrived. He built barracks and purchased supplies. He had a report on the military needs of the colony ready for Leclerc. He heard only indirectly that France had sold the colony to the United States. On July 28, 1803, Laussat wrote to the French government that a rumor that the colony had been sold was going around New Orleans. He had branded the rumor a lie and was trying to do what he could to stop it. Shortly afterward, a French ship came with the official news that the colony had been sold to the United States.

While he was ill with yellow fever, Laussat received official word that war had been declared between France and England on May 18, 1803. He finally received a letter from Napoleon giving his reasons for the sale. Laussat was ordered to deliver the colony to the United States on the same day that he received it for France from Spain. The colony was to be turned over immediately because Napoleon did not have any French troops to support Laussat.

At this time Casa Calvo, the former Louisiana governor, returned from Cuba to assist in the formal ceremonies. He caused trouble from the time he arrived in the colony on May 10, 1803. In order to get rid of him, Laussat decided to accept the colony from Spain as soon as possible. Spain and France were ready, but the United States was not. There would be a delay in the acceptance by the United States because no plans were yet made for the transfer.

Transfer Ceremonies. At last the time came for the transfer of the colony from Spain and France. On **November 30, 1803,** formal ceremonies took place at the public square, or Plaza de Armas, transferring Louisiana to France.

The transfer of Louisiana was conducted with all the pomp possible. French and Spanish soldiers stood at attention in the square while officials exchanged documents in the Cabildo. Salcedo and Casa Calvo delivered the colony to Laussat. They then walked together to the balcony. As they stood, the Spanish flag, flying high on the staff, was lowered. The Spanish regiment accepted it. Then the flag of France was raised. Cheers came up from the

The American flag was raised in transfer ceremonies on December 20, 1803.

crowd. The cold, stormy weather did not dampen the spirit of the crowd.

Days of partying, dancing, and dining followed. Laussat described one of the events:

Seventy-five people came for dinner. There were as many Spanish and Americans as Frenchmen. They began gambling before dinner.... There was all sorts of tomfoolery. They continued until eight o'clock the next morning. Two big servings were interrupted by three toasts. [The toasts were made to the French Republic and Napoleon, then to Spain and Charles IV, and, finally, to the United States and Jefferson.] With each of these toasts, there were three salvos of twenty-one guns fired....

French Government. Laussat then went about his business of governing the colony as though he had no knowledge of the imminent transfer to the United States.

Laussat abolished the Cabildo and set up a French government. He improved the city's police force. He created two adjutants and a municipal court for New Orleans. He published a new code of French law based on the **Napoleonic Code**. For the first mayor of New Orleans, he chose Etienne de Boré. He named the son of Joseph Villeré to the council. Members of the council included such well-known names as Derbigny (der BĒN yē), Fortier (fore SHAY), and Destrehan (dess TREE ähn). Laussat explained his actions.

I wanted some merchants, some Americans, and some experienced businessmen. I intended . . . to honor the memory of the Frenchmen who had been sacrificed under O'Reilly. . . . I wanted a municipality . . . that would do me honor and hold its own with dignity before the Americans. This being the dominant act of my short-lived reign and the one to which I attached the greatest importance . . . for the future of Louisiana.

En Partie 3 (Studying a Part). 1. Describe the general confusion in the government of Louisiana from 1800 to 1803. 2. Who was Laussat? 3. Describe the transfer of Louisiana from Spain to France. 4. When did the transfer take place? 5. Give reasons for the delay in the transfer. 6. What were some official actions of Laussat after the transfer?

Transfer to the United States

France's dream of a colony in the Mississippi Valley was forever ended. On December 20, 1803, Louisiana was transferred to the United States. The procès-verbal of transfer, the official document, was read aloud. **General James Wilkinson** and **W.C.C. Claiborne** accepted the territory for the United States from France. Laussat recalled the ceremony:

I handed over the keys to the city, tied together with the tricolor [the colors of the French flag] to Monsieur Wilkinson. Immediately afterwards, I [excused] from their oath of allegiance to France the inhabitants who chose to remain under the [rule] of the United States.

In this room of the Cabildo, the Louisiana Territory was formally transferred from France to the United States.

Various marching groups camped outside the city. At a designated time they moved in parade formation to the public square. Militiamen from Ohio, Kentucky, and Tennessee received a twenty-one-gun salute when they arrived. The military forces of both France and the United States participated in the ceremonies. The dignitaries appeared on the balcony to watch the flag ceremony. The French lowered their flag as the American flag ascended the flagpole. When the two flags met, a gun sounded. Every cannon in the vicinity answered. More parties, dances, and state dinners marked the second transfer of Louisiana.

Laussat had business for France to complete. He left Louisiana on April 21, 1804.

Many Spanish officials had French Creole wives. They had made their homes in the colony. The Spanish officials claimed to be boundary-adjustment agents or church officials. They aroused the suspicion of Claiborne. Casa Calvo received a passport from Claiborne with a note hinting that he leave. Finally, over two years after the transfer of the colony, Casa Calvo departed.

Louisiana now belonged to the United States. Only a few Spanish settlers had settled in Louisiana. These Spaniards had not developed deep feelings for the colony. The French people did not have the deep loyalty to France that had earlier existed. There were rumors that Napoleon planned to get the colony back. A few French hoped that France would regain the colony. The colonists did not know the Americans. They would need many years before they would appreciate their new country. The customs and language remained the same.

En Partie 4 (Studying a Part). 1. Give details about the transfer of Louisiana to the United States. 2. What was the attitude of most Louisianians toward the change in ownership?

In twenty days three flags flew over Louisiana. The country was still French in language and spirit. Spanish customs also had become a part of the life of Louisiana. Cultural borrowing of French, Spanish, English, Indian, and African roots included the entire population.

Territory of Orleans

Territorial Government. The territory was left without a government. **William Charles Cole Claiborne** was instructed to take charge until Congress could provide for a government. He directed the civil affairs of the colony. During that time Gen. **James Wilkinson** commanded the army. He spent weeks assembling a military force. Both men had held similar positions in the Mississippi Territory.

Claiborne was appointed on a temporary basis while Jefferson tried to make a permanent appointment of a more prestigious or well-known person. Jefferson hoped to appoint officers who could speak French. He was unable to do so. The ability to speak French was a rare accomplishment among people in the United States at that time. Jefferson first tried to persuade General Lafayette to come from France to serve as governor of the territory. When Lafayette declined, he next tried James Monroe. Monroe declined also. He then appointed Claiborne, who knew no French.

The Territory of Orleans. On March 26, 1804, Congress passed a law that divided the Louisiana Territory into two parts. Below the thirty-third parallel was the land that now constitutes most of the state of Louisiana. It was called the Territory of Orleans. This area contained most of the population. It was a very small part of the land area known as

Governor William C. C. Claiborne.

Louisiana under French and Spanish control. North of the thirty-third parallel was the **District of Louisiana.**

The status of Louisiana was that of an **unorganized territory** of the United States. A territory with more than five thousand white males was eligible to become an organized territory. The difference between organized and unorganized territories was in the participation of citizens in the government. The people in an unorganized territory had no voice in the government. Local leaders bitterly resented Louisiana's unorganized status. They felt that the territory met the population requirement. Perhaps Congress did not think that Louisianians could govern themselves.

The government for the Territory of Orleans included a governor, secretary, and legislative council. A superior court of three judges was also included. All were appointed by the president. The governor was appointed to serve three years. He was given all executive powers. The secretary and judges had four-year terms. The secretary kept the territorial records. The thirteen members of the legislative council were given one-year appointments. The legislative council assisted the governor in making laws. The laws had to be submitted to Congress for approval. In reality, Claiborne made nominations and the president approved them. Claiborne had difficulty finding people to accept the appointments.

Dissatisfaction of the People. The people complained that the governor had too much power. Claiborne was almost a dictator. There was no appeal from his decisions.

Even in Spanish Louisiana they were allowed to appeal to the captain general in Havana. The Creoles particularly resented that they were unable to govern themselves. They had heard about the **rights** of citizens in the United States. They were indignant when they did not receive the rights enjoyed by the people of the Mississippi Territory. The treaty provided that the people living in the former colony should have all the rights and privileges enjoyed by the citizens of the rest of the country. The people of Louisiana did not get these rights in 1804.

Other American actions aroused the ire of residents. The Louisiana Purchase Treaty forbade the bringing of **slaves** into the territory from foreign countries. Smuggling of foreign slaves into the territory resulted from this restriction. Only citizens moving into the territory could bring slaves from older sections of the United States. Elsewhere, slaves were still imported from Africa. According to the United States Constitution, Congress could not forbid the importing of slaves from foreign countries or obtaining them from other states until 1808.

The people of the Orleans territory did not like to see their great province divided geographically. Residents of the territory were dissatisfied with the **naming** of their **land.** They felt that the name Louisiana belonged to the southern portion of the former colony. They wanted that section to become a **state** immediately.

The Creoles were also angry because **English** was the **official language.** Governor Claiborne's inability to speak French was considered an insult to Louisiana's French population. They said that the use of English made them feel like foreigners in their native land. The people accused Claiborne of showing a preference for the English-speaking Americans. Some pointedly refused to cooperate with him or even serve in the new government. Etienne de Boré resigned as mayor of New Orleans to show his opposition.

The actions of Congress reflected most United States citizens' fear of **foreigners**. The Louisiana citizens were of French and Spanish heritage. To the English-speaking people, Louisianians had a foreign language and strange customs. Congress felt there was a danger in allowing too much freedom to people in Louisiana. Louisianians resented being regarded as foreigners.

To make matters worse there was a **scarcity of money**. The Spanish had brought large amounts of silver coins from Mexico. These were used to pay the expenses of government. When the flow of coins ceased, money became scarce. Claiborne established the Bank of Louisiana to solve the problem. Its purpose was to furnish the currency and credit needed by the planters and merchants. The bank was of limited value at first because people did not trust it.

Mass Meetings. The discontent led to several mass meetings in New Orleans. The group asked Congress to give the people more involvement in government. A group went to Washington to present the case before Congress. The spokesmen of the group were Pierre Derbigny, Jean Noel Destrehan, and Pierre Sauve (sov). The men impressed Congress and raised the image of so-called foreigners. The Orleans territory enjoyed a more representative government after Congress heard the case. They asked that the territory be admitted as a state. The request was not granted. Provisions were made, however, for its admission when the population amounted to sixty thousand.

Organized Territory. A new act relating to Louisiana was passed on March 2, 1805. It named Louisiana an **organized territory**. At last the people had the same rights as those in the Mississippi Territory. This form of government lasted until Louisiana became a state.

No changes were made in the **executive**

Creoles.

and **judicial** branches of the government. Claiborne remained as governor. The most important change was in the **legislative** branch. The new government had both a legislative council and a house of representatives. Membership in the legislative council was reduced to five. Congress was to appoint the five from a list of ten names. Councilmen were to serve five-year terms. The house of representatives was to be composed of twenty-five members. They were to be elected by qualified voters for two-year terms. A voter had to own fifty acres of land. Voters had to be residents for two years. A representative had to own two hundred acres of land. They had to have been residents for three years.

The legislative council divided the Territory of Orleans into twelve **counties** for purposes of local government. These were Orleans, German Coast, Acadia, Lafourche, Iberville, Pointe Coupee, Atakapas, Opelousas, Natchitoches, Rapides, Ouachita, and Concordia (kon KÔR di ə). A system of local government was provided for each county. This system did not meet with popular approval.

The second session of the legislature created nineteen **parishes** in 1807. The first parishes were Orleans, St. Bernard, Plaquemines, St. Charles, St. John the Baptist, St. James, Ascension (ə SIN shun), Assumption, Lafourche Interior, Iberville and Galveztown, Baton Rouge, Pointe Coupee, Concordia, Ouachita, Rapides, Avoyelles, Natchitoches, St. Landry, and St. Martin. The original twelve counties of 1804 were preserved. Counties continued to exist for certain purposes. They were abandoned by the state's second constitution in 1845.

Death mask of Napoleon.

The city of **New Orleans** presented totally different problems from the rest of Louisiana. New Orleans required a different structure for its government. It had a port dealing in world commerce. New Orleans was incorporated on February 17, 1805. A complete plan of government was provided.

Claiborne made **changes** only gradually. He continued to use those Spanish laws that conformed to the laws of the United States. He was careful to retain what had worked in the past.

In 1805 the English common law was used in criminal cases. Claiborne had a new civil code drawn up and put into effect in 1808. It was based on the **Napoleonic Code** of France. It remains the basis of Louisiana's civil law. A new **slave code** based on Bienville's 1724 *Code Noir* (Black Code) was prepared. Provisions from Carondelet's code were also added.

All laws and legal papers had to be written in both French and English. When cases came before the courts, both languages were used. The evidence of witnesses and the judge's charge were interpreted in both languages for the jury. The membership of the juries had to be composed equally of English-speaking and French-speaking men.

Claiborne's Accomplishments. Claiborne realized that his first job was to gain acceptance of himself. He was openly resented because he was not French. Since he could not speak French, some considered him inadequate as governor.

He was very unpopular during the early years. However, the young governor achieved amazing success in spite of the language handicap and other problems. The legislature and Claiborne were in conflict constantly. All legislation was a compromise between American and Creole views. During the entire territorial period, the leaders of the colony criticized Claiborne. The twenty-eight-year-old governor displayed unusual ability in handling people with such different backgrounds.

Claiborne took action in much-needed areas. He organized a local militia. He started inoculation against smallpox. In 1806 fees of doctors were fixed by law. Physicians, surgeons, and apothecaries all had to be licensed.

Louisiana education was in a sad state at the time of the Louisiana Purchase. It was estimated that only a few hundred people could read and write well. The Ursulines had seventy boarding students. There were about one hundred day-pupils at the convent. Claiborne was a strong supporter of public education. During this period the seed for a free public school system was planted.

As many American ideas as possible were introduced. The first Protestant church—Christ Church of New Orleans—was organized. Protestant Claiborne, as well as many others in Louisiana, enjoyed freedom of worship under the United States government. This privilege was very important to the happiness of the citizens. The natives had not anticipated that the new American government would work so well. Claiborne's work must have pleased the officials in Washington. He received numerous appointments from Presidents Jefferson and Madison.

En Partie 5 (Studying a Part). 1. Trace the development of the government of Louisiana as a territory. 2. List problems in obtaining statehood. 3. Why did the people want statehood? 4. Who was appointed to govern the territory? 5. Why were the people dissatisfied? 6. What were some of the problems that resulted from Creole-American differences? 7. What did Claiborne accomplish?

Boundary of the Louisiana Purchase

Exploration of the Louisiana Purchase Territory. The people of the United States knew very little about the newly purchased land. President Jefferson sent expeditions to find out what the territory was like. Lewis and

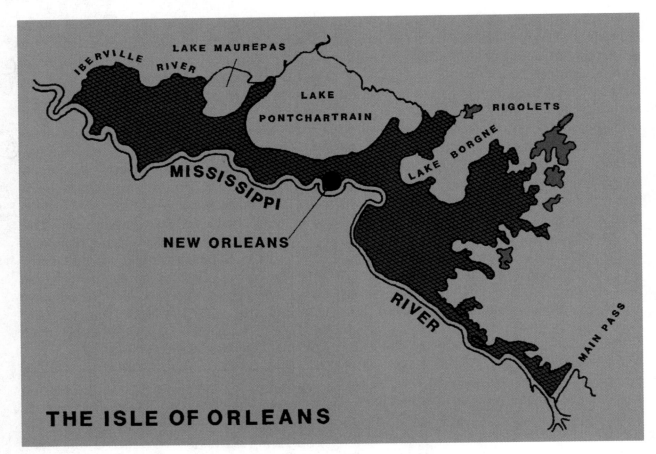

THE ISLE OF ORLEANS

Clark in 1804 and Zebulon Pike in 1805 began expeditions. In 1807 Pike was arrested by Spanish authorities for taking military possession of some of their territory. The Spanish escorted Pike to the United States boundary near Natchitoches and released him. Members of the Freeman and Hunter expedition explored the Ouachita and Red rivers. These explorers described the land, animals, plants, and Indian tribes in the new territory. They gathered information about the inhabitants. When the report was sent to Washington, the president and Congress had a better understanding of local conditions. The exchange of information worked to better relationships between the American government and the inhabitants of the Territory of Orleans.

Boundary Disputes. The boundary of the Louisiana Purchase was in dispute. The papers drawn up at the Louisiana Purchase were not clear. Its boundaries to the north, west, and south were vague and undetermined. The French ministers did not know for sure what France had sold. They said that they were selling what Spain owned at the time of the transfer. Spain insisted that the United States owned only the Isle of Orleans east of the Mississippi River and land extending to the Calcasieu River to the west.

There was a suspicion that Napoleon caused the confusion on purpose. In other words, he left the boundaries vague to provide future trouble between the United States and Spain. For two decades they had a strained relationship because of undetermined boundaries. Napoleon sided with Spain in the boundary disputes. He did so to try to make up for the transfer of Louisiana to the United States.

Trouble in the Felicianas. The United States claimed that West Florida was part of the Louisiana Purchase. However, Spanish officials still held that area. Spain had a military post at Baton Rouge. The district above Baton Rouge was called New Feliciana ("Happy Land") by the Spaniards. It had been settled since 1763 by English-speaking colonists. After the purchase more Americans poured into the area. They lived across the Mississippi River from the Territory of Orleans and communicated frequently with the English in the Natchez area. English settlers, especially those from Natchez, Mississippi, moved down the Mississippi River and settled on the fertile land in the Felicianas. They formed a strong wedge of English culture in the Spanish colony. They settled on plantations a mile or so apart and formed plantation settlements very much like those around Natchez.

When Louisiana was purchased by the United States, these English-speaking Americans were still in Spanish territory. They wanted to become United States citizens. Some leading planters were not satisfied with life under the Spanish government.

Rebellion of 1810. Finally, a rebellion began in West Florida. The people demanded more voice in the government. This uprising was called the West Florida Rebellion.

Fourteen men from plantations near St. Francisville gathered to discuss their quarrels with the Spanish officials. The convention held its first meeting on July 26, 1810. Officers were elected and complaints were organized.

They complained that desirable citizens were not allowed to reside in West Florida, but fugitives from justice and exiled French from Cuba were permitted to do so. They protested their inability to obtain titles to their lands. Too, assault and battery of citizens carried no penalty in the law. There was a neglect of laws respecting roads, slaves, and livestock in the country. There was no uniform standard of weights and measures in use. Citizens were charged exorbitant fees for services.

The planters wrote their demands for government reform and presented them to the Spanish governor. The governor pretended to cooperate, but he quickly requested help to end the rebellion. The people were not fooled and made plans to capture the fort at Baton Rouge.

This was done. Spanish casualties included one killed and two wounded. The

The flag of West Florida (Bonnie Blue Flag).

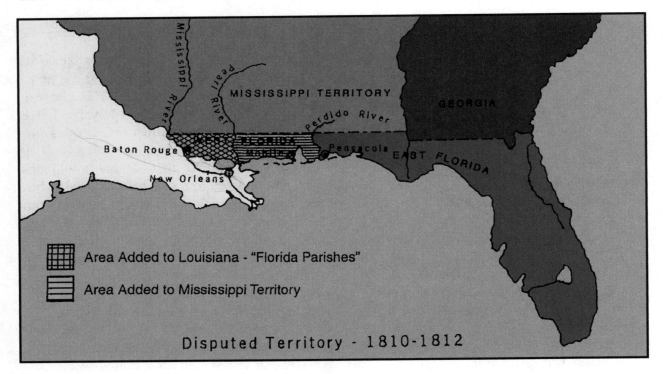

Area Added to Louisiana - "Florida Parishes"

Area Added to Mississippi Territory

Disputed Territory - 1810-1812

Americans had no casualties. The rebels took down the Spanish flag and replaced it with their own flag, the Lone Star flag. They proclaimed West Florida to be a free and independent state.

Leaders wanted the United States to annex the area promptly. In the meantime the rebel leaders proclaimed a new nation called the **Republic of West Florida.** They organized a government. They drew up a constitution and held an election. The legislature of the little republic met in St. Francisville in November 1810. Fulwar Skipwith was elected president of the Republic of West Florida.

They planned to continue their drive against the Spanish. A force of four hundred was raised before the federal government put a stop to their activities.

Annexation of the Republic of West Florida. On December 10, 1810, President James Madison ordered Governor Claiborne to occupy West Florida and govern it. Madison completely ignored the existence of the Republic of West Florida. The annexation document did not mention the rebels. The area became a part of the Territory of Orleans as the County of Feliciana. The Orleans territory and the Mississippi Territory both wanted to annex West Florida. Governor Claiborne offered a compromise. The Mississippi Territory got the land east of the Pearl River. The land west of Pearl River became a part of the Orleans territory. On December 22, 1810, four parishes were made out of this territory. They were Feliciana, East Baton Rouge, St. Helena, and St. Tammany. The area is still referred to as the

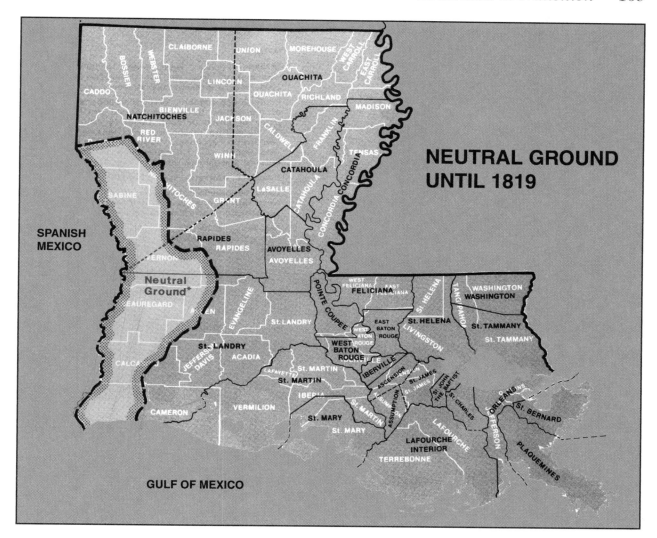

NEUTRAL GROUND UNTIL 1819

SPANISH MEXICO

Neutral Ground*

GULF OF MEXICO

Florida parishes. Even though the United States took over the territory, Spain did not give up its claims until 1819.

Aaron Burr's Conspiracy. Aaron Burr was the former vice president of the United States who had killed Alexander Hamilton in a duel. Naturally, Burr lost the status he once enjoyed. He had plans to regain his position. Burr made his plans because he thought the United States was going to war with Spain over the Louisiana Purchase boundary dispute.

Aaron Burr went to New Orleans in 1805. It was known that he courted a group which hoped to separate Mexico from Spain. The group was headquartered in New Orleans.

In 1806 Burr claimed that he was planning to settle the Baron de Bastrop grant on the Ouachita River. Burr collected provisions,

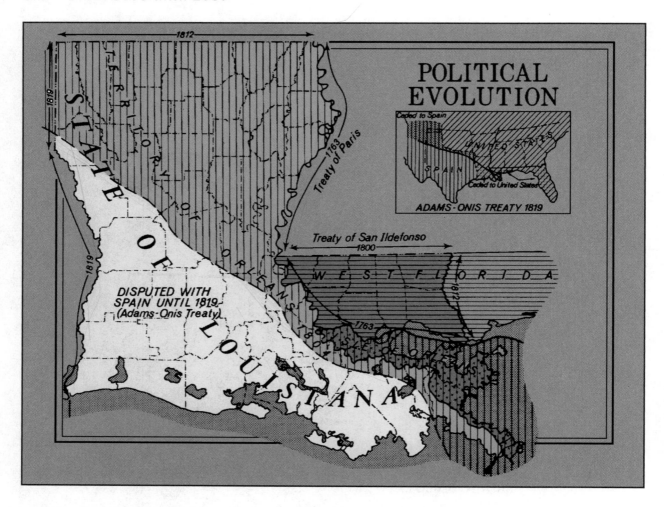

tools, and arms. He had a number of flatboats to take his men and supplies down the river.

Before he reached his destination, he was arrested as he came down the Mississippi. He was stopped by Mississippi authorities at Bayou Pierre, about thirty miles above Natchez. He was released on bail. Later there was an order for his arrest.

When Burr heard that he was being sought by United States officials, he tried to escape in disguise to Spanish West Florida. A reward was offered for his capture. He was arrested at Fort Stoddard, Alabama. He was tried for treason in Richmond, Virginia. He was acquitted. There was no proof that he was guilty of any treacherous acts against the United States.

The conspiracy caused much excitement in the Territory of Orleans for many months. It showed the Spanish in Texas and the Floridas that the western country would not be separated from the eastern states. The results of the conspiracy helped Claiborne, too. Some of the same prominent citizens who were suspected of supporting Burr also opposed Claiborne. After the incident, Claiborne's opposition in New Orleans subsided.

"No Man's Land." There was no definite western boundary of Louisiana. The Spaniards in Texas considered it to be the Red River. The Americans claimed it to be the Trinity River, or at least the Sabine. Finally, a neutral strip was created in 1806 when no decision was forthcoming. This area between the Territory of Orleans and the Spanish to the west was known as the **Neutral Ground.** It was also known as the **Sabine Strip** and **No Man's Land.** Gen. James Wilkinson, representing the United States, met with the Spanish commander at Los Adais to make this agreement. Neither country would claim the land between the Sabine River to the west and the Calcasieu River to the east. The boundary line was not finally determined until the United States bought Florida in 1819.

Neither the laws of the United States nor Spain applied to this forty-mile-wide region. There were five thousand miles of ungoverned territory. It attracted all kinds of people. Outlaws of both nations settled in the area. It was also used as a place for slaves to hide. Outlaws enticed slaves to the area with the promise of freedom. Then the outlaws sold them. Lafitte, the pirate, took stolen slaves up the Sabine River and into the strip. Judges sometimes sentenced criminals to the Neutral Ground. Holdups were frequent for migrants heading west through the strip. There were people other than outlaws in the area. Some were former outlaws trying to start a new life. Others were simply Americans or Spaniards desiring to live within the area.

When the agreement for the territory was made, someone said, "This area will be the stepping off place of all kinds of smuggling and outlawry known to mankind." It proved to be so. Even after it was no longer a lawless area, the tradition of violence remained.

En Partie 6 (Studying a Part). 1. How was information about the new territory obtained? 2. Why was there confusion about the boundaries? 3. (a) Describe the formation of the Republic of West Florida. (b) When did that section become part of the United States? (c) How? 4. (a) Describe Aaron Burr's involvement with the Territory of Orleans. (b) What were the results of this conspiracy? 5. (a) Why was "No Man's Land" created? (b) Why did that area develop into a land of lawlessness?

The young nation had been tested on several occasions shortly after the Louisiana Purchase. Each time the United States government gained the respect of the new Americans.

LOUISIANA: STATEHOOD (1803-1815)

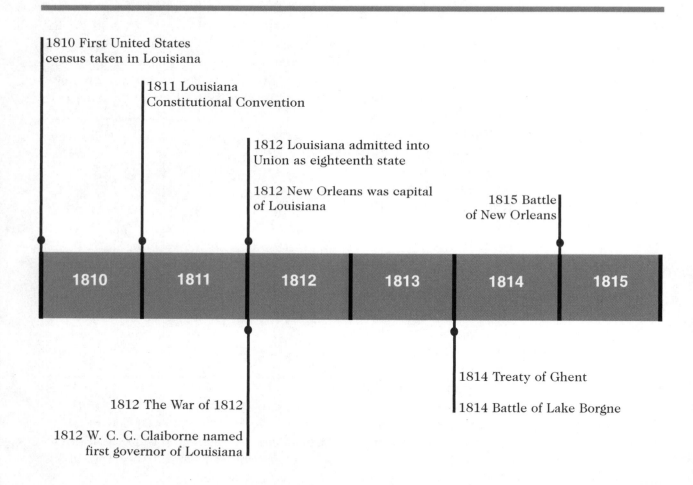

1810 First United States
census taken in Louisiana

1811 Louisiana
Constitutional Convention

1812 Louisiana admitted into
Union as eighteenth state

1812 New Orleans was capital
of Louisiana

1815 Battle
of New Orleans

| 1810 | 1811 | 1812 | 1813 | 1814 | 1815 |

1814 Treaty of Ghent

1814 Battle of Lake Borgne

1812 The War of 1812

1812 W. C. C. Claiborne named
first governor of Louisiana

LOUISIANA: STATEHOOD

Settlement in the Territory

Population. After the Louisiana Purchase the population increased in the territories. In 1804 there were about fifty thousand people living in the present state of Louisiana. These people were settled mostly in the southeastern quarter of the state. The majority were clustered around New Orleans, the only city. There were ten thousand in the city. Baton Rouge, Opelousas, St. Martinville, Natchitoches, and Monroe were small villages. In the rural areas along the Mississippi there were planters and farmers. Many settlements had developed along the important bayous. There were scattered isolated homes on the Red and Ouachita rivers and in the wilderness.

Many French **colonists** from **Cuba** joined the settlers in the Orleans territory. These people had gone to Spanish Cuba during the great slave rebellion in Santo Domingo. There they grew sugarcane. When the war broke out between Spain and France, they had to flee again. This time they chose to come to Louisiana. Nearly six thousand persons arrived by the middle of 1809. About one-third were slaves. New arrivals to Louisiana could not bring in slaves legally, but they were allowed to do so nevertheless. About ten thousand refugees filtered into Louisiana. A large number of free blacks were among them.

United States citizens ordinarily continued to think of Louisiana as populated by foreigners. These "foreigners," they thought, would not prove loyal to the United States. When Louisiana was purchased, most white residents were either French or Spanish. However, **English-Americans** poured into the area. Migration rose after 1812. Large family groups left Virginia, South Carolina, Alabama, and Georgia. Others poured into the state from North Carolina, Tennessee, Kentucky, Ohio, Pennsylvania, and New York. Some were waiting across the Mississippi River in the Mississippi Territory for Louisiana to become a state. It was the beginning of a period when the lure of cheap lands to the west kept many people on the move.

Settlements. Early settlements were made along the waterways. In the colonial period French and Spanish settlers located on the biggest river of them all, the Mississippi. Choice land was that facing the stream on either side. Land holdings were laid out stretching from the river. Each settler held a share along the stream so he could ship his crop out to market. This location was also necessary to receive needed goods.

After 1763 the **English** settled on their plantations on the east side of the Mississippi. The English had a different settlement pattern from the French and Spanish. The English homesites were scattered and apt to be an average of a mile-and-a-half apart. The English worked at building their plantations to be as self-sufficient as possible. When the English joined the territory, they offset the French majority. Many members of Congress felt better about the territory's becoming a state because of the English people in West Florida.

Settlers constantly searched for inland bayous where they could settle. Soon most of the richest land in Louisiana was claimed. That land was the alluvial soil along the

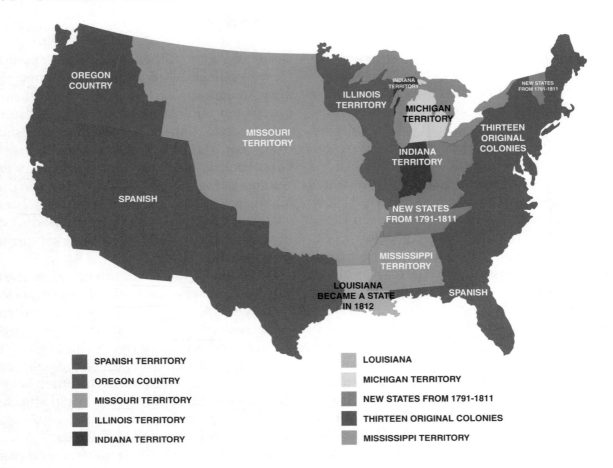

SPANISH TERRITORY

OREGON COUNTRY

MISSOURI TERRITORY

ILLINOIS TERRITORY

INDIANA TERRITORY

LOUISIANA

MICHIGAN TERRITORY

NEW STATES FROM 1791-1811

THIRTEEN ORIGINAL COLONIES

MISSISSIPPI TERRITORY

rivers and largest bayous. Creek bottoms were also desirable locations.

The problem of **land claims** immediately arose. Congress undertook to adjust all land claims fairly and legally. Those actually settling the land had little difficulty in establishing their titles. The absentees who claimed vast tracts of unsettled land had greater difficulties. Squatters who had settled illegally also had trouble. They were later granted relief under the preemption laws. They were allowed to keep the land because they had occupied it before the Louisiana Purchase. Not all land claims were settled in Louisiana during the territorial period. Some had trouble determining the exact boundaries of their property.

The first to join settlers already on the streams were the **traders** and **speculators**. Frequently they traded the Indians out of their land for a few dollars worth of groceries, tobacco, and other supplies. The speculators secured the land from the Indians in order to sell it to incoming pioneers.

Livelihood. Commerce and **agriculture** were fairly well established. Rice, sugarcane, indigo, tobacco, and cotton were the main crops. Sawmills produced shingles and cypress, cedar, and maple boards. These were shipped to the West Indies.

New Orleans had developed into a trade center. It was little more than the Vieux Carré. Ships and boats with their cargoes were sometimes two or three deep. A stockade enclosed the city. Four gates were used to enter and leave the city. At night they were guarded. Five forts provided protection. Present-day Canal Street was a ditch, or moat. Wooden gallows and public pillories stood in the public square. New Orleans had a naval yard and a customhouse. Branches of eastern stores were among the wholesale and retail establishments.

En Partie 1 (Studying a Part). 1. Where was the population of Louisiana centered in 1804? 2. Which towns existed? 3. Describe New Orleans in 1804. 4. How did the French and Spanish settlements differ from the English settlements? 5. Why were there problems with land claims? 6. Why were Louisianians considered foreigners?

Eighteenth State: 1812

Population. The United States **census** was taken every ten years beginning in 1790. It was taken for the first time in Louisiana in 1810. At that time there were 76,556 people in the Territory of Orleans. Of these, 34,660 were slaves. There were 7,585 free persons of color. The census showed that 77.5 percent of the population was rural.

The census showed that the territory had more than the sixty thousand residents required to become a state. A memorial was sent from the Orleans legislature requesting statehood. Claiborne had sent a letter giving his reasons for opposing statehood. After heated debate, Congress refused statehood in March 1810. In December 1810, Julien Poydras, the delegate from the Territory of Orleans, again asked for statehood. In early January 1811 debate began on a bill for admitting the Territory of Orleans. Some members of Congress opposed the measure—some on constitutional grounds. It was argued that Congress had no right to make new states from a territory that was not a part of the United States when the Constitution was adopted. Some feared that new states would outnumber old ones. Then the new states would gain control of the government. In spite of the opposition, the bill for statehood passed in February 1811.

It provided that all qualified free white male voters could elect the members for a convention. The convention was to write a constitution. The constitution had to be consistent with the United States Constitution. It had to guarantee citizens civil and religious liberty and the right of trial by jury. Congress also required that all laws and other important official documents be in English.

The convention met in New Orleans at Tremoulet's Coffee House in November 1811. Julien Poydras was president of the convention. Only twenty-eight of the forty-five delegates were present. The convention immediately adjourned for two weeks. The time allowed for a yellow fever epidemic to subside. The work was finished in January 1812. The convention gave the new state its name—**Louisiana**—and drafted the **constitution**.

The state's first constitution stated that no citizen could become governor unless he owned five thousand dollars worth of property. The people would vote for the governor. The legislature would then choose from the two who received the highest number of votes.

On April 8, 1812, President James Madison approved a bill passed by Congress admitting Louisiana to the Union. On April 14, 1812, West Florida was made a part of the state. The effective date of the act was **April 30, 1812.** That was the day Louisiana officially became the eighteenth state admitted to the Union.

The Capital of Louisiana: 1812. Almost a century old, **New Orleans** was a French and Spanish city. It was the capital of Louisiana in 1812 and the only city in the state of any important size. The population of New Orleans was eighteen thousand.

In the city the most important public buildings were made of brick and were at least partially fireproof. These buildings were erected after the great fires that swept the city in 1788 and 1794. The finest houses of the well-to-do were often made of brick. Because the native bricks were soft, posts were placed between them for support. There were many more modest dwellings of ordinary citizens and the rude huts of the poorest people. The poorer class had frame houses raised off the ground eight to fifteen feet. This was done because of high water and snakes. *Bousill-age*, mud mixed with deer hair or Spanish moss, was still common. It was plastered between the logs and kept the inside of the houses snug and dry. Some roofs were tile or slate. Most were cypress shingles.

Architecture was predominantly Spanish, with houses built flush with the plank walks (sidewalks), or *banquettes* (ban KETS). An enclosed outdoor living space, or courtyard, was the center around which the rooms were built.

Street lights brightened the intersections with pools of soft oil light in the darkness. A few streets were carefully laid with adobe bricks (handmade and dried in the sun). These were the short city streets. Most streets, like the country roads, were dirt trails. They were dusty in summer and muddy in winter.

Garbage disposal presented a street problem as well. New Orleans had no system for waste disposal. The people allowed garbage and sewage to get into the ditches. When flooding occurred, the waste matter washed out into the narrow streets. The river and streams were also used for dumping.

Fire protection consisted of a supply of sturdy buckets to be used in a bucket brigade. In 1807 New Orleans passed a bucket ordinance. Each householder was required to keep two buckets on hand. A watchman on the roof of the city hall was to ring a bell at the cry of "fire." The city kept increasing the numbers of buckets available for use when there was a fire. No doubt the men of New Orleans knew to race to the fire when the warning bell sounded. There every man was needed to pick up the buckets and form a line beginning at the water supply. The buckets of water could be passed rapidly from one man to the next down the line toward the location of the fire. The men nearest the fire kept dashing the water on the flames.

New Orleans was made up of two rival groups: the Creoles and the Americans. In this setting the first state government was assembled.

First Governor. Claiborne was elected as the first governor of the state of Louisiana. He took the oath of office July 30, 1812. The first business he conducted with the general assembly was to annex the West Florida parishes. Among other business were plans for a system of public education. There were plans for organization of the court system and for a more efficient organization of the militia. There was yet a more urgent matter. The United States Congress had declared war on England on June 18, 1812.

En Partie 2 (Studying a Part). 1. Why was there opposition to statehood for Louisiana? 2. When did Louisiana become a state? 3. What star represents Louisiana on the American flag? 4. Describe Louisiana's first state capital. 5. Who was the first elected governor? 6. What were some of the first items of business for the government?

The War of 1812

Invasion of Louisiana. In June 1812, six weeks after Louisiana entered the Union, the United States was at war. The purposes of the war were to defend American rights on the high seas and to put an end to the Indian troubles in the West promoted by the English. This war has been called the "Second American Revolution." Many

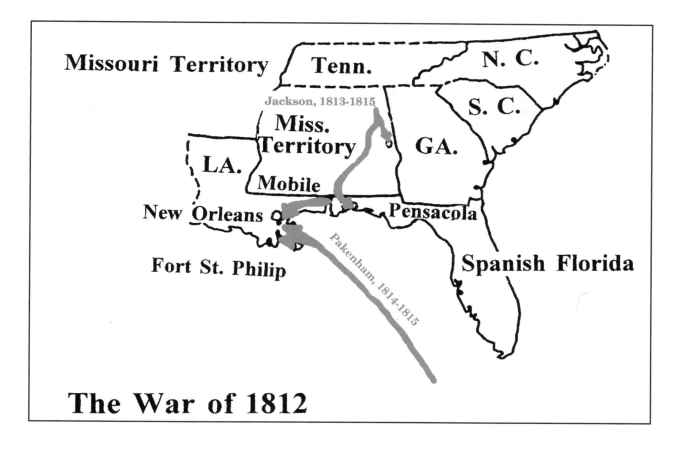

The War of 1812

Americans felt that England had never given up the idea of getting back its lost colonies.

Trouble had been brewing for some time. Congress had adopted the Embargo Act in December 1807. It was designed to prevent seizure of American ships by keeping them off the high seas. It was supposed to punish England and France. They were going to be deprived of American goods. Instead, it injured the United States most of all. The people of the Orleans territory were greatly affected. All foreign trade was stopped except that carried on illegally. There was so much protest that the act was repealed in 1809. England continued to be the main obstacle to neutral commerce. By 1812 controversies with England led to war.

For almost two years of the War of 1812, daily lives of Louisianians were untouched. However, Governor Claiborne had organized the state militia as soon as statehood was declared. All the fighting up to that time was done on the high seas and in the far north near the borders of Canada.

The Baratarians. During the War of 1812,

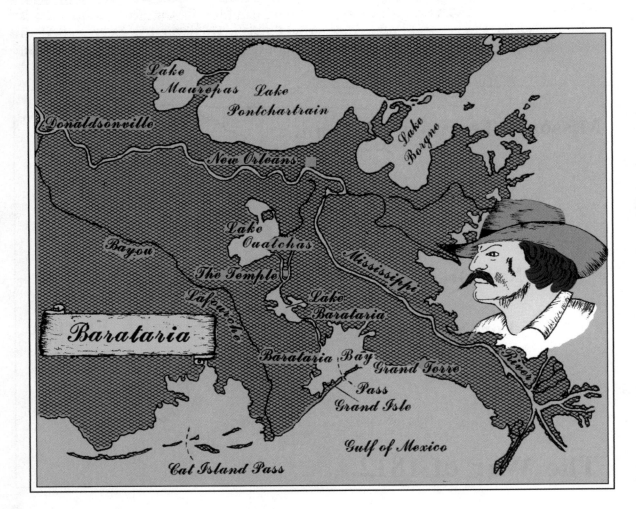

E. H. Suydam
1930

Jean Lafitte.

Jean Lafitte and his older brother **Pierre** became famous. They were known for their smuggling operations centered at Barataria Bay. The smugglers' hideout was on the island of Grand Terre. There they built storehouses for the goods from their plunder. Cafes and gambling houses were a part of the establishment. A fort at the entrance of the bay defended their quarters. They used light, fast sailing vessels to go into the shallow waters. Large ships chasing them could not go into the bay.

The Baratarians got their goods by overpowering Spanish and British merchant vessels. They carried papers called **letters of marque.** These letters were obtained from countries at war with Spain or England. The documents gave them authority to attack ships as an ally of the warring nation that issued the letters. Without the letters of marque, they would have been considered pirates. With them, they were not. The vessels sailing in this manner were called privateers.

The Baratarians violated the law when they brought the captured goods into the country. The smugglers avoided payment of import duty on the goods. They secretly took their goods into New Orleans and sold them at very low prices. Beginning in 1806 a blacksmith shop served as a front for their business. A fleet of barges shuttled to and from Barataria. Much of the stolen goods was sold to merchants and planters along the route. Local merchants could not compete with Lafitte on any item. Public officials received a portion of the profit to keep them quiet about Lafitte's operations. Lafitte's activities involved so many officials and merchants that it was not easy to prosecute him.

Many people of Louisiana did not consider the actions of the pirates to be a serious offense. Instead of condemning Lafitte, many saw him as a most glamorous man. He built himself a mansion of brick and stone with money he accumulated.

Reward for Lafitte's Arrest. Governor Claiborne tried to stop the capture of vessels under the flag of Spain. Spain was friendly with the United States. The governor ordered the bandits to disband. They simply ignored his orders and threats.

The Lafitte brothers were eventually arrested, but they were not punished. Some

This building is said to have been the headquarters of Jean Lafitte in New Orleans.

of their smuggled goods were seized by government officials. The smugglers fought a battle with the officers in broad daylight and recovered the goods.

Governor Claiborne offered a reward. Five hundred dollars would be given for the arrest of Jean Lafitte. Jean Lafitte countered with his own offer of much more for Claiborne. The governor asked the legislature to help destroy Lafitte's organization. The legislature would not provide the required funds. Pierre Lafitte was arrested and sent to jail in New Orleans.

British Offers. While the Lafitte struggle continued, the British were planning to capture New Orleans. Col. Edward Nicholls was sent with two warships to find guides and pilots for the British ships. They hoped to maneuver a big fleet of warships into Lake Borgne.

Nicholls heard about the Baratarians and their troubles. He sent a written offer to Jean Lafitte, proposing to make him a captain in the British navy if he would help the British in the coming battle to take New Orleans. A large sum was offered as additional bait. In another document, Nicholls had an order to destroy the Baratarians' hideout. This was intended to punish the Baratarians for damage done to British ships during their piracy at sea. Nicholls gave Jean Lafitte a choice of documents. In other words, Lafitte could either help the British or be attacked by them.

Lafitte requested two weeks to make his decision. He informed his friend in the legislature, Jean Blanque (blänk), about the British offer. As his reward for the information, Lafitte requested that Pierre be freed from prison. Blanque then told Governor Claiborne what he had learned.

Shortly afterward Pierre "escaped" from prison. Lafitte offered Claiborne the services of his Baratarian pirates. Claiborne was ready to accept his offer. Leaders of a United States expedition against the pirates were not. Instead, the expeditionary force destroyed the Baratarian settlement. The brothers escaped and joined friends on the German Coast.

By 1814 the war was not going very well for the Americans. The British officer, Nicholls, made an offer to the people of the state. He would free Louisiana from the United States. Perhaps the British thought that the people of the new state did not really have any feeling of belonging to the new country. Most Louisiana citizens had lived in the colony when it belonged to Spain or France. The people rejected Nicholls' offer.

1814. Meanwhile, Gen. **Andrew Jackson** was in charge of the defense of the Gulf. He received a message from Governor Claiborne about the crisis at New Orleans. With this news Jackson moved west along the Gulf coast, arriving in New Orleans in December.

A week after Jackson arrived, British troops anchored off the coast of Louisiana. The fleet was commanded by Vice Adm. Sir Alexander Cochrane (COCK rain). The soldiers were led by Gen. Sir Edward Pakenham. The British came in through Lake Borgne and reached the Mississippi River a few miles below New Orleans.

The first clash between American and British forces took place on December 14, 1814. The British won the **Battle of Lake Borgne** and controlled the lake. They lost more men than the Americans.

The available American troops were many days' march from New Orleans. Jackson had to gather troops to defend the city. Frenchmen in Louisiana complained that they were not really Americans and therefore had no intention of getting into the fight. The town officials simply did not trust Andrew Jackson. The rugged Jackson paid no attention.

Jackson went below New Orleans—almost to the Gulf of Mexico. He inspected Fort St. Philip and such troops as Governor Claiborne had assembled. Jackson then set to work training them. He posted them along the river below New Orleans. He planned fortifications and placed guns to greet the British invaders at two points. These were at the Rigolets (RIG uh lēēz) and at Bayou St. John.

On December 22 1,600 British soldiers started moving toward New Orleans. They traveled along a canal to General Villeré's plantation. On the way they captured a few Americans who had been out to secure information about the invading army. The prisoners told the British that Andrew Jackson had sixteen thousand troops in New Orleans. They had been instructed to tell this to the enemy.

Major **Villeré** was the son of General Villeré. The major and his brother were sitting on the gallery of the plantation home when the British invaders were suddenly upon them. Major Villeré managed to free himself and jumped out of a window. He escaped through the thick woods, which he knew well. In this way he was able to avoid the gunfire of the guards who ran after him. He climbed up a big oak tree to hide. The British rushed past him. Major Villeré got down quickly and continued his trip to let Andrew Jackson know the location of the enemy. They rode horses as fast as they could into New Orleans to find Andrew Jackson.

When Jackson got the news of the British invaders, he assembled troops at Fort St. Charles. The Louisiana militia was "called to the colors." Frontiersmen all over Louisiana came to defend New Orleans. A battalion of free men of color was among the troops. Jackson had assembled there one of the strangest armies that any general had ever faced. There were Indians in war paint and backwoodsmen in coonskin caps, as well as trained and polished soldiers.

When Jackson learned that the British were near the city, he quickly called two thousand of his troops into action. They marched down the Mississippi River. Commodore Patterson, on the armed schooner *Carolina,* moved down the river also, and anchored in the darkness opposite the British. Campfires clearly marked the enemy's position.

In the cover of darkness, the *Carolina* opened fire. General Coffee's Tennessee sharpshooters and General Jackson's troops of assorted origins arrived soon afterward. They quickly and forcefully fell upon the British. Both sides fought savagely in the darkness with muskets, tomahawks, knives, and bare hands. It was difficult to distinguish friend from foe. When a heavy fog descended on the battleground, both sides withdrew. The Americans had lost two hundred men— the British three hundred. Neither side could claim a decisive victory.

Jackson moved his troops two miles toward New Orleans. He selected a place where a canal separated the Chalmette and Rodriguez (rō DRĒ gez) plantations to set up his defense. This place was about fifteen hundred yards wide between the Mississippi River and the swamp. Jackson ordered his men to establish earthworks on the New Orleans side of the canal. (These earthworks, between the river and the swamp, stand today.) The defenders took their stations behind the wall of dirt. Fifteen cannons were pulled into place by the defenders.

The Americans received reinforcements. The pirates from Barataria sent word that they were ready to join in the fight against the enemy. Among Lafitte's men were many who were trained to handle heavy cannons. They were all used to fighting and danger. Jackson received others who were raw recruits who had never seen fighting. His total forces now reached four thousand.

Christmas came, and both sides paused to celebrate. Neither side knew that the war in which they were fighting had actually already ended. A **peace treaty** was signed on **Christmas Eve** in Ghent, Belgium, by the Americans and the British. But travel was slow. News came so slowly across the sea that it was weeks before most Americans knew about the signing of the peace treaty.

The British were strengthening their position. Their forces reached eight thousand. On **December 28,** the British **attacked.** The

Chalmette National Park, where part of the Battle of New Orleans was fought.

American riflemen and artillerists were so accurate that the advance of the British toward New Orleans was stopped.

1815. A major clash occurred on January 1, 1815. The British shelled Jackson's earthworks. Again, the British gained nothing.

For a week the British were busy with preparations for battle. They cut the Villeré Canal through to the Mississippi River. This was a distance of about two miles. The canal was to serve as a waterway over which they moved soldiers and guns. Jackson decided the best protection for his defenders would be an embankment of earth. When completed, the earthworks were nearly twenty feet thick in some places. Jackson also flooded the canal in front of the earthworks. Jackson placed troops at various other points around New Orleans lest the British attack from another direction. Just before the beginning of the battle, Kentucky and Tennessee sharpshooters arrived. It could not have been more timely.

The big battle—known in history as the **Battle of New Orleans**—was fought on January 8, 1815. British General Pakenham ordered a full-scale attack on the American line.

There was a heavy fog over the flat, marshy battlefield. The British knew that the Americans were lined up behind the earthen wall to block their march into New Orleans. The attackers' plans to move their troops through their canal to the battle area had failed. The banks of the canal caved in. Only about half of the soldiers were transported over it. The strong current took the troops farther downstream than they had planned to go. Pakenham decided that they would make a frontal attack on the Americans. That is, they would march straight into the fire of the Americans.

The battle began about six o'clock in the morning as the British moved a solid mass of soldiers toward the American lines. The Americans opened fire with artillery and muskets. The British responded. British soldiers who survived the artillery fire were cut down by the sharpshooters firing from behind the earthworks.

After little more than an hour, the slaughter ended. General Pakenham was among the more than two thousand British who lay dead on the battlefield. Behind their barrier the Americans counted only six dead and seventy-one wounded.

Aftermath. The British would not give up after the Battle of New Orleans. Maybe they could not believe that their highly trained veteran troops could not defeat a group of American irregulars. The British continued to attack. After a few weeks, they finally admitted defeat and left.

Henry Miller Shreve steamed up the Red River in his boat, the *Enterprise,* returning veterans of the Battle of New Orleans to their homes. Earlier he had used his boat to haul supplies for the war. He took women and children away from the war zone. The use of steamboats for routine transportation on the Red River was still a few years away.

Andrew Jackson.

A Question of Justice. Andrew Jackson kept New Orleans under martial law another two months after the battle. He received biting criticism from some of the people for this action. Jackson felt that martial law was needed until it was certain that the British were not planning another attack.

A man named Louis Louaillier (LOU el yē) was so insistent that martial law be ended that Jackson ordered his arrest. A judge of the federal district court ordered his release. The feisty Jackson then ordered the arrest of the judge and the attorney general. On March 13, 1815, Jackson declared the end of martial law. News had come at last from Belgium that a peace treaty had been signed. The attorney general, released from jail, sued Jackson. This was in the court of Judge Dominick Hall, whom Jackson had also ordered arrested. Hall fined Jackson one thousand dollars. Years later Congress returned Jackson's money with interest.

Results of the Battle of New Orleans. Although the war was officially over before the battle began, it served important purposes. First, Jackson's call for troops brought response from all over Louisiana. The French, Spanish, Indians, pirates, blacks, and big planters—they were there together fighting to defend their country. There would never again be a question of their loyalty to the United States. And the people of Louisiana themselves had a new feeling of belonging. The people in and around New Orleans had only been in the new nation a short while and felt no real kinship with the United States. Fighting together to defend their home against an enemy made them realize that they were a part of the United States of America. They were proud that they were citizens. Secondly, the battle also united the nation and broke the bonds that Americans had with Europe. It was the final defeat for Britain's colonial ambitions in the New World.

Thirdly, the victory at the Battle of New Orleans was needed by the United States. It bolstered the country's claims at the peace table. The truth was that the United States had won too few victories during the War of 1812. In the negotiations that followed the peace treaty, this victory gave United States representatives more influence. The battle has been described as "the most conclusive battle in American history."

The public square in front of St. Louis Cathedral had its name changed again. When the block was laid out under the French it was christened **Place d'Armes.** The Spanish changed its name to **Plaza de Armas.** Now, under the Americans, it became known as **Jackson Square.**

Jackson's monument was placed in position in the square with appropriate ceremony in 1856. The Baroness Pontalba, who had constructed the apartment houses on the sides of the square, had furnished most of the money for the statue. She had a request. She wanted

Jackson Square, with the statue of Andrew Jackson.

Jackson placed so that he seemed to be looking up at her window. Later, someone observed that both front feet of Jackson's horse are lifted off the ground. This is a posture reserved for the horses of heroes who died in battle. Nobody seemed to mind this mistake. Few monuments in Louisiana are more deserved.

Later, Fort Jackson was built on the Mississippi River below New Orleans. The star-shaped masonry fort was built between 1822 and 1832. It was constructed to keep invaders from threatening New Orleans again.

En Partie 3 (Studying a Part). 1. Identify the causes of the War of 1812. 2. What was unusual about the Battle of New Orleans? 3. (a) Describe the Lafitte brothers. (b) What part did they play in the war? 4. Why was New Orleans important to British strategy? 5. Why were the Americans able to win even though they were outnumbered? 6. What were the results of the battle? 7. Explain how the role of Louisiana in the war helped to unite the people of the state.

Coup de Main
(Completing the Story)

Jambalaya (Putting It All Together)

1. Summarize the conditions existing in Spain, France, England, and the United States at the time of the Louisiana Purchase.

2. How did the Louisiana Purchase affect the United States in (a) size, (b) wealth, and (c) population?

3. Map work. Outline (a) the boundaries of the Louisiana Purchase territory, (b) the part the United States was originally interested in buying, (c) the part of present-day Louisiana obtained by the purchase, (d) the two rivers that formed most of the boundaries of the Louisiana Purchase territory, (e) the part of the United States controlled by the Americans before 1803, and (f) the present states that were part of the purchase.

4. Identify (a) Andrew Jackson, (b) Casa Calvo, (c) Claiborne, (d) Jefferson, (e) Laussat, (f) Monroe, (g) Morales, (h) Napoleon, and (i) Wilkinson.

5. Compare the two transfer ceremonies.

6. Compare the contributions of France with those of Spain to the Louisiana colony.

7. Discuss the political career of W. C. C. Claiborne.

8. What factors contributed to Louisiana's Americanization?

9. Map work. On a Louisiana map show (a) the Territory of Orleans, (b) "No Man's Land," and (c) the Florida parishes. (d) Show the part included in the state in 1812. (e) Give the dates each section became a part of the state.

Potpourri (Getting Involved)

1. Get a cross-section of opinions and

reactions to the Louisiana Purchase. "Interview" the people in 1803: (a) Creoles, (b) government officials of the United States, France, Spain, and England, and (c) the American settlers.

2. Reenact (a) the Louisiana Purchase from the time of the negotiations to its financing, or (b) the transfer ceremonies. Do research to bring out facts not previously mentioned.

3. According to some historians, the Louisiana Purchase is rated second to the winning of American independence and formation of the Union as the most important event in the history of the United States. Support this position.

4. Summarize Jefferson's actions to explore the territory after the purchase. Give reports on information obtained.

5. Prepare a chart showing the various nationalities represented in Louisiana.

6. Write an entry in the diary of a young American who has moved to Louisiana. Relate how you are treated by the native Louisianians. Express your opinions about your strange new surroundings.

7. Make a diorama illustrating (a) line villages, (b) the battle plan for the Battle of New Orleans, or (c) Lafitte's smuggling operations.

Gumbo (Bringing It Up-to-Date)

1. Compare (a) the price of the Louisiana Purchase with the present value of the land that was purchased, and (b) the interest rate paid for the loan with the interest rate on such a loan today.

2. Pretend that the United States was purchasing Louisiana today. If the same circumstances existed except that modern methods of transportation and communication were available, what changes would be made in the activities surrounding the purchase?

3. Compare life in Louisiana in 1803 with today.

4. Compare Louisiana in 1812 with Louisiana today in size, population, cities and towns, means of making a living, transportation, communication, government, and the ways of producing goods.

5. Contrast smuggling in Lafitte's day with smuggling today.

RURAL LOUISIANA (1800-1860)

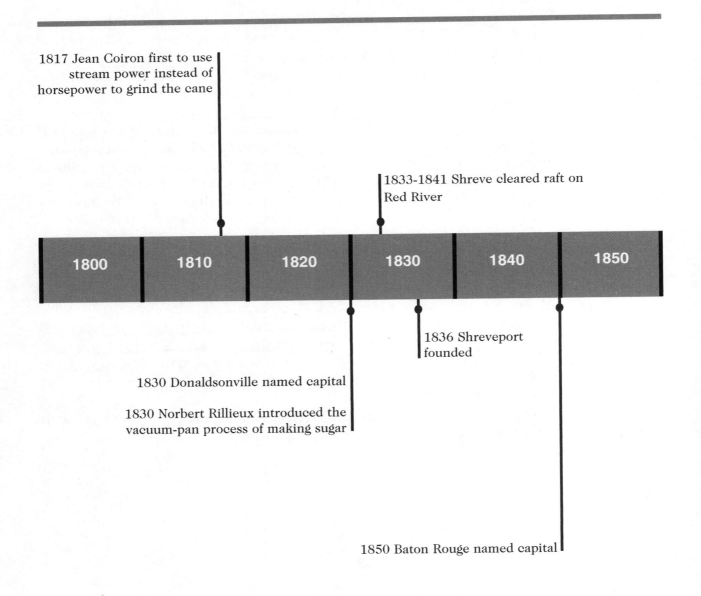

1817 Jean Coiron first to use stream power instead of horsepower to grind the cane

1833-1841 Shreve cleared raft on Red River

| 1800 | 1810 | 1820 | 1830 | 1840 | 1850 |

1836 Shreveport founded

1830 Donaldsonville named capital

1830 Norbert Rillieux introduced the vacuum-pan process of making sugar

1850 Baton Rouge named capital

RURAL LOUISIANA

The Plantation System

Between 1800 and 1860 Louisiana was predominantly a land of **plantations** and farms. Plantations were farm operations which involved a certain lifestyle and abundant cheap labor. Some farmers only raised crops to fill the needs of their families. Others raised a cash crop of a few bales of cotton in order to buy flour, sugar, and coffee. Some farms contained as many acres as plantations. Farmers maintained a different lifestyle from that of planters.

The plantation system had been a part of Louisiana life since its beginning. The French, Spanish, and English used plantations to settle Louisiana.

Plantations were economic institutions planned to produce staple crops. (**Staple crops** are those sold on the world market.)

The plantations of the United States were based on slavery. In the South black slaves were used as labor on the plantations.

The planter (like early governors) was the final authority on the plantation. Each plantation had different rules according to the man who was the "Boss." The Boss lived in "the Big House," where all plantation business was conducted and orders given.

Planter Control. The plantation existed in a nation dedicated to democracy. From the time of the writing of the U.S. Constitution planters were challenged regarding the status of their laborers. The historic wrangle between North and South began over the way the slaves should be counted in the population. The challenges to the plantation grew as the nation grew.

Planters were outnumbered in the population both by blacks and by the masses of whites. Votes of the masses could destroy the power of the planters. For that reason planters were forced into a pattern of interlocking controls. They sought to control Louisiana through its government. It was planters who became the majority in the legislature. The planters became governors.

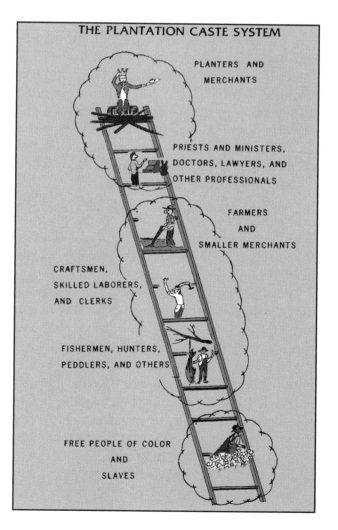

THE PLANTATION CASTE SYSTEM

PLANTERS AND MERCHANTS

PRIESTS AND MINISTERS, DOCTORS, LAWYERS, AND OTHER PROFESSIONALS

FARMERS AND SMALLER MERCHANTS

CRAFTSMEN, SKILLED LABORERS, AND CLERKS

FISHERMEN, HUNTERS, PEDDLERS, AND OTHERS

FREE PEOPLE OF COLOR AND SLAVES

In every walk of life planters made themselves or their associates leading figures. In politics, in churches, and in social life, the authority of the planter prevailed. Socially, the planter class, the aristocrats, dictated fashion and manners. Since the planter class dominated the government and set the standards, everyone was directly or indirectly under its control.

The Unwritten Plantation Code. For centuries planters maintained a pattern of interlocking controls that were defined in an unwritten code. The plantation code described acceptable behavior of both whites and blacks. These rules kept people "in their places" within the class society. This code was stronger than law. Its enforcement depended mostly on community sanctions, positive and negative. The planter had to maintain order and discipline over his labor force. Quite as important, the laborer produced best when he felt comfortable with his life.

There were two primary controls: education and ridicule. The underlying premise was that blacks were inferior to all whites. Non-planter whites were all inferior to the planter class.

Work Schedule. The workday on a plantation for both whites and blacks usually began just before sunrise. The plantation bell was rung several times during the early hour. First it was to wake the sleeping workers. The second was a signal to have the work animals harnessed and ready to be taken to the fields. Black slaves, living in the "quarters," reported to work at daylight and worked until sunset. During the summer heat two hours were taken off from the fields at noon.

There was always work to do. When rains fell, some work was done indoors. Saturday afternoons and Sundays were free. There was free time between the harvest of the crops in the fall and around March when it was time to start the new crop. "Lay-by" time came in the summer when the crops had been cultivated and left to mature before harvest.

The Base of the State's Economy. Every resident, however remote he felt from everyday plantation work, was involved in the plantation system. All livelihoods earned in Louisiana came directly or indirectly from agriculture. Plantations were the base of the economy. They represented the financial support for the entire population. Crop failures not only affected those on the farms

Parlange Plantation, New Roads.

and plantations but also the secondary businesses serving agriculture.

Differences in Farmers and Planters. Most Louisiana farmers cultivated small **acreages** of land. This was not true of all farmers, however. But what distinguished the farm from the plantation was the lifestyles on the two operations. Whether it was a large or small farm, it was a self-sufficient unit. The labor employed was mostly the farmer and family members. The major difference lay in the management of the labor forces.

Farmers relied primarily on family **labor**— their wives, their children, and themselves. The farmer himself did as much of the work as he could. A farmer financially able to operate a large farm usually had sons working with him. If need be, he hired help, often during harvest. He and his neighbors exchanged work. Occasionally there was a farmer who owned a slave or two.

The idea that all farmers dreamed of becoming planters has little to do with reality. Farmers more often despised the lowland lifestyle of those who owned slaves. Farmers often felt that planters represented an immoral society.

The farmer believed in relying on himself. He honored work, and he had no liking for the planter class, who, as he viewed it, depended upon others to "wait on them." Most farmers were skilled in many crafts. They were not only farmers but carpenters, bricklayers, blacksmiths, and, often on Saturday nights, fiddle players. A typical farmer took pride in the amount and quality of his work.

Most **farmers' wives** appeared as truly liberated women. They were usually working partners with their husbands in the fields. Having babies and nurturing them were a part of the routine in the primitive household.

These women sometimes plowed. They

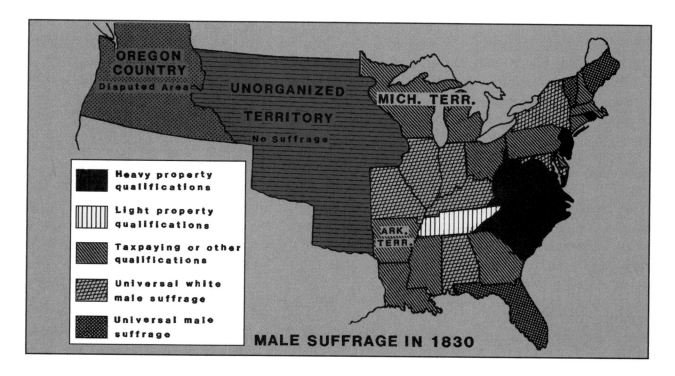

MALE SUFFRAGE IN 1830

helped chop the grass out of their few acres of cotton. They made gardens. They worked at making quilts. They sewed garments for the family.

The **planter's wife** did work equal to her hill country sisters. The difference was in the kind of work. She also bore many children. Most might have a black woman helper when there was no work in the fields. Contrary to the myth, most planters would not think of purchasing high-priced slaves to work in the Big House. (The fields had priority. Slaves were bought to help make money by working in the cotton fields.) The planter's wife was responsible for sewing for the family. She was in charge of clothing needed for the slaves. Making cotton sacks was the planter's wife's responsibility also. Weaving cloth, a necessity on the frontier, was also her job. She was usually the gardener. She was accustomed to long visits throughout the year by large numbers of family and friends. She was often responsible for whatever education her children received.

The planter had usually had more opportunity to secure more education than the farmer. This was not always the case. Most planters spoke the French or English of a better educated class.

Financial Arrangements. Financing a big plantation took a large amount of money. Typically, planters borrowed money for each new crop. Louisiana planters borrowed the money in New Orleans. Planters handled their financial arrangements through agents called factors. The factor borrowed money from a New Orleans bank or financiers in New York or Boston. A lien on the unplanted crop was security against the loan. The factor received the crop shipped from inland Louisiana. It was up to him to sell at the highest price on the New Orleans market. The factor acted as purchasing agent for practically everything the planter and his family bought. He made shipments from New Orleans of everything from harnesses to corsets, seed to hoes, and shovels. In payment the factor received 2 percent of the crop or slightly more.

The farmer was proud of "owing no man." Instead, he and his family spent little cash and saved their money. A simple lifestyle in a moderate climate helped. The two hundred dollars or three hundred dollars from his cotton crop was often more than the family used. The farmer's cotton was often sold to the store owner from whom he bought his supplies. Or he could sell to a planter, who added the farmer's bales to his own before shipment to New Orleans.

Businesses. Each plantation was its own little world. Most of the work was done by hand. There were few machines of any kind. Corn was raised for food for farm animals, poultry, and the family. Corn was ground into meal for bread at a gristmill, often on the plantation. Others took corn to the gristmill. A small portion of the cornmeal was given in payment for milling. Carpen-ters were often on the plantation payroll. During the early decades of the 1800s there were always coopers in the plantation community. Coopers manufactured products from wood secured in the nearby forests. Barrels, buckets, "dough bowls," spokes for wheels, hoe handles, and other items were made by coopers. A blacksmith on the plantation was a necessity. It was he who hammered the cutting edge on plowpoints and kept hoes sharpened and ready for use. Skilled blacksmiths made many useful objects. Often there were sawmills that made boards from the logs cut from the trees on the back of plantations. Cotton gins for separating seed from the cotton stood at about five-mile intervals among the plantations. The gins became increasingly efficient as the decades passed. Crude sugar mills were a part of sugarcane plantations in the early decades. Syrup mills converted the sugarcane into syrup, a very popular food.

Among the farmers there were the same kind of mills. Gristmills and blacksmith shops might be small businesses serving the public. A large farmer might have small mills. A syrup mill for making syrup from sorghum might be operated.

It was often a planter who owned the largest general store serving the community. The post office was located in such stores.

En Partie 1 (Studying a Part). 1. Describe the plantation system. 2. Relate it to the state economy. 3. Describe the position of planters. 4. (a) List some of the unwritten plantation rules. (b) List any unwritten rules you live by. 5. Compare planters and farmers. 6. Describe the (a) role of women, (b) financial arrangements, and (c) work routine. 7. Explain: every resident was involved in the plantation system.

Slavery

With the two new continents to settle, mind-boggling amounts of manpower were necessary. Slave traders appeared to buy slaves from Africa and sell them in the New World. Slavery was an acceptable practice in much of the world at that time.

Arrival of Slaves. Boston developed its "Triangular Trade" of slaves. They were brought from Africa and traded for sugar in the Caribbean islands. The sugar was brought to Boston for producing rum. New England made most of the slave ships.

The first slaves came to Louisiana in the first decades of the 1700s. By 1724 so many slaves were in Louisiana that Bienville produced the historic *Code Noir.* Slaves who had been in the Caribbean working on sugar plantations were especially valuable on sugar plantations in Louisiana. These were said to be "seasoned," or experienced, workmen. Others came into Louisiana with planters moving west to raise cotton in this "Cotton State." Every plantation cut out of the wilderness brought new demands for more slaves.

The Louisiana Purchase treaty prohibited the **importation of slaves** from foreign countries after January 1, 1804. A federal

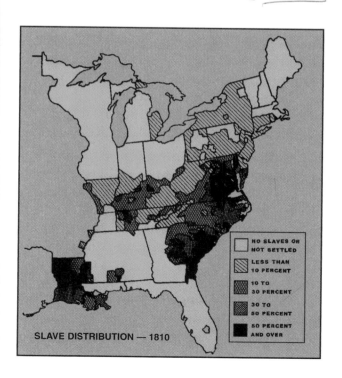

SLAVE DISTRIBUTION — 1810

☐	NO SLAVES OR NOT SETTLED
▨	LESS THAN 10 PERCENT
▩	10 TO 30 PERCENT
▦	30 TO 50 PERCENT
■	50 PERCENT AND OVER

Solomon Northup.

law forbade the importation of slaves from overseas, that is, Africa, after January 1808. Such a law made smuggling of slaves highly attractive to pirates such as the Lafitte brothers. Offspring of slaves added to the numbers available for plantation work. As the demands grew, smuggling grew.

Lagniappe—*Northup's Story.* Solomon Northup was a free man of color kidnapped from a train and sold at auction barns into slavery. The story of his life as a slave in Rapides and Avoyelles Parishes is written as related to a lawyer and is now a documented book, *Twelve Years a Slave, 1841-1853*. The **Northup Trail** is marked through his time owned by William Prince Ford and by Edwin Epps and the restoration of his freedom in 1853 at the Avoyelles Courthouse in Marksville. A duplication of the Epps house

now stands on the campus of LSU-Alexandria. Northup's version of life in plantations in the 1840s reveals much about daily life and survival as a slave and how masters conducted themselves. The book identifies the families living in Rapides and Avoyelles in those years and their lifestyles.

Price. The price of slaves doubled and tripled over the decades before the Civil War. As more cotton plantations were established, the prices of slaves rose. The kidnapping of slaves from northern states established a Reverse Underground Railroad. Criminals, such as the New York kidnappers of Solomon Northup, formed secret alliances with slave auction barns. Those kidnapped were sold into areas where it was almost impossible for contact back home.

Numbers of Slaves. Almost the same number of slaves lived in the State of New York as in all of Louisiana in 1803. By 1810 Louisiana had twice as many slaves as New York. That number more than doubled by 1820. Between 1800 and 1850 slaves in Louisiana increased from forty thousand to 330,000.

In 1860, the year before the Civil War, Louisiana (and the rest of the South) was not filled with vast plantations and many, many slaves. A false image has been created by writers and moviemakers regarding plantations. Most Southerners owned no slaves. One family out of four owned slaves. There were 1,600,000 families in the South in 1860. Only about four hundred thousand owned slaves. Thirty percent of the families owned only one slave. The large slaveholder was the exception among slave owners in Louisiana.

During this period there were as many

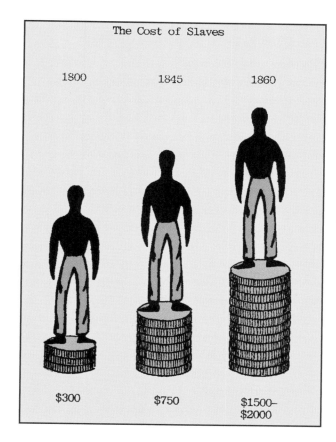

The Cost of Slaves

1800   1845   1860

$300 $750 $1500–$2000

seers. Therefore, the planter himself supervised the work of the slave. In some cases slaves lived almost as if they were freemen. As a general rule, they were not allowed to leave the plantation without permission. Unauthorized white persons were forbidden to visit the slaves for fear the visitor might cause trouble.

A fact difficult for modern people to understand is that slaves were **property**. They represented the largest investment the planter had. Plantations could not exist without a plentiful supply of labor available on the land. It was in the owner's best interest to treat his valuable property well. They produced more work when they were reasonably comfortable.

How much violence there was is difficult to assess. Such archives as were left by planters came from a relatively few Southern planters. Since most of the entire population could neither read nor write during that period, little firsthand information is available.

Contrary to the image, blacks and whites working together on their plantations mostly lived in peace. Although there were exceptions, there were many **family units** among slaves. Plantation legal records often list slaves as parents and their children. Slaves were sometimes sold away from their families. This was not usually true. Many slaves, their children, and children's children lived and died on the same plantation.

Resistance. Fugitive, or runaway, slaves were common in Louisiana. In 1850 there were ninety fugitives. In 1860 there were forty-six. In times of anger over punishment by the owners slaves would hide in a nearby swamp or forest. Usually the situation ended with the slave either being captured or voluntarily returning because of hunger and discomfort. Newspapers of the time carried

blacks as whites in Louisiana. The black population was not distributed equally around the state. At least 90 percent of blacks in the nineteenth century lived on plantations or farms, mostly on plantations. Almost all blacks in the state were slaves. In the hill country there were usually either no blacks at all or very few.

Description. No single description can cover either the role of the master or the treatment of slaves—or the institution itself. Slavery was as humane—or as inhumane—in Louisiana as in any other state. The **treatment** of slaves depended entirely upon the character and attitude of masters and overseers. Probably no two masters treated their slaves identically.

Probably most plantations had no over-

Number of Slaves	1000 & over	500 to 999	100 to 499	50 to 99	20 to 49	10 to 19	5 to 9	2 to 4	one
Number of Slaveholders in Louisiana in 1850	0	4	316	728	1,774	2,652	4,327	6,072	4,797
Number of Slaveholders in USA in 1860	1	13	2,278	8,366	35,616	61,682	89,423	109,588	76,670

Number of Slaveholders in Louisiana in 1850 and the United States in 1860

The numbers for Louisiana changed little between 1850 and 1860

advertisements for runaway slaves.

In order to maintain order and to prevent runaways, parish police juries organized patrols of citizens from the plantations. In times of violence in other areas of the country such as that of John Brown or Nat Turner, the patrols operated.

Rumors of planned slave uprisings were circulated from plantation to plantation. Only a few are mentioned in newspapers of the time. Encouraging slaves to revolt was severely punished.

Lagniappe—*Slave Plot.* The fear of rebellion from the slaves was a constant problem on the plantations. One such organized plan came to light on Bayou Boeuf in Rapides Parish in 1827. The plot was exposed and several slaves were hanged in public exhibition in Alexandria. Supposedly the leader who revealed the plot, **Lew Cheney,** was given money and freedom and allowed to flee the state. The dreadful punishment was supposed to stop any future efforts by slaves to escape and gain freedom. Patrols of citizens from the plantations worked to prevent runaways or uprisings. Stocks, whippings, shackles and deprivation of food were some of the punishments, as well as confinement in some sort of jail. Slaves were valuable assets and were maintained, fed and cared for as such but punishment from the owner

was swift and sure if rebellion or disobedience to orders arose.

Punishment. Large plantations had a jail for confinement for serious violations of the rules on the plantation. Slaves might be sold as a result of breaking the planter's rules. Fugitives might suffer whippings when caught. Stocks were the most common method of punishment. Arms and legs could be stuck through holes placed so that the person punished was unable to free himself.

Manumission. Emancipation was relatively common in Louisiana. In 1850 Louisiana was the fourth state in number of slaves freed or manumitted. In 1860 only one state freed more. Manumission was often given for devoted service. Many slave owners had kinsmen among the slaves. Many of them were freed after the death of the owner. Sometimes slave owners had two families, one white and the other by a black slave woman. In some cases a slave owner freed his own children and legally claimed them as his own.

Lagniappe—*Free Persons of Color.* As time passed in the colonies, people of mixed ethnic heritages were produced. Some were black-white, some were Indian-white. They were griffe, mulattoes, quadroons, half-breeds and soon constituted another class of people to be dealt with. Men and women (at one time numbering around eighteen thousand in New Orleans) established themselves as **Free Persons of Color**. Many of these people were freed or granted manumission by slave owners. Louisiana slave owners granted many manumissions in the 1800s. Novels about Louisiana and plantation culture often feature Free Persons of Color as glamorous and mysterious. Many were a big part of the social life in New Orleans with its balls, theaters and entertainment. Today, they are often identified as Creoles and their history is being documented.

En Partie 2 (Studying a Part). 1. Relate the role of slaves to the plantation economy. 2. Why can't the typical (a) slave, (b) master, or (c) relationship between slave and master be described? 3. Give the relationship among these words: resistance, punishment, and rewards. 4. What percentage of the people owned slaves in 1860? 5. Relate slave life to supply and demand.

The Plantation Class System

Status was an invisible fact of life in plantation country. It was not something that could be abandoned. Louisiana had a rigid class system, the arrangement of society in layers. There were actually two parallel societies which developed side by side. Both the

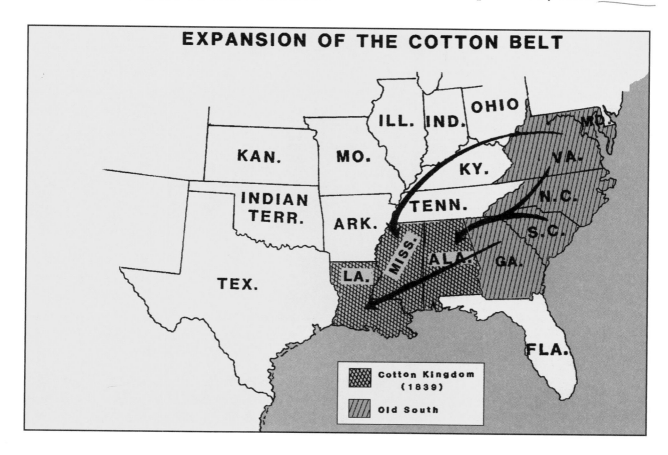

EXPANSION OF THE COTTON BELT

Cotton Kingdom (1839)

Old South

black and the white were very complex societies. Both included a wide variety of people with varying lifestyles.

At the top were the planters, who considered themselves aristocrats. Besides the planters, the aristocracy included bankers, merchants, lawyers, and doctors, as well as other well-to-do businessmen. Members of the planter elite felt superior to other whites as well as blacks. Between the aristocracy and the lowest class were the remainder of the white people living in the state. These people might be designated as "plain people." By far this largest class of white people included farmers, small businessmen, townspeople, clerks, tanners, coopers, and persons in a variety of trades. Somewhere, sandwiched just above the slaves, were the free people of color. Free people of color, often people of mixed ethnic groups, held themselves aloof from slaves. At the bottom of the social ladder were the slaves, who numbered as many as all others who lived in the state. There were layers of classes among slaves, also.

Status was directly related to the way people made a living. Skills earned respect and status just as they do today. On plantations such skills as those of smiths, carpenters, and sugar makers were highly valued. Whites or slaves exhibiting these skills performed these tasks, according to who excelled at the tasks. The only white employees on plantations were often overseers and storekeepers. Most plantations had a skilled blacksmith, who welded broken plow parts, sharpened plow points, and the like. A cooper, who made barrels and other wooden containers, and carpenters were often on the planter's payroll. Others were hired as sugar makers. On many plantations skilled slaves performed these different crafts. Extra

skilled labor was hired during the sugarcane grinding season. Planters sometimes relied on Irish laborers for clearing land, ditching, and other types of plantation work.

The men employed in handling the boats plying the waters of the state had a status hierarchy of their own. These ranged from river pilots to pilots on bayou boats to oarsmen who stoked the furnaces of steamboats.

Some redemptioners, or indentured servants, were used on plantations in Louisiana. After statehood they continued to come. The Germans proved to be the most dependable of the group. Many served their terms and became independent farmers. Some continued to live very much like the black slaves. Their status depended upon their owners.

The class system grew with the necessity of controlling the slave population. The idea of a superior people who had a right to command those beneath them was essential in a slave society. The first rule for controlling slaves was to use the idea that people who were slaves were born inferior. This had to do with the prime goal in any plantation society: to maintain its labor supply.

En Partie 3 (Studying a Part). 1. Explain Louisiana's social class system. 2. Describe life for each of the groups. 3. Why did it develop? 4. Did it exist only in the white community? Defend your position.

Settlements

New Orleans. The port was **the largest city in the South by 1840.** It was the **third largest**

city in America at that time. New Orleans was at its peak of prosperity and growth from 1835 to 1852. It was the largest cotton market in the world. The levee and the streets were piled high with cotton. In the 1830s steamboats arrived and departed every hour. As many as fifty steamboats lined the docks at one time. Fifty thousand bales of cotton waited for shipment almost every day.

New Orleans served as the outlet for the goods of most of the Mississippi Valley. This **river traffic** on the Mississippi was at its peak from 1840 to 1861. The port also served as the outlet for goods from Europe, Mexico, and the Caribbean islands. It led the nation in exports and tonnage on the wharves. In a short period New Orleans doubled the tonnage of New York.

Almost a three-mile stretch of the levee at the river's crescent was an unbroken line of **businesses**. There were storehouses, cotton presses, and shops. Slave gangs loaded and unloaded merchandise of every description.

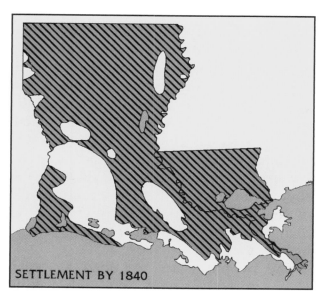

SETTLEMENT BY 1840

Furs, sugar, molasses, rice, mules and horses, tobacco, corn, pork, barrel staves, wheat, oats, and flour were some of the products. Of course, cotton far outweighed other products.

New Orleans developed as the leading **financial center** of the South. New Orleans banks were the largest among those of the fifteen slave-holding states. They financed cotton crops for Louisiana and other Southern states.

The city gained the nickname "Queen City of the South." Its **population** grew rapidly. Many nationalities from all over the world were represented in the city. In fact, almost 40 percent of the city's population was foreign-born. In 1850 New Orleans had forty thousand people residing there.

New Orleans was the place to which the most affluent planters and professional men in rural Louisiana took their families for the **social season** and during the winter months. Some planters lived in New Orleans and provided homes for their overseers on their plantations. Many people came from other states to visit New Orleans.

The city became divided between the Americans and the Creoles. Creole supremacy had been a major problem since the Louisiana Purchase. For years the issue in all elections was **Creole versus American.** Canal Street became the dividing line between the factions. The wide median strip became known as the Neutral Ground. The Creoles built up the French Quarter. American exporters and importers and sugar and cotton brokers built their own city on the other side of Canal Street. The more Americans came the more the supremacy of the Creoles was threatened.

Commercial prosperity led to **economic** and **social improvements** on a large scale. By 1835 the city invested nearly five million

Pontalba Apartments, New Orleans.

dollars improving streets, drains, and banquettes. The city was lighted with gas lanterns. Even after the improvements were made, only 25 percent of the city was paved. Paving stones from Europe and the North were used for the project.

A building boom in the 1830s produced many new **hotels** and boardinghouses. Two of the most famous were the majestic St. Charles Hotel and the St. Louis Hotel.

In 1850 and 1851 two apartment buildings were built flanking Jackson Square in the French Quarter. There were shops on the ground floor. The buildings were erected by Micaela Leonard Almonester, Baroness de Pontalba. They became known as the **Pontalbas.** These two buildings and the three built by her father—the St. Louis Cathedral, the Cabildo, and the Presbytere—are historical landmarks.

Louisiana's booming city developed quite a **reputation.** New Orleans was described as having the worst sanitation in America. The only sewers were open drains. They were clogged with garbage, refuse, and human waste. When it rained, the city's streets flooded. The debris was scattered everywhere. In the dirty city, the life span of its residents was said to be the shortest in the country. The proud people of New Orleans resented any criticism of their city. They denied that it was less healthy than other places.

The people were described as being obsessed with **having fun** and making money. There were more alcoholics and gamblers there than in any other city in America, according to reports. The city was supposed to have had the longest social calendar in the nation. Balls, ballets, and operas were regular features on the calendar of the elite.

New Capitals. New Orleans was the capital of Louisiana until 1830. From its beginning in the French colonial period, the city had been the center of Louisiana's population. However, some people felt that New Orleans represented the French and the urban capital population too much. The legislature wanted to move the capital to a rural area. It chose **Donaldsonville**. If New Orleans had provided too much entertainment for the legislators, Donaldsonville was too small and provided too little. Finally, in 1850, the capital was moved to **Baton Rouge**.

Other Settlements. Most of the towns developed on the rivers and bayous as trading centers for the surrounding area. The country towns grew gradually as their neighboring trade territory developed. Baton Rouge developed after the capital was moved there. It took unusual occurrences to speed up the development of any antebellum Louisiana town.

Towns and settlements of Louisiana in the 1840s were quite different in appearance from our cities today. Many were merely collections of scattered cabins and shacks. Streets were unlighted and unpaved. The streets became mudholes when it rained. The parish seats often had only a courthouse, a jail, a few stores, and a few private buildings. Churches, courthouses, schools, and other public buildings advanced in architectural appearance as the years went by.

Crossroad villages developed mostly around the numerous small bayou and river ports. They met the needs not met on the plantations. Although almost every plantation had its own dock where barges stopped, usually a larger point for depositing freight was necessary. From these places, wagons were used to distribute supplies to other points. The area doctor, a schoolmaster, a church, and a general store often formed a center around which community living revolved. The church became a central gathering place for people. The general store was also a favorite gathering place, and usually there was a post office in the store.

Outside the New Orleans area, Louisiana was part of the western frontier of the United States. The northern part of the state was sparsely settled until after the Civil War. Great virgin forests still covered thousands of acres of land.

Lagniappe—*What was "the West"?* As people arrived in the New World and began to investigate, the definition of West changed. The Appalachians were one great boundary. The Mississippi was another. Then across the Great Plains to the Pacific over the Rocky Mountains became a journey some sought. The trip from the Carolinas through the Black Swamp of Georgia Territory to the Gulf and the Mississippi was the journey of many to Louisiana. Forts established as people moved West became safe havens for stopovers. It is hard to imagine that territories were our West long after Louisiana became a United States possession.

Westward Movement. Moving west was always a thought in the minds of the people of Louisiana, as elsewhere. Migrants from the states across the Mississippi River moved into

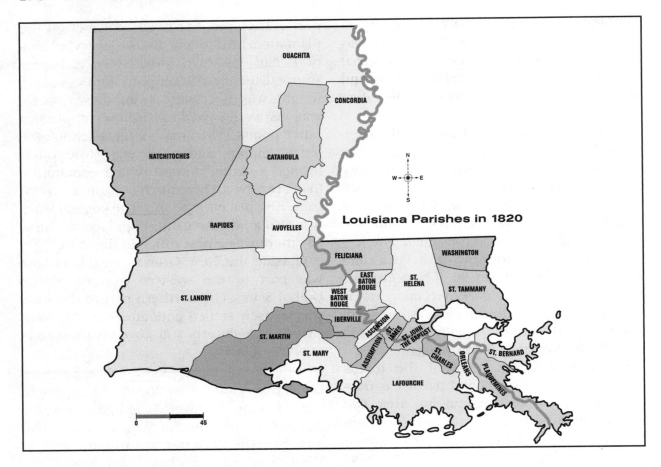

Louisiana Parishes in 1820

Louisiana in their covered wagons. No sooner did some of the immigrants get to Louisiana than they decided that things sounded better a little farther on. This was the mysterious appeal of the westward movement. Although many thousands moved through Louisiana, many others became permanent Louisiana settlers. Most of the immigrants who came to Louisiana were farmers. Thus, the population rapidly increased as the people moved westward.

After the Louisiana Purchase Louisiana's **population** increased greatly. Most of Louisiana's population at that time was French and Spanish. Many foreigners came to the state after 1830. Ireland and Germany contributed the largest numbers. Most of these foreigners settled in New Orleans. The Irish became very active in politics. Their participation gave rise to the American movement that opposed the Creoles.

The greatest influx from the other Southern states came after 1840. This was the time when the region north of the Red River was settled. Americans came into Louisiana before 1860 mostly from these states: Alabama, Georgia, Mississippi, North Carolina, South Carolina, Tennessee, Virginia, Kentucky, New York, Pennsylvania, Ohio, and Texas.

The **Black population** was concentrated on plantations along the rivers, bayous, and creeks. If there were any blacks in the hill country, they were usually free people of color. Most of these people lived in the old French sections. Many free people of color lived in Natchitoches and New Orleans.

The Great Raft. The presence of the Great Raft delayed the exploration and settlement of North Louisiana. The raft was a logjam about 165 miles long that filled the bed of the Red River. The raft obstructed navigation above Natchitoches to the Arkansas border. The westward movement in the early 1830s led to an increasing demand to clear the raft. The development of the steamboat influenced the decision to try to clear the waterway.

Funds were provided by Congress to remove the **log jam.** The work was not progressing when an extraordinary pioneer in the development of water commerce, **Capt. Henry Miller Shreve,** made suggestions. Shreve showed how to use his snag boat *Archimedes* to loosen the logs so that they could be removed. He started his work April 11, 1833, at Campti. By June 27, 1833, he reached Coates' Bluff, located in present-day **Shreveport.** The worst part of the jam was above the site of Shreveport. He continued

Henry Shreve cleared the Red River of the 160-mile-long Great Raft.

to work until 1841. Though there was great improvement, the logjam began to re-form in later years. United States engineers finally cleared the channel in 1873.

Founding of Shreveport. Shreve and seven other men formed the Shreve Town Company on May 27, 1836. They obtained the land given to Larkin Edwards by the Caddo Indians. Then they laid out eight streets. On March 20, 1839, the legislature granted a charter to the town of Shreveport. Thus, a river settlement developed to serve North Louisiana and East Texas.

The settlers of Texas looked to Shreveport for their supplies. It was a market for their cotton, hides, and furs. Caravans of ox teams, bringing the produce, traveled the Texas Trail to the riverfront.

Many American immigrants finding their way to Texas came to Shreveport. The town became the point toward which this migration moved. People traveled by stagecoach from Alexandria through Natchitoches to Shreveport. Others came by stagecoach from Monroe through Mount Lebanon and Minden. Some came by covered wagon with an ox team or by horseback or muleback. Others came up the river from New Orleans.

Shreveport grew steadily during the twenty-four years before the Civil War. The war checked the city's growth and prosperity.

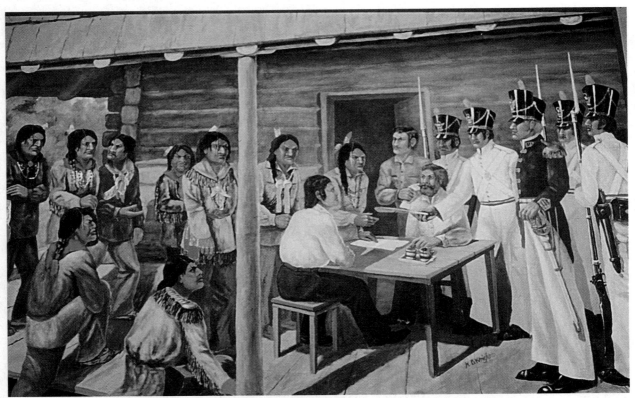

Caddo Indians in 1835 ceded land (the site of Shreveport) to the United States.

1820 . . . 1830 . . . 1840 . . . 1850 . . . 1860.
. . . During these decades, for the most part the state was being settled. **Agriculture** was still the leading industry. Most of the agricultural holdings were small or large farmers rather than plantations. In the rich delta soil along rivers and bayous there were many plantations that were producing large cotton and sugarcane crops.

There was a rush for land to build more plantations. Many planters or their sons from the Carolinas and Virginia were looking for new land. Plantations were expanded backward into the swamps. New areas of virgin soil were constantly being brought into cultivation. The small farmers along the Mississippi sold out to the planters and moved to the western prairies and the hills of North Louisiana. Land prices went from $1.25 in the first decade of the 1800s to fifty dollars an acre for delta land. North Louisiana hill country lands were still sparsely settled. The number and size of plantations increased. There was an unbroken chain along the Mississippi.

Sugarcane was a major crop in south Louisiana. Sugarcane had become an important staple on the lower Mississippi before the Louisiana Purchase. Several advancements caused the growing of sugarcane to spread. In 1817 **Jean Coiron** (KWÄ ron) was the first to use steam engine power instead of horsepower to grind the cane. In 1830 a free person of color, **Norbert Rillieux** (RILL lou), introduced the vacuum pan process of making sugar. It revolutionized the sugar industry. These improvements quickened the making of sugar and increased the profits. At the same time it meant that planters had a great expense erecting the sugarhouses and supplying the necessary equipment.

Tobacco was produced as a staple crop in some sections of the state. Large amounts were raised north of the Red River. Perique tobacco was grown in St. James Parish. Frequently, cotton and tobacco were raised on the same plantation. These crops were harvested at alternating periods.

As wave after wave of land-hungry **cotton** planters and farmers moved into Louisiana from the eastern United States, the production of cotton increased. By the middle of the 1830s more than a half million bales of cotton were produced every year. Cotton became a valuable commodity on the world market. Louisiana was becoming dependent upon the cotton economy. New types of cotton were introduced. The states bordering on the Gulf of Mexico were found ideal for growing short staple cotton. Methods of cultivation improved. Louisiana became one of the five leading cotton-producing states. It was largely from these Gulf coast states that the image of the plantation South emerged.

It is necessary to understand life in antebellum Louisiana to picture the setting before the Civil War.

En Partie 4 (Studying a Part). 1. Describe New Orleans during the antebellum period. 2. Trace the change of the location of the capital. 3. Describe settlement outside New Orleans during this period. 4. How did the westward movement affect Louisiana? 5. What was the West in 1812? 6. How did the Great Raft affect settlement? 7. Who was Henry Miller Shreve? 8. How did plantations change between 1820 and 1860?

LIFE IN ANTEBELLUM LOUISIANA
(1800-1860)

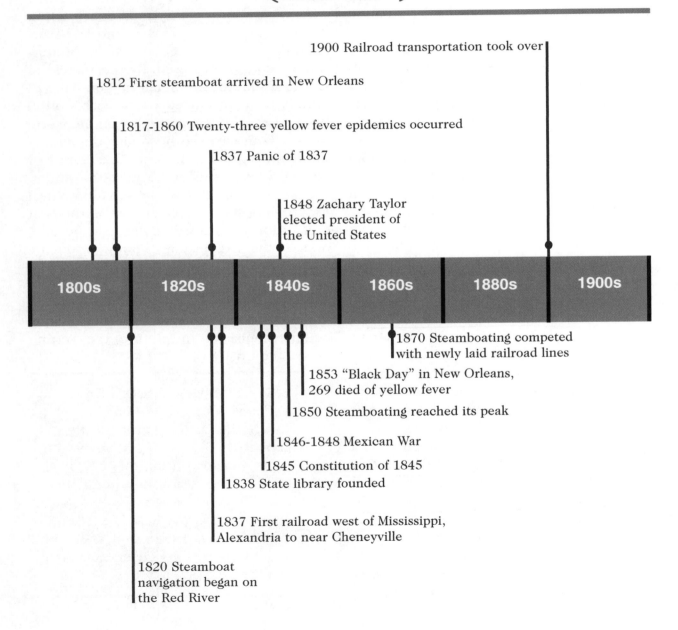

1900 Railroad transportation took over

1812 First steamboat arrived in New Orleans

1817-1860 Twenty-three yellow fever epidemics occurred

1837 Panic of 1837

1848 Zachary Taylor
elected president of
the United States

| 1800s | 1820s | 1840s | 1860s | 1880s | 1900s |

1870 Steamboating competed
with newly laid railroad lines

1853 "Black Day" in New Orleans,
269 died of yellow fever

1850 Steamboating reached its peak

1846-1848 Mexican War

1845 Constitution of 1845

1838 State library founded

1837 First railroad west of Mississippi,
Alexandria to near Cheneyville

1820 Steamboat
navigation began on
the Red River

LIFE IN ANTEBELLUM LOUISIANA

Most people living in Louisiana before 1860 lived on farms or plantations. Their lives were hard and simple, if we measure them by today's standards. That does not mean they were not rewarding.

Food, Clothing, and Shelter

Work Responsibilities. Every member of the large farm families was expected to do his part of the work. To survive it was necessary for every able individual to become skilled in many tasks and work long hours. The men cleared the land, built the houses and furniture, grew the crops, tended the livestock, and hunted and fished. Women cooked, made most of the clothing, and reared the children. They washed, ironed, made soap, and performed many other household chores. They milked cows and gardened while the menfolks were occupied with the crops that provided what cash the family had. The more ambitious ones even found time for a flower garden. The children did their part, too. Boys plowed, milked, hunted, fished, and gathered produce from the garden. They worked alongside their fathers. Girls cooked, sewed, and tended to the younger children. By helping their mothers, they learned the art of housekeeping. Some fortunate girls learned to play the piano or organ. Boys and girls were expected to be able to manage a farm or household by the time they were mid-teens. Marriages occurred at early ages.

Adobe brick cabins on Augusta Plantation in St. Landry Parish were constructed in the early 1800s.

Houses. Building a house was one of the first tasks when a family moved to a new location. The husband often set up a tent or pole shelter for temporary use by the family. Then with the help of the family he cleared the land and cut the timber. A simple log cabin was built. The logs were held together with pegs. New "pens," or rooms, were added to log cabins as more space was required.

Both small and large farmers lived in almost stark simplicity in their unpainted dogtrot houses. During the decade before the Civil War most planters built big, unpainted farmhouses made from the lumber brought from the woods at the back of the plantations. Only a few built the type of plantation homes shown in movies and described in books. A few were made of brick usually produced from clay found in the area. Most houses were made of rough squared timbers. Spaces between boards were filled with mortar, and the house was whitewashed.

Some of the early houses had dirt **floors** while others had puncheon floors. Puncheon floors were made from short sections of heavy squared logs set on end in a bed of sand or soft dirt. The end forming the floor's surface was made as flat and smooth as possible.

Plain wooden shutters covered the **windows.** Sometimes greased paper or thin rawhide covered window openings to keep out mosquitoes and flies. Rarely was glass used. Even if obtainable, it was too expensive.

Most slaves lived on the plantations in cabins lined up close together called **"the quarters."** These cabins were often made of unpainted cypress or adobe brick. ("Adobe" means the bricks were handmade, poured into molds, and dried by the sun.) Many South Louisiana plantations formed small villages with the cabins arranged along the banks of a stream. Usually they were near a bayou, the source of the slaves' water supply. All had fireplaces to use for both heating and cooking.

Furnishings in the homes were often simple. Wood-burning stoves gradually replaced the fireplaces for cooking. After 1835 such mansions as there were might be equipped

Cooking was done mostly on fireplaces until a decade or so before the Civil War.

with gaslights. Only a rare few imported furniture, draperies, and luxuries from Europe.

Almost all Louisiana people depended upon what they could make from the materials found around them. Fine hardwoods were plentiful in the swampland. Ordinary carpenters built solid furniture for their houses. In fact, for most families the skill of the carpenters in the family determined the type furnishings they had. Pioneers built their beds, tables, and armoires, or ornate cupboards, to last. Homemade tables, stools, and wooden chairs with deerskin or cowhide seats furnished most homes. Spinning wheels and looms for making homespun cloth were necessary.

Ordinarily **mattresses** were stuffed with moss or corn shucks. Moss was hanging from the trees, available along the bayous for picking. Those who could afford it preferred other materials for stuffing their mattresses such as cotton and duck feathers. They considered the moss unsightly and dirty.

Fireplaces were the center of home life. They were essential for cooking, heating, and lighting. Cranes and hooks made the open fireplace useful for cooking. Families and friends gathered around the fireplaces to keep warm during cold weather. Firewood was plentiful from the forests nearby. Most families had only two or three pots and utensils that they used for cooking at the fireplace.

Blacksmiths contributed to household needs as well as the needs of the farmers. Skilled men made coffee mills, corn grinders, and sausage grinders.

Candles lit the houses, and almost all families made their own. Candles were made by dipping a string into hot wax over and over again before molds were available. Later hot melted wax was poured into candle molds into which wicks had been placed. Some families had lamps that burned lard.

Plumbing facilities were not available in the country. Outhouses stood in the backyards of rural homes. Indoor plumbing was not introduced in the cities until very late in this period.

Clothing and Linens. Mostly, clothing was homemade until late in the period. The farmers grew the cotton. The women and girls spun it into thread on a spinning wheel. Women then made the threads into cloth on a loom. The cloth was cut out and sewed into clothes for the family. A few decades before the Civil War, cloth could be bought in rural stores.

Ready-made clothing for men and women was available in the stores of the larger towns shortly before the Civil War. Yet most clothing was still homemade.

Shoes for those who could afford them were almost always made to order. Ordinarily

Plantation family buys goods from a peddler.

shoes were sold in large lots. There was no distinction between shoes to be worn on the left or right foot. Many people made their own shoes. Leather was made from animal hides. The shoemaker was a familiar figure.

Women knitted socks, braided straw hats, and embroidered pieces. They made sheets, pillowcases, towels, blankets, and quilts from their homespun cloth. In addition, it was necessary to mend everything. The planter's or farmer's wife was responsible for making cotton sacks.

It was in the best interest of owners to see that **slaves** were adequately **dressed**. A variety of garments was worn by slaves. Their clothing included worn garments of whites, clothing purchased by slaves from their earnings, and clothing received from allowances of the owners.

Food. From the beginning food in Louisiana was of extraordinarily fine quality. The French, Indians, Spanish, blacks, English, Germans, and others had contributed to an unbeatable blend of seasonings and food mixtures. There was plentiful game in the woods, and there was a wealth of fish and seafood. Bear oil, the colonial shortening, was available for frying. Pecans and other nuts and berries were also plentiful.

Providing food for the family was a major task. Farmers raised most of the food they needed. Quantity was important because these hardworking people used so much energy. In the state's mild climate, Louisianians were able to raise two crops of vegetables, one in the spring and one in the fall. Fruit trees—plums, peaches, figs, pomegranates, and pears—were planted. Muscadines and berries were available for picking.

Gathering vegetables from a garden, cleaning them, shelling peas and beans, and peeling cushaw or Irish potatoes were a few of the many tasks in **preparing** food. **Preserving** food for winter was a necessity.

Cattle and **hogs** were raised for a meat supply. A milk cow was kept by almost everyone. The small farmer often herded livestock over open or timbered land. Meat was prepared for family use in a variety of ways. Some was ground and made into sausage. Sometimes meat patties were fried and stored between layers of grease in a crock. A smokehouse constructed near the house was used for curing ham and other meat. Salt meat and bacon were mainstays. Poultry was raised for home use and for sale in the town markets.

All **dairy products** had to be prepared at home. Milking cows, churning butter, and making cheese were jobs that had to be done. Storing butter and milk in a semitropical climate where there was no ice was a problem. It was secured in tight jars or crocks and lowered into the cool water of a well or underground cistern or the cool waters of creeks and springs.

It was up to the owners to furnish **food** for their **slaves**. The slaves had to be fed well. The slave mother often cooked the food in a big pot in the fireplace. On some plantations food for all the slaves was cooked at one central place in great black pots. In such arrangements, slaves ate together, serving themselves from the pots.

The **diet** of most of the rural people was simple and monotonous. Sweet potatoes, pork, strong coffee, and cornbread were basic parts of the diet. Wheat bread cost as much as meat so it was not a part of the diet of rural people. Cornbread was eaten almost every day, and pork seemed to have been more frequently used than beef or mutton.

Slaves found game, such as the opossum and coon, fun to hunt and a fine source of food. Rabbits, squirrels, and wild birds were also hunted.

Obtaining **water** for the household required considerable effort. Some families had wells. Water had to be pulled by a rope from a shallow well or pumped from the depths of an underground cistern into buckets. If a drought came, the cistern, which might be an above-ground one, might dry up. Gutters, or shallow troughs that ran around the eaves of the house, had to be kept clean to let rainwater into the cistern. In times of water scarcity, cistern-owners hauled water in barrels or buckets from the nearest stream or creek. In some wooded areas cool spring water was available the year round. Water was brought to the house in buckets from the bayou or creek, and gourd dippers were commonly used to enjoy a drink. If hot water were needed, it was heated on the wood stove.

In New Orleans the water that could be obtained was often unfit to drink. The drinking water was carted from the Mississippi River. Youngsters spent hours filtering it through porous stone or cleaning it with lime, alum, or charcoal. It was sold for two cents a bucket.

Country Stores. All over the state men gathered at crossroads stores. They were located close enough to be reached by horseback or wagon. Men sat around the potbellied stove, chewing tobacco and talking. All the news of the countryside came up for discussion. There they exchanged news with neighbors, talked about their crops, and heard the latest cotton prices from New Orleans.

These rural stores, wherever located, became a focal point for a large area. The merchandise included a variety of items. Medicines, plows, Christmas toys, seed, horse collars, laces and ribbons, the materials needed for burials, wagons, buggies, pants, flour, coffee, sugar, fruit, shoes—everything came from the general store. All of these supplies arrived by boat from New Orleans.

En Partie 1 (Studying a Part). 1. Define the term "antebellum." 2. Describe the food, clothing, and shelter of the period. 3. What responsibility did each member of the family have in providing the essentials?

Communication and Transportation

Mail. Mail service was slow and uncertain. After the Louisiana Purchase residents expected regular mail service. This was impossible for decades. Roads had to be improved, if not made. Ferries and bridges had to be provided.

As the migrants moved west, letters became extremely important in keeping in touch with people back home. Distances that could be traveled in less than an hour by automobile today presented problems for families wanting to visit each other. Letters then were often the only means of communication. Most had to be hand-delivered from settlement to settlement by chance meetings with migrants headed west and willing to deliver a letter.

Mail riders on horseback, stagecoaches,

and boats delivered mail. Many communities in the state were totally dependent on regular steamboat lines for mail. In the early antebellum days steamboats did not make trips regularly. Mail service was irregular throughout the antebellum period.

Transportation. Horses or **wagons** and **carts** drawn slowly across the wilderness by animals provided **overland** transportation. There were no state highways during this time. There were some **trails** that followed Indian trails. All road construction was the responsibility of the parishes or individuals.

Each landowner along a river or bayou was required to maintain a public road in front of his property. Most of these roads were impassable except when it was dry. In some places where land was swampy and timber was cheap and abundant, plank roads were built.

Land routes were less important in the transportation of mail, freight, and passengers after the **steamboat** became active. More regular ship connections with the Atlantic seaboard also reduced the demand for land transportation.

Most long distance travel was by **boat**.

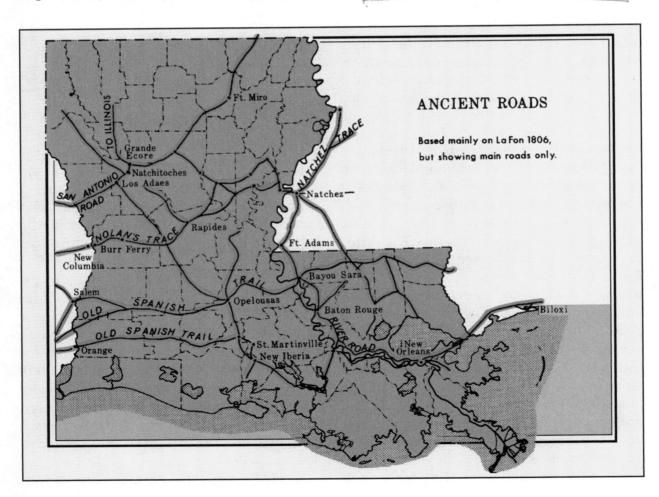

ANCIENT ROADS

Based mainly on La Fon 1806, but showing main roads only.

Ferry at Morgan City in mid-nineteenth century.

Canoes, pirogues, and dugouts were used for transportation by water. Rafts, arks, and broadhorns carried larger cargoes than the smaller craft. Keelboats came later and were faster. All types of boats—flatboats, brigs, clippers, sloops, and schooners—went in and out of New Orleans. Many of these kinds of boats could also be seen on inland streams.

No matter in what part of the state one settled, there was the problem of **getting the crop to market** in New Orleans. For this reason plantations were usually located close to the banks of the river in reach of steamboats. Transportation was an expensive and time-consuming operation. For instance, a cotton planter on the Ouachita River had to ship his cotton crop to New Orleans through a route

that involved the Old River, the Red River, and finally the Mississippi River.

The first **steamboat** to arrive in New Orleans came down the Mississippi River in 1812. Nicholas I. Roosevelt and his wife took the *New Orleans* from Pittsburgh to New Orleans. People all along the way lined the riverbank to view this new invention. Many could not believe what they saw. Some doubted that it could make the return trip.

The first steamboats did not have enough power to make the return trip. They had to stay in the lower Mississippi. **Henry Miller Shreve** designed a boat that could go anywhere it could float. Later Captain Shreve designed a boat that needed only three feet of water to keep it afloat. It was a sternwheeler.

In his boat the *Enterprise,* he made the

Steamboats loaded with cotton bales carried Louisiana's crop to market in New Orleans.

first return trip up the Mississippi. He went to Louisville. He also made the first trip in a steamboat up the Red River.

The *Enterprise* was seized by agents of Robert Fulton and Robert Livingston. Fulton and Livingston had sponsored Roosevelt's trip. The Louisiana Legislature had granted Fulton and Livingston a monopoly to steam navigation on Louisiana streams. Shreve challenged this grant. He believed that the river was free for everyone's use. Shreve took his case to the United States Supreme Court and won.

This decision greatly affected the future of steamboating. If only one firm had been allowed to operate steamboats, the progress of Louisiana would have been delayed unduly. Steamboats had changed travel time from St. Louis to New Orleans from many months to eleven days. Steamboating was as important to navigation in Louisiana as cotton and sugarcane production was to agriculture.

Steamboating reached its peak about 1850. By 1860 steamboat travel could be had on all rivers in the state on regular lines, except when bad conditions temporarily stopped it. By 1870 steamboating was competing with the newly laid railroad lines which gradually replaced them.

Cattle boats were common sights on the rivers of the state. Texas longhorns were driven to Shreveport and held in stock pens on Cross Bayou until shipped down the Red River on cattle boats.

Refinements came in the steamboat as man depended on it regularly for transportation. Each year steamboats were built larger, faster, and more luxurious. However, some problems remained the same. Passengers had to contend with the heat, mosquitoes, sandbars, and ever-present dangers of fire and explosions. A steamboat blew up almost every week on some river. On occasion these steamboats were also the instruments for the spread of the dreaded yellow fever. Even with all the problems, though, steamboat travel was much better than the other methods available.

Steamboating gradually disappeared as the chief means of transportation. **Railroad** transportation took over by 1900.

The railroad boom came when the **canal-building** era in Louisiana had just started. There was a constant demand for clearing waterways and cutting canals to connect them with each other. Louisiana had only thirty-six miles of canals by 1860.

Railroad development in Louisiana began in the early 1830s. The early lines were short. They were not united in a great system as today. The first railroads in the state were built at New Orleans. They linked different waterways. The Pontchartrain Railroad connected New Orleans to Lake Pontchartrain. Other short lines linked inland towns with rivers. The Panic of 1837 put an end to the first railroad-building boom in the state. The panic caused many of the railroad companies to go into bankruptcy. The federal government finally made land grants to several railroads in the 1850s. After 1850 the second era of railroad-building got underway. Railroads gradually became the chief type of land transportation.

En Partie 2 (Studying a Part). 1. How did the people communicate? 2. Trace the history of transportation during this period. 3. What gave a great boost to transportation in 1812?

Different Facets of Life

Private Education. Children of planters, merchants, and professional people became more acquainted with books. The governing planter class felt that it was the responsibility of every man to take care of the education of his own children. Many of these children were taught in their homes by **private tutors** during their early years. For girls, this was often considered enough schooling. Parents able to afford it were apt to send their boys

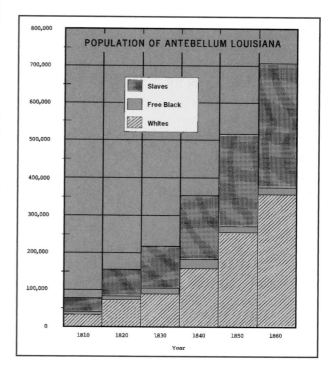

POPULATION OF ANTEBELLUM LOUISIANA

Slaves
Free Black
Whites

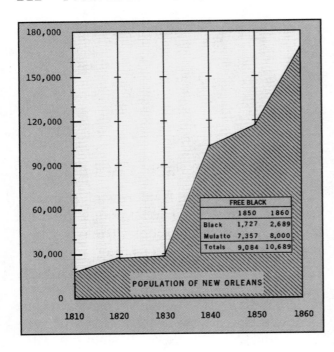

FREE BLACK		
	1850	1860
Black	1,727	2,689
Mulatto	7,357	8,000
Totals	9,084	10,689

POPULATION OF NEW ORLEANS

In the **Constitution of 1845** there was a **plan** for a public school system. It remained on paper. The Constitution of 1852 also affirmed the interest in public education. Little or nothing was done to convert the interest into schools. One historian wrote that Louisiana had the best public school system in the South, but it was only on paper. Little progress was made in the development of free public schools before 1860.

Higher Education. During the antebellum period higher education was almost entirely for men. Some of the French who were able to afford it sent their sons to France. Some were sent to northern and eastern colleges for advanced work. As hostilities increased between the two sections, this pattern stopped. There were very few doing work of today's college level in antebellum Louisiana colleges. Much of the higher education was vocational. The colleges in Louisiana compared favorably with those in other states, however.

Church Schools. There were schools of the **Roman Catholic Church,** mostly designed for children preparing for their first communion. A few colleges were maintained by the church. Schools like **Grand Coteau** (kə TŌ), established in 1838, and some New Orleans schools provided more advanced education.

Two **schools** for **free people of color** existed in New Orleans. Funds for them were provided by the great philanthropist John McDonogh.

off to boarding school, or occasionally, even abroad to study. **Private academies** were also established by the elite.

In short, only those who had the money to afford private schools or tutors received a formal education before the Civil War. Some private schools had high standards for their studies. Many did not.

Public Education. The **reputation of public schools** caused proud people in Louisiana and the rest of the South to reject them. Early public schools were called **paupers' schools.** In the society of that day to be a pauper, or a poor person, was a disgrace. It was considered the fault of the individual that he was poor. The poor were considered **lower class.** The people outside the planter class refused to send their children to public schools for that reason. The idea of paupers' schools came to Louisiana with those migrating here to make new homes.

Lagniappe—*McDonogh's Schools.* John McDonogh claimed 610,000 acres of land and amassed a vast fortune in the Louisiana of the early 1800s. This enabled him to establish two schools in New Orleans for **free people of**

color and at his death to leave millions to New Orleans and Baltimore. Thus thirty-five schools bearing his name were funded. McDonogh was a major contributor to the public school system for Louisiana. The inclusion of free people of color in schooling added to the class distinction in New Orleans. John McDonogh had a unique policy in dealing with his slaves. He freed all three hundred after fourteen years of service and equipped them with tools, clothes, and money for free lives. Setting them up as free men also set a precedent for others to follow in granting manumission and freeing slaves to establish lives of independence.

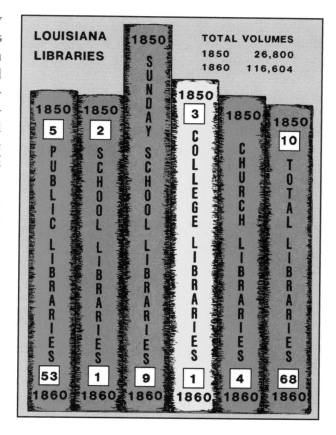

Slave Education. The education of slaves depended upon the attitude of the master. After 1830 teaching blacks to read and write was generally prohibited under severe penalties. It was feared that they might read abolition literature and cause trouble. There were always some slaves who could read and write in spite of the laws.

Libraries. The state library was founded in 1838. By the end of the antebellum period the larger towns had some sort of library facility. In 1842 in New Orleans B. F. French opened his extensive private library to public use. In 1846 it contained 7,500 volumes. Many private citizens had large collections.

Recreation and Amusement. The variety and character of recreational activities depended upon the population and the locality. New Orleans had theatrical performances, opera, and musical concerts. Only when the rural population could get to town did they enjoy these offerings. That was, unless the town were situated on a river where boats visited.

The **rural** population usually depended upon **homemade** amusements. Since people in Louisiana lived mostly on farms, the amusements fitted in with their way of living. Fishing, hunting, and swimming were important forms of recreation. Fish fries and gatherings after a hunt were joyous occasions.

Having sugarcane "chews," popping corn, and pulling taffy at syrup mills were things boys and girls enjoyed. Some men and boys liked to carve wood. Some types of work were social occasions. Neighbors got together for a house or barn raising or a quilting bee. Telling tales was a big part of the fun. Weddings, christenings, rail splittings, wood choppings, and election days were festive occasions.

The people enjoyed other activities. Billiards was a favorite indoor sport for both men and women. This pastime was usually confined to the upper classes. Card playing was a popular pastime for both sexes. Cockfights and boxing were popular, too.

While the affluent hosted balls, the less well-to-do danced to the music of a fiddler. Musical instruments were made by skilled whittlers. The Virginia reel was danced by old and young. Minstrel shows and plays by amateur theater groups added some variety to the entertainment.

Slave Recreation. Owners usually looked after the recreation of their slaves. Most slaves enjoyed regular rest days and vacations. Some were given extra vacation time as reward for faithful work. These vacations came after the crop was harvested. Some plantations even provided places for holiday dancing.

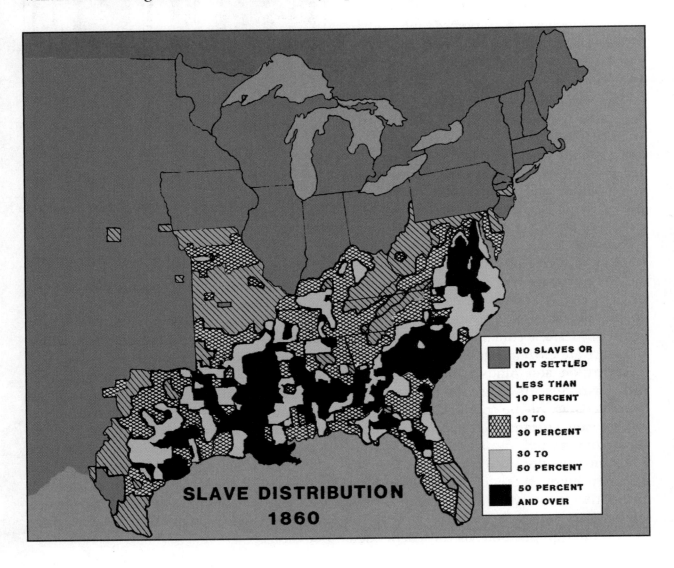

SLAVE DISTRIBUTION 1860

NO SLAVES OR NOT SETTLED

LESS THAN 10 PERCENT

10 TO 30 PERCENT

30 TO 50 PERCENT

50 PERCENT AND OVER

Rural Mardi Gras in Louisiana dates from the 1830s.

Slaves usually enjoyed their own type of **amusements.** Boys and girls played in the open areas of the quarters. There were many children to join the singing and dancing games. The black children enjoyed the same types of homemade games as the white children. However, as soon as black children were old enough, they worked in the fields with their parents.

Mardi Gras. Another widespread activity was Mardi Gras. This was a celebration among the South Louisiana French left over from the days when Louisiana belonged to France. New Orleans had been celebrating Mardi Gras in various ways for many years. In 1838 the first formal parade was held. Maskings and balls were a big part of the Mardi Gras season.

Rural Mardi Gras was not celebrated the way it was in New Orleans. The men of rural communities gathered the night before Shrove Tuesday, a day of celebration before the forty days of Lent in which Roman Catholics fasted. The men made plans that night to "run the Mardi Gras." They decided which roads the group would follow the next day.

By daylight the next day, the men met again. This time they were all on horseback. They wore colorful costumes and homemade masks made by their wives or sweethearts. They wore tall, pointed hats. Their plan was to ride through the countryside and collect materials to make gumbo, a heavy soup.

The night's entertainment began with eating gumbo and drinking and ended with a *fais-do-do* (fā dō DŌ), a dance for everybody.

Music. North Louisiana residents were much more strict than people of South Louisiana in their attitude toward amusements. For many Protestants, drinking, dancing, and other amusements were forbidden. Therefore, other sports and festivities entertained many North Louisianians. Community sings were organized for groups to sing gospel songs. Ability to sing or play the piano or organ was much prized. Quartets, duets, and soloists performed for the songfests, also. Camp meetings, as well as religious events, were social.

Music was used by the slaves to express their sorrow at being slaves. Nobody could reprimand them for music, which was a way of saying what they really felt about the loss of their freedom. There was a distinctive "moanin'" that told, without a word, the slave's feelings. There were happy songs and dances also that told of the joys they still found in living. Our American heritage of the great black spirituals came out of the black slave experience.

War and Courage

Men, especially in the planter class, felt that one proved his courage in war. A boy's training prepared him for war. A boy was expected to become an excellent horseman. In those days, when wars were fought by men on horseback in face-to-face combat, this skill was important. The use of guns was an important part of a boy's training. To become a fine marksman was the goal of every man. Guns were hung in places of honor over the mantle and over the front door. No household was without them for protection and hunting.

Lagniappe—*A Louisiana President*. General Zachary Taylor, who served as president of the United States in 1848, is the only president Louisiana can claim. He was first stationed at Fort Jessup and recruited troops for the Mexican War. Then he commanded the United States troops of the Southwest, headquartered in Baton Rouge in 1827 and 1828. In 1840, he lived in a house that had been built by the Spanish on the banks of the Mississippi and commanded the army post at Baton Rouge. He owned a Louisiana plantation and held 300 slaves. Louisiana was his home from the 1820s until he went to the White House so Louisiana proudly claims him as a son.

Religion

Catholicism was the only religion legally present in Louisiana at the time of the Louisiana Purchase. The church grew steadily during the antebellum period. Many **non-Catholic** churches became a part of Louisiana as Americans moved in. Baptists and Methodists gained a strong position by 1830 and continued their development. They became particularly strong in North Louisiana. The Episcopal, Presbyterian, Lutheran, and Disciples of Christ churches were fewer in number. There were **Jewish** synagogues as well. Before 1850 there was one in New Orleans. By 1860 there were five Jewish synagogues in the state.

Protestant churches were built wherever enough people settled to support them. Louisiana was considered a missionary field throughout the antebellum period. Camp

Mt. Olive Episcopal Church, Pineville, built in 1857.

meetings held in the open air were common as the hill country became settled by small farmers from the seaboard states. Churches played social, religious, and even political roles.

Slaves usually attended the churches of their owners. Some of these churches were built with special balconies for the slaves, or else segregated space was set aside on the same floor. Planters sometimes engaged ministers to preach in the slave quarters.

Slaves were usually given religious instruction. After 1830 this was mostly done by white preachers. Some slaves began to preach and formed "invisible" churches on the plantations. They were called invisible because they were often secret.

It was considered sinful not to belong to a church, but this did not mean that all people attended church regularly. In New Orleans the priests complained that the people did not attend church regularly. The priests said that the women usually went to mass every day, but the men did not attend. The same situation prevailed in Protestant churches.

Attending church was apt to require slow travel by horse-drawn carriage or wagon for rural families. Five miles was a long distance. Roads were mostly muddy trails, and church members often lived far apart on

Typical plantation cabin, now restored, at the LSU Rural Life Museum.

farms. The circuit-rider preachers served many communities. The children and young people got much of their religious training at home. Matters relating to the Bible were debated frequently. The family Bible was the one book that almost every family owned.

En Partie 3 (Studying a Part). 1. Why did education make so little progress? 2. Describe education in antebellum Louisiana. 3. How did recreation vary for the different groups? 4. What part did music play in their lives? 5. What skills were important to boys? 6. Explain the role of religion. 7. How did religion for slaves differ?

Health Care

Sickness. Illnesses were frequent during the antebellum period. There were many fearsome **epidemics**. The death rate in New Orleans was twice that of most large urban areas. The rate for Americans was higher than for blacks and Creoles.

New Orleans suffered from epidemics of **yellow fever, malaria,** and **typhoid fever** from time to time. During these epidemics boats were prohibited from going to and from New Orleans to keep the fever from spreading into other parts of the state. Despite this precaution, the fevers seemed to spread. Bedding and clothes were burned. Sulphuric acid was used to try to keep the disease from spreading. New

Orleanians refused to drink river water. They drank their cistern water instead. They did not know that cistern water was a good breeding ground for the *Aedes aegypti* mosquito, the unknown carrier of yellow fever.

Yellow fever was the unsolved mystery of the nineteenth century. From 1817 to 1860, there were twenty-three yellow fever epidemics in Louisiana. During these forty-three years there were 28,292 deaths. After the 1822 epidemic an ordinance forbade the tolling of church bells and chanting of priests during funerals. The ringing of bells was very depressing. In 1853 one of the worst, if not the worst, epidemics struck. It had been six years since New Orleans had had an epidemic. That year about half of the population was stricken. More than forty thousand cases were recorded. At least fifty thousand people left the city that summer. About ten thousand of those who remained died. From twelve to fifteen died every hour.

Other epidemics plagued the Louisiana population. In 1832 there was a **cholera** epidemic. Malaria was prevalent among Louisiana residents. It was at its worst every summer. Unidentified deadly fevers spread through communities killing many people. **Typhus** and typhoid fever took their toll. Yellow fever and cholera remained the diseases that people dreaded most. People died by the dozen in a day's time when these epidemics came. Infantile paralysis (poliomyelitis)—which was not yet identified—was common. *Polio*

There were few **doctors**. Trained doctors could be found in New Orleans and some of the other towns. Some of them were educated in the best medical schools in the United States and abroad. Most rural doctors were simply men who felt that they had the knack of healing. A few obtained some training in northern medical schools. Would-be doctors served as apprentices to doctors until the twentieth century. A doctor's education up to that point was often no more than grade school. It was said that doctors who had been to college charged more. All doctors did a large amount of charity work. **Charity Hospital** rendered a great service to the poor of New Orleans. Charity services also took care of people who became ill while traveling in the state. The parish police juries took care of the poor who could not afford to pay.

The **life expectancy** in antebellum Louisiana was short in comparison to that of modern times. People died at an early age. Many did not live to be thirty or forty years old. The infant mortality rate was unbelievably high. Many things contributed to this short life expectancy. Superstitions, poor sanitation, polluted water, and lack of trained doctors all had an effect.

Doctor's office, located at the Pioneer Heritage Center, LSU-Shreveport.

Most sick people were treated with **home remedies**. Laxatives, like castor oil; quinine; other medicines that caused vomiting; and medicinal tea, such as sassafras, were favorite treatments. Hot cane juice, tar, honey, egg whites, spices, mineral oils, and alcohol were used by housewives as medicines. Herbs were often used for medicine. These were recommended by Indians. Cobwebs to stop bleeding and prickly-ash bark for toothaches were remedies. Occasionally, an individual might have to set a broken bone or perform simple surgery.

The health of the labor force was very important to the planter. The planter was responsible for the health of his **slaves**. The larger plantations provided hospitals and regular medical attention for the slaves. Most slaves probably remained in their own cabins, and medicine was taken to them there. Slaves in the swampy regions were somewhat more sickly than those in the upland regions. Working in sugarcane was particularly hard on slaves. Sugarcane was harvested during cold, and often wet, weather. The cold, sticky cane juice and the sharp flags of the cane added to the discomfort of the workers.

Burials. Women made shrouds while men made coffins of wood to bury the dead. The services were conducted at home. In the rural areas burial was in a family graveyard near the house or cabin.

In New Orleans people were buried above the ground. The ground was soggy. Water was about eighteen inches below the surface. Graves filled with water shortly after they were dug. New Orleanians therefore adopted the Spanish custom of above-ground burials. These "cities of the dead" soon became filled with magnificent granite and marble structures designed by funerary architects.

Care of Criminals

Louisiana had a penitentiary system that was above average for all the states. The state jail was located in New Orleans until 1832. Then it was moved to Baton Rouge. Each parish maintained a jail for prisoners who were awaiting trial for serious offenses.

In the early years in New Orleans, convicts were employed on the streets. In Baton Rouge convicts worked in industries located in the prison. After 1842 black convicts were assigned to the state board of public works. They built levees, cleared bayous, and built highways. After 1844 the state penitentiary was leased to private individuals. The convicts then worked in industries within the prison walls for these individuals. The practice was criticized throughout the state. It was felt that the use of the penitentiary was unfair competition since the convict labor was free.

Voodoo

Voodoo had been a part of life in the West Indies since the 1500s. The original name of the Afro-Caribbean rite, religion, or cult was *vodu*. Later it was called other names, including *hoodoo*. The people were also called voodoos.

The first slaves who came to the Louisiana colony brought their voodoo with them. During the time Spain owned Louisiana, Governor Gálvez prohibited the importation of slaves from Martinique. The white settlers were scared of voodoo. They felt that more voodoo worshipers would make the colony unsafe. In 1788 slaves from Santo Domingo were banned for the same reason.

Refugees fleeing the revolution in Haiti brought their voodoo to New Orleans with them in 1791. It had existed in Louisiana from the time the slaves came to the state, but it was not organized. Between 1790 and 1840, the black magic was organized for the first time in New Orleans. For a century it was a powerful force in the lives of many blacks and whites.

Voodoo was first mentioned in legal records in the **gris-gris** (grē grē) case of 1773. A *gris-gris,* or a voodoo powder, was made of alligator innards and herbs. It was supposed to have been used by three blacks to poison their overseer. The leader of the group was never released from prison. The other two were freed.

Marie Laveau, the Voodoo Queen, was a free woman of color. In 1809 at age fifteen she moved to New Orleans from Santo Domingo. She married Jacques Paris, a freeman. They had fifteen children. One was a daughter, Marie, who looked like her mother. Her mother used her to pretend to be two places at one time.

Marie's voodoo ceremonials included Zombi snake worship, black cats, and blood drinking. She was supposed to have had a twenty-foot snake. Later she borrowed incense, statues, and holy water from the Catholic religion and added them to her ceremonies. Marie invited the press, the police, and others to special functions. She conducted the annual rites of St. John's Eve on Bayou St. John.

The Voodoo Queen placed curses, removed them, told fortunes, and distributed gris-gris. For a price she could get someone a lover, hold the lover, or get rid of the lover. While common people paid ten dollars for a visit, the rich were charged much more for her advice.

Marie became so powerful that she gained the title "the Boss Woman of New Orleans." She was described as an angel of mercy and a she-witch.

Marie gave up voodoo in her last years. She was supposed to have practiced Catholicism after that. She died in 1881.

Louisiana voodoo is usually associated with New Orleans. Associations of magic and casting spells came naturally in the big port city. Yet, voodoo has been just as much a part of the lifestyle of rural Louisiana people as it has been with the people of New

Voodoo practitioner prepares for ceremony in New Orleans, about 1930.

Orleans. In fact, voodoo existed all over the state.

Drugstores throughout rural areas sold love potions, good luck powders, and the like. Special candles were thought to give luck at cards.

En Partie 4 (Studying a Part). 1. Relate diseases and health care of the period with that of today. 2. Describe a yellow fever epidemic. 3. What was the life expectancy then? 4. How did burials differ from today? 5. Summarize the treatment of prisoners during this time. 6. Compare the privatization of prisons then and now. 7. Trace the history of voodoo. 8. Describe voodoo.

Coup de Main
(Completing the Story)

Jambalaya (Putting It All Together)

1. Explain Louisiana's plantation economy system.

2. Relate the role of slaves to the state's economic development.

3. Cite differences in groups of people during this period.

4. Describe the role of (a) women and (b) children in antebellum times.

5. Explain the reason for the steady and rapid growth of the state in antebellum times.

6. What type of immigrants came to the state?

7. Trace the population growth of whites and blacks.

8. (a) Give characteristics of life in antebellum Louisiana. (b) Cite problems.

9. Why did the plantation system in some way affect everyone in the state?

10. Describe the government at this time.

11. Describe the position of planters in antebellum society.

12. Note the role of New Orleans.

Potpourri (Getting Involved)

1. Role-play the escape of a slave. Show the reaction of the slave, owner, sympathizers, and law-enforcement officers.

2. Research one of the following topics and present the results in a mural, diorama, chart, or other visual form: mail service, clothing, housing, food, transportation, recreation, social life, health care, farm tools and implements, country stores, the Bank of Louisiana, westward migration, voodoo, a steamboat trip from New Orleans to some other Louisiana location, or the settlement of a town.

3. Draw a cartoon to depict the movement of Louisiana's capitals up until 1850.

4. Compare (a) life on the farm with life in the city, (b) life on a small farm with life on a plantation, (c) the life of a Louisiana boy or girl with that of a cousin from the North, (d) the life of a slave with that of a free person of color, or (e) education of blacks with that of children of small farmers or planters.

5. Dramatize (a) a cotton farmer who has just seen the new cotton gin at work, (b) a slave auction, (c) a private tutor conducting a class, or (d) a yellow fever epidemic.

6. Make a model of (a) a plantation, (b) the first cotton gin, (c) a steamboat, or (d) pioneer tools, utensils, or furnishings.

7. Make a chart showing how everyone was affected by and depended on agriculture.

8. Compare the romantic view of plantation life with the real view.

Gumbo (Bringing It Up-to-Date)

1. Give an account of an imaginary trip from St. Louis to New Orleans in 1810. Then take the same trip in 1840, 1850, and 1990.

2. Compare Louisiana's position in the nation in the antebellum period to its position today.

3. Compare (a) the number, size, and appearances of Louisiana cities today with cities of 1850 and 1860, (b) life for blacks during the antebellum period with life today, or (c) antebellum agricultural practices with modern agricultural practices.

4. Show how Louisiana's social class system of today compares with the social class system of the antebellum period. Include status symbols of each period.

5. Relate the bilingual conditions of that day with present bilingual Louisiana.

6. Compare and contrast the social and cultural life in antebellum Louisiana with that in the French colonial period, the Spanish period, and today.

Overleaf: *Admiral David Porter's gunboats passing the dam on the Red River.*

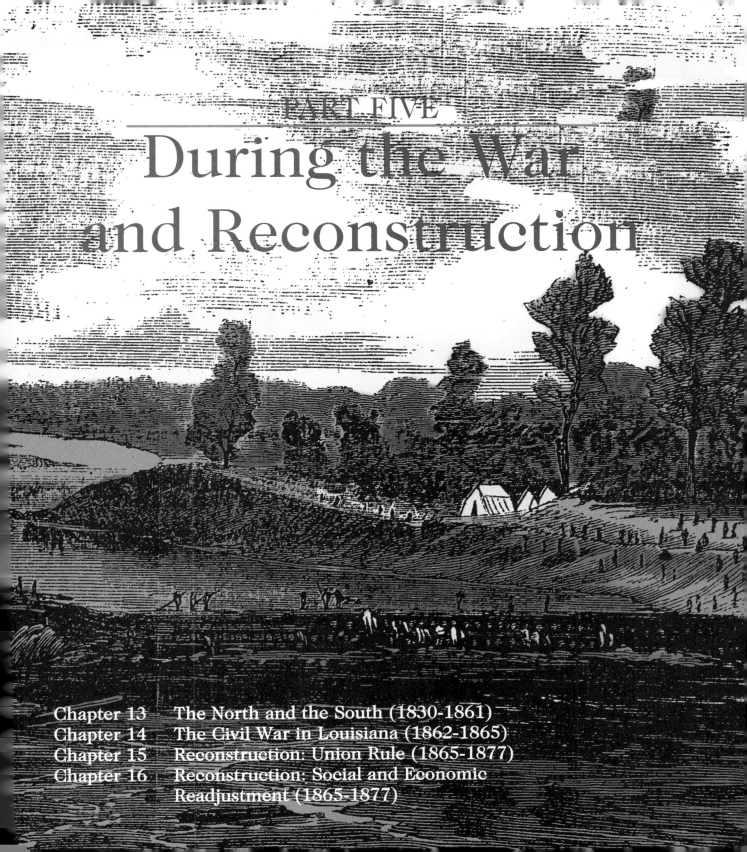

PART FIVE
During the War and Reconstruction

THE NORTH AND THE SOUTH
(1830-1861)

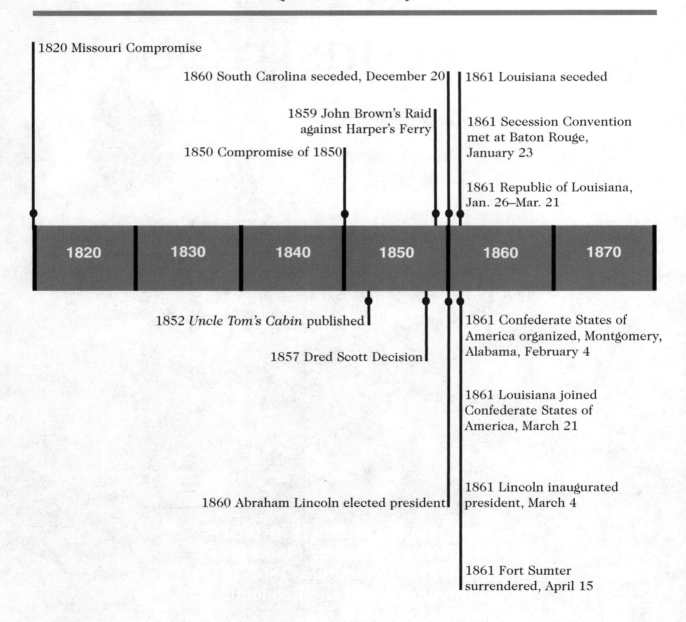

1820 Missouri Compromise

1860 South Carolina seceded, December 20

1861 Louisiana seceded

1859 John Brown's Raid against Harper's Ferry

1861 Secession Convention met at Baton Rouge, January 23

1850 Compromise of 1850

1861 Republic of Louisiana, Jan. 26–Mar. 21

| 1820 | 1830 | 1840 | 1850 | 1860 | 1870 |

1852 *Uncle Tom's Cabin* published

1861 Confederate States of America organized, Montgomery, Alabama, February 4

1857 Dred Scott Decision

1861 Louisiana joined Confederate States of America, March 21

1860 Abraham Lincoln elected president

1861 Lincoln inaugurated president, March 4

1861 Fort Sumter surrendered, April 15

THE NORTH AND THE SOUTH

Different Cultures

Differences. People in the **agricultural South** and the **industrial North** had many differences. From the beginning of the English settlement of this nation there were two different lifestyles among the settlers. The South developed plantations so that they could produce staple crops that provided a livelihood. The North developed shipbuilding and commerce, including the selling of slaves, mills, and factories. New England developed textile mills. The North developed mining and industries. Louisiana, like most of the South, did not have the necessary metals beneath the earth to trigger an industrial economy. It had little industry beyond that needed on the plantations. Plantations, then, shaped the outlook of Southerners the way that the factory shaped the outlook of Northerners. The North was involved in the South's plantations through the building of ships to transport slaves, slave trading, and finance.

Plantations were self sufficient, and towns did not develop in the South. In the North there were many towns. As factories increased, people from Europe were attracted to the North. Cities developed.

New York and Boston, as well as other cities, became financial centers. Many Southerners borrowed money from the Northern financial centers at high interest rates to finance cotton production. A row of factors in New Orleans were middlemen lending money to planters to make their crops. Most of the money came from Northern financiers.

Louisiana, like the rest of the South, bought most of its manufactured goods from the North. The Northern commercial interests pressed the government to pass **protective tariffs** to keep cheaper European goods from the United States. That way Southerners had to pay whatever price the North demanded for its goods. Southerners resented this.

With the coming of **railroads** more problems developed between North and South. From the beginning of the 1850s railroads were becoming a vital part of the nation's economy. Railroads further stimulated the building of factories in the North. Surplus products were being shipped rapidly from one part of the country to another. Railroad rates eventually favored large shippers with cheaper rates. The North benefitted from this. The North prospered with new factories and the growing demand for manufactured products.

Like other cotton-growing states, Louisiana felt its economy based on cotton plantations was secure. New England textile mills needed the cotton.

The South gambled everything on the growing of cotton. **Cotton was "king."** The South prospered as the price of cotton rose, and the annual production more than doubled. With the profits, goods were imported from elsewhere. The entire state of Louisiana was tied to the arrangement.

New States. As the West was being settled, the South felt its power in the government dramatically decreasing. They felt that they were strictly in the minority in the national government. Other areas did not

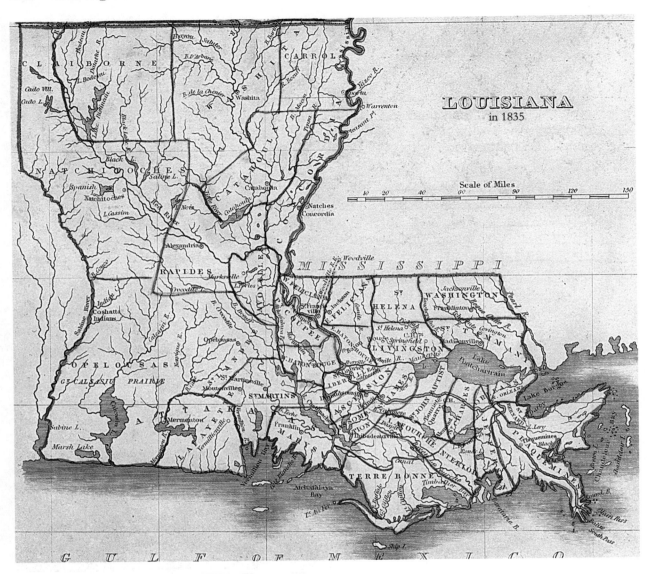

have plantations. They did not need slaves. As new territories applied for statehood, a sharp division arose between the sections as to **slave or free states**.

In 1820 the conflict flared out into the open. New states were being formed to the west. Those protesting slavery did not want slavery allowed in new states. In 1820, when Maine and Missouri applied for statehood,

the fight began in earnest. The famous **Missouri Compromise** was made. Missouri would have slavery. Maine would not. This satisfied both North and South. Each time the question arose about whether a state should be slave or free, the tension mounted. When California applied for statehood, the conflict reached another crisis. There was a dispute over slavery in Kansas that became

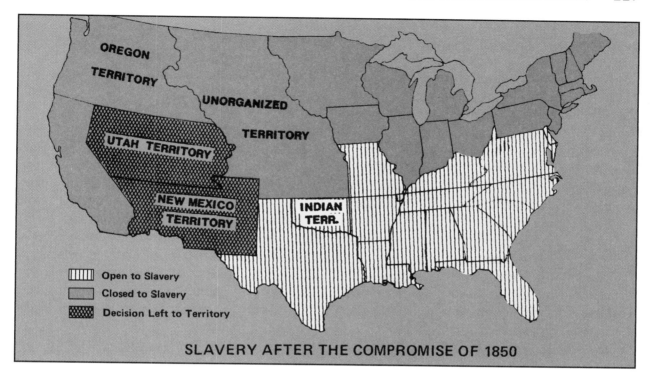

OREGON TERRITORY

UNORGANIZED TERRITORY

UTAH TERRITORY

NEW MEXICO TERRITORY

INDIAN TERR.

|||| Open to Slavery

Closed to Slavery

Decision Left to Territory

SLAVERY AFTER THE COMPROMISE OF 1850

increasingly bitter. It affected every action of the United States Congress.

In the 1850s the number of free states in the Union was becoming larger than the number of slave states. The worst fears of the South were being realized. Representatives of free states in Congress would work to abolish slavery. That would be an end to plantations. Plantation production supported all of the Southern people.

States' Rights. There was a lot of talk about states' rights in Washington and in Louisiana. This was the right of states to control their own society, including slavery. The Southerner's way of life included a strong belief in states' rights.

Abolitionists. When Northern abolitionists began to demand an end to slavery, a Northern press often painted the South as evil. The protests against slavery from the North angered Louisiana's planter-leaders. Any criticism of slavery came to be regarded by planters as an attack on their right to grow cotton and earn a living. The planters argued that slaves lived more healthfully and happily than Irish workingmen and others in the Northern factories. They argued that those who wanted to do away with slavery were troublemakers. The South reminded the North about its part in the slave trade that brought slaves to America. The North had not found slavery practical on their farms and in their factories.

Abolitionists urged blacks to revolt or escape from the plantations. They made speeches. They wrote books and pamphlets. They also published newspapers. The abolitionists urged that slavery be abolished. A series of escape routes, called the **Underground Railroad,** was devised to help slaves escape. By 1850 the antislavery movement had become a strong force.

Uncle Tom's Cabin. A book published in the North in 1852 added to the sectional differences. *Uncle Tom's Cabin* was written by Harriet Beecher Stowe. Stowe wrote her book from collections of stories she had heard from her own servants and those of others. She made the Red River Valley in Louisiana the setting for her fiction. Her emotionally-charged fantasy set an image of the South and Louisiana that has never been overcome. Louisianians felt that the book was unfair to planters.

Other Contributing Factors. There came word that the Republicans had nominated **Abraham Lincoln** for president. In Louisiana there was quick reaction. If Lincoln were elected, there would be war. That seemed clear. Louisianians strongly disliked the **Republican Party,** which nominated him. It had been organized in 1854 to prevent slavery from becoming legal in the territories.

Added to the other problems was a **power struggle** going on in Washington, D.C., between North and South. Four of the first five presidents of the United States were from Virginia. All were planters. Northern political leaders wanted to direct the course of the nation, also. The two groups represented two separate lifestyles. Both wanted power. The North wanted to claim as much of the West as possible. Slavery was an issue, but not the only issue.

En Partie 1 (Studying a Part). 1. What were the two different cultures that developed? 2. What were the political issues of the period? 3. Identify reasons for Louisiana's position. 4. Why did the Republican party develop? 5. Describe the abolitionist movement. 6. What were some of the events leading to the war?

Confederate States of America

Time of Decision. Lincoln's election united Southern planters in an almost solid opposition. Lincoln had not received one vote in Louisiana. Nevertheless, public opinion in Louisiana was sharply divided about what the next course of action should be. The planters felt that there had to be a showdown. Most **favored** immediate **secession.** One group of Louisianians wanted to wait until after Lincoln's inauguration to take a stand. Still another proposed a convention of the Southern states.

News came in December 1860 that South Carolina had seceded from the Union. People over the South were divided. Cooperationists believed that Louisiana should cooperate with the other Southern states. This group believed that the Southern states should act together after they decided on a course of action. Those who favored immediate secession opposed the cooperationists. Many of the state's leaders showed support for secession.

With the news of Lincoln's election, Governor Thomas Overton Moore called a **special session** of the **legislature** at Baton Rouge for December 10, 1860. A bill was passed that called for an election of delegates to a state convention on January 7.

An election for convention delegates was held in January 1861. Many qualified voters did not vote. Twenty-nine parishes were for secession. Nineteen were not. The details of the vote were not known until the convention. Only the names of the successful candidates to the convention were announced.

The crisis sent an electric shock through the non-planters. They felt that the state was rushing toward war. The planters were speaking for the state. Most people who did not own slaves felt that the state was going to war to save slavery.

The Secession Convention. The Secession Convention was held at the capitol in Baton Rouge on January 23, 1861. Former Governor Mouton presided over the excited gathering. Judge Taliaferro made an eloquent speech against secession. In a speech Governor Moore reported that after the January 7 elec-

A cotton steamer.

tion he had seized some United States government military property. After much debate, the Ordinance of Secession was adopted by a vote of 113 to 17.

Four days after the convention started, Governor Moore declared that Louisiana was out of the Union. A delegation was elected to attend the convention of Southern states called to assemble at Montgomery, Alabama, on February 4. The purpose of the convention was to form a Southern confederacy.

The Republic of Louisiana. The Louisiana republic existed for fifty-four days. Louisiana was an independent nation from January 26 until March 21, 1861. Governor Moore served as president. The state legislature and the Secession Convention, meeting in New Orleans, continued to function. These bodies handled most of the republic's business. Louisiana's senators and representatives in Congress withdrew in February 1861.

In January and February 1861, Governor Moore took over all the remaining property of the United States in Louisiana. This included over six hundred thousand dollars in the United States Mint in New Orleans.

The Confederacy. Louisiana was not independent long. The Southern states voted to bind themselves into the **Confederate States of America.** On March 21, 1861, the Secession Convention ratified the state constitution.

The Southern states wanted to form a new nation that would allow them to live as they wished. They would be bound to each other very loosely.

In the North Louisiana hill country there was often anger at the move. Many residents were determined not to take part in a war to oppose the abolition of slavery. They pointed

North and South - 1861

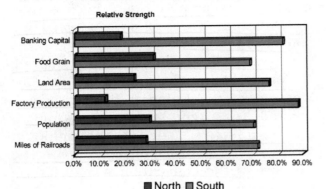

Relative Strength

out that they had no slaves. In other parts of the state there were joyous celebrations. Many felt that a war was justified to defend states' rights.

> **En Partie 2 (Studying a Part)**. 1. What were the two opposing views about the action the state should take? 2. (a) Which view did the planters take? (b) non-planters? 3. Give the details of the Secession Convention. 4. Describe the Republic of Louisiana. 5. When did Louisiana join the Confederacy?

The Beginning of the Civil War

Gen. Pierre Gustave Toutant **Beauregard** (BŌ rē gärd), was in charge of troops at Charleston, South Carolina, in April 1861. It was General Beauregard who demanded the surrender of Fort Sumter on April 12, 1861. The seizure of the fort began four years of war between North and South.

"In Defense of My Country." Louisiana contributed more than its share of **fighting men**. Within three months, by June 1861, sixteen thousand Louisianians volunteered for military service in a great burst of enthusiasm. In the first six months of the war, twenty-four thousand troops left Louisiana for Virginia. The Louisiana Tigers made themselves famous at the first battle, Manassas, or Bull Run. Altogether about sixty thousand men joined the military service. So many able-bodied men of the state were sent elsewhere to fight that Louisiana suffered serious defense problems.

Planter Participation. Planters quickly showed their power during the war. The Confederacy instituted a **military draft** in 1862. This was the first in the nation's history. A despised law of the Confederate government provided exemption from military service for owners of twenty or more slaves. Planters often entered the war as officers.

Non-planter Participation. As events developed, war between North and South ended the waiting for other Louisiana whites as well. These were the white people outside the planter society. Some men in Winn Parish left to go north and join the Union forces. Others simply vowed that they would never fight for the slave owners.

Participation of Blacks. Many free blacks and slaves joined the Union forces. Over four thousand blacks enlisted in the Union army at New Orleans. By the end of the war nearly twenty-one thousand more Louisiana blacks had joined them.

Leaders. During the course of the war, Louisiana supplied the Confederacy with some of its most prominent leaders. Outstanding generals of the state, other than Beauregard, included Braxton Bragg, Leonidas (lē ON ə dəs) Polk, and Richard ("Dick") Taylor, son of Zachary Taylor and

The Arsenal Museum, State Capitol Grounds.

brother-in-law of Jefferson Davis. Taylor distinguished himself at the Battle of Mansfield. Leonidas Polk, although not a native, was closely associated with Louisiana. He was the cousin of a former United States president, James K. Polk. He was killed in battle in 1864.

Other Confederate leaders from Louisiana included Judah P. Benjamin, John Slidell, Duncan F. Kenner, Pierce A. Rost, and former governor A. B. Roman. Benjamin served as attorney general, secretary of war, and then as secretary of state in the cabinet of Jefferson Davis.

False Optimism. Outside of New Orleans, Louisiana was primarily a rural society. With the Southern attachment to the idea of a mil-itary life, marksmanship, and the handling of horses, most felt that the North did not have a chance. The general feeling was that the war would be over soon.

Winning the Battle of Bull Run added to the South's overconfidence about winning the war. Except for the Northern drive ending in the defeat of Gettysburg, it was the South that was devastated by the invading enemy troops.

Preparations for War. In Louisiana Gov. Thomas O. Moore **seized** the United States **arsenals** in Baton Rouge, **Forts Jackson** and **St. Philip,** and other federal properties. The Louisiana Legislature **appropriated** approximately **1.5 million dollars** during 1861 for military equipment and supplies. Steamboats were sent into the rivers and bayous of the

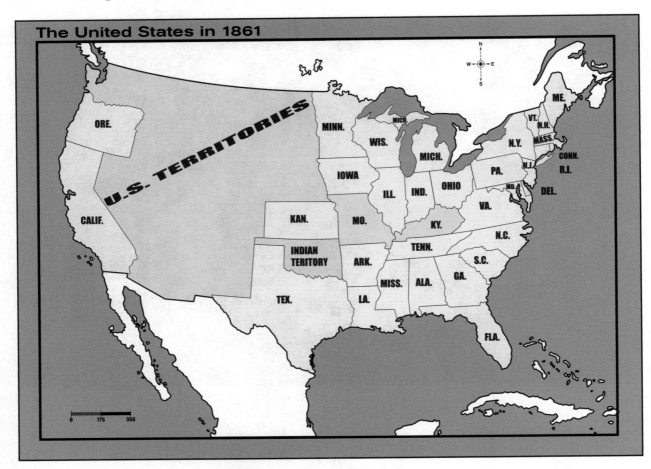

The United States in 1861

state to **collect scrap iron** to be used for making the tools of war.

Below New Orleans men were put to work **building barricades** to keep Union ships out of the mouth of the Mississippi River. The two forts, Fort Jackson on the west side and Fort St. Philip on the east side, were reinforced to prohibit the use of the river by Union forces. Heavy **iron cables with rafts** attached were placed between Fort Jackson and Fort St. Philip. Sharpshooter lookouts guarded the Mississippi River for signs of Union boats. **Gunboats** were fitted out on the Mississippi River to aid in resisting attack.

Concerns about Louisiana's Defense. By the end of 1861 Governor Moore was worried about the defense of Louisiana. Before General Beauregard left for Charleston, he cautioned the military to take care of the defense of New Orleans. He told them to arm Forts Jackson and St. Philip with the heaviest guns possible because he feared an attack on the city. Confederate leaders in Richmond ordered Louisiana to supply more troops and supplies for the Confederate armies to the east. They ordered two ironclads being readied in New Orleans to proceed up the Mississippi. Gen. **Mansfield Lovell** was in charge of Department I of the Confederacy, which was Louisiana. He was convinced that the Federals would attempt to capture New Orleans. Even though he warned the Confederate leaders, plans were not changed. It was unbelievable how casual the Confederacy was about defending its largest city. Lovell and Governor Moore attempted to defend New Orleans as best they could. Lovell had only three thousand troops.

After some months, Louisiana defenders were left with neither guns nor ammunition. Governor Moore wrote repeatedly to President Davis asking for war supplies. Some small factories were built to make war supplies. Supply depots were set up. Most Louisiana soldiers left to guard the state had only wooden sticks with which to drill. Privateers were outfitted at the Algiers shipyard so they could help.

Union Plans. The Union plan to win the war fitted somewhat the idea of one of Lincoln's generals. Like a great snake, the Union forces would wrap themselves around the Confederacy. Yankee troops would capture the Mississippi River and cut the Confederacy in two. Union armies would march south through the border states. The Union would **blockade** the coasts of Southern states and stop commerce. The blockade was ordered one month after the war started. No vessel could enter or leave any harbor in the Confederacy without risk of being captured by a Union vessel. The blockade greatly crippled the Confederacy.

Louisiana was a key target in Union plans. The great port of New Orleans was the largest city in the South, and its commerce was one of the main targets of the blockade. By the summer of 1861 effects of the blockade were being felt. Common commodities became scarce. Prices on ordinary necessities soared. Foreign commerce had been destroyed. This created financial problems in New Orleans.

Blockade Response. "Running the blockade" was the Southern response to the Northern blockade. On dark nights fast-sailing Confederate vessels that could navigate in shallow bays and inlets would slip out. They were loaded with cargoes of cotton for the West Indies. On return trips they brought such things as cannons, rifles, lead, blankets, shoes, coffee, and medicines. Some took their cotton to Mexico and returned with badly needed goods.

War did not come to Louisiana until 1862.

En Partie 3 (Studying a Part). 1. What was this war called? 2. When and where did the war begin? 3.(a) What was the involvement of planters? (b) Non-planters? (c) Blacks? 4. What was done to prepare the state for war? 5. Why was 1862 a fateful year for Louisianians? 6. What was the Union plan? 7. How did the blockade affect Louisiana? 8. How did Louisianians respond?

THE CIVIL WAR IN LOUISIANA
(1862-1865)

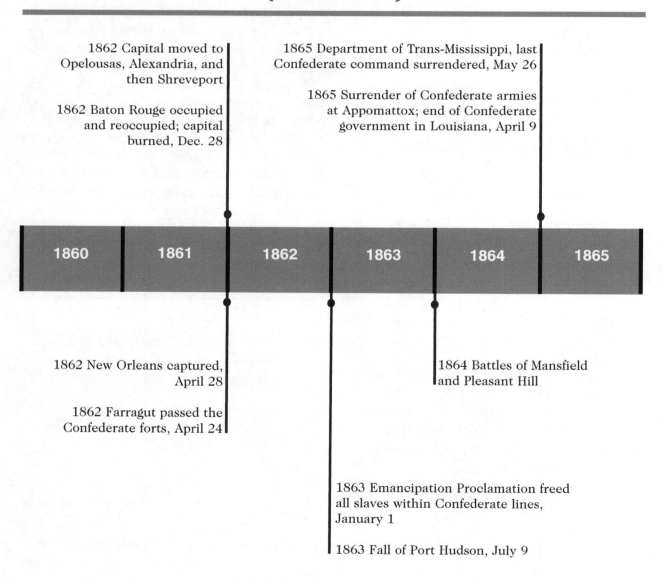

1862 Capital moved to
Opelousas, Alexandria, and
then Shreveport

1862 Baton Rouge occupied
and reoccupied; capital
burned, Dec. 28

1865 Department of Trans-Mississippi, last
Confederate command surrendered, May 26

1865 Surrender of Confederate armies
at Appomattox; end of Confederate
government in Louisiana, April 9

| 1860 | 1861 | 1862 | 1863 | 1864 | 1865 |

1862 New Orleans captured,
April 28

1862 Farragut passed the
Confederate forts, April 24

1864 Battles of Mansfield
and Pleasant Hill

1863 Emancipation Proclamation freed
all slaves within Confederate lines,
January 1

1863 Fall of Port Hudson, July 9

THE CIVIL WAR IN LOUISIANA

1862-1863

1862: Capture of New Orleans. On April 7, 1862, frightening reports reached the city of a Union invasion. A federal expedition of fifteen thousand troops under **Gen. Benjamin F. Butler** and forty-seven ships under Flag Officer **David G. Farragut** were headquartered at Ship Island. It took three weeks to get the gunships over the bar at the river's mouth.

A year after the war began, the Union was ready to capture New Orleans. On April 18 Farragut began bombardment of Forts Jackson and St. Philip. The Union had seventeen warships and twenty mortar schooners commanded by Capt. David Dixon Porter. The Confederacy had sixteen gunboats and a large number of fire-rafts of flatboats loaded with pine knots. There was a fierce battle as men on the ships tried to bombard the forts into submission. The Union had twice the firepower of the two forts. Over thirteen thousand shells rained on the Confederate bastions, but there were only four casualties.

After five days Farragut changed his plans. The Confederates were not surrendering as he had thought they would. He camouflaged some of the ships with black paint. Branches and brush tied against the sides disguised them. During the night of April 24 a heavy fog concealed the Union fleet. The ships appeared as "black shapeless masses." In the wee hours of the morning the Union fleet slipped by the forts and was on its way to New Orleans. Farragut encountered only a token Confederate naval force.

The next day Farragut demanded of Mayor John T. Monroe that he surrender New

LOUISIANA GOVERNORS DURING THE WAR	
CONFEDERATE LOUISIANA	**OCCUPIED LOUISIANA**
Thomas Overton Moore (1860-1864)	George F. Shepley (1862-1864)
Henry Watkins Allen (1864-1865)	Michael Hahn (resigned) (1864-1865)
	James Madison Wells (succeeded as lt. governor) (1865-1867)

Orleans. Lovell, with too few men to defend the city, had already taken his troops northward. Before leaving, Lovell had burned immense quantities of timber, cotton, coal, and other provisions. Mayor Monroe spoke for the desperate residents. He could not surrender the city.

On **May 1, 1862,** the army troops brought by Farragut to **occupy New Orleans** did just that. Gen. Benjamin F. Butler was in command. The Confederacy lost its largest city and its much-needed factories.

After the capture of New Orleans, General Shepley occupied strategic points of approach to the city to prevent Confederates from reoccupying it.

Butler in Command. New Orleans began seven months under Butler's rule. He established his headquarters at the St. Charles Hotel. He became bitterly hated by the people of New Orleans. He gained the title "Beast Butler." When he thought the women of New Orleans were not showing proper respect to his soldiers in the street, he issued General Order No. 28. It said that "Hereafter when any female shall, by word, gesture, or movement, insult or show contempt for any officer or soldier of the United States, she shall be regarded and held liable to be treated as a woman of the town plying her avocation." This caused great indignation throughout the civilized world, including the north and the west. When Mayor Monroe protested, he was arrested and confined to Fort Jackson along with his secretary, the city judge, and the chief of police.

New Orleans papers refused to publish Butler's orders. He then seized the office of the *True Delta* and had his orders printed in the May 2 issue. There was no freedom of the press afterward. Butler prohibited the further circulation of Confederate money. He confiscated the property of prominent secessionists. On June 7, 1862, Butler had William B. Mumford hanged for tearing down the American flag from the United States Mint on April 26. All inhabitants were disarmed. On September 24, 1862, Butler ordered all Americans in his department to renew their allegiance to the United States. At the same time he ordered them to register all their real and personal property. Failure to follow these orders resulted in severe penalties. This brought the sobriquet "Spoons Butler" since he stole the silverware once it was located.

Not all of **Butler's** actions were bad. He reopened the port to commerce for all

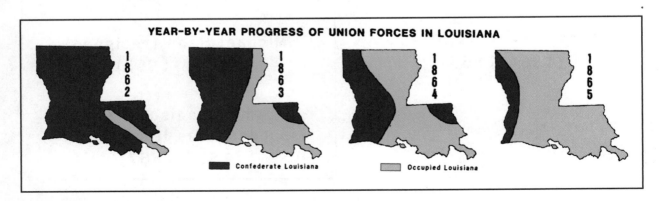

YEAR-BY-YEAR PROGRESS OF UNION FORCES IN LOUISIANA

1862   1863   1864   1865

■ Confederate Louisiana   ▨ Occupied Louisiana

friendly nations. Butler issued very strict quarantine orders to control the yellow fever threat. He did this to protect the Union troops, but it helped clean up the city. Strict orders against drunkenness were issued as well.

Baton Rouge. Farragut sailed on from New Orleans to Baton Rouge and took that city. He left Commander Porter in charge of two ships at Baton Rouge. Guerrillas fired from the riverbanks as his boats proceeded to Vicksburg and Natchez. Commander Porter abandoned the city on August 23, 1862. He went to Port Hudson and Bayou Sara. On August 31, 1862, he shelled and set fire to Bayou Sara, an important port.

Governor Moore had moved the **capital** to **Opelousas** before the Union took control of Baton Rouge on May 7, 1862. Later it was moved to **Alexandria** where it remained for a very short time. From there the capital was moved to **Shreveport.**

On August 5, 1862, Confederate general **John Breckinridge** and about three thousand men were encamped on the Amite River. He planned to recapture Baton Rouge. The ironclad *Arkansas* was to disperse the federal gunboats while Breckinridge took the garrison. Plans were made so that Breckinridge would march on Baton Rouge when he received word that the *Arkansas* had passed Bayou Sara. Breckenridge entered Baton Rouge from the east and drove out the federal troops. Gen. Thomas Williams, who was in command in federally occupied Baton Rouge, was killed. The *Arkansas* did not arrive. Five miles before it reached its destination, its engines failed. To keep it from becoming the property of the Union, the crew destroyed it. Breckinridge was unable

to hold Baton Rouge, so he withdrew about thirty miles north. His new location was Port Hudson. Port Hudson then became the Confederate defense port and the point for receiving supplies.

On December 17, 1862, **Gen. Nathaniel Banks,** commander of the Union army in Louisiana, reoccupied Baton Rouge. Eleven days later Union troops burned the state capitol. The fire destroyed most of the state's official records.

Other Activities. In October 1862 Union general **Godfrey Weitzel** (WĪT səl) led an expedition in the **Bayou Lafourche area.** The federal troops succeeded in capturing Napoleonville, Labadieville (la ba DE vil), and Thibodaux (TIB ə dō). Weitzel continued on to the **Bayou Teche country** to attack troops under **Gen. Alfred Mouton** (mōō TON), son of former Louisiana governor Mouton.

General Butler, on November 9, 1862, declared all **property** of disloyal citizens in Lafourche Parish to be **confiscated** or taken over by the Union. The next month General Butler was replaced by **Gen. Nathaniel Banks** in occupied New Orleans.

1863: Invasion of the Red River Valley. In the spring of 1863, while **Gen. Ulysses Grant** was working on his attack of Vicksburg, Banks led an invasion of the Red River Valley.

Banks took Brashear City (**Morgan City**), Franklin, Patterson, and New Iberia. From there he marched up Bayou Teche. He captured **Opelousas.** Then he marched his troops six miles northwest to the little inland port of **Washington.** From there his soldiers marched along the narrow, winding Bayou Boeuf to **Alexandria.** Alexandria was captured on May 7, 1863.

When Banks wired Washington, D.C.,

about the capture of Alexandria, he received orders to move his men to help Grant take Vicksburg. Orders were given to other soldiers on this first invasion of the Red River Valley to turn around and retrace their steps back to the Gulf of Mexico.

Banks took some of the soldiers through **Simmesport** and **Bayou Sara** to lay siege to **Port Hudson**. Port Hudson was located in rolling hill country between Baton Rouge and St. Francisville on a river bluff. Port Hudson and Vicksburg were the last Confederate strongholds on the Mississippi River. At that time the Union controlled all of the great river north of Vicksburg and all of it south of Port Hudson. Grant laid siege to Vicksburg from May 22 to July 4. Confederates had strongly fortified Port Hudson against attack by river or land. Port Hudson was needed to protect transportation of supplies from the Red River Valley to Confederate forces east of the Mississippi.

Taylor's Activities. In March 1863 the federal forces occupied a large portion of the Florida parishes. **Confederate general Richard Taylor** went to **Berwick Bay**. There he captured seven hundred men, guns, ammunition, medicine, and other supplies. He proceeded to **Donaldsonville**. Taylor prevented federal troops from reaching Banks and Grant to reinforce them. His troops captured **Kenner**.

Invasion of Northeastern Louisiana. A number of men from Union Parish were in the Twelfth Regiment of Louisiana Volunteers. They were among the Confederate soldiers sent to Cairo, Illinois, on the Mississippi River in 1861. Their job was to stop Grant. No matter how hard they fought, Grant captured one important Confederate fortification after another as he marched down the Mississippi.

Grant had not been able to capture Vicksburg in 1862. Union plans called for control of the Mississippi River. By the end of this second year of the war, United States forces controlled the river from occupied Baton Rouge to the Gulf of Mexico. General Grant, who had been in charge of troops coming down the river from the north, reached as far as Vicksburg, Mississippi. He was determined to capture Vicksburg and push on down to Baton Rouge. The fight to close the river by capturing Baton Rouge would take place at Port Hudson thirty miles upstream. This would close the river completely.

During the winter of 1862-1863, Grant and his lieutenant, **William Tecumseh Sherman**, laid the groundwork for the capture of Vicksburg. The determined general decided on a totally different approach for attacking Vicksburg than the one he had used earlier.

He landed his men on the Louisiana side of the river at **Lake Providence** opposite Vicksburg. His ships, traveling from north of Vicksburg to the south, were subjected to the murderous fire from Confederate batteries on the high bluffs rising above the river on the east. To avoid this, Grant planned to dig a canal to run across De Soto Point. He could then safely move his troops to points below Vicksburg. Grant's plan was to make a crescent-shaped waterway on the Louisiana side of the river. The new route would allow the Union troops passage around the city. The canal would connect waters that would lead to the river below Vicksburg. The ships could then approach the Confederate stronghold from the south. Grant had his men begin digging a canal a mile-and-a-half long and sixty feet wide. After months of working on the canal, Grant decided that it was impractical and abandoned the idea.

Grant had allowed the troops to add to their rations by plundering. Much property was destroyed in northeastern Louisiana that winter.

Summer of 1863: The Turning Point. That summer of 1863 was a grim time for the people of Louisiana, as well as the rest of the Confederacy. **Vicksburg,** just across the Mississippi from the state, fell after a month-long siege, on July 4, 1863. As the bad news drifted back to Louisiana, it was known that **Gen. Robert E. Lee,** in his deepest penetration of enemy territory, had also been turned back on that same day at **Gettysburg.**

Capture of Port Hudson: Last Confederate Stronghold on the Mississippi. One of the most dogged battles of the war took place at Port Hudson. About five thousand Confederates under the command of **Gen. Frank Gardner** guarded the fort at Port Hudson. Banks had over twenty-five thousand troops for the attack.

After the 145 days of battle with twenty-one days of hard fighting, the defenders were exhausted. They heard that Vicksburg had surrendered. These Confederates, "digging in" on the bluff above the river, finally had to surrender, too. On July 9, 1863, just five days after the fall of Vicksburg, Port Hudson fell.

With the surrender of Vicksburg and Port Hudson, the very last segment of the Mississippi River remaining in Confederate hands came under the control of Union

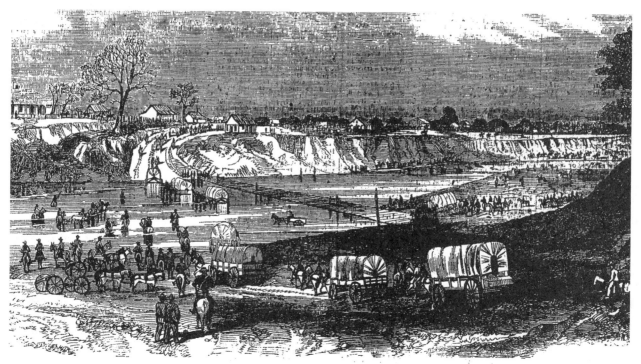

General Albert Lee's Union troops crossing the Cane River in 1863.

forces. After the fall of Port Hudson, Lincoln said, "The Father of Waters goes unvexed to the sea." Much of Louisiana was occupied by the United States soldiers. The Blues held the Mississippi River and a strip of territory from New Orleans westward to Berwick Bay.

Louisiana did not see much activity in the last half of 1863. The reason was that Banks spent the latter part of 1863 on an expedition from New Orleans against Texas by sea. Confederate general Richard Taylor now held all the region of Louisiana west of the Mississippi River. In 1864 the federal troops planned complete occupation of Louisiana.

Government. In January 1863 the capital of Confederate Louisiana was moved to **Shreveport.** In that part of Louisiana that remained under the Confederacy, a new governor was elected in the fall of 1863. He was **Henry Watkins Allen,** a disabled veteran who was on crutches when he took office.

Many sections of Louisiana were occupied off and on. New Orleans was occupied from April 1862 until the end of the war. Two governments existed during the war.

On December 15, 1862, officers for the United States Provisional Court for the state of Louisiana arrived in New Orleans from New York. The court went into operation early in 1863. It lasted throughout the remainder of the war. Under General Banks, a movement started in February 1863 for the reorganization of a loyal government in Louisiana.

Battle of Port Hudson on the Mississippi.

A mural depicting secession and the carnage of war.

Emancipation Proclamation. President Abraham Lincoln issued his Emancipation Proclamation for January 1, 1863. He knew that England and France would like to help the Confederacy but knew that the proclamation could influence them to lean toward the Union. The Emancipation Proclamation declared free all slaves held in parts of the United States not in the possession of the Union armies. In other words, Lincoln proclaimed that on January 1, 1863, all slaves within the Confederate lines were free. Lincoln had no jurisdiction over Confederate territory. He could not free slaves in the Confederacy. All slaves under Lincoln's control remained slaves until after the war, when the Thirteenth Amendment to the Constitution took effect.

En Partie 1 (Studying a Part). 1.(a) Why was New Orleans a key target? (b) Describe the battle. (c) Analyze the effects of the results. 2. Why did Butler arouse so much hatred? 3. Describe the major battles and campaigns in Louisiana. 4. Why was the location of the capital changed? 5. Why did the Union want to capture the Mississippi River? 6.(a) How did the Emancipation Proclamation affect Louisiana? (b) Why was it issued?

The Home Front

Almost all of Louisiana was in the battle zone. Union invasions wreaked havoc in the

Nottoway Plantation.

invasions into much of the state. Invaders moved up the Mississippi River to Baton Rouge, up the Red River twice, and into northeast Louisiana across from Vicksburg.

The cavalry and the infantry of both armies pounded the land with thousands of marching feet, hundreds of horses, and wagonloads of supplies. Long lines of heavy artillery were pulled across plantation fields. Untended lands grew up in switch canes or weeds. Shade trees in groves were cut for firewood. Houses and buildings were burned.

Fortunes were lost, families ruined, and valuables stolen. The blockade prevented the sale of cotton, and the purchase of clothing, tools, and household necessities.

Families grieved over the **death** of a beloved father, brother, son, or husband. Approximately one-fifth of the Louisiana men who had gone to war died in battle or hospitals.

Transportation. The Red River Railroad was destroyed during the war. Some of the rails and metal from the cars were used in building the Red River wing dams in 1864. In some cases the tracks provided iron for the Confederate war effort. Several miles of track near Shreveport were used for construction of the Confederate ironclad *Missouri*.

Life behind the Confederate Lines. Life during the Civil War was very grim. Nearly all able-bodied men went to the army. The homefront provided the fighting men with food and arms. There were times when the soldiers ran out of food, however. The South managed to keep the men in weapons. Many of their weapons were taken from the enemy.

Louisiana citizens were proud of the **sacrifices** they made. Matches, nails, writing paper, soap, needles, cutlery, glassware, and starch were among the scarce items. Clever Louisianians created substitutes to make life easier.

The scarcity of food created untold problems. Both armies "lived off the land." They took all the food they found. Flour and coffee were rarely found except in the federally occupied areas. Parched corn, peanuts, and thinly sliced sweet potato toasted brown and crisp were substituted for coffee. Salt was very scarce until 1862 when a mine was found. Great quantities were mined at Avery Island and distributed in the state. Hominy, cornmeal, and pork were usually found in areas not occupied by the Union. Rice, sugar, and syrup were available in the southern parishes.

Clothing. Leather for shoes became scarce. Shoes were then made of heavy canvas with soles of wood. Persimmon seed or pieces of gourd became buttons. Women made canvas and other kinds of cloth. Spinning wheels were put to use. Women learned the art of spinning and weaving. They made dyes at home. Old garments were ripped apart, turned inside out, and made into another garment.

Destruction by the Enemy. Women and children were often alone on the plantations. Slaves were restless with talk of armies coming to free them from slavery. There were promises of better lives by abolitionists and Union army officers. The people at home feared slave uprisings or military invasion. Some slaves left. The contents of plantation houses were often taken by the Union soldiers or guerilla fighters. The slaves showed great moral character by not harming the defenseless women and children. The Union soldiers and their leaders believed that destroying Southern property would help win the war.

Economy. Louisiana's economy stagnated during the war. The federal blockade along the Gulf of Mexico practically stopped commerce in New Orleans. Shipping to inland Louisiana by waterway ceased with the war. There was no money to buy anything. Confederate bonds were worthless. Confederate currency was worth less and less as time passed. Banks were in unsound conditions. To help the situation, Governor Moore stopped the banks from making payments in gold and silver. Confederate money had to be accepted at face value. By the end of 1864 Confederate money was worth nothing. Eventually, this worthless money ruined many banks in New Orleans. Merchants could not provide credit. Louisianians lost millions in Confederate currency. Approximately 170 million dollars invested in slaves had vanished. The labor supply was gone. Crop production dropped drastically. The crops that were raised could not be sold. Goods were scarce. Prices soared.

Government Programs. Gov. Henry W. Allen added life to the war effort when he started new programs. He established a rope factory; a cotton factory; a factory to produce turpentine, alcohol, and castor oil for medicines; and a cotton-card factory. The cotton cards were used by housewives to make cotton soft and free of tangles. He also stopped the use of corn and sugarcane in making home brew—intoxicating liquors.

Citizens' Plans. After the Union captured New Orleans, aroused citizens in the state above New Orleans went into action to plan against further invasion of the state. It was a frightening time. In Rapides Parish, as in other places over the state, men met to form **Committees of Public Safety.** They had to decide what was to be done should the enemy invade inland communities.

In the crisis, with troops occupying New Orleans and Baton Rouge, the committee met frequently to make plans. Their work included such projects as authorizing collections of food and clothing for the needs of suffering people in the occupied city of New Orleans. They also planned to punish persons ridiculing or reflecting adversely on Confederate currency.

Escape to Texas: 1862-64. From the fall of New Orleans to the second invasion of the Red River Valley, residents of Louisiana fled to Texas. Texas was a haven for young men avoiding the draft. Many gathered all of their possessions—livestock, farm tools, poultry, and slaves—and moved to Texas.

Many of the displaced Louisiana citizens remained in Texas after the war was over. Some refugees got no farther than the banks of the Sabine River. There they camped.

Cotton Sales. Refugees from Louisiana with wagons and mules found that they could rent out their equipment to the Confederacy for hauling cotton across the border to Mexico. Cotton was used as a medium of exchange with foreign countries in place of Confederate money. There the cotton could be shipped aboard Mexican ships. These ships could evade the blockade of the enemy. In this way the South secured

WAGON TRAIN HAULING COTTON TO MEXICO TO HELP FINANCE THE WAR.

desperately needed war supplies from such countries as France and England.

En Partie 2 (Studying a Part). 1. How did fighting on Louisiana soil affect the state? 2. How did the war affect the economy? 3. What were government plans to help? 4. What were the citizens' plans? 5. (a) Why did some people escape to Texas? (b) What did they do there?

1864: Second Invasion of the Red River Valley

Last Major Campaign. In 1864 **Banks** executed his second and largest invasion of the Red River Valley. It was the last major campaign of the Civil War in Louisiana.

Banks took the same route from Brashear City (**Morgan City**) that he had taken in

1863. Union soldiers marched up the Teche. From **Washington** they went north up the winding Bayou Boeuf to **Alexandria**. This time they were aided by ten thousand soldiers released from Vicksburg. These came into central Louisiana at **Simmesport** on transports under **Gen. A. J. Smith**. General Banks had twenty-six thousand troops. Another fifteen thousand troops were expected to come from Arkansas to attack **Shreveport**. In a fleet of nineteen warships, Admiral **David Porter** headed up the Red River. Union naval gunboats and transports entered the Red River through Simmesport.

Maj. General Richard **Taylor** was in command of Confederate troops south of the Red River. With him was Brig. Gen. Alfred **Mouton**, member of a well-known family from Lafayette. As Banks advanced toward **Alexandria**, Taylor's troops were also headed north, advancing to meet him. Taylor had only 8,800 men, commandeered from all the area. Union forces were more than three times greater.

Near **Marksville** a fort had been constructed. It had been built by slaves. This was **Fort de Russy** (deh RUSS see), an earthworks barricade. Confederates hoped that it would stop any invasion up the Red River. Fort de Russy lasted only a couple of hours or so before the big guns from the Union ships brought its surrender on March 14. After that the Union's fleet of ships had clear passage up the river to Alexandria.

Banks captured Alexandria and set up controls. About five hundred Jayhawkers came to Banks's headquarters and joined the Union army. Porter headed upstream. Banks led his army toward Shreveport. Taylor's and Mouton's troops moved at the same time in the same direction. There were

Banks's army crosses Cane River, March 31, 1864, in the advance on Shreveport.

Mansfield State Commemorative Area.

skirmishes along the way between the small groups of the two armies. There was wholesale destruction of houses, fences, crops, and other possessions. All the land over which the invaders traveled was a battleground. Everything in the path of the invaders was in the war zone.

Natchitoches was captured. Since Porter was increasingly concerned about the low-water stages of the Red River, it was decided that the fleet would go no farther than about six miles beyond Natchitoches. This was at **Grand Ecore** (e CORE).

Banks's route did not follow the river closely. Banks followed the beaten trails that ran through the pine-covered hill country to Shreveport. Banks arrived at Mansfield. The village was located on a stretch of flat land among gently rolling hills. Taylor decided to challenge the invaders at this point. On April 8, 1864, the **Battle of Mansfield** was fought. The Union was soundly defeated.

Banks moved his tired soldiers eight miles south to **Pleasant Hill**. On April 9, 1864, a second major battle was fought. The Union won as decisively as the Confederates had won at Mansfield the day before. There were heavy losses on both sides. To the complete surprise of the Confederates, Banks then retreated. Banks was apparently discouraged from going on to Shreveport. His weary troops were driven in disorder back toward Alexandria with Taylor close behind.

It was the third effort that Banks had mounted to invade Texas. Why did he change his mind at this point?

The defenses were so weak at Shreveport that **"Fort Humbug"** was arranged atop a

General William Tecumseh Sherman, the first president of LSU.

bluff. Union boats on the Red River were expected to believe that there were huge cannons aimed toward the river below. Actually, the only "big guns" were large logs painted to resemble cannons. Shreveport and the surrounding area were never invaded, however.

Porter began to return south to **Alexandria**. The Red River was very shallow at some places. Getting to Alexandria was an enormous job. The water level was falling every day.

General Sherman had taught at Louisiana State Seminary at Alexandria. He knew the problems of navigating the Red River. He had cautioned Admiral Porter about the rapids in the river a little above the city. Sherman warned Porter that the river waters might

fall dangerously low for the big boats. That is exactly what happened.

Bailey's Dam. There was near-panic. The fleet could not possibly get by the rapids. Col. Thomas Bailey, a Wisconsin lumberman, presented his plan for a wing dam to General Banks.

The dam would force the water into a narrow but deeper channel through which the fleet could escape. The idea sounded fantastic. Since all else had failed, Bailey was finally told to build his dam.

Bailey was assigned three thousand soldiers to assist him. Union men scoured the country for what remained of old buildings, iron kettles, the tracks of the old Red River Railroad—whatever! All of the material was placed in the river along with trees cut from Pineville hills. It was done in a manner that restricted the flow of water and caused the surface level to rise. The incredible feat was accomplished in record time.

The moment came to see if the dam would work. The first attempt to get a boat through the new channel failed. The banks of the river were lined with Union soldiers and sailors laughing at the effort. This changed to cheers quickly when the entire fleet of sixteen boats, boat by boat, crossed to safety.

The Burnt District. General Banks's steamboat was waiting for him to give the signal to leave. Nobody knows who gave the order—or if one was given. Each side blamed the other. **Alexandria** was burned to the ground. Eyewitness accounts taken later by Louisiana governor Allen told something of the story:

The Court House was the only building on the square. It fronted the river, the three other sides facing blocks of

The levee at New Orleans.

buildings, all of which had been consumed, and had fallen down in smoldering ruins, and yet the Court House stood uninjured. It was fired in the interior and was consumed with every record of the Parish.

There were now no records of who owned the land. There were no defined boundaries of property. There were no marriage records. These and more turned to ashes. The area became known as the "burnt district."

Buildings were burned along the river all the way to Natchitoches. A person who saw the wrecked countryside described it: "His [Banks's] march from five miles outside of Natchitoches had been illumined by the glare of burning homesteads."

After this second invasion of the Red River Valley, disheartened people began to make plans to defend themselves against a third. Plans were made for forts to be constructed at Alexandria. These included two forts on the Pineville side, Fort Buhlow and Fort Randolph. A third, much larger fort was planned on the Alexandria side. The first two were earthworks. The third was never built.

> **En Partie 3 (Studying a Part).** 1.(a) Describe the Second Invasion of the Red River Valley. (b) Compare it with the first. 2. Describe (a) Bailey's Dam and (b) the burnt district.

1865

Bedlam. The collapse of government in Confederate Louisiana began during the

Alexandria in 1863, before it was destroyed.

spring of 1865. There was no enforcement of the civil law in the state. There was very little military enforcement. As soon as the Rebels knew that they were defeated, many deserted. Since the fall of Vicksburg and Port Hudson, desertion had increased. Deserters were shot if they were caught.

Wild disorder prevailed as lawless groups robbed and took what they wanted. Storehouses were pillaged by both civilians and soldiers. Maintaining order became impossible.

Surrender. There was practically no military activity in the state in 1865. On May 26, 1865, the Department of Trans-Mississippi under **Gen. Kirby Smith** was the last Confederate command to surrender. Smith had moved the headquarters of the department from Shreveport to Houston. Gen. Simon Buckner, acting for Smith, signed the surrender papers in New Orleans. Smith signed the official documents for surrender of his army at Houston, but the final phase of the surrender took place on June 11, 1865, in Shreveport.

Governor Allen delivered a farewell address to the people at Shreveport on June 2, 1865. Then he went across Texas into voluntary exile in Mexico. He died there in 1866.

Long before then, many a Louisiana soldier, defeated and near exhaustion, was making his weary way home after the surrender at Appomattox on April 9, 1865.

About six hundred military engagements had taken place in Louisiana. Most of these were just skirmishes. Louisiana had suffered more destruction and casualties than any of the other Confederate states except Georgia, Virginia, and South Carolina. The fighting was over, but the war continued.

En Partie 4 (Studying a Part). 1. Describe the ending of the war. 2.(a) Which department of the Confederacy was the last to surrender? (b) When? (c) Where did the last phase of the surrender of the Confederacy take place? (d) When?

Coup de Main
(Completing the Story)

Jambalaya (Putting It All Together)

1. Identify:
(1) Abraham Lincoln
(2) Alfred Mouton
(3) Bailey's Dam
(4) Benjamin Butler
(5) Blue
(6) Committee of Public Safety
(7) Confederate States of America
(8) David Farragut
(9) Emancipation Proclamation
(10) Gray
(11) Henry W. Allen
(12) Jayhawkers
(13) Kirby Smith
(14) Mansfield Lovell
(15) Nathaniel Banks
(16) Occupied Louisiana
(17) Order No. 28
(18) P. G. T. Beauregard
(19) Rebels
(20) Richard "Dick" Taylor
(21) Robert E. Lee

(22) Thomas O. Moore
(23) Ulysses Grant

2. Map work. On a United States map, color the Confederate states gray, the United States blue, and the border states red. Outline the cotton states. On a Louisiana map, label the capitals of Louisiana during the Civil War. Give the date for each capital in parentheses. Label major Louisiana battles. Underline Union victories in blue and Confederate victories in gray.

3. How did the war affect the following: (a) slaves, (b) free people of color, (c) planters, (d) small farmers, (e) housewives, (f) merchants, (g) teenagers, (h) manufacturers, and (i) bankers?

4. Describe the economic conditions in the state before and during the war.

5. Chart the course of the war in Louisiana and relate it to the rest of the war.

6. Compare life before the war with life during the war.

7. Trace the development of Louisiana government from the time of secession until the war ended.

8. Cite ways Louisiana was devastated and destroyed.

9. Why did the Confederacy's defensive war result in so much fighting in the South?

10. Since the Northern advantages were so much greater then the South's, why didn't the North win quickly?

Potpourri (Getting Involved)

1. Research the background of *Uncle Tom's Cabin*. Relate the book to Louisiana. Give an oral review. Read excerpts.

2. Conduct a panel discussion on the causes of the war. Include political, social, and economic factors.

3. Dramatize a scene involving a discussion of Louisiana's secession.

4. Describe the procedures followed and dangers encountered in your work on the Underground Railroad. Plan an escape route for a runaway slave. Research the Reverse Underground Railroad.

5. Make an illustrated timeline of events from 1861 to 1865.

6. Write a series of letters as a Confederate teenager in Louisiana to a friend describing hardships endured during the war. Relate not only physical sufferings but also injuries to pride and reaction to unjust treatment by Union soldiers.

7. Construct a mural to depict (a) home-life during the war, (b) activities of the Jayhawkers, (c) a certain battle, or (d) any of the happenings leading to the war.

8. Tell Civil War stories to the class. Read aloud a selection of diary accounts of the war in Louisiana.

9. Research the role of (a) the Black, (b) cotton, (c) Louisiana troops, or (d) Louisiana leaders in the war.

10. Contrast the (a) life of Billy Yanks with Johnny Rebs, or (b) the homemaker in the North with the homemaker in the South.

Gumbo (Bringing It Up-to-Date)

1. Pretend that you were a Northern sympathizer in Louisiana opposed to slavery. Imagine what life would have been like during the war if your neighbors had known your feelings. Compare your life then with life today for someone who does not go along with the popular thinking on racial issues.

2. Relate the geography of the United States to the lives of the people. Show how the thinking of the people then and now is influenced by geography.

3. Compare (a) the states' rights issues of the period with the modern states' rights issues, (b) Northern and Southern advantages and disadvantages of the Civil War period with those of today, or (c) abolitionists' actions with civil rights activists' methods.

4. Compare presentations of the Civil War on television with the factual information in your text. Analyze them for bias. Were they presented from one viewpoint? Which one? Justify your answer.

5. Research the treatment of deserters during the Civil War, Vietnam War, and today.

RECONSTRUCTION: UNION RULE
(1865-1877)

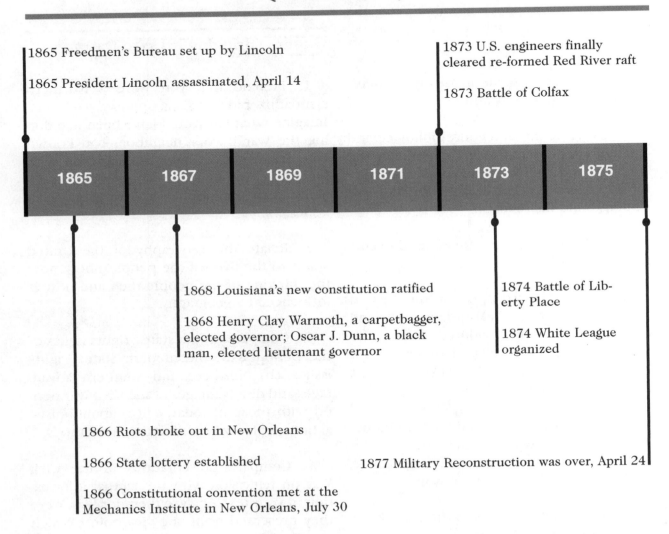

1865 Freedmen's Bureau set up by Lincoln

1865 President Lincoln assassinated, April 14

1873 U.S. engineers finally cleared re-formed Red River raft

1873 Battle of Colfax

1865	1867	1869	1871	1873	1875

1868 Louisiana's new constitution ratified

1868 Henry Clay Warmoth, a carpetbagger, elected governor; Oscar J. Dunn, a black man, elected lieutenant governor

1874 Battle of Liberty Place

1874 White League organized

1866 Riots broke out in New Orleans

1866 State lottery established

1866 Constitutional convention met at the Mechanics Institute in New Orleans, July 30

1877 Military Reconstruction was over, April 24

RECONSTRUCTION: UNION RULE

THE MASSIVE TASK OF REBUILDING

The war was over. Survivors headed home. Louisianians, still in their gray uniforms, trudged along dusty roads toward their loved ones. For four years most of them had been away from their families. Now, despite the hardships and suffering, the hated Yankees occupied and controlled the South. The way of life the Confederacy had fought to save was destroyed. Louisianians returned to fields grown up in canes and without fences. Such buildings as were left were badly in need of repair. No work animals were left to rebuild the run-down farms and plantations. The countryside was overgrown with weeds, and the workers were gone.

In the regions where Banks's army had been, and that included most of Louisiana, the men came home to devastation. Burned cotton gins and sugar mills lay in charred ruins. No barges plied the bayous. Steamboats were gone. The few railroad lines were destroyed. Louisiana was a sad sight. Everything they had built from the wilderness over the decades was destroyed. Some simply did not have the heart to start again the lifelong job of rebuilding.

The victors were collecting federal taxes that would have been due during the years Louisiana was out of the Union. The land was confiscated if these were not paid by a deadline. After four years of war, there was no money. A cotton tax was imposed as a penalty for the war. A few planters chose to go to Mexico, Brazil, or Europe. Most Louisianians—both the veteran soldiers and the home folks—waited anxiously to find out what their fate would be under the Union conquerors.

Presidential Reconstruction

The Union won the war. It was now up to the victors to decide how the defeated South would be treated. Soon very different ideas surfaced in Washington. They ranged from treating the South as conquered territory with no mercy in its punishment "for starting the war" to the ideas of Abraham Lincoln.

Lincoln's Plan. On December 8, 1863, President Lincoln presented his idea of how the South should be restored to the Union. Some conditions had to be met. First, full pardon would be granted to all Southerners except some Confederate civil and military leaders. Southerners had to promise to accept the federal laws and proclamations dealing with slavery. When at least 10 percent of the people voting in the election of 1860 took the oath of allegiance to the Union, then a state could draw up a new constitution, elect new officials, and return to the Union on a basis of full equality.

Andrew Johnson, President. When President Lincoln was assassinated on April 14, 1865, Andrew Johnson became president. Johnson was a Southerner from Tennessee. He had not worked for the Confederacy, but he sympathized with the South's problems after the war. He led the planters to believe that there would be no penalty for being defeated in the war. He followed Lincoln's **policy** with few exceptions. Property seized by federal troops was restored to those taking the loyalty oath. He promised the former Confederate states that they would be readmitted into the Union and granted full self-government. Before the citizens of the state could elect their own officials, they had to elect delegates to a state convention to write a new constitution. In turn, these constitutions had to provide for the end of slavery, acknowledge that a state had no right to secede, and declare that the money borrowed by the state from its citizens to fight the war would not be repaid.

Johnson was aware of the opposition to this plan in Congress. He tried to get all the Confederate states to meet the conditions immediately. Louisiana did so. The people of the state were able to run the government for two years before the Radical Republicans again took control.

The Radical Republicans. Not all leaders of the Republican party agreed with the president's plan for reconstruction. One group called the Radical Republicans wanted to **punish** the South. The South had lost the war, and the Northern victors had won the right to impose penalties on the South. The Radicals in Congress bitterly opposed what they considered as being too easy on the South. They thought it the right of Congress, not the president, to plan reconstruction.

1865—The Freedmen's Bureau. The

A symbolic representation of the role of the Freedmen's Bureau.

Freedmen's Bureau was set up by President Lincoln in 1865 strictly to provide welfare services to the needy of both races after the war. A hostile Congress under President Johnson extended the bureau a year later but shaped it into a radically different organization. It was an **arm** of the **Republican party**. The **functions** in the 1866 bill included supervision of labor contracts between the freedmen and the planters, assistance with voter registration, and the education of the freedmen.

Carpetbaggers and Scalawags. After the war many people from other sections moved into the South, including Louisiana. The newcomers were Republicans. Southerners called them **carpetbaggers** because they carried their possessions in a bag made of a coarse piece of carpet. Some were trying to make money in the war-torn section. Others were missionaries who wanted to educate the former slaves. Some thought they would teach the South how to live in the modern world of industrial expansion. Others came for political advantages. Some men had met Louisiana women and wanted to marry them and settle in the state.

Louisiana had a carpetbag government throughout the period of Military Reconstruction ordered by Congress. That is, the state government was controlled by these newcomers from other parts of the country.

Scalawags were native Louisianians who joined the Republican party. Most were sugar planters. These planters supported the industrial North's position on the protective tariff. The protective tariff included sugar. The importing of cheap foreign sugar would hinder the sales of Louisiana sugarcane crops.

Scalawag Governor James Madison Wells.

When the Union won the war, it took over the government of the Southern states, including Louisiana. The old Confederate government was out of business. The United States government in New Orleans, supported by the United States military, was Louisiana's only government. Michael Hahn, a New Orleans lawyer, and James Madison Wells, a Rapides planter, were elected governor and lieutenant governor of occupied Louisiana on February 22, 1864. Hahn resigned on March 4, 1865, when elected to the United States Senate. President Johnson then recognized Wells as governor.

Wells was a member of a family of early settlers in Rapides Parish. He was a big planter and slave owner. He had strongly opposed secession and had taken no part in the Civil War. Wells had opposed the Confederate government of Louisiana during the war. He was a scalawag. Perhaps in favoring the Union, Wells' position is best explained by his feeling that the South was committing a tragic mistake in seceding from the Union and fighting against the North. Wells had spent much of his early life in Kentucky and attended college in Washington, D.C. He knew the great advantages in the North's large population, railroad lines, and factories that could turn out war materials. He had felt from the beginning that the South could never win a war against the North.

Governor Wells altered his views enough to gain support from Confederate sympathizers. In May 1865 Governor Wells ordered a new registration of **voters**. Only men could vote, and they had to be white men over twenty-one years of age. They had to have lived in the state a year and had to have taken the oath of allegiance to the Union.

The Louisiana Constitution of 1864, written for occupied Louisiana, empowered the governor to extend the suffrage, or voting rights, to some blacks. Governor Wells refused to do so.

Louisiana Democrats. The Democratic party met in New Orleans the fall after the Civil War ended. Representatives to the **Democratic Convention** were from the planter-merchant class, which had always controlled Louisiana government. The Democrats claimed the right to ask the government for compensation for the slaves freed by the war. Before the war this proposition had been advanced by abolitionists. However, nothing had come of it. Now that the war was over there was small chance that anything would be done about the planters' losses. Over the South the value of slaves amounted to two billion dollars. Louisiana's slave losses amounted to one-third of its total wealth.

The Black Code. When the legislature met in 1865 after the war ended, the planters proceeded to pass legislation "to put the Negro back to work." As in all Southern states, this set of laws was called the Black Code. Louisiana's Black Code gave the freedmen only slightly higher status than they had as slaves before the war. Freedmen were not allowed to serve on police juries or bear arms. A freedman could not testify against a white man in court. If not working, the freedman could be charged with vagrancy. In that case a fine was levied, which he likely could not pay. If not, he was placed under the authority of a planter or assigned to public work.

Louisiana and the Fourteenth Amendment. In June 1866 the Fourteenth Amendment was sent to the states for ratification. It granted citizenship to all persons born or naturalized in the United States. This constitutional amendment was passed by Congress after Johnson vetoed their Civil Rights Bill. President Johnson advised the South that it did not have to ratify the Fourteenth Amendment. President Johnson kept assuring the officials that people sympathetic toward the South would be elected in the fall of 1866. That was not true. As it turned out, even more Radical Republicans were elected to Congress. Louisiana did not ratify the Fourteenth Amendment.

New Orleans Riot. Governor Wells decided that a new constitution was needed to replace the 1864 constitution. He called for a **constitutional convention,** but the former Confederates voted it down. He then decided to reconvene the constitutional convention of 1864. The group included black leaders.

The convention met at the Mechanics Institute in New Orleans on July 30, 1866. The mayor of New Orleans, John T. Moore, called upon the police and citizens to stop the convention. Federal police had been scheduled to help protect those attending the convention, but they arrived too late. A riot broke out, and the Metropolitan Police sided with Moore and the protesting whites. In the riot thirty-four blacks were killed and 119 wounded. Three white Unionists were killed and about seventeen were wounded. Among the wounded was Michael Hahn, former Republican governor of occupied Louisiana and senator-elect.

A riot also occurred in Memphis, Tennessee, during the summer of 1866. These two riots in major Southern cities and the Black Codes passed by all the Southern legislatures under the Johnson administration brought angry protests from Northern people. This added to the determination of the

Radical Republicans to place the South under Congressional control.

En Partie 1 (Studying a Part). 1. Describe conditions at the end of the war. 2. How did Lincoln plan to treat the South? 3. What was Johnson's viewpoint? 4. What political groups were competing for leadership? 5. What was the original purpose of the Freedmen's Bureau? 6. Why did the carpetbaggers come to the state? 7. What was the penalty for not ratifying the Fourteenth Amendment? 8. Identify: (a) Abraham Lincoln, (b) Andrew Johnson, (c) Black Code, (d) Carpetbaggers, (e) Democratic party, (f) Fourteenth Amendment, (g) Freedmen's Bureau, (h) James Madison Wells, (I) New Orleans Riot, (j) Radical Republicans, (k) Republican party, and (l) Scalawags.

Congressional Reconstruction

Military Reconstruction. The first Southern congressmen elected after the war went to take their seats in December 1865. They were not accepted. Instead, Congress took matters into its own hands regarding the defeated South. A joint committee from the Senate and House of Representatives was appointed to visit the South. The committee was to find out if the South had accepted defeat. The status of the freedmen was to be examined. Finally, the committee was told to come back with a Congressional plan for Reconstruction. This they did.

In 1867—two years later—Congress passed its own Reconstruction Acts, Military Reconstruction. The **South** was treated as **conquered territory**. It was divided into five military districts. Each district was

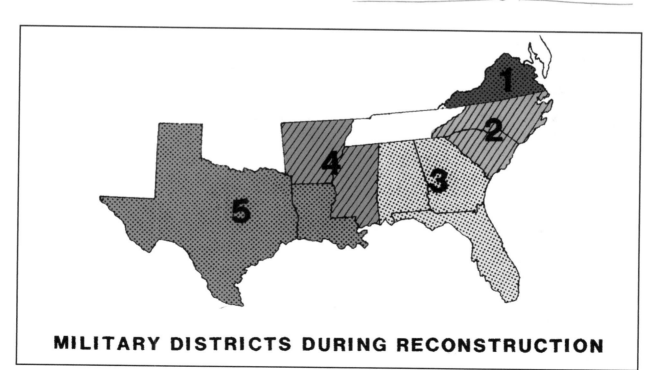

MILITARY DISTRICTS DURING RECONSTRUCTION

placed under the rule of an army general backed with federal troops. Under the new laws Louisiana would have to write a new constitution. Blacks had to be given the right to vote and hold office. The ruling generals would then register voters, including blacks. The right to vote was taken away from high-ranking Confederate military men and officials. Certain other provisions were laid down under which Louisiana might reenter the Union.

Gen. Philip H. Sheridan, famous Union cavalryman, was briefly in command of **District 5.** This district included Louisiana and Texas. Sheridan removed Governor Wells and appointed a former schoolteacher, **Benjamin F. Flanders,** as governor.

Sheridan was also involved in racial troubles in New Orleans. In the city there were about twenty thousand black people who were free before the Civil War. They were willing to fight for equal rights. The **first civil rights demonstrations** took place in New Orleans in 1867. A black man, William Nichols, tried to ride an all-white streetcar. He was removed. This incident encouraged other demonstrations. About five hundred blacks hurled stones at "star cars" (so called because

A bloody race riot in New Orleans brought General Sheridan and his troops to restore order.

The lithograph on the facing page hung in thousands of black homes.

a star designated them all-white cars). One demonstrator took over an empty streetcar and drove it through the city. General Sheridan ended the situation. He met with the mayor and officials of the transit company. Sheridan announced that the streetcars would be desegregated immediately.

Sheridan was replaced by Winfield S. Hancock in command of the state. Hancock appointed Joshua Baker governor. Baker governed for only a short period.

Constitution of 1868. The constitutional convention met at the Mechanics Institute in New Orleans on November 23, 1867. Forty-nine blacks and forty-nine whites wrote the new constitution. It incorporated the principles of the Thirteenth and Fourteenth Amendments to the United States Constitution. It contained a bill of rights. Black males over the age of twenty-one were given the right to vote. The constitution required that public places and public conveyances be open to all people, regardless of race. Public education was also open to all. This constitution was unenforceable without federal troops.

Election of 1868. After the constitution was written, people elected officials. They ratified the constitution by a large vote in 1868. For the first time blacks voted. **Henry Clay Warmoth,** a twenty-six-year-old carpetbagger, was elected governor. A black, **Oscar J. Dunn**, was elected lieutenant governor. The elections increased the anger of the planters toward the Republicans. Nothing so irritated the planters as allowing their former "properties" to vote.

General Ulysses S. Grant, hero of the Union army, became president in 1868. He served a term that was remarkable for its scandals.

Gov. Henry C. Warmoth. Warmoth was the first governor elected by the voters under the Reconstruction Acts. Therefore, he actually began Radical Reconstruction in Louisiana.

Warmoth was one of those rare individuals who possessed so much charm that even his political enemies saluted him. He believed as much as any Southerner in white supremacy. He was an artist at wielding political power. Through the offices of sheriffs throughout the state, he gained a hold on the state's power structure. In time Warmoth became practically a dictator. He controlled the legislature.

For the first time in history, ordinary people

Governor Henry Warmoth.

held office. They sought public services—education, levees, roads, and the like. Partly because of these extras the **expense of government rose** much higher. Dishonesty in public spending was another cause. Under Warmoth and Military Reconstruction, the state debt increased. In less than three years Warmoth's administration added three million dollars to the state's debt.

More blacks than whites **voted** in Louisiana during this period of Radical Reconstruction. Under the laws 82,907 blacks and 44,732 whites registered to vote. Even with the heavy casualties of the war, the numbers of white and black males over twenty-one should have been about equal. The registrars eliminated many whites. The registrars had the right to deny them the right to vote. They did this on the grounds that the white men were not sincere in their loyalty oaths. A large number of white men did not try to register. They felt it an indignity to submit to the black registrars, or they wanted no part of the new government, or there were other reasons. The fact that black voters were in the majority enraged the planters and merchants.

Blacks were not allowed to vote in all Northern states. After black males were voting in the South, a movement began to secure passage of an amendment allowing all adult males to vote. This movement resulted in the **Fifteenth Amendment** to the United States Constitution. The Fifteenth Amendment granted the right to vote to all male citizens, regardless of race or color.

Changes in Louisiana Government. Reconstruction brought radical change. **Universal male suffrage** (the right of all male adults to vote) was only one of the ways that Louisiana government had changed. Former

slaves could not only vote, but, as officeholders, could cast votes to tax the property of their former masters. A "propertyless" class in control of the state government chilled the hearts of men who had long felt that their ownership of property gave them the right to govern.

The **ideas of democratic government** were introduced. The ordinary people now in positions of power in Louisiana government felt that they were in the state's politics to stay.

In 1868 there were, according to Warmoth, sixty-five Republicans and thirty-six Democrats in the legislature. Thirty-five of the Republicans were black. None of the Democrats were black. The House of Representatives was nearly 50 percent black in its membership. Of twenty-three Republicans

---

Louisiana's 1868 Legislature

Senate	House of Representatives
23 Republicans	65 Republicans
7 Blacks 16 Whites	35 Blacks 30 Whites
13 Democrats	36 Democrats
13 Whites	36 Whites

in the Senate, seven were black and all thirteen Democrats were white. The new situation presented a totally different government. This group ratified the Fourteenth and Fifteenth amendments to the United States Constitution.

The former ruling class scoffed at the officials who had taken their places in government. They pointed to their lack of education. They ridiculed their manners and their language. Opponents of the government at this time found that there were no gentlemen in the legislature. The fact horrified them.

The Redeemers. The former Confederate leaders deeply resented the Reconstruction government forced upon them. They were determined to do something about it. They began a **movement** to undermine the government imposed by the North. The leaders of the movement were called the "Redeemers." They planned to redeem, or restore, the South as they thought it had been before the Civil War. Sadly, the Redeemers saw the pre-war society through rose-colored glasses. What they wanted to redeem had never existed. It was merely a dream. Yet, the Redeemers felt that the prosperous cotton kingdom with a planter aristocracy and armies of happy slaves was real. They did not understand that there had always been a resentment of the aristocracy by the people of the piney woods and prairies.

The Redeemers made a practice of wrecking elections. Freedmen were threatened. The threats were often carried out. Blacks and whites opposing the Redeemers were too often found among the missing. A number of blacks working with the Republicans were killed. White men whose political beliefs were not agreeable to the Redeemers were often tarred and feathered, or worse. The Republicans responded to election frauds with the Returning Board and with tricks and violence of their own.

In order to accomplish their goals, the Redeemers went **"underground."** That is, things were done in secret. Many joined groups like the Ku Klux Klan. The identity of members was known only to other members. The most popular underground group in Louisiana was not the Ku Klux Klan, however. It was the Knights of the White Camellia. This white supremacy group began in Franklin in St. Mary Parish. It spread throughout the state. Leading citizens were among its members. This organization was dedicated to preventing the election of blacks. The **Bulldozers** were another such underground group. Bulldozers operated in the Felicianas. Both of these organizations soon disbanded. Lawless people in disguise continued to commit ruthless acts for which the KKK was blamed.

The Union League. The Republicans had organized the blacks into the Union League during the war. It was organized to enlist the freedmen into the Republican party.

The Returning Board. The Republicans reacted to the stealing of elections by the Democrats by creating the Returning Board. The board, in effect, monitored elections. If the Returning Board decided that there had been fraud or intimidation of voters, the election could be cast out. This, in effect, gave Republicans control of elections. The Returning Board was Warmoth's idea.

En Partie 2 (Studying a Part). 1. What happened to Louisiana representatives sent to

Congress in 1865? 2. Who was charged with vagrancy? 3. What was the conflict between Congress and Johnson? 4. When did Military Reconstruction begin in Louisiana? 5. Describe Military Reconstruction. 6. Which groups arose to challenge Military Reconstruction? 7. Describe the changes in government and voting during Reconstruction. 8. Identify: (a) 1868 constitution, (b) Fifteenth Amendment, (c) General Philip Sheridan, (d) Henry Clay Warmoth, (e) Knights of the White Camellia, (f) Ku Klux Klan, (g) Metropolitan Police, (h) Reconstruction Acts, (i) Redeemers, (j) Returning Board, and (k) Union League.

The End of Reconstruction

The Louisiana Lottery. The planter legislators of 1866 had established a state lottery. When Military Reconstruction was imposed, this lottery was no longer in effect. In 1868 a second lottery called the Louisiana Lottery was chartered to last for twenty-five years. This lottery was the **brainchild** of the **Republicans.** Lottery tickets were sold all over the United States. The sales amounted to a figure somewhere under thirty million dollars a year. About half of these funds were paid in prizes to holders of the lucky tickets. Every month there was a drawing for a prize of thirty thousand dollars. Twice a year the prize was one hundred thousand dollars. The owners of this monopoly paid Louisiana forty thousand dollars a year. They paid no taxes. Thousands of poor people who hoped to get something for practically nothing spent their hard-earned money for lottery tickets.

Anti-lottery societies sprang up shortly

Louisiana State Lottery Building.

after 1868 to rid the state of the menace. The company that operated the lottery had become nearly as powerful as the legislature. The lottery added to the terrible corruption of the state. A man named **E. A. Burke** was in charge of political deals for the lottery. In effect, Burke was the state's political boss for the years of the existence of the lottery.

Republican Factions. About 1872 a group of leading Republicans had broken away from the party on the national level. The scandals of the Grant administration repelled this splinter group of Republicans. They opposed Grant as a candidate for reelection. Henry **Warmoth** joined this **group.**

The split was evident in Louisiana. The

Debate in the Louisiana legislature during Reconstruction sometimes led to violent disagreements.

Republican group in the state favoring Grant was led by United States Marshal Stephen B. Packard. The center for the **Packard Republicans** was the customhouse in New Orleans. For this reason, followers of Warmoth ridiculed the Packard group as the "Customhouse Ring." Lieutenant Governor Dunn left Warmoth to join the Customhouse Ring. His reason for this move was disgust over Warmoth's racism. Warmoth had much the same attitude as the Redeemers toward freedmen.

Election of 1872. Warmoth did not get the nomination for governor for a second term. William Pitt **Kellogg**, a carpetbagger, was nominated. C. C. **Antoine,** a black from Caddo Parish, was nominated for lieutenant governor.

Warmoth shifted his support to the Redeemer-Democrats. This group nominated John **McEnery** from Ouachita Parish for governor and Davidson **Penn** for lieutenant governor.

The Republicans claimed their candidate, William Pitt Kellogg, won the election. McEnery supporters proclaimed his victory. Warmoth, as "lame-duck" governor, was a major influence in the election. He was in control of the Returning Board. This board itself was a creation of Military Reconstruction. Now its use was as wild and corrupt as the election itself. It supported McEnery.

Kellogg turned to the federal courts to support him as winner of the election. There was no way to know who won. This was true of every election of the Reconstruction period. Both sides claimed victory. The 1872 election reached a new low in fraud, corruption, and trickery.

Warmoth's Administration. Warmoth was **impeached** by the Kellogg legislature. He was impeached on charges of fraud in counting votes in the presidential election of 1872. The House of Representatives brought him to trial.

Under the Constitution of 1868, the governor, if impeached, was removed from office until after his trial. Warmoth did not recognize his suspension from office. He was never convicted.

According to most historians, Warmoth used his office to become very wealthy. He earned eight thousand dollars his first year in office. He admitted that he accumulated one hundred thousand dollars that same year.

Joanna Moore, a Yankee missionary, organized the Old Folks Home for Negroes in New Orleans and later taught at Leland College.

Warmoth made his money by manipulating state treasury notes and securities. He also had majority ownership in the New Orleans *Republican,* a newspaper. The newspaper did the official printing for the state. Men in and out of public office were using the government for private profit. Scandals like Warmoth's did not exist only in Louisiana.

P. B. S. Pinchback: Governor. In accordance with the Louisiana constitution, the lieutenant governor became governor until the trial took place. Pinchback had become lieutenant governor after the death of Dunn in 1871. Pinchback, the son of a white Mississippi planter and one of his slaves, served only one month as Louisiana's only black governor.

Two Governors: Two Legislatures. Both Kellogg, the Republican, and McEnery, the Redeemer-Democrat, claimed election in 1872. The two governors proceeded to organize separate governments. Each side elected members of the legislature.

The Kellogg government had the legal backing of President Grant and the federal courts. Kellogg was inaugurated on January 13, 1873, at the Mechanics Institute in New Orleans. John McEnery was inaugurated on the same day at about the same time at New Orleans's Lafayette Square. Two governors and two legislatures operating a block apart in New Orleans were the climax of Reconstruction turmoil.

Most of the people of Louisiana, being Democrats, recognized McEnery as governor. With the strength of popular support, McEnery formed a militia under Gen. Fred N. Ogden. Using the militia, McEnery attempted to take control of the New Orleans police. This resulted in the **Battle of the Cabildo** on March 5, 1873. General Longstreet was in control of the Metropolitan Police (actually the state militia) and arrested sixty-five of the McEnery militia.

White League. The White League was organized in June 1874 to rid the state of carpetbag government. The group, dedicated to returning control to Louisiana white men, grew rapidly. Because of the support of the Radicals by federal troops, the White League was convinced that it was necessary to fight to regain control. Its members were organized into military companies. The group was not a secret organization. They did not hide their identity with robes or other disguises.

Violence. This period of constant lawlessness and political turmoil resulted in many riots and conflicts. Some were gruesome. **New Orleans** was hit harder than the rural areas. Planters enforced their own authority on their plantations.

The state was peppered with fresh outbreaks every day, and the tension mounted steadily. In such political tension explosions were sure to come. One of the worst was the **Battle of Colfax** in 1873 in newly created Grant Parish.

One of the largest former slave owners in the South lived at Colfax. His name was Meredith Calhoun. It was at Colfax in Grant Parish that a clash between opposing political groups erupted. Each faction claimed that its candidates for election as judge and sheriff of Grant Parish had been elected. Both sets of officers were given commissions by Kellogg. Both thought the positions were theirs. One pair, supported by McEnery, was white. The other set was black. They were supported by Kellogg.

Whites and blacks gathered from a wide area of Louisiana. Troops of both sides were drilled for the forthcoming battle. On Easter Sunday 1873, a pitched battle occurred at Colfax. The black men had taken over the offices in the courthouse. A trench was dug by the defenders. The white men, supported by McEnery, moved a small cannon from a steamship to the site. It was aimed at the courthouse. The black forces were trapped inside the courthouse when the building was set on fire.

This was no riot but a planned battle. Once the conflict began over seating the officials, both sides gathered support. No records were kept of the number of blacks killed. Local tradition has it that hundreds died. Survivors from the burning courthouse were taken to a Calhoun sugar warehouse. That night they were shot. Three white men died during the battle. Nine white leaders were captured and taken to federal prison in New Orleans. Some time later, the survivors were released. They were welcomed as heroes when they returned to Grant Parish.

A year after the Colfax Riot, there was the **Coushatta Massacre.** Red River Parish, in which Coushatta is located, was tense with rumors of conflict. In August 1874 the rumor was spread that the blacks were going to attack the white Democrats. The White League arrived. White Republican leaders had ruled the parish during Reconstruction. They agreed to leave the state if they were protected. Five office holders and one of their friends with an escort left for Texas on August 30. A mob soon killed all six Republicans. Apparently the mob attack was prearranged. The clash that occurred there and others across Louisiana kept the people on edge.

Two weeks after the Coushatta Massacre, the **Battle of Liberty Place,** or Canal Street, occurred in New Orleans. This battle has been referred to as the Revolution of 1874. It involved the securing of arms from the North by the White League. The Metropolitan Police made a stand to prevent a shipment of supplies from reaching the volunteer army of the Redeemers. A battle was fought between the two groups on September 14, 1874.

Notices appeared in New Orleans newspapers on September 13, 1874, about the meeting on Canal Street. The following day, people closed their businesses, and large numbers assembled. The steamboat *Mississippi* had arrived in New Orleans with weapons and ammunition for the Leaguers. Kellogg's Metropolitan Police, mostly blacks, were ordered to stop the leaguers from getting the shipment. Streetcars were overturned and used for breastworks. Camp Street was blocked off with logs and barrels. Thousands watched and cheered. The Metropolitan Police blocked the levee. The Leaguers used a moving freight train to shield their maneuvers. The Metropolitan troops withdrew. Kellogg fled to the customhouse under the protection of federal troops. Many of the guns brought in aboard the *Mississippi* were seized by the White Leaguers. Eleven of the policemen were killed and sixty of them were wounded. From the White League sixteen were killed and forty-five wounded.

The White League took possession of state government for the McEnery administration. For two days McEnery was governor. The White League celebrated with a victory parade. The federal government stepped in to support Kellogg. President Grant restored the Radical Republicans to office. The Leaguers did not confront the federal troops.

On September 17, 1874, **McEnery retired** from the contest. For almost two years the two rival administrations had functioned. **Kellogg** held power only with the **backing** of **federal troops.**

Home Control. The goal of the Redeemers to regain local control of Louisiana government was in sight by the fall of 1876. More and more resistance to Military Reconstruction had been felt during Kellogg's administration. The over-

A statue commemorates the Confederate soldier in front of the Claiborne Parish Courthouse.

throw of Radical Republican rule in local government was accomplished parish by parish. The Democrats had regained control of most of the parishes along the Mississippi River by 1872. By 1876 the Democrats were in control in all North Louisiana parishes. By then they controlled enough parishes in the state to be a threat to the Republicans.

1876 Election. It was election time. The leader of the Republicans in Louisiana was Stephen B. **Packard.** He was candidate for governor on the Republican ticket. The Redeemers nominated a Confederate war veteran. He had been so shot up in battle that he was a physical wreck. An arm and leg had been amputated, and his eyesight was impaired. He was Francis T. **Nicholls.**

The 1876 election was conducted according to the grim pattern that had been maintained throughout Military Reconstruction. "The end justifies the means" was the battle cry on both sides. Stuffing ballot boxes and casting dead persons' ballots were tricks used by both political parties to steal elections.

Again both candidates claimed victory. Strangely enough, it turned out that the Confederate veteran, Nicholls, had been aided by funds from the Louisiana Lottery. Its owners wanted to be on the side they knew would be winning control of the state. Nicholls accepted their money and thereby committed himself to support the corrupt lottery.

Both men were **inaugurated** in New Orleans in separate ceremonies on January 8, 1877. The state again had two governors, indeed, two entire rosters of officers. Nicholls had the support of the native whites. About ten thousand of his enthusiastic supporters watched the swearing in. Packard claimed support of the white Radical Republicans, many of them carpetbaggers.

The Weary North. By now, however, the Northern population was weary of what appeared a hopeless task. That task was to reconstruct the South according to ideas developed in the North. Many Northerners believed that the South needed to work out its own problems of government and race relations. When several thousand men from the White League, now called the Continental Guards, marched into New Orleans and took over police stations, the arsenal, and the Cabildo, there were no federal troops to support Packard. President **Grant,** at last, **gave up.** There would be no more federal troops. Packard offered no resistance.

The **Republican legislature,** which had been holding its sessions within a short distance

A Louisiana resident in the late nineteenth century.

from the Democratic legislature, **disbanded.** Governor Packard resigned. Francis Tillou Nicholls was unchallenged in his position as head of the state government. The situation remained tense, however, until the March 4, 1877, presidential inauguration.

A Compromise. There had not been an honest election in Louisiana—or probably anywhere else in the South—since Military Reconstruction began. In early 1877 there was still no way of knowing which candidate for president of the United States had received winning votes in three Southern states. Either a Republican, Rutherford B. Hayes, or a Democrat, Samuel J. Tilden, would become president of the United States. Louisiana's **electoral vote** would help decide the winner. Louisiana sent two different sets of results for the presidential election. Louisiana agreed to go with Hayes if certain conditions were met. A compromise was reached to give the presidency to Hayes, although Tilden probably won the election. One condition was that military troops be withdrawn from the South.

Hayes also agreed to give federal support to Southern Democrats and the Nicholls government. After President Hayes was inaugurated, on March 4, 1877, Louisiana governmental affairs, tangled as they were, changed swiftly.

Two months after Hayes' inauguration, all federal **troops** were at last **withdrawn** from the state on April 24, **1877**. Military Reconstruction was over. Nicholls was finally established in power. He was the first native of Louisiana to serve since the Civil War. Louisiana had lived under military government longer than any other Southern state. New Orleans had been under federal domination for fifteen years.

Louisiana: Part of the Solid South. Since the Republican party was formed to keep slaves out of the territories, the South rejected the party. Planters felt that the Republicans brought on the war to free slaves. The people of Louisiana, like the rest of the South, hated the Republican party. The Republicans were responsible for Military Reconstruction. Voters were determined to rid the state of the Republicans. This is the reason Louisiana became a part of the Solid South. The Solid South voted the Democratic ticket. It took nearly a hundred years to overcome the bitterness resulting from the war and Reconstruction. The first Republican elected governor of Louisiana since Reconstruction was elected in 1980. *Dave Treen*

En Partie 3 (Studying a Part). 1. (a) Who organized the Louisiana Lottery? (b) Why? (c) How did it work? 2. Describe the elections that resulted in two sets of officials. 3. Describe Warmoth's administration. 4. How did the cost of state government change? 5. Relate violence and Reconstruction. 6. What was the compromise made in 1877? 7. How long was Louisiana under federal control? 8. Why were Louisianians bitter about Republican control? 9. Identify: (a) C. C. Antoine, (b) Colfax Riot, (c) Francis T. Nicholls, (d) home control, (e) impeachment, (f) P. B. S. Pinchback, (g) Solid South, (h) Stephen Packard, and (i) White League.

RECONSTRUCTION: SOCIAL AND ECONOMIC READJUSTMENT (1865-1877)

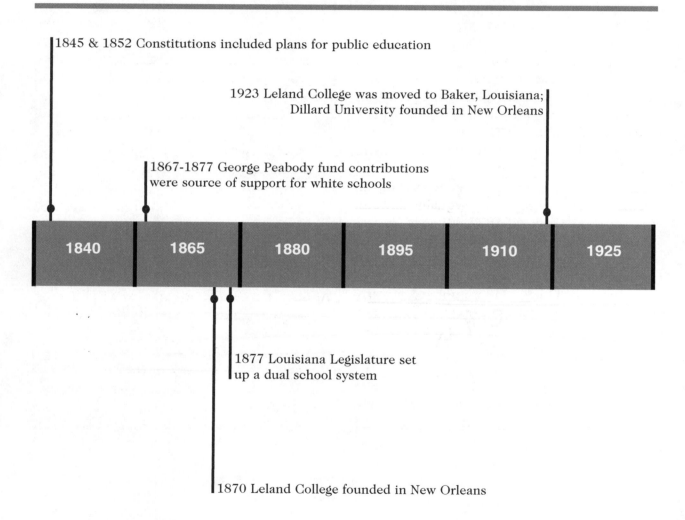

1845 & 1852 Constitutions included plans for public education

1923 Leland College was moved to Baker, Louisiana;
Dillard University founded in New Orleans

1867-1877 George Peabody fund contributions
were source of support for white schools

| 1840 | 1865 | 1880 | 1895 | 1910 | 1925 |

1877 Louisiana Legislature set
up a dual school system

1870 Leland College founded in New Orleans

RECONSTRUCTION: SOCIAL AND ECONOMIC READJUSTMENT

Slavery was ended at the close of the Civil War. The North was convinced that the Union victory had destroyed plantations forever. The North thought the victory in war would force the South to accept the same way of life as their own. Meanwhile, in defeat, the South was struggling to maintain the plantations as the only way they knew to make a living.

The idea of treating the South as conquered territory, which ultimately prevailed after the war, was self-defeating. It left problems that would fester forever.

The political changes in Louisiana were not the only changes to follow the Civil War. Louisiana faced social and economic adjustments as well. These were equally difficult for Louisianians. The people of the plantation lowlands in the state, along with the New Orleans commercial interests, were hardest hit.

The end of slavery and the impact of the war meant that there could be no complete return to the prewar ways of life. New ways of living were necessary. The state and its citizens had to make these adjustments with desperately limited financial resources.

Freemen and Freedmen

Identity. Two groups of black people still existed in the state after the war. The people who had been called "free persons of color" before the war were freemen. They were

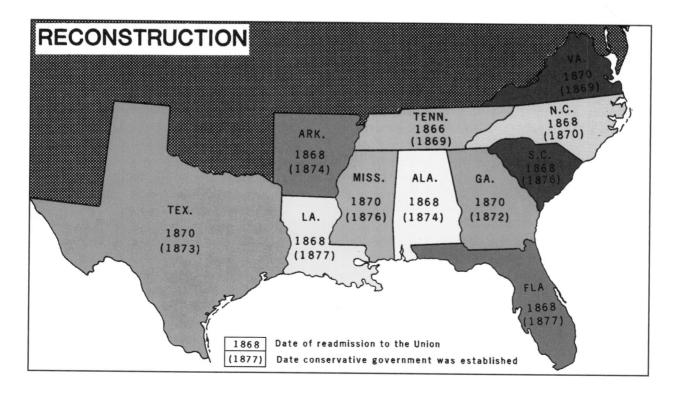

RECONSTRUCTION

VA.
1870
(1869)

N.C.
1868
(1870)

TENN.
1866
(1869)

S.C.
1868
(1876)

ARK.
1868
(1874)

MISS.
1870
(1876)

ALA.
1868
(1874)

GA.
1870
(1872)

TEX.
1870
(1873)

LA.
1868
(1877)

FLA
1868
(1877)

| 1868 | Date of readmission to the Union |
| (1877) | Date conservative government was established |

free before the war. Others were freedmen. These were freed by the war. Both groups faced social and economic adjustment problems, but the freedmen were the hardest hit.

Problems. The freedmen found themselves in a desperate situation after the war. Some migrated to the North and West. A few found jobs off the plantations. Some found work as day laborers. Jobs in the crossroad villages were few. New Orleans held the promise of jobs loading and unloading ships and various other work. Most jobs were still on plantations or farms. Work was scarce in impoverished Louisiana. Money was even more scarce.

To some freedom meant that they did not have to work anymore. They expected the Freedmen's Bureau to provide them with food, shelter, and medical care. Later the Bureau would give them land of their own, they thought. They did not want to return to the plantations when they were expecting to be given a farm of their own from the government.

The North supplied no solution to the freedmen for the fundamental problem of earning a livelihood. Although critical of the South, the North had no answers. Federal officials, especially those of the Freedmen's Bureau, made it clear that former slaves would have to find jobs. All but a handful of the freedmen had no skills except those related to farming. The Bureau did try to arrange for jobs. It was the Bureau's responsibility to see that blacks received fair treatment.

Relocation. It is small wonder that the freedmen were confused. One thing was certain: the North did not want the freedmen. Most Northerners felt that former slaves should remain in the South.

For some freedmen it meant leaving the plantations for good. They crowded into New Orleans or relocated in the villages. There they believed that they might be both safer and more likely to find employment.

Some did change plantations. This choice of which planter they wanted as employer came with the newly found freedom. The planter himself figured in that decision. However, freedmen had no money, no land, and no way to earn a living. Slaves who had lived on a prosperous, well-run plantation before the war had better living conditions than they did after the war. Not all desired to undertake the hardships of those beginning life anew in shacks thrown up in the woods. The truth was that the Louisiana economy was based on cotton. The cotton plantations at least offered food and shelter in a familiar setting. The skills learned on the plantations could be used to secure a living.

Most of the freedmen, sooner or later, found themselves back on the plantations. There were few choices. Moving to the North or going to work at such menial jobs as could be found in Louisiana villages or New Orleans were the options. Most of the former plantation slaves went back to the same plantation routine often working for the same planters as before the war. There were few different arrangements.

Land Allotments. The promised land allotments which never came contributed greatly to the confusion. The rumor was that on New Year's Day 1866, each former slave was to receive forty acres and a mule from the United States government. Instead of working, many waited around the Bureau offices hoping that the rumor was true.

There were threats that the United States

government would seize all plantation land and redistribute it as small family farms to the freedmen. Actually, a Freedmen's Bureau act of March 3, 1865, provided for allotting confiscated property to former slaves. However, during 1865 most of the 65,528 acres of farmland that the Freedmen's Bureau had seized and leased to freedmen was restored to the original owners. Eighty-six buildings confiscated by the Freedmen's Bureau in New Orleans had been restored to their former owners.

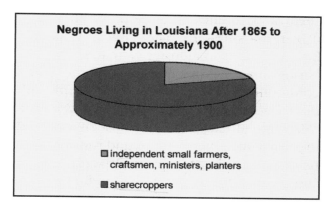

It was during this period that planters hustled off to the legislature to pass Black Codes. These laws clearly pointed out the manner in which planters expected to deal with the former slaves.

The Black Codes applied to the **black planters** also. Black planters were few in number, but there were some with large landholdings. Although they were well-to-do, they did not possess any political power. They held themselves aloof from other blacks. On Cane River, for instance, they did not attend church with either the blacks or whites.

Rural Black Communities. Some freedmen worked to save money for land of their own. The women took in washing and ironing for white families. The men found jobs such as cutting wood. Many of mixed black and white heritage received land from their white planter parents. However the land was acquired, a number of independent black farm communities developed. These were often on marginal (unfertile) or uncleared land.

The public was hardly aware of the large number of black men and women on their own small farms. Entire communities of blacks settled in several different locations in

North Louisiana. In marvelous bootstrap operations they built churches and schools. They carried on community functions in a similar pattern to the white communities. These communities were scattered throughout the state. Perhaps the number of northern settlements was due to the vast unsettled pine-covered hills. Land was cheap. Some could be homesteaded. In the beginning men and women worked under circumstances in which they had to subsist on minimum food in order to pay for their small plots of land. The entire family provided the labor needed on these farms.

Almost hidden in isolated areas, these blacks meant to be free to handle their affairs as they pleased. Many growing up in the black world had little contact with "the other race," as they referred to the white man. This worked both ways. Whites often did not know this class of black people.

Urban Black Communities. Cities like New Orleans had sections where freedmen gathered. Those who had learned crafts as slaves now used them as freedmen. They worked as brickmasons, carpenters, wagonmakers, blacksmiths, and tanners. Barber shops, funeral homes, general stores, and countless other small black businesses developed within black urban communities. The largest group of blacks working in industry were found in lumbering. Blacks crossed daily into the white community where most were employed. Blacks sometimes did manual work in the "Main Street" stores, banks, post offices, and the like, which were owned and run by white people. Handymen, draymen (drivers of carts), and drivers of teams were able to find a livelihood in the towns. Women were almost always assured employment as domestics in the homes of white people on the "other side of the track."

When railroad tracks were laid across the state around 1880, the urban black communities almost invariably expanded on one side of the tracks. The trains needed porters and other employees. These were often black. A parallel white community grew on the other side. "On the other side of the track" took on different meanings according to whether you were black or white.

Freemen. Before the war free blacks were scattered throughout the state. Some had their own farms. Some were planters. The largest group of freemen were in New Orleans. According to some historians, before the war this cultured, free-black group had reached a higher level of living than any other black group anywhere in the world. Some were highly educated and well-traveled. Approximately twenty thousand were in New Orleans before the war started. Many of them owned their own businesses. After the war their trade increased with the presence of the Union military occupation forces. Many of the wealthy freemen received political recognition during the occupation period.

Black Leadership. The independent communities were cradles of outstanding black leaders. The role of the community black church in developing leaders can hardly be overestimated. These leaders were thinkers and planners. Many of the black leaders were ministers, but deacons and others also became leaders. The roles of these church leaders extended far beyond religion to the uplifting of the race. They were usually educators as well.

Among the black leaders of the Reconstruction period were a few well-educated men. They were mostly from New Orleans.

Governor P. B. S. Pinchback.

Descendants of the important group of blacks educated in schools provided by John McDonogh were some of these leaders. The New Orleans environment stimulated leadership. Some of them had white fathers who had sent them to the North or to France to become educated. Now they returned home to take the lead in black civil rights work. Two brothers in the wealthy freemen group, Dr. Louis Roudanez, (rō DAN ez) and Joseph B. Roudanez published the Republican *La Tribune de la Nouvelle-Orléans,* the first black daily newspaper in the United States. Dr. A. P. Dostie (DOS tee), P. B. S. Pinchback, and C. C. Antoine were among these leaders.

En Partie 1 (Studying a Part). 1. Cite the position and problems of the freedmen and the freemen. 2. How were some of the problems solved? 3. Describe a (a) black rural community and (b) black urban community.

Planters

Ezra Bennett, one of the most outstanding planters in Rapides Parish, had remained at "Bennettville" throughout the Civil War. Later he took a job working at a store at Eldred's

Oak Alley.

Bend and found that he liked that much better. He married Sarah Eldred, daughter of the planter who owned the plantation on which the store was located. He eventually bought the store and his father-in-law's plantation. He became a valued agent for New Orleans factors, or financial agents, who financed all the crops grown on neighboring plantations on both sides of Bayou Boeuf.

In 1865 everything was gone. The Union blockade of the port of New Orleans quickly stopped the flow of goods to such inland stores. Bennett's store had closed early during the war. Factors, who supplied the all-important money, were out of business. The waterways connecting inland Louisiana with New Orleans money and the New Orleans market were given over to the war. Soldiers of both armies moved over his land in 1863 and 1864. Both took whatever of his possessions they wanted. All of his neighbors fled to Texas. Sarah Bennett wrote in 1865: "This is a very lonesom[e] country now. So many have left. Old Mrs. Ford and me has to do our visiting among our selves. . . ."

So much was gone that Ezra, at the age of fifty-seven, had no thought of rebuilding. Back taxes owed to the United States government were due on his property as soon as the war was over. There was no money with which to pay them. The old Confederate money and the war bonds issued by the Confederate States of America were worthless. In addition the victorious United States had imposed a cotton tax as a penalty. Planters and farmers were required to pay a tax of fifteen dollars on every bale of the new cotton crop that they grew. With no money at all to pay obligations, Ezra Bennett was sick from worrying about how he would pay the cotton tax and back taxes. The federal government demanded that all taxes owed since the state left the Union be paid promptly.

Changes. Under such circumstances many plantations were seized and sold for debts at sheriffs' sales. A large number changed hands. Planters, who had little if any cash to hire farm laborers, began to sell portions of their plantations. As a result of the breakup of some of the large plantations and the opening of new lands, the number of small farms increased. But within a decade or so plantations were usually larger than ever. Some planters changed to subsistence farming. They provided for their families from their own land.

Outcome. Somehow, Ezra and others managed to pay the delinquent taxes owed to the United States. Somehow, too, they managed to pay the cotton tax. Some gradually rebuilt their homes and outbuildings. Ezra Bennett himself, like many other planters of this generation, could not face the destruction of everything he had worked for over the decades.

En Partie 2 (Studying a Part). 1. Cite the position and problems of the planter class. 2. How were some of the problems solved?

Farmers

The farmers had a different **philosophy of life** from that of the planters. Their lifestyle was simple. They were accustomed to providing their own labor force—mainly their large families. The Civil War changed none of their arrangements.

Independent farmers, both white and black,

spread out over the North Louisiana hills. They felt the damage of the war. Some lost their land when railroads were given the right-of-way to lay tracks. Some farmers "squatted" on public land. There was no record of their homesteads in the courthouses. Later, this neglect resulted in the tragedy of a number of Louisiana small farmers and plain folk losing their land. This was the land that they had cleared and farmed for years. Most of all they considered these homesteads their homes. Yet, there were no legal records. The railroads received their land.

Much of the North Louisiana population consisted of subsistence farmers. That is, they were **self-sufficient** people who supplied almost all of their needs from their farms. Most of the farmer's energies were used to grow corn and other grains. He and his family planted a garden and raised barnyard animals. Eggs, milk, corn, and other produce were traded to neighbors or to the merchants in town. In other words, the barter economy of the pioneering days resumed shortly after the war. But times were changing.

The farmer and the planter had one thing in common—cotton. After the Civil War there were several years of such heavy rains that no crops were made. Caterpillars devoured large portions of crops. The Panic of 1873 and the depression that followed added to the problems.

Some farmers saw little reason to grow commercial farm crops such as cotton.

The Wells House, built in 1776 in Natchitoches.

There was no way to market them. Many changed from commercial farming to subsistence farming. Louisiana farmers did not begin a sizable return to growing cash crops until the problems of finance and transportation were eased.

The farmer had always added to the small amount of money received from his cotton crop by taking **odd jobs**. One was to gather pine knots and stack them on the river banks to sell to steamboat captains as fuel for the boats. There were occasional jobs hauling materials for planters or merchants. Some raised range cattle in the woods. A few set up small "wildcat" sawmills to cut timber.

The farmer continued to live simply. He lived off his farm except for a few purchases elsewhere. The Civil War had brought new ideas and new desires into the piney woods. The situation of the war opened up new possibilities. People wanted more.

After the war the hill farmers, along with artisans and other wage earners, talked of ways to better themselves. They knew the country was not going to remain a frontier forever. More people were coming into the hills. They were clearing land, building homes, and starting farms. The simple life in the new country was changing.

The Civil War brought a **new thinking** to the mass of white people regarding Louisiana politics. Many had been against secession and felt they had no opportunity to vote to keep Louisiana in the Union. The war some viewed as a war over slavery brought the realization that they must break the monopoly of the ruling class. The privileges assumed by the planter-merchant class was not lost on small farmers, craftsmen, and small businessmen. They began to explore ways to get their voices heard in reform. Life on the small farms was no longer as satisfying as it had been. The farmers sought to make changes.

En Partie 3 (Studying a Part). 1. Cite the position and problems of the small farmers. 2. How were some of the problems solved?

Financial and Work Arrangements

Crop-Lien System. The crop-lien system developed. Land was no longer good security for a loan. Land value had depreciated greatly. The creditor chose instead to lend money on the unplanted crop, usually cotton. The creditor took a lien, or mortgage, on the producer's crop. Because farming is so risky, interest rates were extremely high. Cotton was so much in demand after the war that cotton farmers could get credit. Sugar planters had a much harder time securing loans. Sugar plantations required much more capital than cotton plantations.

Planters went in debt for not only one but often two and three years of making crops. Once a planter began to borrow, it was very difficult to break the chain of indebtedness. This year's profit was used to pay last year's debts. It was necessary to borrow again to make the next year's crop and pay living expenses. The credit system had always been part of the plantation system. Living was always on credit—with interest.

Small farmers were less often in debt and in debt for less. They did not own sufficient collateral to borrow money in the amounts the planter did. They were more likely to seek advances at a planter's store against the small crops they expected to harvest in the fall. Then, too, the farmer's lifestyle was much simpler and less demanding of cash outlays.

Sharecropping. The freedman had his work to offer. The planter had nothing but his land and such buildings as remained. He had no money. The only solution for him and the freedman was to pool their resources and make a crop. This was how sharecropping developed. The freedman received a share of the crop. How much he received depended upon the particular arrangements between each cropper and planter. Sharecropping had different features from one section of Louisiana to the other.

The sharecropper reported to work in the same way he had before the war. On the plantations he more often furnished nothing but his labor. The equipment used for plowing and harvesting was basically the same as it had been for centuries. The planter or overseer issued work orders the same as he had under slavery. The sharecropper received wages for his work on the land reserved for the planter's crop. The wage was credited against the charges for necessities bought at a plantation store. He received a weekly quota of rations from the plantation store. He also got a cabin, seed, tools, and a mule.

The freedmen and his family had the **use of a small strip of land** to farm as their own. The

Typical transportation in the late 1800s.

sharecropper plowed his land. He and his family planted, chopped grass out of the cotton, and harvested the crop. The planter sold it, and the sharecropper received one-fourth to one-half of the value of the cotton produced on his acre or two. He kept a portion of the corn for himself and his poultry and animals, usually hogs.

"Settlin' up time" in the fall was the time that the sharecroppers and planter figured what was due. If the planter were an honest man, he followed a simple procedure. This was a matter of adding up purchases made by the sharecropper and credits for the cropper's labor. The sharecropper was given credit for his part of the income from the sale of the cotton. If the planter were not honest, there might not be any settlement at all. In other words, the planter's word was the last word in any disagreement.

The sharecropper could not **move** without the creditor's permission. The laws of the state had been quickly changed to protect the planter or merchant to whom the sharecropper owed money. On the other hand, there was strong competition among planters for labor. The more desirable workers received better treatment and working arrangements. The sharecropper was not without options. He could leave and deprive the planter of critically needed labor. The planters' unwritten rules were even stronger controls in maintaining fair relations between planters and laborers.

The Freedmen's Bureau's supervision of labor contracts of sharecroppers added to the problems. The supervision was done with little understanding of the blacks with whom they were dealing. The result was that

such a provision as the croppper remaining on the plantation until the crop was harvested was often disregarded. If the freedmen decided to leave, they left.

The average **cash income** of the sharecropper was less than two hundred dollars a year. This can be compared with the income of the average white independent farmer of the piney woods. His annual income from two to three bales of cotton ranged from one hundred dollars to two hundred dollars. Also, the world in which the sharecropper and other plain folks lived used very little money. They produced little, if anything, to sell. Money was needed for sugar, flour, and coffee. Clothes were homemade. The lives of the planter families were not a great deal different.

Every year more and more blacks became sharecroppers. Ninety percent of the freedmen in the state eventually became sharecroppers. Life on the plantations after the war was little changed from life on plantations before the war.

Right after the war the fears of not having labor to produce the cotton crops influenced the **treatment** that the black sharecropper received. The more desirable blacks received better treatment and working agreements. Those blacks who were politically active or particularly outspoken about their civil rights were not able to find a planter willing to employ them. Those who voiced their displeasure could not find land to rent. Without land there was little hope for gaining even the bare living sharecropping provided. In other words, sharecropping became both a social and economic factor in the lives of black Louisianians.

Other Labor Sources. Some planters felt that the problems of dealing with the freedmen were so great that they searched for other sources of labor. Efforts were made to replace blacks with Chinese, Italians, and other peoples. Agents were sent to locate white families in other states to become sharecroppers on the plantations. None of these tactics worked.

Some workers were hired. Sugar plantation workers were paid from fifteen to eighteen dollars per month. These wages went to prime men. If they fed themselves, they made twenty-five to thirty dollars per month. Women, children, and older men were paid wages according to the contribution the planter thought they could make. The planter always furnished a cabin. He usually provided credit at the plantation store. Of course, the goods were usually highly priced.

Tenant Farming. Many blacks and whites entered into a tenant relationship with a large landowner. A planter usually rented portions of his land to several tenants. The tenants supplied their own seed, mules, and provisions. They were charged yearly rent without a percentage of the crop being involved. Usually only small acreage was involved in the tenant arrangement. Most tenant farmers rented only the amount of land that their families could work.

En Partie 4 (Studying a Part). 1. Describe sharecropping and tenant farming arrangements. 2. What was the crop-lien system?

The Role of the Church

Blacks and whites turned to the churches.

White Churches. Membership in white churches grew steadily. The Catholic church was still the dominant church in South Louisiana. The small Protestant churches of North Louisiana were community centers for whites. The Protestant churches were, first of all, places for religious worship. After that, they were private church schools mostly for the primary grades. By a decade after the Civil War these schools were established at almost every church. The churches also served as welfare centers. Fellow church members provided sources of help and relief

Rosedown Plantation.

Grace Episcopal Church in St. Francisville was heavily damaged during the Civil War.

in emergency situations, and the church was the place where beginning political organizations were formed. The first organizations of white farmers were get-togethers at the church buildings where mutual problems were discussed. The Farm Alliance movement came through the North Louisiana churches. The church was a social center as well. Revivals, or protracted meetings, were important in the white Protestant churches of North Louisiana.

Black Churches. Whether in New Orleans, on plantations, in villages, or in communities of independent farmers, blacks all had one center in their lives: the church. Since so many other avenues were closed to blacks,

the church played an especially important role in everyday life.

As soon as blacks were free, they set up churches whenever they could. **"Invisible"** churches that had operated under cover on some plantations sprang to life. Under the strict controls of slavery, the right of assembly of slaves had been denied. This depended upon the planter. Often gatherings of blacks had been held secretly. These gatherings were mostly in plantation quarters in the homes of members or in a vacant cabin.

The black freedmen's church became the headquarters of **benevolent associations** that handled inexpensive burial insurance for members. It was also a **welfare agency** where the orphans and elderly could find help. The church was the **political center** for sharing black problems. Blacks discussed among themselves conditions on different plantations. It was also the **educational center**. The black church gave the members an opportunity to work together in a formal organization. Very importantly, the church developed leaders. Here with their own kind they had identities as respected human beings. The church was also the center of social activities. The black churches had social and fraternal organizations, political organizations, and self-help organizations. These self-help groups were designed to aid blacks in securing land or finding employment.

These **black** churches were **non-Catholic**. Almost all were **Baptist**. The Baptist organization had no hierarchy of superior officers over the local church. Although whites sometimes offered assistance, only the black members were directly involved in the church. Therefore, in the Baptist church they were free to develop a church to fit their needs. The Methodists had the second largest number of black churches. The Catholic churches continued with integrated membership for a short time. By the 1890s Louisiana Catholics did not welcome black members. Eventually, with their large numbers, black Catholics in Lafayette and other places had their own segregated churches. The Catholic, Episcopal, and Presbyterian churches eventually lost almost all of their black members.

In some cases white ministers helped freedmen get their churches started. In order to attract workers, planters granted land for black churches. Blacks ordinarily built their churches and used them as schoolhouses. They sometimes built small schools on the church grounds. The planter may have lent teams and mules to haul logs from the woods and to a sawmill. All the work was done by members of the black congregation.

Whites were eager to have the freedmen out of white churches. As slaves, blacks had been under unquestioned white control. Freedmen were a different matter. Stories of violence between the races added nothing to the comfort of white church goers who had blacks in segregated seats of their congregations. At the same time, blacks were more than eager to secure their own meeting places. Again, however, there were exceptions.

En Partie 5 (Studying a Part). 1. Compare the role of the white and black churches. 2. (a) What were "invisible" churches? (b) Trace the history of these churches.

Education

By the mid-1870s it was clear that the federal government was withdrawing from the policy of protecting black rights. The black organizations then became even more important. The freed blacks soon realized that they were going to have to develop their own solutions. Thus, the black community turned inward. They insulated themselves within their own subculture. Black Louisianians adapted themselves to the second-class citizenship imposed on them by the majority of whites. They turned to education as a ladder on which they could climb.

Education was a prime goal of black people. Legally, it had been denied them as slaves. Blacks felt that they could overcome their inferior position in the society through education. They worked hard to establish schools of their own so that they could help each other become educated.

Public Education. The Union army first brought public education to Louisiana. Gen. Nathaniel Banks set up public schools in New Orleans during military occupation. These schools were primarily to educate the freedmen. However, they were open to whites as well. Many freedmen enrolled in the classes.

The idea of public education was not new to Louisiana. Plans for public education were outlined in both the 1845 and 1852 constitutions. Neither plan was ever put into effect. There was no public education, as we know it, in Louisiana until after the Civil War.

The Freedmen's Bureau was to provide public schools. At first Northern missionaries and philanthropists helped with these schools. During the 1870s attempts were made to integrate schools in New Orleans. Whites and blacks were to attend schools together. There were disturbances, and the integrated schools lasted only a few months. The remarkable fact about the first schools was the great enthusiasm with which the blacks greeted the schools. Actually, only a small percentage of blacks in the state attended school during this entire period. Even fewer whites enrolled in the first years of public education.

In 1877, soon after Pres. Rutherford B. Hayes was inaugurated, the Louisiana Legislature set up a dual school system. There were segregated schools for blacks and whites.

Louisiana had not recovered from the great financial losses resulting from the war effort. There was little money to fund schools. When the funds were divided, neither school system had nearly enough. The schools that did exist were of very low quality. New

The mail was delivered by horse-drawn coach.

Orleans had the best ones. As the years passed and children from the mass of both black and white people enrolled in public schools, more public money was needed. The black schools received what was left after minimum needs of the growing white schools were met. That amount was very small, and black schools were poor indeed.

Private Academies. By the time military troops had withdrawn from Louisiana, many blacks had completed their early education. They were ready for high schools. They knew that the Redeemers would not provide public funds for black secondary education. Blacks set about securing this for themselves. Groups of churches sponsored private academies. These were modeled after the private academies of the planters. The same architecture, goals, and courses were used.

The Redeemers were so busy perfecting their controls over society that they were unaware of the black educational movement going on around them. Blacks made every effort to keep their schools unnoticed by whites for fear of opposition. The academies were largely camouflaged within the church programs and attracted little attention from whites.

Leland College.

Leland College. Northern churches and interested citizens sent money, supplies, and missionaries to help the freedmen. Mr. and Mrs. Holbrook Chamberlain were visitors to New Orleans after the Civil War. The Chamberlains gave funds to found a college in New Orleans that would help educate black leaders. The American Home Mission Society gave financial support. The Chamberlains helped with more funds as the years passed. The name of the college was Leland, named for Mrs. Chamberlain's family. It was founded in 1870. Leland was moved to Baker, Louisiana, in 1923. Leland College educated many leaders who poured out over the state. Its faculty in the early years was all white. They were highly qualified persons from Harvard, Brown, and other great colleges and universities. Leland College continued to serve the black community until it closed after World War II.

Black Universities. New Orleans University was founded the following year by Methodists. Straight University, which later became Dillard, was founded during the same period.

En Partie 6 (Studying a Part). 1. Describe the status of education for both blacks and whites. 2. Name schools of higher learning established during this period.

Business and Trade

The operations of business and trade had greatly deteriorated during the war. Many people had placed their savings in Confederate bonds. Now the bonds were worthless. Businesses had sold goods to the Confederacy on credit. Those debts would never be paid. There was little gold money in the state. Confederate paper money had no value. Many businesses were closed. Cotton gins and sugar mills had been destroyed. Sugar production was almost at a standstill. The business owners had nothing to sell. The federal military control and the success of the Union navy's blockade had ruined business.

The movement of goods and products had all but ceased. Poor means of transportation and impassable roads made it difficult to obtain what was needed to rebuild and repair. Also, crops could not be shipped to market. The Mississippi River had been reopened after 1862 when New Orleans was occupied. Some river traffic continued, and New Orleans began to revive. After the war, when the Red and the Arkansas rivers were reopened, there was more traffic. New Orleans remained the main outlet for American cotton and grain being sent abroad. Railroads were gradually rebuilt. New lines were added.

Business for the state was no longer concentrated in New Orleans. Planters tended to do business closer to home. This change caused towns to grow. Baton Rouge and Shreveport grew rapidly. One big difference between the antebellum towns and the post-bellum towns was the growth of the merchant class. New Orleans factors quickly declined in importance. Many were bankrupt. The disastrous crops of 1866 and 1867 put some out of business. The commercial class of New Orleans gained with the increasing commercialization of agriculture.

The Panic of 1873 caused another major economic crisis. It brought a halt to economic development of every type in the whole nation. Louisiana suffered a setback in the slow process of regaining economic stability.

All people felt economic hardships. In one way or another the war had disturbed the lives of everyone. Life was extremely hard for many for years afterward. Families sometimes lived on short rations. The quality of life over the entire state was not high.

Reconstruction was a period of resistance and readjustment in Louisiana to Republican regulations imposed as punishment for defeat in the Civil War. The era of Reconstruction was among the unhappiest periods of Louisiana history. The old plantation system had undergone many changes. There was the slow process of the Louisiana population working out lifestyles acceptable to themselves. New lifestyles had developed for merchants, planters, white farmers, and blacks. By the end of 1877 Louisiana had again found a measure of stability and peace.

En Partie 7 (Studying a Part). 1. What was the economic picture in Louisiana during Reconstruction? 2. Why did the role of New Orleans change?

Coup de Main (Completing the Story)

Jambalaya (Putting It All Together)

1. (a) Analyze the problems facing the state after the Civil War. (b) Which problems grew out of the war? (c) Which had their roots in Southern life? (d) Which were common to all parts of the United States?

2. If Lincoln had lived, would there have

been conflict between him and Congress over Reconstruction policies? Justify your answer.

3. How did each of these groups view the situation in Louisiana after the war: (a) carpetbaggers, (b) scalawags, (c) Redeemers, (d) freedmen, and (e) Radical Republicans?

4. What complications confronted the Democratic legislature in dealing with the freedmen?

5. What caused tension between races and between Louisiana citizens and the federal government?

6. Describe the different attitudes toward national legislation passed and presidential orders issued that affected Louisiana.

7. What struggle occurred for control of the state?

8. Discuss: Congressional Reconstruction was so bitter and humiliating an experience that Southerners found it hard to forgive and even harder to forget.

9. Why were graft and corruption so widespread after the war?

10. Evaluate the Reconstruction period. Prove that it was a tragic era. Give any constructive achievements.

Potpourri (Getting Involved)

1. Conduct (a) a Ku Klux Klan meeting or dramatize their activities, (b) a meeting of the legislature under the carpetbaggers, (c) a confrontation between the two governments, or (d) a debate for or against a harsh or lenient plan for Reconstruction.

2. Compare (a) the returning soldier with the freed black, (b) the black's life before the Civil War with that after the war, or (c) violence during the war with that after the war.

3. Report on the private black academies or black colleges established during this period.

Gumbo (Bringing It Up-to-Date)

1. Explain the Fourteenth and Fifteenth amendments. Point out implications of the amendments to Louisianians during the time in which they were passed and today.

2. Compare the Civil Rights Movement with the rights of blacks after the war.

3. Compare voting rights and procedures of this period with those of today. Include the number of registered black voters for each period. Include methods used today to try to get a greater voter turnout.

4. Compare education conditions of this period with integration in education of modern times.

5. Relate the Republican party's influence on the Reconstruction period to its influence today.

PART SIX

Under Redeemer and Bourbon Rule

UNDER THE REDEEMERS AND BOURBONS: POLITICAL LIFE (1877-1927)

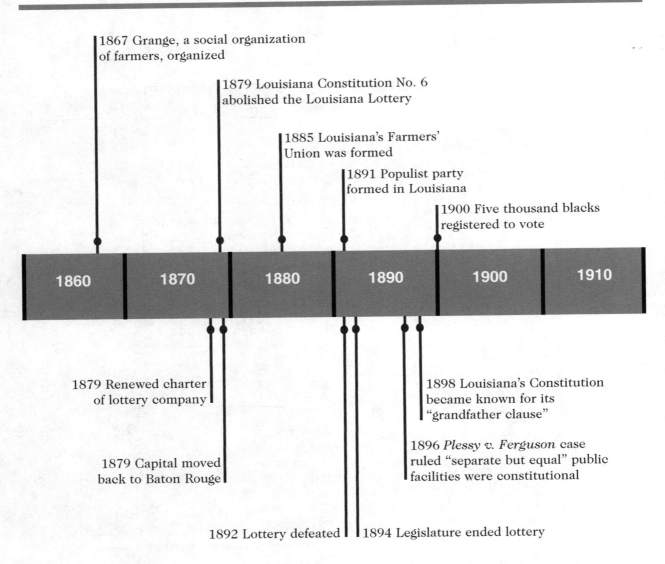

1867 Grange, a social organization of farmers, organized

1879 Louisiana Constitution No. 6 abolished the Louisiana Lottery

1885 Louisiana's Farmers' Union was formed

1891 Populist party formed in Louisiana

1900 Five thousand blacks registered to vote

| 1860 | 1870 | 1880 | 1890 | 1900 | 1910 |

1879 Renewed charter of lottery company

1879 Capital moved back to Baton Rouge

1898 Louisiana's Constitution became known for its "grandfather clause"

1896 *Plessy v. Ferguson* case ruled "separate but equal" public facilities were constitutional

1892 Lottery defeated   1894 Legislature ended lottery

Overleaf: *Early automobile enthusiasts at Libuse in Rapides Parish about 1920.*

UNDER THE REDEEMERS AND BOURBONS: POLITICAL LIFE

1877-1879

By March 1877 there was no question about the final victory in the struggle for political control. The Redeemers won. After four years of war and twelve years of Reconstruction, control of the state government was returned to Louisiana. Redeemers were the political leaders of the state at that time. The shape of things to come was almost altogether up to the Redeemers—but not quite.

The "Understanding" with the North. Leading to the compromise, which gave Republican Rutherford B. Hayes the presidency, there were "understandings" between the Republicans and the Redeemers. Much was written down, but some matters were understood above and beyond the written agreements. These "understood" matters were the cautious reminders regarding the freedmen.

Northern officials wanted assurance that the freedom of the former slaves would not be limited. The understanding with the South was that political freedom and equality were to be assured all state residents. Much of this was written into law, but there was no guarantee of the civil rights of freedmen. Equal opportunity for education was a promise.

The unwritten code of the planters had always had more force in directing the actions of people in Louisiana than those written down in laws. This understanding with the North shaped the course of action of the Redeemers. If the Redeemers had felt completely free of the North, they would have limited the freedom of the blacks more than they did in 1877. Only the fear of provoking Northern interference against their policies toward blacks kept the Redeemers from taking immediate action.

Action of Redeemers was delayed in two areas. The Redeemers felt very strongly about both areas—**black suffrage** (voting) and **black education.** They could not tolerate black suffrage. It was the final blow to the planter outlook on white supremacy. Education for plantation labor would destroy plantations in the future. The planter dedication to near private education for whites had provided planters with a monopoly on the tools of formal education. It should not be overlooked, however, that many self-educated whites and blacks had existed all along in the population.

The Status of Freedmen. By 1877 freedmen were voting. Some held political offices. They had the freedom to obtain an education, and they had the right of assembly. The status of the freedmen was not the same as that of white citizens, however.

Redeemers wanted to return to controls

PROBLEMS IN 1877

Enormous State Debt

High Taxes

Bad Agricultural Conditions

Little Money

Poor General Business Conditions

used before the war for slaves on plantations. Controls were needed to keep cheap labor available and dependable for critical work in the fields.

There was also the matter of money. The war had left most people impoverished. It would take decades to rebuild what had been destroyed by the war.

Redeemers in Triumph. The Redeemers acquired a new look after 1877. "Redemption" was not something in the future. Redemption was accomplished. Rapidly the planter-businessman-Democrat became even more visibly in control of the state than before the war. These men wore the airs of kings. They were called **"Bourbons"** because of their arrogance. The absolute monarch, Louis XIV, for whom Louisiana was named, was a Bourbon. Some linked the planters and Bourbon kings with a saying, "They never learned anything and never forgot anything." Another phrase from a Bourbon king fits the governing group even better. That was the statement of Louis XIV, who said, "I am the state." The Bourbons of Louisiana held the same views except that they believed not in a single ruler, but in the rule of an **elite**, a select few. Their idea was that, by nature, the better-educated people with property were meant to govern men with less education and less property. They were the state.

Bourbon Control. The Bourbons managed to dominate Louisiana government as if they were kings. Yet, this was within the United States where the people are supposed to rule. Before the war planters had been in control. They were now joined by an increasingly large merchant class. The planter-merchant elite—the Bourbons—felt it even more important to dominate politics completely. The disasters of war and military must never happen again. Bourbon Democrats must remain in power forever. Or so they thought.

Nicholls' Administration. Francis Nicholls was governor of Louisiana. He was a planter, and he shared the attitudes of planters. He was the kind of man who would rule the state for decades. Like most whites, North and South, he believed in white supremacy. He was rejected by some planters for being what they considered too liberal toward

Governor Francis T. Nicholls.

blacks. Perhaps the difference was that Nicholls felt times were changing and that some concessions must be made.

Marshal Packard left with the federal troops. Some of Packard's legislators remained in the new Louisiana Legislature. Money from the Louisiana Lottery was used to silence anyone who might cause trouble. Maj. E. A. Burke, the corrupt Republican who headed the Louisiana Lottery, supported Nicholls. Burke was state treasurer.

A special meeting of the Louisiana Legislature was called in 1877, as soon as President Hayes was inaugurated. A great deal of work was done in reshaping the state government the way the Bourbons wanted it. Government expenses were cut. State services started for the first time during Reconstruction were reduced. The public education system was restyled.

The legislature adopted new election laws and destroyed the Returning Board. These boards had been instituted in answer to the tactics of Bourbons to control elections. These included intimidation of black voters, violence, stealing ballot boxes, and the like. Now there was no penalty for falsifying election returns. Bourbons did what they could to decrease Republican votes.

Election Controls. The Bourbons set up a system to control elections similar to the one that had existed during Reconstruction. They feared that not only blacks but many whites would be denied the right to vote.

One prospect that quickly proved a reality was the planter control of the black vote. Individual planters cast ballots for the share-croppers on their plantations. Ballots were printed. Voters marked their choices by hand. Planters either supervised or actually marked the ballots for the sharecroppers. A handful of white planters, voting blacks employed on their plantations, dominated the state.

These Bourbon Democrats called their government "a taxpayers' government." Yet the elite paid little or no taxes. Large planters and businessmen received tax reductions. Governor Nicholls complained that "men of large means" did not pay their taxes and that something should be done about it. Nothing was. Protest voters from the hills had no chance of outvoting the planters and their black votes. White voters among non-planters greatly outnumbered planter votes. Planter use of the Republican law for blacks to vote simply added to planter power.

Louisiana Constitution No. 6: 1879. Governor Nicholls signed a bill passed by the legislature in 1879 to abolish the Louisiana Lottery. Maj. E. A. Burke, Louisiana political boss and state treasurer, engineered action to destroy Nicholls politically and save the lottery. An order from a federal judge kept the law that would abolish the lottery from going into effect. He issued a temporary restraining order. The lottery company had only begun. Lottery officials produced, in quick order, the calling of a constitutional convention.

Nicholls was out of office with the passage of the new constitution. The convention shortened the terms of office by a year. That vindictive action was taken because Nicholls dared to oppose Burke's lottery.

The 1879 constitution increased the power of the governor. The power of the legislature and local officials was reduced. The **capital** was **moved** back to **Baton Rouge** from New Orleans. Southern University was established. The University of New Orleans was created for blacks. Louisiana State Agricultural and Mechanical College (1873) and Louisiana State University (1860) were merged.

Louisiana Lottery Company. The new constitution, after eight days of debate, included an article to give the Louisiana Lottery Company a charter to last twenty-five years.

Lottery Leadership. All of this effort was the work of Maj. E. A. Burke. Burke had demonstrated just how powerful both he and the lottery were. Burke owned the *New Orleans Times.* When the *New Orleans Democrat* was going bankrupt, Burke purchased the paper. The **Democrat** was the chief newspaper that opposed the lottery. Burke received help from the lottery to purchase the paper. He then combined the two newspapers. The newspaper praised the great benefits of the Louisiana Lottery.

Kansas Fever. Times were hard, and plans for the new 1879 constitution disturbed blacks. They feared that the Redeemers planned to take away their remaining civil rights. Under these conditions, "Kansas fever" affected many Louisiana blacks. A rumor spread through the state that better opportunities awaited blacks in Kansas. How many blacks actually left in the mass movement from this state to Kansas is unknown. But many thousands tried. "Kansas landings" remain, like one on Boeuf River near Rayville. It is a sad reminder of the planned exodus to a promised land. Many groups of frustrated blacks waited at such landings to catch rides on steamboats that passed them by. It was strongly suggested that the failure of the boats to stop was arranged by the planters. Planters were greatly concerned over this movement among their plantation workers. They tried to prevent the freedmen from leaving.

Typical dress around 1880.

Many of those who made it to Kansas soon returned. They did not find the "heaven on earth" they were seeking. The people of Kansas did not welcome them as they thought they would. The migrants lacked the skills needed for wheat farming as well.

En Partie 1 (Studying a Part). 1. What was the "understanding" with the North? 2. (a) Identify the Bourbons. (b) How did they control the government? 3. Which two privileges did the Bourbons not want to give the freedmen? 4. Describe "Kansas fever."

Bourbons and the Lottery

Bourbon Government. A new governor, Louis Wiltz, was elected at the same time the constitution was ratified. Wiltz was a New Orleans Democrat who had served as chairman of the 1879 constitutional convention.

The lieutenant governor elected was Samuel McEnery, brother of a former governor. When Wiltz died two years later, McEnery became governor. He was elected to the office in 1883. He served as governor from 1881 until 1888. McEnery's chief asset was his willingness to allow Burke, the man running the lottery, to run the state.

During McEnery's governorship the Bourbons ruled the state. A state Democratic convention nominated candidates for office. Delegates were elected according to the population. Due to the large numbers of black sharecroppers on the plantations, the big planters won elections. The planters controlled the votes of their black sharecroppers as long as blacks voted after 1877. The New Orleans ring controlled elections in the city. The Republican party was gradually being eliminated from the state. The strong Democratic party gave the Bourbons complete control of the government.

Governor Nicholls became governor a second time in 1888. The people had become dissatisfied with the Burke-McEnery government running the state. Burke went out of office.

The Lottery Question. The Louisiana Lottery received bets totaling between twenty million and thirty million dollars annually by 1890. Of this gross amount, 40 percent was profit.

The 1879 constitution renewed the charter of the lottery company for twenty-five years. There was great concern among lottery officials that those opposing the lottery would destroy it at last. Feverish activity began by 1890 to secure another renewal of the charter.

An election for governor fell in 1892. That year the Louisiana Lottery Company offered the state thirty times as much as it had been paying. That would amount to 1.2 million dollars.

The Anti-Lottery League's efforts to destroy the lottery equaled those of the Louisiana Lottery Company to extend it. The Farmers' Union was persuaded to join hands with the Anti-Lottery League. Out of all this, Anti-Lottery Democrats, or Reform Democrats, nominated Murphy J. Foster of St. Mary Parish for governor. Foster led in efforts to reach the goals of the Bourbons.

There were five political parties in Louisiana in 1892. These were the Anti-Lottery Democrats, the Regular Democrats, the Populists, the Anti-Lottery Republicans, and the Regular (pro-Lottery) Republicans. Each nominated a full slate of candidates. The contest was so heated that fistfights and even duels erupted. Murphy J. Foster, the Anti-Lottery Democrat, won the race for governor.

The lottery was **defeated.** The people did not want it even if there would be enough money from it to pay off the state debt. The lottery company moved to Honduras. However, it continued to sell lottery tickets in Louisiana. It took another act of the Louisiana Legislature to prohibit the sale. In 1894 the legislature finally legally ended the entire lottery business throughout the state. It existed illegally for many more years. For over twenty years it had dominated the government of the state.

Foster's Administration. Governor Foster led a movement to take the right to vote

Governor Murphy J. Foster, whose grandson was also elected governor a century later.

from those he termed "the ignorant and unpropertied" in the state. This was mainly an effort to take suffrage from the blacks. This disenfranchisement of freedmen represented the Bourbon response to the outcry of the non-planter whites. The whites resented the common practice of the Bourbons controlling the black vote.

En Partie 2 (Studying a Part). 1. Explain the one-party system. 2. (a) Define disenfranchise. (b) How were people disenfranchised? 3. (a) List the effects of the lottery. (b) What happened to it?

Frontier Violence, Change, and Reform

Lynchings. Between 1882 and 1903, there was a total of 285 lynchings reported in Louisiana. Most of the victims—232—were black. How many lynchings went unreported is unknown, but there were undoubtedly many.

Violence was a part of the lifestyle of people on the frontier, and Louisiana was still a part of the frontier. Only a handful took part in the beatings, burnings, and lynchings that were carried out. Yet, it was clear that little could, or would, be done to stop those who did.

Services. Very little was done by the government to provide for the health needs of the people. The **asylum for the insane** at Jackson was a disgrace. The mentally ill in New Orleans were locked up in a prison. The disabled, the blind, the deaf, and the mute occupied an inadequate building in Baton Rouge. After 1880 many parishes established **poor farms** to care for those in financial need. Private citizens or religious organizations took care of some of the unfortunates. **Charity Hospital** in New Orleans provided services for people from all over the state. In 1894 the **leprosarium** at Carville was opened. In 1921 the Carville institution became the responsibility of the federal government. The Gillis W. Long Hansen's Disease Center was the only inpatient facility in the United States devoted primarily to Hansen's disease (leprosy) when it closed in June 1999.

Yellow Fever did not affect the state during the Civil War. As soon as ships from the tropical countries returned to New Orleans, the deadly fever returned. In 1878 another epidemic swept over the country. New

Orleans had nearly four thousand victims. Finally the state set up a system of quarantine. After this system began, there were fewer epidemics and fewer victims.

In 1905 New Orleans suffered an unusually severe epidemic of yellow fever. Approximately one thousand people died in Louisiana in 1905. This was the last time yellow fever was reported in North America until 1996. By then it was established that mosquitoes were the carriers of the disease. Great efforts were made to get rid of mosquitoes.

One person who greatly aided the victims of yellow fever in New Orleans was Margaret Haughery (HAW er i). A statue raised to her memory is said to be the first ever to honor a woman in this country.

The **convict lease system** of Louisiana was a disgrace. Since before the war, prisoners were leased to private companies. About three-fourths of these convicts were black. One company, S. L. James and Associates, had a monopoly on the lease of convicts. People who wanted to lease convicts had to deal with James. James rented convicts to contractors for much more than he had paid for them. Huge profits were made from this business. The courts provided a steady flow of convicts. There were always replacements for the convicts who did not survive the cruel treatment they received. The convict-lease system stayed in existence until W. W. Heard became governor in 1900.

Farmers' Organizations. Life for the small farmer changed radically after the war. The farmers began to meet together to discuss their problems. In 1867 farmers of the United States formed a social organization called the Grange, or the Patrons of Husbandry. By 1874 there were about ten thousand members in

Margaret Haughery.

Louisiana. The Grange sponsored gatherings, picnics, and retreats to provide more entertainment and social life. Meetings were often held in community lodges.

The Grange recognized the mutual **problems** of black and white farmers. The first Grange lodge included both races. The farmers' group worked for racial cooperation in agricultural reform. It became a pioneer in its goal of instilling an appreciation of the dignity of the farmer's role. Grange members tried to get lower freight rates on rail and steamboat shipments. Better schools and clean government with honest elections were among their goals. They provided training for leaders who would operate future farm organizations.

The Grange introduced **farm cooperative stores** for purchasing supplies and marketing produce. Goods were obtained wholesale through a state agency. In the 1870s most of the co-ops in Louisiana were closed. The economic depression in the midst of the political and social chaos caused them to fail.

Louisiana farmers felt that the lottery was indirectly responsible for the lack of attention to their problems. If the government had not been involved with the lottery, they believed there would have been more time to handle farmers' problems.

The Grange did not prove to be an effective vehicle for these early reformers. Perhaps it served its purpose in laying the foundation of the reform movement. The Grange died out by the end of Reconstruction. The interest and attention to reform among these people was still alive. There was, however, little if any formal organization of farmers for a decade.

In 1885 J. A. Tetts organized the **Louisiana Farmers' Union** in Lincoln Parish. By 1887

Rural home about 1900.

there were ten thousand members in this state. At that time, the Louisiana organization combined with the Texas Farmers' Alliance. The new organization was the largest national farm organization ever to exist. Its name was the **National Farmers' Alliance and Industrial Union,** or Southern Alliance. It had over three million members in 1887.

Populists. The Farmers' Union (the Farm Alliance groups) of the 1880s lasted until the 1890s. After the merger of the Farmers' Alliance and the Anti-Lottery League, those who opposed the merger left the group.

In October 1891 the splinter group met in Alexandria. A new direction proved more appealing. This produced the People's party—the Populists. No matter what name it was called, the discontented rural people were bent on reform. The movement had begun in the Midwest and gained national importance. The Populists organized in Winn and other hill country parishes. They bitterly resented the Bourbon Democrats. They wanted a government that responded to the people.

The Populists wanted the federal **government** to **establish warehouses** and **storage facilities** for their crops. They demanded **public ownership** of **railroads.** Crops were shipped by railroad. Northern industry received favored railroad rates. Populists wanted public ownership of utilities as well.

The Populists did not want a handful of party members electing candidates. The people wanted to elect the senators to Congress. At that time they were elected by the State Senate in Baton Rouge. There were also demands, such as a **secret ballot,** the Populist party was making in other states.

They wanted other things. Populists

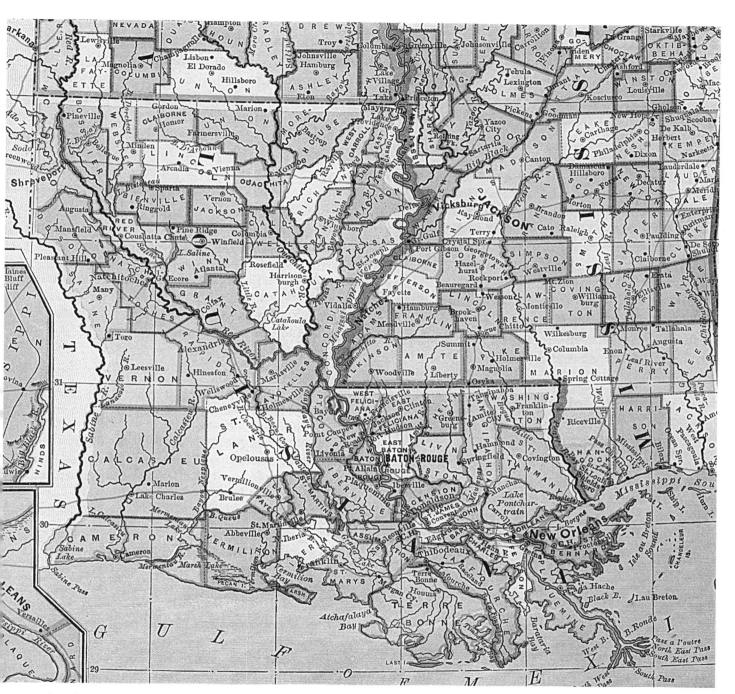

Louisiana in 1885.

wanted a **graduated income tax.** They wanted a **way to put forth legislation.** They wanted to be able to **recall** undesirable officials. They demanded **equalization** of **tax assessments** in the state. They also wanted the **unlimited production** of **silver coins.**

The hostility against the Bourbon Democrats increased. Populists formed a group whose voice was heard among the many people who were non-planters. There were few Populists in South Louisiana. The Republicans were in a similar situation. Louisiana sugar planters' need for the protective tariff was the same as the need of Northern manufacturers who voted Republican. For this reason the sugar planters voted the Republican ticket.

The "lily-white" Republicans and Populists formed a "fusion ticket" in 1892. John N. Pharr, a rich sugar planter from the coast, was the candidate of the Fusion party. He came in last in the election. However, this action produced evidence of Populist strength in the state.

The Populists were led by leaders from the hotbed of reformers, Winn Parish, the center of the hill country. Hardy Brian published a newspaper, the *Winnfield Comrade.* With the support of the people of the parish, he expressed the feelings of most of the people of his area about the government.

The **Populist** party in Louisiana **disappeared** after the **1896** election. Only the formal organization of the Populist party was gone. The mass of people still shared a hunger for a voice in the government and a redistribution of unequal wealth. Their desires did not disappear. They would find new expression for their dissent and work toward reform.

The Bourbon Democrats countered the Populist-Republican vote in their own way. They felt that any means were justified to save the state from the Populists and Republicans. The Bourbons had controlled the sharecroppers' votes for a long time. There was no way for them to lose an election as long as they did it their way. They felt the heat of mass hostility so warm against them that they resolved not to endure such a risk again.

1898 Constitution. After the 1896 election, plans were made to elect delegates to write yet another Louisiana constitution. This constitution completed the planters' movement. It was written by Bourbon delegates. There was only one Populist delegate. The constitution was not submitted to the electorate for approval. The 1898 constitution was very much like the 1879 constitution. The major difference was in the restrictions placed on voting.

The Bourbons, however, insisted on provisions to limit the vote. A voter had to own property worth three hundred dollars or had to know how to read. A **poll tax** of one dollar per year was imposed. A receipt for two years' payment of taxes had to be presented at the polls to qualify to vote.

The inconvenience and cost of qualifying to vote eliminated many more potential voters. Horseback riding or vehicles drawn by horses were the means for people to ride to the polls. For many people courthouses were a day's ride away.

The Louisiana Constitution of 1898 has long since become known for its famous **"grandfather clause."** Those whose father or grandfather had voted prior to 1867 did not have to meet literacy requirements. The chief

School buses were pulled by horses near the turn of the century.

purpose of the "grandfather clause" was to eliminate the black vote instituted after the Civil War.

The Bourbons were not so sure of their power that they totally disregarded the hostility of the Populists. Continued great excesses in power might bring about the downfall of even the powerful Bourbons. They thought it wise to make some concessions.

The provisions of the 1898 constitution were concessions to the common people. A **railroad commission** was **created**. It later became the Public Service Commission. Utilities were included in its jurisdiction. The State Department of Agriculture and Immigration was expanded. A **state primary system** was planned for the nomination of candidates. The way was paved for school districts to vote bond issues for construction of buildings and maintenance of schools.

Jim Crow Laws. "Drawing the color line" was a phrase used to describe separation of blacks and whites. This was the goal of the Bourbons. The dual school system became the first legal action in **segregating the two races.** Such laws separating blacks and whites came to be known as "Jim Crow" laws. The name came from a comic character in Broadway minstrel shows.

In 1891 Louisiana passed a law requiring separate coaches on railroads for blacks and whites. This law was the first of a series of segregation laws that divided the races in all public places. After trains were segregated, the next step was to furnish separate rest rooms at the depots. Such laws included public drinking fountains and eating places.

Segregation laws were passed to ensure that the black and white races were separated in every aspect except the workplace. Laws were passed segregating the races in mental institutions (1902), in streetcars (1902), in saloons (1908), at circuses (1914), and in prisons (1918).

In 1896 the United States Supreme Court gave its decision on the ***Plessy v. Ferguson*** case. Homer Plessy (PLES sē), a Louisiana black man, had challenged the law requiring separation of the races. The court ruled that "separate but equal" public facilities were constitutional. This decision settled for half a century the legal right of the state to provide segregated schools for blacks and whites.

Political Power. The Republican party remained active in political campaigns until the early 1900s. In 1900 Bourbon **Democrat W. W. Heard** of Union Parish was elected **governor** by a large majority. The Republican party was no longer a threat. The one-party system was assured.

The Bourbons now had no party to challenge them. On January 1, 1897, 130,000 blacks were registered to vote. By early 1900 only about five thousand black voters were

Registering to vote in Shreveport in 1894.

registered. Even that number decreased within a few years. Within a few years, too, the number of white registered voters declined to a little more than half of the number in 1897.

Now that the 1898 constitution kept blacks from voting, the planters no longer had black votes to add to their own. Now they felt Bourbon power was so secure that they did not need their sharecroppers' votes any longer. Louisiana was now a one-party state. It belonged to the Democratic party.

En Partie 3 (Studying a Part). 1. Identify (a) "grandfather clause," (b) "Jim Crow" laws, (c) Populists, and (d) suffrage. 2. How many lynchings took place between 1882 and 1913? 3. (a) Why did farmers begin to organize after the Civil War? (b) What was the effect of these organizations? 4. How did the *Plessy v. Ferguson* case affect education? 5. Explain the significance of the 1898 constitution. 6. Which party controlled the state?

UNDER THE REDEEMERS AND BOURBONS: INDUSTRY AND AGRICULTURE (1877-1927)

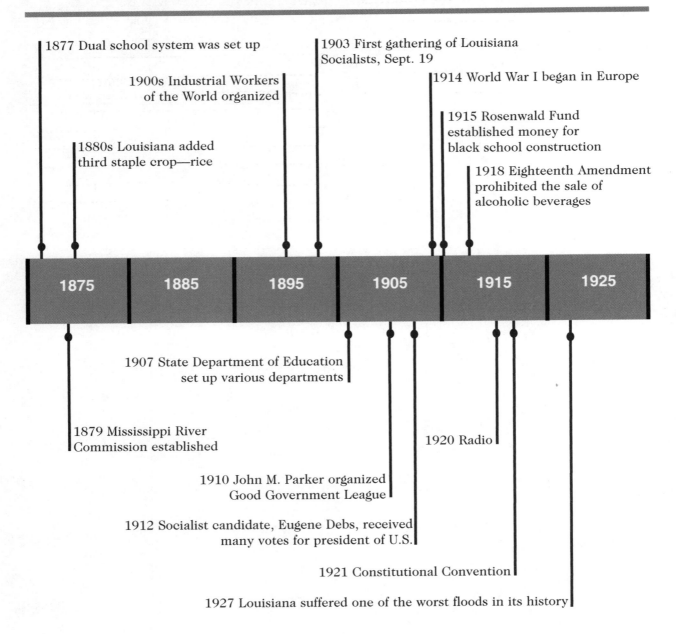

1877 Dual school system was set up

1903 First gathering of Louisiana Socialists, Sept. 19

1900s Industrial Workers of the World organized

1914 World War I began in Europe

1915 Rosenwald Fund established money for black school construction

1880s Louisiana added third staple crop—rice

1918 Eighteenth Amendment prohibited the sale of alcoholic beverages

1875   1885   1895   1905   1915   1925

1907 State Department of Education set up various departments

1879 Mississippi River Commission established

1920 Radio

1910 John M. Parker organized Good Government League

1912 Socialist candidate, Eugene Debs, received many votes for president of U.S.

1921 Constitutional Convention

1927 Louisiana suffered one of the worst floods in its history

UNDER THE REDEEMERS AND BOURBONS: INDUSTRY AND AGRICULTURE

Lumber Industry

Sawmill Invasion. Miles of railroads were laid in Louisiana between the 1880s and 1900. As soon as the railroads were laid, investors arrived. They were eager to convert Louisiana's vast forests into lumber. The forests still covered approximately seventy-five percent of the state. For nearly two decades lumbermen came into the state. The investors included Midwesterners and Northeastern financiers and Texas and Oklahoma lumbermen.

In the early 1900s huge **mills** operated twenty-four hours a day all year. By 1904 Louisiana was leading the South in lumber production with 2.25 billion board feet per year. By 1909 the state had reached its peak of over sixteen billion board feet per year. The Great Southern Lumber Company of Bogalusa (bō gə LŌŌ sə), established in 1908, had become the largest lumber mill in the world. By 1925 many of the great forests were gone.

Company towns sprang up in the forests almost overnight during the time of the sawmill invasion. Boomtowns grew up all over the state. The life of these sawmill towns probably averaged fewer than twenty years. One and all of the lumber companies had the policy: **"cut out and get out."** Lake Charles, Winnfield, and Bogalusa survive today.

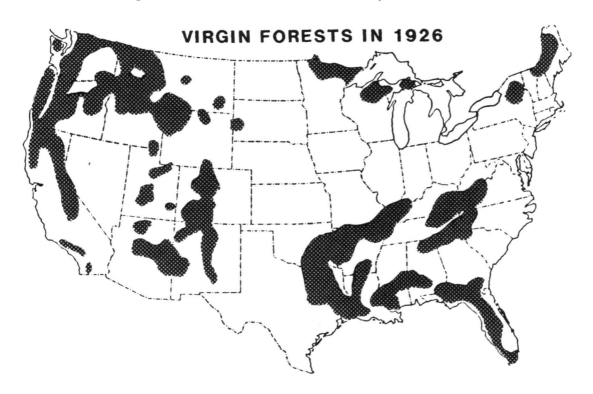

VIRGIN FORESTS IN 1926

These sawmill towns were built in the center of the timber holdings. They had company-owned houses, churches, and commissaries (company stores). They also had the big mill with its log ponds in which the logs were unloaded from the rail cars.

The hill-country farmers sold the timber off their land, if not the land itself. They themselves became employees of the sawmill. Many people, including Indians, found employment for the first time. The Northern owners managed their employees with an iron hand. Excitement over the sawmills faded into the grim reality of the ruthless lumber companies. Farmers soon realized that the invaders forever destroyed not only the vast pine forests but also the simple life on the frontier. Indeed, as the timber was cut wild game had a smaller habitat. **Wages** at the sawmill appeared small for the long hours that practically eliminated family life. Ten- and eleven-hour work days continued six days a week.

Wages ranged from $2.50 a week for the least skilled to ten dollars for the most skilled. Even these wages were often not paid in cash. Instead, the workers got **"scrip."** Scrip was a certificate of money owed the workers. Prices were higher at the company store. Scrip was only redeemable in making purchases at the company store.

Unions. There were many workers from all over the nation who poured into Louisiana with the sawmills. They brought new ideas from these other sections.

Labor unions were organized in the sawmill communities. This was not done without bloodshed. The mill owners were supported by considerable public feeling. Most people had never faced the idea that labor had rights.

Nineteenth-century sawmill in Winn Parish.

Railroads reaching out into the isolated sawmill communities brought newcomers. Ideas spread to Louisiana from California, Kansas, and other states regarding fundamental changes in the social and political life of the country. The nine-hour workday, higher wages, elimination of child labor, nationalization of railroads and utilities, accident and unemployment insurance, survivor's benefits—all these new ideas were causing working people to think of a way to obtain some of the material blessings enjoyed by the more prosperous.

Reforestation. By the 1900s the state was left with endless acres of cutover land. Such land sold for as little as ten cents an acre.

The priceless timber resources were gone. Louisiana had paid a terrible price for the brief years of employment afforded by the invading lumber companies. Many thought that there would never be anything more than the bleak land without trees. Some men thought differently. Through their replanting and other efforts Louisiana's important industry was developed anew.

En Partie 1 (Studying a Part). 1. Describe the invasion by the sawmill owners. 2. (a) Trace the organization of sawmill workers' unions. (b) What new ideas did they introduce? 3. Analyze the impact of the sawmill industry on the state.

Introduction of New Ideas

Labor Organizations. Violence flared between the sawmill employees and the mill owners during the first decade of the new century. The years of labor disturbances in southwestern Louisiana before World War I were known as the "Louisiana Lumber War." In 1910 owners of the largest mills in Louisiana, Arkansas, and Texas met to discuss the organizing of labor. The owners organized into the powerful Southern Lumber Operators' Association. They vowed not to hire anybody who belonged to a union or anyone who would join one.

The sawmill owners tried to enforce their rule. The laborers felt that they were free people and would join unions if they chose to do so. Laborers called the contract that owners required of them a "yellow dog contract." Any worker who signed one was a "yellow dog."

The group called the **Industrial Workers of the World** (the "Wobblies") and the Socialist party were closely allied. Often the same leaders appeared in both. The same was true

Early logging industry used mules for heavy labor.

of the Brotherhood of Timber Workers.

When the **Southern Lumber Operators' Association** declared war on the Union, eleven sawmills near DeRidder were closed. Three thousand men lost their jobs.

The **union goals** included an eight-hour workday, an end to forced trading at company stores, and a $2.50-per-day minimum wage for common laborers.

Political Choices. It was no accident that the Louisiana voters of 1912 gave the Socialist **candidate,** Eugene Debs, many votes for **president** of the United States. One out of every fourteen who voted in Louisiana voted for Debs. He received more votes in the state than the Republican Taft. In Winn Parish in 1912 Socialists elected almost the full slate of parish officers. The Socialists were a threat to the Democrats' one-party political monopoly.

In the first years of the new twentieth century, the **Democratic party** dominated Louisiana politics. For nearly three decades the state was run by that party alone. Only Democrats could vote in a Democratic primary. Since almost everyone was a Democrat, this was the only election that counted.

The simmering discontent of laboring people and hill-country farmers burned at white heat. Hostility and disgust had been expressed in the **Populist** party.

The sawmill owners and planters were exactly alike in their attitudes toward workers. Sawmill owners had no such feeling of responsibility toward their workers. The planters and sawmill owners became allies. The Choctaw Club of New Orleans found both groups to be political friends. The great oil companies and Union Sulphur Company took the side of management. These groups controlled the government.

Plowing often was work for young boys.

Other Industrial Development. Louisiana's industrial development of minerals began in the 1900s. Abundant natural resources discovered throughout the state formed the basis for industry. **Salt, sulphur, oil,** and **natural gas** were first produced commercially during this period. The fur, seafood, moss, and other industries also developed at this time.

En Partie 2 (Studying a Part). 1. Trace the development of the Socialist party. 2. What were some of the goals of the protesting people? 3. Describe the industrial development of this period.

Postwar Agriculture

Status. The agricultural **picture** in Louisiana

was very **bleak** during this entire period. This was true for the entire United States between 1865 and 1900. Overproduction contributed to falling prices. The rapid growth of new farmlands, the development of new farm machinery, the use of commercial fertilizers, and improved methods of farming increased production. Prices fell drastically. Cotton sold for sixty-five cents a pound in 1860. In 1895 it sold for five cents. With the South out of the Union during the Civil War other countries began growing cotton. At the same time farmers had to pay high prices for the goods they needed. The value of farmland and equipment fell.

Yet, the Bourbons, with the sharecropper labor, **rebuilt** the **plantation system**. Plantations continued to dominate life in Louisiana. Factors were again in business in New Orleans. Planters secured money necessary to produce crops at high interest rates through factors. Again, goods were shipped by water from New Orleans to various points in the state. Warehouses and the hauling business continued.

Many former aristocratic planters were trying to restore their old places to their pre-Civil War conditions. The small farmers barely managed to provide the essentials for their families. The economy improved little.

For two decades after the Civil War the sugarcane industry barely survived. It was three decades before the industry recovered to the 1862 level of production. In 1861 the value of sugar planters' property

THE COTTON PRESS.

Plantation cotton press in the nineteenth century.

Sugarcane workers, about 1887.

reached nearly two hundred million dollars. By the end of the war the value amounted to about sixteen million. The sugar industry would never again contribute to the prosperity of the state to the extent it had before the war.

Sharecropping was not used for sugarcane production. Large labor gangs were needed during certain periods of the season. Wages stayed relatively high. Planters were afraid to try to reduce wages for fear of losing their labor force.

The sugarcane **workers** went on **strike** during the 1880s. Some of the strikers protested wage cuts. Most wanted higher wages. Strikes were not successful.

Before the end of the nineteenth century **sugarcane operations** had changed. Corporations bought out plantations and built better sugar mills. Sugar-making was taken over by the corporations. Planters sold their cane by the ton. They organized cooperatives. Either the co-ops or the corporations ground the cane. Blacks still formed most of the labor force.

Cotton continued to be the most important single crop in Louisiana. It was in demand briefly after the Civil War, but prices fell. Cotton farmers struggled. Cotton did not reach the pre-war level of production. There are those who contend that the world demand for cotton reached its peak about the time of the Civil War. During four years of war other areas of the world found that they could grow cotton.

Rice. During the 1880s Louisiana added a third staple crop—rice. The introduction of this crop to southwestern Louisiana was directly related to the **railroad**. The Watkins Railroad made a dramatic slash through the western Louisiana wilderness. This railroad was first called the Louisiana Western Railroad. In 1865 it joined the Southern Pacific system. A Kansas banker, Jabez B. Watkins, owned the company. The new railroad ran through forests from Lake Charles to Alexandria. Lake Charles had begun as the site of a large sawmill. Watkins saw the value of attracting migrants into southwestern Louisiana. He promoted the area among Midwest grain growers. They came in large numbers. **Seaman A. Knapp** (nap),

Cotton gin scales at Frogmore Plantation.

the president of Iowa Agricultural College, was persuaded to come. The name Knapp became famous in Louisiana because of his pioneer work in rice development. Knapp discovered that the hardpan of the Louisiana prairies could be used to hold the water to irrigate rice. Within a few years the grain farmers of the Midwest transformed southwestern Louisiana into the "Rice Capital of the World."

Agricultural Progress. After 1900 Louisiana farm production recovered. Plantations developed in the valleys between North Louisiana hills. Many of these were made by combining small farms. New varieties of sugarcane contributed to increased production. The agricultural experiment station at Kenner helped spread new knowledge about agriculture. Farmers learned scientific methods from government agencies and other groups. Prices of farm products and consumer goods were more in balance than they were before the war. By 1920 Louisiana agriculture had reestablished itself as a force in the American economy.

En Partie 3 (Studying a Part). 1. What problems did farmers face? 2. What was the economic picture in agriculture in the early 1900s? 3. Cite changes in agriculture.

Transportation

Louisiana's economic development depended on good transportation. Water transportation was extremely important, especially for commercial traffic. **Water navigation** on the Mississippi was greatly improved by James B. Eads, a noted engineer. The maintenance of a channel at the mouth of the river deep enough for large ships was a big problem.

Steamboats finally disappeared from the rivers and bayous of the state. **Trains** provided long-distance traveling. Most of the state was rural. **Horses and carriages** were the chief mode of transportation in local areas.

There was no system of state **roads**. Roads were built by parishes or by towns. Louisiana roads were still mostly muddy trails. There was a growing need for better roads.

The stagecoach ride was a rough one. It cost fifteen dollars per passenger. If it rained and the stagecoach bogged down in the clay hills, everybody, including passengers, had to get out of the coach to help push it out of the muck. Sometimes robbers bolted out of the woods in Ouachita Parish to waylay the coach. They robbed the passengers and stole any valuable goods that might be aboard. They even took the team of horses or oxen.

> **En Partie 4 (Studying a Part).** 1. How did James B. Eads help transportation? 2. What were the chief means of transportation during this period? 3. (a) What means were used for local travel? (b) Long-distance travel?

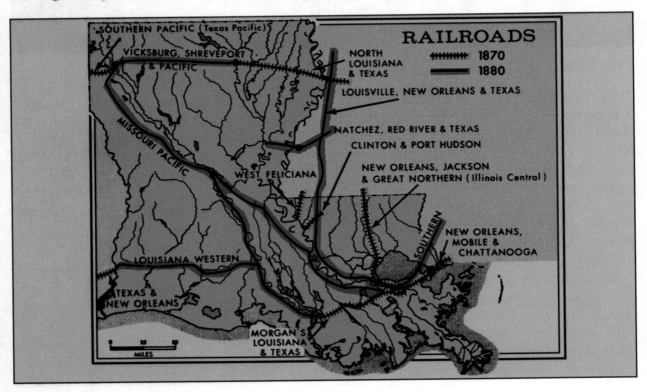

RAILROADS

SOUTHERN PACIFIC (Texas Pacific)
VICKSBURG, SHREVEPORT & PACIFIC
NORTH LOUISIANA & TEXAS
LOUISVILLE, NEW ORLEANS & TEXAS
NATCHEZ, RED RIVER & TEXAS
CLINTON & PORT HUDSON
NEW ORLEANS, JACKSON & GREAT NORTHERN (Illinois Central)
NEW ORLEANS, MOBILE & CHATTANOOGA
MISSOURI PACIFIC
WEST FELICIANA
SOUTHERN
LOUISIANA WESTERN
TEXAS & NEW ORLEANS
MORGAN'S LOUISIANA & TEXAS

+++++++ 1870
━━━━━ 1880

MILES

Flood Control

Another big problem for the state during this period was the floods along the Mississippi River. Some **levees** had been constructed by parish governments before the Civil War. However, the levees were not maintained during the war. Consequently, when the river rose, the water flowed through. The flooding made it impossible to cultivate the fertile land. The government claimed to have spent about eleven million dollars on repairs. If so, little improvement was made.

Some **federal aid** was received in 1879 when the government established the Mississippi River Commission. During the administration of Governor Nicholls a state board of engineers was begun. The engineers were to be responsible for the levee work. Little was done due to the lack of funds.

In 1882 over a hundred thousand people were driven from their homes by the Mississippi River. After that **flood** the federal government helped the state keep the river under **control**. The Louisiana Legislature in 1885 divided the state into levee districts. Plans were made to build large systems of levees along the rivers and bayous of the state. Not nearly enough was done. **Floods** came again in 1912, 1913, and 1916.

In 1927 Louisiana suffered one of the worst floods in its history. It was the most disastrous in the history of the Mississippi River Valley up to that time. It covered an area of about

The crevasse of May 1927.

twenty-six thousand square miles. It was mainly in north and south-central Louisiana. There were 637,000 driven from their homes. Two hundred fourteen people were killed. Crops were ruined, and hundreds of animals drowned. Property damage amounted to about 236 million dollars. Business was at a standstill. The federal and state governments and the Red Cross came to the aid of the stricken people. After the water receded, it took months to restore the area. The Flood Act of 1928 followed this 1927 disaster.

En Partie 5 (Studying a Part). 1. Describe the damage by floods. 2. (a) When did the federal government offer assistance? (b) What kind?

Education

Education had never been a priority for people on the frontier. For most of the nineteenth century Louisiana was being settled. Louisiana was the only state in which white **illiteracy** increased between 1880 and 1890. Black illiteracy remained about 70 percent. Some progress was made after 1900. Even then Louisiana's educational system was very poor.

After 1877 a **dual school system** was set up—one for blacks and one for whites. The planters conceded the need for primary schools for blacks. The small plantation schools usually included grades one through three. Some went as high as the sixth or seventh grades. That did not mean the planter class expected to allow blacks the right to higher education without a challenge. They would simply find ways to limit opportunities for blacks.

Not only was there little money, but also neither the public nor their representatives in government were sold on public education. One reason was the stigma that planters had attached to public schools. Planters did not believe in public schools. The rest of the public had largely accepted their view. At one time persons whose children went to public schools had to sign papers acknowledging that they were paupers. Although this was done before the Civil War, the ugly image remained. People unable to afford private schools preferred no schools to paupers' schools or public schools.

The truth was that these public schools, begun after the war, were public in name only.

Charles P. Adams, founder of Grambling State University.

They were more private than public. School patrons had to furnish the building and the fuel for heating. They bought books and supplies. Patrons supplemented the tax money that paid a teacher for a few weeks or a few months of the school year. Patrons ordinarily extended the school term by paying the teacher's salary for the added time. Teachers bore the expense of institutes or summer college courses. Even school officials were unpaid volunteers.

Generally speaking, the schools were of poor **quality.** The teachers were usually not qualified for the job. Schools were only in session for a few months each year.

In New Orleans education was more advanced. Free textbooks were first given to the needy in New Orleans in 1898. There was a state compulsory attendance law, but it was not enforced. Those with any means received some education. In New Orleans and elsewhere in South Louisiana there was a tradition of Catholic church schools.

Planters continued to use **private education** for their children after the Civil War. Their proud claim to "aristocracy" required social distance from the white masses more than ever. Private schools of many types flourished in the 1880s. Numerous private teachers were employed.

Although some whites in rural Louisiana may have resisted efforts to educate black freedmen, blacks nevertheless were being educated. Some blacks dedicated themselves to work with their private academies. These schools generally kept a low profile.

It is doubtful that the public school system of Louisiana would have continued but for the white masses who poured into public schools. Gradually, the stigma of pre-Civil War days faded. The scant **funds** provided by tax monies were distributed by parish police juries. The money was never divided equally between the schools for whites and schools for blacks.

Improvements made after 1900 included lengthening the average school term from one month to three or four months a year. All children between seven and fifteen years of age had to attend school at least 140 days a year. This was in accordance with a law passed in 1916. Funds were also provided for libraries.

Tax monies granted for public schools increased from 1.5 million dollars in 1904 to 3.5 million in 1908. More students were in school than ever before. In 1907 the State Department of Education set up various departments. The state teachers organized in 1884. T. H. Harris began a long term as state superintendent of education in 1908. Many changes took place under Harris so that schools gradually improved.

By the School Act of 1888 parish school boards were authorized to establish central or **high schools.** By the 1890s all larger cities and towns had opened a public secondary school. High school courses were standardized. By 1900 there were thirty-five white secondary schools. There were no black secondary schools.

By the end of World War II, the concept of black high schools was firmly established. After Booker T. Washington made public his support of vocational training in the 1890s, black schools above the elementary level were called **training schools.** None was called a high school. By 1919 there were seven parish training schools established.

En Partie 6 (Studying a Part). 1. What improvements were made in education during this period? 2. Chart the development of the dual school system. 3. What were training schools?

World War I

World War I broke out in Europe in 1914. The war stirred strong feelings of **patriotism** in Louisiana. "Uncle Sam Needs You" war posters found plenty of response. Louisiana contributed 80,834 men to the army. Blacks were among those who enlisted in the military service. Louisiana's most distinguished serviceman was Maj. Gen. John A. LeJeune of Pointe Coupee Parish. He rose to commander of the United States Marines. Many soldiers were trained at Camp Beauregard near Alexandria. Aviators trained at Lake Charles. Several other **military** camps were established in the state.

The **home front** again was very supportive of the war effort. Local organizations raised money and furnished war supplies. Women made bandages and knitted clothes for the servicemen. Meatless days and wheatless days were observed every week. About 150 million dollars worth of Liberty loan bonds were bought by Louisianians.

World War I songs were sung from New Orleans to every rural school and church in the state. The catchy tunes caught the ears of Louisianians. This was before radio and decades before television. The songs reflected the spirit of a people who fervently believed in their country. They believed in the rightness of "stopping the kaiser." They believed heartily in themselves as Americans. There was a contagious optimism and a cheerfulness about the old songs such as "Over There." They were whistled, sung, and "banged out" on pianos across the state.

En Partie 7 (Studying a Part). 1. How did Louisiana participate in the war? 2. Describe the patriotism displayed by the people during World War I.

Lagniappe—*Jazz.* New Orleans and jazz music are closely bound. The music is a compilation of joy, grief, mixed cultures and a definition of

World War I soldier, from Cheneyville.

old New Orleans. **Louis "Satchmo" Armstrong** and every bugle man prancing with a funeral procession all pour out the emotions spoken in jazz. The bugle, the saxophone, the trombone, the clarinet, the drums lend that creative interpretation of the South, the city, the climate and the life. It made Louis Armstrong known and loved around the world. Following his death in New York in 1971, all New Orleans turned out for a traditional jazz farewell to express the grief and mourning felt. Tour the French Quarter and hear that jazz ringing out alive and well! New Orleans holds collections of the works of jazz artists since the early 1900s and many assorted lots are being reproduced. Offers for purchase of jazz collections appear on public television for the love of jazz continues. **Al Hirt, Pete Fountain,** and many others are recognized worldwide as major contributors to the wonderful world of New Orleans music. To feel the soul of jazz and Louisiana's music, participate—listen to Louis Armstrong.

Postwar Changes

Social and Political Changes. Automobiles were introduced before World War I. After the war there were more. By the 1920s the Model T was traveling over the muddy or dusty roads of the state. The car made it possible for the farmer and his family to make trips to town more often. Women cut their hair. Skirts became shorter. In 1920 some citizens heard the first presidential election returns to be broadcast over radio. In 1918 the Eighteenth Amendment to the United States Constitution was passed. This amendment prohibited the sale of alcoholic beverages. The Nineteenth Amendment passed the next year. It gave women the right to vote. The first tractors were brought to plantations on trial. They were tried as experiments. These machines could replace men and mules. More tractors and more trucks were brought to plantations and farms. Blacks sought better living conditions. A great wave of black migration to Chicago and other northern cities took place. More Model T Fords and other cars appeared on the scene. Roads in the state were still poor. The state was still rural in character, but Louisiana was changing. It was changing slowly through **new machines and new technology.**

Reform had been sweeping over the nation since 1900. Socialist Walter Dietz said that both the Democrats and Republicans took over the ideas of the socialists. In 1910 John M. Parker organized the Good Government League. This was meant to get rid of the Choctaws, a **political ring** in New Orleans. The

Governor John M. Parker.

ring candidate, J. Y. Sanders, had won the race for governor in 1908. The candidate of the Good Government League had won in 1912. The ring had elected their man in 1916. He was Ruffin G. Pleasant. Parker, of the reform league, carried the state in 1920. He was a representative of the planter-urban alliance. This group pledged themselves to subdue the Choctaws. Parker, known as the "gentleman reformer," made no basic reforms. He did support the building of better roads and led in getting legislation passed to provide more funds for Louisiana State University. It was he who called for the Constitutional Convention of 1921. A new **constitution** attempted to bring the state laws more in line with the times. The 1913 constitution had not served the state well.

Political Discontent. The Bourbons were politicians. They never represented the majority of the people of Louisiana. They were keenly aware that times were changing. They could not entirely ignore the discontented people they governed. Only a fraction of the people voted. Members of the upper class held office. That was the planter class and New Orleans political leaders. In a free country the common people never forgot the promise of equality and freedom for all men. The Bourbons' claim to aristocracy and a right to govern had never been accepted by the mass of people. The highhanded action of the Bourbons was resented. Even the Bourbons knew that severe discontent existed among the people. It could not be ignored.

An important reason for the feeling that Bourbon government could not last was public education. Most of the whites had the opportunity for a generation to obtain such public education as Louisiana afforded. The schools were not of highest quality, but, even so, they were creating change. The voting citizens of the state in the 1920s were more educated than their forebears.

The Bourbons were not going to risk another crisis like the Civil War, which had destroyed their fathers' way of living. Therefore, laws were designed without apology to maintain the control that the Bourbons held in 1900 and for twenty-eight years afterwards. They were made strong with as few loopholes as possible. But deeper problems were brewing for the Bourbons. Their time was passing.

Governor J. Y. Sanders.

En Partie 8 (Studying a Part). 1. How did life change for most Louisianians after World War I? 2. What problem did the Bourbons have to face?

Coup de Main
(Completing the Story)

Jambalaya (Putting It All Together)

1. Which party dominated Louisiana politics completely for the first three decades of the twentieth century?

2. Summarize social and political controls of the party.

3. Explain how Louisiana become a one-party state.

4. Which class of people were in control?

5. What were the beliefs of the Bourbons?

6. What was happening in each of these areas in the early 1900s: (a) transportation, (b) education, (c) industry, (d) agriculture, and (e) services for the people?

Potpourri (Getting Involved)

1. Map Work. (a) Show the section of the state flooded in 1927, or (b) show World War I Louisiana camps and other government installations.

2. Research (a) the women's rights movement, including their efforts to obtain the right to vote, or (b) the development of unions in Louisiana.

3. Compare (a) the development of the Populist party or Socialist party in Louisiana with their development in the rest of the United States, (b) life before with life after the inventions of this period, or (c) patriotism during World War I with that during the Vietnam War.

4. Compare (a) the 1898 constitution with the 1974 constitution, or (b) the Cotton Exposition with the 1984 World's Fair.

Gumbo (Bringing It Up-to-Date)

1. Compare the women's voting rights movement with the present women's rights movement.

2. Relate (a) the Louisiana Lottery of the 1800s to the present lottery for Louisiana and lottery systems being used today in other states, or (b) the "Jim Crow" laws to current racial problems.

THE REVOLT AGAINST
THE BOURBONS (1928-1940)

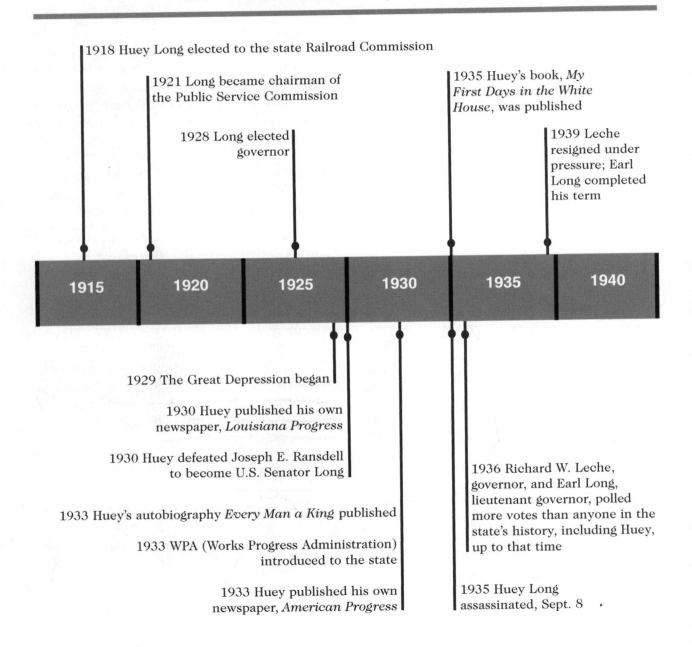

1918 Huey Long elected to the state Railroad Commission

1921 Long became chairman of the Public Service Commission

1928 Long elected governor

1935 Huey's book, *My First Days in the White House*, was published

1939 Leche resigned under pressure; Earl Long completed his term

| 1915 | 1920 | 1925 | 1930 | 1935 | 1940 |

1929 The Great Depression began

1930 Huey published his own newspaper, *Louisiana Progress*

1930 Huey defeated Joseph E. Ransdell to become U.S. Senator Long

1933 Huey's autobiography *Every Man a King* published

1933 WPA (Works Progress Administration) introduced to the state

1933 Huey published his own newspaper, *American Progress*

1936 Richard W. Leche, governor, and Earl Long, lieutenant governor, polled more votes than anyone in the state's history, including Huey, up to that time

1935 Huey Long assassinated, Sept. 8

THE REVOLT AGAINST THE BOURBONS

Huey Pierce Long

From 1928 to 1935 Louisiana's government was dominated by Huey Pierce Long. He has been described as the state's most colorful political figure. He has also been described as a demagogue and as Louisiana's most original and aggressive governor. Long called himself "the Kingfish."

Background. Huey's background was not like that of the poor people he represented. He was born in 1893 at Winnfield in Winn Parish. He was seventh in a family of ten children born to Huey Pierce Long Sr. and Caledonia Tison Long. Huey's parents owned their 340-acre farm. They belonged to a very proud group of people living in the hill country. They had a very different lifestyle from the planters.

Huey's **family** was unusual in many ways. His mother and father worked hard to see that their children were educated. Six out of the nine children who grew to adulthood attended college. The family included, besides Huey, a lawyer, a dentist, a United States representative, a Louisiana governor, and a college professor with a master's degree from Columbia University.

Huey was brash, ambitious, and highly intelligent. He annoyed adults with his questions and opinions. Huey was an extraordinary child who presented problems. He did not fit into the small rural school. In fact, he did not graduate from high school. There was a mix-up about graduation over which Huey did not have control.

Huey always found an outlet for his **sharp mind** and **abundant energies**. Once he had a chance to sell books. At first he and his friend Harley Bozeman helped a peddler selling books at the Winn Parish

Four portraits of Huey P. Long.

Courthouse. Later they rode the train to sawmill towns nearby and sold more books. The boys' pay for their sales was a selection of books, but that was what they wanted.

Huey decided that he could stop the crowd if he played a banjo and sang. He decided that when he saw a banjo player near the place where he planned to sell his books. The only problem was that he could not play a banjo. He asked the man playing one to sell him his. The man agreed. In the sale Huey made an agreement for the man to teach him to play. Huey learned so quickly that right away he started **playing** and **singing** to attract crowds. After that he performed to attract people to buy his books. The amount of his sales surprised everybody. Huey never quit using catchy songs as a selling tool. He always included musicians among his associates. From an early age he worked at being a **good salesman**. He became one of the best. After selling books, Huey sold cooking oil. He became so good at selling that people could not believe it. At age nineteen he became sales manager for the Faultless Starch Company sales office in Memphis, Tennessee. Years later his selling experience helped him sell his political ideas. It also gave him an understanding of people. It developed his ability to persuade them.

Huey Pierce Long grew up in a hotbed of **political discontent**—Winn Parish. It is referred to as the "Free State of Winn." This was the same area that opposed secession before the Civil War.

Listening to his elders talking about politics, he heard about Bourbons. The adults he knew mocked these people who thought that they were better than others. They felt strongly that they themselves were not getting a fair share of opportunities. They were angry.

Harley Bozeman and Huey Long, both bright boys, formed a **debate** team. They were young students at Winnfield High School. They were invited on at least one occasion to debate against a Socialist speaker from the North. The subject was "Democracy versus Socialism." A crowd of hill country farmers was the audience. "Huey and Harley were just boys in knee pants. But they held their own. They really won that debate," an old socialist recalled admiringly.

Huey got much of his education from **listening** to older people. Sometimes he tried to join in their conversations and was rebuked. He was also very **well-read**. Books were not as plentiful as they are today. There was no public library. His mother made arrangements for him to read books in the library of a senator from the area. It was said that Huey possessed almost total recall of his reading. Huey supposedly said, "There may be smarter men in the United States, but they ain't in Louisiana."

When Huey set a goal to succeed in politics, he decided that he needed to prepare. His older brother, Julius, a lawyer, financed a year in Tulane University for Huey. Julius outlined everything Huey needed to know to pass the state law exam. Huey entered Tulane University Law School as a special student. He did not have a high school diploma so he could not attend as a regular student. With careful instructions from Julius he attended for less than a year before he **passed** the **bar exam.**

Huey began his practice as partner of Julius in Winnfield. They soon parted ways. Then Huey set up a practice for himself. To supplement his income, he sold containers for kerosene. His law practice grew as his cases involving timber companies increased. He and his wife Rose moved to the home of Rose's parents in Shreveport. There he started his career. He developed a very successful practice.

Beginning of Huey's Political Career. Huey's political career began in 1918. He became a candidate for membership on the state **Railroad Commission.** The commission had been established by the Constitution of 1898. Its purpose was regulating railroads, steamboats, pipelines, telegraph, and telephone companies. The commission had done little up to this time.

Long campaigned with the support and help of his family and the people his family knew. He had a large number of friends in the Third Commission District. Many of these friends were made during his selling days.

He carefully made **campaign plans.** These included becoming acquainted with those who had run and those who had been elected since the commission started. One method he used was unusual for that time. He conducted a very successful direct-mail campaign. His wife mainly took care of that part of the campaign. Huey hit the campaign trail. He spoke to as many as he could on a one-to-one basis. He went to the voters wherever they were. Some heard a candidate for an important office for the first time. He spoke to crowds. He told them that the commission would be an agent of the people. It would be against big corporations. Huey displayed his posters everywhere. He sold himself so well that he won the election.

Huey started his new job in December 1918. He concentrated on serving the public interest. This meant that he had to represent the people against large corporations. This issue caused him to split with Governor Parker, whom he had supported earlier. Standard Oil Company had managed to get written into law its own version of a bill levying a severance tax on gas, oil, and other natural resources. Long's objections were heard throughout the state. He fought an unsuccessful campaign to put Standard Oil's operations under the control of the commission. Even though he did not win, he gained a lot of publicity. In 1921 Huey became chairman of the commission. It had a new name: the Public Service Commission.

His election to the Railroad Commission and later the Public Service Commission gave Huey the opportunity he wanted to lay a foundation for election as governor at some future time. From the beginning he took advantage of the privilege that went with the position to ride the trains in Louisiana free. He used it to learn every whistle stop in the state. He made key political contacts at each stop. He talked endlessly to people he met.

It was probably at this time that he introduced himself to a network of socialists. They were mostly those who had belonged to the party before World War I when the party had been shut down in Louisiana. That was because people associated it with communism. When it was revived in the state, it did embrace communism. Consequently, most of the early reformers no longer belonged, but they were dedicated to the principles of socialism. Huey Pierce Long became their standard bearer. They entertained him when he was making speeches in their areas. They actively worked to get votes for him.

Governor's Election: 1924. By the end of 1922 Long started his campaign for governor. On his thirtieth birthday, in 1923, he filed as a candidate for governor. He used some of the same plans he had used in the commissioner's election. Two of his most effective methods were **statewide circulars and speeches.**

Huey went directly to the people. He called them by name. He made them feel important. This was the first time that campaigning had been taken to them in their small country towns. He made them feel that he was one of them. He spoke to the farmers about the wealthy. He told them what they wanted to hear.

Huey was a master at making a political speech. He attacked his opponents in his humorous manner and in plain language. His use of ridicule was one of his striking characteristics. He labeled his political enemies with such names as "Turkey Neck" and "Kinky." The Bourbons had long poked fun at people they considered to be of lower social status. Now they themselves were the objects of biting ridicule and caricature.

Long made it very clear where he **stood** on **most issues.** He opposed the concentration of wealth, corporate interests, and banking. He supported the right of labor to organize. In labor disputes, he opposed the use of injunctions. Huey was not racist. In his sense of timing, however, he knew that he must not try to take the mass of people

faster toward a more democratic order than they were willing to go.

One issue that he treated lightly might have caused him to lose the election. The Ku Klux Klan was active again. It was strong in North Louisiana and southwestern Louisiana. The organization opposed blacks, Jews, and Catholics. Two of his opponents strongly opposed the Ku Klux Klan. Long said little about it. He finished third in the race. The Klan issue might have made the difference. He received seventy-four thousand votes. Rains had kept many of the poor—the Long supporters—away from the polls.

Governor: 1928. Huey had prepared for the 1928 campaign for governor to gain support where he needed it. He did not support either candidate in the 1924 runoff election. He did support a Catholic, Joseph E. Ransdell, in his successful race for United States senator in 1924. Ransdell probably owed his victory to Huey's support. Long also supported Edwin Broussard against J. Y. Sanders for the United States Senate in 1926. Broussard was a very popular French Catholic from rural South Louisiana. Long actively campaigned for Broussard. Broussard won. Long had gained support for himself in French Catholic South Louisiana.

Long emphasized his carefully **planned programs** during the 1928 campaign. The programs were tailored to take care of problems that existed in the state. Louisiana had only three hundred miles of paved roads, so he promised more and better roads. There wasn't a bridge over the Mississippi. He promised to remedy this problem. Louisiana had the highest illiteracy rate in the United

States. Textbooks were worn out and out-of-date. Huey promised better schools and free textbooks. More care for the blind, deaf, aged, and sick was another of his pledges. New Orleans was promised natural gas.

Huey made the people aware of their needs. He did this in his campaign speech made under the Evangeline Oak at St. Martinville. This speech has been described as the greatest speech he ever made. In the following part of the speech, he demonstrated his ability to appeal to the people.

Where are the schools that you have waited for your children to have that have never come? Where are the roads and the highways that you spent your money to build that are no nearer now than ever before? Where are the institutions to care for the sick and the disabled? Evangeline wept bitter tears in her disappointment. But they lasted through only one lifetime. Your tears in this country, around this oak, have lasted for generations. Give me a chance to dry the tears of those who still weep here.

Long did not receive a majority in the first primary. However, his impressive showing caused his opponent to withdraw. Since there was no Republican ticket, he was declared the winner.

Huey gave a new feeling of confidence to the mass of people. He was one of them. They identified with the first of their kind to be elected governor of Louisiana. About twenty thousand of his followers traveled to Baton Rouge for his inauguration.

Break from Bourbon Rule. This unusual man seemed destined to break the Bourbon rule. He was never a Socialist, but the cries of the common people were in his ears all of his life. The break from Bourbon rule came in 1928 when Huey was elected governor of Louisiana. Joe Gray Taylor said, "What the Jacksonians, the Radical Republicans, the Populists, and the Socialists had failed to do, Huey Long accomplished." He did more than simply defeat a political party. His election marked the end to the plantation system's hold on the state as far as the government was concerned. Huey put an end to the one-party aristocratic rule that had gripped the state. Gentlemen, as defined by the Bourbons, were out-of-date in Huey Long's Louisiana. These "gentlemen" had been concerned with preserving their position, status, and wealth. Elitism had no place in Huey's world.

Long **flaunted convention.** He made jokes about the Bourbons' insistence on formal manners. He knew that the defeated Bourbons were cringing when he was pictured serving "pot likker" in Washington, D. C., or receiving a foreign official while he was clad in green pajamas. He spoke in the language of the backwoodsman. Yet, he was a well-educated man and could speak as correctly as any Bourbon when he chose to do so. He chose to speak in the language of the mass of the state's people. They were not educated. He wanted to identify with the common man. These people in Louisiana understood exactly what Huey Long meant.

Long's Program. As governor, Huey set about putting into action the program he had promised for the public good. He did not have an easy job getting his programs carried out. He had to wheel and deal to win. He managed to get **natural gas** piped to New Orleans homes and businesses. He managed to get a small bond issue for **road** and **bridge construction**. This program became a constitutional amendment. Since good roads were a prime goal, Huey began a program of hard-topping roads. New **bridges** were built. Louisiana State University was a pet project. A crash **program** to **teach** people to **read** and **write** was started. Huey started the **free school books** program.

Huey had many other programs. A **graduated income tax** became law. He got the **poll tax** repealed. **Homestead exemptions** were made so that most homeowners paid no state or parish taxes on their houses. **Charity Hospital** in New Orleans received more **funds** to expand its services to poor people. The **Louisiana State University Medical School** was **started** to provide more doctors for the state. Schools received more funding. A new **governor's mansion** and a new **capitol** were part of his program. More **care** was given the **unfortunate** people of the state. He adopted a motto, "Share Our Wealth," which might have come directly from the theme of the old Socialists.

Huey Long became noted for his bitter **enemies**. He made some of his enemies by using a spoils system. He removed political opponents from key jobs and replaced them with his own supporters. He then asked for contributions from his appointees for his political campaign fund. Eventually Huey became heady with power that amounted to almost a dictatorship. He seemed to want power more than anything else. He became ruthless as the job of getting his programs into motion became more difficult. He, like the planters before

The state capitol under construction, 1931.

him, felt that the ends justified the means.

When Long called a special session of the legislature to increase the tax on oil production, his opponents resisted. The president of Standard Oil set up his headquarters in a hotel in Baton Rouge. He directed a program to oppose Long. Lobbyists fought Long's tax. When the anti-Longs showed an increase in strength, some former Long followers joined his opponents.

Impeachment. An attempt to impeach Long followed. Before April 6, 1929, the House of Representatives adopted an article of impeachment. That was the date set for the end of the special session. Later they adopted six more charges. Long questioned their legality. The Senate rejected

Long's argument by one vote. Then before the impeachment trial was to start, fifteen senators signed a very important statement. It said that they would not vote to convict Long under any circumstances. It took two days to get enough legislators to vote Huey's way. Huey said, "I buy 'em [legislators] like sacks of potatoes. I used to try persuasion and reason and logic. From now on, I'm a dynamiter. I dynamite 'em out of my way." The remaining members knew that it was pointless to proceed. Long was forever indebted to those fifteen senators. Some feel that the experience brought drastic changes in his behavior. It made him more vicious in his attacks against his opponents.

The Great Depression. The nation was hit by the Great Depression at about the time that Huey Long became governor. The economic crash came in 1929. The creeping slowdown of business added to the despair of the people. The depression in Louisiana was as dreary as elsewhere across the nation. Everyone was affected. Probably the city dwellers suffered from lack of essentials more than the people who lived in rural areas. Most of the people in Louisiana still lived on farms.

Prices of **farm products** had been **dropping** since the mid-1920s so that farmers had not shown a profit for some years. When the Depression hit, prices dropped even lower. Cotton sold for as low as five cents per pound.

All farmers—planters, small farmers, large

Share Our Wealth parade.

farmers, and sharecroppers—were joined in a desperate situation. Crops could not be sold for enough money to pay for the seed. Much less cash was available for the farmer's family. Yet, most farmers were not used to much cash, so they were able to manage without it. They were able to raise almost all of the food they needed as they had done before the Depression. Through credit at the country stores they were able to buy some of the things they could not produce on the farm. Flour, coffee, and sugar were three items that they desired but could not produce.

In response, the federal government began a program of **price supports** in 1933. Under this program farmers were required to limit their crop production. In return they were guaranteed a minimum price for their crops. This federal program begun by Pres. Franklin D. Roosevelt provided for subsidies, a payment for following this program. The government programs gave a new measure of security. Acreages were regulated in an effort to secure higher prices for farm products by making them less plentiful.

The idea of **work-relief** was introduced to the state. The WPA (Works Progress Administration) included both blue-collar and white-collar jobs. In New Orleans a large number of urban workers were employed on work-relief projects. Many of these agencies had their headquarters in New Orleans. Blue-collar workers were employed to improve roads. Others worked on reforestation and drainage projects. The Historical Records Survey and the Federal Writers' Project were among white-collar projects. Other New Deal programs were the CCC

Share Our Wealth rally at the state capitol.

(Civilian Conservation Corps) and the NYA (National Youth Administration), which provided student jobs.

In Huey's autobiography *Every Man A King,* published in 1933, he offered a program to end the Depression. Not all were satisfied with Roosevelt. Long gained a big following with his program. This program would redistribute the country's wealth. Every head of a household who did not already have five thousand dollars would receive that amount. Family personal income was to be limited to one million dollars per year, and family fortunes limited to five million dollars. The people were ready to listen to a new radical program such as Share Our Wealth.

Huey's Newspaper. Since Huey received such bad press, he published his own newspaper, *Louisiana Progress*. It was first published in March, 1930. He printed it in Mississippi to prevent any legal problems. The paper was another tool to get his message across. Many of his subscribers were on the state payroll. In 1933 he again published his own paper, *American Progress*. This paper was intended for a national audience.

United States Senator. In 1930 Huey Long defeated Joseph E. Ransdell to become a United States senator. Ransdell had been one of his supporters. Long did some clever "politicking" to retain control of the state while he was in Washington. Lt. Gov. Cyr and Long had become bitter enemies. Cyr said that Huey had vacated the governor's office. Cyr argued that Huey could not hold two offices at the same time. Therefore, Cyr had himself sworn in as governor. The National Guard under orders from Huey prevented Cyr from entering his office. Then Huey took steps to disqualify Cyr's actions. With political maneuvering he prevented Cyr from becoming governor. Huey declared Cyr's office vacant. In time the courts supported Long. Huey finally took the oath of office as senator in 1932, two years after the election. Alvin King, the president of the Louisiana Senate, became governor for the short time left in Huey's term.

Long maintained close contact with the state government from Washington. His political machine controlled every aspect of state government. The machine also controlled many of the parish governments.

Huey's Political Ambitions. Senator Huey Long quickly became a national figure. He left the national Democratic party and broke with President Roosevelt. There was talk that Huey wanted to be president of the United States in 1936. He had even written a book—*My First Days in the White House*. It laid out in detail his program if he became president. Also "Huey Long for President" posters were distributed.

Most historians agree that Huey Long posed a threat to Pres. Franklin D. Roosevelt. Of course, there were other political figures of the period who were also threats. Some say that it was Long who caused Roosevelt to search for a program like Share Our Wealth to appeal to the people. This turned out to be the first Social Security Act, passed in 1935. No doubt, the Roosevelt administration was determined to "get Long." Huey knew about the situation and its implications.

Huey's Death. Those opposing Long were as ruthless as he was. His enemies felt very strongly, and he had many enemies. His followers felt that he could do no wrong. People were either intensely for Huey Long or intensely against him. There was no middle ground. Any means used to win this "biggest fight yet" were all right in Huey's mind. Huey must have felt that he was right because he thought he was fighting for the common man. He developed a large following of devoted common people. Voters listened to him so that even Roosevelt feared him. Yet, even people who supported Long repeated, "Power tends to corrupt and absolute power corrupts absolutely." That, many thought, was the story of Huey Long.

There was mounting tension in Louisiana by 1935. There was talk that somebody was going to kill Huey Long. He often acted like a

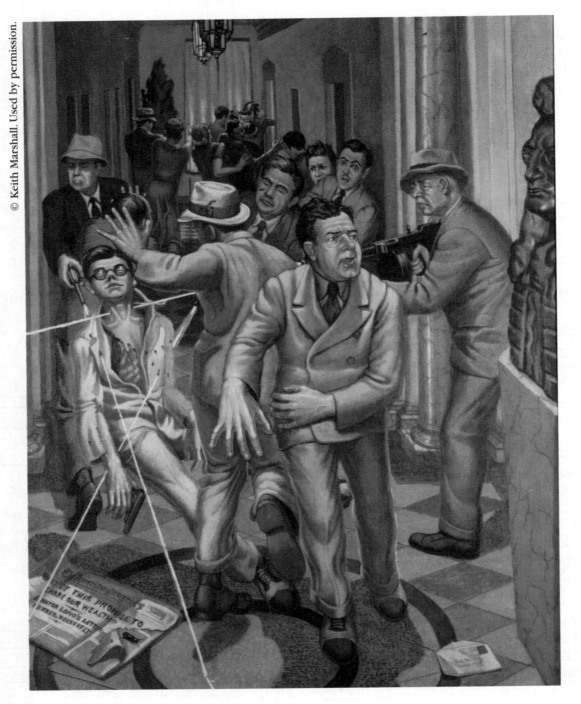

"The shooting of Huey P. Long," as depicted in a famous portrait commissioned by Life *magazine in 1939.*

dictator with high-handed methods that offended many. Fear of assassination caused him to shield himself with armed bodyguards.

Senator Long ordered a special session of the legislature in September 1935. One of his goals was to remove Judge Benjamin Pavy from office. Pavy was a very popular anti-Long judge who had held his seat twenty-eight years. By gerrymandering judicial districts Pavy would have been put out of office. Huey got a call that he was needed at the session. On Sunday night, September 8, 1935, Huey left the house chamber in the capitol.

The story of what happened next is controversial. Although it is generally believed that the version that follows is correct, there are other theories. As Huey walked down the hall, Carl Austin Weiss, Judge Pavy's son-in-law, shot him. Weiss fired one shot at Huey at close range. Long's bodyguards killed Weiss with at least twenty-six bullets.

Huey was taken to Our Lady of the Lake Hospital with a bullet wound in the upper part of his abdomen. Surgery was delayed while Dr. Urban Maes, chief of surgery at LSU Medical School, and his young assistant Dr. James D. Rives made the trip to Baton Rouge. They had an accident just outside New Orleans and never made it. This left Dr. Arthur Vidrine to operate. He was a doctor whom the New Orleans medical establishment had labeled incompetent. Huey disagreed. He had made the country doctor Vidrine head of Charity Hospital over the

Dr. Carl Weiss, named as the assassin of Huey Long in the capitol shooting in 1935.

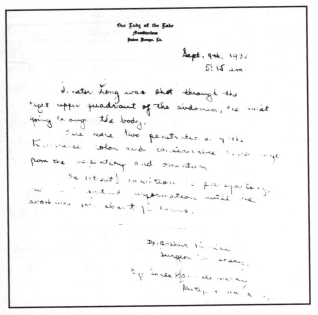

Medical report on Governor Long.

objections of the New Orleans group. Dr. Vidrine operated, but a blood vessel was not tied off properly, and Huey slowly bled to death. He died September 10, 1935.

Trainloads of sobbing people attended his funeral on the lawn of the capitol he had built. At least one hundred thousand mourners viewed his coffin. Their grief was genuine. Their reason for mourning him was real. Long had established the white masses as people of dignity, deserving respect. They were people whose voices in government should be and would be heard. Henceforth,

the Bourbons' claim that they had the right to govern would be a myth of the past. All white people of Louisiana would now walk together at the same level. Minorities, including the state's blacks, had a way to go before achieving equality. The supporters of Huey P. Long loved him for making a move in this direction. Many ordinary white men and women felt that Huey Long was their deliverer from the oppression of the Bourbons.

Others felt that he was a disgrace. For many years after his death the fight would continue. Long and anti-Long factions of the Democratic party would struggle for power.

Aftermath of the Kingfish

Louisiana Scandals. The Louisiana scandals erupted a few years after Huey Long's death. The scandal-ridden five-year period following used for the personal gain of some of Long's followers.

Among the most prominent of Huey's "rascals" to be convicted was Gov. Richard Leche (lesh). Others were Dr. James Monroe Smith, president of Louisiana State University; Seymour Weiss, president of the Roosevelt Hotel in New Orleans; and Monte Hart, a prominent contractor. At least a dozen others were involved. Using the mails to defraud, income tax evasion, and other charges were filed against at least eight men. Seven, including Leche and Smith, went to jail. Four people involved in

Governor Richard Leche, a key figure in the Louisiana scandals.

his death has been called the Louisiana Hayride. In 1939 there was a series of startling federal indictments against some of the leading political figures of the state. The scandals shocked the entire nation. It was referred to as the "most systematic theft upon an American state" to ever take place. Long's followers had all too frequently helped themselves to public monies and properties. There had been too many opportunities for personal profit for the weak men Long left in power. These men had come to terms with the Roosevelt administration. As a result, federal money flowed into the state. By one means or another, much of it was

Lieutenant Governor Jimmie Noe (left) with Governor O. K. Allen.

The capitol gardens surround the statue of Huey P. Long.

the scandal committed suicide. Many were discredited. The cost of the scandals has been estimated at one hundred million dollars.

Governors: 1932-1940. Huey Long was governor officially until January 25, 1932. The president *pro tempore* (prō TEM pə rē) (for the time) of the Louisiana Senate, Alvin O. King, then became governor briefly. Oscar K. Allen was the next governor elected. Allen was handpicked by Long. He continued Long's programs until his death in 1936. James A. Noe finished his term. In 1936 Richard W. Leche, governor, and

Huey's brother, Earl, lieutenant governor, polled more votes than anyone in the state's history, including Huey, up to that time. Leche resigned under pressure in 1939. Earl Long completed his term.

During all these elections there were two big factions: Longs and anti-Longs. North versus South Louisiana, rural versus urban (or New Orleans), and Protestant versus Catholic were other confrontations. The Long forces won in all the elections for governor. All of these people continued the policies started by Huey P. Long, but none could replace him.

The Goldurndest Gang Ever Seen Anywhere!

(from *The American Progress*, Sept. 22, 1939)

Coup de Main
(Completing the Story)

Jambalaya (Putting It All Together)

1. (a) Who headed the revolt against the Bourbons? (b) What was the difference between Long's philosophy and that of the Bourbons? (c) How were they alike?

2. How did Long reshape Louisiana's political system?

3. (a) Explain the ideology of Share Our Wealth. (b) Support using his plan or not using it today.

4. Trace the personal and political life of Huey Long.

5. (a) What did Long call his autobiography? (b) Relate it to his philosophy and to the Depression.

6. (a) How did Long maintain control of the state? (b) Could his tactics be used today? (c) Justify your answer.

The Great Sideshow of Freaks, Fakes and Frauds

(from *The American Progress*, Sept. 29, 1939)

7. (a) What kind of government did Long's political machine provide? (b) What effect did the machine have on the state?

8. List Long's contributions to the state. Divide your list into negative and positive contributions.

9. Discuss Huey Long as perhaps the most controversial figure in all of Louisiana history.

10. Cite reasons Long's influence continued after his death.

11. (a) What was the Great Depression? (b) When did it begin? (c) End? (d) Give its effects on the state.

12. Trace Huey's role in U.S. politics.

13. What important federal legislation did Long influence?

14. What were the work-relief programs introduced?

15. (a) What was called the Louisiana Hayride? (b) Give details.

16. Interpret the cartoons on pages 337 and 338.

Potpourri (Getting Involved)

1. Stage (a) a debate between the Long and anti-Long factions regarding Huey's chief issues, (b) a political rally typical of the day, (c) a speech Huey Long-style, presenting your platform, or (d) a debate on Huey Long's merits and demerits.

2. Interview someone who remembers the Depression, or pretend that you lived here at that time. Report on problems, help received from the government, and job opportunities.

3. Compare (a) the political career of Huey with that of his son, Russell, (b) Huey's contributions as governor with those of any other Louisiana governor or with all others, or (c) opinions of Huey Long by noted writers.

4. Interview someone who lived during Huey Long's time. Ask what their feelings were about his programs. Try to discover little-known facts about the man.

5. Report on Louisiana political machines.

6. Role-play or illustrate campaigning for governor, impeachment proceedings, the assassination, or any other significant event in Huey's life.

7. Examine (a) Joe Gray Taylor's statement: "Huey Long may have been the most remarkable American of the twentieth century," or (b) the statement: "Huey P. Long seemingly left behind him a permanent political organization that entailed radicalism, reaction, and reform."

Gumbo (Bringing It Up-to-Date)

1. Compare (a) the role of the government during the Depression with its role today, or (b) Huey's welfare programs with welfare programs of modern times.

2. Report on Long's political influence during his lifetime, in the 1960s, and in the 1990s.

3. Stage a "Meeting of the Minds" between Huey Long and later governors. Include Edwin Edwards, Murphy J. "Mike" Foster, and Kathleen Blanco. Discuss how each would have handled the problems of each period.

Overleaf: *The Louisiana Superdome.*

PART SEVEN
In Recent Times

CHAPTER 20

MODERN LOUISIANA: 1940s-1970s

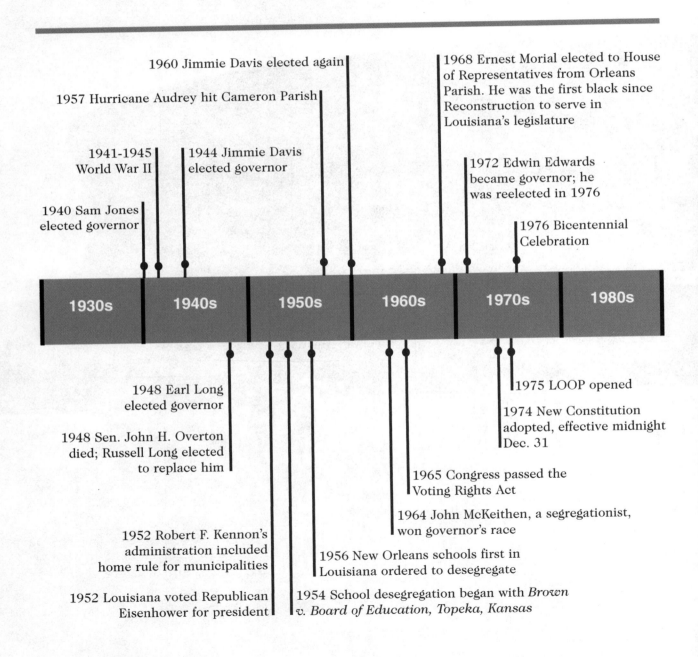

1960 Jimmie Davis elected again

1957 Hurricane Audrey hit Cameron Parish

1968 Ernest Morial elected to House of Representatives from Orleans Parish. He was the first black since Reconstruction to serve in Louisiana's legislature

1941-1945 World War II

1944 Jimmie Davis elected governor

1972 Edwin Edwards became governor; he was reelected in 1976

1940 Sam Jones elected governor

1976 Bicentennial Celebration

| 1930s | 1940s | 1950s | 1960s | 1970s | 1980s |

1948 Earl Long elected governor

1948 Sen. John H. Overton died; Russell Long elected to replace him

1975 LOOP opened

1974 New Constitution adopted, effective midnight Dec. 31

1965 Congress passed the Voting Rights Act

1964 John McKeithen, a segregationist, won governor's race

1952 Robert F. Kennon's administration included home rule for municipalities

1956 New Orleans schools first in Louisiana ordered to desegregate

1952 Louisiana voted Republican Eisenhower for president

1954 School desegregation began with *Brown v. Board of Education, Topeka, Kansas*

MODERN LOUISIANA: 1940s-1970s

World War II marked four years of turmoil that ended with spectacular changes in the world, the United States, and Louisiana. In many ways its legacy was like the Civil War of the century before. People in the time of the Civil War (1861-1865) spoke of "Before the War" when describing earlier life. "After the War" was the phrase used for the years which followed the war. It was the same for people living during World War II (1941-1945). "Before World War II" refers to a time that seems separated from the post-World War II period by many more years than those of the war. Louisiana, like the rest of the world, entered an awe-inspiring new era. This war brought even greater changes, perhaps, than had the Civil War.

Louisiana in the 1940s

World War II. Louisianians responded to the call of their country in World War II in many different ways. Many did so by serving in the military, working in factories, and making sacrifices on the home front. The collection of scrap iron and rationing of sugar, tires, and gasoline were a part of life during wartime. So was the use of substitutes for such things as nylon stockings and butter. Such activities as Mardi Gras were canceled for the duration of the war.

More than 325,000 Louisiana men and women volunteered or were drafted into the **military** ranks. Louisiana became almost an armed camp. Five large military training camps and ten flying fields appeared. Other military and naval establishments mushroomed within the state. Louisiana was the site of maneuvers, or mock battles, to train soldiers for the overseas battles. Many of the nation's great generals were in Louisiana during the war at one time or another because of the state's role in these training exercises. These leaders included Gen. Dwight Eisenhower, who later became president of the United States. Gen. George Patton also came here.

Gen. Claire Chennault (shə NÔLT) of Waterproof led the famous Flying Tigers, a group of daring volunteers who flew against the Japanese.

Louisiana had German and Italian **prisoner-of-war** camps. Prisoners were used on the plantations to meet the problems caused by labor shortages. They were also used to build levees and to do numerous other jobs. Many Louisianians were prisoners of war in camps in Japan and Germany. Some returned to tell the horrors of their experiences.

Shipyards constructed much-needed seagoing vessels. Andrew Jackson Higgins employed forty thousand workers in his assembly-line production in New Orleans that turned out ships very rapidly. Henry J. Kaiser made national headlines with the astounding speed with which he turned out ships. A merchant ship was built in ten days, a liberty ship in two weeks.

Much was going on during the war years than was visible. **Women** went to **work** outside the homes. They were often trained for skills, such as mechanics, that they thought that they would never master. Some rose to higher positions in a variety of fields than would have been possible if men had not been away at war.

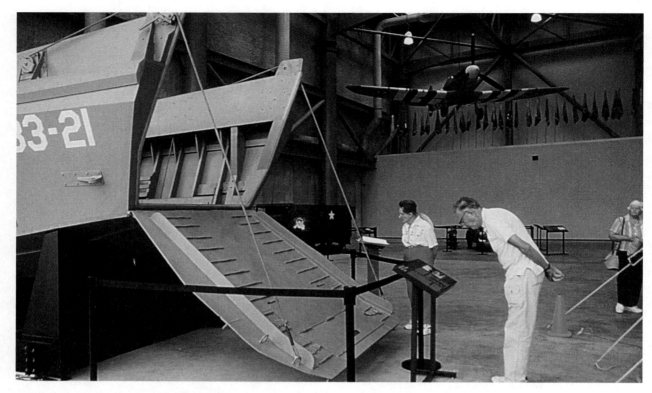

A Higgins craft at the National D-Day Museum, New Orleans.

From the beginning of the war **blacks** began the efforts to establish equality that would grow into the Civil Rights movement after the war was over. Blacks served in the military, both as volunteers and as draftees.

Sam Jones. Sam Jones led the state through almost all of the war years. The lawyer from Lake Charles was elected governor of Louisiana in 1940. He was the first anti-Long governor elected after Huey Long's death. He was opposed by Huey's younger brother, Earl.

The state was divided into the Longs and the anti-Longs. There was an outpouring of ridicule from both sides. The Long followers dubbed Jones "High Hat Sam." They wanted the voters to link Jones to the Bourbons of the 1890s. The anti-Longs ridiculed the Longs as uncouth, uneducated hillbillies—people with no manners. It seemed that the more the former Bourbons poked fun at the Longs' image, the more fervent Long supporters became. The anti-Longs won.

Sam Jones' style as governor was completely different from that of Huey Long. Jones led in passage of laws that repealed powers of the government. Changes made by Jones included reducing auto license fees. He created twenty departments to take over the duties of 175 boards and commissions and reduced the expenses of government. Eight thousand people were removed from

Governor Sam Jones.

the state payroll. A **civil service program** for state employees was established. Louisiana's debt was eliminated. Jones left a surplus of fifteen million dollars. However, Jones did continue the welfare services started by Huey Long. Taxes were increased some to improve the school hot-lunch program. He also increased old-age pensions.

Jimmie Davis. In 1944 Jimmie Davis of Jackson Parish was elected governor. Davis came from the same North Louisiana hill country from which the Longs came. Indeed, he had a close relationship with many people in Winn Parish. Oddly enough, despite his background, Davis was allied with Sam Jones and the anti-Long forces.

There was little to distinguish his administration. His time as governor was dominated by the war and the postwar adjustment period. Davis's administration left a fifty-million-dollar surplus.

Davis became famous for his country music. He and Charles Mitchell wrote **"You Are My Sunshine."** He used his hillbilly band on a campaign tour of the state. Davis acted in minor roles in Hollywood movies while he was governor.

Postwar Adjustment. World War II was finally over in 1945. The new world that waited brought dramatic changes in Louisiana life.

In the nineteenth century and for several decades afterwards, most of the population outside New Orleans had made their living from **agriculture**. Modern machines and technology changed the old farming methods. Wartime pilots became "crop dusters" with small airplanes loaded with fertilizers, herbicides, and insecticides.

The armies of **laborers** used on plantations were no longer needed. Long before the war black plantation laborers had realized that machines would replace them. When war brought new opportunities for employment to blacks, many of them relocated. After the war, more moved to the cities in other states, especially California and Illinois, as well as in Louisiana. Los Angeles, Detroit, and Chicago were favorite new locations. The state's black population continued to decline.

There were many other adjustments that had to be made when the war was over. **Colleges** were overcrowded. Returning servicemen used their G.I. (government issue)

Jimmie Davis (third from right), Louisiana's singing governor.

benefits and went to college. Veterans of ages far beyond that of the traditional college freshman poured into the colleges and universities. Gradually older women and men embraced the idea that securing a higher education could extend over a lifetime. The huge postwar influx of students into higher education brought the need for expanding colleges and universities and establishing others.

Classes to train veterans in every kind of **vocational training** flourished. Skilled carpenters enrolled groups of veterans. There were classes in unnumbered fields aimed at providing assistance for veterans returning to the work place.

Women gained a new feeling of equality and independence when they joined the work force. After the war they wanted to keep their jobs. There were more divorces, and more women were head of the household. War brides from many different countries had come to live in the United States.

Population. In 1940 Louisiana's population had been nearly sixty percent rural. By the end of the decade the state's population was 49 percent rural. People were moving to the cities.

Industrial Development. Louisiana experienced the greatest industrial boom in its history after World War II. Wartime factories turned to making peacetime products. The backlog of consumer products that had not been available during the war created an enormous market. New industry created thousands of jobs. There was a period of a flourishing economy after the war.

Earl Long. In 1948 Earl Long became governor of Louisiana. For eight years the "Long machine" had been out of office. Earl had a deep person-to-person appeal that Huey did not have. Even his enemies agreed that Earl had a sincere desire to uplift the mass of people. Many were in need of employment, education, and training for jobs. His campaign slogan was "Service to the People." Earl labeled Sam Jones, his opponent, with "do-nothingism." His critics felt that Long tried to do everything for everybody.

Earl expanded welfare programs already in existence and contributed his own. He provided a fifty-dollar monthly pension for the aged. He added fourteen trade schools, two charity hospitals, and bonuses for veterans. He experimented with free hot lunches for all school children. The state

Aerial view of rice farms.

Governor Earl Long goes hog hunting on horseback.

had medical programs that were similar to Medicare and Medicaid of today three decades before the rest of the nation. Earl added free ambulance services for charity hospitals and free dental clinics that traveled the state. During his administration large sums of money went for improvement of roads and for road-building.

Earl raised teachers' salaries to a minimum of twenty-four hundred dollars per year. Black teachers, for the first time, received the same salaries as white teachers. There was "a massive step taken to begin equalizing educational opportunities." Other state employees were not as happy. Earl abolished their civil service system everywhere except in New Orleans. (The Long forces did not control New Orleans.)

Earl needed money to carry out campaign promises. A sales tax bill was passed by the legislature. Taxes were placed on beer and cigarettes. In 1948 a two-cents-a-gallon tax was added to gasoline. Oil and gas producers showed their disapproval by wearing black armbands. Gasoline pumps were covered in black. Citizens complained loudly about taxes. For the first time the state's per capita taxes were the highest in the United States. Up to this time the natural resources had borne the tax burden.

Russell Long. When United States Sen. John H. Overton died in 1948, two years of his term were left. Overton had been a Long supporter. Anti-Long forces tried to win the vacated seat, but they were unsuccessful. Russell Long, Huey's son, was elected over Robert Kennon. He served as senator well into the 1980s and became one of the most powerful national political leaders. He became chairman of the Senate Finance Committee and at one time served as Senate Democratic Whip. His powerful influence in Congress served to the state's advantage.

Louisiana Hayride. Between 1948 and 1958 a radio show, the "Louisiana Hayride," spawned a number of entertainers. The most famous was Elvis Presley. The "Hayride" provided a stage in Shreveport for unknown talent to perform before a weekly live audience. The listeners could tune in from as far away as Canada,

Australia, and New Zealand. In addition, the Hayride was carried by CBS Radio and the Armed Forces Radio Network.

Offshore Oil and Gas Industry. On November 14, 1947, an event of worldwide significance occurred within the Louisiana oil industry. About forty-five miles from Morgan City, in the Gulf of Mexico, the Kerr-McGee Corporation brought in the first commercial oil well out of sight of land. This nine-hundred-barrels-per-day well gave birth to the offshore oil and gas industry. The impact of the offshore oil industry on the state's economy can hardly be overestimated.

News Stories of the 1940s. In 1940 the bridge across the Mississippi River at Baton Rouge was completed . . . **Lyle Saxon**, well-known Louisiana author, died in 1946 . . . WDSU-TV in New Orleans brought **television** to Louisiana in 1948 . . . That same year the International Trade Mart opened at New Orleans . . . In the late 1940s **Dudley LeBlanc** (leh blawn) designed one of the most spectacular promotions to ever sweep the country. He became a millionaire when his patent medicine **Hadacol** made such a hit. Bob Hope was hired to advertise the new product.

En Partie 1 (Studying a Part). 1. (a) What did Louisiana contribute to the war effort? (b) What military operations were located here? 2. Identify: (a) Claire Chennault, (b) Earl Long, (c) Jimmie Davis, (d) Russell Long, and (e) Sam Jones. 3. What postwar adjustments had to be made? 4. (a) When did Louisiana experience its greatest industrial boom? (b) Why did it happen?

Louisiana in the 1950s

Industrial Expansion. The 132-mile stretch of Mississippi River banks between New Orleans and Baton Rouge attracted a vast cluster of industries in the 1950s. Two nationwide surveys done in 1956 showed this strip to be the fastest growing industrial area in the country. This was the time of the greatest plant-building and relocation of industry in our history.

Population Changes. In 1954 for the first time in our history, Louisiana became more urban than rural. There were more people living in towns of two thousand or more than in the country.

New patterns of living appeared rapidly. People moved to industrial areas where the jobs were. Suburbs multiplied. All over Louisiana, as over the rest of the nation, old-time Main Streets were deserted. Businesses created shopping centers on the fringes of the cities. Schools and churches moved from downtown areas. Homes were almost always built away from the hearts of cities and towns. Real estate on Main Streets declined in value. The prices of land on the fringes skyrocketed. Downtown areas were neglected. Chambers of commerce all over the state worked hard to reverse the trend, but there was no use. It was a permanent change. As a result of this postwar change, Louisiana cities have sprawled out over large areas.

Transportation Changes. Increasing industry and a swelling population brought problems for the state highways as well. The number of vehicles, including big commercial trucks, increased at a phenomenal rate. The state's highways and bridges were not capable of handling the heavier loads. Gravel roads had to be resurfaced. Two-lane highways had to become four-lane ones. In some places six and eight lanes were required. The modern highway systems—both state and federal—were developed.

Tidelands. Louisiana lost a major lawsuit over the money pouring in from tidelands oil and gas. Millions and millions of dollars worth of mineral rights off Louisiana's coast were involved. The state had sued the federal government for its share of the mineral rights of the submerged lands. In 1950 the decision was in favor of the United States.

Oil Leases. Over ninety-eight million dollars poured into the state from its offshore oil leases. Spending rose to keep up with this bounty. A law was passed requiring the votes of two-thirds of elected members of the legislature for the passing of bills to raise taxes or to levy new ones.

Korean War. There was never any real peace after World War II. Russia, ally of the United States in the war, became a threat. A "cold war" developed between these two nations. As a result of the Cold War, fighting began only a few years after World War II ended. The Korean War started in 1950. It lasted through 1953. This war upset the lives of Louisiana people. It cost the lives of some and left more wounded.

Robert F. Kennon's Administration. Robert F. Kennon became governor in 1952. Kennon had defeated Carlos Spaht of Baton Rouge, who made a good showing. Race had been the big issue. There was much tension over the forthcoming United States Supreme Court decision on segregation. The conservative Kennon, from North Louisiana, was a States' Rights Democrat. This was the party of

Governor Robert Kennon.

Southerners who wanted firm commitments against integration of the races.

Robert F. Kennon's administration is noted for several accomplishments. These include the reinstatement of state civil service. Permanent registration of voters was authorized. Provision for voting machines in every precinct in the state was made by Kennon. His reforms also included **home rule** for municipalities. He made an effort to remove politics from the operations of four major state departments. These included the departments of highways, welfare, institutions, and wildlife and fisheries. Kennon established boards that were not under the control of the governor. Kennon's reforms included blasts at **gambling,** both organized and unorganized. The law reached all the way to church bingo games. Smashing of slot machines by the state police was a part of the movement.

Republican Movement. Louisianians voted in large numbers for Dwight Eisenhower in his successful bid to become president of the United States in 1952. This was the beginning of the Republican movement in the state.

Labor. In 1954 another major issue was before the Louisiana people. A **right-to-work** law was a threat to union power. The law allows any person to work for an employer without having to join a labor union. Members united to get the right-to-work law repealed. Victor Bussie, president of the AFL-CIO, led the fight to repeal the law. His efforts failed.

The Civil Rights Act of 1957. Congress passed the first civil rights act since Reconstruction. The first civil rights bill passed after the Civil War became the Fourteenth Amendment to the United States Constitution in 1868. Even with these safeguards civil rights had never been respected as law. Nearly one hundred years later, this history-making law was to be enforced. The law marked a milestone in the achievement of this country's ideal of equal rights for all citizens. In some parts of the state there were more blacks than whites in the 1950s, also. After World War II about one-third of the state's population was black. The civil rights movement changed relations between the races in Louisiana.

School Desegregation. School desegregation had its beginning in 1954. With the ***Brown v. Board of Education, Topeka, Kansas*** case the United States Supreme Court decided the fate of the state's dual school system. After 1877 the state had one system of schools for whites and one for blacks. In 1896, in the ***Plessy v. Ferguson*** case, the Supreme Court had ruled that "separate but equal" facilities were legal. Black schools had never been equal to white schools. After the 1954 decision the Supreme Court ordered school desegregation. It directed school boards to make a "prompt and reasonable start toward full compliance." The federal government did not enforce the rule in Louisiana for several years.

Education. Lack of education was a handicap in the changing world of the 1950s. In Louisiana formal education had not been valued to the extent that it had been in New England, for instance. Whether to get a formal education had been a personal choice. The type of work done by most Louisianians prior to World War II required skills not learned from books. The demands of industrialization and modern technology made formal training necessary. The lack of a large pool of trained laborers had its effect on continued industrial expansion within the state. Louisiana faced a rethinking of the value of formal education.

Education was one of the major concerns of the state in the 1950s. In 1956 New Orleans schools were the first in Louisiana ordered to desegregate. In 1957 the Russian **Sputnik** was launched and the space program started. The craft was the first man-made satellite to orbit the earth. It led the way in a giant worldwide effort to explore outer space. As a result, Louisiana schools, like others across the nation, were ordered to provide more science courses for students. In 1958 Gov. Earl Long, in a special session, got a law passed reducing state subsidies for free school lunches. This restricted these lunches to the needy. That same year Louisiana State University at New Orleans opened. The next year a branch of Southern University opened in New Orleans. Louisiana State University at Alexandria was located on the grounds of the state agricultural experiment station. It opened its doors the following year.

Public Welfare. Public welfare became a way of life for many people in the state. The money spent for public welfare in Louisiana during the years after World War II rose to 24 percent of the total spent by the state for all purposes. In the 1954-1955 fiscal year it amounted to nearly 108 million dollars. About 60 percent of federal funds received by the state went to welfare programs. There were three types of charity hospitals in the state—general, mental, and tuberculosis. Louisiana's welfare programs surpassed all other states.

Earl Long's Third Term. Earl Long won a third term as governor in 1955. It was the first time since colonial days that a governor served three terms. It was the last Long/anti-Long state election held. Race was again the issue. All candidates had declared themselves in favor of segregation.

Long had killed civil service in 1950. He did not attempt to kill it when it was reinstituted by Kennon. Earl proposed tax increases, but they failed to pass. He worked with all his political skill to assist blacks without destroying himself among white voters. At the time he remained faithful to the national Democratic party. Many white voters had become members of the States' Rights Democratic party. The big issue that separated the two parties was race. States' Rights Democrats fought to keep blacks segregated.

Long fought efforts to remove blacks' names from the rolls in North Louisiana. He made his feelings on the issue clear. Some people felt that it was a confusing change in Earl.

He suffered some kind of illness during his last years in public office. His illness worsened, but he remained in the political limelight. He embarrassed both Louisiana and himself with some of his antics. At one time he had his picture taken with a pillow case over his head. The picture was seen all over the world. Reporters followed him and recorded his escapades. His term was spent going in and out of hospitals. He was absent from Baton Rouge much of the time. Noticeable signs of a change in Earl's behavior indicated the beginning of his personal tragedy.

Two Parties. For the first time since Reconstruction a Republican for president of the United States carried the state in 1956. When Dwight Eisenhower ran for president for his second term, Louisiana voted for him. It was a sign that the two-party system would be revived in Louisiana.

Racial Organizations. The Ku Klux Klan appeared at various places in the state. An old law designed for use against the Klan was revived. This time it was used to try to destroy the National Association for the Advancement of Colored People (NAACP) in the state. The law required that all organizations list their membership with the secretary of state. White Citizens' Council officials spoke before citizens' groups. They organized some groups in Louisiana. Other groups opposing integration were formed.

LSU Football. Louisiana State University grabbed the limelight with its winning football team of 1958. The "Bayou Bengals," officially the "Tigers," became national champions that year.

Hurricane Audrey. Audrey, the first hurricane of the 1957 hurricane season, blew in from the Gulf of Mexico and hit the Cameron Parish coastal area on June 28, 1957. Between four and five hundred people lost their lives. Many of them were children. Over 150 million dollars in damages resulted. Many people might have been saved had they understood the language of radio announcers urging them to move to higher ground. Many people thought this meant that they should move to the cheniers in the area. The cheniers were only slightly higher than the surrounding land. After Audrey, specific language was used to make any future warnings clearer. Storm-tracking by the National Weather Service was greatly improved, too.

News Items of the 1950s. In 1951 Angola, the state prison, gained national attention for the state. The convicts there protested the inhumane treatment they were receiving. It was called the worst prison in the nation. . . . In 1952 Governor Kennon had penologists help correct the problems at Angola. . . . In 1955 the two hundredth anniversary of the coming of the Acadians to Louisiana was celebrated. Festivities centered around St. Martinville. . . . About half of the people in Louisiana in 1956 were watching the news on their own television sets. . . . That same year the legislature created the **State Archives and Records Service.** The purpose of this state agency is to preserve the state's historical documents.

En Partie 2 (Studying a Part). 1. What development took place in industry? 2.

How did the Civil Rights Act of 1957 affect Louisiana? 3. (a) What had been the attitude toward formal education? (b) What caused a change in attitude toward formal training? 4. What was the status of public welfare? 5. Identify: (a) Republican movement, (b) right-to-work, and (c) Robert F. Kennon. 6. What was the tidelands issue? 7. What was different about Earl Long's third term?

Louisiana in the 1960s

Earl Long's Death. Earl Long came in third in the race for lieutenant governor in the 1960 election. It was the first time that a Long candidate had failed to make the runoff since Huey's time. In the fall of 1960 Earl ran against incumbent Congressman Harold McSween for the United States House of Representatives from the Eighth District. Long was the nominee of the Democratic party in the second primary. Long's illness became worse with the pressures of the campaign. He was near collapse. Personal problems bedeviled him. The night before his victory over McSween, Earl Long had a heart attack. He died a few days later in a hospital in Alexandria.

Jimmie Davis's Second Term. Jimmie Davis was elected governor again in 1960. He declared himself to be a segregationist. Integration was the big campaign issue. Ironically, "Peace and Harmony" was his campaign slogan. His four years in office were noted not for peace but for turmoil. School desegregation orders for East Baton Rouge and St. Helena parishes brought unrelieved conflict. Leander Perez, the symbol of Louisiana segregationists from Plaquemines Parish, strode across the state's political stage. His fiery approach to segregation in the parish over which he ruled made national headlines. The debate over state aid to private schools began.

A law was passed requiring the withholding of state income taxes. It was under Jimmie Davis that a new governor's mansion was constructed. Governor Davis's "Sunshine Bridge," built halfway between Baton Rouge and New Orleans, became the subject of much ridicule. Opponents argued that it had no value. Davis argued that it was needed for industrial expansion.

In the midst of financial troubles, threats of war, and desegregation problems, Governor Davis diverted the attention of Louisiana people with his own brand of showmanship. He led his horse Sunshine up the capitol steps and into his office. A Baton Rouge legislator was not amused. He sent Davis a bale of hay. He suggested that there were others, as well as the horse, who needed the hay.

Improvements under Davis included a constitutional amendment. It provided for a legislative auditor. A capital budget law and a law to invest idle funds were both passed under Davis. The first college student loan law was passed during his administration.

Toledo Bend Reservoir. The Toledo Bend Reservoir project was completed in 1960. This was a joint project with Texas. It provides

Toledo Bend Reservoir.

Louis Armstrong New Orleans International Airport.

electrical power, navigational facilities, water for industrial uses, and recreational opportunities for thousands. It is the largest man-made reservoir in the eastern two-thirds of the United States.

DeLesseps S. Morrison. Mayor deLesseps (del ES seps) S. Morrison of New Orleans was an extraordinary reform mayor. He was first elected in 1946. Morrison unseated Robert S. Maestri (MAY stree), who had been mayor from 1936 to 1946. Morrison was mayor of New Orleans four times. He was in office fifteen years. He ran for governor unsuccessfully three times. In 1964 he was killed in an airplane accident in Mexico. Mayor Morrison left behind many civic improvements. He left a new city hall and civic center, a network of expressways and boulevards, a new bridge over the Mississippi, and the Moisant (MOI sänt) international airport (in 1960,

the official name of the airport was changed from Moisant Field to New Orleans International Airport. In August 2001, the airport was renamed the Louis Armstrong New Orleans International Airport). These remain as monuments to his administration. Even these accomplishments do not loom so large as his success in securing an amendment to the Louisiana Constitution. It allowed metropolitan **New Orleans** to operate under **home-rule charter** drafted by a citizens' committee.

John J. McKeithen. John McKeithen of Columbia took a stand as a segregationist in the 1964 race for governor. He won the election. A member of the Long political circle, McKeithen surprised Louisiana voters with his reforms. Major reform bills were passed to improve state government. The powers of the governor were reduced. One of the changes included reduction in the power of the governor to appoint local officials. In 1966 a bill was passed making it possible for a Louisiana governor to succeed himself. The law on investing idle state funds was made stronger. An amendment dedicating tidelands revenue to pay off state debt and finance capital construction also passed. A code of ethics for government officials was approved. A central list of state employees was compiled. An inventory of public property was begun. Tax disadvantages for industry were removed. An industrial boom followed. McKeithen personally made efforts to attract industry to Louisiana.

McKeithen was reelected governor in 1968. He was the first Louisiana governor to succeed himself in the twentieth century.

Hurricanes. During the 1960s portions of Louisiana were laid waste by three hurricanes. In 1964 Hurricane Hilda took the lives of thirty-two persons in the Lafourche Parish area. It did one hundred million dollars in damages to property. Hurricane Betsy, in 1965, claimed fifty-eight lives. The damage amounted to 1.2 billion dollars in the Grande Isle area. Plaquemines Parish received the brunt of Hurricane Camille in 1969. Nine lives and 322 million dollars worth of property were destroyed.

Desegregation. Congress passed the **Civil Rights Act of 1964**. This time desegregation began in earnest. The years 1960-68 were landmarks in the dying of an era in which blacks were controlled to provide an army of plantation labor. This new law brought many changes for Louisiana. The act provided that "all places serving the public" should be open to all the public "on an equal basis." This included voting booths, public schools, parks, and hotels.

The civil rights movement took many forms in Louisiana. Federal voting registrars were sent to parishes in the state where blacks could not register. The federal government stepped in after Congress passed the Voting Rights Act in 1965. That year Bogalusa was the scene of much racial conflict. Governor McKeithen earned respect for his handling of the tense racial situation there. McKeithen formed a biracial committee to work on current problems. Integration brought lawsuits among school boards and private citizens as well. Many delaying tactics were tried. There were various plans used to implement the orders of the court. There were even more plans to get around these orders. When the federal open housing law passed in 1968, it became illegal to refuse to rent or sell homes to people because of their race or color. Problems arose. Whites found ways to get around this law.

Federal programs became a dominant part of Louisiana. Many of these brought much desired federal funds into the state. Desegregation was required for the state to be eligible for federal funds. This proved effective in completing the process of integration.

The Youth Rebellion of the 1960s. The clash of pre-World War II and post-World War II ideas may have been most visible among the youth in the 1960s. Louisiana, like the rest of the nation, suffered through probably the most painful crises of the nation's past. Suddenly it seemed all of the old familiar values of the pre-World War II generation were questioned. The Vietnam War caused the loudest protest. Yet, the rebellion went much deeper. The right of the United States to draft young men for military duty was challenged. Draft cards were burned. Some young men fled to Canada to escape the draft. Many rejected the value of material possessions.

In many ways it was a tragic era. The use of alcoholic beverages and drugs brought early deaths and countless lost years of life to many young people in the state. New music, new dance styles, and new literature expressed the chaos, idealism, problems, and tragedy of the youth rebellion. It was a time of questioning of values all over the nation.

Decline in Industry. In 1967 Louisiana was enjoying an industrial boom. The peak was reached in early spring. By fall a downhill trend had started. Labor troubles of every kind developed. New construction was shut down, and the industrial boom fizzled for awhile.

News Items of the 1960s. The 1960s brought a variety of other important developments. The Freeport Sulphur Company completed a large half-mile-long steel island. It rose above the water of the Gulf of Mexico. The company began the **first offshore sulphur production** on April 14, 1960.

From 1961 to 1965 the **Civil War Centennial** was celebrated in the state.... In 1963, many Louisiana Democrats did not like John F. Kennedy and called for **free**

Separate drinking fountains gradually disappeared during the 1960s.

presidential electors. Democratic electors would be free to vote for the candidate of their choice. . . . Louisianians again voted **Republican.** This time it was for Barry Goldwater for president. . . . In 1967, Louisiana made national news when *Life* magazine printed a three-part story on **organized crime** in the state. . . . The **New Orleans Saints** became the state's professional football team to the delight of the many football fans. . . . In 1968 Ernest Morial (MŌ RĒ al), a black man, was elected to the House of Representatives from Orleans Parish. He was the **first black** since Reconstruction to serve in Louisiana's legislature. . . . In 1964 the **first black undergraduate** enrolled at Louisiana State University. . . . In 1965 **Shirley Ann Grau** won a Pulitzer Prize for *The Keepers of the House,* and **Jack R. Thornton** won one in photography in 1967. . . . A **Board of Regents** was created in 1968 as an agency to supervise the state's higher education program.

En Partie 3 (Studying a Part). 1. What was the key political issue in the governors' races in the 1960s? 2. How did desegregation affect the state in the 1960s? 3. Describe the youth rebellion. 4. When did the first offshore sulphur production begin? 5. Identify: (a) deLesseps Morrison, (b) Ernest Morial, (c) free presidential electors, (d) John McKeithen, (e) New Orleans Saints, and (f) Toledo Bend Reservoir.

Louisiana in the 1970s

Pete Maravich. In 1970 "Pistol Pete" Maravich played basketball at Louisiana State University. He not only broke college records but also helped make basketball a more popular game in Louisiana.

Edwin Edwards. Edwin Edwards, a native of Avoyelles Parish, became governor in 1972 and again in 1976. Although this Crowley lawyer had an English surname, Edwards had a French background. He spoke French fluently. He spoke of his lowly background during his campaign, but in fact Edwards's family produced several judges in Avoyelles Parish. Edwards's charm matched that of Huey Long. He quickly gained a huge following. He was elected with votes that included those of most blacks and organized labor.

Constitutional Convention. Edwards had made a campaign promise to rewrite the

Governor Edwin Edwards.

cumbersome 1921 constitution. In 1970 voters had to decide on fifty-three amendments to the constitution. The Constitution of 1921 had become the most often amended of all state constitutions except that of Georgia. It was extremely long with over 225,000 words. Popular opinion favored the writing of a new constitution.

Edwards kept his promise. A constitutional convention convened January 5, 1973. It did not adjourn until a year later on January 19, 1974. The convention was composed of 132 delegates. There were 105 elected by the people from the House of Representatives districts. Twelve were appointed by the governor to represent special interests. Fifteen were appointed by the governor from the public at large. Meetings were open to the public. E. L. "Bubba" Henry served as chairman of the convention.

The proposed constitution was submitted to the voters and approved. It became effective at midnight December 31, 1974. It was Louisiana's **eleventh constitution,** more than any other state. This one is brief, as constitutions go. It contains 30,000 words.

Superport. A Superport Authority was created during Edwards's administration. This authority planned the construction, maintenance, and operation of Louisiana's Superport. This project was funded entirely by private capital provided by a group of major oil companies, Louisiana Offshore Oil Port (LOOP). The Superport is an offshore oil terminal in the Gulf of Mexico. It loads and unloads oil tankers, thereby relieving them of the need to go inland.

Superdome. In New Orleans in 1975 a hotly debated Louisiana Superdome opened for business. Many Louisiana citizens were annoyed. Others praised its construction. This huge structure has been the site of many sporting events. It is also used for concerts, conventions, trade shows, and other events. Its vast, completely enclosed arena seats 19,678 for basketball. It seats 67,650 for baseball and 81,187 for football. Over 95,000 can be seated in the Superdome when it is used as an auditorium. The dome's major tenants include the New Orleans Saints and Tulane University with its various events. The annual Sugar Bowl events are staged in the dome.

The Superdome was the home of the former New Orleans Jazz, a professional basketball team. In the opening year, the Jazz played before 26,500 in the Superdome. This was more than its ordinary seating capacity. It was the largest crowd ever to see a National Basketball Association game in the history of the sport.

The 1976 Bicentennial Celebration. In 1976 the Bicentennial of the Declaration of Independence was celebrated. Patriotic programs and events refreshed pride in Jefferson's moving words of the Declaration.

One of the lasting results of the 1976 celebration was a focus on historical preservation. Since 1976 the movement to restore prized buildings has grown rapidly. Many buildings have been placed on the National Register of Historic Places. Historic districts have been designated. Emphasis on genealogy and respect for the past have grown as by-products of the celebration. Some Louisiana groups dedicated to preservation were very active in the celebration. Local historical groups were organized in many communities. The value of the past has been emphasized.

Women's Rights. After World War II

women joined in the movement for equal rights and equal pay for equal work. Southern states of the plantation system, including Louisiana, kept women in a subordinate status. The women's rights movement was hotly resisted. While times were changing, they had not changed enough for the state to ratify the Equal Rights Amendment.

King Tut Exhibition. Increased interest in cultural events was seen with the exhibit of the priceless art and historical objects of King Tut. The Treasures of Tutankhamen were exhibited in New Orleans. Huge crowds waited to view the treasures.

Lagniappe—*Art*. Clementine Hunter was born at Cloutierville, Louisiana, in 1887 and grew up living in the black quarters. At fifteen, she worked at Melrose Plantation and lived in a cabin on the plantation. Her first paintings were done after watching some of the artists residing in Mrs. Annie Henry's colony at Melrose Plantation. Her primitive interpretations of plantation life and black culture have been exhibited everywhere in Louisiana, California, New York, and Alabama, and were eagerly sought after by collectors. The primitive figures in ***The Baptismal Scene, Cotton Picking, Wash Day, A Funeral, A Wedding,*** and ***Going to Town*** are executing rites she had witnessed growing up in the plantation world. Her sponsors soon protected her and marketed her work for the world to learn from and enjoy. Some of early pieces were done on paper sacks, old boards, cardboard from boxes and then she was provided with canvases and paints. The moving scenes of daily live are an astounding record of life in rural Louisiana

Clementine Hunter, internationally known primitive artist.

until the 1940s. The cabins, the quarters, the churches, the fields of cotton, cotton sacks, and old gins are gone as a way of life.

Desegregation. The struggle over desegregation continued in the 1970s. School system after school system received orders from the federal courts. School officials spent long hours working out plans to satisfy federal requirements. Faculties and student bodies were integrated. The traditional school system of old disappeared. Completely new programs

The African House at Melrose Plantation.

were started in an effort to solve problems generated in the desegregation of schools.

During the course of desegregation and a resulting "white flight," a number of private schools were founded in the state. ("White flight" became a popular description of the various designs of whites to maintain a segregated society in spite of the law.) These were similar to the earlier plantation academies. The expense of maintaining such schools became overwhelming. Many of these private schools were associated with churches. Few of these schools survived.

Busing of schoolchildren became a highly emotional issue linked with school desegregation. From time to time judges would order certain children bused over long distances to achieve "racial balance." Some schools were closed. Others were forced to change their functions to another type school. Only one factor remained constant—the courts were in control. Few people were happy with the results of court orders, whatever they were.

Black Officials. In 1976 more than 98 percent of black officials were still elected from all-black districts. In 1978 Louisiana had more elected black officials than any other state. That year Louisiana had 333 black officials, fifty-seven more than in 1977. These included nine state representatives, one state senator, seventy-four members of parish governing bodies, eleven mayors, 102 justices of the peace or magistrates, ninety-three school board members, three judges, and nine police chiefs or marshals.

Natural Disasters. Nature took its toll during this decade. In 1971 Hurricane Edith did fifteen million dollars in damages when it reached the coastal land east of Cameron. Much more property damage was done when Carmen entered the state through the Atchafalaya Bay in 1974. In 1977 Babe swung through St. Mary, Iberia, and St. Martin parishes. A path of destruction and damage was left behind. Flooding of the Ouachita, Tensas, Black, Red, Atchafalaya, and Mississippi rivers in 1973 caused thousands to leave their homes. Damages amounted to millions. Floods in South Louisiana in 1977 caused much damage.

News Stories of the 1970s. The **Louisiana Educational Television Authority (LETA)** was created by an act of the state legislature in 1971. In that year 95 percent of all Louisiana families had television sets....The **Rock Festival of Life** at McCrea in 1971 attracted thousands of youths from all over the nation....That year eight blacks were elected to the House of Representatives. Louisiana ranked ninth in the nation in the number of **black legislators**.... **Ernest J. Gaines,** a black novelist from New Roads, won the 1972 Louisiana Literary Award for *The Autobiography of Miss Jane Pittman*. . . . The North-South toll road bill passed in 1974....The economy of the entire state was affected by the strike of dock workers in New Orleans during this period. When the port closed down completely, millions of dollars were lost....The **Independence Bowl** in Shreveport hosted McNeese State University and the University of Tulsa in its first game ever....In 1975 the flagship **public television** station began broadcasting in Baton Rouge. . . . In 1975 **Fort Polk** at Leesville became the permanent home of the First Brigade, Fifth Infantry Division (Mechanized). Fort Polk is the largest military installation in Louisiana....In 1976, a **right-to-work bill** was passed. . . . In 1976 Louisiana elected its **first woman state senator,** Virginia Shehee from Shreveport.... In 1977 New Orleans elected Ernest Morial as its **first black mayor**. . . . Louisiana passed a **first-use tax** on natural gas in 1978....In November 1978 Richard Nixon

Ceremony at Fort Polk.

came to Louisiana to visit his old friend **Joe D. Waggoner**. . . . Brian Weber took his case to the Supreme Court. He sued Kaiser Aluminum and the United Steelworkers on reverse-discrimination charges. Weber lost. Private industry was allowed to set up many kinds of **affirmative-action** employment programs. . . . Louisiana led all states in 1978 in industrial expansion. . . . Dr. Andrew Schally won the Nobel Prize in medicine in 1977 for his work in isolating and synthesizing hormones of the hypothalamus. Dr. Schally was born in Poland, educated in Great Britain, and became a U.S. citizen in 1962. He held positions at the VA Medical Center in New Orleans and was on the medical faculty at Tulane University.

En Partie 4 (Studying a Part). 1. (a) Who wrote Louisiana's eleventh constitution? (b) When? (c) When did it become effective? 2. What were some of the permanent benefits of the bicentennial celebration? 3. What was the status of desegregation in the 1970s? 4. Identify: (a) Clementine Hunter, (b) Edwin Edwards, (c) Ernest Gaines, (d) Superdome, and (e) Superport.

MODERN LOUISIANA: 1980s-1990s

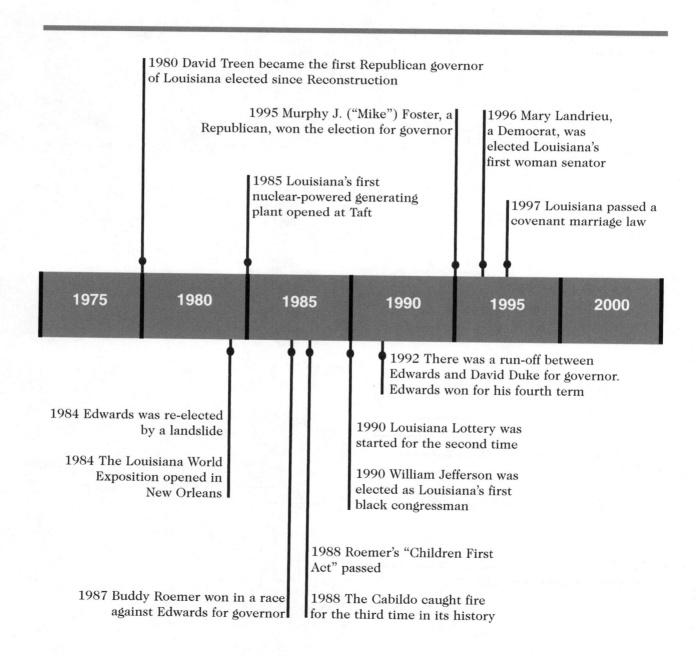

1980 David Treen became the first Republican governor of Louisiana elected since Reconstruction

1995 Murphy J. ("Mike") Foster, a Republican, won the election for governor

1996 Mary Landrieu, a Democrat, was elected Louisiana's first woman senator

1985 Louisiana's first nuclear-powered generating plant opened at Taft

1997 Louisiana passed a covenant marriage law

| 1975 | 1980 | 1985 | 1990 | 1995 | 2000 |

1992 There was a run-off between Edwards and David Duke for governor. Edwards won for his fourth term

1984 Edwards was re-elected by a landslide

1990 Louisiana Lottery was started for the second time

1984 The Louisiana World Exposition opened in New Orleans

1990 William Jefferson was elected as Louisiana's first black congressman

1988 Roemer's "Children First Act" passed

1987 Buddy Roemer won in a race against Edwards for governor

1988 The Cabildo caught fire for the third time in its history

MODERN LOUISIANA: 1980s-1990s

Louisiana in the 1980s

David Treen. In 1980 David Treen became the first Republican elected governor of Louisiana since Reconstruction. He made a good record in office. Treen was handicapped by the popular Edwards getting ready to reclaim the governor's chair in 1984. There was the deep recession that had settled over Louisiana and the rest of the nation in 1981 that continued into 1983. State revenues from the idle oil industry as well as other tax monies had been severely slashed.

Governor David Treen.

Edwards' Reelection. In 1984 Edwin Edwards was reelected by a landslide. He got 64 percent of the votes. Edwards was the first person ever elected governor of Louisiana three times. The 1983 race between Edwards and Treen was far more expensive than races in any other state.

Edwards soon put a $97 million package of new tax bills through the legislature. He contended that the state's revenue from natural resources had dwindled so that heavier taxes were necessary to maintain state services. The new tax package shifted the burden from Louisiana's oil and gas industry to other businesses and individuals. After this tax-raising session, the voters became negative toward the governor, the legislature, and state government in general.

Governor Edwards became the subject of several federal investigations. These brought the number of investigations into the affairs of Edwards to eight. On February 28, 1985, Governor Edwards was indicted by a federal grand jury on fifty-one counts. Charges included racketeering, conspiracy, mail fraud, and wire fraud. Charges were made against his brother Marion and others. Edwards remained under investigation in the Texaco case.

In less than a year after he started his third term, Edwards suffered the most dramatic shift in popularity in the state's political history. A survey showed that only 37 percent of the voters were pleased with his performance. The polls gave him his lowest rating in his thirty years in public office. A recall petition was started. The necessary number of signatures was not obtained by the deadline set by law.

Multibanking. The legislature approved multibanking in 1984. Multibanking holding companies could form statewide banks. Louisiana banks could now branch into other parishes. Louisiana Bankshares, the state's first holding company of this kind, opened in the mid-1980s.

World's Fair. In 1984 the **Louisiana World Exposition** opened in New Orleans. The fair opened one hundred years after New Orleans hosted the World's Industrial and Cotton Centennial Exposition. The theme for the 1984 World's Fair was "The World of Rivers—Fresh Water as a Source of Life." The major attractions included an exhibit from the Vatican and Louisiana's own exhibit. The fair was a glowing cultural achievement. Visitors praised the attractions and exhibits.

Financial troubles plagued the fair from the start. Louisiana World Exposition (LWE), a private company, received loans from the state before the fair opened. A state committee took charge of the firm's finances in July 1984 after LWE was unable to pay the bills. There was considerable division over Governor Edwards' decision to bail out the World's Fair with state funds. The fair cost Louisiana taxpayers about sixty-five million dollars. Just five days before closing, the fair filed for bankruptcy. The fair was more than one hundred million dollars in debt. One reason for the financial disaster was the failure to draw the expected eleven million people. Barely seven million attended. The World's Fair was a complete financial failure.

Blacks in Government. In 1987 Louisiana and Mississippi were the two states with the highest numbers of black residents holding elected positions in legislatures, town halls, and other offices. There were 505 black elected officials in Louisiana, reflecting the large percentage of blacks among the voting age population—26.6 percent.

Edwards' Third Administration. Edwards remained governor while he was indicted. He was the first to remain in office while under indictment but the second to be indicted. In the end he was cleared of all charges against him. Toward the last months of his second administration, he was shocked when legislators rejected his gambling proposals and balanced the budget on their own. They made cuts of $400 million and added new taxes.

During his tenure in office Edwards engineered the writing of the 1974 constitution. The new constitution initiated some much-needed changes in government. He reduced the inflated state bureaucracy by reducing hundreds of departments. Edwards changed the method of levying all severance taxes to provide Louisiana with fairer compensation. The state police system was reorganized. More investment in higher education was made.

The 1987 Election. Despite the indictment and trial, Edwards ran for a fourth term as governor. He was figured by the voters to be the inevitable winner. This conclusion was based especially on his personal charisma and numbers of diehard supporters. U.S. Representative Buddy **Roemer** (roam er) of Bossier Parish was considered one of three candidates least likely to win. Only 9 percent of the votes were for him.

Education was top priority with all candidates. It was thought to be the issue uppermost in the minds of voters. Edwards supported a lottery. The lottery was violently opposed by different groups, especially by church groups.

In the primary election Roemer was the top candidate. He had 33 percent of the votes while Edwards had 28 percent. Before the general election for voters to decide between the two, Edwards stood on the balcony of a New Orleans hotel and conceded defeat and withdrew from the race. Roemer became the governor with the lowest percentage of support from voters ever recorded for a winning candidate.

"Lame-Duck" Governor. In the months between the October election and the inauguration of the new governor in March, Governor Edwards remained in power. At first he agreed to make cuts asked by Roemer. Roemer was trying to avoid bankruptcy for the state. Instead, Edwards decided to make only half of the proposed cuts that Roemer had requested. Roemer was left to face a $500 million deficit and an increased threat of bankruptcy.

The public had lost faith in Edwards already. He drew more criticism with his last minute signing of pardons to criminals. He also shortened the terms of thirty-four. Altogether Edwards took executive action on more than two hundred criminal cases during his last two months in office.

Charles "Buddy" Roemer III, Governor. Roemer was inaugurated on March 14, 1988, with high public expectations for progressive change. Harvard-educated, Roemer came into office intensely dedicated to staging a "Roemer Revolution."

He immediately called a special session of the legislature. Then he asked for emergency budget powers. Many legislators were bitterly opposed to giving the governor the budgeting and borrowing power he asked. This was a power exceeded only by Gov. Huey P. Long. However, the outlook was grim. The legislators voted Roemer the power due to the emergency financial situation of the state.

The state could not afford to issue bonds since the state debt limit had been reached. Commission of Administration Brian Kendrick said that New York markets advised Louisiana to issue no bonds in 1988. They simply would not sell. Louisiana in 1989 also ranked at the bottom of the nation in national bond ratings. The poor bond ratings resulted in taxpayers paying more interest on bond issues. In that year the state's general obligation debt totaled $930 for each Louisianian.

Governor Charles "Buddy" Roemer III.

The severe cash flow problems called for drastic actions. In January 1988 refunds on state income taxes were withheld as a "cash saving" measure. In May 1988, near the end of the fiscal year, a policy of delayed paychecks of state employees was put into effect. Such pay was withheld during the two months before June 30 and was to be paid by October 1, 1988.

In regular session, the governor was able to get legislation providing for the reforms he sought in elementary and secondary education. His "Children First Act" passed in 1988. It emphasized education reform. Legislation was passed to fund the reforms with tax increases. Roemer was able to get legislation passed for business reforms as well. Increased funding was afforded the Department of Environmental Quality. In 1989 a four-cent tax on motor fuel was used to set up the Highway Trust Fund. The fund was approved by the voters.

Fortunately by spring 1988 observers detected a slightly hopeful feeling regarding the state's economy. There were still major problems, however. A recession, creeping across the nation, added further gloom to Louisiana.

Oil and Gas Crisis. Shock waves hit Louisiana with the oil and gas crisis, the worst recession in the history of the industry. The petroleum industry began a five-year slump in 1981 and continued its downward trend. In good years the petrochemical industry had contributed up to one-third of the revenue collected by the state. The crisis brought plunging prices of crude oil and the rapid reduction of offshore drilling rigs. Thousands of residents lost jobs. Expensive unused equipment was abandoned. It was plain that the state could no longer depend upon these dwindling natural resources.

Deep Recession. The protests that this state of things did not constitute a recession did not mean a thing to the residents. They could see for themselves. The second quarter of 1987 was the all-time low point for Louisiana's economy. Bankruptcies listed in the columns of newspapers were routine. **Bankruptcies and bank failures** continued to rise. Twenty-six banks failed in 1986 with sixteen more added in 1987. Twenty-one more banks failed in 1989. Seven Louisiana savings and loans institutions were counted among the one hundred worst nationwide in 1989. Two were among the ten worst. Of ninety-four Louisiana thrifts, twenty-three had negative net worth. Businesses were closing at an appalling rate. **Migrations** out of the state to seek employment became commonplace.

At the same time that Louisiana was coping with a deep recession it had the highest **unemployment** rate in the nation. The recession caused slower retail sales, lower home values, and reduced tax collections. The minimum wage was to be increased from $3.35 an hour to $5.05 over a given period. Meantime, the per capita income of Louisiana had fallen from $12,559 in 1981 to $12,296 in 1988.

Offshore Settlement. In 1986 Louisiana at last received a long-shot $640 million settlement on its **tidelands oil claims** against the federal government. Money from the massive offshore settlement with the federal government (the "8(g) settlement") was dedicated in the constitution by the voters. It included a $50.5 million permanent trust fund (PTF) and a support fund (SF) for education from the elementary to university levels. Future windfall revenues from the settlement will also be diverted into the fund.

Inspector General. Governor Roemer tapped a top-notch investigative reporter, Bill Lynch. He was hired to investigate allegations of waste, corruption, and inefficiency in state government. This was the first time such a position had been included in the state government. It was a controversial move by the governor. Lynch's investigations revealed payroll abuse, use of drugs for race horses, lack of discretion in the licensing of companies involved in horse racing, and other abuses in the business. Phone irregularities involving state offices were also cited.

In the 1980 "Brilab" investigations, federal agents posed as insurance executives to obtain state contracts from Louisiana officials. The federal agents offered bribes. The planned action resulted in indictments and convictions.

Cabildo Disaster. About 5:30 P.M. on May 11, 1988, the Cabildo caught fire for the third time in its history. A spark from a welder's torch started a fire on the third floor. Firefighters fought desperately to save the building, where the final formalities of the Louisiana Purchase took place. Luckily, the fire was confined to the third floor. While insurance covered the cost of rebuilding the structure, the exhibits which were damaged by the smoke, water, and fire had to be replaced by private funds. The renovations were completed in the early 1990s.

Panama. Task Force Bayonet, undertaken in Panama in 1989 to oust President Noriega included Louisiana soldiers and airmen. About seven hundred soldiers from Fort Polk's 5th Infantry Mechanized Division and airmen from Barksdale Air Force Base were sent to Panama.

News Stories of the 1980s. In 1980 Louisiana abolished its **head-and-master** law. Until this time the husband was considered head and master of the household. He had total control of community property. . . . Sonya Landry became managing editor of the *Shreveport Sun* in 1982. Her grandfather started this newspaper. It is the **oldest weekly black newspaper** in Louisiana. . . . In July 1983 the **International Special Olympics** were held in Baton Rouge. . . . Also in 1983 Louisiana State University received a donation of $125 million. This was the largest single donation ever made to an educational institution in the nation. C. B. ("Doc") Pennington donated the entire fund to build and operate a nutrition and preventive medicine **research center** at LSU. . . . That same year, **Barksdale Air Force Base** in Bossier City celebrated its fiftieth anniversary. . . . In 1984 the legislature passed a **child-restraint law** requiring that children of certain ages wear safety belts while in moving vehicles. . . . **Grambling coach Eddie Robinson** achieved a milestone in his career in 1984. He chalked up his 315th win in football and then surpassed the legendary Bear Bryant in career wins. . . . In 1984 at the Cabildo an extraordinary exhibit, *The Sun King,* displayed artifacts that belonged to Louis XIV. Original documents relating to Louisiana history were on display. . . . In 1985 Ruston got a new **biological technology research** facility. It was the first major facility of its kind to locate in the state. . . . In July 1985 **Lake Charles** was designated the port of one navy oiler and two minesweepers. . . . Louisiana's first **nuclear-powered** generating plant opened at Taft in

Sports Museum of Champions, Shreveport.

1985.... Sen. **Russell Long** retired after he completed his thirty-eighth year in 1986.... **Pope John Paul II** visited New Orleans in September 1987.... The **Louisiana State Archives building** was dedicated on April 27, 1987.... In March 1988 two swarms of **killer bees** were brought into the port of New Orleans on a leaking shipment of honey from Guatemala. They were quickly destroyed.... The **Republican National Convention** was held in New Orleans, August 15-18.... In 1988 **Poverty Point** was designated a national monument.... The **Oakdale Federal Detention Center,** virtually destroyed in the 1987 riot by Cuban inmates, was changed to a prison for aliens convicted of crimes and other federal

prisoners. After the rebelling Cubans burned out the federal detention center, Oakdale citizens at first were fearful of the rebuilding of the facility. The facility was rebuilt, but no Cubans are to be housed in the Oakdale facility.... **Cockfighting**—a brutal sport in which two spirited fowls fight until one dies— remained legal in 1988. Efforts to make these fights illegal were killed in the 1974 and 1983 legislatures.... A Shreveport race riot made national news in 1989. Dick Gregory, entertainer-entrepreneur-activist, Coretta Scott King, Ben Vereen, and several other celebrities came to Shreveport to lead in a project to make the area drug-free.

Making news in the 1980s were terrible

Poverty Point State Historic Site, Epps.

accidents. In 1980 the Jefferson Island Salt Dome caved in after being punctured by oil drilling equipment. Another accident in 1980 threatened the seafood industry. This disaster was a chemical spill in a river in St. Bernard Parish. The crash of Pan American Airline Flight 759 in Kenner was the second worst commercial aviation disaster in United States history at that time. In 1982 forty-three tank cars carrying toxic chemicals derailed near Livingston. Explosions spread toxic vapors over a wide area. Almost three thousand people were forced to leave their homes.

The loss of many famous Louisianians made news in the 1980s. Dr. **Ralph Waldo Emerson Jones,** Grambling State University's president for forty-one years, died in 1981. . . . Louisiana's native-born son, author **Truman Capote** (kə pōT Ē), died in 1984. . . . **Clifton Chenier** (shuh near), King of Zydeco, died in Lafayette in 1987. He is credited with having done more for Louisiana's international music reputation than any other entertainer in the state but was little known in Louisiana. . . . On January 1, 1988, **Clementine Hunter,** internationally-known primitive painter of black plantation workers like herself, died at age 100 at Cane River. . . . Former Governor **Robert Kennon** died January 11,

1988. . . . **Ernest Morial**, first black mayor of New Orleans, was the first black delegate to the Democratic National Convention in 1968. In the 1988 Democratic National Convention half the Louisiana delegation of seventy-three were women and 40 percent were black. Morial died December 24, 1989. . . . **Joshua Logan**, seventy-nine, famous Mansfield playwright and director, died in July 1988.

En Partie 1 (Studying a Part). 1. Why was the 1984 World's Fair considered a financial failure but a cultural achievement? 2. Identify: (a) multibanking (b) David Treen and (c) Buddy Roemer. 3. What caused the drop in Edwin Edwards's popularity? 4. What caused the poor economic picture in the 1980s?

Louisiana in the 1990s

Reapportionment. The 1980 Louisiana population was 4,206,116. The state had a population of 4,499,000 in 1986. The population on April 1, 1990, was 4,219,973. The 1990 census figures revealed to Louisiana residents what they knew all along. People had moved out of the state in large numbers since 1986.

The increase between 1980 and 1990 was not enough to keep pace with increases in many other states and with the country as a whole. These population figures meant the loss of one representative in Congress. Since representatives are elected from congressional districts, one district was lost. Louisiana was one of thirteen states to lose a seat in Congress. The state would have needed sixty thousand more people than at least one of the states that gained in population to keep its eight seats.

How the state selects the seven representatives is determined by the state legislature. Originally, congressional districts were decided mostly on the basis of geographic considerations. Gerrymandering was done to provide an opportunity for the election of blacks in the 1991 reapportionment plan. After bitter debate, the Senate and House plans were signed into law. The wrangling was not over, though. The complicated process of getting approval from the U.S. Justice Department had to be undertaken. Because Louisiana has a history of discrimination, the Voting Rights Act was applied. It declares that any changes that would affect voters' rights must be approved by the federal government. The federal ruling has now been made that race, culture, and ethnicity can't be the only criterion for mapping a congressional district.

The Lottery. The bitterly contested issue of the lottery, which Edwards had proposed, won 69 percent of the popular vote in 1990. By that time, Roemer had reluctantly given it his support.

With the creation of the Lottery Board, the lottery got under way in 1991. This marked the first state lottery in Louisiana since the corrupt one created during Reconstruction.

Problems. Louisiana citizens in 1991 responded to a problems poll by ranking drug abuse number one. Crime was a close second. Other concerns measured included the economy, education, environment, political corruption, and unemployment.

David Duke. In spite of much controversy, former Ku Klux Klan member David Duke won a seat in the Louisiana House from Metairie in 1989. By the time he got 40 percent of the vote in the 1990 race for U.S. senator, Duke had gained international fame. He was the first state legislator to do so from performances in his own state. The winner of the race was the incumbent, J. Bennett Johnston. He announced his retirement in 1996.

First Black Congressman. November 6, 1990, was a historic day for the state of Louisiana as the people of New Orleans elected the state's first black congressman since Reconstruction. **William Jefferson** replaced U.S. Representative **Lindy Boggs**. The event ended the Boggs family's fifty-year hold on the congressional seat. It also ended the one-race character of Louisiana's delegation.

Desert Storm. In Desert Storm (August 1990-1991) Louisiana had more than its share of young men and women in the Persian Gulf. With less than 2 percent of the population, Louisiana furnished 10 percent of the National Guard forces in Saudi Arabia. There was a reason for the large number of Louisiana units being called. Louisiana's National Guard was rated as having greater combat readiness of any Guard unit in the nation. Louisiana's participation roughly compared with the fact that military recruitments from Louisiana had been among the highest in the nation.

Theft of Art Works. Priceless Audubon prints were among 108 fine art works stolen from the Louisiana State Museum and sold to dealers scattered from the United States and Canada to France. Sixty of the 435 prints of John James Audubon's *Birds of America* were among those stolen by a former volunteer at the museum. These prints were originally sold to the Louisiana legislature in 1838 by the artist. The loss of the art has been estimated at a dollar value of $750,000.

Forty of the rare prints were returned by a Chicago art gallery. Only two of the sixty Audubon prints have not been returned. The museum has received one extra Audubon print. The extra was printed nineteen years after the museum's rare 1838 set. Of the forty-nine non-Audubon prints stolen, forty-four have been returned.

Edwards' Fourth Term. David Duke, Edwin Edwards, and Buddy Roemer were among the hopefuls fighting it out for Louisiana's top office in 1992. The runoff was between Edwards and Duke. Edwin

Lindy Boggs.

The Mississippi Queen.

Edwards won for the fourth time. He returned during another crisis in the oil business. When the price of a barrel of oil fell to between $16 to $17 a barrel, there was a crisis. The state had been dependent on oil and gas revenues from royalties on state lands as well as taxes. Governor Edwards had been accustomed to enormous revenues from these sources in prior terms. There had to be another source of income.

Gaming. Edwards felt the answer to the state's reduced financing was gambling. The fact that the Louisiana Constitution forbids gambling would be no problem. He convinced the state legislature and the Louisiana Supreme Court that only a change of name was needed. Gaming was not prohibited by the Louisiana Constitution.

The Louisiana Lottery, illegal for ninety years, was reinstituted in 1990. "Powerball," a multi-state lottery game, was added. "Progressive mega jackpot bingo" was introduced in 1995. That year the state's single land-based casino in New Orleans failed. The casino operator declared bankruptcy. In 1994-95 there were 16,074 video poker devices in over 3,961 establishments. By January 1, 1996, twelve of the fifteen licenses for riverboat gaming had been issued.

Native American tribes recognized by the federal government have jurisdiction over their territory. With a treaty with Louisiana, Native Americans started opening huge casinos. The Chitimacha tribe's Cypress Bayou Casino at Charenton opened in 1993. The Tunica-Biloxi Grand Casino complex in Avoyelles Parish opened in mid-1994. In 1995 the Grand Casino Coushatta opened at Kinder. In 1996 the Jena-Choctaw were waiting for approval to open a fourth casino.

Many people in Louisiana opposed the reintroduction of legal gambling (gaming). The legalization has brought problems. The political involvement was one. Debates over the issue have brought divisions among groups of people. Bankruptcies have increased. Homes have been lost. Savings and money needed for necessities have been gambled away. Gambling addiction has wrecked marriages. It has even led to suicides and murders.

However, the gambling industry has provided thousands of jobs. It has brought in considerable tax money. Much-needed construction jobs have come with the new hotels and other support industries. The casinos are providing entertainment programs featuring well-known performers. Gaming has attracted tourists in large numbers. Gaming was one of the principal issues in the gubernatorial campaign for 1995.

Governor Murphy Foster. Foster, then sixty-five, won the election in 1995 with over sixty percent of the vote. His opponent was Cleo Fields, then thirty-two, a Democrat. Foster switched from the Democratic to the Republican party shortly before qualifying. The contest was termed as a conservative white candidate against a liberal black. Foster was pictured as Mister Everyman and a working man's governor. His hard-boiled independence appealed to large numbers of the

Governor Murphy J. "Mike" Foster.

reform-minded electorate. His campaign promised that he would run the government as a business.

Mike Foster is the grandson of Governor Murphy James Foster (1896-1900), a Bourbon. He is from one of the richest and most prominent families in the state. Foster, a sugar planter, enjoys a huge legacy from sugar planters going back generations. He lives at Oaklawn Manor in old sugar-plantation country.

Governor Foster's first executive order in 1996 was to order an end to affirmative action and set-aside programs for minorities and women. It was not effective since both kinds of programs are protected under state and federal laws. Foster then took on gaming. After a struggle, he was able to institute two elections for the people to vote for or against gaming. The lottery and horse racing were excluded. The governor and his anti-gaming followers wanted a constitutional amendment outlawing the practice. The legislature changed the amendment to allow voters in each parish to decide the issue of any new gaming and the amendment passed.

U.S. Supreme Court Rules. Louisiana's legal problems were taken to the U.S. Supreme Court. In 1997 Louisiana's **statutory rape** law, which allowed the death penalty in child rape cases, was upheld. . . . The court okayed the Bossier Parish School Board **Redistricting** Plan of 1992. The decision was seen as reassertion of the Tenth Amendment. The justices felt that the Justice Department should not have brought the case to the Supreme Court. They felt that it was a crystal clear law. . . . In Agostoni vs. Felton, generally called the Jefferson case, the judge ruled that the federal government could provide computers and other instructional materials to **parochial schools**. . . . The court struck down the populist so-called "blanket" **primary election rules** used in various states. The court noted that Louisiana's unique primary system was the only new election innovation to meet the test of the Constitution. The U.S. Supreme Court ruled in 1998 that Louisiana could not finally elect a senator or congressmen before the national election day in November. In all elections that do not include federal elective offices the state sets the date. All absentee voting by mail must be received by the registrar of voters on or before election day.

Uniformed and overseas citizens are included in this ruling. This makes Louisiana the last state to elect national senators or representatives if there is a runoff election.

News Stories of the 1990s. Walker Percy, one of the giants of twentieth century American literature, died in 1990 at Covington. . . . That year, 1990, one out of four people living in the state lived below the national **poverty** level. . . . In 1990 Governor Buddy Roemer was in the national news when he vetoed legislation that would have given Louisiana the strictest **abortion law** in the nation. With the division of voters on both sides of the abortion issue almost exactly equal in numbers, the highly emotional issue faced the 1991 legislative session. . . . Only four Louisiana **banks** failed in 1990. . . . In 1991 Standard and Poor's Corporation upgraded the state's **bond rating** from BBB-plus to A. This move saved millions of dollars in interest costs when the state issued bonds for over two billion dollars. Much fiscal reform remained to be done. . . . **Roemer**, the nation's first sitting governor to switch parties, left the Democratic party for the Republican party in 1991. He became the second Republican governor to serve Louisiana since Reconstruction. . . . Governor Roemer proclaimed a state of emergency in Caddo, Bossier, and Webster parishes after the **floods** of April 15-17, 1991. The flood-ravaged area was declared a disaster by President Bush. . . . In 1991 the closing of **England Air Force Base** and the cutting back of **Fort Polk** by 25 percent was announced. . . . The "**temporary sales tax**," voted two years earlier in the midst of crisis, was renewed by the legislature in 1991. . . . In 1994 the Cabildo reopened. The exhibition in the Cabildo now traces the history of the state from precolonial times to the later nineteenth century....The much awaited interstate connecting north and south Louisiana was completed in 1996.

En Partie 2 (Studying a Part). 1. How did reapportionment affect the state? 2. Who was Louisiana's only four-time governor? 3. Describe the gaming industry. 4. How does Foster differ from other Louisiana governors? 5. What significant decisions concerning Louisiana were made by the U. S. Supreme Court?

Coup de Main (Completing the Story)

Jambalaya (Putting It All Together)

1. How did the governors of the 1980s and 1990s attempt to solve the problems faced by their administrations? Evaluate their success.

2. (a) How did the people of these decades at first react to solving the financial problems of the state with a lottery or gambling? (b) Why did enough of them change their minds to approve it? (c) How was it accomplished within the law? (d) Predict how gaming will be viewed by the people twenty-five years from now.

3. How did multi-banking make better banking representation all over the state?

4. Trace the ups and downs in the oil business of the 1980s and 1990s and relate it to the economy of the state, businesses, and individuals.

5. Why was Roemer, who was elected by such a small percentage of voters, able to attain so much power? Evaluate how he used the power.

6. (a) What are indications of a recession? (b) How deeply did the recession depress the economy? (c) Did this recession affect the whole nation? Research to get the answer.

Potpourri (Getting Involved)

1. Explain this statement: The scandals of politicians had far-reaching effects for the state. Document your answer by doing a newspaper search of the period to locate news articles from around the country. Draw conclusions about the effects of scandals.

2. Do an in-depth study of a Louisiana governor. Relate the personal life and the political life of the governor.

Gumbo (Bringing It Up-to-Date)

1. Check available sources to determine if the oil and gas industry is following the fluctuation pattern of the 1980s and 1990s today.

2. Update the information about the lives of any of the important people of the 1980s and 1990s to determine what course their lives are presently taking.

LOUISIANA IN THE 2000s

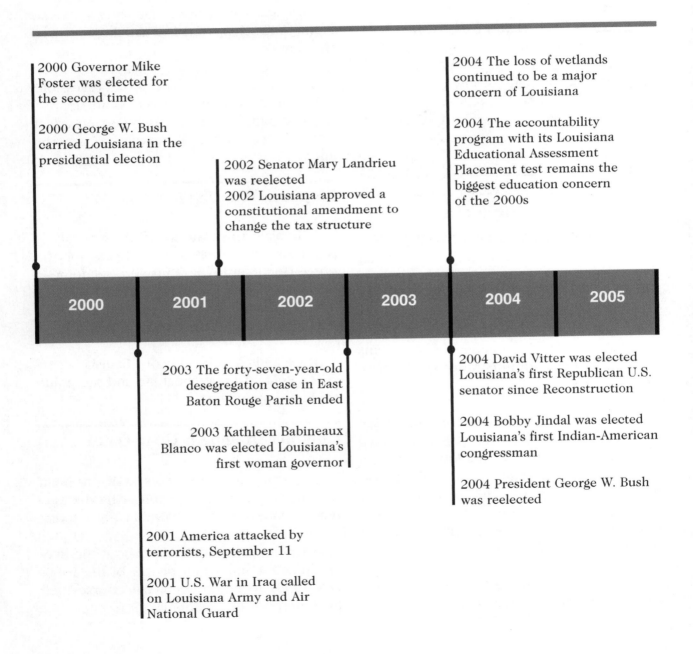

2000 Governor Mike Foster was elected for the second time

2000 George W. Bush carried Louisiana in the presidential election

2002 Senator Mary Landrieu was reelected
2002 Louisiana approved a constitutional amendment to change the tax structure

2004 The loss of wetlands continued to be a major concern of Louisiana

2004 The accountability program with its Louisiana Educational Assessment Placement test remains the biggest education concern of the 2000s

2000 2001 2002 2003 2004 2005

2003 The forty-seven-year-old desegregation case in East Baton Rouge Parish ended

2003 Kathleen Babineaux Blanco was elected Louisiana's first woman governor

2004 David Vitter was elected Louisiana's first Republican U.S. senator since Reconstruction

2004 Bobby Jindal was elected Louisiana's first Indian-American congressman

2004 President George W. Bush was reelected

2001 America attacked by terrorists, September 11

2001 U.S. War in Iraq called on Louisiana Army and Air National Guard

LOUISIANA IN THE 2000s

Louisiana's Population. According to the 2000 U.S. census, the population of Louisiana was 4,468,976. Louisiana's growth rate was less than half of the national average and smaller than other Southern states. The state's growth was attributed to the positive birth to death rate and the influx of foreign immigrants, including Vietnamese, Indians, and Latin-Americans.

The decrease in the population in the cities continued with much out-migration in Orleans and Jefferson Parishes. Many families moved to the suburbs and this was reflected in the growth in St. Tammany, Ascension, Livingston, and Tangipahoa Parishes. Job seekers moved to industry locations, following the oil and manufacturing industries.

Louisiana Economy 2005. Louisiana's economy responds positively to the rise of the international price of oil. As oil and gas prices move up and down, so does the Louisiana economy. As oil prices peak, per capita income increases. However, the oil and gas industry has not seen a similar influence on employment. The energy production and exploration have not expanded in response to worldwide price increases. The reasons for this are based upon input and output from the offshore oil and gas fields. While there has been some repair work done because of various climatic conditions in the Gulf, which has boosted some employment, this is short term. The longer outlook for Louisiana remains tied to renewed oil and gas explorations and drilling.

Employment in the manufacturing sector will continue to be sluggish with further employment decline because of foreign competition and increased technology. There will be some positive spots in the manufacturing economy, such as shipbuilding and oil and gas pipeline construction and repair.

The real estate market will hold steady through 2006. Professional and business service employment will continue at the same rates. However, because of budget cuts, hospital areas will continue to grow, but at slow rates.

Agriculture, fisheries, and forestry will continue at steady rates with foreign competition becoming more significant in all areas. This is based on future trade agreements, especially with Latin America.

Casinos. The impact Native American casinos has had on the economy has led to Nevada-type operations moving into the state. Casinos greatly alter the area where they are located. Other businesses open to meet the needs of the casinos, the visitors, and the performers. The casinos offer jobs to many for their round-the-clock operations. The Native American casinos are freed from much taxation. Major tax concessions may offset costs of police protection, highway access and maintenance, and general services provided. It has not been determined if this is profitable to the state, with the exception of increased employment. Much of the gambling takes place at I-10 truck stop casinos, the slots at racetracks, and riverboats. When thirty-three parishes outlawed video poker, relocation began. It seems no one wants gambling in the neighborhood. The addiction to gambling has far-reaching negative effects. Programs have been set up to handle this problem with counseling and control.

Oil and Gas Sector. The September 11, 2001, attacks shifted the focus from energy policy to dangerous international concerns of foreign oil production. This invigorated domestic production of oil and gas and brought Louisiana to the forefront.

The newly reopened eastern region of the Gulf of Mexico was bid by oil and gas companies. Drilling in federal waters of the Gulf adds greatly to Louisiana's economy by jobs and services required. The economy of many coastal towns is based on these services.

Louisiana in 2003 ranked second in the nation in natural gas production and fourth in crude oil, which are so critical to the national economy. Louisiana oil and natural gas reserves (meaning undeveloped resources) are the highest in the nation except for the prohibited areas of Alaska.

In 2005 there were about six hundred drilling rigs and platforms operating in the Louisiana Gulf. The great complex of platforms, service boats, drilling rigs, and maintenance safeguards provided many jobs. Refineries and petrochemical plants offered highly desirable jobs. A great increase in employment was created by emphasis on secondary recovery, pipeline safety, and environmental protection practices.

Ports. The New Orleans port lost business when the import tax on foreign steel was levied. This tax was to protect U.S. steel manufacturers, but it became a political trade issue. The tax was withdrawn in 2003. The issue affects the nation's steel manufacturing businesses and accounts for many lost U.S. jobs. In the first half of 2004 Louisiana ranked tenth among the top exporting states. Exports passing through the state's ports increased by 9.2 percent compared to 2003.

These exports covered the products created in Louisiana and goods produced in other states and exported through Louisiana ports.

Medical Research. A research team at LSU Pennington Biomedical Research Center in October 2003 announced an important discovery. The center got a patent on a promising drug treatment that killed cancerous tumors in mice. The drug must go through extensive human testing. Further work is needed before the U.S. Food and Drug Administration will approve that testing. The Pennington is heavily endowed and is a major contribution to the world.

Terrorists. America was attacked by terrorists on September 11, 2001. The aircraft attacks hit New York City early in the morning. The first one hit the World Trade Center, the next the South Tower, and the last hit the Pentagon in Washington, D.C. Three thousand people were killed in these attacks. President Bush was in Florida when he got the word. His plane was rerouted to Barksdale Air Force Base in Shreveport for the return trip to Washington. Louisiana Air National Guard F-15 fighter jets escorted Air Force One from Florida to Louisiana. All airports were closed immediately nationwide. They reopened on September 13.

Immediately an attack plan was put into effect for the entire state. Security was tightened at New Orleans' port of entry, oil refineries, chemical plants, and the capitol. National Guardsmen began patrolling area airports and the River Bend nuclear facility.

Aftershocks from the September 11 attack caused the National Football League to change the date of the Super Bowl game from January 27 to February 3, 2002. New Orleans gained national attention for managing to

An editorial cartoon showing the nation's reaction to the September 11, 2001, terrorist attacks.

make the change. A convention of the National Automobile Dealers Association, already scheduled for the February date, met at a later date. Mardi Gras krewes had to reschedule parades. For a nation hesitant about traveling and being in a large crowd, the game proved to be uplifting and reassuring. The high security at the game was accepted as necessary. This was the first major event of a huge crowd. It helped the country to realize that the country must not give in to fear.

Louisianians responded to September 11 with an outpouring of patriotism. Displays of the American flag or red, white, and blue banners were everywhere. A flag was painted on the roof of a new building. The demand was so great that local stores quickly ran out of flags. People did more than show their colors. Hundreds of people donated blood and/or participated in fundraisers for the Red Cross or assisted families of the victims. Some volunteers went to New York to help.

Another scare followed with the mailing of anthrax-laced letters to congressmen and media figures. The anthrax scare spread to Louisiana in 2001. Mail handlers throughout the state donned gloves and masks as a precaution. Threats and reports of possible mailings proved to be hoaxes. An LSU bioterrorism expert was considered a "person of interest" in the probe of anthrax mailings. No charges were filed against him. An unusually large number of bomb threats occurred. Unclaimed packages or suitcases were treated as potential bombs. All proved to be harmless. Increased precautions continue to be taken with careful screenings at airports.

War in Afghanistan and Iraq. In the fall of 2001, war broke out in Afghanistan after the terrorist attacks on the World Trade Center and the Pentagon. The goal was to destroy Al Qaida, the terrorist group blamed for the 9-11 attacks. This effort was named Operation Enduring Freedom. Military units and thousands of Louisianians in the National Guard or reserves got the call. Some headed overseas right away, and others provided security in airports. In the spring of 2003, they were called up for Operation Iraqi Freedom, the United States war in Iraq. Many men and women left jobs and families for new assignments. Families were disrupted as many mothers and fathers left their children to fight the war. Many were sent to Iraq or nearby countries. Others were assigned inside the United States. The Iraqi war, along with the ongoing U.S. presence in Afghanistan, put a strain on many of Louisiana's part-time troops (National Guard and Reserves). Some were deployed for a second time since 2001. To date, nearly

eighty-five hundred men and women in the Louisiana Army and Air National Guard have been deployed in support of both wars. All of them have flown out of England Airpark in Alexandria to head overseas. They also return to the same airport when they come home. As the war continued, Louisianians watched as Saddam's statue was toppled. On December 13, 2003, they saw Saddam captured. Local media featured pictures and stories of units leaving for war and returning to happy families.

The local media also covered the deaths and funerals of servicemen and women from Louisiana. In January 2005 the state lost eight Louisiana National Guard troops in a very short period.

Fort Polk and the Joint Readinesss Training Center. Fort Polk is a major defense center for our nation. It is located in Leesville. Its stated mission is to provide advanced training for U.S. contingency forces under tough, realistic conditions. Since 1993, Fort Polk has become home to the Joint Readiness Training Center (JRTC). It is also home to several units with early deploying wartime missions. Medical and dental personnel and military police are also assigned to the post.

The JRTC has a multimillion-dollar mock city, an airfield facility, and a military compound. These facilities provide realistic training in third-world urban warfare scenarios. The Military Operations on Urbanized Terrain complex is a one-of-a-kind facility. It provides joint and combined arms training for soldiers and leaders. Units from the Air Force, Army, Navy, and Marines are involved in training here along with military units from foreign countries.

The training is based on a U.S. task force

being sent to a mythical small island nation. The task force is to help them face an invading force. Tough, demanding, realistic, real-time combat operations follow. There are live-fire exercises where company and platoon-size units engage realistic targets.

The Fort Polk operation uses almost two hundred thousand acres. Some the army owns; some the U.S. Forest Service owns. The annual economic impact is over $950 million. The total effect on the state's economy is enormous. It directly affects over 132,000 of Louisiana's population. With a post population of over ten thousand, with sixty-two hundred civilian jobs, plus families, civilians, and retired military families, the impact is felt locally as well as statewide. Fort Polk additions of $13.2 million for the mock-city urbanized terrain facility, and $9.2 million for targetry and audio-visual networking add to the hundreds of millions already invested.

***Columbia* Disaster.** The shuttle crew's sixteen-day research mission ended sixteen minutes short of touchdown February 1, 2003. All crewmen were killed. Investigators said the cause was a chunk of insulation that broke off the fuel tank and pierced the left wing on launch day. The Lockheed Martin Space Systems' Michoud facility in New Orleans made fuel tanks for the shuttle. The foam was applied to tanks. It was determined that the method used to apply the foam was wrong, but investigators did not blame workers at Michoud for the accident. Michoud followed NASA's orders. The *Columbia* disintegrated into fiery debris over western Louisiana and Texas. Authorities recovered dozens of pieces in Louisiana, including three engine parts from two craters at Fort Polk. The Louisiana

The launch of the Columbia *shuttle.*

State Police, assisted by Louisiana National Guardsmen, helped manage efforts to investigate reports that poured in from people who believed they might have found pieces of the shuttle. Recovered pieces were taken to Barksdale Air Force Base and Camp Beauregard Louisiana National Guard Training Headquarters in Pineville.

Environmental Problems. The Department of Health and Hospitals in 2001 discovered vinyl chloride in drinking water. It was found at high levels near Plaquemine. Lawsuits resulted, and the complaints were satisfied.

In 2002 the Industrial Zeolite Ltd. at their plant at Meeker in central Louisiana was charged with illegal dumping. The plant first dumped eighty-four thousand gallons and then one million gallons of a highly acidic water. The acid was used in processing zeolite. It is a key ingredient in detergents to make them clean better and the water softer. The modern plant is located on the banks of Bayou Boeuf. This is a major waterway for drainage and irrigation and ditches that lead to the Chatlin Lake Canal and Avoyelles wetlands. The problem came to light when someone reported the incidents to environmental agencies. The company received a $1.5 million fine. The individual responsible for the dumping received a high fine and jail sentence for his irresponsible decision.

Toxic mold problems arose in the state in 2002. The mold spawned lawsuits and raised homeowners' concerns. Mold was discovered in the Plaza Tower in New Orleans. There were many thousands of dollars in damage.

Asbestos and lead paint found in buildings and on bridges had to be removed. Government rulings required inspectors to look for both items. Much money was spent in the removal of asbestos in office buildings, schools, and other public buildings. Bridges had to be scraped, treated, and repainted as part of environmental protection practices.

Health Care. The West Nile virus broke out in Louisiana in 2002. Health officials reported twenty-four confirmed deaths from the mosquito-borne disease and more than three hundred cases. Louisiana had 114 cases of West Nile virus in 2004, seven of them fatal. The disease appears to be firmly established in the state. Louisiana led the nation in the number of West Nile deaths for a while, but eventually was surpassed by other states as the disease spread.

The West Nile outbreak prompted local governments and the state to dip into emergency money to step up spraying from planes and trucks to kill mosquitoes. Mosquitoes, once the dread source of yellow fever, malaria, and other tropical diseases, have regained force with the government ban on DDT.

The state hospitals for the low-income population are threatened by state budget allocations. These hospitals were established by Huey P. Long to take care of the poor. The closures would be devastating to the no-insurance children, elderly, and mentally ill of Louisiana. The number of those without health insurance has crept up. The uninsured rose from 18.6 percent in 2002 to 19.4 percent in 2003. This was the second highest percentage in the nation. There are over 830,000 in the state without health insurance. Eighty percent of the adults and 70 percent of the low-income earners were uninsured in 2003.

Formosan Termites entered New Orleans in the 1940s at the Coast Guard station on the West Bank and have spread along the Gulf Coast. The French Quarter has suffered much damage. It is believed that the termites are transplanted in wood products. In the spring of 2000 the Louisiana Department of Agriculture and Forestry, under the direction of the Formosan Termite Task Force, launched an extensive tree treatment program in Greater New Orleans and Lake Charles to stop the invasion of the termite. In 2004 the Formosan termite ate away at a cost of about five hundred million dollars.

Weather. The three-year cycle (1998-2000) of drought and extremely hot summer temperatures finally ended in March 2001. The rains started, and in some areas it was too much. Tropical storm Allison drenched the Louisiana-Texas coast in July 2001, and two storms hit Louisiana in October 2002. Crop damage amounted to more than $440 million. The double-whammy coupled with a rainy fall kept farmers from harvesting their crops. Many of them were left deep in debt. The closing of businesses, layoffs, loss of homes and businesses, and other costs by government agencies, such as police protection, affected the state's economy.

Tropical storms affect all activities in the Gulf area, including the oil industry. The chain of economic effects of a shutdown include individuals, businesses, the state, the nation, and the world.

Safety Measures. The National Weather Service now uses the technology advancements to prepare Louisiana with storm warnings and alerts to protect life and property. Natural disasters like hurricanes have forced Louisiana to develop specific expertise in disaster management.

In 2004 Louisiana learned that the evacuation plan of New Orleans had to be reexamined. For national home security, major changes must be made.

Because the oil supply of the nation is vulnerable to attack, the Louisiana Offshore Oil Port (LOOP) is now being protected by the Department of Homeland Security. It has been designated as one of the top possible terrorist targets in the nation. The state participates in cooperation with the federal agencies with securing the port. Louisiana's state and local agencies received nearly eighty-six million dollars from the federal government for homeland security.

Other safety measures have been taken to reduce deaths and injuries on Louisiana's highways. Changes in the speed limit and traffic regulations have been made for congested areas. The Louisiana legislature mandated helmets for all motorcycle riders in Louisiana.

Conservation. At no time have wetlands in general and coastal wetlands in particular received more attention and interest from our state and our nation. Voters in 2003 approved constitutional amendments to help finance efforts to preserve and restore the state's dwindling coastline. Some estimates show that Louisiana is currently losing twenty-four square miles of coastal wetland every year. With the combined effects of sea level rise and subsidence (land sinking), water levels in coastal Louisiana may rise. The rise could be as much as one inch every two years. This is the rise rate during recent times. In the next fifty years, the average sea level at the present Gulf coast will be at least two feet higher than it is today. Dramatic changes in coastal Louisiana would take place. Coastal communities and the state's multi-billion-dollar fish and wildlife resources would be at risk. Oyster beds and shrimp and crab production are already threatened. Also at risk is the state's oil and gas infrastructure, which is important to the energy security and economy of the entire nation. Significant reductions in wetland loss will require major actions and great expense.

Education. In 2003 *Education Week* ranked Louisiana among the top states in the country for its efforts to improve schools and school performance. Concentration in education has been on the accountability program with its Louisiana Educational Assessment Placement test and meeting the requirements of the 2001 "No Child Left Behind" Act. *Education Week* in 2004 ranked Louisiana's Accountability System first in the nation. The testing involved changed many aspects of public schooling at all levels.

Louisiana Scandals. Louisiana's politics continues to be full of scandals. After many conflicts and investigations, popular four-term governor Edwin Edwards in 1998 was charged by a federal grand jury. He was charged with racketeering, extortion, and fraud in dealing with casino licenses. In 2003 Edwards was sentenced to ten years in prison. The seventy-five-year-old served time at the Federal Medical Center in Texas until he was moved to the Oakdale Federal Detention Center.

Other politicians were also involved in scandals. Jim Brown, Louisiana Commissioner of Insurance, was indicted for lying to the FBI about the Cascade Insurance Co. and its dissolve. He was sentenced to ten months in prison. Brown was the third Louisiana Commissioner of Insurance to be indicted for bribery. Agriculture Commissioner Bob Odom was indicted in 2002. He faced counts of bribery, theft, money laundering, and filing false public records. While under indictment, Odom was overwhelmingly reelected to his position. The charges were all dropped.

Louisiana's First Woman Governor. Kathleen Babineaux Blanco, a Democrat, was elected governor in November 2003. She defeated Bobby Jindal, a Republican, to become Louisiana's first female governor. Blanco, who had served as the state's lieutenant governor since 1996, replaced

Governor Kathleen Babineaux Blanco.

Governor Murphy "Mike" Foster, who had been elected to his second term in 2000. Her program includes creating a stronger economy, having better management of state government, being committed to educational excellence, and having better health and safety programs for Louisiana citizens.

Congress. In 2002 Louisiana's first woman U.S. senator, Mary Landrieu, a Democrat, was reelected in a runoff with Republican Elections Commissioner Suzanne Terrell. State Rep. Rodney Alexander, a Democrat, was elected to the Fifth Congressional District seat after a bitter runoff battle with Lee Fletcher in 2002. In 2004 Alexander changed parties and was reelected as a Republican without a runoff. John Breaux, Louisiana's senator for the past eighteen years, chose not to run for reelection. The Democrat replaced another long-time senator, Democrat Russell Long. Breaux had already served in the House for fourteen years. He was elected to the House in 1972 to replace Edwin Edwards when he became governor. David Vitter, who replaced Breaux, became the first Republican U.S. senator from Louisiana since Reconstruction. Vitter avoided a runoff by earning nearly 52 percent of the vote. W. J. "Billy" Tauzin, a Republican,

chose to leave Congress at the same time. Tauzin was elected as a Democrat in 1986. He changed parties in 1995. In the December 2004 runoff between Tauzin's son, Billy Tauzin III, a Republican, and Gerald Melancon, a Democrat, Melancon won. Bobby Jindal, who lost the governor's race to Blanco, had an easy victory in his election to replace Vitter in Congress. Jindal, the son of immigrants from India, is the first Indian-American from Louisiana and the second in the nation to serve in Congress. Other representatives reelected in 2004 include Richard Baker, a Republican, and William Jefferson, a Democrat. Republican Jim McCrery was unopposed for reelection in his northwest Louisiana district. In the Seventh District in the December 2004 runoff Charles Boustany, a Republican, beat Willie Mount, a Democrat.

Political News Stories of the 2000s. George W. Bush, a Republican, carried Louisiana in the 2000 presidential election. He defeated Al Gore with 52.6 percent of the votes. In 2004 President Bush got 57 percent in his defeat of John Kerry in the state.... In 2003 the Bush **tax cut** passed. . . . **Russell Long**, Louisiana's powerful U.S. senator from 1948 to 1986, died in 2003. He was the son of Huey P. Long. . . . After the 2000 census, new U.S. Congressional districts were drawn by the state legislature. Three times the state legislative districts were changed before the map was finalized in 2003.

"Tax Swap" Plan. Louisiana in 2002 approved a constitutional amendment to change the tax structure. The plan calls for cutting state sales taxes and increases income taxes for many wage earners. The plan banned state sales taxes on groceries, home utilities, and prescriptions drugs. It

Senator Mary Landrieu.

increased the income taxes for higher-income wage earners. This was done by compressing tax brackets. It also eliminated state income-tax deductions on federal excess itemized deductions.

This "Stelly Plan" was pitched as an overall tax cut for most people. It was described as the first step in reforming the state's tax system. Louisiana is one of few states with a personal income tax and inheritance tax.

Bankruptcies. Bankruptcies soared. In 2001 Harrah's New Orleans Casino filed for Chapter 11 bankruptcy. The casino negotiated a fifty-million-dollar tax break with the state. In exchange, Harrah's pledged not to cut more than 10 percent of its jobs or payroll. Even with that help the casino laid off 5 percent of its work force. It also cut 10 percent of its table games. . . . In 2002 one of the state's largest health maintenance organizations (HMOs), the Oath, went broke. The health plan, launched in 2000, left health care providers with millions in unpaid bills. It forced ten thousand Medicare members to find new insurance coverage. . . . Jazzland Theme Park in New Orleans failed also. Six Flags agreed to buy the park. . . . In 2002 the Delta Queen Steamboat Co. was bought out of bankruptcy. The Delta Queen's three Mississippi River steamboats resumed operations.

Tourism. In 2005 the Department of Tourism continued to promote the history and culture of the state to lure visitors. Tourism is a major contributor to the state's economy. In 2003, 25.5 million visitors spent 9.4 billion dollars in Louisiana. The budget for the office was seventeen million dollars.

News Stories of the 2000s. In 2000 the Saints won the team's first-ever playoff victory against the Super Bowl champions, the St. Louis Rams. In 2001 the Saints and the state made an agreement to keep the football team in the Superdome for ten years. The state agreed to guarantee $180.5 million in additional revenue. . . . The *Princeton Review* rated **LSU** the top party school in the nation. . . . In 2001 the **sixtieth anniversary** of Louisiana's **National Guard** was celebrated. . . . According to the Milken Institute's

Visitors to New Orleans may view Clyde Connell's Dancer *at the Ogden Museum of Southern Art.*

Inside the Superdome.

New Economy Index in November 2001, Louisiana was among the most improved states. . . . The NBA **Hornets** moved to New Orleans in 2002. . . . The federal judge overseeing the East Baton Rouge Parish school desegregation case for twenty-two years quit. In August 2003 the forty-seven-year-old case ended. . . . The Associated Press named Tiger's coach **Nick Saban** the college football coach of the year in 2003. In December 2004 Saban left LSU to be the head coach for the Miami Dolphins. . . . Louisiana State University at Alexandria (**LSUA**) gained a four-year status in June 2001. This enables many central Louisiana students to work and commute to LSUA. . . . In 2002 New Orleans received kudos for handling the **Super Bowl**. The twelfth-ranked **LSU** beat seventh-ranked Illinois in that **Sugar Bowl** game. . . . The **Louisiana Purchase**

Bicentennial's official opening ceremonies were held in Alexandria on December 20, 2002. More than six hundred bicentennial-related events were held in 2003. . . . That same year the Baton Rouge area failed to meet federal **clean air** standards. . . . **LSU** won the national college football championship in 2003. . . . Tax assessors were ordered to reassess taxes on households in 2004 to bring in more revenue. . . . Louisiana led the nation in incarcerations in 2004. . . . In 2005 Pollock had three federal penitentiaries. . . . In 2005 Louisiana continued to face threats to the state's **aquatic environment.** Hydrilla is more threatening than the noxious water hyacinth. . . . In 2005 Mink, deep in the Kisatchie Forest in Natchitoches Parish, made national news when the small community got telephone service for the first time ever.

LSU won the national college football championship in 2003.

En Partie (Studying a Part). 1. What part did Louisiana play in national events during this period? 2. What were the major contributors to the state's economy? 3. How does the weather affect the economy of individuals; businesses; the world; local, state, and federal government? 4. What is being done to conserve Louisiana's wetlands? 5. Why is it important that these wetlands be conserved? 6. Who was the governor elected to serve until 2008? 7. Who were the state senators serving in 2005? 8. Who were the congressmen representing Louisiana districts in 2005?

Coup de Main (Completing the Story)

Jambalaya (Putting It All Together)

1. Summarize the reactions of the people and the government during World War II, after the World Trade Center attack on September 11, 2001, and after the wars that followed.

2. Does the forecast for the Louisiana economy affect your family's future in choosing education, automobiles, homes, or relocation? What is considered when making these decisions?

3. (a) Outline a program for your personal safety in your life's activities. (b) Should you be dependent on others, especially the government, to make sure you are safe?

4. (a) What has been the traditional role of the Louisiana National Guard? (b) What role did the National Guard have during the Afghanistan and Iraq wars? (c) How did the change in roles affect the National Guard? (d) Is the enrollment in Louisiana's National Guard meeting its goal today? (e) Suggest any changes that you would make to attract new enlistments.

5. Cite the changes in the lives of Louisianians brought about by information technology, changing attitudes, and new approaches in management.

6. Select the ten most important events of modern Louisiana. Justify your answer.

7. Relate the present population data to your life, your area of the state, and the country.

8. Interpret the political cartoon on page 381.

Potpourri (Getting Involved)

1. Show how the following differed: (a) the political issues of each decade: 1940s, 1950s, 1960s, 1970s, 1980s, 1990s, and 2000s (b) the inauguration of all Louisiana governors from 1940 to the present time (c) the political careers of Huey Long and Earl Long.

2. Compare Louisiana maneuvers during World War II and the training of the military during the Afghanistan or Iraq wars.

3. Conduct research to discover changes that have taken place in any of these areas since World War II: clothing, transportation, art, films, interior design, architecture, advertising, music, entertainment, housing, food, education, and government programs. Include present trends in any of these areas.

4. Summarize steps taken in Louisiana in the field of civil rights.

5. Cite evidence to show that journalists, writers, and/or television commentators exert an influence on the thinking of the people of the state by using techniques of propaganda.

6. (a) Interview a veteran of World War II, the Korean War, the Vietnam War, or the war in Afghanistan or Iraq. (b) Interview a war bride or a civilian who lived during any of these periods. (c) Interview a U.S. citizen with dual citizenship from Iraq or Afghanistan. Describe his/her views about the war.

Gumbo (Bringing It Up-to-Date)

1. What new programs are being proposed for the state? How will they be financed? Who will be held accountable to evaluate their effectiveness? How will these programs involve your generation?

2. Trace the historical background of participation in the military. Compare feelings then with feelings now.

3. Select the ten most important items that have occurred since this book's copyright that you would include if you were updating this book. Justify your selections.

CURRENT LOUISIANA CHALLENGES

Meeting challenges and working out solutions to them is always on the agenda of Louisiana residents and its officials.

Economic Issues

City Concerns. Louisiana's cities are being forced to evaluate great changes that have come to them. Crime, racial strife, falling property values, drugs, and gangs have hastened the move away from the cities, especially the downtown areas or inner cities.

Despite expensive movements to revitalize downtowns, downtowns mostly remain relics of a not-so-distant past. Local citizens and visitors are difficult to entice to downtown areas. When the public changed its shopping habits and moved from downtown shopping to the malls and strip centers with free parking, city planners had to accept the fact that locating business and government downtown is risky business. Problems of housing and clean air, lack of parking space, the effect of interstates, the dominance of large chain stores, and crowding are some of the problems changing the faces of our cities.

Many of Louisiana's smaller towns have become "bedroom communities." Residents commute to urban centers for employment because these communities do not have supporting industries. Interstates have cut off traffic from many of the state's small towns so survival of these towns is a challenge. Government programs are necessary to provide such things as utilities.

Financing Our Government. Financing of Louisiana's government is a major concern. Neither oil nor agriculture will supply the state with the revenues of the past. The state's financial base must be redesigned. New sources must be found to keep Louisiana on a sound financial footing. Controversial gaming is certainly no guarantee of income. Louisiana must make persons who spend government money accountable.

Today's global economy demands new techniques in economic development. International marketing must be a major focus. Chemical production, water transportation, agriculture, and tourism must be made even more productive of revenue.

Highways. Louisiana has over sixty thousand miles of public roadways. Of this total, 28 percent are part of the state's system. Louisiana has one of the highest percentages of roads under state management. Therefore, the state bears a proportionally higher share of road maintenance costs than most other states. The dedicated Highway Trust Fund will finance the repairs and new construction. This constitutionally established fund dedicates all state fuel taxes to transportation and public works.

More highways are needed. The greatest problems exist on the rural state system. Lane width, shoulder conditions, and operating speeds need attention. Road repairs consume a big part of the money assigned for highways. Bridge projects, signs, and traffic signals are continuing expenses of the state.

The interstate system's life expectancy was based on the projected volume of traffic. The volume has been much greater than predicted; therefore, problems of maintenance came sooner than expected. Making the interstates user-friendly while satisfying environmentalists is another problem. Supporters of a scenic highway demand minimum and restricted markers for towns and attractions off interstates. These highways are criticized for the disappearance of many of the state's small towns.

For several years the state has been near the top of national rankings in auto fatalities per year. However, these fatalities are not

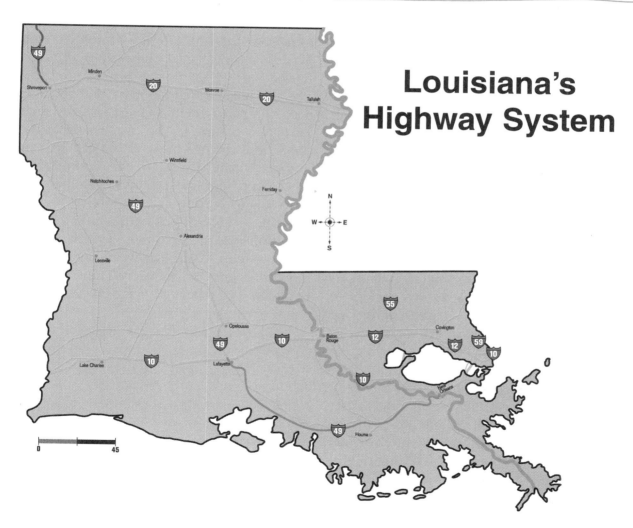

Louisiana's Highway System

attributable to the state's highways. Except in rare cases, the deaths are due to the weather, terrain, alcohol involvement, and many unskilled drivers.

Industrial Expansion. The state must attract job-creating industries. The Louisiana Office of Commerce and Industry tries to attract industry. Many city and state organizations constantly pursue the attraction of industry.

The enormous Red River project is expected to provide exciting possibilities for industrial expansion. Five lock-and-dam structures designed to make the Red River navigable from the Mississippi to Shreveport have been completed. Red River now affords a nine-foot-deep and two-hundred-foot-wide navigation channel.

Quality of Government. Louisiana has suffered throughout its history from the poor image of its government. Unfortunately, the state is frequently viewed elsewhere as being highly corrupt and backward. Louisiana has had its share of flamboyant politicians. Often they have had a flair for dramatic and sometimes outlandish actions. Even so, they have been attractive to voters of the state. Charges and counter charges concerning politicians have brought the distrust of government to an all-time high. There is a perception that the government is not run efficiently. Accusations of waste, kickbacks, irregular business dealings, and corruption of all types deeply concern Louisiana citizens.

Political scientists speculate about the situation. They say that our unique blend of cultural heritage and political economics are largely responsible for our low rating of government performance. The modern, post-oil-boom, taxpaying voter is now looking for a more serious, sober-minded, business-like politician.

Unemployment. For many years the unemployment rate in Louisiana has been excessive. Between 1994 and 2004, Louisiana's average annual unemployment rate fell from 8 percent to 5.7 percent, ranking the state thirty-ninth in the nation. In 2004 the national unemployment rate was 5.4 percent. The state employs more workers than the national average. It pays less, too. The employment in 2004 showed an increase of over two thousand positions. In Louisiana in 2003, 13 percent of teens aged sixteen to nineteen did not attend school or work. That was the second highest percentage in the nation.

Louisiana's skilled labor has left the state, seeking employment in industrialized areas. The state is now in the process of training the workforce in various fields of high technology to meet today's needs. Technical colleges have been enlarged and changed their curricula to accomplish the job.

While United States employment in construction has gone down, Louisiana's has grown. Much of the Louisiana construction is in the chemical industry. The industry is expanding to meet the overseas demand.

En Partie 1 (Studying a Part). 1. What problems have Louisiana's cities and towns encountered? 2. (a) Why does the state's economic base have to change? (b) What are the possibilities for state income? 3. How does our highway system affect our economy? 4. Relate the quality of government to the economy. 5. What are problems with labor?

Environmental and Preservation Issues

Conservation. The conservation of our soil, vegetation, water, air, and minerals is the duty of everyone. Numerous groups in government and business offer education in ways to conserve our natural resources and enforce government regulations.

Conservation is practiced for all of our resources. Waste in production is prevented. Highly trained biologists work protecting endangered species. Wildlife management areas and refuges are set aside. Various techniques are used to conserve our soil, forests, minerals, and water.

Lagniappe—The Atchafalaya River Basin. The Atchafalaya River Basin in South Louisiana is forested with hardwoods. Almost one million acres makes this the largest wetland in the United States and a most valuable natural resource. In this vast acreage are swamps, bayous, and lakes providing great recreational and commercial fishing. Within its great forests are many species of wildlife—bear, puma, fox, coon, possums, deer, squirrels, and many migratory birds.

The Atchafalaya River Basin is part of a carefully engineered flood control plan to handle the overflows of the Mississippi and Red Rivers. During the rainy season and the

Wildlife abounds in the wetlands.

spring thaws north of Louisiana, the Basin must serve as a giant catch basin to hold and absorb water and silt and control ground water to prevent flooding.

The Basin is open for tourists with boats and guides to go deep into the forests and see alligators, birds, moss and experience the heat and humidity of the tropics. Controversy over the federal government taking over privately owned lands, over wilderness preservation, over cattle grazing leases have come to the forefront. The state Legislature has authorized funds to match federal funds for some preservation work to be completed in 2014.

Leases for cattle grazing on this vast acreage are offered to local cattlemen but their cattle have to be moved when the flooding and flood control work comes into play. Levees have to be maintained.

Environmental Quality. Louisiana's record in 2004 for providing a clean environment was very good. Finding a way to control **air pollution** for the state presents a challenge. Regulations aim at controlling emissions in urban areas, the major sources. Louisiana's air quality in local areas has improved over the last twenty years. In 2004 there was only one five-parish area that did not meet the standards of air quality as opposed to twenty in 1984. Louisiana's air quality standards are more stringent and comprehensive than forty-seven other states. The Environmental Protection Agency (EPA), the agency that protects the environment in the United States, stated that Louisiana has met the air quality standard of fine particulate matter. The state reported that since 1991, the releases of toxic substances into the air declined about 43 percent.

The Department of Environmental Quality (DEQ) is the state agency with jurisdiction over certain environmental and health issues, including abandoned service stations and agricultural chemicals. The agency's waste tire program has cleaned up over 5.5 million waste tires and tire sites in Louisiana since 1970. Today used tires are recycled, so there are no waste sites. Over 65 percent of the state's sites of contamination have been completely cleaned up and made reusable. The costs of recovering these sites are covered by the superfund tax from the chemical and petroleum industries and individuals responsible for the contamination. DEQ has increased its surrounding water monitoring sites from just over one hundred in 1984 to more than six hundred in 2004.

Laws have been enacted and are enforced for the protection of wildlife—both animals and birds—our parks, roadsides, and forests. Some conflict has arisen about the recreational use of our parks where damage can be done during periods of excessive rainfall or drought. Forest fire protection, including controlled burning and harvesting, is included in the responsibility of government agencies. Injection wells will no longer be used, and toxic chemicals will not be buried in the ground. Wetlands will be protected.

Few states can match Louisiana in **litter** and **illegal dumping of roadside trash**. A small percent of the public causes thousands of dollars in needless expenses each year. This is done daily by littering the highways and forests that cover the state. The cleaning and hauling necessary to remove the litter is a heavy financial burden on the state and a needless waste of money. Currently, more than three thousand miles of roadway are being regularly cleared of litter by volunteers. Trash Bash, Adopt-a-Road, and recycling are other successful projects. Some cities have found success by making dumpsters available to everyone.

Land Use. If we are to grow the best crops and have the highest yields, then we must use prime farmland. It is estimated that twelve million acres in Louisiana are considered prime. Many acres of prime farmland are shifted to other uses every year. Should the government require Louisiana's prime farmland be preserved for future generations? Should prime farmland be used for industry and residences? Should the land be used for producing minerals or for agriculture? Should the wetlands be reserved for wildlife? Or should oil companies be allowed to drill there? Should oil companies be allowed to drill offshore in the Gulf? Forestland or farmland—which shall it be? Should this be decided by law?

Wetlands. Louisiana ranks second only to Florida in the amount of wetlands. Wetlands are most often associated with the Louisiana coast. Louisiana measures approximately four hundred miles from the Texas border to the Mississippi line. From this coastline up to Interstate 10 lies about fifty-three hundred square miles (or 3.4 million acres) of coastal

Louisiana cypress trees at Lake Bistineau State Park.

wetlands. The northern parts of the state also share in this natural resource.

Why are the wetlands considered so valuable? These lands have been called the state's most valuable real estate. No other similar sized geographic area of the United States impacts the nation's aggregate economy like this vital Wetlands Energy Corridor. The brackish marshes are critical to the life cycle of 95 percent of the one-billion-dollar seafood industry, upon which the economy of the Gulf states depends. The area provides a crucial wildlife habitat to more than five hundred rare, threatened, or endangered plant and wildlife species. This includes an estimated five million ducks and geese that use the central flyway as their principal feeding grounds. The wetlands also serve as protection against floods. They stabilize water tables and reduce pollution. The barrier islands protect the coastline from waves generated by high winds and storms.

Louisiana is losing its wetlands through both natural and man-made causes. The state partly inherited this problem, with the benefits, coming from the basic facts of its geography. Restraints were put on the Mississippi River to stay confined within its banks. This was done chiefly to prevent its flowing out into the countryside. In this continued gigantic effort, the fresh water that originally poured out over the marshlands has been forced to continue to the Gulf of Mexico. There it is dumped. The same is true of the sediment that built up the seven million acres of wetlands.

Erosion is eating away at thousands of acres of marshlands at an alarming rate. The state has lost an estimated nineteen hundred square miles of land since the 1930s. In the past hundred years, the total barrier island landmass in Louisiana has declined by 55 percent. Drainage to allow the use of the land in agriculture, logging activities, construction of roads, oil and gas explorations in the area, and the dredging out of ship channels take a toll in these wetlands. Such a loss is a national concern, as 90 percent of the coastal marsh loss in the lower forty-eight states occurs in Louisiana.

Many bold and innovative coastal restoration projects have been proposed. Much debate goes on about them. Some feel that a major diversion of the sediment-rich waters of the Mississippi is necessary. Others argue for a limited diversion to the wetlands in order to refurbish them. Plans for restoring the coastal zone include refurbishing barrier islands and created barriers. Modifications of some major navigation channels are planned. Some plans are already underway. Canal dredging has been significantly reduced within the Louisiana coastal zone. Sediment from maintenance dredging operations is being used more and more for the beneficial creation of new marsh or the replenishment of deteriorated marshes. Conservation includes using old Christmas trees for filler to hold the loose soil.

The effort to restore and protect our state's coastal wetlands and resources is now at a critical juncture. Unfortunately, roughly half of our original wetlands are gone. Restoration will require the effective and efficient use of all technology currently available. A number of problems hinder the progress. These include funding, property rights questions, and user-group conflicts. Users of traditional coastal resources may be impacted. Commercial and recreational fishery harvest patterns, wildlife habitat, coastal vegetative patterns, and land configurations will change. Restoration will not be cheap. It will affect the state's economy. The effect on individuals will vary.

There must be careful studies in understanding and preserving this valuable real estate. Louisiana voters in 1989 approved a coastal wetlands preservation fund. It will pump at least five million dollars and up to twenty-five million dollars each year into projects aimed at stopping the loss. In 1990 the U.S. Congress passed the Breaux Act, which provides approximately forty million dollars annually to the state to restore wetlands.

Conservation of Lands. Other Louisiana lands have received attention, too. In early 1990, efforts were begun to restore Louisiana's **prairies**. Scientists at LSU-Eunice are responsible in some measure for restoring the prairies. The Nature Conservancy and General Motors collaborated on the preservation of hardwood bottomland in the **Tensas Basin**.

Preservation. Interest in historical preservation has been stimulated by the creation of the National Register of Historic Places. Art exhibits and cultural activities have been included on a parish level. Exciting projects in the arts have brought opportunities for participation to many state residents. Federal agencies have contributed to all forms of art.

Louisiana began building its first adequate state archives building in mid-1984. Up until that time the state's valuable archives were not properly cared for or preserved. The state's archives are scattered across the nation. Priceless archives were purchased before the state recognized the value of its documents of the past. Much has been destroyed. Thousands of precious documents rotted in an old lumberyard warehouse in Baton Rouge while legislators debated the archives building issue. Louisiana was the only state in the United States without a state archives building.

The four-storied, 118,920-square-foot archives building has impressive exhibit galleries. A research room and a record center contain some of the finest equipment available for preserving documents and for microfilming. A conservation laboratory is part of the fine building.

In Baton Rouge, there is a Center of Political and Government History in the Old State Capitol. A research library houses a definitive collection of political memorabilia.

Water Management. Despite an abundant water supply, the state is not immune to water problems. **Water shortages, flood prevention and control, water pollution, saltwater intrusion, drainage**, and maintenance of channels are the most critical of these problems.

Water pollution is one of the biggest problems for Louisiana today. Supplies of good quality water are necessary to the development of the state. Cities have a hard time finding a good water supply. This problem worsens as the population increases. Oilfield wastes, industrial wastes, agricultural chemicals, and sanitary landfills cause water pollution. Seawater near the places where streams enter the Gulf of Mexico may become polluted by the contents of the river. Oysters grown on shallow sea bottoms near shore may be unfit for human food. Offshore petroleum spills may pollute seawater to the point of killing oysters, shrimp, and many fish.

Both the federal and state governments have passed laws to control water pollution and to protect wildlife at all locations. New methods used by industries prevent most of

Old State Capitol Building.

the problems of the past.

The salty water of the Gulf of Mexico creeps up the Mississippi River for weeks during low-river stage. Lack of rain causes the water level of the river to drop. This weakens its powerful flow south to the Gulf.

Navigation of the Mississippi and inland rivers poses a challenge. The **maintenance of deep channels** at the mouth of the Mississippi has been a problem since the French first colonized the state. Large ships must be able to enter the river.

Over six million acres of the land in the state have some degree of drainage problems. **Drainage** is really a small part of flood control.

Another water problem is caused by beautiful flowers—**water hyacinths**. These pretty purple flowers completely choke and clog many of the state's waterways. Because they double their number every two weeks, they present a big obstacle. So far nothing has stopped them. Meanwhile, they have cost the state untold millions. **Hydrilla** is presently the second most threatening plant found in Louisiana's aquatic environment.

Flood control problems plague the state. Man has long tried to control the Mississippi River. Many doubt that it can be done, should the river decide to change its course. Every control devised by man has been put in place when no floods exist. Yet these controls can only be tested by floods. Years intervene before sufficient floodwaters pour out from rivers to test the holding power of such structures as the Morganza Control Structure. Another great floodway is that of the Atchafalaya Basin.

Levees extend from the Mississippi and Red Rivers almost to the Gulf near Morgan City. The Atchafalaya was deepened and widened so it could carry a greater load. The amount of water the Mississippi had to carry past Baton Rouge, Donaldsonville, and New Orleans was reduced.

The Bonnet Carre (BON nay ka RH RAY) Spillway was built near Laplace. When the spillway is opened, great quantities of water flow through it from the Mississippi to Lake Pontchartrain.

During periods when major flooding threatens Louisiana from swollen waters of the Mississippi River, questions rise again.

Typical terrain along coastal Louisiana.

What would happen if the Old River Control Structure failed? To understand the problem, it is necessary to know the history of the Atchafalaya River. It is a unique story. About a century and a half ago the river was little more than a ditch. Here and there its channel was filled with logs and debris. The stream was once a distributary of both the Mississippi and Red Rivers. The Atchafalaya River was once connected with the lower channel of the Mississippi.

In 1831 Captain Henry Miller Shreve cut off one of the great loops of the Mississippi to form a straight and shorter channel. Old River, a seven-mile-long stream, was formed by the Shreve cutoff and connected the Mississippi with the Atchafalaya and Red Rivers. The Atchafalaya became swollen with water from the Mississippi. Gradually enough water from the Mississippi flowed into the Atchafalaya to make it the major river it is today.

The Atchafalaya flows from near Simmesport on the northern boundary of Pointe Coupee Parish to the Gulf. At the coast it flows into Atchafalaya Bay, 170 miles from its beginning.

In 1950 an important study was begun when the threat of the Mississippi changing its channel became a terrifying possibility. The conclusion drawn by the engineers' study was that this would happen if the Mississippi were left alone.

The Mississippi River Commission made a detailed plan it hopes will prevent the river from changing its course. A project was begun in 1954 and completed in 1963 to

Old River Control Structure.

dam Old River. The Old River control locks are designed to control the flow of water from the Mississippi through Old River into the Atchafalaya.

Engineers disagree whether the controls will prevent the Mississippi from changing its channel to claim that of the Atchafalaya. Some believe it will. Others think that the powerful Mississippi will do as it pleases when and if it is ready to change course.

En Partie 2 (Studying a Part). 1. (a) Which environmental problems are caused by individuals in their daily lives? (b) By industries? 2. What is being done to protect our environment? 3. Which government agencies are responsible for protecting our environment? 4. Answer the questions in "Land Uses." 5. Describe the wetlands problems and the reasons for concerns about them. 6. Why should Louisiana protect its heritage? 7. What are the major water problems the state faces?

Social Issues

Crime and Violence. Crime is one of Louisiana's greatest problems. More than nine hundred agencies work together to control crime in the state. In 2002 Louisiana had the highest **incarceration rate** (the number of state prisoners with a sentence of more than one year per one hundred thousand population) in the nation. In 2004 there were 36,564 inmates incarcerated in Louisiana. Louisiana is on pace to have over thirty-eight thousand inmates by the year 2013. Louisiana has the highest juvenile incarceration rate at a cost of more than twenty-six thousand dollars a year for every juvenile housed in a state facility. The state was first in murder and rape in 2002 and had the seventh highest overall **crime rate** among all states. The state's violent crime rate ranked sixth highest in the nation. The crime rate is higher in cities but no rural area is immune.

Overcrowded conditions in jails and prisons exist at city, parish, and state facilities. More buildings are badly needed. More personnel are needed for rehabilitation work.

Youth services and adult corrections have been separated, and efforts have been made to improve **juvenile justice** for the state. Many children end up in the juvenile justice system as the result of mental illness or substance abuse. Various programs are underway to improve services and treatment for youth with these two treatable, preventable problems. In 1994 Louisiana became the first state in the nation to initiate the U.S. Army's literacy/job training program. This is part of the rehabilitation programs for incarcerated youths and adults. In 1996 another program, Louisiana Youth Academy Boot Camp, had its beginning. The Boot Camp supports the gap between detention and shelter care for non-adjudicated juveniles who need structure and behavioral modification training. These juveniles chose this method of getting their needed help when the judge gave them a choice in their treatment.

The state's spending per **prisoner** in 2002 was $16,174, with $578 million being spent that year. The average daily **cost** per inmate in 2002-2003 was $33.61. Louisiana ranked forty-fourth in spending for prisoners. The staggering cost of crime, of which prison costs are only a part, can be compared with funding for education and other needs of citizens.

Vandalism destroys road signs and defaces property. Markings on bridges, buildings, and other public property cost countless dollars. In addition, the graffiti mars the beauty of the state.

Violence is recognized as a law enforcement and criminal justice problem. It is also a public health problem. Stress associated with the fear of violence presents a growing threat to the health and well-being of Louisianians. As a result, many people report that they have made significant changes in the way they lead their lives.

Drug and Tobacco Use. Alcohol is clearly the most abused drug in Louisiana. Alcohol was involved in 45 percent of the fatal wrecks in Louisiana. Drug crimes were the second most serious commitment crime at 31 percent in 2002-2003. About half of all juvenile offenders had some level of substance abuse history. Louisiana students used alcohol, cigarettes, and marijuana more than other substances according to a 2002 survey. The use of cigarettes, the most commonly used drug in Louisiana and nationwide, increased with grade level. Use by Louisiana students was higher than the national survey.

The government, churches, schools, special organizations, and families warn people about the dangers of substance abuse. Both state and national programs have been developed to reduce risk factors and to fight drug

Mural depicting medical research.

and tobacco use. Health services and rehabilitation for substance abuse are costly to all participants, including the state and national governments.

Louisiana's location on the Gulf of Mexico makes it a popular point of entry for drug smugglers. Most operate from South and Central America or Mexico. Some fly the drugs in under cover of darkness. Others transport drugs in ships. Preventing the smuggling of marijuana and other drugs presents a challenge. In addition, the growing of marijuana in heavily forested Louisiana is also a problem.

Gangs. A 2002 seven-state study showed that gang involvement for all grades in Louisiana was significantly lower than the norm, and it has been decreasing since 1998. Gangs include males and females, elementary through high school students, as well as young adults, especially dropouts. Minor and major disruptions by gangs happen in schools. Violence and drugs usually accompany gang life.

Health Care. The facilities that provide health care throughout the state include a wide variety of hospitals and clinics, including the state **charity hospital** system. Other programs such as school-based health centers, community care, and health maintenance organizations (HMOs) also serve Louisianians.

Louisiana has the only charity hospital system in the nation. This system is operated by the Louisiana State University Health Science Center. Most of these hospitals are teaching hospitals to train medical, graduate, and postgraduate students from LSU's Schools of Medicine and Nursing, as well as other professional educational institutions.

In its **Rural Health Care** Initiative, the state has appropriated money to support rural hospitals suffering financial distress. Parish health units and clinics provide a wide range of services including immunizations, prenatal care, testing and monitoring of infectious diseases, and health education, as well as other services.

Because **death rates** due to trauma are 40 percent higher than the national average, the state created the Louisiana Emergency Response Network (LERN), a patient care data system designed to help trauma centers better communicate with each other so that acute patient care needs can be matched with available hospital resources in a timely manner.

Another program was made to provide care for Louisiana's uninsured adult population. The **LaCHOICE** program allows more opportunities for uninsured workers to have access to private insurance coverage. In 2004, over one hundred thousand children in Louisiana had health insurance as a result of the **LaCHIP** program.

These services are very expensive. In 2003, per capita public health **spending** declined from thirty-five dollars to twenty-two dollars per person. Louisiana's ranking in 2002 in support for public health care was forty-eighth. In 2001-2002, 833,230 Louisiana residents benefited from Medicaid and 691,195 residents were enrolled in Medicare.

Scholarship **programs** are available for students who return to areas with a shortage of health professionals. Programs for medical professionals to practice in shortage areas in exchange for payment of professional education loans have been set up. These programs have been provided with state and federal funds. The funds for these programs have decreased in recent years, but the State Repayment Program has continued.

The United Health Foundation's state health **rankings** in 2004 put Louisiana in the fiftieth position. Louisiana ranks in the bottom five in a high rate of uninsured population (20.6 percent), a high rate of cancer deaths, and a high premature death rate. The state also ranks in the bottom ten states in a high incidence of infectious disease, low support for public health, high rate of motor vehicle deaths, and a high total mortality rate. Studies seem to indicate that the relative health of the population will remain at current levels in the future.

The **HIV/AIDS** epidemic will make growing demands on health and social service systems in Louisiana for many decades as rates rise steadily. The 2001 HIV detection rate among blacks was over six times higher than the rate among whites, and two times higher than the rate among Hispanics. Black women accounted for 84 percent of all new HIV/AIDS cases among those detected with the virus in 2001. The lifetime medical cost for caring for a person with AIDS is over one hundred thousand dollars, most of which is paid for by the government. Every year new infections obligate Louisiana to approximately $120 million in future medical costs.

Louisiana had the fourth highest chlamydia rate and the highest gonorrhea rate nationwide in 2001. The syphilis rates declined between 1998 and 2002. In 2001 Louisiana was eighth highest in the nation.

For many decades, Louisiana's death rates from **cancer** have been much higher than the national average. To try to understand why and to reduce the impact of cancer in the state, the Louisiana legislature passed a law in 1983 creating the Louisiana Tumor Registry, which monitors the incidence of new cancer cases diagnosed or treated in the state each year.

The tumor registry has discovered that in general incidence rates are about the same as the nationwide rates or even lower. A notable exception is lung cancer, as the rates are higher throughout the state than nationally. The registry has also documented that Louisiana residents tend to be diagnosed with more advanced disease than the national population, thus they are more likely to die from their cancer. The Louisiana Cancer Control Partnership was inaugurated in 2004 to encourage and help people make healthy lifestyle choices and participate in early detection screenings for cancer.

Other health problems exist. The **elderly** in Louisiana have the same problems as elderly all over the nation. Regulating and enforcing rules for the management of nursing homes is a government responsibility. Inflation has caused social security and other retirement plans to be inadequate. How to ensure a more secure and dignified old age is a problem for everybody.

The problems of **children** are of particular concern, too. A 2002 survey asked students about delinquent behavior. Antisocial behaviors most often engaged in by students were being suspended from school and attacking someone with the intention of hurting them. Carrying a handgun to school was another antisocial behavior measured. Of all students surveyed in these studies, rates peaked in the eighth grade. The rate for students going to school while drunk or high increased with grade level. The rates in all of these studies have decreased since 2001.

Louisiana's **poverty** rate was 20.3 percent in 2004. This was the highest rate in the United States, according to the U.S. Census Bureau's American Community Survey. More than 26 percent of Louisiana children live in poverty, the second highest rate in the nation and the highest in the South. Over 60 percent of students under age ten in Louisiana public schools were Medicaid-eligible. In 2003, 14.6 percent of the state's population received food stamps.

The state's primary strength is access to adequate prenatal care, which is eligible to 79.2 percent of **pregnant** women. Only 69.1 percent of pregnant black women receive adequate prenatal care compared to 86.5 percent of pregnant white women. In 2000 Louisiana ranked nineteenth in pregnancy rate, seventh in birthrate, and forty-fourth in abortion rate per one thousand women aged fifteen to nineteen. In 2002 the teenage birth rate in Louisiana was 58.1 births per one thousand teenage women, the sixth highest rate in the United States. Louisiana had a high infant mortality rate of 9.7 deaths per one thousand live births in 2004. Ten percent of the babies born in Louisiana are at low birth weight.

Louisiana has the highest percentage of families with children headed by a single parent— 35 percent—compared with the Southern average of 29 percent. Thirty-five percent of children in Louisiana live with parents who do not have full-time, year-round jobs. That's the second worst rate in the nation. The nationally recognized Better Homes Fund cited Louisiana as the state where children are the most at risk for homelessness.

Housing. The goal of the federal Housing and Community Development Act of 1974 is to provide every family with a decent home and suitable living environment. It is very difficult for the state to meet this goal. Low-cost housing is offered through government programs. There is controversy about the location of such housing. Housing is far from adequate in many areas of the state. Government controls of mobile home locations and safety standards have to be met.

Race and Ethnic Groups. Negative attitudes between races and ethnic groups are not limited to blacks and whites. Native Americans have confronted enormous difficulties. Jews, Italians, and the Irish have also met opposition. Hispanics, whose numbers in the population are increasing rapidly, encounter obstacles, too. Vietnamese, Japanese, Chinese, Thai, and other Asians often encounter cautious acceptance in the population. Racial discrimination overtones arise from fear, envy, and different lifestyles.

Racial problems are not simply Louisiana problems. With the large numbers of people of different ethnic groups, the situation may, if anything, be more promising in Louisiana than in other sections of the country.

Basket making at the Louisiana Folklife Fest, Monroe.

En Partie 3 (Studying a Part). 1. What conclusions can you draw from the facts about crime and justice in the state? 2. What type rehabilitation programs are available in your area? 3. What is poverty? 4. (a) What are the chief health concerns of Louisianians? (b) What programs are handling these concerns? 5. (a) Analyze race relations as they exist in the state today. (b) Give your solutions for improving relationships.

As Louisiana approaches the future, there is more reason for optimism for the future than ever before. Yes, there are many challenges. These a resourceful people can tackle. By learning the lessons of the past, an educated public can use that past as a springboard for planning a better tomorrow.

Coup de Main
(Completing the Story)

Jambalaya (Putting It All Together)

1. Select a challenge discussed in the text or one not mentioned which now faces the state. Update the problem. Give solutions and causes listed as well as your own. Classify your challenge as a Louisiana problem only or as a United States one, also.

2. Who must take the responsibility for solving these challenges?

3. List specific contributions that you could make to help Louisiana solve her problems.

4. Describe the punishment you would impose if you were in a position to do so for the following: (a) participation in gang activities (b) vandalism (c) littering (d) truancy or (e) drug abuse.

5. Rank the state's challenges on a scale of one to ten with ten being the most important. Include problems not previously mentioned, or reword the ones in the text in any way.

6. What advice would you give the state's leaders to help them solve or prevent a particular challenge?

7. (a) Do you present a challenge to your family, school, or community? (b) In what way are you a valuable contributor to the welfare of your family, school, or community?

8. (a) What measures of preventive health care and maintenance do you take? (b) When should emergency rooms be used? (c) How does preventive care of individuals affect the economy?

9. (a) What do you do to protect your personal environment? (b) Are you guilty of damaging the environment? (c) What might you do to help preserve the beauty of our state?

Potpourri (Getting Involved)

1. List teen age problems of different periods of history. Base your list on your knowledge of life during those periods.

2. Trace the historical background of today's challenges.

3. Should the landowners or the government win the debate over the control of the Atchafalaya Basin? Research to bring the information up to date. Justify your conclusions.

4. Make a record of land use in a given area. Trace the history of land use in that area and government regulations of its use.

Gumbo (Bringing It Up-to-Date)

1. Record evidences of conservation practices in the state today.

2. Make your own list of teenage problems that exist in your school, community, the state, or the country. Propose solutions.

3. Cite evidence that progress is being made toward solving a challenge. Document your evidence with newspaper clippings, magazine articles, or interviews.

4. Interview an employer about the qualifications he is looking for in an employee.

Which rules of dress and courtesies are important to him? Why have some people not been successful in his employment? What does "work ethic" mean?

5. Trace the historical background of some programs designed to take care of unemployment. Find out how successful the programs have been. What current programs to reduce unemployment are being used? How is unemployment defined? Has it always been defined according to the present definition?

6. Relate some lessons that can be learned from events in our state's history to a current challenge.

7. Conduct a survey to determine whether Louisianians are content with the state of the state. Use any research available to support your conclusions.

8. Make a study of the causes of automobile accidents in your area. Keep a record of the reported causes from the local news reports. Draw conclusions about the causes. Set up your own hypotheses to investigate. Would better signs avoid some of these accidents?

CHAPTER 24

OUR PEOPLE AND OUR CULTURE

Louisiana people include those from almost every land around the globe. The great mixture of races and ethnic backgrounds of the state's people is related to its rich history. Even though the state's people have come from widely different lines of descent, a respect for differences has developed among them. It is this potpourri of the world's peoples that gives our state a special quality and excitement.

Racial Composition

Before the Europeans came, Louisiana belonged to the Indians alone. During the colonial period French, German, Swiss, English, Spanish, African, and Indian people lived here. Italians, Belgians, Czechoslovakians, Hungarians, Irish, Orientals, Scots-Irish, and others have come in waves of settlers to Louisiana. Today's society is a mixing of these different peoples and cultures producing a unique population. The daily lives of some of these people continue to reflect many "old country" heritages.

Life in Louisiana is far richer because of the many cultural groups with each adding its flavor to the state. Protestant churches blended with a primarily Catholic region and brought standards and rules of their own. Different cultures have exchanged ideas drawn from every corner of the world with economic and cultural impact. This exchange of ideas is referred to as "cultural borrowing." Cultural borrowing has gone on for such a long time that it is impossible to establish the original source of many of our foods, traditions, and other aspects of our lives.

The chronological study of the state's history has included the migrations of these people as they occurred. For this treatment of Louisiana's people, migrations are divided into major periods. During the period from 1702 until 1803 Louisiana was under the French and the Spanish. From 1803 until 1861 people of different races and ethnic backgrounds crossed into the eighteenth state from other states. After the Civil War in 1865 through 1910, migrations of people swelled Louisiana's population. From 1911 until the present, people have continued to come to the state.

Industrial, sociological, and economic changes have caused infiltrations into Louisiana's population. World War II brought hundreds of thousands of soldiers to train here and many found brides. Some came back to settle here. The oil boom brought engineers, technicians, and investors from nearby states. The GI bill brought Pan American scholars to our schools and universities to further diversify our culture.

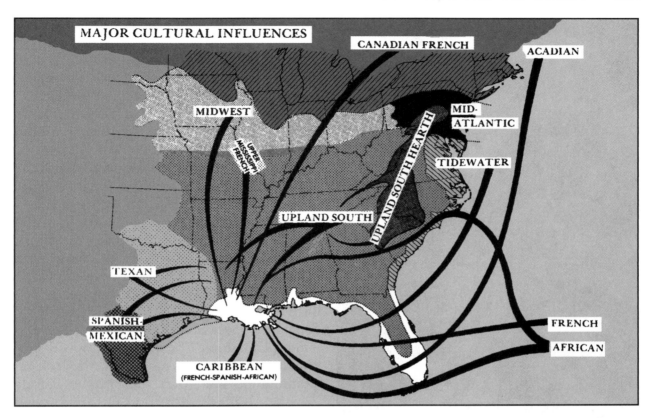

MAJOR CULTURAL INFLUENCES
CANADIAN FRENCH
ACADIAN
MIDWEST
MID-ATLANTIC
UPPER MISSISSIPPI FRENCH
TIDEWATER
UPLAND SOUTH HEARTH
UPLAND SOUTH
TEXAN
SPANISH-MEXICAN
FRENCH
AFRICAN
CARIBBEAN
(FRENCH-SPANISH-AFRICAN)

En Partie 1 (Studying a Part). 1. Were the Indians or Native Americans migrants? 2. Should "native" be applied to any group of settlers? 3. What is cultural borrowing? 4. How did migrants change colonial Louisiana?

Migrations: 1702-1803

The migration of the French **Acadians** from Nova Scotia to Louisiana occurred during the Spanish reign. The Acadians established small farms along the Mississippi River, Bayou Teche, Bayou Lafourche and other streams in the southern part of the region. Fishing and trapping villages were established in the swampland.

Cajun country today lies within a triangle whose base is the Louisiana coast and whose apex is near Alexandria in the central part of the state. The triangle contains twenty-two parishes. The region's principal city, Lafayette, is the unofficial capital of "Acadiana." The Cajun French spoken in this area is a patois different from standard French or the French from France. The Acadians adapted their skills to rice growing and crawfish cultivation, suitable to the lands on which they settled. The Cajun cottages with a sleeping loft and outside stairs were their chosen architecture. The Cajuns work hard and play hard. They are intensely

Mardi Gras in New Orleans.

loyal to their church, their community, and to each other.

Cajun cooking has gained world-wide fame. Favorite Cajun dishes include *jambalaya*, gumbo, turtle sauce *piquante* (pea kont), *andouille* (ähn DOO ē) sausage, *boudin* (BOO dan) (a pork and rice sausage), *cochon du lait*, stuffed crab, a hundred shrimp dishes, crawfish *etouffee* (ay two FAY), crawfish *bisque* (bisk), crawfish pie, and dozens more.

Historians writing of peoples from the **British** Isles rarely distinguish those from England, Scotland, Ireland, or Wales. From the colonial period through the 1800s and early 1900s **English**-speaking people came to Louisiana. The Irish, often seamen, settled in the swamp areas of the Florida parishes. Many were Catholic. A person of English descent is an Anglo-Saxon. A person of Irish, Scots-Irish, Scots, Welsh, Cornish, or Breton descent is a Celt.

People from Great Britain pushed into the unsettled territory along the Mississippi River above New Orleans in the early 1770s. They infiltrated Spanish Louisiana from the Natchez District. That is what the British called the settlements along the entire east bank of the Mississippi River between Baton Rouge and Natchez. It was occupied by 247 British grantees.

English speakers came to the rich soil and built plantations. The planters moved into the areas around St. Francisville, the Jackson community, and other sites in the Florida parishes. Both English and Celts established their culture there. Thirty-seven percent of them remained on their grants after 1781. Others moved west or returned to the east.

Other groups settled in Spanish Louisiana. Their identities were sometimes lost in the vast wilderness. During the American Revolution English loyalists took refuge in Louisiana. Men like Englishmen Samuel Levi Wells of Ville Platte and Robert Tanner of the Rapides settlement surveyed land in the 1790s and early 1800s and were handsomely paid with incredible acreages of rich lands.

In 1780 the settlers from the British Isles moved into Acadiana. English speakers managed to get deep into South Louisiana by settling in Attakapas District, and along with some French, settled in the Ouachita area during the Spanish period. By early nineteenth century they became dominant in the Ouachita area.

The food the English preferred was not so highly seasoned, and they prepared their food differently. The English common law and the English trial by jury were different from the French or Spanish law. Most of the early settlers belonged to the Episcopal church. Grace Episcopal Church and its churchyard at St. Francisville symbolize the English in Louisiana before the United States owned the territory. The English built their log houses, but they were different from the French. The English laid their logs horizontally, rather then vertically like the French. The English built their chimneys inside the house, rather than on the outside. Great colonial houses were built in the 1800s, and many still stand, relics of an age of grandeur.

The British lived quietly, worked hard, and most established cotton plantations. The British made valuable contributions to the state in both North and South Louisiana. In addition to churches and schools, they advanced the construction of railroads, levees, and road systems.

The first Europeans to settle this land were the **French**. Many of the French settlers were forced to come to the Louisiana colony. Few Frenchmen wanted to leave their homes in France for life in swamps and virgin forests. They came from different parts of France and varied in lifestyles and occupations.

St. Denis and Iberville and Bienville Le Moyne were cousins from French Canada. The Le Moyne family had migrated from Normandy in Northern France. Normandy, with its rocky shores, was not a land of farmers but of craftsmen, fishermen, and seamen.

The French first settled near the mouth of the Mississippi. In moving northward up Red River, the French left their French language and French culture in North Louisiana. The French they spoke was different from that of the Acadians. From the little village of Natchitoches the French Catholic influence spread out in all directions. Many attended St. Joseph's Catholic Church on Cane River. The descendants of these settlers, mostly a mixture of many ethnic groups, reflect their French origins.

Farm villages, as those of Bordelonville or along the Lafourche, strung out alongside a stream. The streams provided water for the household. Many took their clothes to the bayou or riverbank to wash them. The stream and forests provided the food basic to their diet.

French-speaking people have formed wave after wave of migrants to Louisiana over the centuries, thus enriching the tradition.

Lagniappe—*French Heritage.* At one time Louisiana avoided being known as a French state. The language was forbidden in public schools in the 1930s, to the confusion of children who spoke French at home. In some parishes, courts and business were conducted in French. Today, Lafayette has French-English radio stations and the news is regularly presented in both languages. Music, song lyrics, and menus are all offered in French in several parishes. The Council for the Development of French in Louisiana (**CODOFIL**) is working to preserve the French language and unique culture. LSU and its branches sponsor student programs, including an exchange program with France for high school and college students. Scholarships and state funds are offered for these programs. The French culture makes Louisiana unique and adds to its appeal to its citizens and to visitors. French is offered in public and parochial schools now as a regular part of the curriculum. The charm of the language and of Louisiana's French people must not be lost.

Hundreds of **German** families were recruited in 1719 to come to the French colony of Louisiana. The Germans, along with the small numbers of **Swiss** and **Alsatians**, settled upriver from New Orleans along a section of the Mississippi River called Cote des Allemands (German Coast). Even before leaving Europe, some of the Germans changed their names to sound like French. Even the pronunciation of their German family names was changed to French or Spanish. Many early German migrants were completely absorbed by the French. They achieved a special distinction for themselves as hardworking farmers dedicated to tilling the soil with uncommon skill.

About fifty thousand Germans came to Louisiana between 1820-1850 in almost equal numbers to the Irish. About 11,425 settled in New Orleans. In 1834 a German settlement was made near Grand Ecore in Natchitoches Parish. In 1835 the small group moved to a new site near Minden where they carried on the colony to 1871. Germantown, as this area is known, also includes a cemetery with German names on the tombstones.

More Germans were lured into the state in the 1870s and 1880s. Military conscription and religious persecution against Catholics in Germany brought settlers to Roberts Cove in the prairie of Acadia Parish. Both the communities of Fubacher and Roberts Cove were promoted by Germans who sought to bring their countrymen into the area. A Roberts Cove German priest established a Catholic church and a German school with German teachers. There was even a German newspaper, *Das Echo von New Orleans*. About eight colonists first settled in the community, and most became rice farmers. Other Germans from the grain-growing Midwest later joined them. In time they became interested in politics.

Descendants of the early German settlers have migrated to other parts of the state. In Hammond, the influence of German architecture is clearly evident in the major restorations of the old city.

Jews with centuries of commercial skills slipped into the French-owned wilderness as peddlers when Protestants and Jews were not legally allowed in the Catholic colony. Spanish and German-speaking Jews came in great numbers. In 1828 the first synagogue was founded in New Orleans.

Jews made an impact on New Orleans commerce. Many Jews spread out over Louisiana to become the owners of large stores in plantation areas. In these places they also established the beginning of banking in rural Louisiana where no banks existed until late nineteenth century.

As all over the United States, Jews hold positions of political and social prominence. Many are identified with mercantile businesses and fields of medicine. Their synagogues are established in every major community. Their contributions to the arts and education

Judah Touro.

support Louisiana's cultural development. The first public school in Rapides Parish was established by Leon Blum.

Lagniappe—*Outstanding Jews.* The great Touro Hospital was named for Judah Touro whose generosity to charities benefited both Jews and Christians everywhere. The Touro Infirmary and the Jewish Children's home were built from his contributions. His money was made from a commercial cargo ship business and from real estate investments, largely in Plaquemines Parish. Also of great economic importance in Louisiana's history is **Etienne de Boré,** who developed a method of producing granulated sugar. From his sugarcane plantation operation came the nucleus of the sugarcane industry important in Louisiana's economy today. Early-day schools, particularly, benefitted from the vision and support of Jewish citizens. Many others made outstanding contributions in medicine, in architecture, and in building commercial enterprises all over the state.

Soon after the French established their settlement, there were **slaves** from Africa and the Caribbean. The number of slaves increased rapidly as more settlers came to the Louisiana colony.

The principal areas of the state in which **blacks** located included parishes bordering the Mississippi River, the Red River, and the Atchafalaya. The Teche and Lafourche areas included plantations and many blacks.

Blacks do not have a common background. Not all came directly from Africa. Those who did come from Africa came from various tribes. Many Louisiana blacks arrived speaking French. Others may have spoken Spanish, Portuguese, Dutch, or other languages of plantation owners in the Caribbean islands, Barbados, Trinidad, and Santo Domingo. Many slaves coming into the state after the Louisiana Purchase spoke English. They were descended from generations of slaves living among English-speaking planters on the east coast, and they spoke English.

Slaves brought their cultural baggage with them, as all of the settlers did. The blacks brought memories, traditions, customs, languages, and religious ideas from their native land. They added new customs, new languages, and new religions in their new experiences. Music, art, and folklore bear strains from the riches of the Caribbean and Gulf islands. Words like "obie" came from Africa. This was a good luck piece. There were many other words. The Africans added foods, dance, folk practices for ailments, and much more to the Louisiana mixture. Gumbo developed from African game soup. The mysteries of voodoo with tokens and amulets cling to Louisiana today.

Free blacks, called Creoles de Couleur (KRĒ ōl de kə lair), were settled mainly in New Orleans and on South Louisiana plantations. Many came to Louisiana between 1790 and shortly after the War of 1812. They were from Santo Domingo and other islands of the West Indies. The group in New Orleans included Thomy Lafon, a philanthropist. He was a "patron of the arts and charitable causes." Those in New Orleans included among their achievements supporting a symphony orchestra, founding the world's first anthology of black poetry, producing plays, and developing composers and orchestra conductors. People who identify themselves as Creoles are located in various areas of the state. Senator Bennett Johnston achieved a large grant for the study of the Creole culture. This project is headquartered in Natchitoches.

The mechanization of agriculture, the draft, and World War II freed blacks from the rural jobs and caused a migration to cities. Some

A jazz funeral in New Orleans.

went to Detroit and California, seeking a better life. Nostalgia for the home state has brought many home to become private business owners, mayors, and city councilmen. Technical schools prepare many for non-agriculture jobs.

Today's blacks have become independent homeowners with modern churches and life styles. Where requiring assistance, they live in rental or public housing in towns and cities. Their distinction in athletic accomplishments, law, politics, and the arts has overcome the years of segregation and deprived education.

The first **Spaniards** to live in Louisiana came from Mexico. They moved within thirteen miles of Louisiana French at Natchitoches. The Spanish military post became the heart of a Spanish community that spread out over the low lying hill country. Many in the community owned land in the Nacagodoches, Texas, area across the Sabine River. In 1838, when there was a revolution of the Spanish against the Texas government, large numbers of the men involved were forced to leave Texas. Some moved south or west of Natchitoches.

Spain was anxious to have more settlers in the sparsely settled land. The policy of encouraging new settlers, whether the Acadians or other Spanish, to come to Louisiana was maintained. Spanish settlements were made in Lafourche, Sabine, and Iberia parishes.

The Spanish influence lives on in western Natchitoches Parish and in parts of western Louisiana. Spanish-**Mexicans** established the range livestock industry. From there ranching spread into the prairies of Louisiana. Branding, cowboy lore, and a swing quality in Cajun music are credited to these people. Robeline and Zwolle are noted for their hot

tamales and Spanish foods. Descendants of early Spanish settlers retain some of their Spanish cultural heritage. Like all other groups, the Spanish have intermarried with people of other ethnic origins.

Other Spanish settlements included the settlement of New Iberia in 1779 by the **Malaguenos** (mal ə Qwan nos) from Malaga, Spain, and those of the **Islenos** from the Canary Islands. The first Islenos came to Louisiana in 1777. Gálvez selected a site on Bayou Lafourche at the location of present-day Donaldsonville and the Church of the Ascension. There was already a settlement of Acadians there. Gálvez ordered a community, Valenzuela, to be established farther down the stream. Galveztown was settled at the junction of Bayou Manchac and the Amite River by British refugees and early Americans. Islenos joined them. Below New Orleans on Bayou-aux-Boeuf in St. Bernard Parish, another community was planted on land given by Pierre de Marigny (mä rē NYĒ). Galveztown and Valenzuela later failed, but the Islenos flourished on Bayou Lafourche among the Acadians. There were twenty-eight hundred people with fewer than four hundred slaves. The bayou "was lined with farms, only one deep, along its bank for forty miles."

In the 1820s plantations came to Bayou Lafourche, and some Islenos moved to the interior. There were altogether about two thousand Islenos in Louisiana.

By 1900 most Canary Islanders had moved to Baton Rouge. After the Civil War, the settlers left the area, and few returned.

About one thousand descendants of the Islenos continue to live on Delacroix Island in St. Bernard Parish. These people still live in

Participants in the Junior Heritage Program stand in front of the Islenos Museum.

a line settlement today. Almost all are Catholic and cherish their Spanish traditions. Some speak both English and Spanish. Others speak English, Spanish, and French. They live by trapping, hunting, and fishing. These skills are passed on from father to son.

Spanish influences on Louisiana architecture are shown in wrought iron balcony rails, gates, adobe, and stucco treatments in Natchitoches, New Orleans, and New Iberia.

En Partie 2 (Studying a Part). 1. Who were the first Europeans to come to Louisiana? 2. Where did they settle? 3. Which settlers came against their will? 4. Which settlers came during the Spanish period? 5. Give a significant fact about each group.

Migrations: 1803-1861

After the Louisiana Purchase in 1803, new settlers poured into the hill country during the westward movement. Most came from Southern states to the east. English, Scots-Irish, and some German migrants chose the hill country for their homes. Many of them settled on small farms. Most of the choice plantation lowlands had already been taken by the French and Spanish planters when the English-speaking Americans arrived. These residents share similar folkways, mores, religion, speech, politics, and culture in general with the older southeastern states.

From 1840-1860 the English-speaking Protestants from Mississippi, Alabama,

Georgia, North and South Carolina, Virginia, Kentucky, and Tennessee poured into North Louisiana. These pioneers settled in Bienville, Bossier, Caddo, Claiborne, Jackson, Lincoln, Union, and Webster parishes. The English, Scots-Irish, Irish, and the Welsh often took their slaves with them in their westward movement. The pioneer settlement of the hill country ended with the coming of the railroads and the advent of the great lumber companies beginning in the 1880s.

The Scots-Irish had a tradition of establishing churches as they moved westward. The stern Protestant religion gave an image to these English-speaking people that was not altogether accurate. They frowned upon gambling, alcohol, and cards and did not approve of dancing, but these people had their frolics and their fun. Some of these occasions were fish fries, hog killings, and sewing bees, which were little different from those of the fun-loving French of South Louisiana.

Fishing in the Gulf waters attracted migrants during the antebellum period. It was the **Croatian** immigrants to St. Bernard and Plaquemine parishes who developed the oyster industry.

In 1809 about ten thousand refugees from Saint Domingo arrived in New Orleans by way of Cuba. These **Haitian** migrants were from the richest sugar island in the Caribbean and reinforced the French influence in New Orleans. The newcomers continued their caste system by division into whites, free persons of color, and slaves. The background of sugar planters and workers contributed to the increase in sugar planting in the territory.

The **Irish** have spread throughout Louisiana. Their St. Patrick's Day—March 17—is a day of celebration. New Orleans had its first celebration of the holiday in 1909.

The first migrations of groups came after 1798 when a great rebellion broke out between the United Irishmen and the British government. The Crown owned the land and taxation and conscription to service were demanded of the Irish. There were, of course, Irishmen already in Louisiana as the name of the Spanish governor O'Reilly suggests. O'Reilly was a Spanish citizen, but his parents had migrated to Spain from Ireland during one of the ever-going disturbances.

Because of its significance in Irish migration, historians have divided the Irish migrations into before the Great Potato Famine (1803-1830) and after the Great Potato Famine (1830-1860). Between 1820 and 1860 approximately three hundred thousand Irish swelled the population of New Orleans. In 1840 one out of every five residents was Irish.

New Orleans was divided into three municipalities. The Irish and Germans were concentrated in the Third Municipality. The Irish were predominant in the part that extended to the St. Bernard Parish line.

They lived in slum conditions and found "rough manual labor awaiting them, their brawn being needed for the internal improvements and industrial growth of the nation." Many Irish worked at low-paying menial jobs. The Irish adapted to their lives in Louisiana through their social and political clubs, hard work, and gradual improvement of their lifestyles.

Most of the early Irish, outstanding businessmen and well-trained professionals, migrated to New Orleans. Oliver Pollock became a purchasing agent for the Continental Congress. He was a businessman living in New Orleans during the Spanish colonial period. Daniel Clark accumulated a fortune in trade up the Mississippi River. His son, Daniel Clark, Jr., became a merchant prince and was appointed consul. Maunsel White was a highly successful merchant and land speculator. Schoolmasters, journalists, and writers contributed to the little city's growing cultural life. Judge James Workman had a distinguished legal career, led in promoting cultural and philanthropic organizations, and served as president of banks.

Italians make up the largest group of foreign white stock in Louisiana. The majority live in New Orleans, but there are other large Italian-American communities. Two are in Tangipahoa Parish. Independence, known as "Little Italy," and Tickfaw are on the Tickfaw River. Another group lives along the Mississippi River in the upper portions of St. Charles, Jefferson, and Plaquemines parishes. There are other smaller communities of Italians scattered throughout the sugar and trucking regions of South Louisiana. Shreveport has a large population from the Cefalu area of Sicily. Baton Rouge also has many Italians.

Many Italians started grocery stores, bakeries, and restaurants. In Italian settlements, it was customary for the family to live above the store.

Most Italians in the remote colonial frontier left no records of their presence. One lone settler, an Italian, went down in history, however. The legendary Italian peddler named Garibaldi came up Red River and along Bayou des Glaises (d GLAZE) in Avoyelles Parish to sell to the Indians. So delighted were the Indian children with the coconuts the Italian peddler sold that they renamed Garibaldi "Mister Coco." His descendants to this day go by the name of Coco.

Nearly three million Italians, mostly Sicilians, arrived in the United States between 1880 and 1920. They were all searching for more economic opportunity than existed for them in their homeland. About half of them chose to stay in New Orleans. Others spread out into the villages and in rural areas. By 1850 New Orleans had

Ponchatoula hosts the annual Strawberry Festival.

the largest urban Italian population in the United States. In 1890 the first Italian migrants arrived in Independence.

In 1901, five hundred thousand Italians left for the United States. Many came to Louisiana. By 1910, 39 percent of the Louisiana population was Italian. Over 90 percent came from Sicily. Italian migrants during 1880-1914 left to evade military service or criminal prosecution or because of social and political conditions. Mostly these migrants wanted to escape the abject poverty of the feudal Sicilian society and the dominance of landowners.

These were hardy peasants, thrifty and hardworking. Many eventually went to Tangipahoa Parish to work on strawberry farms. They worked on sugar plantations farther in South Louisiana during the rest of the year. Over five hundred Italians commuted from New Orleans from the middle of March to the middle of May to work during the strawberry harvest. Hundreds of these people eventually decided to live permanently in Tangipahoa. Many came to own their strawberry farms. At one time, the school term was adapted to fit in with the strawberry harvest requirements.

Many were stone masons and built villa-like structures that are still standing in Tangipahoa and Livingston parishes.

Urban Italians supported opera and Italian-American theater. The Catholic church became the social centers of their communities in Tangipahoa Parish. They became known through the 1920s-1940s for their religious festivals. Italians look to the things that are distinctively theirs: close knit families, devout Catholicism, family activities, the work ethic, pride in home, and encouragement of a good education. St. Joseph's altars are a tradition of Sicilian-Americans. Italians are probably being assimilated faster than any other ethnic group into the larger society. Status is associated with Americanization, so Italians do not cling to the old world culture as much as other ethnic groups.

A St. Joseph's altar.

En Partie 3 (Studying a Part). 1. Give distinguishing characteristics of each of these groups of people: (a) English (b)

Irish and (c) Italians. 2. Who developed the oyster industry? 3. Who were the Haitians and Sicilians?

Migrations: 1865-1910

Belgians settled mostly in Rapides Parish. Some settled in Caddo and La Salle. A colony of Belgians live at Many. They are no longer recognized as a distinct group.

As early as 1834, a small Belgian-Flemish community existed in Rapides. However, most came in the late 1800s. These hardworking people were lured into Louisiana by people selling cutover land. This new settlement worked at truck-vegetable farming and maintained a conservative, frugal lifestyle. They have produced many doctors, lawyers, nuns, priests, teachers, politicians, and wealthy landowners.

After the Civil War, Louisiana planters, like others throughout the defeated South, tried desperately to find labor to work the plantations. Recruiters were sent to other states to attempt to find workers. They were sent to Europe to bring back indentured servants, who promised to work the land. Among the overseas recruits were a few Chinese.

On October 6, 1869, a ship from Hong Kong arrived in New Orleans with 222 Chinese recruited as laborers for a plantation belonging to two Williams brothers. About half of the Chinese were placed on their plantation. Others were hired by neighboring planters. The experiment did not prove particularly successful. A few Chinese were recruited by agents from Cuba. They worked briefly on a Natchitoches plantation and on one in the Lafourche area, but they were not well adapted to plantation work either. There is a **Chinese** settlement at Bayou Defon. This small community is still the home of shrimp fishermen.

Czechoslovakians in a large group migrated to the Midwest between 1900 and 1912. They were from the part of Czechoslovakia called Bohemia. They wanted to establish a Bohemian village of their own. A committee was appointed to locate a desirable site. Land in central Louisiana was advertised in a Nebraska newspaper. This was ten thousand acres of cutover land about five miles east of Pineville. It could be bought at costs ranging from twelve dollars to eighteen dollars an acre. It could be occupied with a small down payment. The Czechs established colonies at Kolin and Libuse near Alexandria.

The Czechs, or **Bohemians**, were a hardy people, and they had to be to deal with their disappointment when they arrived at Kolin and Libuse. They found roads from Alexandria to Pineville nearly impossible in Louisiana rains. In the advertising they had seen pictures of a school and church in the city of Kolin. There was no school, no church, no city. Unstoppable, the Bohemians dedicated themselves to building all three. The 186 families that arrived at Kolin simply went to work. They shocked the people of the surrounding countryside because they worked seven days a week. If Kolin did not become a city, it became a lively center of a remarkable people.

Their colorful dances, folk music, and costumes live on through their descendants. Their history, which includes passing on Old Country legends and folkways, provides a continuing enrichment to the lives of each new generation of these people. The Czechs have achieved an enviable reputation for their baked foods, such as kolaches, poppy seed buns, and oat cakes. An annual festival carried on with the same zest for living that has always distinguished the Bohemians has brought much respect and admiration. With their work ethic and sound financial practices, many of their descendants have become community leaders.

The **Hungarian** community in Livingston Parish was settled by people who answered advertisements in Hungarian language newspapers. An advertisement appeared in a Hungarian newspaper in Ohio called *Szabadsog* (*Liberty*). In 1890, when Brakenridge Lumber Company advertised for laborers in its Louisiana sawmill, the first Hungarians came to Louisiana. By 1900, ten families settled in a town called Maxwell. The Hungarians came to better themselves.

A farming community grew up around the sawmill near Hammond. The Hungarian settlement was then called "Arpadhad." It was named for a legendary Hungarian hero. In time the little village was renamed Albany by English-speaking settlers also living in the area. By 1908 the Albany community was well established by descendants from the peasant class in Hungary.

They worked hard to buy land, and about 90 percent were farmers. Many soon owned their own farms of about thirty acres. The women and children worked in the fields. The Hungarians found the raising of strawberries, which were already being produced in the area, a profitable crop. They extended their crops to include many vegetables. A traditional Hungarian dance performed under an arch decorated with vegetables at harvest time became an annual event. Young people in colorful Hungarian costumes performed. Folk music from the Old Country was played to accompany the dance.

Seventy-five percent of the people were Catholics, 25 percent were Presbyterians. The two churches cooperated with each other to better the community. The recreational and social life centered around the church. The children attend public schools today, but at one time they attended a school organized and run by the Hungarians.

There were at least three generations of Hungarian settlers living in Albany in 2005. Today this area has great pine tree plantations, strawberry farms, and alligator and dairy and nursery operations fully into the technical age. Their special breads and sausages are sought after and shipped everywhere.

Other Hungarian settlements are located near Albany. In the area along the Amite River and Highway 22, pine plantations are carefully tended for Louisiana's future. Near Springfield, a wonderful walking park has been established among the giant bamboo and ancient cypress trees. The area is the protected breeding spot for wood ducks, blue heron, and the white tufted egrets.

Evidence of the old cultures prevails along Highway 22, skirting Lake Maurepas. Churches, houses, clubs, and cafes define Hungaria, French Settlement, and Sorrento. Shiny white churches and clean cemetery yards lie between new houses with satellite dishes. Life is water oriented with fishing and playing.

Toward the end of the nineteenth century, **Lebanese** began coming to the United States. The early wave of Lebanese immigrants in the 1890s came for better economic opportunities. The Lebanese desired to escape the

Ottoman Turks, and the decline of the Lebanese silk industry brought financial problems. By 1924, about 123,000 came to Louisiana. About 80 percent were Arabic-speaking immigrants from Lebanon and Syria. Lebanon had been associated with France over the centuries, and many Lebanese were French-speaking Catholics. Their cuisine, with its parsley and cinnamon-flavored kibbi, is both distinctive and appealing.

A Lebanese circle folk dance used at weddings and receptions is revived on special occasions with distinctive Lebanese instruments: the oud, a round-backed string flute played with a pick; the derbukki, a bongo-like hand drum played between the keys; and the flute. The most famous resident of Lebanese descent was Dr. Michael DeBakey, who pioneered heart surgery.

En Partie 4 (Studying a Part). 1. What brought the Belgians, Czechoslovakians, and Hungarians to Louisiana? 2. Which descriptive words fit all three groups? 3. Why were the Chinese brought to the state? 4. Why did the Lebanese come here?

Migrations: 1911-Present

Southeastern Asians—Cambodians, Koreans, Laotians, Thai, and Vietnamese—started their migrations in the 1970s. Since 1975, when South Vietnam fell to the North Vietnam communist government under Ho Chi Minh, displaced Southeast Asians have come to the United States. Louisiana has the third highest number in the United States of Vietnamese, Cambodians, and Laotians who have become residents. They settled in the coastal fishing areas and in nearly all cities. The fact that Louisiana's coastal area and semi-tropical climate are somewhat similar to the countries they left attracted these people here. The involvement of the Catholic church in resettling the southeast Asians brought many of them to Louisiana. Catholic agencies settled a large number of Laotians in New Iberia. Laotians tended to become laborers or retailers.

Over 30 percent of the Vietnamese in the first wave of these immigrants had backgrounds in the medical, professional, technical, or managerial occupations. Almost 17 percent were in transportation. Another 11.7 percent were in clerical and sales work. Over 70 percent of these were urban in their predominantly rural homeland. About 5 percent were fishermen or farmers.

This immigration was expected to end after 1975. However, refugees continued to come to this country. In 1978, after Vietnam's conquest of Cambodia, publicity was given to the courageous people trying to flee their country in ships unfit for ocean navigation. These were "the boat people." Many reached this country from 1979 to 1981. By 1980, Louisiana had accepted 10,853 of these migrants.

Many Koreans have come to Louisiana. Some groups have formed their own churches and continue to cling to some of the culture of their homeland.

Louisiana has other small groups of people. A religious cultural island of Mennonites lives in Beauregard Parish.

Slavonians and **Dalmatians** came from what is now Yugoslavia. Their descendants live in villages south of New Orleans along the Mississippi near Buras. At one time, the young men went to Yugoslavia to get their brides. These people are hard workers and shrewd businessmen. Raising citrus crops, cultivating oyster beds, and processing shrimp and crabs are areas in which they have expertise.

In the 1950s their settlement became the avenue to the Gulf and the offshore industry. Since these people knew the waterways, the routes, and the climate and had boats, the men made a successful work force for industry.

When the **Filipinos** came to Louisiana they populated Manila Village, Leon Rojas, and Bayou Choulas in the marshes. They built platforms and a dried-shrimp business.

Emigrant Indian innkeepers are now our hotel and motel operators. Many computer technicians and medical industry personnel are emigrant Indians. It is not unusual to see saris, beautiful draped silk trousers and folded headdresses, out shopping with their blue-jean clad neighbors.

Almost all of the migrants have come with hopes of improving their lifestyles. Whether they came out of poverty or from political or religious prosecution, they looked to find better lives for themselves and their children in Louisiana.

En Partie 5 (Studying a Part). 1. (a) Who were the boat people? (b) Why did they leave their homeland? 2. Who is associated with the shrimping industry? 3. Which other groups settled in Louisiana from 1911 to the present?

The traditions of the Old Worlds, whether European, Asian, or African, found their way into Louisiana. Music, dances, festivals, foods, clothing, folklore, work habits, and an endless variety of philosophies of life have been brought together in Louisiana. Most of the ethnic groups have preserved traces of their own identities even though all have intermarried with other groups. Many Native Americans have been absorbed into other groups. Together, the incredibly rich blend of the cultures of all of these people has become an enduring part of Louisiana and gives the state its distinction.

Population in 2004

Single Race	4,420,711	(98.9 percent)
More than One Race	48,265	(1.1 percent)
White	2,894,983	(64.8 percent)
Black	1,468,317	(32.9 percent)
Hispanic (Any Race)	107,738	(2.4 percent)
Asian	64,350	(1.4 percent)
Native American	42,878	(1.0 percent)
Hawaiian/Pacific Islander	3,237	(< 0.1 percent)

Note: According to the U.S. Census Bureau, the numbers and the percentages may add up to more than the total population or 100 percent because individuals may report more than one race.

Jazz and Heritage Festival in New Orleans.

Coup de Main
(Completing the Story)

Jambalaya (Putting It All Together)

1. Why has the combination of different peoples given Louisiana a special quality and excitement?

2. Relate the time of migrations to the impact of the people on our history.

3. (a) Give examples of cultural borrowing in Louisiana culture. (b) What have you shared of your culture with friends and neighbors, and what have they shared with you?

4. (a) Discuss Louisiana languages. (b) What is the state's second language? (c) How has this second language affected the state?

5. (a) Which ethnic group had the most influence in the state? (b) Justify your answer.

6. Locate ethnic settlements on a map.

7. Make a chart showing the contributions of each group.

8. Relate religion and the history of our state.

Potpourri (Getting Involved)

1. Trace your ancestors' migration to the state, or do an in-depth study of your people.

2. Create a poem, collage, or story that illustrates the diversity of our society.

3. Compare the career choices of your ancestors with their educational level and their background in their native land.

4. Name the ethnic festivals that are held in the state. Report on any that you have attended.

5. Relate these words: Muslim, Muhammad, Koran, Islam.

Gumbo (Bringing It Up-to-Date)

1. Investigate to find out what others think of Louisianians and what Louisianians think of themselves.

2. Use the latest available information to summarize the trends in leisure-time activities, church membership, and current migration patterns. What is the significance of these developments?

3. What should be the goals for Louisiana for your generation?

4. Interview people from different ethnic groups to find out their assessments of where the state is, where it is going, and how best to get it there. Draw conclusions. Do the different groups have views that are similar to yours?

5. Interview a migrant of modern times to get the reaction to treatment, needs not met, or any other interesting information about the migrant's new home–Louisiana.

6. Describe migration patterns that exist today.

7. People in other states and in other countries often call anyone from Louisiana a Cajun. Why is this so? Has the state capitalized on the Cajun image? If so, how? Are there adopted Cajuns?

OUR HUMAN RESOURCES

The people represent Louisiana's most valuable resource. Utilization of all our human resources of gender, ethnic groups, and talents maximizes the quality of life for the entire population.

Population Statistics

Population. Louisiana ranked as the twenty-second most populous state in the country in 2000. The population was 4,468,976. Louisiana ranked fortieth of all states in growth. The growth rate was 5.9 compared with the 13.2 rate for the U.S and the South's 17.3 percent. It is predicted to continue this trend for some time. Half of the population is in three areas: New Orleans, Baton Rouge, and Shreveport. The other four major **metropolitan areas** are Lafayette, Lake Charles, Monroe, and Alexandria. Over two-thirds of the people reside in these seven areas. Some parishes do not have large population centers. South Louisiana enjoys the advantage of political power

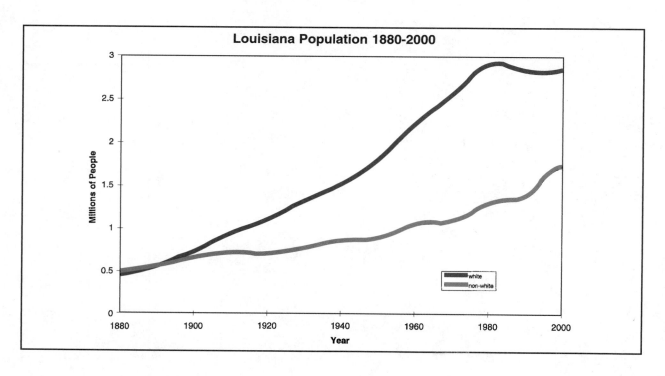

Biedenharn Foundation Home, Monroe.

because of the greater population in that area.

The ethnic distribution in 2000 was 61.5 percent white; 32.5 percent black; 1.2 percent Asian; 0.6 percent Native American; 0.7 percent other race; 1.1 percent two or more races; 2.4 percent Hispanic population (any race). The percentage of blacks in Louisiana is more than twice the national average. Minority populations are largely concentrated in the cities. New Orleans has the greatest difference, with 135,956 whites and 325,947 blacks.

Louisiana is mostly an **urban state**. Orleans Parish is the most urbanized at 100 percent. However, in 2000 there were eight parishes that were considered to be 100 percent rural. They include Caldwell, Cameron, Catahoula, Grant, St. Helena (HEL e na), Tensas (TEN saw), West Carroll, and West Feliciana.

Population Density. In 2000, the residents of Louisiana lived on 42,560 square miles of land. This means that the state's population density is 102.6 persons per square mile. This figure compares with the national average of 79.6 persons per square mile. In 2000 Orleans Parish had 2,684.3 persons per square mile. Cameron Parish is the least densely populated parish. It has only 7.6 persons per square mile.

Age of the Population. A comparison of the year 2000 national and state census counts show that Louisiana and the U.S. have very similar age distributions. Relative to the country as a whole, Louisiana has a larger percentage of population aged five to nineteen years, but a smaller percentage aged twenty to forty-four years.

Income. Per capita income is used to judge the wealth of a state. It is the average income per person—men, women, and children included. In 2000 the Louisiana per capita income was $16,912. The gain was almost 66 percent since 1993. The U.S. per capita income was $21,587. In 2003 the Louisiana per capita income was $25,446. The Louisiana median family income in 2000 was $39,774, compared with the U.S. $50,046. In 2001-2002 the average medium household income for Louisiana was $33,930, which was substantially lower than the national $42,654.

Census 2000: Louisiana Profile

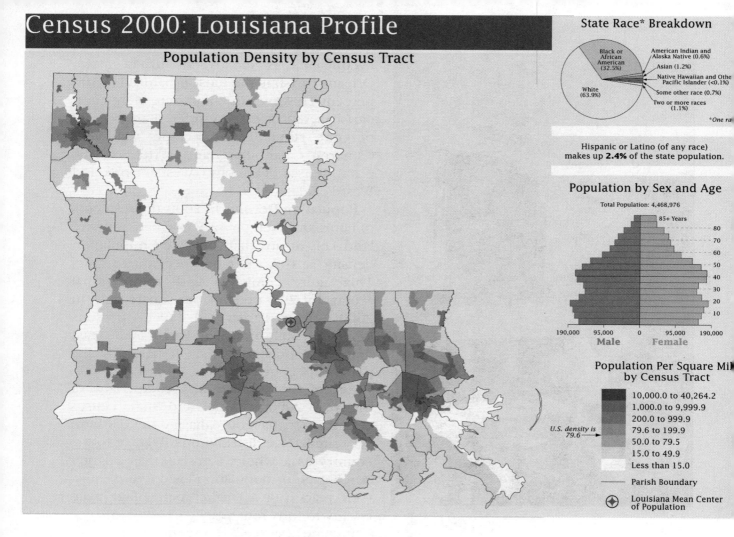

Population Density by Census Tract

State Race* Breakdown

- Black or African American (32.5%)
- White (63.9%)
- American Indian and Alaska Native (0.6%)
- Asian (1.2%)
- Native Hawaiian and Other Pacific Islander (<0.1%)
- Some other race (0.7%)
- Two or more races (1.1%)

*One ra...

Hispanic or Latino (of any race) makes up **2.4%** of the state population.

Population by Sex and Age

Total Population: 4,468,976

85+ Years

190,000   95,000   0   95,000   190,000
Male   **Female**

Population Per Square Mi... by Census Tract

- 10,000.0 to 40,264.2
- 1,000.0 to 9,999.9
- 200.0 to 999.9
- 79.6 to 199.9
- 50.0 to 79.5
- 15.0 to 49.9
- Less than 15.0
- —— Parish Boundary
- ⊕ Louisiana Mean Center of Population

U.S. density is 79.6 →

Work Force. Louisiana had a work force of 2,064,400 in 2003. The distribution included 38 percent in the services sector, doing such jobs as working in hospitals or restaurants. Another 24 percent worked in wholesale or retail trade; 6 percent in federal, state, or local government, including those in the military; 10 percent in manufacturing; 7 percent in construction; 7 percent in transportation or public utilities; 4 percent in finance, insurance, or real estate; 1 percent in farming (including agricultural services), fishing, or forestry; and 3 percent in mining.

In 2003, 7 percent of Louisiana's workers were members of a labor union. In terms of employment, services and wholesale and retail trade are the leading economic activities in Louisiana. The warehouse-type shopping, which has replaced small town stores, accounts for many minimum wage non-union jobs. Health care, hospitals, nursing homes, and assisted living have a constant demand for employees. Food processing plants offer seasonal employment. In 2003 the state employed 120,000 people in tourism. The jobs of tourism are often held

The famed Louisiana Catahoula dog.

by shop owners and homeowners and may not be reflected in the employment statistics of the state.

Louisiana has never had a broad factory base of many assembly line jobs, but the state's efforts to attract new industry are reaping good results. Today, paper mills, detergent factories, and lumber products offer new employment opportunities. Central Louisiana welcomed Union Tank Car Company in 2004. As a result of their major merger, Proctor and Gamble in 2005 made a costly expansion of their facilities. Roy O. Martin Industries increased their capacity and added new mills. These businesses will add greatly to our work force in 2006.

En Partie 1 (Studying a Part). 1. How did Louisiana rank in population in 2000? 2. What is the population of the state today? 3. What are the seven major metropolitan areas? 4. In which three metropolitan areas does half the population live? 5. Relate population density with the lives of the residents. 6. (a) What is per capita income? (b) How does Louisiana's income compare with the rest of the United States? 7. In which area was the largest percentage of the work force employed in 2003?

Facets of Our Culture

Education, art, literature, music, and theater are some of the most visible facets of our culture. To these facets can be added hospitality, sports, craftsmanship, and mechanical skills.

Education. Louisiana has repeatedly ranked among the top states in the country since 2003 for its efforts to improve schools and school performance. Even though it will take years to improve the state's educational system to the standards set by both state and national programs, much progress has been made. Overcoming the poor educational background of the past two centuries will not be easy. The movement toward excellence has caused every problem to be examined for causes and solutions. Steps have been taken to remedy the problems.

The Louisiana Competency-Based Education Program, established by the Louisiana Legislature, began January 1, 1980. At that time, a state curriculum guide in Louisiana Studies was provided, which gave minimum competencies to be attained. Act 146 passed in the 1986 legislative session made

Public education in Louisiana.

government as meeting most of the requirements of the act. Louisiana's system was modified and/or expanded to come into compliance with the law. Private schools are exempt from these requirements because they do not receive federal funding.

Louisiana's accountability program includes high-stakes LEAP tests. The student test results (Iowa and LEAP tests) comprise 90 percent of the accountability scores. The tests are the yardstick for promotion of students from the fourth and eighth grades. If students fail the LEAP tests in grades four or eight, they are retained. High school seniors must pass exit exams to get a high school diploma. State programs for curriculum have been designed, on which the tests are based. The results of the tests are reported on a regular basis. Decisions of all types are based on test results. Schools, subject areas, teachers, and programs are rated and judged.

Much controversy exists about the merits of the program. The controlled curriculum with "teaching the test" is a common complaint. The cost of developing and implementing the accountability program is questioned. The failure to modify testing to allow for emigrant status, cultural background, or opportunities continues to damage the success of the program for Louisiana. There are pros and cons of making judgments on test scores, especially when they are used as the sole basis for judgment for such things as failures.

the minimum competencies grade-level standards. Teachers were required to have daily lesson plans that showed compliance with the requirements.

The current efforts were begun with Buddy Roemer's Children First Act in 1988. The "Progress Profiles" in the program became the basis for Louisiana's Accountability System. The new program was implemented during the 1998-1999 school year. The No Child Left Behind Act of 2001 (NCLB) required each state to be accountable for student performance. Louisiana's Educational Assessment Program (LEAP) was accepted by the federal

The success or failure of the students on these tests determines the rating of schools. In 2003 a constitutional amendment was approved by the Louisiana legislature to allow the State Board of Elementary and Secondary Education to take over the management, supervision, and operation of failing schools. Failures on the exams mean repeated grades. Programs after school and during the summer to offer help for failing students have been started. Failures add to the risk of school dropouts.

Statistics of the results of the accountability tests have shown the state's public schools' strengths and weaknesses. In 1999 the first results of the accountability program were awaited with interest. They showed that nine out of ten primary and elementary schools performed below the national average. The accountability tests for fourth and eighth grades showed marked improvement between 1999 and 2003.

The American College Test (ACT) composite score for Louisiana's combined public and non-public schools in 2003 remained steady at 19.6 for the fifth year—1.2 points below the national average of 20.8. The U.S. score was 20.9 and the state's was 19.8 in 2004. Louisiana's public colleges and universities require ACT scores for admission and to obtain TOPS (Tuition Opportunity for Students). The ACT measures educational development in English, mathematics, reading, and science reasoning. Louisiana's Scholastic Aptitude Test (SAT) math and verbal scores for college bound seniors from 1996-1997 to 2002-2003 were higher every year than the national scores. Since Louisiana public colleges and universities do not require the SAT, only 8 percent of the state's public high school seniors took the SAT in 2002-2003.

A practical measure of student performance is the test given to those who volunteer for service in the armed forces. The test measures ability to handle written instructions, command of the English language, and basic arithmetic skills. Scores from the 1995 test placed volunteers for military service from Louisiana next to last.

The accountability federal and state control of parish and city programs has caused both students and teachers to seek other options. Dissatisfaction with desegregation control of schools is another important factor in making the decisions. Teachers are taking early retirement. This adds to teacher shortages. Enrollment at parochial or private schools has increased. The number of schools has multiplied. There were 371 non-public schools in the state in 2003. There were 6,054 in-state private school students. Some families cannot handle the expense of private schools. They choose another route. Home schooling was selected by 5,958 in 2003 for financial reasons or for other reasons. Home schooling does have restrictions with state requirements and guidelines.

Eight parishes were allowed to start experimental charter schools in 1995 by authorization of the Legislature. In 2004 sixteen charter schools were in place. The eleven-million-dollar Belle Chasse Academy opened in September 2002. It is at the Naval Air Station-Joint Reserve base in Belle Chasse. The Academy is the only charter school in the nation on a military base. It was created to help address a quality-of-life issue for local military families, officials said.

Money for education is one of the state's biggest problems because of the lack of money at all levels of government in the state. Yet the cost of education continues to rise at all levels. School taxes have been rejected time and time again. The new programs and desegregation orders have drained the money from the budget so that the basic needs of the schools are not being met. The Louisiana Education Quality Support Fund (known as the 8[g] Fund) has provided for some much-needed education programs. Federal grants and corporate sponsorships have been used to help provide the needed funds.

In 2001-2002 Louisiana's school districts received on average $6,547 per student from the state. Among the districts, the per pupil revenue ranged from $9,919 to a low of $5,794. In other words, some school districts have much more money to spend than others in Louisiana. In the fiscal year 2002-2003, Louisiana's current expenditures for each **pupil** in public K-12 schools were $6,906 rather than the national average of $7,920. Louisiana ranked thirty-eighth out of fifty-one states, including Washington, D.C., in money spent on instruction. Teachers do not have the materials needed for a good school program and often purchase materials for their classrooms.

A major change to the LEAP program was the requirement about **teachers**, who have to be not only certified but highly qualified. *Education Week* ranked Louisiana fifth in the nation in 2004 for its efforts to improve teacher quality. Louisiana had 337 teachers with National Board Certification (NBC) in 2003. In that year Louisiana was ranked among the twelve states with the highest number of new NBC teachers.

The need for a workable system for upgrading teacher quality, teacher pay, and working conditions is critical. The lack of enough qualified teachers will likely get worse. The state has a low salary scale for teachers compared to that of other states.

In 2001-2002 the National Education Association ranked Louisiana forty-fifth of fifty-one states (Washington, D.C. counted as a state) for teacher salaries. In 2002-2003 state public school teachers earned an average of $37,166. The national average was $45,810.

Louisiana faces many more educational **problems**. One of the state's continuing problems is illiteracy (the condition of being unable to read or write). All studies do not use this dictionary definition. For some studies literacy is defined as the ability to read and write at a certain grade level, usually fourth or fifth grade. Other studies use the term as functionally literate. Reading a newspaper and filling out forms, such as applications for a job, are the functions most often used. Studies of adult literacy have always placed Louisiana at low literacy levels. In 1991 one out of six adults in Louisiana could not read or write. The 1990 census showed that 2.8 percent of Louisianians were illiterate—the highest rate in the nation. Programs are in place to change the statistics by tutoring and adult education opportunities.

Another big problem is the dropout rate. Dropout is defined differently in studies so that the figures do not always mean the same thing. Some studies do not consider persons dropouts if they are in any special programs, such as the GED (General Education Development). In 2001 Louisiana had 6,103 dropouts. The number of dropouts has been decreasing since 1998. Louisiana's ninth through twelfth grade dropout rate for the 2000-2001 school year was 8.3 percent, compared to the national rate of 4.5 percent. In 2002-2003 the dropout rate for Louisiana was 5.4 percent of the high school enrollment. The students who failed to pass the LEAP test in the eighth grade and never entered the ninth grade are not shown in these statistics. Failure continued to be a problem for Louisiana youth, according to a 2002 survey. Alternative curricula and certification of accomplishment at various levels were proposed.

The **political overtones** in education add several problems. The State Department of Education makes regulatory decisions. Since 1985, the state superintendent of education has been appointed by the governor. The legislature passes laws about education that can mandate the teaching of a subject, establish educational programs, and make requirements for such things as tenure. The federal government continues to control much of the Louisiana educational system.

Another problem is maintaining the large number of institutions of **higher learning**. In November 1994, a twenty-year-old lawsuit over the desegregation of Louisiana's public colleges was settled. The plan set up a ten-year timetable to meet the points in the settlement. In 2005, the state was scheduled to be released from the agreement. Among the institutions is Southern in Baton Rouge, with a fully integrated enrollment.

The graduation rate at public Louisiana universities over an eight-year period ending in 2004 was 39 percent. The national rate during the same period was 54 percent. A study showed that in the U.S. fewer than six out of nineteen graduate in six years. In Louisiana it is about four out of ten.

In order to supply a trained and educated work force for incoming industries, Louisiana is becoming a leading edge reform state in workforce education. Since economists predict that service industries offer the greatest job opportunities in this new century, schools are working to prepare students with the required skills.

Art. Portraits—from fine miniatures to immense oils—were probably most representative of Louisiana's art by the early European settlers. Many examples hang in the Cabildo. Collections in private homes, such as Parlange at New Roads, include fine family portraits of mid-eighteenth century. Plantations in the St. Francisville and New Orleans areas feature imported sculpture in formal gardens.

John James Audubon painted his brown pelican in Louisiana.

An example of Newcomb pottery.

Bousillage (mud and moss construction) at the Louisiana Folklife Festival, Monroe.

LePage du Pratz left early-eighteenth century crude drawings of Indians found in Louisiana as early as 1732. Dumont de Montiguy, who was in the Louisiana colony from 1719 to 1739, left crude sketches that he used to illustrate his verse history. A sketch of Kerlerec, the last of the French governors, was made by an unknown artist of the time.

In the early American period, no one is more outstanding than the Feliciana tutor, John James Audubon, who spent his time observing birds of the area. Seventy-five of his *Birds of America* were painted in the fields and woods of the Felicianas.

Two young women from Natchitoches brought their Newcomb college professor from New Orleans to paint. This was the beginning of Carmelite ("Miss Cammie") Henry's writers' and artists' colony. Not only were artists encouraged to produce, but the excitement of attending this colony inspired interest in the arts all over rural Louisiana. Their effort triggered activity in the arts that lasted for decades. The influence spread over the state. Clementine Hunter, the celebrated black primitive painter, began at Melrose Plantation on Cane River.

From Newcomb in New Orleans came great potters' work with distinctive floral forms and colors that is highly sought after today. Another prized pottery was made by Ellsworth and William Woodward.

Robert Rucker's landscapes, George Rodrigue's Blue Dog, Juanita Courtney's works that capture Louisiana at home, C. C. Lockwood's and Philip Gould's photography—all interpret Louisiana through the eyes of artists.

From the earliest settlement of Louisiana, the state has had wonderful examples of architecture and landscape architecture. Today, there is no more meaningful contribution to the arts of Louisiana than the restoration and preservation of antebellum homes and gardens. Because restorationists worked with the National Historic Register, many of the monuments to the grandeur of a past era remain. Louisiana represents architecture from the early bousillage of French settlers to the fine houses of Greek revival. The Shadows on Bayou Teche, the Ellerslie in the Tunica Hills, the Des Hotel House in Washington, Louisiana, and the Acadian House from 1765 with its eighteen-inch thick walls and its double fireplaces tell the story of Louisiana and our forebears.

From these origins, the state's tradition of fine design continues. The work of landscape architect Dr. Robert Reich, the founder of the program in landscape architecture at LSU, and the houses of architect A. Hays Town, and the buildings of John Desmond define Louisiana today.

New Orleans was the cultural center of all Louisiana from the beginning of its settlement. The New Orleans French Quarter, the Vieux Carré, became a magnet that attracted some of the nation's outstanding writers and artists. It continues to be an artist attraction with museums, grand shops, and entertainment.

Literature. Until the twentieth century, Louisiana writers came almost entirely from New Orleans. Writing fiction and poetry carried low esteem. The Protestant religion had

The Acadian House.

its work ethic, and in a frontier land that meant only physical effort. If an individual wrote and published, the author used a pseudonym. To use one's own name so publicly was considered bad taste. The first writings by Louisianians were, naturally, in French since the colony belonged to the French until 1762. The French segment of Louisiana produced notable literary works in French up to the time of the American Civil War. Because much of Louisiana literature was in French, it was not in the mainstream of American literature.

In 1779 Julien Poydras, a planter from Pointe Coupee Parish, wrote a long epic poem. It celebrated the capture of Baton Rouge by Gálvez during the American Revolution. Such writings as that of Le Page du Pratz came from French colonial

Cammie Henry.

Louisiana. Dr. Alfred Nercier wrote novels, and there were a number of French poets.

In history there were outstanding works by Louisianians in French. Two histories of the state have become classics. Judge Francis Xavier Martin of New Orleans wrote his caustic *History of Louisiana*. It was published in 1827. Charles Etienne Gayarre (gäh yə RĀ), grandson of Etienne de Boré and the Spanish governor, Ulloa, published his four-volume history. It remains one of the chief references on Louisiana history.

New Orleans nurtured many writers, including Lafacadio Hearn. He is mostly remembered for *Chita*. George Washington Cable is famous for his *Old Creole Days*. Alcee (AL say) Fortier left a four-volume

Louisiana history. Grace King wrote about the life of Bienville and the New Orleans French.

When Cammie Henry founded her writers and artists colony at Melrose Plantation near Natchitoches in the 1920s, Lyle Saxon, a gifted New Orleans *Times Picayune* writer, was her first recruit. He wrote seven of his eight books while a resident. Roark Bradford, Sherwood Anderson, William Faulkner, Ross Phares, Caroline Dormon, Francois Mignon, and many others were guests at one time or another at the colony. While many of these writers were either already published or established with a reputation before association with the Melrose group, the total effect of Miss Cammie's contribution can never be measured.

Kate Chopin of Cloutierville (KLŌŌ shay vil) became recognized a half century after the publication of her novels and short stories. She was an early-day liberated woman. James Rice is the illustrator of *Cajun Night Before Christmas,* the most famous children's book about Louisiana ever written. The most prolific children's book writer/illustrator in Louisiana history, he produced fifty-five books.

Two Louisiana writers won Pulitzer prizes writing books about Louisiana's colorful governor, Huey Long. T. Harry Williams wrote *Huey Long*. He was teaching history at Louisiana State University when he wrote the book. Robert Penn Warren, who taught English at LSU, wrote *All the King's Men* based on Huey Long and set in Louisiana. In 2005 a multi-million-dollar film, based on the novel and also called *All the King's Men*, was produced in the state with an all-star cast.

Louisiana proudly includes writers Truman Capote, Ernest Gaines, John Kennedy Toole, and Shirley Ann Grau. Other Louisiana successes are Kathleen Woodweiss, Harnet Kane, Francis Parkinson Keyes, and Ellen Glasgow. Playwright Lillian Hellman wrote many plays for Broadway. *Steel Magnolias* was written by a Natchitoches native, Robert Harling, and was filmed in his hometown. It gave accurate glimpses of Louisiana life. It played later on Broadway.

Music. Like a great gumbo, the music of Louisiana is a blend of wonderful ingredients gathered from a variety of sources. The various ethnic groups that comprise the people of the state have each added flavor to the mix. Blues, jazz, zydeco, country, rhythm and blues, rock and roll, funk, gospel, classical, and other forms contribute to the musical heritage of the state. Each influences and builds upon the next, creating the marvelous variety of sounds that we enjoy. No matter the occasion, when the good times are rolling in Louisiana, there will be music.

From the first settlers came the first French folk music. Folk songs go along with the Mardi Gras riders. Music swells from the *fais-do-dos* and at festivals in Acadiana. It is not unusual to eat catfish in a sawdust-floored spot and be entertained with a live band including a singer. Louisianians of all ages dance, sometimes with babies on pallets alongside.

"Frere Jacques" and "Clair de la Lune" are part of all South Louisiana repertoire. "Jolie Blonde" could almost qualify as an official anthem, so identified is it with French gatherings. "Lache Pas la Patate" (losh pah la tot, meaning "Don't drop the potato," which is to say "Hang in there") and songs that reflect Spanish and African influences are popular. One such is "Les Haricots Sont Pas Sales."

Ninety percent of the Cajun music has never been written down. Yet everyone from the youngest to the oldest in a gathering will be singing the words. It takes more than words to convey the tempos and sounds of the instruments that distinguish Cajun music. Cajun music has only two beats—a slow, gliding waltz and a breathtaking, fast shuffle. Cajun music is represented by such groups as Beausoleil.

Country music is very popular with many local participants. In southwestern Louisiana, the cowboys across the Sabine River bordering Texas have added their influence to French folk songs. In 1948, country music came into prominence. It was not only acceptable, it became very popular. Radio station

Mary Alice Fontenot, acclaimed author of Clovis Crawfish books.

The French influence on music is still apparent.

KWKH of Shreveport created the sensational Louisiana Hayride. Their very first show presented stars. Twenty of the Hayride artists are represented in the Country Music Hall of Fame. Among the stars were Elvis Presley and Hank Williams, Sr. Louisiana is represented in country music today by artists Tim McGraw and Kix Brooks of the duo Brooks and Dunn.

Louisiana's fame in the national music world has come from the fabulous creations of blacks. Jazz is said to have begun in New Orleans in the 1920s. It is likely jazz was present among blacks in Louisiana long before that date. The talent of a people expressing the gamut of human emotions is felt in their music. The New Orleans Jazz and Heritage Festival is an annual event that draws huge crowds. Louisiana has contributed many artists in the jazz world including Louis Armstrong, Al Hirt, Professor Longhair, the Marsalis family, and Harry Connick, Jr.

Zydeco (ZY de coh) is a uniquely Louisiana creation. It is a mixture of Afro-Caribbean rhythms and French-European melodies. The rhythm is said to lie between traditional Cajun music and modern rock. Clifton Chenier was but one of the many musicians who have popularized zydeco.

Gospel songs created in the numerous black churches of the state are classics. Words were mostly unwritten, and singers created many variations. The gospel music of white North Louisiana was equally vital to their congregations. Singing conventions and even week-long camps brought families together to sing. Robert McGimpsey recorded the spirituals as his lifetime work. Threads of the spirituals appear in the new world symphony performances at Lincoln Center.

The marching bands of Southern and Grambling thrill the crowds each year at the Bayou Classic in New Orleans. The Golden Band from Tigerland appears at LSU games.

Louisiana has made and continues to make innumerable contributions to the development of American music.

Theater. New Orleans became the cultural center of Louisiana during the nineteenth century. The first professional theatrical performance in Louisiana was given in New Orleans in 1791. In 1796 New Orleans hosted the first opera performance ever held in America. In 1859 the French Opera House was built in the French Quarter. Louis Morean Gottschalk, a New Orleans native,

Zydeco Music Festival, Plaisance.

facilities for concerts. Thespian or dramatic groups are found throughout the state. Southern University sponsors an active group with works of local writers. Lake Charles has an outstanding group and LSU in Alexandria offers classes and performances. The restoration of the Saenger Theatre in New Orleans now enables major Broadway shows to appear there. Alexandria recently dedicated the Coughlin Sanders Auditorium as a center for performing arts, and Shreveport's restored Strand Theater is the center for many performances.

En Partie 2 (Studying a Part). 1. Analyze Louisiana's offerings in one of these areas: (a) art (b) education (c) literature (d) music (f) theater. 2. Relate Audubon to Louisiana. 3. How does early Louisiana literature differ from that of other states? 4. Identify the types of music for which Louisiana is best known.

---

was the first American concert artist to win recognition in Europe. He was a child prodigy born in 1829. A second child prodigy from the Crescent City was acclaimed Earnest Giraud, born in 1839, who wrote an opera performed at Orleans Theater.

During the 1800s the word "opera" was used for performances other than grand opera. Traveling shows were presented in "opera houses" in villages. Ventriloquists, magicians, popular singers, and comedy acts might be seen at such opera houses.

Today, most of the major cities and larger towns in the state have playhouses and

Contemporary media brought cultural influences to Louisiana homes and in turn has taken Louisiana culture to the world. Louisiana can be a model for how a great diversity of people work and play together and produce the incredibly rich culture for which the state is famous.

Coup de Main
(Completing the Story)

Jambalaya (Putting It All Together)

1. (a) How does music contribute to the

state's economy? (b) How much do you contribute to the economy with the purchase of instruments, equipment, concert tickets, CDs, and other music-related purchases? (c) How much time do you devote to your interest in music?

2. (a) Why is hospitality included as a facet of our culture? (b) Describe Southern hospitality. (c) Relate it to the image of the South and Louisiana in particular.

3. How does contemporary media bring cultural influences to Louisiana homes and, in turn, take Louisiana culture to the world?

4. Describe the problems in Louisiana schools at the present time.

5. Give the details of the accountability program that affect you.

6. Why do dropouts often present problems for the community and the state?

7. Evaluate your education in the arts, music, and theater. Did you gain an appreciation for art, music, or the theater after a study of the topic?

8. Explain what it means to say that Louisiana music is like a gumbo.

Potpourri (Getting Involved)

1. Explain this statement: Visionaries spur on this society to achieve new goals for the betterment of the people.

2. Research any type of Louisiana literature.

3. Do an in-depth study of a Louisiana author, artist, educator, musician, actor, actress, playwright, or athlete. Should this person be in a Louisiana Hall of Fame? Justify your answer.

4. Make a study of any type of Louisiana music. How has Louisiana been viewed in song?

5. Where are Louisiana's Halls of Fame located? What are the requirements for becoming a member?

Gumbo (Bringing It Up-to-Date)

1. Investigate careers in Louisiana and predict possible future careers in the state.

2. What is the part played by the federal government in your local public school today? Interview a leader in education to find out what federal programs are a part of your system.

3. Use the latest available information to summarize the trends in major occupations, distribution of income, leisure-time activities, school and college enrollment and achievement, and the relationship of the labor force to the total population. What is the significance of these developments?

4. What should be the goals for Louisiana for your generation?

5. List Louisiana living artists, musicians, authors, actors, actresses, or television journalists who enjoy nationwide fame.

6. Report on Louisiana's official poet, artist laureate, or historian. Who selects them? How much are they paid? What do they do? Who has held these titles in the past? Who holds them now?

7. Compare public schools before and after federal intervention. What is the part played by the federal government in your local public school today?

OUR NATURAL RESOURCES
AND INDUSTRIAL DEVELOPMENT

Louisiana is rich with a wide variety of natural resources. It has been said that these resources would allow the people of the state to live comfortably even if we were isolated from the rest of the world. The state has benefitted greatly from mineral resources. Other resources are equally important. The state's farm products, fur industry, livestock and dairy, forests, and the various products from the waters are all important to the economy of the state. Almost every section of the state has been industrialized with a natural resource being used as a base.

Lagniappe—*Renewable and Nonrenewable Resources.* Any natural resource that can be restored to its original state after use is a renewable resource. One of Louisiana's most important renewable resources is lumber. Restoration programs help restore renewable resources to their original condition. Nonrenewable resources cannot be restored. Once a nonrenewable resource is used, it can't be replaced. Petroleum, gas, sulphur, and salt are nonrenewable resources.

Agriculture

Agriculture is a major contributor to the state's economy. Mechanization and technological advances have dramatically changed agriculture, which provides essential raw materials for industries. Today's highly mechanized farms are larger with fewer laborers. Less than one-fourth as many people work on Louisiana's farms as work in the industries.

This state occupies an important place in the nation's agriculture. Louisiana in 2003 was among the top ten states in the **production** of sugarcane (second), sweet potatoes (third), rice (third), cotton (seventh), and pecans (fifth). The state ranked eighteenth in soybean production. Specialty crops grown in the state include strawberries, peaches, peppers, and tung nuts.

Crops accounted for 65 percent of farm **income** in 2002, with livestock and livestock products accounting for 35 percent. Poultry and eggs are the most economically important livestock products. Poultry, cattle, calf, and hog production and dairy farming are leading sources of revenue in agriculture. Exotic animal farms are new additions to the agricultural picture. In 2004 the three million pounds of honey produced had a return of about four million dollars. The racehorse industry significantly contributed to Louisiana's economy in 2004. Louisiana's nursery industry is important in Central Louisiana and in the Florida parishes.

In 2003 **farmland** covered nearly a third of Louisiana's land area or 7.85 million acres.

Bees gathering pollen to make honey.

The state is a leader in diversified agriculture. Extremely fertile soils are the state's basic resource. Almost every kind of farm produce grown in the Western Hemisphere can be produced in the Pelican State. Louisiana has the climate, soil, and rainfall that combine to produce bountiful farm products.

Crops are raised on 65 percent of all farmland in Louisiana. Most of the remaining farmland is used for pasture. There were 27,200 farms in the state in 2003, averaging 289 acres in size. The largest farms are the highly mechanized farms located in the Mississippi Alluvial Plain and in the sugar and rice-producing areas of the West Gulf Coastal Plain.

Louisiana continues to have cotton, rice, and sugarcane as its major crops. Corn and soybean acreage has declined because of disease invasion. The severe drought of 1998 brought aslatoxin to invade the cornfields. Soybean rust, a wind-borne fungus that restricts plant growth, hit Louisiana crops in 2004. The boll weevil control program, so carefully enforced, has reduced that cost and peril to cotton farmers. The sugarcane industry faced changes in 2005. Two small co-op refineries closed. New harvesting methods with expensive equipment and high costs of transportation to distant mills may force cane growers to reconsider cane production in a fluctuating market. Crop selection is also dependent upon the competitive developing foreign growers.

In the nineteenth century and for several decades afterwards, most of the population

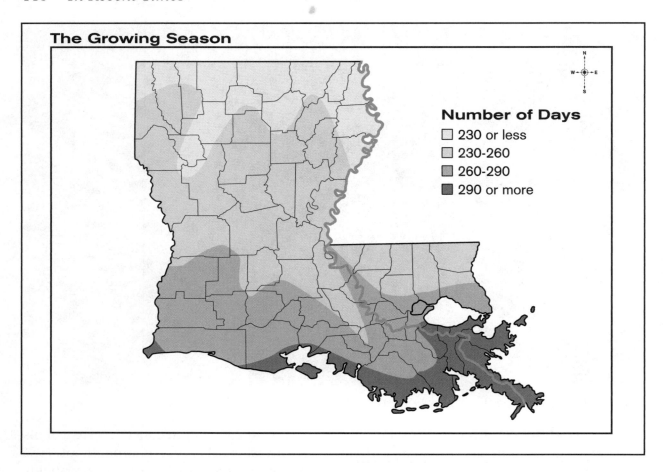

The Growing Season

Number of Days
- ☐ 230 or less
- ☐ 230-260
- ☐ 260-290
- ■ 290 or more

outside New Orleans made their living from agriculture. Agriculture, along with oil and gas, continues to contribute greatly to the state's economy. It remains a major part of the society of this state as well.

Changes. Agriculture has changed dramatically since World War II. Machines and agricultural chemicals brought the end to the old plantations. Plantations have been replaced by commercial farms. Plantations involved large numbers of field workers. Many of the commercial farms have no individual living on the land. Instead of one-owner operations, big corporations have now taken over many farm operations. The family farm has almost disappeared.

The Revolution in Agriculture. A great industrial revolution changed factories around the world dramatically in the late 1700s and 1800s. The Agricultural Revolution began in the early 1900s with the first motorized buggies. In a few decades these became automobiles. Tractors were introduced in the 1920s. By World War II tractors had replaced both men and mules plowing the fields. Work to develop machines to pick cotton and cut sugarcane increased rapidly with the crisis of World War II. Cotton pickers and cane cutters replaced people in both crops by the early 1950s. Corn pullers, potato diggers, milking machines—the list of farm machines created to replace human labor goes on and on. Modern cotton gins replaced large numbers of small gins. These gins compress the bales into compact packages.

Lines of plantation cabins and small armies of black **workers** disappeared. Only skilled or semiskilled workers find work on large farms today.

Airplanes for planting, spraying, defoliating, and fertilizing became part of the revolution. Effective herbicides, insecticides, and fungicides added to the new agricultural methods. Weed control by chemicals accounted for a vast reduction in labor.

The improved variety of crops, new fertilizers, new methods of farming, and other factors greatly increased production. Government **farm programs** dating from the 1930s affected the acreage planted and value of crops produced in the state.

As a result, government programs to control production, conservation, and protection of land were developed. The character of farming changed as controls were put into effect. What and how much the farmer planted were often determined by government controls. Government controls were intended to prevent overproduction and to educate farmers in methods to handle chemicals.

In 1996 the Farm Bill was passed, which set up certain government control programs for agriculture. In 2002 modifications were made to the bill. Further modifications are expected to affect cotton, sugarcane, and corn.

Much work is being done to change the application of **insecticides** and **herbicides**. Far lower costs can be obtained by farmers in pinpointing the areas where these are needed. Some insecticides and herbicides are applied close to the ground. This is in contrast to the broadcast method where pesticides are applied by airplanes.

The **lifestyle** of modern farmers has radically changed from the past. Many farmers live in town. Their families go to the farm only on occasional visits, if at all. Some farmers fly their own airplanes. Pickups and heavy farm machinery are apt to be air-conditioned. With the communication explosion and rapid transportation the farmer is no longer isolated.

Research. Many of these changes have come about as a result of research. Research is constantly underway by the government and private businesses. Louisiana is a leading state in agricultural research. Attempts to apply scientific knowledge to farming have gone on for many years. It began with the creation of the United States Department of Agriculture in 1862. Our land-grant university, Louisiana State University, is the state's center of agricultural research. Much of the research is done at the fourteen agricultural experiment stations scattered throughout the state. Many trained scientists in a number of fields work to produce a better variety of crops, improve farm practices, and introduce better methods of livestock and crop production.

The Louisiana Cooperative Extension Service extends research findings from Louisiana State University throughout the state's population. It passes on helpful information from the United States Department of Agriculture, other farm people, and other researchers as well. Specialists and agents work in each parish. A series of adult education courses, workshops, and short courses are held throughout the year.

Marketing. A well-planned promotion program advertises Louisiana products. Fairs and festivals promote farm products. These play an important part in economic development. This is combined with important cultural contributions. Over the years, fairs have created interest in improving the quality and yield of livestock, sugarcane, cotton, yams, rice, dairy products, and many other farm products. The annual state fair is held in Shreveport. Parish fairs are held throughout the state. Louisiana celebrates with more fairs and festivals than any other state.

The Louisiana Department of Agriculture and Forestry sponsors competitions among different groups. Future Farmers of America (FFA), 4-H members, and adults compete in exhibitions. These include

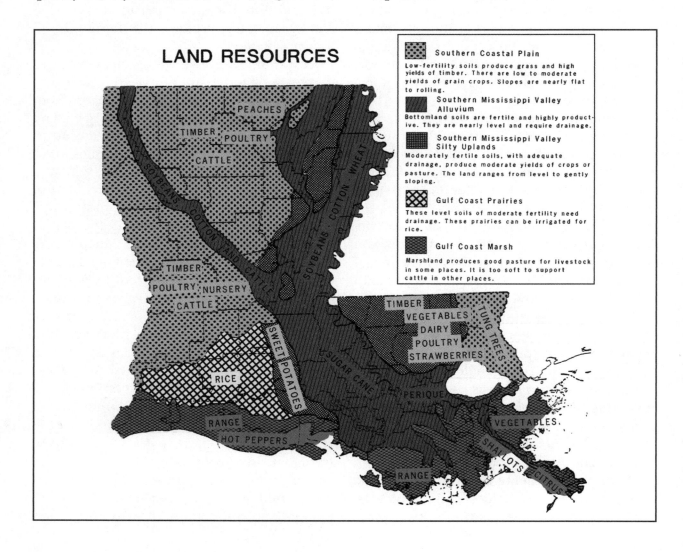

LAND RESOURCES

Southern Coastal Plain
Low-fertility soils produce grass and high yields of timber. There are low to moderate yields of grain crops. Slopes are nearly flat to rolling.

Southern Mississippi Valley Alluvium
Bottomland soils are fertile and highly productive. They are nearly level and require drainage.

Southern Mississippi Valley Silty Uplands
Moderately fertile soils, with adequate drainage, produce moderate yields of crops or pasture. The land ranges from level to gently sloping.

Gulf Coast Prairies
These level soils of moderate fertility need drainage. These prairies can be irrigated for rice.

Gulf Coast Marsh
Marshland produces good pasture for livestock in some places. It is too soft to support cattle in other places.

displays of livestock, poultry, and the other farm products grown in the state.

Promotion is a vital part of marketing crops. Promotion of Louisiana products has made the state's crops known around the world. Louisiana has long supported an aggressive foreign marketing program. Such promotion will increase with the expanding world markets.

Farm-related industries increased production. Between 1965 and 1985 the cottonseed oil industry (margarine, cooking oil, and cosmetics) became one of the most important in the state. Eight factories in New Orleans process cottonseed oil and its by-products. In 1990, 80 percent of the cottonseed went to the cottonseed oil industry and the rest went to the feed market. In 2004 the seed market changed so that a greater percentage was in the dairy feed market. By 1990 the value of the business was over seven million dollars, and in 2004 the value was a little over thirty-five million dollars. The 2004 value of the United States market was $925 million.

Agribusiness. Major changes in the outlook of agriculture are revealed in a word that has come into use: **agribusiness**. Agriculture, aquaculture, and forestry, as well as marketing, processing, and transportation of agricultural products, are included in the agribusiness. Many agribusiness firms are located in urban areas.

Today's farmers must be knowledgeable businessmen. The farm people in the rural areas have become part of the vast economic system. The differences in life on the farm and in the city have become fewer. The future of agribusiness seems to promise that these differences will continue to disappear.

Future. Agriculture will continue to be one of the most important sectors in the state's economy. When agriculture prospers, the entire state prospers. It has a multiplier effect on the state's economy. This means that related businesses create jobs and provide income for the state. Such businesses involve storing, shipping, processing, packaging, and merchandising of farm products.

The future of Louisiana agriculture will be shaped by the world's growing needs. Many changes may be in store for Louisiana agriculture with the world outlook. The need to feed the world is magnified with growing populations. Crop production will fluctuate with demands of the world market.

En Partie 1 (Studying a Part). 1. Why is Louisiana a good agricultural state? 2. How does Louisiana rank in agricultural production? 3. How does this agricultural production affect our economy? 4. Describe the revolution in agriculture. 5. What part have research and promotion played? 6. Describe the agricultural picture in Louisiana today. 7. How does the current agricultural picture in the state affect your life?

Forest Industry

Louisiana's Number One Crop. Entering the twenty-first century, Louisiana's number one crop is its forests. Forestry is the largest single land-use industry. The state ranked among the foremost producers of timber in the nation in 2004. It ranked high in the nation in production of pulpwood and southern pine plywood and developed new mills that produce innovative products including engineered lumber. In 2003 about 1.3 billion board feet of saw timber was harvested along with almost seven million cords of pulpwood. Over four million cords of pine pulp came out of state forests in 2003. There are 148,000 landowners of forests. The annual sales of timber amounted to six hundred million in 2003.

History. If the first settlers had measured, they would have found that almost twenty-six million of the thirty-one million acres in this land were covered with trees. This was three centuries ago. Today forests occupy between 45 and 50 percent of the state's total nonmetro land area. In the 2000s there are 13.8 million acres of forest in the state.

The newcomers found almost 150 species of native trees. From **hardwoods**, like oaks, to the **softwoods**, like pine, the settler had his choice. The forests yielded lumber for every possible need. Tall pine trees seemed to reach the sky. The hills were covered with these pines. Four kinds of pines were felled for making lumber and other wood products. The trees included cypress, which the new settlers put to use in their first homes. Cypress grows in the deep swamps. The cypress flares at its base to form buttresses to support the tall trees growing in wet, insecure soil. Its many strange knees, or roots, come out of the water. These roots are used for decorative purposes and crafts today.

The forests of Louisiana were among the first of the state's natural resources to be developed. Today they produce the raw materials for one of the state's chief industries.

Reforestation. This multibillion-dollar industry has developed from the cutover lands of the early "cut out and get out" days.

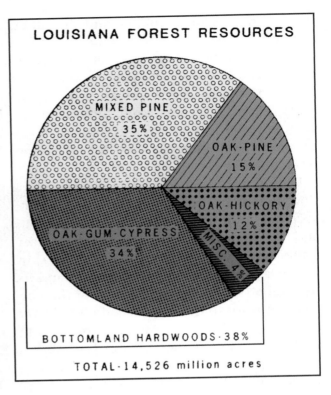

LOUISIANA FOREST RESOURCES

MIXED PINE 35%

OAK-PINE 15%

OAK-HICKORY 12%

MISC. 4%

OAK-GUM-CYPRESS 34%

BOTTOMLAND HARDWOODS·38%

TOTAL·14,526 million acres

After those days, lumbering began a steady decline. The native forests had been cut, especially the giant longleaf pines and the cypress. These two varieties make fine lumber, but they grow very slowly. By the early 1930s and the Great Depression, Louisiana lumber production had fallen drastically. Most major sawmills and lumber companies had ceased operating. A carefully planned conservation program was started in the early 1900s.

Outstanding among men dedicated to saving the forest industry was **Henry Hardtner** of Urania. He believed that Louisiana could have a second crop of trees. Hardtner is now known as the "Father of Forestry in the South."

Hardtner organized the Urania Lumber Company in 1898. He devoted himself to finding ways of making new crops of timber grow. He sought the advice of the United States Forestry Service in 1910 and became a strong supporter of reforestation in the state. Hardtner wrote the general conservation laws for Louisiana as a member of the legislature. He helped pass the Reforestation Act of 1910. Under this act landowners could sign an agreement to reforest their lands and be guaranteed a fixed amount of money for as long as forty years. This act did not work very well, however.

Not only did Henry Hardtner prove that Louisiana's forests could be rebuilt, but he also proved that forests themselves worked at making a second crop. Largely as a result of his effort, the trees gradually began to grow again.

It is believed that Hardtner's project at Urania was the beginning of the reforestation movement in Louisiana. His project served as an example to other companies, and its fame and influence spread to other states. Yale University sent students to study Hardtner's methods. The contributions by Hardtner and the Urania Lumber Company are still being felt in Louisiana.

Other efforts helped in the **conservation** of our forests. President Theodore Roosevelt had started an enthusiastic forest conservation movement across the nation. Louisiana's legislature created its department of forestry in 1904. The public schools were told to teach forestry. Arbor Day, tree-planting day, was set aside for special recognition. These actions and similar legislation brought an increased awareness of the value of the pine forests. Even then they were being stripped by out-of-state and in-state lumber interests.

Acres and acres of cutover land, which had seemed useless, were planted. Gradually, the trees began to grow again. It was a slow process to which government agencies and laws greatly contributed. During the 1940-1950 period the tree-farm movement began. The Timber Severance Act after World War II actually created the program of reforestation in Louisiana. More than two million acres of forestlands were restored to production by a massive reforestation effort. The thriving industry it is today has come through dedicated work.

Related Industries. New related industries have developed. The old ones have continued to expand. For many years, Louisiana forests have supported an industry that is a mainstay of the state's **economy.** Altogether, the wood industries add billions of dollars to the Louisiana economy each year. Louisiana's forest products feed our sawmills, Kraft paper and fine-paper mills, plywood and particle board plants, liner board and container board factories, paper bag plants, pulp mills, veneer plants, cooperage plants, and plants treating wood products with chemical preservatives. The naval stores (products such as turpentine or pitch, originally used to caulk wooden ships) industry is a money-maker dependent upon Louisiana trees. Furniture and flooring manufacturers get their raw materials from Louisiana's forest.

The **Spanish moss** industry developed very early. The moss was used in upholstered furniture and mattresses. Today moss is marketed to the florist industry.

Other Products. Forty-seven parishes have wood-using industries. Poles, pilings, crossties, barrels, veneer, baskets, handles, crates, charcoal, fence pickets, golf tees, and boat paddles are all made from Louisiana timber. Louisiana still produces wooden matches but not in the

Spanish moss.

same quantities as were done before industries moved overseas.

Problems. Although demands for more and more forest products are expected, the amount of land with forests has declined since 1965. This reduction has been due largely to the destruction of forests for construction of roads, houses, and businesses. There has also been the use of forestlands for farming, particularly for growing soybeans. However, some of these lands are being returned to forests or other uses. Land use patterns are changing.

Since the recession beginning in 1981, the forest industry has faced setbacks. The high interest rates caused homebuilding to decline. Many plants closed. In the mid-1980s some of these plants returned to production.

Since that time, forest products have demanded greater prices than ever before because of curtailed operations in forests due to environmental regulations. The 1990s were good years for the forest industry. Because a high percentage of Louisiana forests are owned by individuals and companies instead of the government, the industry has not been as greatly affected as it has been in other states. In the 2000s timber prices have fallen from peaks in the 1990s but remain at a level that is profitable for forestland owners while allowing Louisiana forest industries to remain competitive.

Conservation. Today, Louisiana forests are restored. Trained foresters tend the state's great resource. Laws protect against waste.

The business of restocking goes on steadily. The "second forest" replaced the virgin forests. It will be replaced by the "third forest," which is already beginning to evolve. Plans have been made for the third forest to meet expected needs in the future. The third forest is growing on fewer acres with greater production. It has required the united efforts of government, industry, and landowners.

Both the government and private industry have spent much time and effort to ensure the future supply of timber. Seedlings are planted where mature trees have been cut. The Office of Forestry provides seedling trees. The government helps small landowners with **tree planting**. It also assists landowners with forest management plans and aids in **prescribed burning**. Special attention is given to **insect** and **tree disease control**. As a result of all these efforts, the basic forest resources of Louisiana will be available to support the many forest industries in the future.

A **fire control system** of observation towers and lookouts is part of the conservation program. Even though Louisiana does not have the giant forest fires seen in Western states, it has a large number of more contained fires. It is a sad fact that woods arsonists are responsible for over three-fourths of these fires.

Future Expectations. Forest growth potential in the state is as great as that of any other southern state. The contribution of forestry to the economy is expected to vastly increase. The optimism is due to expected developments in many areas, including secondary forest project manufacturing. New techniques, improved equipment, new products, and more efficient production are in the plans for the future. Pine tree farms are a big business in Louisiana today. Forests will remain a major crop.

Lagniappe—*Caroline Dormon.* Caroline Dormon was the first woman employed in the forestry industry in the United States. She worked with Louisiana and U.S. Forest Service leaders to establish **Kisatchie National Forest**, which is comprised of 600,000 acres and includes seven parishes.

Kisatchie Bayou.

Caroline was born on July 19, 1888, to James Alexander Dormon, a lawyer, and Caroline Trotti Sweat Dormon at their summer home in Natchitoches Parish. She later renamed the retreat Briarwood. She graduated Judson College in Marion, Alabama, and began her career as a public school teacher before serving on the legislative committee to study the state's forestry laws.

Caroline's work was well known. Her first book was *Arbor Day Program for Louisiana*, published in 1928. In 1965 she was awarded an honorary Doctorate of Science degree from Louisiana State University for her achievements in botany and horticulture.

Before she died in Shreveport in 1971, she willed Briarwood to the Foundation for the Preservation of the Caroline Dormon Nature Preserve. For more information on Caroline Dormon, visit the Web site http://www.explorenatchitoches.com/outdoors.

En Partie 2 (Studying a Part). 1. Trace the history of the forestry industry in Louisiana. 2. How much and what have our forests contributed to our economy? 3. What methods are used to preserve our forestry resource?

Wildlife and Fisheries

Seafood Industry. Louisiana's fisheries continue to provide abundant resources for both commercial production and recreational enjoyment. The many miles of shoreline and bayous provide an excellent habitat for fish. This feature has enabled the state to take a leading role in this industry. Louisiana's commercial fishing industry in 2004 produces 13 percent of all the seafood domestic landings in America. The state is second in commercial landings by weight and value. It holds the record for the second greatest catch ever, 1.9 billion pounds in one year. No other state surpasses Louisiana in the number of commercially valuable seafood species. There are over one hundred types.

Louisiana is noted for its **freshwater** and **saltwater** fisheries, which make up one of the state's largest industries. These industries add millions of dollars to the state's **economy** yearly. Louisiana has the biggest and most diversified freshwater fisheries production in America. The state leads others in volume of fish and shellfish catch. In 2004 Louisiana is a leader in the nation's production of shrimp (first), blue crab (first in Gulf, third in U.S.), oysters (first), crawfish, tuna, red snapper, wild catfish, black drum, sea trout, and mullet. Bass, catfish, and perch abound. The state's saltwater fish include sheepshead, croaker, mackerel, amberjack, and tarpon.

The commercial seafood industry includes the processing of shrimp, crabs, buffalo fish, catfish, bullheads, menhaden, clams, trout, flounders, and the like. Vast schools of **tuna** from the Gulf of Mexico yield a product that compares favorably with that from other sections of the country. There are more tuna harvested from the waters off the Louisiana coast than on the East Coast or anywhere else along the Gulf coast. Louisiana **shrimp** are known to world markets for both quality and flavor. More shrimp are landed in Louisiana than in any other place in America. **Menhaden** is not a human food fish, but it provides fish meal for

Gulf of Mexico.

animal feeds. It is also used in making some soaps, paints, lipstick, and linoleum. It is even used in the hardening of steel. Louisiana's **oyster** industry provides the nation's finest oysters. Thirty-three percent of the nation's oyster demand is supplied by Louisiana.

Louisiana is the only state with a **crawfish** industry. In both wild and farm crawfish production Louisiana ranks first. In recent years Chinese crawfish imports have threatened the industry. Imports of crawfish tail meat from China jumped 350 percent between 1993 and 1995. China's crawfish made up 70 percent of the U.S. market. The crawfish were sold at half the price of domestic crawfish. In 1996 Louisiana asked two federal agencies to impose a 424 percent tariff on Chinese crawfish coming into the U.S. Louisiana's crawfish industry will be devastated if the foreign market is not curtailed. In 2004 the U.S. placed trade restrictions on imported crawfish; however, enforcement has been limited. Louisiana continues to see global competition erode its crawfish industry.

Other contributors to our economy are **frogs** and **turtles**. Louisiana in 2004 was first in the world in pet turtles (red-eared sliders). The state produced 85 to 90 percent of the world supply.

Louisiana is the only state with a crawfish industry.

In 2005 Louisiana had one of the largest **aquaculture** industries in the nation. The industry includes crawfish, oysters, catfish, alligators, turtles, and baitfish as well as bass and other freshwater and marine fish.

The **Artificial Reef Program** continues to enhance the marine fisheries along the Gulf coast. Artificial reefs provide a base for many small organisms that, in turn, provide a food source for larger fish. Obsolete oil and gas platforms are being converted to reefs. In 2004 these platforms are the destination of over 70 percent of offshore fishing trips leaving Louisiana ports. Some of these reefs use obsolete military vehicles and vessels.

Lagniappe—*Snakes*. Only six of Louisiana's forty-two species of snakes are poisonous. Stay away from the **copperhead, coral, cottonmouth moccasin, pygmy rattlesnake, canebrake rattlesnake**, and **eastern diamondback rattlesnake**. Louisiana snakes lay eggs from May to July. They hatch between late July and late September. Live-bearing snakes give birth in August to October.

Fur-producing Industry. Louisiana wildlife provides the raw materials for the fur-producing industry. The state has long been the nation's top fur producer. Louisiana has historically produced more furs than Canada. The state once harvested more than three million pelts annually. Due to the decreased demand in furs, the number of furbearers harvested remains below average. Approximately 356,000 furbearer pelts were harvested during the 2003-2004 season.

Nutria is the most important furbearing species. Nutria accounted for 71 percent of the marketing value of the furbearing animals. **Otter, raccoon**, and **mink** follow. The trees, swamps, and bayous shelter large quantities of **muskrat, opossum, skunk, red fox**, and **gray fox**. The fur industry relies greatly on these and other fur-bearing animals such as the **bobcat, beaver**, and **coyote**. New Orleans has been the shipping center for raw furs since the French first settled Louisiana. The state has never made the finished product.

Alligator Industry. During the 1950s and 1960s alligators were in serious decline. By 1972, scientific management had returned alligators to commercial populations, and the season reopened in Cameron Parish. In 1979 the season was expanded to nine coastal parishes and in 1981 hunters searched for alligators statewide for the first time in eighteen years. The alligator has again taken its place in commercial production. During 2003, 31,571 were harvested for hides and meat, and Louisiana's sixty-one alligator farms produced 271,796 skins and 815,388 pounds of meat. The state in 2003 was first in both wild and farm alligator production. Louisiana's alligator hides bring top prices in both domestic and foreign markets. France imported 40 percent of the wild and farmed alligator skins from this state in 2002.

Recreational Industries. Louisiana's game and fish are in the highest ranks of the state's natural resources. Hunting, fishing, boating, skiing, and observing wildlife are socially and economically important to the state. Licenses, taxes, and supporting industries are part of this recreational industry. Camping, canoeing, and photography add to the impact of the fish and wildlife-related recreational activities.

Hunting and fishing draws many tourists to Louisiana to participate in tournaments, regattas, and sport events. Thousands of the six hundred thousand national forest acres are open to the public. One and one half billion dollars were spent with twenty-five thousand outdoor jobs in 2003. The annual income from state licenses was $16.5 million dollars.

Louisiana naturalist John James Audubon.

Deer herd in North Louisiana reserve.

The average Louisianian spends twenty-five days each year enjoying the state's outdoor recreational resources. Surveys indicate that nearly one-fourth of Louisianians fish, and recreational anglers fish an average of sixteen days per year.

Hunters spend time in the outdoors an average of twenty-three days per year. Hunters know that one-half of the continent's ducks and geese pass overhead on the route of the Mississippi Flyway. The state's abundance of squirrels, rabbits, coyotes, deer, doves, quail, water fowl, and snipe make it a hunter's paradise.

Some industrial enterprises have developed because of a favorite pastime—bird watching. Bird watchers participate in bird watching an average of ten days per year away from home. Birdhouses and bird feed are much in demand in the 2000s. Louisiana ranks in the top ten in number of species of birds in the U.S. with over four hundred. Louisiana is a top destination for birders worldwide with the introduction of a Wetland Birding Trail.

Toledo Bend Reservoir, the Atchafalaya River Basin, and the many other lakes, rivers, and wildlife areas play an important part in the recreational industries.

En Partie 3 (Studying a Part). 1. Describe our wildlife and fish resources. 2. (a) What are the main contributors to the seafood industry? (b) wildlife industry? 3. Define aquaculture. 4. How are these industries important to the state's economy? 5. (a) What problems have been faced in the wildlife and seafood industries? (b) Which problems continue to trouble the industries?

Coup de Main
(Completing the Story)

Jambalaya (Putting It All Together)

1. (a) List Louisiana's natural resources. (b) Classify each resource as renewable or nonrenewable. (c) Why is it important to know this information?

2. What natural resources must we have for existence?

3. What are wise and unwise practices concerning the state's soil, water, forests,

wildlife, and fish that have existed or now exist?

4. How is the state's economy related to our natural resources?

5. (a) Why is the forest fire control system an important part of the environmental program? (b) Have you been involved in or observed the misuse of our forests? (c) If so, how?

Potpourri (Getting Involved)

1. Research the history of a particular industry based on our agriculture, forests, wildlife, or fish.

2. Compare Louisiana with another state. Compare size, population, landforms, rainfall, vegetation, and major ways of making a living.

3. Investigate the fairs and festivals associated with our natural resources. What are their benefits? What are the ways that both service industries and producers are involved? Is the capital investment of the sponsors and participants profitable?

4. On a map locate Alexander State Forest. Research the history of the forest and the current status of the activities that go on there.

5. What is a fish hatchery? Why are they maintained by the state or federal government? Research to find out where they are located in the state.

6. Make a record of farmland crop use in a given area. Trace the history of the land use

and government regulations of its use. If possible, interview the farmer to learn the reasons for crop changes.

Gumbo (Bringing It Up-to-Date)

1. Create your own ideal Louisiana. Identify all changes that you will have to make in the present state. How could these changes be made?

2. Compare Louisiana farming operations of today with those prior to 1930. Compare ownership, management, labor, production, economic value, social life, daily routine, use and sale of goods, and equipment.

3. Research to answer these questions: What famous fishing lures and pleasure boats are manufactured in Louisiana? Where are fishing contests held? What is Ducks Unlimited and what does it protect?

4. Summarize Louisiana's forest, wildlife, and fisheries resources in chart form. Use the following headings: Resource, Location of Resource, Problems Involved, Practices of Conservation, and Current Outlook. Use current information to update your answer.

5. Interview people to locate abandoned sites for syrup mills, cotton gins, blacksmith shops, and sawmills.

6. Use your research skills to locate the answers to one of these questions. How do pulpwood haulers get permits? If you had your own lake, how would you get fish fingerlings to stock it? How are seasons set? Who has to have a license? What becomes of pine needles?

MINERALS AND INDUSTRIAL DEVELOPMENT

Mineral Production

Louisiana's oil and gas are of critical importance to the nation's fuel supply, and much of the nation depends upon the state for salt and sulphur. Another source of energy, lignite coal, is also produced in Louisiana. Other important minerals in the state include gravel, sand, silt, clay, shell, and shale. Peat, limestone, and gypsum complete the list of Louisiana's minerals of significant value.

Oil and Gas. Oil and gas production accounted for 96 percent of the value of the mineral industry in 2004. The impact of petroleum and natural gas on the industrial development of this state is important to comprehend. Nearly 34 percent of the nation's natural gas supply and over 39 percent of the nation's crude oil supply moved through the state of Louisiana and was connected to nearly 50 percent of the U.S. refining capacity in 2004. In 2003 Louisiana's rankings among the fifty states were given in two categories. The energy statistics either include just Louisiana production or Louisiana's plus the production in federal waters, referred to as the Louisiana Outer Continental Shelf, or LOCS, which is the most extensively developed energy area in the U.S. Louisiana, including LOCS, ranked first in crude oil, second in natural gas, and second in total energy. Louisiana excluding LOCS ranked fourth in crude oil, fifth in natural gas, and eighth in total energy. Louisiana ranked second in refining capacity and second in primary petrochemical production.

Louisiana's wetlands are referred to as the energy corridor to the nation. In 2004 Louisiana had the greatest concentration of crude oil refineries, natural gas plants, and petrochemical production facilities in the Western Hemisphere. The state's nineteen refineries include one of the four largest in the Western Hemisphere. Louisiana's facilities are of particular importance because the U.S. has a shortage in refining capacity. No new refineries have been built in the U.S. in the last twenty-five years.

All the major companies have Louisiana production facilities. More than one hundred major chemical plants are located in the state. They are producing a variety of "building block" chemicals, fertilizers, and plastics, plus the feedstocks for a wide array of other products. The state also produces jet fuels, lubricants, and some six hundred other petroleum products.

Lagniappe—*Severance Tax*. A tax is levied on production of natural resources taken from land or water bottoms within Louisiana for market. This tax is called a severance tax. Oil and gas collections account for almost 92 percent of all severance tax collections.

Four-fifths of the severance tax on oil goes into the state public school fund. One-fifth is returned to the parish in which the oil is produced.

Oil or Petroleum Industry. Louisiana has enjoyed incredible wealth from its oil and gas production and from the taxes produced for the state. The exploring, drilling, producing, refining, transporting, and marketing of oil have been leading sources of income and employment since the 1900s. Refineries and other facilities have become features of the Louisiana landscape. Nothing has been more important in changing the face of Louisiana than the discovery and use of petroleum.

The unbelievable riches of Spindletop, a tremendously successful oil strike near Beaumont, Texas, had its effect in Louisiana. It

Kerr-McGee's Gunnison Platform opened in December 2003.

caused much clamoring for oil discovery in the state. In 1901, the same year of the Spindletop discovery, the Heywood brothers brought in an oil well six miles from Jennings. During that year seventy-six Louisiana oil companies were formed to drill for oil. In 1902, five producing wells brought forth 548,617 barrels of oil with a total value of $188,985. Two years later, the Mamou, or Evangeline, Field had a total of thirty-three producing wells. On March 28, 1906, the first Caddo Parish oil well to produce in commercial quantities was brought in. The state's first oil refinery was built near Jennings the same year. The following year what was probably the first water site in the world occurred in Caddo Lake. In 1909 North Louisiana oil wells were linked to Baton Rouge with a pipeline that had its origin in Oklahoma oil fields. Also in that year the Standard Oil Company built a new refinery in Baton Rouge.

By 1916 the oil industry had grown so much that Louisiana ranked fifth among the forty-eight states in the production of oil. By 1919 the state had fifteen refineries.

Until the 1930s, North Louisiana was the site of most of the state's oil and gas production. In the late 1930s drillers with new equipment and techniques began to develop South Louisiana fields.

Louisiana oil production had topped the one-million-barrels-per-day mark. In 1937 the processing of farm products still exceeded industry based on petroleum. Since World War II Louisiana's industrial growth has been stimulated chiefly by the petroleum and chemical industries, which led in value of products produced.

Offshore development started a new phase in 1947. Oil and gas exploration and drilling moved offshore. <u>The first well ever drilled out of sight of land was off the Louisiana coast.</u>

By 1954, fifty-nine parishes in the state produced oil or gas, or both. By the following year the number of offshore wells had risen to four hundred. In 1956, the deepest well in the world at that time was drilled in Plaquemines Parish.

The exploration, development, and production of oil and gas continued at a rapid pace with many improvements in equipment and processes. Drillers moved into deeper water in the Gulf of Mexico. Wells were placed beyond the three-mile limit in the waters controlled by the United States. Production was developed to accommodate the great depths and secondary recovery methods employed to stimulate formations.

Oil production peaked in 1971, but known reserves began to decline. Production in the Gulf began declining in 1972. Oil companies went farther out into deeper waters in search of more oil. The start of a new boom began in 1973. By 1977, sixty-one parishes had a history of petroleum production. Only East and West Feliciana, St. Helena, and Vernon were not involved. Caddo Parish, Rodessa, Haynesville, and Jennings fields reached the charmed circle in oil production. These exceeded a cumulative production of one hundred million barrels. East Baton Rouge and Caddo were two of the most productive parishes.

The energy crisis exploded and energy prices soared. Suddenly all the oil and gas that in the past had been unprofitable to extract now promised profits. There was increased drilling and old wells were reworked with improvements in technology. New areas were opened by federal leasing.

Deregulation of natural gas prices by Congress improved the market.

Lagniappe—*Offshore drilling.* Louisiana's coast is the land base for the Louisiana Offshore Oil Port (LOOP), the only offshore oil port of the United States. LOOP handles about 15 percent of the U.S.'s foreign oil and is connected to more than 30 percent of the total refining capacity in the U.S. More than thirty thousand people are employed offshore.

Port Fourchon is the geographic and economic center of offshore drilling along the Louisiana Gulf Coast. It is twenty miles southwest of LOOP. For more information on Port Fourchon, visit the Web site www.portfourchon.com.

Even though the numbers have been greatly reduced, the offshore routine goes on as usual. This expensive operation is also repeated many times during weather that forces platforms to be shut down. This is a way of life for many. Their "off" days are spent at their homes scattered all over Louisiana, Texas, and other states. The jobs and income are very important to many families.

Offshore workers' jobs are affected by tropical storms. The temporary shutdown of oil facilities in bad weather in the Gulf is costly. Hourly workers lose their pay. Service industries are temporarily shut down. This can be for days. The expense of shuffling workers to the rig is a big expense to the companies. These shutdowns affect oil prices.

Gulf storm systems shut down or restrict the flow of oil to much of the nation. Oil futures surge as refiners warn of possible shortages and prices rise. The amount of oil shut in between September 13 and September 21, 2004, from storm damage totaled about 8.5 million barrels. This amounted to around 1 percent of the annual production from the Gulf. Natural gas shut down totaled thirty-six billion cubic feet, or just less than 1 percent of yearly production. This created shortages for the refineries and caused spikes in crude oil prices, which affected the stock market. Refiners asked the president to dip into the 670 million barrels in the reserves stored in old salt domes in southern Louisiana and Texas. This was not done. Presidents are reluctant to release any of these reserves.

In the 1980s, development of the domestic oil industry declined as the expenses of exploration, drilling, and production increased. Oil companies merged and consolidated operations for efficiency in management and profits. Activity moved overseas where ready reserves were less expensive to locate, drill, and produce. American engineers and scientists developed the Arab oil industry.

In the decline, service companies folded and were absorbed by Schlumberger, Halliburton, AMF, and other major conglomerates. Some petrochemical plants curbed production and had layoffs. Louisiana lost oil company jobs and many offices. Exxon Mobil Corp. consolidated and closed its New Orleans office. Shell also left. Chevron joined Texaco and moved its headquarters to Houston, Texas, the worldwide marketing center for oil and gas.

Geologists are looking for **new sources** of these rich deposits. Studies indicate many barrels of recoverable oil are still to be found in Louisiana. New deposits are neither readily nor cheaply found, and recovery will be costly. Horizontal drilling, shale recovery, new equipment and techniques in recovery must be employed.

Adverse actions associated with oil and gas production have largely been eliminated due to improved drilling technology and a growing environmental awareness within the oil and gas industry.

The **future** of the oil industry in the state should continue to reinforce the state's economy even though the industry suffered some decline in all areas in the last few years due to foreign competition. Known reserves of natural gas and oil should carry Louisiana's production into the next century.

Natural Gas. The production, processing, and transportation of natural gas are vital parts of the state's petroleum industry.

There are records of discoveries of natural gas in the 1800s. However, it was not until the discoveries of oil in the early 1900s that the **natural gas industry** really began. The natural gas pipeline that connected Dixie and Shreveport was laid in 1908. This was the first year that natural gas was used commercially in Louisiana.

This business did not develop to any extent until the development of industrial **uses** for the gas. Heating needs could not consume the large amount of natural gas that was available. Improvements in pipe-laying methods reduced the cost so that more and more people were able to use gas for heating. Gas was sent by pipeline to other sections of the United States. As the uses for natural gas expanded, drillers began to seek out deposits.

Natural gas usually occurs with oil. One of

the largest gas fields ever discovered was the Monroe Gas Field. It was discovered in 1916. Some of the greatest gas production in the world has been in the vicinity of Ouachita Parish. The Haynesville Gas Field started in 1921.

In LaSalle Parish the Olla Field was discovered in 1940. It brought a big boom to the oil and gas industry. By then natural gas was a vital factor in industry and home use. By 1968 the state was producing one-fourth of the nation's supply of natural gas in its 126 plants.

The known natural gas reserves in Louisiana were reported to be declining in 1970. Major developments in the science of geology and in production techniques for the natural gas industry should continue to be an important part of our **economy** for many years. Natural gas is converted to many uses in plastics, petrochemicals, and synthetic fabrics. Pipelines transport Louisiana gas across the nation. Natural gas is used as fuel for power plants and for domestic fuel consumption.

Salt. Louisiana is the saltiest state in the United States. The state's numerous salt domes are pillars of pure salt up to a mile in diameter and fifty thousand feet deep. Louisiana ranks first in the production of salt. In 2003 Louisiana produced six million tons of salt and 12.2 million tons of salt brine.

The **history** of salt in Louisiana dates back to the salt licks found by early explorers. Records of work at Drake's Salt Lick near Goldonna in Natchitoches Parish date back to 1812. Before the Civil War one of the largest sites was the Bistineau Works near Shreveport. Other locations included Price's Salt Works near Drake's and those at Catahoula Lake, Castor, Friendship, and

Negreet Bayou. John Marsh Avery started evaporating brine from Avery Island's salt dome to help the Confederate cause in 1862. In 1889 a new company, International Salt, took over the operation on Avery Island. This company was joined in salt production by other companies. Salt mining was not successful until 1898. In 1894 salt was found on Jefferson Island. Production there did not begin until 1923, however.

In modern times, Louisiana's salt industry has been concentrated on the five **salt domes** strung along the southwest coastline. Avery Island, Belle Isle, Côte Blanche, Jefferson Island, and Weeks Island yield the bulk of the state's salt production. A very small percentage of the state's salt reserves has been taken. Salt is still there—perhaps billions of tons. It is likely that there are many salt domes that we do not know about. Drilling for other minerals sometimes discloses new domes.

Sulphur. The first sulphur mined in America came from Louisiana. Louisiana was a leader in the **production** of sulphur for many years. The world's largest sulphur producer, Freeport Sulphur Company, operated in the state until the 1990s. The world's largest sulphur warehouse was located at Port Sulphur. Sulphur operations located off the coast of Louisiana ceased to produce after 1999. Main Pass in federal waters was the only Louisiana offshore operation in 1996. Louisiana produced **recovered sulphur** after 1996 for its own uses. Since the globalization of the market, beginning in the late 1980s and progressing until the present date, the sources of sulphur have changed to foreign markets.

Louisiana has two towns named for their

sulphur deposits—Sulphur and Port Sulphur. The town of Sulphur in Calcasieu Parish developed around the mining of sulphur. In 1867, drillers **found** sulphur there. The Union Sulphur Company had a near monopoly in the mining of this valuable resource in the state. It was not until Dr. Herman **Frasch** invented a **process** to extract sulphur that the commercial industry started.

In 1894 Dr. Frasch watched the first flow of softened sulphur spill into a wooden barrel from a Louisiana salt dome. It was eight years later before the process was considered a commercial success. The Frasch process has been improved, but the basic idea is still used today.

The Calcasieu Field produced 75 percent of the nation's sulphur supply until 1914. It was exhausted by the early 1920s. During the years 1924 to 1932, sulphur production was at a standstill in Louisiana.

In 1928 the Gulf Production Company discovered sulphur in an oil well in Plaquemines Parish. In 1933 the Freeport Sulphur Company began operations in the Plaquemines Parish dome. Freeport's first mine in the state was at Grand Ecaille (EH ki Oy). Louisiana again ranked second in production when the newly found sulphur was produced.

Increased demand for sulphur resulted in increased production. Sulphur was being obtained at Jefferson Island, Grand Ecaille, and Garden Island Bay.

Sulphur production has slowed down greatly. In the 1970s Louisiana sulphur mines almost ceased to produce. **New sources** of sulphur were found. A process was developed for extracting sulphur from natural gas and oil. The sulphur obtained in this manner is called recovered sulphur. Almost every refinery in the state produces sulphur in this manner. In 1995 Louisiana produced 3.2 million tons of sulphur by the Frasch process and 7.2 million tons recovered sulphur. In 2003 there was no reportable production of sulphur in Louisiana. Sulphur was produced as a by-product of crude oil production.

The production of sulphur is important in attracting other industries that **use** sulphur or sulphur compounds. It is likely that growing needs of farms and factories will require greater supplies of sulphur. Sulphur is used in medicines, insecticides, and feeds. Demands for sulphur to make fertilizer for growing crops to feed an increasing world population make it urgent to find new sources for sulphur. The search for new sources continues.

Other Minerals. Some of the state's mineral resources are not buried deep in the ground. Some are right on the surface or not far below it. **Gravel, sand, silt, clay, shells, and shale** are among these deposits. Centuries-old streams brought them to the state.

Most of the gravel, sand, and shells are used in the construction business, but there are other uses. Some of the state's sand of a special quality is used in the manufacturing of glass. Gravel and sand are also used in making cement and building roads. Silt may be made into bricks, tiles, and the like.

There are large **peat** deposits in South Louisiana. Only a few states have nearly as much peat. Peat is mixed with soil to make a potting soil for plants. It is also used to wrap around the roots of plants being sent from one place to another. Peat is easy to dig and load onto barges with draglines.

In this period of concern about energy-producing fuels, Louisiana's **lignite** coal deposits in North Louisiana hill country were evaluated. This inferior grade of coal, produced by strip mining, now fuels electricity production at new plants. Commercial production began in 1985. In 1993 almost 3.5 million tons of lignite were produced from two surface mines. The same amount was produced in 2003.

Other Louisiana minerals include **limestone**, which is desirable for road building and soil improvement. **Gypsum** is another mineral mined in our state. In addition, tons of **clam** and **oyster shells** are dredged from our waterways and marketed yearly.

En Partie 1 (Studying a Part). 1. What are the minerals the state produces commercially? 2. What role has mineral production played in the state's economy? 3. Trace the development of production of oil, gas, salt, sulphur, and lignite coal.

Industry and Commerce

History. Louisiana's industry was not of major economic importance until the twentieth century. Between 1935 and 1953 the state's industrial growth increased 100 percent. Louisiana's industrial development expanded after World War II. The construction business prospered. Marriages delayed because of the war brought many new homes into being. New buildings were needed for businesses, for the government, and for recreational activities. Hospitals and buildings for professionals provided almost limitless opportunities. New industry created thousands of jobs. There was a period of a flourishing economy after the war.

The backlog of consumer products that had not been available during World War II created an enormous market. During the war household appliances, automobiles and trucks, and many kinds of labor-saving equipment had not been available. New inventions swelled the variety of consumer products. With severance pay from the military service and paychecks from working women, consumers waited to purchase these things as producers worked to satisfy the demands.

In the 1950s Louisiana was spotlighted as the state most likely to become an industrial complex. Industry was favoring locations here as factory sites that would require less fuel for heating than in the North. The state's location at the mouth of the Mississippi River had always provided special advantages. With a view toward water transportation, the industrialists found much to recommend Louisiana. The state's vast natural resources were a decisive factor.

The stretch of Mississippi River banks between New Orleans and Baton Rouge was referred to as the "Miracle Strip." It became the location of a variety of industries in the 1950s. With it came a complete reshaping of commerce within the country to a north and south axis along the Mississippi River. In the Mississippi River the nation gained a "fourth seacoast." This area is important economically and is of great value during times of war.

There were thirty-eight hundred businesses that could be called manufacturers. The value of their products amounted to over three billion dollars. In 1939 the total products manufactured in Louisiana had been valued at $565 million. In the 1950s the largest manufacturing industry in the state was petrochemicals. Food processing was the second largest industry.

The Mississippi River at New Orleans.

Leading Production Industries. In 2004 the petrochemical industry ranked first in production among the state's industries. The oil and gas industry was second. Agricultural and forest products were third. In 2004 the Shaw Group Incorporated in Baton Rouge had the largest manufacturing employment.

General Manufacturing. In addition to its resource-based industries, Louisiana also has a diverse general manufacturing base. Louisiana produces business telephone systems, assembles light trucks, and manufactures electrical equipment. It manufactures pharmaceuticals, glass products, and automobile batteries. Manufacturing specialized vehicles for traveling over marshes, maritime ranging equipment to let boats know where they are at sea, and yachts are big businesses. Louisiana makes playground equipment, mobile homes, clothing, and weapons, plus several hundred other products.

Louisianians are employed in mining, wholesale and retail trade, insurance, real estate, transportation, communication, public utilities, finance, construction, service industries, and tourism. The wholesale and retail trade industry employs more people than any other employer in the state. These represent a high percentage of Louisiana's private non-farm wage and salaried employment.

An important Louisiana industry is **ship**

and boatbuilding. Louisiana shipyards build every kind of seagoing vessel. The vessels range from giant cryogenic ships used to transport liquefied natural gas to some of the largest offshore oil and gas exploration rigs in the world. They also build merchant vessels, Coast Guard cutters, barges, tugs, supply boats, fishing vessels, pleasure craft, and river patrol boats. The largest industrial employer in the state is Northrop Grumman Ship Systems on the Mississippi River near New Orleans. Here vessels are sometimes built upside down and ships are launched sideways into the river. The custom elsewhere is to launch stern first. The manufacturing of equipment for these vessels is important as well. Fishing boats and other smaller boats are built at locations scattered throughout the state. Providing repairs and replacements are other big associated businesses.

The shipyard at Avondale and a sister plant in Mississippi contracted to build nine deep-water vessels for the U.S. Coast Guard in 2002. These vessels, known as landing platform dock ships, have reactivated shipbuilding for the more than sixty-five hundred Avondale workers.

Louisiana has several links to the nation's **space program**. The huge first-stage Saturn C-5 rocket was built in this state. It was used in the Apollo program to land men on the moon. Lockheed Martin in New Orleans is the sole producer of the giant external fuel tanks for NASA's space shuttle program. NASA operates an aerospace computer services center in Slidell. The state also has an emerging aviation services sector. The European Aviation Defenses Systems operates a major aviation maintenance facility in Lake Charles. Workers repair and refit jet aircraft there. Collins Defense Communications, a division of Rockwell International, operates an aircraft modification center in Shreveport.

The first commercial **film production** in Louisiana began in 1908. A silent film, **Faust**, was produced. Over the years many more movies and video productions have been made in the state. In 1974 the Louisiana Film Commission was formed to lure movie dollars to the state. The results have been rewarding. In 2003 Louisiana started a project to give tax-credits for Louisiana-based movie and television projects. Nearly twice the film business was done in 2004 as was done in 2003. In 2004 Louisiana ranked as one of the top ten U.S. locations for this business. The movie industry continues to be a valuable contributor to the state's economy. Production crews spend money for Louisiana services, labor, rentals, catering, hotels, restaurants, and entertainment.

Music was an approximately twenty-billion-dollar business in the state in 2004. Music-related spending, jobs, and taxes are important to the economy.

Tourism is a major Louisiana industry. **Mardi Gras** has made an economic contribution to New Orleans for some time. In 2005 Mardi Gras celebrations continued to bring tourist dollars to many other towns and cities. Other major attractions include the French Quarter, plantation homes, festivals of every description, Cajun Country, distinctive food, music, and sports.

Tax-free Shopping. In 1990 Louisiana introduced a tax-free shopping program. The program is the only one of its kind in the nation. It encourages foreign visitors to come to Louisiana and spend money. The state refunds sales taxes to foreign visitors who buy merchandise at any of the eleven-hundred-plus participating stores.

Louisiana remains a center for **foreign investment**. In 2004 some two hundred foreign companies have invested almost twenty-one billion dollars in the state. This is the largest amount of foreign investment in any southeastern state and thirteenth largest among all states. In 2004 there were seventy major foreign firms in the state. There is an aggressive effort on the part of the state to attract these investments. International investment will continue to be a noteworthy factor in the state's industrial growth.

Transportation. The interstate highways provide fast transportation both north and south and east and west. Interstate 49 connects the state from north to south. Plans include extending I-49 to Kansas City. I-10 connects Houston and places along the coast to Florida. I-20 ties Dallas to destinations in the east.

Louisiana in 2004 had seven air carrier airports and seventy-two public general **aviation facilities**. In addition, there are 294 private airports, 365 heliports, and 17 seaplane bases.

Louisiana's abundant **water** supply has contributed greatly to the state's agricultural and industrial growth. Since early times, water has been one of the state's most important resources. Our largest cities and greatest industrial centers are located on or near important bodies of water. New Orleans and Baton Rouge are on the Mississippi. Shreveport and Alexandria are on the Red River. Lake Charles is on the Calcasieu. Monroe is on the Ouachita River. Lafayette's location near the coast has contributed to its status as the state's oil center. Morgan City, on the Gulf

Ouachita River, Monroe.

coast, is an exit point for people going off-shore.

This water-rich state has much to offer industry in the way of transportation. Louisiana has more navigable waterways than any other state in the nation. Louisiana combines domestic road, rail, and air facilities with five thousand miles of intrastate waterways. These are linked to nineteen thousand miles of the Mississippi River system.

The Gulf Intracoastal Waterway crosses the state near the coast. This waterway is part of the Intracoastal Waterway, which extends along the Atlantic and Gulf of Mexico. This canal is used to carry products from New Orleans westward to points of

The Harvey Lock is located on the Gulf Intracoastal Waterway.

Louisiana and Texas as far as the Mexican border. It is also used for products going eastward from New Orleans to Florida.

In 2003 Louisiana's **ports** played an especially vital role in exporting U.S. crops. There are twenty-five active ports or terminals in the state. The ports of New Orleans, Baton Rouge, South Louisiana, Lake Charles, and Plaquemines are world-class ports. More than 30 percent of the nation's waterborne exports are shipped through these ports. Louisiana is the nation's largest handler of grain for export to world markets. Louisiana's exports are the twelfth highest in dollar value among states. The Port of South Louisiana (Laplace) ranked first, New Orleans fourth, Baton Rouge tenth, Port of Plaquemines eleventh, and Lake Charles thirteenth as the busiest U.S. ports based on tonnage in 2001. The Red River

Waterway has made navigation available to Shreveport and Natchitoches.

In 2005 an automated bag loading computer-controlled facility opened at the Port of Lake Charles. The new system will load more than one hundred tons of cargo an hour rather than the fifty tons loaded by gang labor.

In January 2005 a barge carrying military equipment moved into the Port of Alexandria. The equipment will be used in a training exercise at Fort Polk. On February 9 and 10 another batch of twenty to twenty-five barges loaded with military equipment arrived at the port for unloading. After the exercises are completed, the port workers will load equipment onto barges for transport back to Fort Campbell, Kentucky.

As the nation's reliance on imports has grown, so too has the domestic reliance on increased deep-water production, much of it flowing through the **Louisiana Offshore Oil Port (LOOP)** facility to shore. It is located in the Gulf of Mexico about eighteen miles south of Leeville and Grand Isle at Bay Marchand. The facility became operational in 1981 and operates under both a federal and state regulatory regime. The LOOP handles 12 percent of the nation's daily crude oil imports.

En Partie 2 (Studying a Part). 1. Summarize the history of Louisiana's industrial development. 2. What are Louisiana's industrial centers? 3. (a) How much foreign investment has been made in Louisiana in 2004? (b) Why is the state making an aggressive effort to attract foreign firms? 4. Relate the state's transportation system to industry. 5. (a) What are our major ports, and how do they

The Nashville Avenue Wharf in New Orleans.

rank? (b) What is the importance of these ports? 6. (a) What is the Louisiana Offshore Oil Port? (b) What is its importance?

Outlook. Louisiana's future depends upon the full use of our human, natural, and industrial resources. For a prosperous future we must continue to tap Louisiana's vast resources. Programs and policies will have to be developed to put our resources to good use. We must produce more products and services for the increasing demand. To provide the best Louisiana environment requires skillful management of our soil, water, air, vegetation, minerals, fisheries, wildlife, and industry. The state's future

growth appears to be fairly secure even though the question of whether minerals will be available dims the picture.

Many years ago John Law described what Louisiana had to offer. In 1952 Hodding Carter wrote in *John Law Wasn't So Wrong:*

But now, 250 years since the French first came, Louisiana is proving that John Law was not as wrong as he thought himself in his heart to be. Out of the river god's cornucopia pours as diverse a wealth as can be found anywhere in all the world. It comes from tropic sea and flowing rivers, from sun-blessed farmlands and forests, from the bowels of the earth, from the ingenious

The New Orleans skyline.

minds and skillful hands of a new industrial surging. Today 250 years after John Law's emigrants cursed his trickery and died, their descendants and sons of the later comers, more than two and one-half million of them, are fashioning a purposeful union of city, town, and countryside whose common denominator is confidence.

Coup de Main
(Completing the Story)

Jambalaya (Putting It All Together)

1. (a) Why are minerals classified as a nonrenewable resource? (b) How do resources in this category have to be handled?

2. (a) Are we consuming our natural resources to depletion? (b) What happens to the value of these resources as they become scarce? (c) How can we prevent these losses?

3. Give proof that Louisiana's petroleum-related industries are important to both the U.S. and the rest of the world.

4. (a) What is given credit for being most important for changing the face of Louisiana? (b) What does that mean?

5. What are Louisiana's assets and liabilities at the present?

6. What are wise and unwise practices concerning the state's mineral resources that have existed or now exist?

7. Support this statement: Louisiana has changed from a rural, agricultural economy to an urban, industrial economy.

8. How is the state's economy related to our mineral resources?

9. When did Louisiana industries reach major economic importance?

10. (a) How have foreign goods affected the economy? (b) Do you buy foreign goods? (c) If so, where?

11. What course of study would you follow to preserve our natural resources as your career?

12. What are rules of safety and preservation that you should observe when you engage in recreational activities?

Potpourri (Getting Involved)

1. Research the history of a particular industry. Name the companies and people involved with the history.

2. Compare Louisiana with another state. Compare size, population, landforms, rainfall, vegetation, and major ways of making a living. Include the differences in form of government, language, customs, and career opportunities.

Gumbo (Bringing It Up-to-Date)

1. Research the topic of tax incentives offered to businesses.

2. What is the outlook for each of our minerals? Support your answer with the latest facts available.

3. Explain this statement: Inventions and technological advances have changed and continue to change every aspect of Louisiana life. Cite changes made in one area in your lifetime.

4. Are there closed factories in your vicinity? How have the closings affected the economy? Does your area have a new industry? How does the industry affect your community?

5. Summarize the use of our mineral resources—oil, gas, sulfur, lignite, and salt. Complete a chart with the following headings: Resource, Location of Source, Problems Involved, Practices of Conservation, and Current Outlook. Use current information to update your answer.

OUR LOUISIANA GOVERNMENT

The government of Louisiana does not differ to any great extent from that of other states. It is different, however, in one important respect. Its judicial system is unique. Louisiana is the only state that uses **civil law**, also called written law or code law. The basic law evolved through the century of French and Spanish rule. Both France and Spain use civil law.

All other states use common law, or unwritten law. Common law judgments are made on the basis of the results of previous legal cases. The common law is associated with English custom. Today Louisiana's judicial system shows some influence of English common law.

The supreme, or final, reference law is the state constitution. All Louisiana's constitutions have safeguarded basic civil law.

Branches of Government

There are three branches of government: the **executive**, the **legislative**, and the **judicial**. These same three branches exist in our United States government. The duties of each branch are listed in the Louisiana constitution. The executive branch manages the state's business and carries out the laws. The legislative branch enacts laws and sets policy. The judicial branch interprets the laws. The three branches are part of a system of **checks and balances**. This term means that each branch stands watch over the other to prevent any branch from doing anything that it is not authorized by law to do.

Executive Branch. The executive branch administers our state government. The governor as our elected leader points the direction and forms goals to be carried out. It is the governor who holds the final authority over the executive branch. This branch includes other officials and as many as twenty departments.

Members of this official group are elected by the people at statewide elections. They serve terms of four years. They are paid an annual salary. A candidate for election must be a qualified voter. He must have been a citizen of the state for five years and must be at least twenty-five years old. The attorney general must have practiced law in the state for at least five years before the election.

All state officials except the governor and lieutenant governor appoint first assistants. These executive assistants must possess the same qualifications required of the state officials. Their appointments must be approved by a majority vote of the Senate. If the elected official for some reason vacates his post with less than a year left, first assistants may fill the office. If there is more time left, the vacancy must be filled at the next statewide election.

According to the Louisiana Constitution of 1974 some officials in the executive

The state capitol.

branch may be appointed by the governor. Approval by two-thirds of the Senate is required. Officers that may be appointed if the legislature approves include the commissioners of agriculture, insurance, and elections. The same two-thirds vote would be needed to combine any of these offices.

Louisiana's **governor** is the chief executive of the state. He manages the state government. He appoints many top officials to state agencies, boards, and commissions. With the advice and consent of the Senate he makes appointments for nonelective offices. The governor serves as a member of the most important boards and commissions. He is responsible for preparing and presenting an annual operating budget to the legislature.

The governor is commander in chief of the state militia. In this role he may call out the National Guard. The governor alone has the right to grant pardons and paroles, commute sentences, or remit fines. He has the power to grant reprieves for crimes against the state upon recommendations of either the pardon board or the parole board.

Governors propose legislation in messages to the legislature. They take an active part in getting desired legislation passed. The governor may draft bills. He has supportive legislators introduce them. The governor may veto or approve a bill passed by the legislature. He does not sign and cannot veto any resolutions of the legislature. The governor can call special sessions of

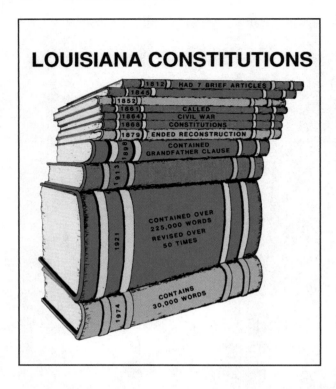

LOUISIANA CONSTITUTIONS

1812 HAD 7 BRIEF ARTICLES
1845
1852
1861   CALLED
1864   CIVIL WAR
1868   CONSTITUTIONS
1879   ENDED RECONSTRUCTION
1898   CONTAINED GRANDFATHER CLAUSE
1913
1921   CONTAINED OVER 225,000 WORDS REVISED OVER 50 TIMES
1974   CONTAINS 30,000 WORDS

the legislature to consider specific matters.

The governor presides at strictly ceremonial occasions. This includes welcoming celebrities who visit the state. He congratulates Louisiana citizens for outstanding accomplishments in various fields. Entertaining important people who come to the state is one of his jobs. Dedicating memorials and monuments is yet another task.

The governor may succeed himself for one term unless he has already served a full term and half of another. He lives in the governor's mansion in Baton Rouge. In addition, he is paid all household, office, and travel expenses.

The **lieutenant governor** acts for the governor in case of his absence. He also serves as an ***ex officio*** member of various boards and commissions. This means that he is a member of certain boards and commissions

because he holds his position as lieutenant governor. In case of a vacancy in the office of lieutenant governor, a successor is named by the governor. The appointee must be approved by the majority of both houses of the legislature.

The **secretary of state** is the custodian of the Great Seal. He imprints this seal to all official laws, documents, proclamations, and commissions. He serves as the chief election officer of the state. He prepares and certifies the ballots for all elections and announces election returns. His other duties include supervising the publication and distribution of the acts and journals of the legislature and Supreme Court reports. He also administers and preserves the official archives of the state. It is his job to maintain and register trademarks and labels. He issues extradition papers, which give legal surrender of an alleged criminal

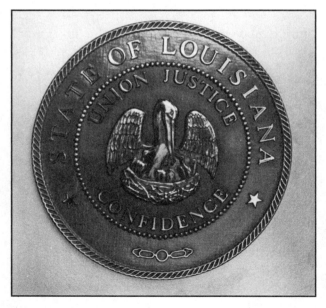

State seal.

THE GOVERNOR'S OPTIONS ON A BILL

 **1** He may sign it, and it becomes law.

 **2** He may veto it. He shall then return it to the Legislature with his veto message. This has to be done within 12 days after delivery to him if the Legislature is in session. If the Legislature adjourns, he shall return it as provided by law.

 **3** He may pocket veto. The bill becomes law if the governor fails to sign or veto it within 10 days after delivery to him, if the Legislature is in session. It must be returned within 20 days after delivery to him, if the Legislature is not in session.

to another state, country, or government for trial. The secretary of state records and files articles of incorporation.

The **treasurer** is the keeper of all public monies. He manages the receiving and spending of state funds. He reports annually to the governor and the legislature.

The **attorney general** is the state's chief legal officer. He is concerned with all legal matters in which the state has an interest. He serves as an advisor. He determines the meaning of Louisiana laws and explains them when called upon. The attorney general supervises lawyers throughout the state. He represents most state agencies as legal counsel. He also represents the state in all criminal cases on appeal.

The **commissioner of agriculture** advances, protects, and promotes agriculture in the state. Under him are the Department of Agriculture and thirteen agribusiness-related agencies.

The **commissioner of insurance** supervises the insurance laws of the state—the Louisiana Insurance Code. He serves as *ex officio* member of the Louisiana Insurance Rating Commission. He examines all insurers doing business in the state. He also approves insurance contracts used in the state.

The **superintendent of education** heads the department of education. It is his duty to carry out the policies of the State Board of Elementary and Secondary Education. It is he who carries out the laws of the state affecting schools under the board's jurisdiction.

The **commissioner of elections** administers the laws relating to elections. This involves voter registration and the physical arrangements for elections. He purchases voting machines and sees that they are kept in perfect working condition. He is custodian of the voting machines at all times. They must be stored between elections. They are delivered to the many voting precincts throughout the state. Then they are returned to storage after elections.

En Partie 1 (Studying a Partie). 1. Where is Louisiana's capital? 2. (a) What is Louisiana's supreme law? (b) When was the current one written? 3. (a) Compare civil law to common law. (b) Which does Louisiana use? 4. (a) What are the three branches of our state government? (b) What is the duty of each branch? 5. Explain the system of checks and balances. 6. Who heads the executive branch? 7. List the other executive officials. 8. (a) What are the duties of each of the executive officials? (b) What are the qualifications of each? 9. What is the term of office of members of the executive branch?

Legislative Branch. The Louisiana Legislature is composed of two houses: the **Senate** and the **House of Representatives**. There are thirty-nine members in the Senate. The House of Representatives has 105 members.

Lawmaking is the basic function of the legislature. It passes laws on any matter. It proposes amendments to the state constitution. These duties are outlined in the constitution. Since it passes the laws, the legislature sets the policies of the state on all-important issues. It decides the level of spending for various services of the state. Since this is so, it also sets the level of taxation required to finance these services. The Senate must confirm many of the people nominated by the governor to fill public office. The same is true for the governor's appointees to serve on boards and commissions.

When the legislative sessions are held for voting to confirm or deny appointees, no visitors are allowed. This type of session is called an **executive session** or **closed session**. This means that the sessions are closed to all persons except the members of the Senate and

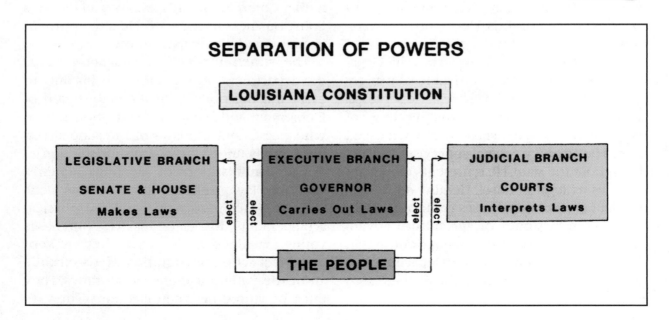

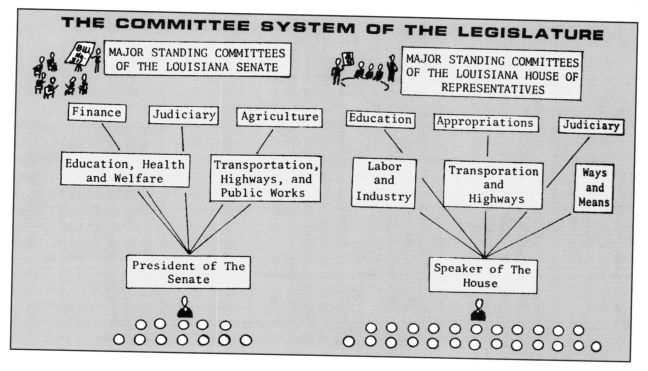

THE COMMITTEE SYSTEM OF THE LEGISLATURE

MAJOR STANDING COMMITTEES OF THE LOUISIANA SENATE

MAJOR STANDING COMMITTEES OF THE LOUISIANA HOUSE OF REPRESENTATIVES

Finance · Judiciary · Agriculture · Education · Appropriations · Judiciary

Education, Health and Welfare · Transportation, Highways, and Public Works · Labor and Industry · Transporation and Highways · Ways and Means

President of The Senate

Speaker of The House

certain necessary Senate personnel. This includes secretaries recording the session. All public bodies are allowed executive or closed sessions under certain circumstances.

Representatives and senators must be at least eighteen years old. They must have been citizens of the state for at least two years. They must be residents of the district from which they are elected for one year before their election to office.

They are elected from single-member districts for four-year terms. Terms begin the second Monday in March. After each census the legislature must reapportion itself on a population basis. Membership in the House is based on the numbers of people being represented. Increases and decreases in population have to be taken into consideration. If the legislature does not reapportion according to changing population figures, any voter may challenge the census. A voter may petition the Supreme Court and demand that this be done. The Supreme Court may then make the reapportionment itself.

Members are paid for each day spent at legislative sessions. They are allowed mileage and monthly expense allowances. They are permitted to hire either a secretary or a legal assistant. They receive a limited amount for furnishings and equipment for their parish offices. They also receive pay to cover rent and utilities for the office.

The legislature is a part-time agency. Unlike the executive and judicial branches, the legislature meets for not more than sixty legislative days during its regular annual session. This begins the third

Senate Districts

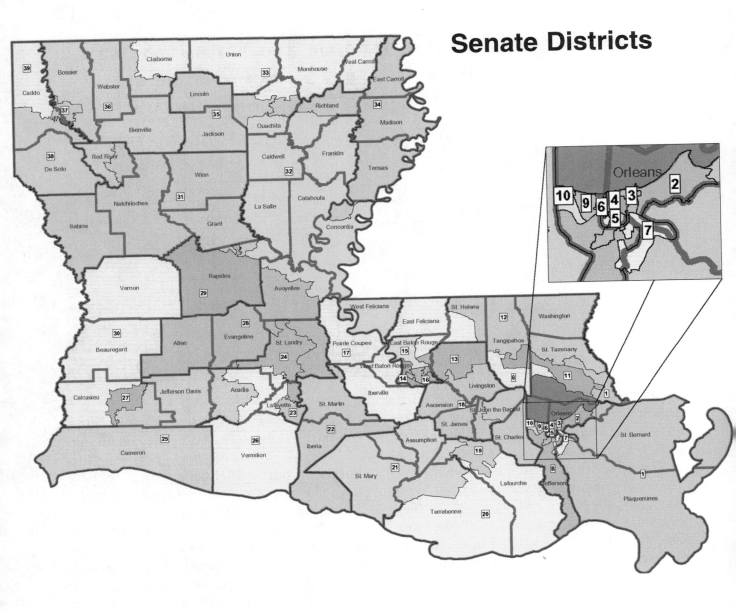

Monday in April. The sixty-day session is held during a period of eighty-five calendar days. The twenty-five extra days included in this span are to allow the legislature a **split session**. The legislature may meet for part of the sixty-day session, take a break, and return home. This is important for the law-makers. It allows them to return home and talk to the voters they represent. They are able to learn the voters' wishes on certain issues that must be voted on during the last part of the session. It also permits a more thorough study of bills being considered.

The legislature may also meet in extra

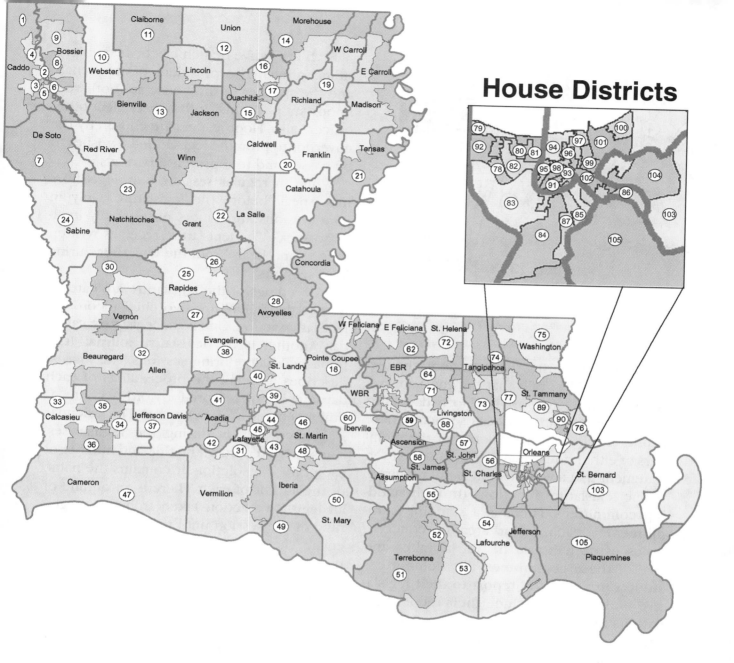

House Districts

sessions. **Special sessions** or extraordinary sessions of no more than thirty days may be held. The governor or the presiding officers of both houses may call a special session. The presiding officers of the Senate and House are authorized to call these special sessions only by majority votes of each house. Special sessions are limited to subjects listed in the call for the session. Certain procedures must be followed. In the event of a public emergency the governor may call the legislature to convene without prior notice.

Veto sessions of the legislature are held

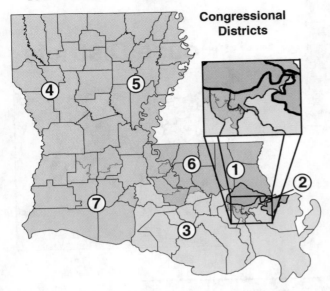

Congressional Districts

automatically. During these sessions, the legislature considers bills that the governor has vetoed. Veto sessions are held forty days after the end of regular or special sessions. There is one exception. The majority of the members of either house may declare in a written statement that a veto session is not required.

The legislature functions through **standing committees**. There is a standing committee for each major area of concern. Rules of each house fix the number and size of these committees. The committees study a problem and report to their legislative bodies. They include their recommendations for action. The presiding officer of each legislative branch appoints members to the committees. The fate of a bill is often decided by the committee. For this reason there is much competition among legislators to be named to these very influential committees. Usually a senator serves on no more than three committees. A representative serves on no more than two.

Each legislative branch elects its own presiding officer. The president of the senate and the speaker of the house are both very important positions. Both houses elect other officers also. Floor leaders are chosen by the governor to promote legislation he wishes to be passed and to represent his views.

While in regular session, only legislators may speak before the legislature. Only in joint sessions are visitors occasionally invited to speak. The legislature receives written reports and hears from the governor during joint sessions.

Proceedings of the legislature are carefully recorded. There are two chief records of legislative action. One is the **legislative calendar**. Another is the **legislative journal**. It is published daily during sessions. The journal describes in detail the proceedings of each day but is not a word-for-word account. It omits debates or assignments. The calendar is printed weekly during the regular sessions. It is a record of the title and number of each bill or resolution. It contains the name of the author of each. There is an outline of all legislative action taken from the beginning of the session until the date of the calendar. The official newspaper of the state prints the acts and constitutional amendments. After a session the calendar, acts, and journal are available in bound volumes.

A number of legislative agencies contribute to the work of the lawmakers. The **Legislative Council** was established in 1952 to assist lawmakers with research. The council provides clerical assistance to the legislators in drafting bills and resolutions. The Office of the Legislative Auditor has the important concern of the state's fiscal, or financial, affairs. It studies the budget, revenues, and expenses. It advises the legislature on financial issues. The **Legislative Fiscal Office** and **Legislative Budgetary Control Council** are other important agencies assisting the legislature. The **Louisiana State Law Institute** aids in revising statutes and in amending the constitution.

To be considered for passage, each bill or joint resolution must be introduced by a member of the legislature. Each bill must meet the requirements of the United States and Louisiana Constitutions. Some bills require a two-thirds vote and some three-fourths to pass. A bill must be delivered to the governor within three days after it passes both houses of the legislature. The governor has ten days after he receives the bill to approve or veto it.

Lobbying is the best known and most commonly used method of trying to influence the legislature. It is a part of the legislative process. There are both professional and volunteer lobbyists. Usually it is the professionals to whom people refer. These people give assistance to legislators because they are able to supply information on issues of particular concern to them. Lobbyists represent one viewpoint—the one they are paid, or volunteer, to represent. Since there are two sides to most issues, there are usually lobbyists representing both sides.

Lobbyists are required to register with the Senate at each session. They are required to reveal whom they represent and who pays them.

Citizens who wish to get their side heard often volunteer as lobbyists on special issues. Such citizen-lobbyists include teacher groups. Some represent art groups and museums. There are people representing many other groups.

Lagniappe—*Congress*. Louisiana is divided into seven districts and elects a representative from each district to serve in the House of Representatives. Two people are elected to serve in the Senate. Since Louisiana is represented in the United States Congress by a total of nine people, the state gets nine electoral votes in presidential elections.

En Partie 2 (Studying a Partie). 1. What are the duties of the legislature? 2. What are the two houses of the legislature? 3. (a) What are the qualifications of members of the legislature? (b) What is their term of office? 4. What is the procedure for passing a bill? 5. What is lobbying?

Judicial Branch. The judicial branch of the government is composed of many courts. Both federal and state judicial systems function in Louisiana. The federal court system deals with violations of the federal constitution and federal statutes. The state system handles violations of the state constitution and state statutes. This discussion is limited to the state system.

Each of these courts falls into a category, or type, of court. The type depends on its function and jurisdiction. Some courts handle misdemeanors. Others handle felonies. Only one, the Supreme Court, is alone in its category. It is the only court of final, or last, appeal in the state judicial system.

There are other types of courts in the state's judicial system. These are courts of appeal, district courts, juvenile and family courts, city and municipal courts, justices of the peace, and miscellaneous courts. The powers of these various courts are defined by the Louisiana Constitution. Each court handles certain types of cases.

Lagniappe—*Crime and Punishment*. A felony is any crime punishable by death or hard labor. The defendant (the person accused of the crime) is entitled to a trial by jury in felony cases. The death penalty is called **capital punishment**. A **misdemeanor** is a lesser crime than a felony. Conviction usually carries a maximum penalty of a five-hundred-dollar fine and six months in jail. The defendant in a misdemeanor case is entitled to a trial by a judge alone.

The Supreme Court is headed by the chief justice. He is the member who has served longest on the Supreme Court. The court holds yearly sessions in New Orleans. It hears cases that have been heard in lower courts. These cases have been "appealed to

LOUISIANA DISTRICT COURTS JUDICIAL DISTRICTS

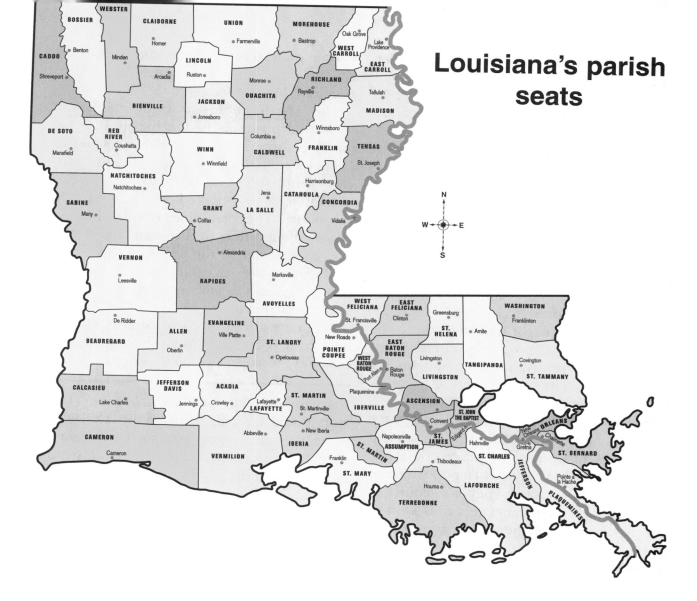

Louisiana's parish seats

this higher court." In this way the Supreme Court acts as a court of appeal. It also has a few cases that begin with the Supreme Court itself. Decisions of the Supreme Court are final. They cannot be appealed to any other state court.

Courts of appeal have no authority to try criminal cases. A unanimous agreement by a court of appeal is essential to reverse a judgment of a district court. The court of appeals is often the highest court for civil cases.

District courts are the general trial courts. These have broad jurisdiction. They handle civil, criminal, and probate matters. There are thirty-three judicial districts. Each has its district court. New Orleans has two district courts—one civil and one criminal. The number of parishes included in a district and the number of judges for each vary.

District court judges serve as juvenile court judges in parishes without a separate juvenile court. Juvenile courts handle matters involving children. If the juvenile is fifteen years old or older and is accused of having committed a capital offense, these courts do not handle the case. Juvenile and family courts also handle cases involving action for divorce, separation, annulment, and child custody. Civil cases from juvenile courts are sent to courts of appeal.

Parish and city courts are two other types of courts in Louisiana's judicial system. There are three parish courts in the state. Every parish seat has a city court. Every ward that has over five thousand inhabitants is entitled to a city court. These city courts have authority to handle certain cases.

Mayor's courts and justices of the peace courts handle any violation of municipal ordinances. Justices of the peace courts are located mostly in wards with a population of less than five thousand. They are "courts of no record." No permanent record is kept of the proceedings of these minor courts. In courts of no record the judges may be removed by recall elections.

The Louisiana **attorney general** is the top official in the state's judicial system. **District attorneys** are elected in each judicial court district. Each of these district attorneys is in full charge of every criminal suit started or pending in his district. He determines when, whom, and how he shall prosecute. He also serves as legal advisor to the police jury.

Each parish elects a **clerk of the district court**. The clerk records court proceedings, preserves court records, and performs certain judicial functions when the judge is absent. The clerk of court has other assigned duties also.

The **sheriff** holds one of the most respected positions in the parish. It is his job to enforce state and parish laws and to collect state and parish taxes. He must also carry out district court rulings.

Constables are elected for each ward in the parish. The constable acts as the law enforcement officer for the ward and as officer of the justice of the peace courts.

Marshals are elected officers of city courts. They act as law enforcement officers for a municipality.

Coroners are licensed physicians elected by each parish to hold inquests, order autopsies, and investigate suspicious deaths.

Lagniappe—*Unusual Punishment.* The story is told, unverified, that in the late 1800s some prisoners were punished by having them lay bricks in Shreveport streets, instead of fines or jail time.

Each parish except Orleans has a **jury commissioner**. It consists of the clerk of court or his deputy and four members appointed by the district judge. The jury commission is responsible for selection of juries for the two kinds of juries in Louisiana. These include **grand juries** and **petit**, or **trial, juries**. The jury members are selected by drawings from a jury list compiled by the commission.

The **grand jury** is a group of twelve persons who serve for six months. It is their duty to investigate all crimes punishable by death, election frauds, charges against public officials, conditions in private prisons, and other causes for public concern. **Petit** (PET i) juries are divided into those for the trial of civil cases and those for the trial of criminal cases. Petit, or trial juries, hear cases and issue verdicts.

Lagniappe—*Edward Douglass White.* White, son of a former Louisiana governor, served as chief justice of the United States Supreme Court from 1910 to 1921. He served with distinction.

En Partie 3 (Studying a Partie). 1. What makes up our judicial system? 2. What is the rank from bottom to top of Louisiana's courts? 3. Which courts handle cases concerning federal constitutional questions? 4. What is the difference between a grand jury and a petit jury?

Local Government

Local government includes parishes, municipalities, and special districts. Louisiana has three classes of municipalities. They are **villages** (population between 150 and 999), **towns** (population between 1,000 and 4,999), and **cities** (population over 5,000). Parishes and municipalities are allowed to exercise any power and perform any function necessary and proper in the management of their affairs. They have all powers except those prohibited by the Louisiana Constitution or state laws. Parishes are divided into **wards**. Wards are divided into **precincts**.

The power of local political units to govern themselves is called **home rule**. The voters in a parish determine what form of government shall be used. Voters may decide to change the existing form. They do this by forming a parish charter commission. Ten percent of the voters (or ten thousand—whichever is the lesser number) petition the parish governing body to form such a commission. The goal of the commission is the study of a new plan of government for the parish. After the plan is presented, voters must decide by majority vote whether they prefer the new form.

Most parishes have the **police jury** form of government. Members of the body are elected for four-year terms. They represent districts in the parish. Police jurors are paid a monthly salary. Some receive travel expenses.

To qualify as a police juror, the citizen must be a registered voter and resident of the district he wishes to represent. If a vacancy occurs, the remaining members of the police jury select a replacement. This individual serves only until an election can be held.

Other parishes have home-rule charters. They are developed and approved by the people in the parish. A home-rule charter is a parish constitution. It usually provides for a legislative and executive branch of parish government. A few parishes, usually the largest metropolitan parishes, use this system. It is a commission form of some type. This form resembles the jury system except the number of individuals serving on the commission is smaller. In some cases each commissioner heads a department of government.

The **municipalities** operate under several different types of charters and forms of government. They have the right to draft and adopt their own charters unless the population is less than twenty-five hundred. The **mayor-alderman** type government is the plan these small towns must follow. Almost all of the cities in the state have the **mayor-council** form of government. Some use the **commissioner** form. The voters elect the officials who have terms of varying lengths. Each commissioner is head of a separate department. The commissioners act as a body to determine policy. Another form is the **council-manager plan**.

The **school board** administers the local school system. Members are elected for six overlapping terms. The local system is supervised by the state board of education. These systems are organized on a parish basis except for Monroe and Bogalusa. Members of the local school board are elected by the voters according to seats allowed on the basis of population. The board, with approval of the voters, levies property taxes. These taxes support the school system. The board appoints the local superintendent, makes contracts, and issues bonds. The parish school board orders and maintains public school buildings in the parish. It manages school lands. It also approves public school teachers, supervisors, and all other parish school personnel. It carries out the laws pertaining to schools passed by the State Board of Education and such local laws as are made by the parish school board itself. The school board also determines the number of schools. It creates, consolidates, or abolishes school districts. It prepares an annual budget that must be approved by the state school budget committee.

Louisiana has **special districts** created to perform certain services that existing government units are unwilling or unable to administer. The powers of these districts are limited to a specific purpose or purposes. The most common special districts are the drainage, sewerage, road, fire, levee, garbage, and school districts.

En Partie 4 (Studying a Part). 1. What are the units of local government? 2. Who determines the form of government for a parish? 3. What is the police jury? 4. What is home rule? 5. What is the population range of (a) a village, (b) a town, and (c) a city? 6. Who administers the educational system?

Lagniappe—*PAR*. The public representative in government reform is PAR, founded in 1950. Its goal is to correct the government of Louisiana, end the scandals, and make the public aware in a non-partisan fashion. It is a nonprofit research organization with volunteer members, who attend meetings and report findings.

Finances

Taxes are the major **source of the money the state spends**. The state also obtains money from licenses, fees, state land leases, oil royalties, and federal funds. Parish revenues are obtained from local taxes, court fines, leases and royalties on parish-owned lands, and state funds. The Louisiana Constitution or statutory law sets limits on parish tax levies, court fines, and parking and license fees. Revenues from some sources are dedicated to specific purposes and to a particular branch of government.

Louisiana has different kinds of **taxes**. They include sales, severance, income, petroleum products, beverage, tobacco, corporation franchise, property, gasoline, and a number of minor taxes.

Louisiana in 2003 had a net state tax-supported debt per capita of $661, ranking it twenty-eighth among states. Louisiana had less debt per capita than the national average of $701.

Over the last decade, management of Louisiana's state finances has been concerned with some added problems. One of these is the growing drain on state funds caused by federal mandates.

The state legislature decides how the state's money is spent. Each fiscal (financial) year, a balanced operating **budget** for the state must be prepared. The budget must show the estimated funds that will be available. Also, plans for spending these funds must be shown. The state often uses bond sales as a means of borrowing money to meet the major costs that cannot be met out of current state revenues. The state usually issues bonds for permanent improvements. This includes public buildings and state highways. A vote of two-thirds of each house is necessary to authorize bond issues.

> **En Partie 5 (Studying a Part).** 1. What are Louisiana's main sources of money? 2. Who determines how this money will be spent?

Citizens' Participation

Registration and Voting. The Louisiana Constitution provides for the permanent registration of voters. It provides for the secret ballot and for the conduct of all elections.

To register to vote, a person has several options. One is to appear before the parish registrar of voters. The registrar of voters is located in the parish seat. Other options include registering at any federal social agency, such as food stamp and welfare offices, or at the driver's license locations if some change has to be made in the driver's license. Other optional sites include participating banks, libraries, post offices, town halls, and some other public places. It is also possible to register by mail if certain conditions are met. For instance, United States service personnel are permitted to register by mail.

The voter must prove his identity. When the registrar secures the needed information, the voter's name is placed on the official list of voters.

Certain people are entitled to vote by mail. Provisions are made for those who are homebound, are hospitalized, or have just been released from the hospital and are unable to go to the polls. Those who are out of town because they are away at school, work outside the state, work offshore, or with the military may vote by mail. Special arrangements are made for those whose religion conflicts with voting on Saturday. Any registered voter who expects to be out of town on voting day may vote absentee by going to the registrar's office at the appointed time.

Failure to vote at least once during a four-year period cancels the registration of a voter. In Orleans Parish the voter is disqualified after only two years of failing to vote.

To be eligible to vote, a person must be at least eighteen years of age. He or she must be a citizen of the United States. The person must be a bona fide resident of the state, parish, municipality, and precinct in which he is registered as a voter. Louisianians are required to live in the state thirty days before they may register. This requirement is the same as the residence requirement for voting in the national presidential elections.

The right to vote is not given to prisoners in penitentiaries. Nor is it given to those declared mentally incompetent. Persons under an order for imprisonment for conviction of a felony or indicted do not have the right to vote. Deserters from military service

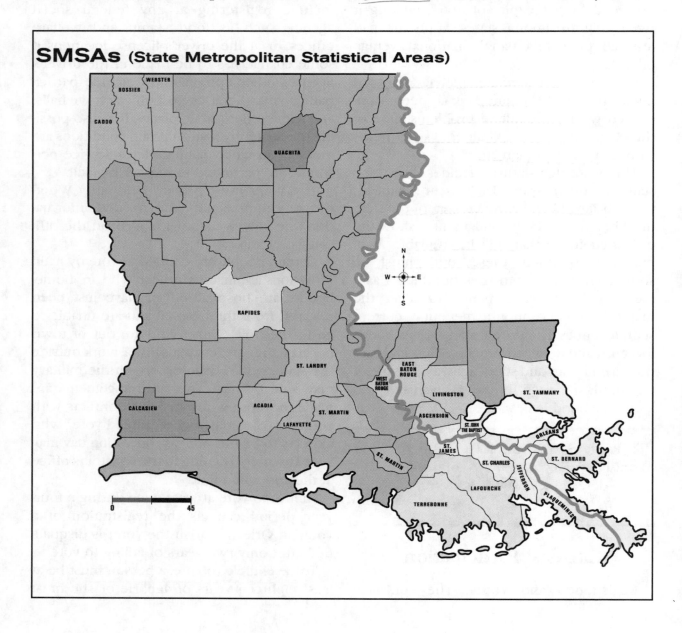

SMSAs (State Metropolitan Statistical Areas)

or persons dishonorably discharged from the service may not vote.

Political Parties. Provision is made for political parties. A person can declare himself a member of any party or no party. A person does not have to be nominated by a party to run for office. State elections are by an open primary. The top two candidates, regardless of their party, enter a runoff unless one of the candidates has gained over 50 percent of the vote. Federal elections are between all party candidates. The candidate with the most votes wins.

Elections. Louisianians vote between 6 A.M. and 8 P.M. They vote in primary, general, special, property, and bond elections. Voting machines are provided at polling places in geographical precincts as drawn by ordinance by the parish governing authority.

Commissioners open and close polls. They determine whether voters are qualified. They keep order in the polling places. They maintain and complete election forms. They also record the vote as shown on machines and announce election results in their precincts. **Citizens** make a statement at the polls. Their voting reflects their values. Less than 50 percent of the registered voters vote in most elections. Therefore, a minority decides the issues for everyone. Through the years Louisianians have developed a reputation for not taking their part in government seriously. The more the citizens bear the cost of government through taxes the more likely they are to take an active part. They are then likely to make their wishes known. They will then demand efficiency and honesty from the officials they elected. It is up to the people to decide through their votes what Louisiana is and will become.

En Partie 6 (Studying a Part). 1. What are the qualifications for voting? 2. Who cannot vote? 3. (a) How do you register? (b) How often? (c) Where? 4. When and where do you vote? 5. Why should you vote?

Coup de Main
(Completing the Story)

Jambalaya (Putting It All Together)

1. What is there about Louisiana's government that sets it apart from that of other states?

2. Define:
a. Capital Punishment
b. Checks and Balances
c. Civil Law
d. Common Law
e. Executive Assistants
f. Executive Branch
g. Executive Sessions
h. Felony
i. Joint Sessions
j. Judicial Branch
k. Legislative Branch
l. Legislative Calendar
m. Legislative Council
n. Legislative Journal
o. Misdemeanor
p. Municipalities
q. Political Parties

r. Polls
s. Precincts
t. Registrar
u. Severance Tax
v. Special Sessions
w. Split Sessions
x. Standing Committee

3. Describe the form of government used in (a) your parish and (b) your village, town, or city.

4. Who are your parish officials?

5. (a) Name Louisiana's United States senators and United States representatives. (b) Which ones represent you? (c) Name the state senators and representatives who represent you in the legislature.

6. Give your location: (a) state senatorial district, (b) state representative district, (c) United States senatorial district, (d) United States representative district, (e) your ward, (f) your precinct, and (g) your voting station.

7. (a) How many electors does this state have? (b) How are they selected?

Potpourri (Getting Involved)

1. Investigate the Napoleonic Code and its influence on the Louisiana constitution. Is Louisiana the only state in the U.S. that uses the Napoleonic Code?

2. Reenact (a) the Constitutional Convention of 1973, (b) a town meeting in which a proposed law is being debated, (c) a session of the legislature, or (d) the passage of a bill.

3. Compare (a) the government of Louisiana with that of another state or (b) the civil service system with the spoils system.

4. Trace (a) the constitutional changes that have taken place in Louisiana, (b) the forces that have changed Louisiana's political structure throughout its history, (c) steps the government has taken in response to crises that reflect the traditions, customs, and values of the state, or (d) political pressures that have influenced major decisions made by the state's leaders.

5. Evaluate the role of specific government leaders. Relate the leadership to the progress of the state.

6. Report on the relationship of state, parish, and city governments.

Gumbo (Bringing It Up-to-Date)

1. Report on how and when Louisianians vote. Evaluate Louisiana's voting system.

2. Report on ways that citizens may (a) voice disagreement about our government, (b) communicate with state leaders, and (c) lobby.

3. Study some controversial laws of Louisiana such as forced heirship or blue laws or proposed laws that are being debated. Report your findings to the class.

4. Investigate salaries and special privileges

or benefits of current government officials. Compare these with those of private businesses and/or those of government officials in other states.

5. Research juvenile law enforcement. Who in law enforcement handles child abuse, neglect, or missing children? What are the punishments for children in violation of the law?

6. How are petit jurors selected? Who can be excused? Who excuses potential jurors? Are there problems in finding people to serve?

CHAPTER 29

HURRICANES KATRINA AND RITA

The National Weather Service on August 23, 2005, referred to a disturbance in the Caribbean as Tropical Depression 12. The warm waters of the Caribbean permitted intensification, so that by August 24 its winds were at 35 mph. The depression continued to move slowly, with moisture and heat building up its center. The satellite reports stressed that the depression was "getting better organized."

The storm continued to move west-north-west, with nothing in its path to weaken it. Once the winds reached 45 mph, it was named Tropical Storm Katrina. It was now approximately 135 miles east of the Florida Keys. The tropical-storm-force winds extended out 70 miles, and the power of this storm continued to increase. A hurricane watch was issued on August 25 for Florida's southeast coast, west coast, and the Florida Keys. Katrina became a Category 1 hurricane by 5 p.m., with sustained winds of 75 mph that extended out for 15 miles. Within an hour and a half, the storm reached the Florida coast with 80-mph winds and a storm surge of two to four feet.

Katrina cut a wide area of destruction as it moved southwest across Florida. It dropped back to tropical-storm status before entering into the **Gulf of Mexico**. Katrina was expected to hug the coastline, moving northward toward the Florida panhandle. The meteorologists did not expect Katrina to weaken. The storm, within hours, regained hurricane strength, veering northwest into the open waters of the Gulf of Mexico. Katrina slowly passed directly over the "loop current," a great deep patch of tropically hot seawater, which fed the storm's force like high-octane fuel.

The United States watched as Katrina quickly became a Category 4 hurricane with sustained winds of 145 mph, and by August 28 it was an unbelievable Category 5 hurricane packing winds up to 175 mph. Katrina was now a massive storm, about 1,000 miles across, with a storm surge predicted up to 28 feet.

Katrina, within 72 hours, had become a **"Monster Storm,"** a killer capable of unimaginable destruction, on a collision course with the coasts of Louisiana and Mississippi. A near-direct hit was predicted for New Orleans, a city built below sea level. An aging levee system and massive loss of protective wetlands made it and the surrounding coastline extremely vulnerable to the approaching monster.

August 28, Sunday. The National Hurricane Center at 8 a.m. in Miami upgraded Katrina to a Category 5, the highest rating on the Saffir-Simpson scale. Pres. George W. Bush by 9 a.m. called Louisiana governor Kathleen Blanco and encouraged an evacuation of New Orleans. At 10 a.m. New Orleans mayor Ray Nagin ordered a mandatory evacuation, the first for the city of 485,000 residents. "We're facing the storm most of us have feared," Mayor Nagin stated.

Governor Blanco urged residents to leave New Orleans. She stated, "I have determined that this incident will be of such severity and magnitude that effective response will be beyond the capabilities of the state and the affected governments."

Michael Brown, the Federal Emergency Management Agency (**FEMA**) director, and Department of Homeland Security (DHS) secretary Michael Chertoff at 11 a.m. prepared the daily briefing for President Bush. National Hurricane Center officials warned that Katrina's storm surge could overtop New Orleans' levees.

The Regional Transit Authority at noon sent buses to 12 New Orleans locations to transport people to the Superdome, one of 10 city shelters. About 550 members of the Louisiana National Guard were assigned to provide security and distribute food and water in the giant arena. By 1 p.m., traffic congestion and weather delays turned the standard two-hour drive from New Orleans to Baton Rouge into a 10-hour ordeal.

Governor Blanco by midafternoon activated 3,500 of the 6,000 National Guard troops under her command. About 40 percent of the state's National Guard troops were serving in Iraq. The Louisiana National Guard requested 700 buses from FEMA to assist coastal evacuation. Only 100 buses arrived, for reasons that are still unclear.

President Bush declared a federal state of emergency for Mississippi and Alabama and declared a major disaster in Louisiana. Governor Blanco asked the president to boost emergency financial aid from $9 million to $130 million.

This satellite photograph shows Hurricane Katrina making landfall on August 29, 2005.

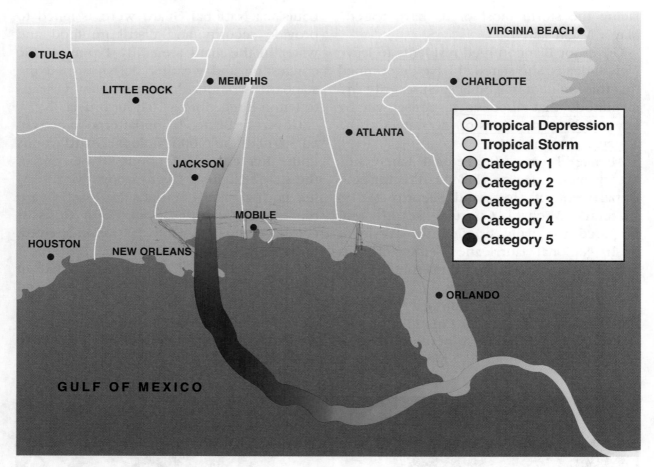

The legend on the map reads:

- ○ **Tropical Depression**
- ○ **Tropical Storm**
- ○ **Category 1**
- ○ **Category 2**
- ○ **Category 3**
- ○ **Category 4**
- ○ **Category 5**

Map labels: VIRGINIA BEACH ●, ● TULSA, ● MEMPHIS, ● CHARLOTTE, LITTLE ROCK, ● ATLANTA, JACKSON, MOBILE, HOUSTON, NEW ORLEANS, ● ORLANDO, GULF OF MEXICO

The path of Hurricane Katrina.

By 9 p.m. over 20,000 people had gathered at the Superdome. The National Guard had stocked the arena with three trucks of water and seven trucks of meals ready to eat (MREs). This was sufficient for 15,000 people for three days, a Guard spokesman stated.

August 29, Monday. Katrina, by 6 a.m., veered to the east of New Orleans, and its winds slowed to 145 mph. The storm made landfall at Buras, Louisiana, 70 miles southeast of New Orleans. The first photos from Buras showed it was completely destroyed.

By dawn the Superdome lost electricity and began running on generator power. The 20,000 people there had reduced lighting and no air conditioning.

At 6:30 a.m., a storm surge from the Mississippi River-Gulf Outlet began to flood eastern New Orleans and St. Bernard Parish. The levees along the north side of the Intracoastal Waterway were soon disintegrating. The Industrial Canal levees were overtopped at 6:50 a.m. on both sides, and water began spewing through a breach to the east, into the Lower Ninth Ward of New Orleans.

The surge that made its way up the

Homes stand damaged following Hurricane Katrina.

Mississippi River-Gulf Outlet and the Intracoastal Waterway slammed into the Industrial Canal, causing a loud boom at 7:45 a.m. The concrete floodwall shattered. At 8:15 a.m., a barge started to slam against the Industrial Canal floodwall, sending more booming sounds through the neighborhood. As 100- to 140-mph winds blew through the Industrial Canal, the levee breach lengthened to 300 feet.

Lagniappe—*Mississippi River-Gulf Outlet (MR-GO)*. This is a 76-mile shipping canal that was opened in 1963. The use of this outlet peaked in 1978. As of 2004, an average of four ships per week used it. The MR-GO's future would be reevaluated after Hurricane Katrina. Its presence has eroded 27,000 acres of marsh that stood between St. Bernard Parish and Lake Borgne.

Katrina's eye passed over the Mississippi Gulf Coast at 9 a.m., moving at 15 mph. Destruction resulted from wind speeds of 135 mph and a storm surge of 26 feet.

By 9:30 a.m., two pieces of metal tore loose from the roof of the Superdome and rain poured in. Electrical and phone systems in New Orleans began to go offline. Floodwaters continued to rise above six feet in Orleans and St. Bernard parishes. The St. Bernard Parish Web site posted at 1 p.m.

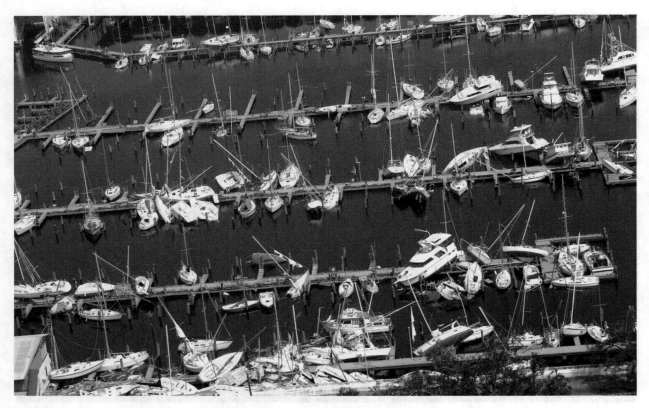

Boats in a New Orleans marina lie in disarray due to the powerful winds and waters of Katrina.

a bulletin in red: *Estimated 40,000 homes are flooded.*

New Orleans officials confirmed by 2 p.m. that the levee along the 17th Street Canal, on the northwest side of the city, had failed. The city was filling with water from Lake Pontchartrain, just like a bowl.

Lagniappe—*Lake Pontchartrain.* This is the second largest saltwater lake in the United States. It is 4 miles across east to west and 24 miles across north to south. The Lake Pontchartrain Causeway is considered the longest over-water span in the world, connecting New Orleans to Mandeville.

The last breaches in New Orleans' barriers occurred at 4 p.m. Both levees along the London Avenue Canal failed.

Early news reports that focused on the Garden District and French Quarter stated the city's damage was far lighter than expected. These tourist areas are built on the natural higher ground.

By 5 p.m. the breach in the 17th Street Canal levee was widening, ultimately measuring 200 feet. Most of New Orleans would be underwater within 12 hours.

August 30, Tuesday. President Bush, in San Diego for a V-J Day anniversary celebration, was briefed on the flooding in New Orleans. He shortened his visit and returned to

Parts of Slidell were flattened by Hurricane Katrina.

Washington, D.C., to address the crisis.

DHS secretary Chertoff was told that there was no quick fix for the multiple levee breaches in New Orleans. The rapid flooding continued.

Fires broke out around the city, some of them believed to be the result of arson. Looting of businesses and homes also began, with few police on hand to halt it.

Governor Blanco, that afternoon, visited the Superdome and was shocked by the conditions. Louisiana and FEMA officials argued over who should be supplying buses to evacuate the displaced. The city's water-supply system failed, depriving stranded residents of water.

Mayor Nagin announced at 6:30 p.m. that the **Army Corps of Engineers'** efforts to mend the city's levees had not succeeded. He estimated that 80 percent of the city was underwater and that some areas then dry might soon flood.

The population within the Superdome had swelled to 25,000 and no evacuation plan was in effect. Sanitary conditions were rapidly deteriorating, food and water were scarce, and rumors of violence spread fear.

To relieve crowding at the Superdome, local officials opened the Ernest N. Morial Memorial Convention Center and advised residents to take shelter there. No plans existed for using this facility as a refuge for a large number of people. The conditions at the Convention Center seemed to mirror those within the Superdome.

Katrina forced sections of the Interstate-10 span into Lake Pontchartrain.

Large numbers of evacuees gathered beneath the downtown overpass of Interstate 10. Rescue helicopters dropped off here the people they had plucked from rooftops. The displaced were left in the open for days without shelter, food, water, sanitary facilities, medical aid, or official supervision.

August 31, Wednesday. Emergency generators at University and Charity hospitals ran out of fuel, leaving nearly 500 patients and 1,000 staff in the dark. The conditions in the Superdome worsened. FEMA and Governor Blanco announced a new evacuation plan for the displaced. A convoy of buses would take the evacuees in the Superdome to the Houston Astrodome.

Air Force One flew over New Orleans about noon for 35 minutes at 1,700 feet. President Bush was able to see the Superdome and the flooded neighborhoods. "It's devastating," he remarked.

The Army Corps of Engineers declared that the water levels in the New Orleans area and Lake Pontchartrain had equalized. Efforts to plug the 17th Street Canal levee were hindered by a lack of rocks, sand, sheet piling, and concrete bars.

After a cabinet meeting, President Bush confirmed the scale of the disaster. "The vast majority of New Orleans is underwater. Tens of thousands of homes and businesses are beyond repair. A lot of the Mississippi Gulf

Large parts of New Orleans flooded after levees failed in the wake of Hurricane Katrina.

Coast has been completely destroyed. Mobile [Alabama] is flooded. We are dealing with one of the worst natural disasters in our nation's history."

Mayor Nagin ordered the city's 1,500 police officers off search-and-rescue duty to control looting and arson. However, one-sixth of the city's policemen did not report for duty.

The crowds at the Convention Center swelled to more than 15,000. Local officials said the facility had food for the hungry and buses to evacuate the victims. Both statements were incorrect.

September 1, Thursday. As many as 20,000 people were stranded at the Convention Center amid turmoil. Police chief Eddie Compass sent 88 officers to establish security there. They could not control the crowds.

The Louisiana National Guard sent 300 troops to the Superdome to begin the bus and helicopter evacuation. Within an hour, it was suspended due to rioting outside and sniper firings at the rescuers.

Countries around the globe pledged aid and money. Russia, France, Mexico, Singapore, Afghanistan—from the largest to the smallest, they offered supplies, manpower, and money. *The Chronicle of Philanthropy* later reported that American citizens gave over $27 million for hurricane relief. Former presidents **Bill Clinton** and **George H. W. Bush** would join together to head up an international relief

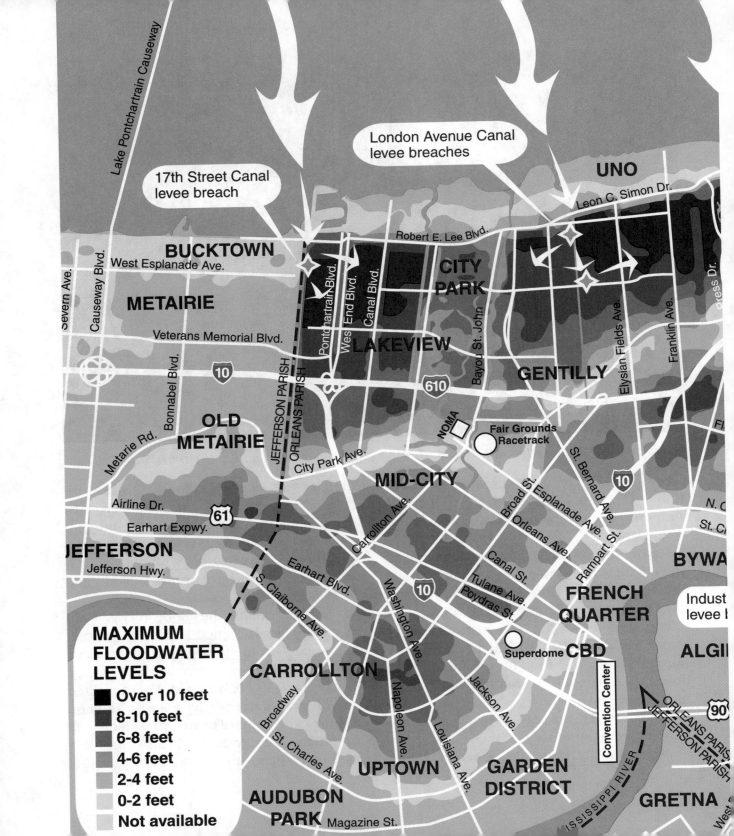

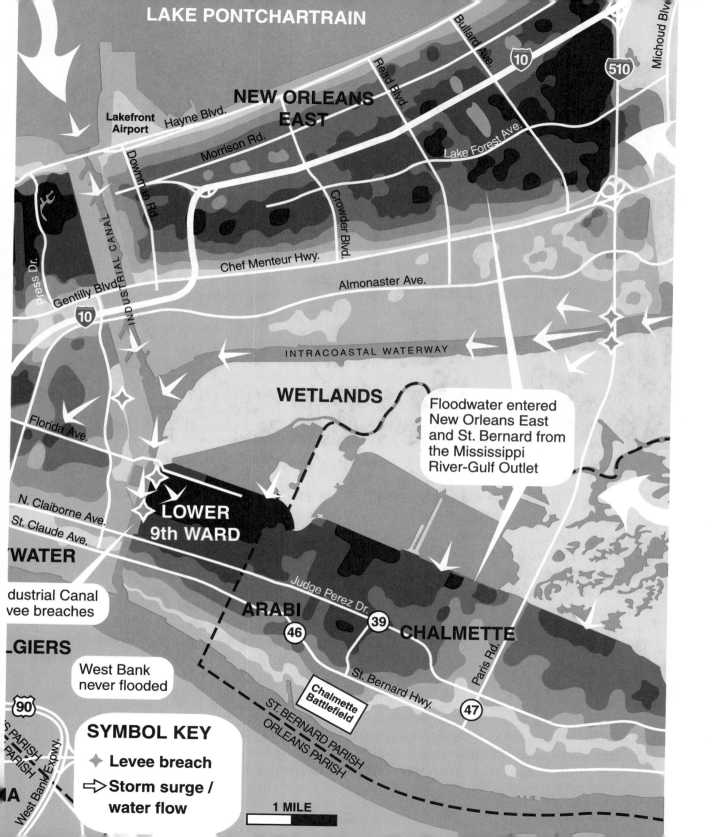

Many New Orleans residents lost their homes and cars after the levees failed.

effort similar to their tsunami fund of 2004.

DHS secretary Chertoff claimed in a press conference that the agency had New Orleans under control and the Superdome was secure. Mayor Nagin, live on television, sent out "a desperate SOS . . . I keep hearing [help] is coming."

Dennis Hastert, speaker of the U.S. House of Representatives, said of New Orleans, "It looks like a lot of that place could be bulldozed." He later apologized.

Attempts to evacuate Charity and University hospitals were stopped by sniper fire. Lt. Gen. Carl A. Strock of the Army Corps of Engineers admitted that his agency could no longer address the breached levees. All available helicopters were working search-and-rescue missions.

Secretary Chertoff, in an interview on National Public Radio, dismissed the idea that there were large numbers of people starving at the Convention Center. FEMA director Brown, on ABC-TV's "Nightline," said he learned about the problems at the Convention Center only hours before.

Lt. Gen. Russel Honore was the newly appointed Joint Task Force commander of all active-duty military forces assigned to the New Orleans area. He planned to have 12,000 National Guard troops in the region by the weekend.

At around midnight, people fleeing the

Evacuees gathered at Interstate 10 near the Superdome, seeking some way out of a flooded New Orleans.

city began arriving in Houston, Dallas, San Antonio, Huntsville, and Atlanta.

September 2, Friday. At 4:30 a.m., New Orleans was rocked by a series of large explosions at a nearby chemical-storage facility. President Bush, before leaving Washington for a six-hour air tour of the devastated coast area, commented about the federal response to Katrina, "The results are not acceptable." Governor Blanco and Mayor Nagin, in a heated meeting with the president aboard Air Force One at the New Orleans airport, attacked the Bush administration's response to the hurricane. President Bush asked Governor Blanco to relinquish control of local law enforcement and National Guard troops. She asked for time to consider the request and later refused it.

By noon, a force of 1,000 National Guard troops and New Orleans police officers arrived at the Convention Center to provide security, food, and water. The crowd was now estimated at more than 20,000. The National Guard had no buses to speed the evacuation. On this day, the evacuation of the Superdome was resumed. It is estimated that 8,000 to 10,000 people were standing in 100-plus-degree heat and wading through knee-deep water and trash to board the buses.

A firefighter holds an elderly woman rescued from the New Orleans floodwaters. The elderly made up a large percentage of those stranded by the hurricane.

From University Hospital, more than 600 people, including 110 patients, were evacuated. Charity Hospital evacuated 2,000 people, including 363 patients. The remaining staff and patients at Methodist Hospital and Tulane Medical Center were evacuated.

Houston mayor Bill White reported that, with 15,000 evacuees inside, the Astrodome was full. He opened the Reliant Center, a convention center, which could hold another 11,000 people.

September 3, Saturday. The evacuation of the Superdome neared the end. About 2,000 to 5,000 evacuees remained. Efforts to retrieve 25,000 people from the Convention Center had barely started. The buses freed from the Superdome were redirected to the Convention Center.

President Bush, in his weekly radio address, said he would send more than 7,000 military personnel to the Gulf Coast over the next 72 hours. The Department of Defense announced that 10,000 more National Guard troops were being sent to the region.

By noon, members of the Texas National Guard cheered as the last person left the Superdome. That afternoon, U.S. Army colonel John Smart, chief operations officer for the Joint Task Force Katrina (West), reported that 42,000 people had now been evacuated from the Superdome and Convention Center.

Army Corps of Engineers officials realized that the type of pumps used to drain New Orleans had not been manufactured for years. The replacement parts would have to be designed and made from scratch. This would delay the removal of the floodwater.

Governor Blanco announced she had hired former FEMA director James Lee Witt, a Clinton appointee, to head the Louisiana relief efforts.

American Airlines dispatched three aircraft manned by volunteer crews to New Orleans. They would fly Katrina evacuees to Lackland Air Force Base in San Antonio, Texas. More than 50 of these missions would be flown over the next five days.

September 4, Sunday. In the past week, 24 people had died in and around the Convention Center. Four bodies had been recovered from inside the Superdome and six more in the immediate area.

The Coast Guard, boating into St. Bernard and Plaquemines parishes, found people in attics and second floors who were exhausted, having endured without food and water for days. Despite the situation, they were unwilling to leave their belongings and pets.

FEMA chartered three Carnival cruise ships to house 7,000 evacuees and emergency workers. Federal officials formally accepted several offers of foreign aid. Sweden, Germany, and other countries in Europe donated first-aid kits, blankets, water trucks, and food rations.

Federal officials acknowledged that the USS *Bataan,* a naval relief ship, had been in the region for four days. This vessel had six operating rooms, 600 hospital beds, food,

water, and the ability to produce 100,000 gallons of clean, fresh water a day.

By the end of this day, Mayor Nagin estimated that Katrina's death toll might approach the thousands. The number of Katrina evacuees in Texas reached 250,000. The Army Corps of Engineers succeeded in closing the breach in the 17th Street Canal.

September 5, Monday. This was a national holiday, Labor Day 2005, a day of rest for working Americans. However, for the citizens of the Louisiana Gulf Coast, it was a day when many wished they still had a job, a house, or a city to work in. As far as the eye could see, it was miles of water or miles of debris in southeastern Louisiana.

The most important change in New Orleans was that the levees had been repaired and pumps were working. The city would be drained in weeks, but bacteria would continue to grow in the water. Mayor Nagin again issued a mandatory evacuation for New Orleans. It is estimated 10,000 citizens remained—many of them elderly, homeless, injured, or mentally challenged.

Jefferson Parish residents could return on this day if they provided a photo ID and proof of residence. The line for entering was eight miles long at 6 a.m. As they arrived at the checkpoints, the residents were greeted by the local police and National Guard. No one was permitted to stay. They could examine their property and search through rubble. The curfew to leave the parish was 6 p.m.

President Bush toured the Gulf Coast again, stopping in Baton Rouge. Governor Blanco would tour the affected areas with the president. Laura Bush would tour many

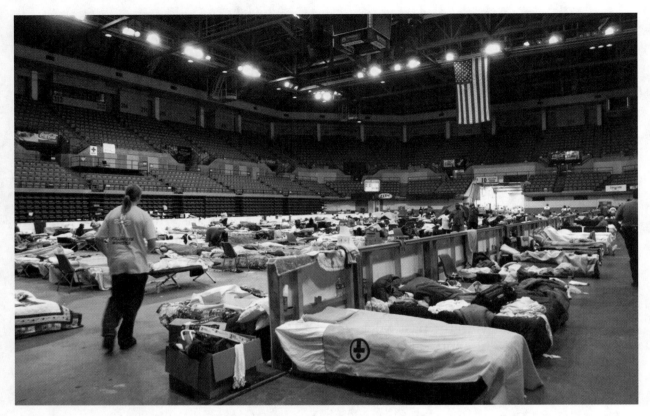

The River Center in Baton Rouge served as shelter for thousands of Katrina evacuees.

schools and shelters in Louisiana.

Despite an early curfew and military occupation, the members of the New Orleans Police Department locked themselves in for the night. Out of the original 1,700-man police force, 400 were now unaccounted for. They fled to look for family members or because their houses were flooded. Some could not cope with the roles of rescuer, law enforcer, and victim.

Thousands of evacuees had been forced to leave something very important behind: their pets. Once the human population was in safekeeping, rescuers had more time to help the thousands of abandoned pets. Some were still tied to porches, trapped on roofs, or hiding in trees. The pets were scared, starving, and isolated from rescuers by water too deep and wide for animals to cross. Trained animal rescuers began to arrive and carry the lost pets to shelters. The American Society for the Prevention of Cruelty to Animals (ASPCA) branches in Louisiana and Texas and the Humane Society of the United States pooled their resources in order to take reports of missing or abandoned pets.

The water in New Orleans was referred to as a witch's brew or toxic gumbo consisting of garbage, human waste, toxic chemicals, and germs. The **Centers for Disease Control (CDC)** tested it for bacterial levels and found it had more than 100 times the amount of fecal coliform usually contained in water runoff into rivers.

The Days That Followed

The morning of September 9, DHS secretary Chertoff relieved FEMA director Brown and placed Coast Guard vice-admiral Thad W. Allen in day-to-day command for the Katrina relief effort. FEMA halted its distribution of debit cards worth $2,000 to Katrina victims; instead, the funds would be directly deposited into their bank accounts.

On September 11, President Bush announced another trip to the Louisiana coast. In a press conference, he admitted for the first time federal failures in responding to Katrina, saying, "Serious problems [were exposed] at all levels of government. And to the extent that the federal government did not fully do its job right, I take responsibility."

In an effort to provide Americans with the answers they deserved, Sen. Bill Frist (R-Tenn.) announced a joint House-Senate panel that would investigate the initial response to Hurricane Katrina. The panel would review "at all levels of government" both the preparation for and recovery from the hurricane.

In a live TV address on September 15 from Jackson Square in New Orleans, President Bush stated, "I offer this pledge of the American people: throughout the area hit by the hurricane, we will do what it takes. We will stay as long as it takes to help citizens rebuild their communities and their lives. And all who question the future of the Crescent City need to know: there is no way to imagine America without New Orleans, and this great city will rise again."

Hurricane Rita

On Sunday, September 18, 2005, the seventeenth named storm of the hurricane season was born and named Rita. This time around, no one was going to be caught by surprise.

On Wednesday, September 21, hovering over the Gulf of Mexico, Rita was upgraded to a Category 3 hurricane. Meteorologists at the National Hurricane Center, later that same day, ranked Rita a Category 5. It set a record for the most Catergory 5 hurricanes in one Atlantic hurricane season. The National Hurricane Center predicted landfall somewhere on the Texas-Louisiana coastline. Officials ordered the evacuation of 1.8 million people from the threatened areas of the Gulf Coast.

On Saturday, September 24, Hurricane Rita came ashore at 3:30 a.m., crossing the coastline east of the Sabine Pass on the Texas-Louisiana border, with winds of 120 mph. The Louisiana coast was decimated once again. Roofs were torn from houses, trees were uprooted from the ground, and floodwaters rose again. Exploding transformers and damaged power lines left more than 1 million people without electricity.

The storm then headed northwest over Orange and Beaumont, Texas. Most of Rita's damage to the east was in Cameron Parish. Winds had gusted to 112 mph, and the Calcasieu River in Lake Charles took on a storm surge of 8 feet. In some areas, Rita raised the Gulf of Mexico waters up to 15 feet. The town of Delcambre was the hardest hit. In Vermilion Parish, rescue workers retrieved citizens from rooftops.

Mayor Randy Roach of Lake Charles requested that citizens not return home for at least two days because of the widespread flooding. The Interstate-10 bridge over the Calcasieu River was closed after it had been struck by barges.

Lafitte, Louisiana, received a storm surge of 15 feet. In New Orleans, the surge broke the repaired Industrial Canal levee. Water rushed through and over the breach, flooding the uninhabited Lower Ninth Ward and the St. Bernard communities of Arabi and Chalmette.

"We are working as hard and as fast as we can," said Col. Richard Wagenaar, the New Orleans district commander for the Army Corps of Engineers. "There's only so much we can do against the forces of Mother Nature. At some point, it just exceeds the capability of man."

Myrtle Grove in south Plaquemines Parish and Jean Lafitte in south Jefferson Parish had levee breaches, flooding areas that were dry during Katrina. A five-foot storm surge from Rita along with heavy rains flooded parts of Orleans and St. Tammany parishes. Lake Pontchartrain also flooded St. Tammany Parish from Madisonville to Eden Isles.

Coast Guard vice-admiral Thad W. Allen, Gov. Kathleen Blanco, and Lt. Gen. Russel Honore gather in New Orleans for a press conference on the evacuation for Hurricane Rita.

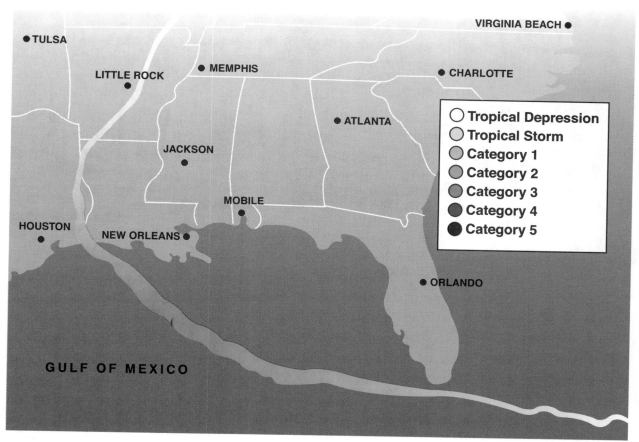

The path of Hurricane Rita.

"We are now fighting on two fronts," Lt. Col. Pete Schneider, spokesman for the Louisiana National Guard, said of the Katrina cleanup in New Orleans and the relief programs for Rita victims in southwest Louisiana.

The Numbers

The official death toll from Hurricanes Katrina and Rita in Louisiana is 1,103. . . . The number of people in New Orleans without privately owned transportation before the hurricanes was 120,000. . . . The poverty rate in New Orleans before the hurricanes was 28 percent. . . . The Humane Society of the United States rescued and sheltered 6,036 animals at the Lamar-Dixon facility in Gonzales and received donations of $15 million. . . . At the New Orleans Aquarium of the Americas, 10,000 fish died. . . . The total number of evacuees from all states threatened by Katrina and Rita was over 1 million. . . . The number of Katrina evacuees in shelters, homes, hotels, and other housing was 374,000. . . . Texas had 250,000 Louisiana evacuees; Arkansas had 50,000; Tennessee had 12,000. . . . Forty-five percent of New Orleans evacuees say they will return to the

Rita's high winds forced down power lines in Lake Charles, cutting off electricity in the area. Many roads in and around the city were covered with debris and impassable.

city.... In Texas, 40 percent of evacuees plan to stay.... Fifteen percent of evacuees state they will move out of Louisiana. . . . Baton Rouge's population increased by 50,000 following Katrina.... FEMA sent 61 emergency-response teams into the area....The National Guard deployed 50,000 individuals to hard-hit areas. . . . The number of active-duty troops deployed in hard-hit areas was 22,000. . . . The United States Coast Guard saved 33,000 lives. . . . Over 125 tons of water, ice, and MREs were brought to Louisiana, with over 3 million MREs delivered to New Orleans....

About 80 percent of New Orleans was underwater at the height of the flood....The United States Coast Guard dropped 350 tons of sand to repair the levees. . . . The Army Corps of Engineers repaired 800 feet of the levees. . . . New Orleans' pumps drained the equivalent of one Olympic-size swimming pool per 1.9 seconds....In Louisiana, 200,000 cars, 75,000 boats, and 1,000 overturned railroad cars would need to be removed from roads, yards, canals, and bayous. . . . Bass Enterprises South Facility, in Cox Bay, Louisiana, spilled 3.8 million gallons of oil; 1.1 million gallons of oil spilled from Murphy Oil Company, in Chalmette, Louisiana; and 18,900 gallons of oil spilled from Sundown

A National Guard helicopter prepares to drop sandbags in Terrebonne Parish into a levee breach caused by Hurricane Rita.

The breach in the 17th Street Canal was closed and pumps worked to drain New Orleans following Hurricane Katrina.

Energy East in Potash, Louisiana....

The number of children displaced in the 2005 hurricane season is estimated at 372,000.... The National Center for Missing and Exploited Children received 4,724 reports of children separated from their families due to Hurricanes Katrina and Rita. ...There were 285,983 names online at the **American Red Cross** "Family Links Registry." ... Since the conclusion of the 2005 hurricane season, 2,523 families have been reunited.... Over 190,000 American Red Cross workers provided relief aid.... The American Red Cross had 1,150 shelters in 27 states and provided financial assistance for 1.2 million families.... Orleans Parish requested 152,000 trailers from FEMA for displaced families, and surrounding parishes requested 120,000.... Insurance claims for the 2005 hurricane season are estimated at more than $25 billion.... The number of households that received a portion of $3.51 billion in disaster assistance was 1,198,000. ...The United States Congress passed a $29 billion package of hurricane aid that included levee and coastal restoration.... Louisiana has received $62 million in national-emergency grants.... The estimated cost of damage to the entire Gulf Coast area is over $200 billion.

This temporary housing site for FEMA trailers in Baker was one of several built for those left homeless by Katrina.

Governor Blanco's Special Legislative Session

Gov. Kathleen Blanco called a 17-day special session of the Louisiana state legislature in November 2005. She asked state lawmakers to support her storm-recovery programs by slashing hundreds of millions of dollars from the state budget. Governor Blanco stated: "I am cutting some of your favorite programs. Some of you will consider these cuts way too painful. . . . Let me warn you: this is just the beginning. Life has changed for us all."

The state of Louisiana faced a $1 billion shortfall in its budget. Lawmakers filed over 152 bills for debate. Sen. Francis Heitmeier, who chaired the Senate Finance Committee, said, "It is going to be a long and gruesome process. I think we are going to be back here two or three more special sessions before it is all over."

Governor Blanco emerged from the 17-day special session with a string of victories on the state budget, business tax breaks, a statewide building code, and a partial takeover of the Orleans public schools. The state legislature also honored her executive order for spending cuts.

The State Budget Act. Legislators cut spending by more than $600 million to rebalance the 2005-6 budgets, which were $959 million in the red after Hurricanes Katrina and Rita. Every department in state government was required to sacrifice. Money from the state's 2004-5 surpluses and "rainy-day fund" was used to make up the remaining deficit.

Tax Cuts on Rebuilding. Companies repairing or replacing equipment damaged by the hurricanes did not have to pay state sales tax on the purchases. And companies borrowing to rebuild from the storms did not have to pay the state franchise tax on debt.

Utility Tax Break. All businesses paid 3.3 percent state tax instead of 3.8 percent on their utility bills and purchases of natural gas. This translated into a savings of more than $20 million for businesses in the first six months after the hurricanes. Paper and pulp companies received an even larger tax break.

Sales-Tax Holiday. The state legislature agreed to a three-day sales-tax holiday, which took place in December 2005. Shoppers around the state were not charged the 4 percent state sales tax for purchases under $2,500.

The New Building Code. All homes that were more than 50 percent damaged by Hurricanes Katrina and Rita must meet the

Hurricane Katrina damaged house roofs in many parishes. The U.S. Army Corps of Engineers operated a "Blue Roof Program," which supplied and installed blue protective roof tarps like the ones seen here in St. Tammany Parish.

new statewide building code if rebuilt. This law went into effect in February 2006 in the 11 coastal parishes hit by the storms. The rest of the state must follow the new code after 2006. The Department of Health and Hospitals worked to establish new building codes for hospitals, nursing homes, and group homes for the disabled in flood-prone areas.

The Orleans Public Schools. The state took over responsibility for 102 of 117 public schools in New Orleans. Every school with a performance score below the state average will be moved into a "recovery school district" run by the State Department of Education and Board of Elementary and Secondary Education (BESE). These two bodies will determine which schools will reopen and how they will operate.

Other Laws Passed at the Session

Property Assessments. A new law required parish assessors to reevaluate storm-damaged property according to its post-Katrina value. Some parishes could choose an automatic assessment of properties at two-thirds of their pre-damage value by calling a vote of the elected taxing bodies within the parish. Orleans, Jefferson, St. Bernard, and Plaquemines parishes did not have this option.

Coastal Restoration. The state will create a new authority to oversee a state plan for coastal restoration and flood control. The federal revenue received from offshore oil and gas production will be deposited into a fund for levee and wetlands improvement.

Elections. The secretary of state, with approval of the governor and the legislature, has the authority to draft a plan to hold elections after a state of emergency has been declared. The plan is limited to consolidating voting precincts and bringing in poll commissioners from other parishes.

Hurricane Recovery Bill

The United States Congress approved a $29 billion hurricane-recovery spending bill in December 2005, including $2.9 billion to repair and upgrade levees in the state of Louisiana. The spending bill also included $1.6 billion for hurricane-ravaged schools as well as schools that took in students displaced by the storms; $11.5 billion in Community Block Grants; $2.75 billion to repair roads, bridges, and other transportation infrastructure; $350 million to NASA to repair space-program facilities; $135 million to repair damage in national parks, wildlife refuges, and forests; $30 million to repair waterways or watersheds; $618 million to help farmers and ranchers affected by the hurricanes; and $441 million for Small Business Administration disaster loans.

Looking to the Future

Hurricanes Katrina and Rita caused extensive unprecedented damage to Louisiana (along with other states). Months after the storm, displaced residents were still debating whether or not to return. New Orleans' tax base fell so much that 3,000 city workers were laid off. Questions remained about which neighborhoods to rebuild. Should the city reduce its footprint, or should it allow all areas to rebuild? If residents were allowed to rebuild, would they need to elevate their homes to the base flood level? If so, who would pay for this? If residents were not permitted to return and their homes were bulldozed and property seized, would they receive just compensation? Would they be relocated to higher areas of the city? What about housing for the city's poor population? What about citizens who did not have flood insurance because they were in a "no flood zone"? The White House opposed a state proposal to bail out uninsured mortgage holders.

Outside of New Orleans, communities affected by the storms also faced monumental challenges. The town of Buras, the first to be hit by Katrina, would never be the same. Boats that supported the livelihoods of the fishermen were destroyed by the storms. The further destruction of barrier islands and wetlands by these hurricanes made South Louisiana especially vulnerable to future devastating hurricanes. What was once a protective area of land is now gone. Damage can increase because there is less wetland to protect inhabited places from approaching hurricanes. Whether or not levees were to be rebuilt to withstand Category 4 or 5 hurricanes was still unknown. Officials saw the need to protect the area, but financing those projects is difficult. Louisiana needed to convince the rest of the country that it was worth saving.

Future hurricane seasons would be interesting. Would those areas in a hurricane's projected path call for evacuations early enough so that everyone had the opportunity to leave? Would officials make certain that those with limited means were evacuated? Would shelters be set up and stocked so that if anyone did stay, they would be able to subsist? Would Louisiana and federal officials learn the lessons of Hurricanes Katrina and Rita?

Coup de Main (Completing the Story)

Jambalaya (Putting It All Together)

1. Select a challenge discussed in the text that the state still faces. Update the problem. Give the causes and solutions listed, as well as your own. Classify your challenge as a Louisiana problem only or as a United States one, also.

2. Who must take the responsibility for solving these problems?

3. List specific contributions that you could make to help Louisiana solve her hurricane problems.

4. Rank the state's challenges on a scale of 1 to 10, with 10 being the most important. Include problems not mentioned here, or reword the ones in the text.

5. What advice would you give the parish leaders to help them solve their problems of devastation from Hurricanes Katrina and Rita?

6. What measures should the parishes take prior to each hurricane season in order to minimize the chance of having the same problems again?

7. Evaluate the roles of specific government leaders during Hurricanes Katrina and Rita. Relate their leadership to the state's progress after the storms.

8. Compare the actions of Louisiana's government with those of another state that was struck by Hurricanes Katrina and Rita.

9. What might you do to help preserve the coastal area of Louisiana from another hit by a Hurricane Katrina and Rita?

Potpourri (Getting Involved)

1. Research the role of a (a) police officer, (b) city mayor, (c) emergency-room doctor, or (d) National Guardsman during Hurricanes Katrina and Rita.

2. Make an illustrated timeline of events from August 28, 2005, to September 5, 2005.

3. Conduct a panel discussion on the failures of the government during the hurricane season of 2005.

4. Write a letter to a friend describing the hardships endured after Hurricanes Katrina or Rita.

5. Interview someone who lived during Hurricanes Hilda, Betsy, or Camille. Ask what their feelings were about the government's aid in the rebuilding of Louisiana.

6. Compare the population and landforms in Louisiana from before and after Hurricane Katrina.

Gumbo (Bringing It Up-to-Date)

1. What should be the goal of Louisiana's state and parish officials for future hurricane seasons?

2. What new programs are being proposed for levee protection in Louisiana? How will they be financed? Who will be held accountable for evaluating their effectiveness?

3. Compare the public schools of Orleans Parish before Hurricane Katrina and after. What role did the Louisiana legislature play in the school system's restructuring?

4. Describe migration patterns that occurred after Hurricanes Katrina and Rita.

5. Cite evidence that progress is being made in the greater New Orleans area. Document your evidence with newspaper clippings, magazine articles, or interviews.

6. Use the latest information to summarize the trends in school and college enrollment, major occupations, distribution of income, and the relationship of the labor force to the total population. What is the significance of these developments?

APPENDIX

Glossary

Acadian. One who came from or a descendant of one who came from Acadia (Nova Scotia) when exiled by the British; an adjective used to describe the culture of the Acadians, such as an Acadian house.

Acadiana. A twenty-two-parish area officially named by an act of the Louisiana Legislature.

Acadian Coast. Land along the Mississippi River north of New Orleans where many of the Acadians settled. It is the center of French Acadians' initial settlements (St. James and Ascension parishes).

Acadian Country. A distinct cultural area influenced primarily by the French.

Algiers. A city across the Mississippi River from New Orleans, noted for its shipyard.

Anglo-Saxon. A person of English descent.

Antebellum. Period before a war, particularly the Civil War.

Aquaculture. Growing crawfish, catfish, alligators, baitfish, bass, and other water-dependent species in a controlled environment.

Ark-La-Miss. The area includes parts of Arkansas, Louisiana, and Mississippi at the junction of these states.

Ark-La-Tex. A circular area including parts of Arkansas, Louisiana, and Texas located near the point where the borders of these three states meet.

Arpent. An old French measure of land, less than an acre, 605 arpents being equivalent to 512 acres; a lineal measure, roughly equal to 192 feet.

Avoyelles Prairie. Relatively high plateau in Avoyelles Parish.

Backland. The land between the frontlands and swamplands.

Backswamp. Flat, wet area in the floodplain beyond the natural levees.

Banquette. A sidewalk.

Bar. A shoal area or area of deposition where material is being deposited from water; a sandbar.

Barataria. Inlet of the Gulf of Mexico on the boundary between Jefferson and Plaquemines parishes; a bay, bayou, and village.

Barrier beach. Beach ridge pushed up against the land.

Barrier island. Beach ridge separated from shore by open water.

Batture. That part of the inner shore of a stream that has been thrown up by the action of the current and that, at certain seasons of the year, may be covered as a whole or in part by the water.

Bay. A body of water partly enclosed by land, but having a wide outlet to the sea.

Bayou. A sluggish stream through lowlands; a term used mainly in the lower Mississippi Basin and the Gulf coast region.

Big House. The residence of the planter and his family and the business center of the plantation operation.

Birdfoot delta. A triangular area at the mouth of a river through which several river outlets pass. The outlets fan out in different angles to form a pattern resembling the footprint of a bird.

Blue Law. Any Puritanical law that forbids certain behaviors or practices, such as banning commercial activity on Sunday.

Blufflands. Areas of considerable relief generally bordering the alluvial valley.

Bottomlands. Lowlands near stream beds.

Boudin. A type of spicy Cajun sausage.

Bousillage. A mixture of Spanish moss or grass and clay used to fill the spaces between the posts of a French cabin; a French shotgun house.

Brackish. Salt water and freshwater mix.

Brake. A wooded swamp; a thicket.

Briquette entre poteaux. Bricks placed between posts of a French cabin.

Cajun. A Louisianian of Acadian descent.

Calinda. An African dance.

Cane River Country. A stretch of land along Cane River Lake, the old channel of Red River.

Capital. Accumulated wealth used to produce additional wealth.

Celt. A person of Irish, Scots-Irish, Scots, Welsh, Cornish, or Breton descent.

Channel. The deepest part of a river, harbor, or strait that affords the best passage.

Chenier. Sand ridges covered with growing oaks. **Cheniere**. An "e" is added when used as a place name.

Chert. A type of flint, common in gravel beds of North Louisiana, used by Indians for making tools.

Claypan. A shallow layer of impervious clay underlying the topsoil.

Coastline. A line along the coast following generally the path of the shoreline but not including every irregularity.

Contour plowing. The practice of plowing on a slope along points of equal elevation rather than up and down the slope.

Coureurs de bois. Early French settlers who hunted and trapped alone in the deep forests of North America, often following Native Americans' ways of life.

Creoles. A white descendant of the French or Spanish settlers in Louisiana during the colonial period. The organization C.R.E.O.L.E., Inc. in 1996 stated that the majority of people who consider themselves Creoles have an African base. See Lagniappe **Creole**.

Crevasse. Point where a river breaks out of its levee.

Crop acreage. Acres of land planted in a crop.

Crop rotation. The practice of changing crop types on a piece of land on a yearly or longer basis so as to restore the soil.

Culture. Learned patterns of thinking and living that have been passed from generation to generation among a people; the characteristic features of a particular group.

Cutoff. A shortening of a river's course caused by water cutting across a loop, or meander, of the river. An ox-bow lake is often formed in this manner.

Cutover land. Land that has been cleared of trees.

Defoliating agent. A chemical used to make leaves drop off plants.

Delta. A deposit of sediment at the mouth of a river where water flow is slower.

Deltaic lakes. See lagoonal lake.

Depression. A period of decreased economic activity.

Disenfranchise. To deprive of citizenship.

Distributary. A river branch flowing from the main stream in a direction away from the stream.

Dogtrot house. A house with a central hall extending the length of the structure and open at both ends.

Drought. Prolonged dry weather that affects the earth's surface and prevents the growth of plants.

Elevation. The height above sea level.

Erosion. The wearing away of rocks and soil caused by water, ice, wind, and other natural forces.

Estuary. An arm of the sea that extends inland to meet the mouth of a river.

Fais-do-do. "Go to sleep"; a dance of the Acadian country; a country or village dance usually held on Saturday nights.

Farm. An agricultural operation carried on by members of a family and/or hired day labor.

Filé. A powder made from sassafras leaves and used to season food.

First bottom. Permanent swamps.

Five Islands. Avery, Belle, Côte Blanche, Jefferson, Weeks; salt domes around Vermilion Bay.

Flatwoods. Flat, timbered lands.

Fleur de lys or **lis**. Lily flower used on the French flag.

Floating land. The top layer of certain marshland or swampland that floats on water beneath it. Because of its instability, floating land wobbles or quivers when walked upon.

Floodplain. The floor of a valley over which a river spreads sediment when it overflows its banks.

Florida parishes. The parishes in Louisiana that were once a part of Florida.

Frasch process. A process of mining sulphur by pumping superheated water into the sulphur bed, which melts and is forced in molten form to the surface.

French Louisiana. Acadiana.

Frontland. Land on the side of the natural levee, sloping away from the river or stream.

Geologic age. The age of natural features of the earth described by reference to past periods of time, always of great length.

German Coast. An area settled by Germans in about 1720 (St. Charles and St. John the Baptist parishes).

Gerrymander. To divide a geographic area into voting districts so as to give an advantage to one party in elections.

Grand jury. Group of twelve persons who investigate all crimes punishable by death, election frauds, and charges against the public.

Grasslands. Lands where grass is the chief native vegetation.

Great Raft. A great logjam in the Red River.

Gris-gris. An object worn as a protective charm against evil, or used for the purpose of inflicting injury; to voodoo, bewitch, or cast a spell over. A favorite gris-gris was, and is, a dime with a hole in it. It was often worn about the ankle.

Gristmill. A mill that grinds grain, especially corn.

Growing season. The time between the last killing frost in the spring and the first killing frost in the fall; the part of the year with warm enough days and nights for plants to grow.

Gumbo. Dialects of Central Africa, probably Negro; any thick soup in which okra is an ingredient.

Gumbo clay. A sticky, clay-like soil found in many low regions of Louisiana, especially in northeast Louisiana.

Gumbo-ya-ya. A get together where people meet just to talk.

Hardpan. A layer of soil made up of clay particles, minerals, and organic matter, which clog the pores of the soil and make it water resistant.

Hill Country. Usually refers to North Louisiana uplands.

Home rule. The power of local political units to govern themselves.

Impressment. To force into public service, especially the British practice of forcing American seamen to serve in the royal navy.

Indentured servant. A person who is bound by contract as servant of another for a designated time and under specified conditions.

Indigo. Plant first grown in Louisiana under Crozat as a money crop, used for making a deep violet-blue dye.

Inlet. A relatively narrow channel or pocket of water.

Isle of Orleans. The land that makes up the Isle of Orleans is bounded on its west, southwest, and south by the Mississippi River; on its southeast and east by the Gulf of Mexico; and on its north by Lakes Maurepas, Pontchartrain, and Borgne, and the Iberville River (Bayou Manchac). See map in text.

Jambalaya. A Spanish-Creole dish made with rice and some other main ingredient, such as ham, shrimp, crabmeat, sausage, or chicken.

Jetty. Man-made structures extending into the sea to influence currents and/or protect a harbor.

Joie de vivre. Joy of living.

Lafourche. A bayou in South Louisiana known as "the longest street in the world," as there have been homes along the bayou banks for two hundred years.

Lagniappe. Something thrown in for good measure; something extra.

Lagoonal lake. Lake formed by wave action beating openings into shorelines, or by sinking of the land. Coastal lakes are formed behind cheniers or natural levees.

Laissez les bons temps rouler (lay zay lay bawn tawn roo lay). "Let the good times roll," the motto of many South Louisianians.

Lamb's quarter. A weed.

Landform. A kind of land. Plains, plateaus, hills, and mountains are all different landforms.

Latitude. Distance north or south of the equator.

Les Rapides. Village on Red River, present-day Pineville.

Line settlement. Houses closely spaced along a road.

Livre. Old French money equivalent to twenty cents in American money.

Lobbying. Part of the legislative process; attempting to influence legislators or other public officials.

Locks. An enclosure placed in streams with a gate at each end, used to raise or lower boats as they navigate the stream.

Longitude. Distance east or west of the prime meridian.

Louisiana's Outer Continental Shelf (OCS). Federal offshore territory adjacent to Louisiana's coast beyond the three-mile limit of the state's offshore boundary.

Lowlands. Scene of river activity—floodplain, delta, cheniers, and coastal marshes.

Mardi Gras. Fat Tuesday; Shrove Tuesday. The last day before Lent. Carnival season is from Twelfth Night to Shrove Tuesday. New Orleans' Mardi Gras celebration is famous.

Marsh. An area of flat, treeless plains dotted with shallow lakes and lagoons. It is often flooded.

Marsh grass. Thick grass that grows in marshlands.

Marshland. Grass-covered land of low elevation that is almost always wet and is void of trees.

Meander. A winding or large curve of a river valley; a winding course; to turn and glide to and fro as a river; one of the loops formed by a river as it cuts its course over the earth's surface. This feature is found in old streambeds.

Migratory birds. Birds that move from one region or climate to another. They usually move south in the winter and north in the summer.

Mortar. A strong vessel used to grind various products such as grain. Indians usually made them of stone or wood.

Mudlumps. Mounds of clay extending above the surface of the water at the mouths of passes of the Mississippi River.

Mulatto. One who has mixed black and Caucasian ancestry.

Natural levees. Ridges along main river channels and their distributaries; the natural outlets.

Natural region. An area within which all of the natural elements or qualities are the same.

Naval stores. Products such as turpentine or pitch, originally used to caulk the seams of wooden ships.

Navigable. Having features that allow the passage of boats or ships.

North Louisiana. Geographically, that part of the state above the thirty-first parallel. Culturally, North Louisiana is identified as that part of the state in which Anglo-Saxon or Celtic Protestant culture is found, although this same culture also exists in geographical South Louisiana.

Outer Continental Shelf. Shallow water between the coastline and deep water of the Gulf or ocean.

Oxbow. A U-shaped bend in a river; a lake,

usually crescent in shape, formed when the meanders of the river are cut off by the action of the stream; also called horseshoe lakes.

Palmetto. Any of various fan palms grown in the southern United States.

Peach Country. Area around Ruston.

Perique. A unique, strong-flavored tobacco grown in St. James Parish.

Pestle. Cut and shaped implement used with a mortar to grind grain. Louisiana Indians made them of wood or stone.

Petit jury. Group that hears cases and issues verdicts.

Pimple mounds. Small elevated mounds scattered throughout Louisiana. Their origin is unknown.

Pirogue. A type of canoe used in Louisiana. It was originally made of a single log.

Pitch. A resin found in certain evergreen trees; a black, sticky substance found in the distillation of coal tar, wood tar, and petroleum, and used for waterproofing, roofing, and pavement.

Plantation. An organized economic system of cheap labor for raising staple crops.

Plantation system. The economic system dominated by plantations.

Planter. The final authority on a plantation, which involved not only farming operations but also often included small manufacturing operations and a store (called a commissary after the sawmills came to Louisiana).

Pleistocene. An epoch in the geologic time scale. It began about one million years ago and was marked by glaciation and continental ice sheets.

Pot likker. The juice or stock from vegetables after cooking.

Prairie. Generally, a relatively flat area of tall grasslands in the west-southwest.

Praline. A type of confection made in Louisiana of sugar paste and nut meats.

Raft lakes. Water impounded in parts of the main tributary valleys of the Red River, commonly attributed to the Great Raft.

Rapids. Part of a river where water moves swiftly as it descends to a lower level, passing over rocks or other obstructions, thereby creating turbulence and sounds usually audible for a considerable distance.

Real. Spanish silver coin valued at ten sols (1 sol=1 penny); worth approximately 12.5 cents and at one time widely used in North American colonies where it was referred to as a "bit." Two bits equals twenty-five cents.

Recent. The period in geologic time from the end of the last continental glaciation (eighteen thousand years ago) to the present.

Redneck. A term of affection applied generally to members of the North Louisiana cultural group. The name originally referred to farmers who had sunburned necks from plowing. In recent times, the term has been given unfavorable meanings which conflict with the original meaning.

Relief. The difference in elevation between the high and low points of a land surface. Relief features are surface outlines of the land, such as plains and mountains.

Rice Country. Rice-producing area of southwest Louisiana. Crowley is the unofficial "Rice Capital."

Ridge. A long and narrow elevation of land or a range of hills or mountains.

Rigolets. The name of the strait that connects Lake Borgne and Lake Pontchartrain.

Rigolet de Bon Dieu. An arm of the Red River that extends from a point about two miles below Grand Ecore to Colfax, where it again unites with the Red.

Riverbed. The bottom of a river.

Roux. A basic brown sauce.

Sagamite. Hominy or porridge of coarse corn made by the early Indians of Louisiana.

Salt dome. A place where salt has pushed up through overlying earth materials into a rounded peak.

Salt islands, or land islands. Elevated domes in the marshy areas of South Louisiana. They were formed by salt plugs being thrust upward.

Sassafras. The dried root bark of a number of related trees of the laurel family, used in medicine and for flavoring.

Sediment. Particles deposited by flowing water, wind, or ice.

Selective cutting. The practice of cutting mature trees and also some young trees when they have grown too thickly.

Shoreline. The line where the water, such as the Gulf, meets the land.

Shotgun house. Type of architecture characterized by all the rooms arranged in a straight line.

Shrove Tuesday. The Tuesday before Ash Wednesday, a day of penitence and confession immediately preceding Lent.

Silt. Fine clay particles deposited by water.

South Louisiana. The part of Louisiana below the thirty-first parallel. It is made up of West Florida, the Mississippi Delta, Acadiana, and the southwest non-Catholic area. The latter area is much like North Louisiana.

Spillway. Emergency outlet for river waters at floodstage.

States' Rights Democratic party. A political party formed by southern Democrats in 1948 who opposed the candidacy of Harry Truman and campaigned on a platform of states' rights.

Strawberry Country. Area around Hammond.

Suffrage. The right to vote.

Sugarcane Country. An eighteen-parish area in the south-central part of the state below the thirty-first parallel.

Swamp, or swampland. Low, wet forested area.

Syndics. Spanish name for justices of the peace.

Tafia. An alcoholic drink made from boiled-down cane juice.

Teche Country. The land along Bayou Teche.

Terrace. A level, narrow plain with a steep front bordering a river, lake, or sea.

Time zone. A geographic area observing the same time of day.

Topography. A description of the surface features of a particular region; the configuration of the natural and artificial features of a particular region, including such things as mountains, rivers, and cities.

Tributary. River flowing into a main river and contributing water to the largest river.

Truck farm. A small vegetable farm that sells its products locally.

Uplands. Hill lands; hills.

Vacheries. Stock farms.

Versailles. City near Paris, France; site of the magnificent palace that cost 150 million francs; King Louis XV lived lavishly there.

Watershed. A dividing ridge between drainage areas; a region or area drained by a river or lake.

Wattle and daub. A method of building whereby a wattle, or frame, of poles and interwoven twigs is covered with mud or plaster.

Weathering. The breaking of rocks into smaller pieces by actions of freezing, heating, and cooling, tramping of animals, or the movement or changing of soil by man.

Wetlands. Those areas that are inundated or saturated by service or ground water at a frequency and duration sufficient to support, and that under normal circumstances do support, a prevalence of vegetation typically adapted for life in saturated soil conditions. Generally includes swamps, marshes, bogs, and similar areas.

Wold. An open, hilly area.

Yam Country. Area around Opelousas, the "Yam Capital."

Governors of Louisiana

FRENCH LOUISISANA

Pierre le Moyne, Sieur d'Iberville 1699
Sieur de Sauvole (died in office) 1699-1701
Jean Baptiste le Moyne, Sieur de Bienville 1701-1713
Antoine de la Mothe Cadillac 1713-1716
Jean Baptiste le Moyne, Sieur de Bienville 1716-1717
Jean Michiele Seigneur de Lepinay 1717-1718
Jean Baptiste le Moyne, Sieur de Bienville 1718-1724
Pierre Dugue, Sieur de Boisbriant 1724-1725
Etienne Périer 1725-1733
Jean Baptiste le Moyne, Sieur de Bienville 1733-1743
Pierre François de Rigaud, Marquis de Vaudreuil 1743-1753
Louis Billouart, Chevalier de Kerlerec 1753-1763
Jean Jacques d'Abbadie (died in office) 1763-1765
Charles Philippe Aubry 1765-1769

SPANISH LOUISIANA

Antonio de Ulloa 1766-1768
Don Alejandro O'Reilly 1768-1769
Don Luis de Unzaga 1769-1777
Don Bernardo de Gálvez 1777-1785
Don Estevan Miro 1785-1791
François Luis Hector, Baron de Carondelet 1791-1797

Don Manuel Gayoso de Lemos (died in office) 1797-1799
Don Francisco Bouligny 1799
Sebastian, Marquis de Casa Calvo 1799-1801
Juan Manuel de Salcedo 1801-1803

TRANSITIONAL PERIOD

Pierre Clement de Laussat ....1803 (November 30-December 20)

TERRITORY OF LOUISIANA

W. C. C. Claiborne 1803-1812

STATE OF LOUISIANA

		Spouse
W. C. C. Claiborne	1812-1816	Eliza Lewis;
		Clarisse Duralde Suzette Bosque
Jacques Villeré	1816-1820	Jeanne Henriette Fazende
Thomas Bolling Robertson (resigned)	1820-1824	Lelia Skipwith
Henry S. Thibodeaux		
(succeeded as president of Senate)	1824	Miss Lejeune; Brigitte Bellanger
Henry Johnson	1824-1828	Elizabeth Key
Pierre Derbigny (died in office)	1828-1829	Felicite Odile de Hault de lassus
Armand Beauvais		
(succeeded as president of Senate)	1829-1830	None
Jacques Dupre	1830-1831	Theotiste Roy
Andre Bienvenu Roman	1831-1835	Aimee Françoise Parent
Edward Douglass White	1835-1839	Catherine S. Ringgold
Andre Bienvenu Roman	1839-1843	Aimee Françoise Parent
Alexandre Mouton	1843-1846	Zelia Rousseau
Isaac Johnson	1846-1850	Charlotte McDermott
Joseph Walker	1850-1853	Catherine Carter
Paul O. Hebert	1853-1856	Cora Wills Vaughn; Penelope Lynch
Robert Charles Wickliffe	1856-1860	Anna Dawson; Anna Davis Anderson
Thomas Overton Moore	1860-1864	Bertha Leonard
Gen. G. F. Shepley (military governor)	1862-1864	None
Henry Watkins Allen		
(under Confederate government)	1864-1865	Salome Crane

Michael Hahn		
(under Federal government—resigned)	1864-1865	None
James Madison Wells		
(succeeded as president of Senate)	1865-1867	Mary Ann Scott
Benjamin Flanders		
(under military authority)	1867-1868	Susan H. Sawyer
Joshua Baker		
(under military authority)	1868	Fanny Assherton; Catherine Patton
Henry Clay Warmoth	1868-1872	Sally Durand
P.B.S. Pinchback		
(lieutenant governor, acting governor)	1872-1873	Nina Emily Hawthorne
John McEnery (elected, but ruled out)	1873	None
William Pitt Kellogg		
(governor de facto)	1873-1877	Mary Emily Wills
Francis T. Nicholls	1877-1880	Caroline Zilpha Guion
Louis Alfred Wiltz		
(died in office)	1880-1881	Mildred Bienvenue
Samuel Douglas McEnery		
(succeeded as lt. governor)	1881-1888	Elizabeth Phillips
Francis T. Nicholls	1888-1892	Caroline Zilpha Guion
Murphy James Foster	1892-1900	Rosa Rosetta Ker
William Wright Heard	1900-1904	Isabelle Manning
Newton Crain Blanchard	1904-1908	Emily Barret; Charlotte Tracy
Jared Young Sanders	1908-1912	Ada V. Shaw; Emma Dickinson
Luther Egbert Hall	1912-1916	Clara Wendell
Ruffin G. Pleasant	1916-1920	Ann Ector
John M. Parker	1920-1924	Cecile Airey
Henry L. Fuqua (died in office)	1924-1926	Laura Matta
Oramel H. Simpson		
(succeeded as lieutenant governor)	1926-1928	Louise Pickett
Huey P. Long		
(qualified for U.S. senator, 1932)	1928-1932	Rose McConnell
Alvin O. King		
(succeeded as president of Senate)	1932	Willie Lee Voris
Oscar K. Allen (died in office)	1932-1936	Florence Love
James A. Noe		
(succeeded as lieutenant governor)	1936	Anna Gray
Richard W. Leche (resigned)	1936-1939	Elton Reynolds
Earl K. Long		
(succeeded as lieutenant governor)	1939-1940	Blanche B. Revere

Sam H. Jones	1940-1944	Louise Gambrell Boyer
Jimmie H. Davis	1944-1948	Alverne Adams
Earl K. Long	1948-1952	Blanche B. Revere
Robert F. Kennon	1952-1956	Eugenia Sentell
Earl K. Long	1956-1960	Blanche B. Revere
Jimmie H. Davis	1960-1964	Alverne Adams
John J. McKeithen	1964-1972	Marjorie Funderburk
Edwin W. Edwards	1972-1980	Elaine Schwartzenburg
David Treen	1980-1984	Dolores Brisbi
Edwin W. Edwards	1984-1988	Elaine Schwartzenburg
Charles "Buddy" Roemer, III	1988-1992	Patti Crocker (divorced during term)
Edwin W. Edwards	1992-1996	Divorced; married Candace Picou
Murphy J. ("Mike") Foster	1996-2004	Alice Cosner
Kathleeen Babineaux Blanco	2004-	Raymond Blanco

Senators to the United States Congress from Louisiana

Name	Home	Dates Served
Allen B. McGruder	Opelousas	Nov. 18, 1812-Mar. 3, 1813
John N. Destrehan	*Destrehan	
Thomas Posey	Attakapas	Dec. 7, 1812-Feb. 4, 1813
James Brown	New Orleans	Feb. 5, 1813-Mar. 3, 1817
Elegius Fromentin	New Orleans	Mar. 4, 1813-Mar. 3, 1819
William C. C. Claiborne	*New Orleans	
Henry Johnson	Donaldsonville	Feb. 26, 1818-May 27, 1824
James Brown	New Orleans	Mar. 4, 1819-Dec. 10, 1823
Dominique Bouligny	New Orleans	Dec. 21, 1824-Mar. 3, 1829
Josiah S. Johnston	Alexandria	Mar. 12, 1824-May 19, 1833
Edward Livingston	New Orleans	Mar. 4, 1829-May 24, 1831
George A. Waggaman	New Orleans	Nov. 15, 1831-Mar. 3, 1835
Alexander Porter	Attakapas	Jan. 6, 1834-Jan. 5, 1837
Alexander Mouton	Vermilionville	Feb. 2, 1837-Mar. 1, 1842
Robert C Nicholas	Donaldsonville	Mar. 4, 1836-Mar. 3, 1841
Charles E. A. Gayarré	*New Orleans	
Charles M. Conrad	New Orleans	Apr. 14, 1842-Mar. 3, 1843
Alexander Barrow	Baton Rouge	Mar. 4, 1841-Dec. 29, 1846
Henry Johnson	New River	Mar. 4, 1844-Mar. 3, 1949
Alexander Porter	*Attakapas	
Pierre Soule	New Orleans	Feb. 3, 1847-Mar. 3, 1847

Solomon W. Downs	Monroe	Mar. 4, 1847-Mar. 3, 1853
Pierre Soule	New Orleans	Mar. 4, 1849-Apr. 11, 1853
John Slidell	New Orleans	Dec. 5, 1853-Feb. 4, 1861
Judah P. Benjamin	New Orleans	Mar. 4, 1853-Feb. 4, 1861
John S. Harris	Vidalia	July 17, 1868-Mar. 3, 1871
William Pitt Kellogg	New Orleans	July 17, 1868-Nov. 1, 1872
J. Rodman West	New Orleans	Mar. 4, 1871-Mar. 3, 1877
James B. Eustis	**New Orleans	
William Pitt Kellogg	New Orleans	Nov. 30, 1877-Mar. 3, 1883
James B. Eustis	New Orleans	Jan. 12, 1876-Mar. 3, 1879
Benjamin F. Jonas	New Orleans	Mar. 4, 1879-Mar. 3, 1885
Randall L. Gibson	New Orleans	Mar. 4, 1883-Dec. 15, 1892
James B. Eustis	New Orleans	Mar. 4, 1885-Mar. 3, 1891
Donelson Caffery	Franklin	Jan. 14, 1893-Mar. 3, 1901
Edward Douglass White	New Orleans	Mar. 4, 1891-Mar. 12, 1894
Newton C. Blanchard	Shreveport	Mar. 12, 1894-Mar. 3, 1897
Samuel D. McEnery	New Orleans	Mar. 4, 1897-June 28, 1910
Murphy J. Foster	Franklin	Mar. 4, 1901-Mar. 3, 1913
John R. Thornton	Alexandria	Dec. 12, 1910-Mar. 3, 1915
Joseph E. Ransdell	Lake Providence	Mar. 4, 1913-Mar. 3, 1931
Robert F. Broussard	New Iberia	Mar. 4, 1915-Apr. 12, 1918
Walter Guion	Napoleonville	Apr. 24, 1918-Nov. 5, 1918
Edward J. Gay	Plaquemine	Dec. 2, 1918-Mar. 3, 1921
Edwin S. Broussard	New Iberia	Mar. 4, 1921-Mar. 3, 1933
Huey P. Long	New Orleans	Jan. 25, 1932-Sept 10, 1935
John H. Overton	Alexandria	Mar. 4, 1933-May 14, 1948
Rose McConnell Long	New Orleans	Feb. 10, 1936-Jan. 3, 1937
Allen J. Ellender	Houma	Jan. 3, 1937-July 27, 1972
William C. Feazel	West Monroe	May 24, 1948-Dec. 30, 1948
Russell B. Long	Shreveport	Dec. 31, 1948-Jan. 2, 1987
Elaine Edwards	Crowley	Aug. 7, 1972-Nov. 13, 1972
J. Bennett Johnston	Shreveport	Nov. 14, 1972-Jan. 1, 1997
John Breaux	Crowley	Jan. 3, 1987-Jan.3, 2005
Mary Landrieu	Baton Rouge	Jan. 1, 1997-
David Vitter	Metairie	Jan. 3, 2005-

*Never qualified for office
**Contested election, no action taken in 44th Congress
***In a closely run senatorial election Nov. 5, 1996, Mary Landrieu received 852,945 votes while Woody Jenkins received 847,157 votes (official count as of Nov. 20, 1996). Citing

claims of election violations and targeting Orleans Parish as the primary source of irregularities, Jenkins filed a lawsuit on Nov. 14, 1996, which asked that the court either declare Jenkins the winner or order a new election on Dec. 10, 1996.

The lawsuit alleged that the initial excess of votes (at the time estimated to be 10,000) were cast by unqualified persons or cast illegally; the precinct sign-in logs were signed by thousands of voters who were allowed to cast their ballots without first being properly identified; the amount of votes registered on voting machines greatly exceeded the amount of people who signed up to vote, accounting for more than 1,500 "phantom votes," which should be nullified.

Three days after filing his lawsuit, Jenkins dropped it because he did not have enough time to complete his investigation. The charge of voter fraud went before the Senate Rules Committee, which found no credible evidence of Election Fraud. The first female elected as a senator from Louisiana, Mary Landrieu, was sworn in as full senator "without prejudice."

The senatorial election was the closest in Louisiana history and the closest in the United States for 1996.

Sources: *Biographical Directory of the American Congress, 1774-1971; Louisiana Office of the Secretary of State*

Representatives to the United States Congress from Louisiana

Name	Home	Dates Served
Daniel Clark[1]	New Orleans	Dec 1, 1806-Mar. 3, 1809
Julien de L. Poydras[2]	New Orleans	Mar. 4, 1809-Mar. 3, 1811
Allen B. McGruder[3]	Opelousas	
Elegius Fromentin[4]	New Orleans	

District 1

Thomas Robertson	New Orleans	Dec. 23, 1812-Apr. 20, 1818
Thomas Butler	St. Francisville	Nov. 16, 1818-Mar. 3, 1821
Josiah S. Johnston	Alexandria	Mar. 4, 1821-Mar. 3, 1823
Edward Livingston	New Orleans	Mar. 4, 1823-Mar. 3, 1829
Edward D. White	Donaldsonville	Mar. 4, 1829-Nov. 15, 1834
Henry Johnson	Donaldsonville	Dec. 1, 1834-Mar. 3, 1839
Edward D. White	Thibodaux	Mar. 4, 1839-Mar. 3, 1843
John Slidell	New Orleans	Mar. 4, 1843-Nov. 10, 1845
Emile LaSere	New Orleans	Jan. 29, 1846-Mar, 3, 1851
Louis St. Martin	New Orleans	Mar. 4, 1851-Mar. 3, 1853
William Dunbar	New Orleans	Mar. 4, 1853-Mar. 3, 1855
George Eustis, Jr.	New Orleans	Mar. 4, 1855-Mar. 3, 1859
John E. Bouligny	New Orleans	Mar. 4, 1859-Mar. 3, 1861

Benjamin F. Flanders[5]	New Orleans	Feb. 17, 1863-Mar. 3, 1863
J. Hale Sypher	New Orleans	July 18, 1868-Mar. 3, 1869
J. Hale Sypher[6]	New Orleans	Dec. 5, 1870-Mar. 3, 1875
Randall L. Gibson	New Orleans	Mar. 4, 1875-Mar. 3, 1883
Carleton Hunt	New Orleans	Mar. 4, 1883-Mar. 3, 1885
Louis St. Martin	New Orleans	Mar. 4, 1885-Mar. 3, 1887
Theodore S. Wilkinson	Plaquemines Parish	Mar. 4, 1887-Mar. 3, 1891
Adolph Meyer	New Orleans	Mar. 4, 1891-Mar. 8, 1908
Albert Estopinal	Estopinal	Dec. 7, 1908-Apr. 28, 1919
James O'Connor	New Orleans	June 10, 1919-Mar. 3, 1931
Joachim O. Fernandez	New Orleans	Mar. 4, 1931-Jan. 3, 1941
F. Edward Hebert	New Orleans	Jan. 3, 1941-Jan. 3, 1976
Richard A. Tonry[7]	Chalmette	Jan. 3, 1976-May 4, 1976
Robert L. Livingston	New Orleans	Sept. 7, 1977-Mar 1, 1999
David Vitter	Metairie	May 29, 1999-Dec. 31, 2004
Bobby Jindal	Kenner	Jan. 3, 2005-

District 2

Henry Gurley	Baton Rouge	Mar. 4, 1823-Mar. 3, 1831
Philemon Thomas	Baton Rouge	Mar. 4, 1831-Mar. 3, 1835
Eleazer W. Ripley	Jackson	Mar. 4, 1835-Mar. 3, 1839
Thomas W. Chinn	Baton Rouge	Mar. 4, 1839-Mar. 3, 1841
John B. Dawson	St. Francisville	Mar. 4, 1841-Mar. 3, 1843
Alcee L. LaBranche	New Orleans	Mar. 4, 1843-Mar. 3, 1845
Bannon G. Thibodeaux	Thibodaux	Mar. 4, 1845-Mar. 3, 1849
Charles M. Conrad	New Orleans	Mar. 4, 1849-Aug. 17, 1850
Henry A. Bullard	New Orleans	Dec. 5, 1850-Mar. 3, 1851
J. Aristide Landry	Donaldsonville	Mar. 4, 1851-Mar. 3, 1853
Theodore G. Hunt	New Orleans	Mar. 4, 1853-Mar. 3, 1855
Miles Taylor	Donaldsonville	Mar. 4, 1855-Feb. 5, 1861
Michael Hahn[8]	New Orleans	Feb. 17, 1863-Mar. 3, 1863
James Mann	New Orleans	July 18, 1868-Aug. 26, 1868
Lionel A. Sheldon	New Orleans	Apr. 8, 1869-Mar. 3, 1871
E. John Ellis	New Orleans	Mar. 4, 1875-Mar. 3, 1885
Michael Hahn	New Orleans	Mar. 4, 1885-Mar. 15, 1886
Nathaniel D. Wallace	New Orleans	Dec. 9, 1886-Mar. 3, 1887
Matthew D. Lagan	New Orleans	Mar. 4, 1887-Mar. 3, 1889
Hamilton D. Coleman	New Orleans	Mar. 4, 1889-Mar. 3, 1891
Matthew D. Lagan	New Orleans	Mar. 4, 1891-Mar. 3, 1893
Robert C. Davey	New Orleans	Mar. 4, 1893-Mar. 3, 1895

Charles F. Buck	New Orleans	Mar. 4, 1895-Mar. 3, 1897
Robert C. Davey	New Orleans	Mar. 4, 1897-Dec. 26, 1908
Samuel L. Gilmore	New Orleans	Apr. 22, 1909-July 18, 1910
H. Garland Dupre	New Orleans	Dec. 12, 1910-Feb 21, 1924
J. Zach Spearing	New Orleans	May , 15, 1924-Mar. 3, 1931
Paul H. Maloney	New Orleans	Mar. 4, 1931-Dec. 15, 1940
T. Hale Boggs	New Orleans	Jan. 3, 1941-Jan. 3, 1943
Paul H. Maloney	New Orleans	Jan. 3, 1943-Jan. 3, 1947
T. Hale Boggs[9]	NewOrleans	Jan. 3, 1947-Jan. 3, 1973
Lindy Boggs	NewOrleans	Mar.28, 1973-Oct. 3, 1992
William J. Jefferson	New Orleans	Oct. 3, 1992-

District 3

William L. Brent	St. Martinville	Mar. 4, 1823-Mar. 3, 1829
Walter H. Overton	Alexandria	Mar. 4, 1829-Mar. 3, 1831
Henry A. Bullard	Alexandria	Mar 4, 1831-Jan. 4, 1834
Rice Garland	Opelousas	Apr. 28, 1834-Aug. 31, 1840
John Moore	Franklin	Dec. 17, 1840-Mar. 3, 1843
Pierre E. J. B. Bossier	Natchitoches	Mar. 4, 1843-Apr. 21, 1844
Isaac E. Morse	St. Martinville	Dec. 2, 1844-Mar. 3, 1851
John Moore	New Iberia	Mar. 4, 1851-Mar. 3, 1853
Roland Jones	Shreveport	Mar. 4, 1853-Mar. 3, 1855
John M. Sandidge	Pineville	Mar. 4, 1855-Mar. 3, 1859
John M. Landrum	Shreveport	Mar. 4, 1859-Mar. 3, 1861
Michel Vidal	Opelousas	July 18, 1868-Mar. 3, 1869
Chester B. Darrall	Brashear	July 6, 1870-Feb. 20, 1878
Joseph H. Acklen	Pattersonville	Feb.20, 1878-Mar. 3, 1881
Chester B. Darrall	Morgan City	Mar. 4, 1881-Mar. 3, 1883
William Pitt Kellogg	New Orleans	Mar. 4, 1883-Mar. 3, 1885
Edward J. Gay	Plaquemine	Mar. 4, 1885-May 30, 1889
Andrew Price	Thibodaux	Dec. 2, 1889-Mar. 3, 1897
Robert F. Broussard	New Iberia	Mar. 4, 1897-Mar. 3, 1915
Whitmell P. Martin	Thibodaux	Mar. 4, 1915-Apr. 6, 1929
Numa F. Montet	Thibodaux	Oct. 14, 1929-Jan. 3, 1937
Robert L. Mouton	Lafayette	Jan. 3, 1937-Jan. 3, 1941
James Domengeaux[10]	Lafayette	Jan. 3, 1941-Apr. 15, 1944
James Domengeaux	Lafayette	Nov. 7, 1944-Jan. 3, 1949
Edwin E. Willis	St. Martinville	Jan. 3, 1949-Jan. 3, 1969
Patrick T. Caffery	New Iberia	Jan. 3, 1969-Jan. 3, 1973
David C. Treen	Metairie	Jan. 3, 1973-Mar. 10, 1980

| W. J. ("Billy") Tauzin | Metairie | May 22, 1980-Dec. 31, 2004 |
| Charles Melancon | Napoleonville | Jan. 3, 2005- |

District 4

John B. Dawson	St. Francisville	Mar. 4, 1843-Mar. 3, 1845
John H. Harmanson	Simmesport	Mar. 4, 1845-Oct. 24, 1850
Alexander G. Penn	Covington	Dec. 30, 1850-Mar. 3, 1853
John Perkins, Jr.	Ashwood	Mar. 4, 1853-Mar. 3, 1855
Thomas G. Davidson	East Feliciana Parish	Mar. 4, 1855-Feb. 5, 1861
Joseph P. Newsham	St. Francisville	July 18, 1868-Mar. 3, 1869
Joseph P. Newsham[11]	St. Francisville	May 23, 1870-Mar. 3, 1871
James McCleery[12]	Shreveport	
Aleck Boarman	Shreveport	Dec. 3, 1872-Mar. 3, 1873
Samuel Peters[13]		
George L. Smith	Shreveport	Dec. 3, 1873-Mar. 3, 1875
William M. Levy	Natchitoches	Mar. 4, 1875-Mar. 3, 1877
Joseph B. Elam	Mansfield	Mar. 4, 1877-Mar. 3, 1881
Newton C. Blanchard	Shreveport	Mar. 4, 1881-Mar. 12, 1894
Henry W. Ogden	Benton	May 12, 1894-Mar. 3, 1899
Phanor Breazeale	Natchitoches	Mar. 4, 1899-Mar. 3, 1905
John T. Watkins	Minden	Mar. 4, 1905-Mar. 3, 1921
John N. Sandlin	Minden	Mar. 4, 1921-Jan. 3, 1937
Overton Brooks	Shreveport	Jan. 3, 1937-Sept 16, 1961
Joe D. Waggonner	Plain Dealing	Sept 16, 1961-Jan. 3, 1979
Claude ("Buddy") Leach	Leesville	Jan. 3, 1979-Jan. 3, 1981
Charles E. ("Buddy") Roemer III	Bossier City	Jan. 3, 1981-Mar. 14, 1988
Jim McCrery III	Shreveport	Apr. 26, 1988-Nov. 3, 1992
Cleo Fields	Baton Rouge	Nov. 3, 1992-Jan. 3, 1997
Jim McCrery III	Shreveport	Jan. 3, 1997-

District 5

W. Jasper Blackburn	Homer	July 18, 1868-Mar. 3, 1869
Frank Morey	Monroe	Dec. 6, 1870-June 8, 1876
George A. Sheridan[14]	Lake Providence	Mar. 3, 1875-Mar. 3, 1875
William B. Spencer	Vidalia	June 8, 1876-Mar. 3, 1877
John E. Leonard	Lake Providence	Mar. 4, 1877-Mar. 15, 1878
John S. Young	Homer	Dec. 2, 1878-Mar. 3, 1879
J. Floyd King	Vidalia	Mar. 4, 1879-Mar. 3, 1887
Cherubusco Newton	Bastrop	Mar. 3, 1887-Mar. 3, 1889
Charles J. Boatner	Monroe	Mar. 4, 1889-Mar. 20, 1896

Charles J. Boatner[15]	Monroe	Dec. 10, 1896-Mar. 3, 1897
Samuel T. Baird	Bastrop	Mar. 4, 1897-Apr. 22, 1899
Joseph E. Ransdell	Lake Providence	Dec. 4, 1899-Mar. 3, 1913
J. Walter Elder	Monroe	Mar. 4, 1913-Mar. 3, 1915
Riley J. Wilson	Harrisonburg	Mar. 4, 1915-Jan. 3, 1937
Newt V. Mills	Mer Rouge	Jan. 3, 1937-Jan. 3, 1943
Charles E. McKenzie	Monroe	Jan. 3, 1943-Jan. 3, 1947
Otto E. Passman	Monroe	Jan. 3, 1947-Jan. 3, 1976
Jerry Huckaby	Ringgold	Jan. 3, 1977-Nov. 3, 1992
Jim McCrery III	Shreveport	Nov. 3, 1992-Jan. 3, 1997
John Cooksey	Monroe	Jan. 3, 1997-Dec. 31, 2002
Rodney Alexander	Quitman	Jan. 1, 2002-

District 6

Charles E. Nash	Washington	Mar. 4, 1875-Mar. 3, 1877
Edward W. Robertson	Baton Rouge	Mar. 4, 1877-Mar. 3, 1883
Andrew S. Herron[16]		
Edward T. Lewis	Opelousas	Dec. 3, 1883-Mar. 3, 1885
Alfred B. Irion	Marksville	Mar. 4, 1885-Mar. 3, 1887
Edward W. Robertson	Baton Rouge	Mar. 4, 1887-Aug. 2, 1887
Samuel M. Robertson	Baton Rouge	Dec. 5, 1887-Mar. 3, 1907
George K. Favrot	Baton Rouge	Mar. 4, 1907-Mar. 3, 1909
Robert C. Wickliffe	St. Francisville	Mar. 4, 1909-June 11, 1912
Lewis L. Morgan	Covington	Dec. 2, 1912-Mar. 3, 1917
Jared Y. Sanders	Bogalusa	Mar. 4, 1917-Mar. 3, 1921
George K. Favrot	Baton Rouge	Mar. 4, 1921-Mar. 3, 1925
Bolivar E. Kemp	Amite	Mar. 4, 1925-June 19, 1933
Jared Y. Sanders, Jr.	Baton Rouge	May 21, 1934-Jan. 3, 1937
John K. Griffith	Slidell	Jan. 3, 1937-Jan. 3, 1941
Jared Y. Sanders, Jr.	Baton Rouge	Jan. 3, 1941-Jan. 3, 1943
James H. Morrison	Hammond	Jan. 3, 1943-Jan. 3, 1967
John R. Rarick	St. Francisville	Jan. 3, 1967-Jan. 3, 1975
W. Henson Moore	Baton Rouge	Jan. 3, 1975-Jan. 3, 1987
Richard Baker	Baton Rouge	Jan .3, 1987-

District 7 At Large

Arsene P. Pujo	Lake Charles	Mar. 4, 1903-Mar. 3, 1913
Ladislas Lazaro	Washington	Mar. 4, 1913-Mar. 30, 1927
Rene L. DeRouen	Ville Platte	Dec. 5, 1927-Jan. 3, 1941

Vance Plauche	Lake Charles	Jan. 3, 1941-Jan. 3, 1943
Henry D. Larcade, Jr.	Opelousas	Jan. 3, 1943-Jan. 3, 1953
T. Ashton Thompson	Ville Platte	Jan. 3, 1953-July 1, 1965
Edwin W. Edwards	Crowley	Oct. 18, 1965-May 9, 1972
John B. Breaux	Crowley	Oct. 12, 1972-Jan. 3, 1987
James Hayes	Lafayette	Jan. 3, 1987-Jan. 3, 1997
Chris John	Crowley	Jan. 3, 1997-Dec. 31, 2004
Charles Boustany	Lafayette	Jan. 3, 2005-

District 8[17]

James B. Aswell	Natchitoches	Mar. 4, 1913-Mar. 16, 1931
John H. Overton	Alexandria	Dec. 7, 1931-Mar. 3, 1933
Cleveland Dear	Alexandria	Mar. 4, 1933-Jan. 3, 1937
A. Leonard Allen	Winnfield	Jan. 3, 1937-Jan. 3, 1953
George S. Long	Pineville	Jan. 3, 1953-Mar. 22, 1958
Harold B. McSween	Alexandria	Jan. 3, 1959-Jan. 3, 1963
Gillis W. Long	Winnfield	Jan. 3, 1963-Jan. 3, 1965
Speedy O. Long	Jena	Jan. 3, 1965-Jan. 3, 1973
Gillis W. Long	Winnfield	Jan. 3, 1973-Jan. 20, 1985
Cathy Long	Winnfield	Apr. 3, 1985-Jan. 3, 1987
Clyde Holloway	Forest Hill	Jan. 3, 1987-Jan. 3, 1993

1. Delegate from Orleans Territory.
2. Delegate from Orleans Territory.
3. Agent only, not voting delegate, granted floor privileges Mar. 6, 1812.
4. Agent only, not voting delegate, granted floor privileges Mar. 6 1812.
5. Took office by resolution of Congress upon presentation of credentials.
6. Took office by resolution of Congress upon presentation of credentials.
7. Resigned because of vote fraud.
8. Took office by resolution of Congress upon presentation of credentials.
9. Seat officially declared vacant.
10. Resigned to enter service.
11. Successfully contested election.
12. Never qualified for office..
13. Never qualified for office.
14. Successfully contested election, took seat Mar. 3, 1875; served one day.
15. Successfully contested election.
16. Never qualified for office.
17. As a result of the 1990 U.S. Census, District 8 was eliminated after 1992.

Sources: *Biographical Directory of the American Congress, 1774-1971* and Louisiana Office of the Secretary of State

LOUISIANA PURCHASE

ONE DAY IN 1803, THIS WAS THE U.S.A.

NEXT DAY ALL THIS WAS!

IT MAKES YOU A WORLD POWER, SON!

THIS WAS THE FAMOUS **LOUISIANA PURCHASE**

Brains and mosquito bites did it..

BRAINS and **MOSQUITO BITES** won an empire!

WE **MUST** CONTROL THE MISSISSIPPI!

THE STATESMANSHIP OF **THOMAS JEFFERSON**.

WE ONLY WANTED NEW ORLEANS, BUT AT THESE PRICES WE'LL BUY THE WORKS

..AND THE COURAGE AND VISION OF **ROBERT LIVINGSTON** MADE THE U.S. GREAT **IN 1803**.

NAPOLEON.. BAH!

NAPOLEON HAD TO SELL. YELLOW FEVER MOSQUITOES DESTROYED HIS COLONIAL ARMY IN HAITI.

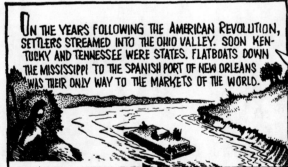

ON THE YEARS FOLLOWING THE AMERICAN REVOLUTION, SETTLERS STREAMED INTO THE OHIO VALLEY. SOON KENTUCKY AND TENNESSEE WERE STATES. FLATBOATS DOWN THE MISSISSIPPI TO THE SPANISH PORT OF NEW ORLEANS WAS THEIR ONLY WAY TO THE MARKETS OF THE WORLD.

IT'S MINE!

ON 1795 A TREATY WITH SPAIN GUARANTEED TO AMERICANS NAVIGATION OF THE RIVER AND FREE USE OF THE PORT OF NEW ORLEANS.

BUT, IN 1801 **NAPOLEON** FORCED SPAIN TO CEDE LOUISIANA TO FRANCE. AMERICANS VIEWED THIS WITH ALARM

ON OCTOBER, 1802 SPAIN SUDDENLY CLOSED THE PORT OF NEW ORLEANS. AMERICANS, UPRIVER, THREATENED TO FIGHT SPAIN, OR FRANCE – OR **BOTH**!

NAPOLEON'S COLONIAL EMPIRE

BUZZ

BUT TWO MONTHS LATER THOSE MOSQUITOS GOT TO NAPOLEON'S 45,000 TROOPS IN HAITI. ALL BUT A FEW DIED OF YELLOW FEVER.

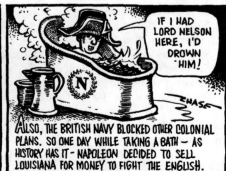

IF I HAD LORD NELSON HERE, I'D DROWN HIM!

ALSO, THE BRITISH NAVY BLOCKED OTHER COLONIAL PLANS. SO ONE DAY WHILE TAKING A BATH – AS HISTORY HAS IT – NAPOLEON DECIDED TO SELL LOUISIANA FOR MONEY TO FIGHT THE ENGLISH.

From Louisiana Purchase: An American Story, *by John Chase.*

List of Maps

Louisiana State Symbols

The following have been designated as official state symbols by legislative action:

Amphibian: Green tree frog
Bird: Brown pelican
Colors: Blue, white and gold
Crustacean: Crawfish
Day: April 30, known as "Louisiana Day"
Dog: Catahoula leopard dog
Drink: Milk
Flower: Magnolia
Wild Flower: Louisiana Iris
Fossil: Petrified palmwood

Freshwater Fish: White perch or crappie, or poxomis anularis, sac-a-lait
Fruit: Tomato (1986), Cantaloupe (1987)
Gemstone: Agate
Insect: Honeybee
Musical instrument: Diatonic or "Cajun" accordion
Reptile: Alligator
Tree: Bald cyprus

Pledge of Allegiance: "I pledge allegiance to the flag of the State of Louisiana and to the motto for which it stands: A state under God, united in purpose and ideals, confident that justice shall prevail for all of those abiding here."

State Songs: *Give Me Louisiana,* by Doralice Fontane; *You Are My Sunshine,* by Jimmie H. Davis and Charles Mitchell

March song: *Louisiana My Home Sweet Home,* by Sammie McKenzie, Lou Levoy, and Castro Carazo

Louisiana Parishes

The following shows the parish, the date the parish was created, and the parish seat.

Acadia (1886)	Crowley	Madison (1838)	Tallulah
Allen (1912)	Oberlin	Morehouse (1844)	Bastrop
Ascension (1807)	Donaldsonville	Natchitoches (1807)	Natchitoches
Assumption (1807)	Napoleonville	Orleans (1807)	New Orleans
Avoyelles (1807)	Marksville	Ouachita (1807)	Monroe
Beauregard (1912)	DeRidder	Plaquemines (1807)	Pointe-a-la-Hache
Bienville (1848)	Arcadia	Pointe Coupee (1807)	New Roads
Bossier (1843)	Benton	Rapides (1807)	Alexandria
Caddo (1838)	Shreveport	Red River (1871)	Coushatta
Calcasieu (1840)	Lake Charles	Richland (1868)	Rayville
Caldwell (1838)	Columbia	Sabine (1843)	Many
Cameron (1870)	Cameron	St. Bernard (1807)	Chalmette
Catahoula (1808)	Harrisonburg	St. Charles (1807)	Hahnville
Claiborne (1828)	Homer	St. Helena (1810)	Greensburg
Concordia (1807)	Vidalia	St. James (1807)	Convent
DeSoto (1843)	Mansfield	St. John the Baptist (1807)	Edgard
East Baton Rouge (1810)	Baton Rouge	St. Landry (1807)	Opelousas
East Carroll (1877)	Lake Providence	St. Martin (1807)	St. Martinville
East Feliciana (1824)	Clinton	St. Mary (1811)	Franklin
Evangeline (1910)	Ville Platte	St. Tammany (1810)	Covington
Franklin (1843)	Winnsboro	Tangipahoa (1869)	Amite
Grant (1869)	Colfax	Tensas (1843)	St. Joseph
Iberia (1868)	New Iberia	Terrebonne (1822)	Houma
Iberville (1807)	Plaquemine	Union (1839)	Farmerville
Jackson (1845)	Jonesboro	Vermilion (1844)	Abbeville
Jefferson (1825)	Gretna	Vernon (1871)	Leesville
Jefferson Davis (1912)	Jennings	Washington (1819)	Franklinton
Lafayette (1823)	Lafayette	Webster (1871)	Minden
Lafourche (1807)	Thibodaux	West Baton Rouge (1807)	Port Allen
LaSalle (1908)	Jena	West Carroll (1877)	Oak Grove
Lincoln (1873)	Ruston	West Feliciana (1824)	St. Francisville
Livingston (1832)	Livingston	Winn (1852)	Winnfield

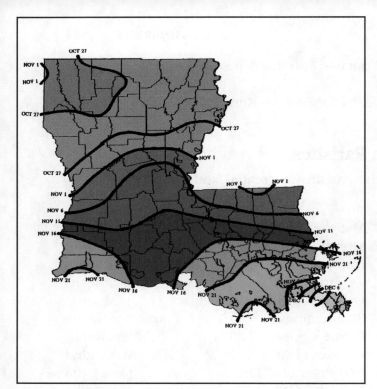

Mean dates of first fall freeze.

Mean dates of last spring freeze.

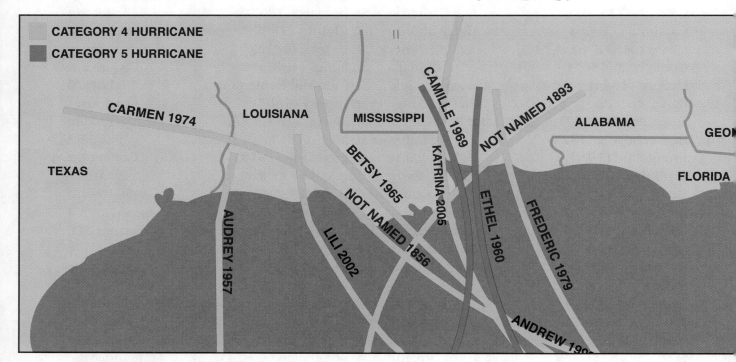

CATEGORY 4 HURRICANE

CATEGORY 5 HURRICANE

CARMEN 1974   LOUISIANA   MISSISSIPPI   CAMILLE 1969   NOT NAMED 1893   ALABAMA   GEO

TEXAS   FLORIDA

BETSY 1965

KATRINA 2005

AUDREY 1957

NOT NAMED 1856

LILI 2002

ETHEL 1960

FREDERIC 1979

ANDREW 199

Category 4 and Category 5 Hurricane paths.

INDEX

CREDITS

Maps and drawings by Jim Culbertson, except as noted below.

P. 1, 2, Pelican Archives; 7, Louisiana Office of Tourism; 8, all photographs courtesy Louisiana Office of Tourism, except frog (Netstate), colors, milk (Pelican Archives), catahoula (Gold Star Catahoulas), fossil (Amy O'Connell), perch (Cornell University), cantaloupe (Terry Callaway), agate (© Aaron Pratt), bee (P-O Gustafsson); 10, 11, Louisiana Office of Tourism.

Part One—p. 12, Architect of the Capitol; 18, *Newton's Atlas;* 23, Pelican Archives; 27, Jon Gibson; 29, detail, New Orleans Museum of Art; 31, Louisiana Office of Tourism; 32, Peabody Museum, Harvard University Photo 41-72-10/27 T1203; 35, Louisiana Division of Archaeology; 37, David Jeane; 42, Louisiana Office of Tourism; 50, Historic New Orleans Collection; 52, Texas Historical Commission; 53, Private Collection.

Part Two—p. 58, Louisiana Office of Tourism; 61, Pelican Archives; 62, Sue Eakin; 64, Louisiana Office of Tourism; 70, Private Collection; 71, Sue Eakin; 74, Louisiana Office of Tourism; 80, Alex Demyan image courtesy of Louisiana State Parks; 81, Sue Eakin; 82, Louisiana State Library; 83, Sue Eakin; 84, 88, 93, Historic New Orleans Collection; 95, 98 (bottom), Pelican Archives; 100, Louisiana Office of Tourism; 101, Louisiana State Museum; 103, Pelican Archives; 104, 105, Louisiana Office of Tourism.

Part Three—p. 108, Louisiana State Museum; 111, Pelican Archives; 112, MarJan Studio, Bunkie; 114, 115, Sue Eakin; 120, MarJan Studio, Bunkie; 121, Louisiana State Museum; 122, 125, 127, Pelican Archives; 129, 131, Louisiana State Museum; 132 (bottom), Louisiana Office of Tourism; 134, Pelican Archives; 141, Historic New Orleans Collection; 142, Louisiana Office of Tourism.

Part Four—p. 146, Historic New Orleans Collection; 149, Sue Eakin; 152, Historic New Orleans Collection; 153, Louisiana State Library; 154, Private Collection; 156, Pelican Archives; 157, Collection of the Louisiana Historical Society, Courtesy of the Louisiana State Museum; 159, Kathleen Balthazar Heitzmann; 160, Louisiana State Museum; 163, 165, Pelican Archives; 167, *Newton's Atlas;* 175, E. H. Suydam, © 1930 The Century Co., © 1950 Robert L. Crager & Co., present owner Pelican Publishing Company, Inc.; 176, 179, Louisiana Office of Tourism; 180, Louisiana State Library; 181, 186, Louisiana Office of Tourism; 190, Sue Eakin; 196, Louisiana Office of Tourism; 198, Pelican Archives; 199, R. W. Norton Art Gallery; 200, 203, Sue Eakin; 205, *Harper's;* 208, *Newton's Atlas;* 209, Private Collection; 210, 215, Louisiana Office of Tourism; 217, Sue Eakin; 218, Louisiana Office of Tourism; 219, Pioneer Heritage Center at LSU-Shreveport; 221, Louisiana State Library.

Part Five—p. 224, Louisiana State Library; 228, Private Collection; 231, Louisiana State Library; 233, Louisiana Office of Tourism; 234, Pelican Archives; 241, Louisiana State Library; 242, LSU Museum of Art; 243, Pelican Archives; 244, Louisiana Office of Tourism; 247, Pelican Archives; 248, Louisiana Office of Tourism; 249, LSU Office of Public Relations; 250, Historic New Orleans Collection; 251, Louisiana State Library; 256, Historic New Orleans Collection; 260, Boston Public Library; 261, *Harper's;* 262, 265, Louisiana State Museum; 266, Tim Tolar; 267, Sue Eakin; 269, Louisiana Office of Tourism; 270, 273, Sue Eakin; 275, Guy Tanner; 276, Pelican Archives; 277, Louisiana Office of Tourism; 279, 281, Sue Eakin; 283, Louisiana Office of Tourism; 284, 286, 287, Sue Eakin.

Part Six—p. 290, Sue Eakin; 294, Louisiana State Library; 296, Louisiana Office of Tourism; 298, Louisiana State Museum; 299, Pelican Archives; 300, Sue Eakin; 301, Private Collection; 303, Sue Eakin;

304, LSU-Shreveport Library; 308, 309, Buck Sowers; 310, Sue Eakin; 311, 312, Louisiana State Library; 313, Louisiana Office of Tourism; 314, *Newton's Atlas;* 315, Pelican Archives; 316, Grambling State University; 318, Sue Eakin; 319, 320, Pelican Archives; 323, Louisiana State Library; 328, Solis Seiferth; 329, *Alexandria Daily Town Talk;* 330, Louisiana State Library; 332, © Keith Marshall; 333 (2), Private Collection; 334 (2), 335 (2), Louisiana State Library; 336, Louisiana Office of Tourism; 337, 338, Pelican Archives.

Part Seven—p. 340, 344, Louisiana Office of Tourism; 345, Louisiana State Museum; 346, Sue Eakin; 347, Louisiana Office of Tourism; 348, Sue Eakin; 350, Louisiana State Museum; 354, Louisiana Office of Tourism; 355, Louis Armstrong New Orleans International Airport; 357 (2), Sue Eakin; 358, 360, Louisiana State Library; 361, Louisiana Office of Tourism; 362, U.S. Army; 365, Pelican Archives; 367, Louisiana State Library; 370, 371, Louisiana Office of Tourism; 373, Louisiana State Library; 374, Louisiana Office of Tourism; 375, Pelican Archives; 381, Mike Luckovich; 383, NASA; 386, Pelican Archives; 387, Office of Mary Landrieu; 388, Ogden Museum of Southern Art; 389, Louisiana Office of Tourism; 390, LSU Office of Public Relations; 393, Pelican Archives; 395, 397, 400, 401, 402, Louisiana Office of Tourism; 404, Pelican Archives; 407, Louisiana Office of Tourism; 411, *Newton's Atlas;* 412, Louisiana Office of Tourism; 415, Louisiana State Museum; 416, Louisiana Office of Tourism; 418, Dot Benge; 420, Louisiana Office of Tourism; 421, Pelican Archives; 426, 429, Louisiana Office of Tourism; 430, U.S. Census Bureau; 431, Gold Star Catahoulas; 432, © Dr. John Shaw; 435, 436 (left), Pelican Archives; 436 (right), Louisiana Office of Tourism; 437, Pelican Archives; 438, Cammie G. Henry Research Center, Northwestern State University of Louisiana; 439, Pelican Archives; 440, 441, 445, Louisiana Office of Tourism; 446, Pelican Archives; 452, 453, 455, 456, Louisiana Office of Tourism; 457, Pelican Archives; 458, Louisiana Office of Tourism; 461, Kerr-McGee; 467, 469, Louisiana Office of Tourism; 470, U.S. Army Corps of Engineers, New Orleans District; 471, © Donn Young/Port of New Orleans; 472, 475, 476, Louisiana Office of Tourism; 480, 481, 482, 484, 485, 490, Pelican Archives; 495, NOAA; 496, Pelican Archives; 497, 498, 499, 500, 501, FEMA; 502, Pelican Archives; 504, 505, 506, 508, 510, FEMA; 511, Pelican Archives; 512, 513, 514, 515, 516, FEMA.

Appendix—p. 538, 542, Pelican Archives.

Front cover: Ceiling of the Old State Capitol, photographed by Taryn Kay. Back cover: The Louisiana State Seal, courtesy Louisiana Office of Tourism.

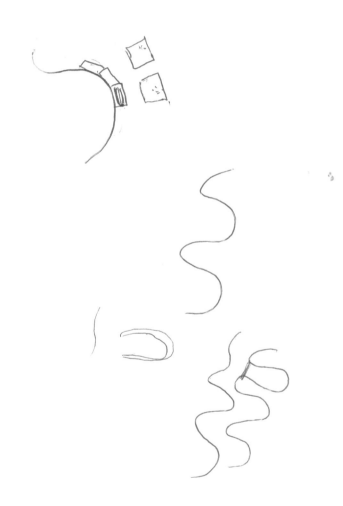